Abnormal and Clinical Psychology

AN INTRODUCTORY TEXTBOOK

THIRD EDITION

Paul Bennett

Open University Press

Open University Press

Open University Press
McGraw-Hill Education
McGraw-Hill House
Shoppenhangers Road
Maidenhead
Berkshire
England
SL6 2QL

email: enquiries@openup.co.uk
world wide web: www.openup.co.uk

and Two Penn Plaza, New York, NY 10121-2289, USA

First published 2011

A catalogue record of this book is available from the British Library

ISBN-13: 978-0-33-523746-3
ISBN-10: 0-33-523746-0

Library of Congress Cataloging-in-Publication Data
CIP data applied for

Typeset by Graphicraft Limited, Hong Kong
Printed in Italy by Rotolito Lombarda, Italy

The McGraw·Hill Companies

Brief Table of Contents

Detailed Table of Contents

—

PART 1

Background and methods

Part contents

Introduction

Chapter contents

This chapter introduces a number of issues relevant to abnormal psychology, many of which are returned to in more detail later in the book. It starts by considering what is meant by abnormality and how this relates to mental health. It looks at how these ideas have changed over time, before considering ways in which mental health problems are now conceptualized. The chapter then examines a number of factors that contribute to the development and differing presentations of mental health disorders, focusing on genetic, biological, psychological, social, cultural and familial explanations. Finally, it introduces the biopsychosocial approach, which attempts to integrate these various factors into one holistic model. By the end of the chapter, you should have an understanding of:

- Concepts of abnormality
- Historical concepts and treatments of abnormality
- Issues of diagnosis: the key diagnostic classification systems and their alternatives
- Models of the aetiology of mental health problems: genetic, biological, psychological, socio-cultural and systemic or familial
- The biopsychosocial approach.

1.1 Concepts of abnormality

This book focuses on factors that contribute to mental health problems and their treatment. Despite its title, it actually excludes many individuals who would be considered 'abnormal'. A number of simple definitions of abnormality may be proposed, none of which captures the essence of what is meant by the term abnormal in the present context:

- *Psychometric abnormality*: Cohen (1981) suggested that abnormality is a deviation from a statistically determined norm, such as the population average IQ of 100. An IQ score less than about 70–75, for example, may define someone as having a learning disability and indicate they may experience difficulties coping with life. However, the problems associated with a low IQ differ widely across individuals depending on their life circumstances. So, even when an individual is defined as psychometrically 'abnormal', this tells us little about their actual condition or problems. Furthermore, if one takes the other end of the IQ spectrum, a deviation of 30 points above the mean is generally not considered to be abnormal or to indicate the presence of mental health problems. Similarly, people who are rich or highly attractive or who engage in dangerous sports differ markedly from the norm. But none would be seen as having a mental health problem.

- *Incomprehensible behaviour*: According to Ahn et al. (2003), the key criterion underlying a judgement of abnormality is the degree to which any behaviour is understandable. Behaviour which is incomprehensible is considered abnormal; by contrast, even aberrant behaviour which appears to be abnormal can be normalized if given a plausible explanation.

- *Undesirable behaviour*: In his subjective values model, Szasz (1960) argued that abnormal psychological conditions are those that are deemed by society to be undesirable in some way. However, many undesirable behaviours or attributes including racism, anger or sexism may be considered undesirable, but are not seen as signs of mental health problems. More dramatically, stealing a car and 'joy riding' may be considered deviant, abnormal, behaviour by many people: but again, it is not a sign of a mental health problem.

None of these simple, one-dimensional, models have provided a convincing definition of abnormal functioning in the context of mental health. Indeed, some authors have contended that concepts of abnormality *cannot* be absolutely defined. In arguing this case, Lilienfeld and Marino (1995) introduced what they call a family resemblance model of abnormality, in which abnormality is seen as an inherently 'fuzzy' concept with 'indefinite boundaries'. Nevertheless, they argued that conditions that may be considered abnormal share a loose formation of characteristics which vary in scope and severity. In their view, conditions that can be considered abnormal in the context of mental health are characterized by:

- statistical rarity
- being maladaptive responses to particular circumstances
- involving impairment
- leading to the need for treatment.

According to Lilienfeld and Marino, although these criteria are subjective (who defines when someone needs treatment?) and difficult to define, there may be sufficient consensus in any one case to allow a judgement whether a particular behaviour or set of attributes could be defined as abnormal. Of course, the very subjectivity of these criteria means that any such judgements may differ across cultures, societies and time. As an example of the latter, homosexuality was considered a mental disorder, removed from being a mental disorder, and then replaced as a mental disorder in various versions of the *Diagnostic and Statistical Manual* – the American Psychiatric Association's guide to clinical diagnosis (American Psychiatric Association 1968, 1987, 1994). Societal norms across countries may also influence definitions of abnormality. In Puerto Rico, for example, a belief that one is surrounded by spirits is common; in the UK, such beliefs would probably result in an individual being treated for schizophrenia. Nevertheless, some behaviours may be so deviant or different to the norm that they are considered abnormal across cultures. Murphy (1976), for example, reported that cultures as widely separated as the Yoruba people of Nigeria and the Inuit in Alaska considered behaviours such as talking to oneself as abnormal.

In some cases, odd behaviour may result in an individual being labelled eccentric – a more benign label than 'mad' or 'mentally ill'. Any label may vary according to the degree to which the individual differs from the norm, how many behaviours are abnormal, and the implications of these behaviours for others. However, the nature of the label has powerful implications for the individual. Perhaps the most extreme example of this can be found in a classic study reported by Rosenhan (1973). In it, he taught a number of students to act as if they were psychotic – by stat- ing they heard one-word hallucinations – in an attempt to study the processes of diagnosis and hospitalization. As Rosenhan predicted, most students were admitted to hospital and assigned a diagnosis of schizophrenia. More worryingly, when the students admitted to the hoax, many of their psychiatrists took this to be further evidence of their 'illness'. It took some weeks before some students were discharged from hospital, some with a diagnosis of 'schizophrenia in remission'.

1.2 Historical overview

Explanations of 'madness' have existed for much of history. Early Chinese, Hebrew and Egyptian writings attributed bizarre behaviours to demonic possession. By the first century BC, biological explanations were predominant. Hippocrates, for example, considered abnormal behaviour to result from an imbalance between four fluids, or humours, within the body: yellow and black bile, blood, and phlegm. Excess yellow bile, for example, resulted in mania; excess black bile led to melancholia. Treatment involved reducing levels of the relevant fluids through a variety of means. Levels of black bile, for example, could be reduced by a quiet life, a vegetarian diet, temperance, exercise and celibacy. Although radical treatment approaches such as bleeding or restraint by mechanical devices were evident at this time, the first-line treatment of both the ancient Greeks and Romans was generally humane, and included providing comfort and a supportive atmosphere.

By the Middle Ages, the dominance of religious thinking resulted in abnormal behaviour once more being considered the result of demonic possession. Treatment was provided by priests and included attempts to rid the individual of the demon through prayer, chanting and administration of holy water. More radical approaches included insulting the devil, starving, whipping or stretching the affected individual. Perhaps the most dramatic treatment of people supposedly possessed by demons was outlined in the Catholic Church's *Malleus Maleficarum* (witches' hammer) which provided a guide to the identification and treatment of witches; women who were blamed for any ills that occurred within society. The manual stated that a sudden loss of reason was the result of demonic possession, and that burning was the only way to expel the devil. Estimates of the number of women burned to death as a result of being considered a witch throughout Europe range from 1 700 to 9 000 000 over a period of 250 years.

Towards the end of the Middle Ages, power again shifted to the secular authorities and biological theories of mental health problems became dominant. Institutions for the humane care of people with mental health problems were established. However, their initial success led to them become overcrowded. As a result, the quality of care they provided gradually deteriorated and became increasingly inhumane. One of the most famous of these institutions was Bethlem Hospital in London. Here, patients were bound by chains and, in certain phases of the moon, some were chained and whipped to prevent violence. Restraints were cruel and inhumane. The hospital became one of the most popular tourist attractions in London, with people paying to see the crazed inmates: hence the term, Bedlam.

The care of mentally disturbed people changed once more in the eighteenth century. William Tuke in Britain and Phillipe Pinel in France re-established more humane treatments. Although asylums remained, their inmates were able to move around them freely. Treatments included working closely with inmates, reading and talking to them and taking them on regular walks. Many were released from hospital as a result of their improved condition. This 'moral approach' was based on the assumption that if people with mental health problems were treated with care, they would improve sufficiently not to need further care. However, success rates did not reflect this optimism, and prejudice against people with mental health problems increased. Long-term incarceration once more became the norm.

Somatogenic and psychogenic perspectives

In the early twentieth century, theories and treatments of mental disorders diverged into two approaches: the somatogenic and psychogenic perspectives. The *somatogenic approach* considered mental abnormalities to result from biological disorders of the brain. A highly influential advocate of this approach, Emil Kraepelin, constructed the first modern typology of abnormal behaviour (Kraepelin [1883] 1981). He identified various clusters of symptoms, gave them diagnostic labels and reported on their course. In addition, he measured the effects of various drugs on abnormal behaviour. Despite the rapid adoption of this approach, many of the interventions it led to, including remedies as diverse as tonsillectomy and lobotomy (see Chapter 3), proved ineffective. More recently, the somatogenic approach has led to the development of powerful drugs used successfully in the treatment of conditions as varied as depression, psychosis and panic attacks.

The *psychogenic approach* considered the primary causes of mental disorders to be psychological. It was initially led by an Austrian physician, Friedrich Mesmer. In 1778, he established a clinic in Paris to treat people with hysterical disorders. The treatment, called mesmerism, involved the patient sitting in a darkened room filled with music. Mesmer then appeared dressed in a flamboyant costume and touched the troubled area of the individual's body with a special rod, a treatment that proved effective in a number of cases. Despite this, he was considered a charlatan and eventually banned from holding his clinics in Paris. Other leading advocates of the psychogenic approach, Jean Charcot and then Sigmund Freud, used hypnotism in the treatment of hysterical disorders. Treatment typically involved hypnotizing the patient before encouraging them to identify the factors precipitating the onset of their symptoms and to re-experience their emotions at this time, a process known as catharsis. Freud later rejected this method in favour of free association and the use of psychoanalysis.

The latter part of the twentieth century saw a dramatic development in the psychological treatment of mental health problems. Humanistic therapies advocated by Rogers added to those of Freud and the analysts, as did the behavioural and cognitive behavioural approaches led by theorists such as Eysenck and Rachman in the UK, and Beck and Meichenbaum in the USA and Canada. These, and even more recent developments, are described in the next two chapters. Modern psychological therapies are now equally, if not more, effective than pharmacological interventions in the treatment of many mental health disorders.

Care in the community

Modern treatments allow thousands of individuals with mental health conditions, who would have required hospital care in the first half of the twentieth century, to be treated in the community. In the UK, the movement of people from hospital to community began in the 1950s, and reached its peak in the 1970s. Over this time, many people who had spent years, perhaps decades, in hospital were gradually moved back into the communities from which they came. This was not an easy process, as many had become totally institutionalized. Their behaviour was determined by the rules of the hospital, which were generally more accepting of deviance than the general population. They had limited self-care skills, as they had not been responsible for cooking, cleaning and other elements of self-care for many years. Often the impact of living in an institution was more disabling than the condition for which they had originally been hospitalized, which could have been as non-problematic as vagrancy or being an unmarried mother. As a result, people discharged into the community had to be taught how to survive outside the hospital environment. Many found this very difficult, ending up as 'rotating door cases'; that is, as quickly as they were discharged into the community, they were readmitted to the hospital.

To avoid these difficulties, modern treatment seeks to minimize the use of hospital facilities and to maintain people within the community in which they live. In the UK, for example, people with relatively minor mental health problems, including most people with anxiety or mild–moderate depression, are treated by their general practitioner in a primary care setting. More serious mental health problems are usually treated in the secondary care system. However, this usually involves outpatient appointments or visits to the individual's home by members of multidisciplinary teams of health care workers. Admission to hospital occurs only at times of crisis, with discharge back to the community as quickly as is reasonably possible.

Multidisciplinary teams are usually led by a consultant psychiatrist who has medical responsibility for the care of their patients. They and the more junior doctors are medical graduates who have specialized in the care of the 'mentally ill'. Nurses within the team have a multifaceted role involving, among other things, monitoring an individual's progress, recommending changes in medication (or in countries such as the USA or the UK, prescribing some medication), providing basic psychological therapies, and acting as advocate for the patient. More specialized professions may also be involved in the provision of care. Occupational therapists can help the individual develop or maintain life skills such as cooking or strategies for coping with stress. Clinical psychologists provide therapy for people with complex problems, and support others in their therapeutic work with clients, through clinical supervision and training in therapy skills. Finally, social workers help the individual deal with social problems including lack of money or employment that may contribute to their problems.

Unfortunately, the evolution of differing foci of clinical work in primary care (general practitioners treating most cases of anxiety and depression) and secondary care (experts from various professions treating complex cases including psychosis, treatment-resistant depression, and so on) has meant that many people do not receive the optimal treatment for their condition. One key problem has been that despite the National Institute of Clinical Excellence (NICE) stating that the optimal treatment for mild–moderate depression and anxiety involves cognitive-behavioural therapy (CBT), most people with these disorders have been treated by their general practitioner using medication. Recognizing this anomaly, the UK government is spending millions of pounds to increase the availability of psychological treatments within primary care through a programme known as Improving Access to Psychological Therapies (IAPT). In this initiative, so-called low intensity workers will provide basic CBT – incorporating computerized interventions, psychoeducational groups, and guided self-help. Only more serious cases or people who do not benefit from this intervention will be referred to a 'high intensity' service, where they are treated by specialists (nurses, psychologists, and so on) for severe anxiety and depression.

1.3 Issues of diagnosis

The medical model

This book is organized around a set of diagnostic labels that can be ascribed to people with common mental experiences or who behave in similar ways – schizophrenia, depression, and so on. This approach is rooted in the 'medical model', which assumes that mental health problems are the result of physiological abnormalities, generally involving brain systems. A disorder is considered as an illness, much as other medical problems are, and is therefore treated with physical treatments, usually medication, that modify the underlying biological disorder. The type of treatment given is determined by a diagnosis, which is itself determined by the presence or absence of various signs or symptoms. This assumes that people with mental health problems are experiencing a state divorced from that of 'normal' individuals: a mental illness.

Classification systems

The historical roots of this approach lie in the work of Kraepelin in the late nineteenth century. He described a number of syndromes, each of which had a common set of symptoms differing from those of other syndromes, in a classification system which later formed the basis of the World Health Organization's (WHO) *International Classification of Diseases* (ICD: WHO 1992). Indicating how such systems have struggled to accurately identify and classify mental health conditions, this is currently in its tenth revision. The American Psychiatric Association (APA) devised its own classification system, known as the *Diagnostic and Statistical Manual* (DSM), which although having much in common with the ICD system, differs in a number of details.

Like the ICD, it has changed over the years and, since its first publication in 1952, is now in its fifth revision (DSM-IV-TR: APA 2000).

The DSM system is 'multi-axial'. That is, it allows an individual's mental state to be evaluated on five different axes:

- *Axis 1*: the presence or absence of most clinical syndromes, such as schizophrenia, mood, and eating disorders
- *Axis 2*: the presence or absence of stable long-term conditions, including personality disorders and learning disabilities
- *Axis 3*: relevant information on the individual's physical health
- *Axis 4*: psychosocial and environmental problems
- *Axis 5*: rating of an individual's global level of functioning: from a score of 1 for persistent violence, suicidal behaviour or inability to maintain personal hygiene to 100, symptom-free.

These classification systems provide clinicans with a dichotomous outcome that fits the medical model of treatment. Whether an individual is diagnosed with an 'illness' or not will determine whether or not they are treated, admitted to hospital, and so on. Proponents of the medical model have argued that a reliable diagnosis that is consistent both within and between countries ensures that:

- any individual presenting with a set of problems will receive the same diagnosis across the world
- they will therefore receive the same treatment wherever they are in the world
- research that informs treatment focuses on the same condition wherever it is conducted.

Diagnoses are particularly important in relation to drug therapies where a diagnosis will determine which class of drugs is used to treat the presenting problem: antidepressants for depression, anti-psychotics for schizophrenia, and so on. An incorrect diagnosis will mean that incorrect medication is prescribed. In the case of research, incorrect diagnosis will result in unreliable results from any treatment trial and will confuse rather than help the development of new treatments.

Before considering how well the present diagnostic systems have achieved these goals, it is important to indicate some fundamental scientific and philosophical implications to this approach:

- The model implies a dichotomy between normal and abnormal mental states. An individual either is mentally ill or is not. This dichotomy is becoming increasingly difficult to sustain. Many 'abnormal' states ascribed to the 'mentally ill' have now been found to occur in large numbers of the 'normal' population; many people who live normal lives and who have never been considered in any way 'abnormal', for example, report having heard voices in their head – almost a defining characteristic of schizophrenia.
- The model implies that when an individual is ill, they behave or experience mental events that are in some way abnormal and different from those of 'normal' people – an argument

rejected by the findings of cognitive psychology. There is increasing evidence that while the thought content and behaviour of people with and without mental health problems may differ from the norm, the cognitive processes underlying them are essentially the same. This issue will be returned to on many occasions later in the book.

● The approach fails to recognize the experience of the individual; they are assigned a diagnosis and the diagnosis is treated, not the individual.

● The model implies that biological factors are primary in the development of mental health problems and that, therefore, biological treatments are also primary. This ignores findings that social and psychological factors appear to be critical in the development of mental health problems and that biological factors involved in mental health problems change as a result of changes in these factors. It also distracts from findings that pharmacological therapies may prove only partially effective in the treatment of a number of apparently biologically mediated conditions and that psychological therapies have proven more effective than pharmacological interventions in the treatment of many conditions.

Diagnostic consistency

Despite the development of clear criteria for each disorder, making a diagnosis is not a clear-cut process and levels of diagnostic agreement may be low. In an assessment of individuals diagnosed using DSM-III (APA 1987), for example, Chen et al. (1996) examined changes in diagnoses among individuals initially diagnosed with schizophrenia who were hospitalized in one US hospital at least four times over a seven-year period. Twenty-two per cent were subsequently given different diagnoses. In addition, 33 per cent of patients with an initial diagnosis other than schizophrenia were subsequently given this diagnosis. Nathan and Langenbucher (2003) noted that while the more recent DSM-IV improved diagnostic consistency of some conditions, such as substance abuse, there were no gains in others, such as personality disorders and disorders within the schizophrenic spectrum. More recently, Barnes (2008) found systematic differences in the diagnosis of schizophrenia across different ethnic groups in all the psychiatric hospitals in one US state. African Americans were less likely to diagnosed with bipolar and major depressive disorders, and more likely to be diagnosed with schizophrenia than white patients. In an interesting contrast to these findings, Mikton and Grounds (2007) found that the ethnicity of the diagnosing physician also seemed to impact on diagnostic decisions. In a UK study in which psychiatrists were asked to give a diagnosis based on a case vignette, Caucasian doctors were nearly three times more likely to assign a diagnosis of personality disorder than African Caribbean doctors.

Diagnostic validity: schizophrenia

Validity of classification labels can also be difficult to achieve. Perhaps the most controversy lies with the diagnosis of schizophrenia. Bleuler (1908) identified four fundamental symptoms of what he termed the group of schizophrenias: ambivalence, disturbance of association, disturbance of affect, and a preference of fantasy over reality. Subsequent diagnostic systems have, until recently, adapted these diagnostic categories, and attempted to develop increasingly unambiguous diagnostic criteria for various sub-types of the disorder. Until the mid-1990s, DSM-III identified four types of schizophrenia:

- *Simple*: progressive development of 'oddities of conduct', an inability to meet the demands of society, and withdrawal from everyday life.

- *Paranoid*: stable, paranoid delusions, frequently accompanied by auditory hallucinations that support these delusional beliefs.

- *Catatonic*: marked psychomotor disturbances, switching between extreme excitement, stupor and waxy flexibility in which the individual may be placed in a position and maintain it for several hours.

- *Hebephrenic*: changes in mood and irresponsible and unpredictable behaviour, accompanied by disorganized thought processes and speech that is frequently rambling and incoherent.

Unfortunately, this categorization disregarded any form of causal theory of linkages between the various symptom clusters, and may have actually inhibited our developing understanding of the nature and treatment of schizophrenia. A more useful classification system has now been derived from consideration of the causes of the symptoms of schizophrenia.

Factor analysis of the signs and symptoms of the various sub-types of schizophrenia has identified three clusters of symptoms, known as disorganized symptoms, positive symptoms and negative symptoms (Liddle et al. 1994) that tend to co-occur. The positive cluster includes hallucinations, delusions, disorganized speech or positive thought disorder. Negative symptoms denote an absence of activation, and include apathy, lack of motivation or poverty of speech. Disorganized symptoms include disorganized speech and behaviour, and flat or inappropriate mood. These may have differing biological and neuropsychological foundations, and prove a more useful way of categorizing the various schizophrenic-type disorders (see Chapter 6). Some of these concepts have now been incorporated into DSM-IV. The new diagnosis of residual schizophrenia, for example, is characterized by the presence of negative symptoms. However, the classification system still does not match onto these symptom clusters. Other areas of discussion include the validity of diagnoses as varied as alcohol abuse and dependence (Harford et al. 2009), sub-types of bulimia (van Hoeken et al. 2009), and various personality disorders (e.g. Huprich 2009).

Cultural relativity

One important goal of DSM is to identify and diagnose mental health problems in a similar way across cultures. The approach assumes that medical illnesses will present in a universal way throughout the world. Whether this is actually the case is questionable. People from different cultures may, for example, report their distress in quite different ways. Somatization involves the presentation or experience of physical problems rather than emotional ones: 'My heart is burning', for example, may imply depression or anxiety. This type of reporting is relatively rare in Western cultures, but very common in Asian cultures, possibly because such cultures disapprove of the strong expression of emotions, particularly negative ones. Interestingly, while many people from non-Western cultures still report predominantly somatic symptoms when reporting psychological distress, the more Westernized the individual the less likely this is to happen (Rao et al. 2007). It seems that the Western model of emotional distress is becoming the dominant model. Nevertheless, this cultural relativism indicates that it may be inappropriate to assume that one set of diagnostic symptoms may be appropriate for all cultures and at all times.

A social critique

In addition to the scientific critique, a number of social commentators have raised ethical objections to the medical model. Farber (1990), for example, argued that the medical model underestimates the individual's capacity for change, and consequently inhibits this capacity. At its most stark, the model assumes that unchangeable biological factors lead to psychological states that are distinct from the mental processes of 'normal' individuals. These may remit, either as a result of treatment or through natural recovery, but the individual is still prone to further episodes of the disorder.

Farber identified two types of medical models: one that assumes that mental disorders are the result of genetic and biological factors and the psychoanalytic model that assumes the adult disorders are the result of psychological, but biologically driven, mental structures that are set down in childhood and are unchangeable over the life course. He saw the ethical danger of the medical model in its legitimization of the health care professions' control, and therefore the state's control, of people considered as disordered. According to Farber, the medical treatment that people with mental health disorders receive prevents them from self-change and serves to reinforce assumptions that they are not capable of self-development and change. He also contended that such treatment is coercive, and that any attempt at self-change is viewed negatively and resisted: the patient who wishes to discontinue medical treatment, for example, is told that this is a sign that they are resisting treatment, and that they do not want to get 'well'. Only the experts know when people who are mentally ill are well enough to make authentic choices.

Having provided such a critique of the medical model, the astute reader may now be asking why the book is organized around a set of diagnoses which may be so seriously questioned. Their use here perhaps reflects one of the reasons for their continued use by psychologists and others that reject the medical model. They provide a shorthand means of orienting the reader to the content of each chapter. However, their use does not imply an acceptance of the medical model – even the 'reality' of the conditions described within them is occasionally questioned – and while biological explanations for each disorder are provided, this certainly does not indicate that these are considered their primary cause.

Alternatives to the medical model

Any alternative to the medical model needs to differ from it on some important dimensions. In particular, it needs to do the following:

- make no dichotomy between abnormal and normal mental states
- consider the social and psychological processes that lead to and accompany any mental health problems
- make the affected individual (and not their diagnosis) the focus of assessment and treatment
- consider non-pharmacologically based interventions as (potentially) primary.

Two alternative approaches that address these issues are the dimensional approach and the psychological formulation.

Dimensional approaches

While accepting the benefits of some form of diagnostic system, a number of commentators (e.g. Clark et al. 1995) have challenged the categorical approach adopted by the DSM. In DSM, diagnoses are based on the presence of a number of symptoms, such as poor sleep, feeling depressed, and so on. It provides a categorical classification: the individual either has the symptoms, and therefore a disorder, or does not. A dimensional approach rejects this all-or-nothing approach and the assumption that the mental states of people with a mental health problem are distinctly different from those of the 'normal' population. Proponents of the dimensional approach argue that categorical models of psychopathology are challenged by a number of problems, including:

- co-morbidity: an individual might satisfy the criteria for more than one diagnosis (see, for example, the discussion of the transtheoretical approach in Chapter 3)
- heterogeneity: two people with the same diagnosis can present with entirely different patterns of symptoms (see, for example, the discussion of diagnoses of schizophrenia in Chapter 6).

The dimensional approach suggests that people who are now diagnosed as having a mental disorder may better be considered to be at the extreme end of a distribution of normality, not categorically different from others. Many of us have been anxious or depressed at one time or another, felt like not engaging with the world, or slept poorly. These experiences are not unique to people with a depressive disorder. Whether or not we consider them to be problematic is dependent on their frequency and the intensity with which they are experienced. Dimensional approaches adopt this approach, and suggest it is the degree to which problems are experienced, not merely their presence or absence, that determines whether or not an individual has a mental health disorder. This approach fits well with increasing findings that some 'symptoms' of mental health disorders, such as hearing voices, are relatively common within the general population, and may never lead an individual to seek help and these symptoms may never impair their everyday living. As a compromise with the diagnostic approach, some proponents of the dimensional system suggest that if an individual scores above a threshold score, based on the severity and frequency of their experiences, they may be given some form of diagnosis.

The dimensional approach has a number of strengths. In particular it highlights which aspects of a person's life are problematic and for which they may require some form of help, and avoids 'forcing' the presenting problems into a diagnostic category into which they do not easily fit. What it does not address is the processes causing or maintaining any problems. This level of assessment is provided by the psychological formulation.

Hankin, B.L., Fraley, R.C., Lahey, B.B. et al. (2005). Is depression best viewed as a continuum or discrete category? A taxometric analysis of childhood and adolescent depression in a population-based sample. *Journal of Abnormal Psychology*, 114: 96–110.

The authors note that current psychiatric diagnostic structures consider the experience of depression to be categorically different to any other mental state. By contrast, a number of researchers have argued that depression may best be viewed as a deviation from the 'norm' – the dimensional view. The goal of their research was to evaluate the extent to which major depression among young people, as defined by DSM-IV, is categorical or dimensional by using a form of statistical analysis developed by Meehl which allows the validity of these differing models to be assessed.

Method

The study sample comprised 845 young people aged between 9 and 17 years from Atlanta, USA. Part of the sample was drawn from a larger study known as the Georgia Health and Behavior Study. A second sample taken specifically for this study was also obtained. For both studies, a stratified random sample of households was selected from the population of addresses in Georgia. Researchers visited each house to screen for the presence of eligible individuals. If a young person lived in the house, they and a carer were asked to participate in the study and were interviewed in the family home. The overall response rate was 74 per cent.

Clinical interview

The young people and carer were interviewed using the investigational version of the Child and Adolescent Psychopathology Scale (I-CAPS), which assessed all of the symptoms of major depression as defined by DSM-IV. Respondents rated the I-CAPS items on a 4-point response scale that ranged from 1 (not at all) to 4 (very much). They rated each symptom according to how well it described their (or their child's) emotion or behaviour, how often such symptoms occurred, and how serious the symptom was over the past 12 months. Several questions tapped each symptom. For example, for the symptom of fatigue or loss of energy, the authors averaged the following I-CAPS items: (a) sluggish and tired, (b) tired out by little things, (c) sluggish and not energetic, and (d) had less energy than usual.

Statistical procedures

This involved an analysis known as Maximum Covariance-Hitmax (MAXCOV or MAXCOV-HITMAX). This analyses the covariance between two variables as a function of a third variable. The function characterizing these conditional covariances is called a MAXCOV function and its shape depends on the status of the latent variable (in this case, each symptom of depression) under study. If the latent variable is categorical (i.e. depressed individuals had the symptom, non-depressed individuals did not), the MAXCOV curves tend to have a mountain-like peak. If the latent variable is continuous (i.e. if the symptoms are present to a lesser or greater degree in both depressed and non-depressed individuals), the MAXCOV curves tend to resemble a flat line.

Results

MAXCOV analyses were conducted on the nine symptoms of DSM-IV major depression. Overall, the MAXCOV curves were more similar to those expected under a dimensional model than a categorical one. Figure 1.1 illustrates the average MAXCOV curves for data based on youth (top row) and parent reports (bottom row). The shaded regions of the graphs show the range of MAXCOV functions that should be observed if the various symptoms were dimensional in nature. The spiked line represents the type of graph that would imply the symptoms were categorical. The data (marked with dots) clearly follows the pattern expected in a dimensional patterning of symptoms.

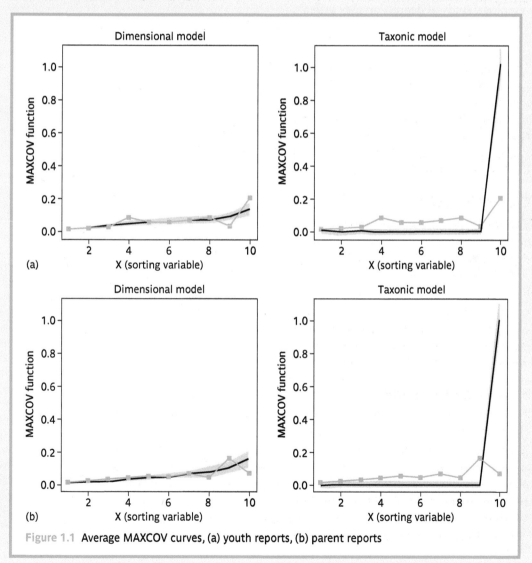

Figure 1.1 Average MAXCOV curves, (a) youth reports, (b) parent reports

Discussion

The findings of this study suggest that depression in young people is continuously, not categorically, distributed. This held for both youth and parent reports, and for all DSM-IV depressive symptoms, and across gender. The current diagnostic system and nomenclature, used by DSM-IV and all other diagnostic systems, assumes that disorders, such as depression, are categorical. The authors' findings, as well as other studies, argue against DSM's categorical emphasis for depression in children, adolescents and adults. They therefore concluded that dimensional approaches may be valuable for studying and assessing depression. Indeed, if individual differences in depression really are continuous, but researchers continue to use categorical measurement models, the empirical study of depression may suffer.

Diagnosis versus psychological formulation

Evidence reviewed earlier in the chapter has shown that diagnostic errors are common. They may, for example, result from a failure to question patients about key issues, a failure to consider all diagnostic possibilities, doctors being overly influenced by dramatic symptoms, or an individual bias towards particular diagnoses. These errors can be minimized by the use of a standardized diagnostic process. To this end, various authorities have developed standardized, structured or semi-structured, diagnostic interview protocols that systematically examine various aspects of the individual's functioning and symptoms, and according to the symptoms identified provide the clinician with a likely diagnosis. These are most commonly used in research studies, where accuracy and replicability of the diagnostic process are paramount. Schedules for adults include:

- *The Structured Clinical Interview for DSM-IV Axis-1 Disorders* (SCID: First et al. 1996): available in a short and long form, with good reliability. The short SCID is relatively brief and applicable to most clinical disorders;
- *The Schedule for Affective Disorders and Schizophrenia* (SADS: Endicott and Spitzer 1978): a semi-structured interview, that is highly reliable in the diagnosis of depression (and now, anxiety; Mannuzza et al. 1986);
- *The Diagnostic Interview Schedule* (DIS-IV; Robins et al. 1995): a diagnostic interview that can be conducted by lay people as well as professionals. It includes a number of modules that can be used as appropriate. Unfortunately, it has poor reliability when compared with clinical diagnoses and is best used in conjunction with other assessments.

These instruments can also be used in day-to-day practice, although their length (the DIS can take 2–3 hours) combined with the requirement for appropriate training and access to diagnostic and scoring protocols means that many psychiatrists do not use them. Instead, many adopt a less formalized, but nevertheless reasonably structured approach, known as the mental state examination. This systematically considers a variety of symptoms and background information that may contribute to a diagnosis, including: physical appearance, behaviour, mood, attitude, orientation, attention and concentration, thought content and processes (to assess delusions), perception (to assess hallucinations), and insight and judgement. The final diagnosis is a subjective judgement based on this information rather than a score resulting from an interview.

A quite different view is taken by psychotherapists. From their perspective, the nature of the hallucinations or conditions that led to a period of depression are of paramount importance, and are the focus of any intervention. The diagnostic label assigned has little impact on the type of treatment given. Psychological formulations attempt to identify the processes that led to and maintain the problems an individual is facing. These may be external: negative life-events, rape, bereavement, and so on. They may be internal: distorted interpretations of the world, hyperventilation leading to panic disorder, and so on. They may be short-term or longer-term sequelae to childhood events such as sexual abuse or poor parental relationships.

Although the content of a formulation will necessarily differ according to the orientation of the therapist, a typical cognitive behavioural formulation would consider:

- The presenting problem(s): what is troubling the individual?
- Predisposing factors: what factors have left them vulnerable to any problems they are experiencing?
- Precipitating factors: why have they developed problems *now*?
- Perpetuating cognitions and consequences: what thoughts are they experiencing and behaviours are they engaged in that are maintaining their problems?

Together, these would lead to a formulation of the problem and a treatment plan that would be acceptable to the individual and within their resources to carry out.

A formulation is an explanatory hypothesis about the nature of the clinical problem. It has two main functions: to guide the therapist in what to do and to help establish criteria for evaluating the effectiveness of the intervention. Formulations are not static, and may change in the light of information emerging over time, as will the focus and form of any intervention. They are necessarily guided by the theoretical perspective of the therapist, which focuses the questions asked and the formulation established. These may be quite different for, say, a psychoanalyst and a cognitive behavioural therapist. This, of course, is both a strength and a weakness. A strength, because it allows the therapist to select – in a relatively parsimonious way from the myriad of potential contributors to a problem – those most likely to be relevant. A weakness, because these theoretical blinkers may focus the therapist too exclusively on what they consider to be important aspects of a client's experience, and too little on what may actually be important. On this basis, some have argued that good therapists are aware of several aetiological models and can either integrate them into a meaningful synthesis or identify which are relevant to particular clients.

While psychotherapists may not comfortably assign a diagnostic label, they may use psychometric instruments as part of the assessment process and to measure changes over time. Frequently used measures include:

- *Spielberger State-Trait Anxiety Scale* (Spielberger et al. 1983): a measure of anxiety measuring both trait (general) and state (how you feel now) anxiety. Each scale comprises 20 items and has norms for clinical patients, working adults and (the children version) high school and college students.

● *Beck Depression Inventory* (Beck et al. 1996): comprises 21 questions relating to symptoms of depression such as hopelessness and irritability, cognitions such as guilt or feelings of being punished, and physical symptoms such as fatigue or lack of interest in sex. It can be used by people aged 13 years and upward, and provides cut-off scores indicating four levels of depression from minimal to severe.

They may also measure processes such as beliefs or meta-cognitions (see Chapters 2 and 3) that contribute to distress or problematic behaviours, including:

● *The Meta-cognitions Questionnaire* (Cartwright-Hatton and Wells 1997): this taps into five relevant dimensions including: positive beliefs about worry, negative beliefs about the controllability of thoughts, and negative beliefs about thoughts in general.

● *Paranoia, Persecutory and Delusional-Proneness Questionnaire* (McKay et al. 2005): a 54-item questionnaire comprises three subscales: persecutory paranoid ideation, non-persecutory paranoid ideation, and non-paranoid delusion-proneness. The questionnaire is suitable for use across both clinical and non-clinical populations.

1.4 The aetiology of mental health problems

There are a number of diverse literatures focusing on factors that contribute to the development of mental health problems. The rest of this chapter provides an introduction to each type of explanation. The chapters in Part 2 of the book examine the issues in more detail in relation to specific disorders.

● *Genetic models* consider how genetic factors influence an individual's risk of developing a mental health disorder.

● *Biological models* focus on biochemical processes, usually involving chemicals known as neurotransmitters, which mediate mood and behaviour. They also consider how damage to the brain can result in a number of mental health disorders.

● *Psychological models* focus on the internal mental processes that influence mood and behaviour. There are a number of psychological explanations of mental health disorders, the best known being psychoanalytic, humanistic, behavioural and cognitive behavioural.

● *The socio-cultural approach* focuses on the role of social and cultural factors in mental health disorders.

● *Systemic models* focus on the role of smaller social systems, frequently the family, in which the individual is situated. Disorders are considered to be the consequence of stressful or disordered interactions with families.

● *The biopsychosocial approach* integrates these various factors into a holistic causal model. This suggests that genetic and other biological factors may increase an individual's risk of developing a mental health disorder. However, whether the disorder will actually develop depends on whether an 'at risk' individual encounters factors such as social or family stress and/or whether they have the coping resources to help them cope with such stresses.

Genetic models

With the exception of egg, sperm and red blood cells, each of the approximately 100 trillion cells of the body contains two complete sets of the human genome: one set from the individual's father, the other from their mother. Each genome comprises 23 pairs of chromosomes. Each set of chromosomes carries the 60 000–80 000 genes that contribute to both the physical and psychological characteristics of the individual.

Each gene in a set of matched genes affecting the same processes is known as an allele. The instructions in the sets of genes from each parent may be the same or quite different, for example, blue versus brown eyes. Where the alleles are the same, the individual is described as homozygotic. Where they differ, they are termed heterozygotic. The expression of these 'competing' genes is determined by whether the genes are dominant or recessive. Some genes, such as those determining the eye colour brown, are described as dominant and are expressed when linked to a gene with other instructions. Recessive genes are expressed only when matched with other recessive genes with the same instructions. The development of most mental health disorders is associated with recessive genes. If they were the result of dominant genes, their expression in each generation would be virtually guaranteed, resulting in continuing disadvantage and limited chances of reproduction.

Genetic studies of the aetiology of mental health problems have used several methods. Family studies measure whether those with genotypes that are more or less similar to the affected individual are at different risk for the disorder. If there is a genetic linkage in a disorder, one would expect someone with identical genetic make-up (a monozygotic (MZ) twin) to be more likely to develop the disorder than a non-identical or dyzygotic (DZ) twin, who has roughly 50 per cent of genes in common, who in turn would be more at risk than a cousin or aunt with even less genetic similarity. Many family studies focus on the degree to which both MZ and DZ twins develop the same disorder. Where more MZ than DZ twins are concordant for the disorder, this is taken to imply some level of genetic risk. This approach has a number of limitations. Critically, not only do closer family members share more genes, they also share a more common environment. MZ twins, for example, tend to be treated more similarly than DZ twins. Any concordance for a condition may therefore be attributable to a shared environment rather than shared genes.

In an attempt to separate out environment from genetic factors, many studies have examined concordance rates in twins brought up in differing environments, usually as a result of adoption. It is assumed that because the separated twins have a common genetic make-up and different environments, any concordance for the condition under examination is the result of genetic factors. However, there are a number of reasons why any heritability coefficient determined by this method may not prove totally accurate. First, even twins that are separated have factors other than their genes in common. If nothing else, they have shared the same prenatal experiences that may determine risk for various disorders. Another factor that can result in overestimation of genetic risk involves any genetic influence on the behaviour of a child, particularly where they are 'difficult' or 'problematic', instigating similar reactions from those caring for them. As a result, separated children may experience both a common genetic heritage and a common family background, despite their separation.

This kind of interpretive problem has resulted in new methodologies in this type of study. Rather than assume the nature of the environment in which the person lives, studies have now begun to measure genetic, environmental, social and other life stresses. These data are then subject to statistical modelling techniques that allow the investigators to determine the degree to which genetic and environmental factors separately contribute to the development of the disorder under investigation.

Work on the human genome now permits more fundamental research – the identification of specific genes responsible for specific disorders. In fact, most disorders are likely to result from a number of genes (that is, they are polygenic), and in some cases problems may arise from the absence of a gene, rather than its presence. There is evidence, for example, of a gene locus on chromosome 4 that may be protective against alcohol problems. Whatever the genetic linkages found, there is a general consensus that genes, at most, influence risk for a particular mental health disorder. Indeed, while risk for a particular disorder may be increased as a result of genetic factors, many if not most people with the disorder may not carry the relevant gene. Eighty-nine per cent of individuals diagnosed with schizophrenia, for example, have no known relative with the disorder. Not carrying the gene that increases risk for a disorder does not mean that you are immune to that disorder.

The potential for testing for genes that confer risk of both physical and mental health problems carries a number of challenges to modern society. At present, screening programmes for genetic risk of disorders such as Huntington's disease are now being widely instituted. These programmes bring with them a whole series of ethical dilemmas and we are now learning how a generation of men and women cope with knowledge of risk for disease. So far, it seems that it is not easy, and testing seems to evoke high levels of anxiety among a significant minority of vulnerable individuals in both the short and the long term (Bennett et al. 2010). At a societal level, the likelihood of genetic screening for medical insurance and even job selection is increasing. Will genetic testing result in an underclass that will find it difficult or impossible to get insurance, buy a house, or even hold a job? Time will tell.

Biological models

Biochemical explanations of mental health problems focus on the biological processes underlying mood and behaviour. Both are regulated by brain systems, whose actions are mediated by neurotransmitters. These allow us to perceive information, integrate that information with past memories and other salient factors, and then respond emotionally and behaviourally. Disruption of these systems as a result of inappropriate neurotransmitter actions results in inappropriate perception, mood and behaviour. The exact nature of the systems and the neurotransmitters involved in different mental health problems are considered in more detail in Chapter 4 and in each of the chapters in Part 2 of the book.

Other biochemical processes have been implicated in some conditions. Hormones such as melatonin appear to be involved in the aetiology of seasonal affective disorder, a type of depression considered in Chapter 9. Other disorders may be the result of problems in the architecture of the brain. Some of the symptoms of schizophrenia, for example, may arise from degeneration or failures of brain development that lead to fundamental errors in information processing, and disordered thoughts and behaviour. Alzheimer's disease results from progressive neuronal damage evident through the deterioration of cognitive functioning in later life.

Biochemical models are often considered to be in opposition to psychological explanations: mental health problems are seen as either psychological in nature or to have a biological cause.

A more appropriate way of thinking about the two approaches is that they provide different *levels* of explanation, somewhat analogous to the levels of explanation provided by physics and chemistry. Biochemical processes underpin all our behaviour at all times. The act of writing this sentence involves numerous sensory, motor and neuronal processes, all of which are mediated by chemical transmissions. But understanding these fundamental processes explains only part of the behaviour: it does not easily account for the motivation for writing the sentence, the process of mental construction of the sentence, or, indeed, my mood as it was written. To understand these, one needs to address the psychological processes driving the behaviour. In this way, both biochemical and psychological explanations of the behaviour are 'correct'.

Psychological models

In contrast to the biochemical and genetic models where most scientists and practitioners believe in a common process through which mental health disorders arise, there are many psychological models. There are a number of 'mainstream' theories of mental health disorders and related treatments. The first of which, psychoanalysis, was first practised in the beginning of the twentieth century, with Freud and his followers being the leaders of this movement. This was the dominant therapy for a number of years and is still practised, albeit with some modifications, over 100 years after its inception.

Psychoanalytic principles were rejected by two therapies, both of which began in the 1950s and 1960s. Behaviour therapy (e.g. Wolpe 1982) rejected the notion of psychic processes influencing mood and behaviour and the unscientific nature of psychoanalysis. Its practitioners argued that behaviour is largely controlled by external events, and based its principles on the 'hard' science of classical and operant conditioning. At a similar time, humanistic therapies (Rogers 1961) rejected psychoanalysis, not because of its psychic nature, but because of the nature of its psychic phenomena. In contrast to psychoanalysis which assumes that behaviour and mood are influenced by past traumas, humanistic therapies are based on the assumption that behaviour is driven by aspirations towards the future, with the potential of self-actualization available to all. Therapy was designed to help the individual achieve their potential, not to resolve the traumas of the past.

The most widely practised therapy is a derivative of behaviour therapy, known as cognitive or cognitive behavioural therapy (Beck 1977). It considers our thought processes, or cognitions, as the prime determinant of behaviour and mood. It makes no assumptions of past trauma or future aspirations and is not based on a model of personality as are psychoanalysis and humanistic therapies. Instead, it focuses on how the thoughts we have at any one time influence mood and behaviour. It assumes that the cognitions that result in mental health problems are somehow 'faulty' and dysfunctional. Therapy focuses on changing them to more functional and less inappropriate ones or learning not to be affected by potentially distressing thoughts. It also retains a strong behavioural focus: distorted cognitions, for example, may be challenged by behavioural experiments designed to illustrate errors of thinking. Each of these models is described and discussed in more detail in Chapters 2 and 3 and the chapters in Part 2.

Psychotherapy versus pharmacotherapy

It is possible to argue that, because biochemical processes underpin behaviour at a fundamental level, altering the levels of neurotransmitters that influence mood through pharmacological processes provides the most direct and effective form of treatment of mental health disorders. While there is some logic in this argument, it certainly does not hold for all cases and it implicitly assumes that psychological therapy does not influence the fundamental biological processes underpinning mental health disorders. This is not the case: there is a powerful reciprocity between the two forms of treatment. Psychological treatments cause changes at the biochemical level: otherwise they would not alter mood. Similarly, pharmacotherapy alters cognitions and behaviour (e.g. Mogg et al. 2004).

One argument favouring the use of psychological therapy is that many of the drugs pre-scribed are effective only while they are being taken. Once a course of drugs has finished, their action stops and the individual's biochemical status, and hence mood and behaviour, may revert to their state before the treatment was commenced. To prevent this, many people are now being prescribed drugs such as antidepressants for much longer than was initially considered to be necessary. In contrast, some have argued that psychological therapy prepares the individual to cope with the stresses they face now and in the future, making them at significantly less risk of relapse once therapy is terminated.

Both arguments may be overstating the case. There is good evidence that many people maintain good mental health following cessation of pharmacological treatments, although the reasons for this may be more psychological than pharmacological. A depressed individual who has with-drawn from family and social life, for example, may benefit from a drug treatment that helps them re-engage with people and enjoy life more. The pleasure gained from this may increase levels of the neurotransmitters that prevent depression (see Chapter 3) and maintain them in a healthy state once drug therapy is stopped. If they had not re-engaged so positively, the risk of relapse might have been much greater.

It is also true that some individuals do not benefit from psychological therapies, or they relapse following successful psychological treatments. They may find it difficult to adopt a psychological approach to reducing their problems. They may forget, be unable to use the new skills they have learned, or feel so overwhelmed by circumstances that they once more experience a deterioration in their mental health. For this reason, some advocates of psychological therapy suggest the need for 'booster' sessions some months after the completion of therapy to help maintain a positive mental state.

Both pharmacological and psychological therapies are effective in treating most mental health conditions. Psychological therapies seem to be more effective than drug treatments in treating conditions such as anorexia, panic disorder, mild–moderate depression, and some sexual problems. In contrast, although psychological treatments are increasingly being used in the treatment of schizophrenia, the mainstay of treatment remains drug therapy. The relative effectiveness of the two forms of treatment for some conditions such as severe depression is still hotly debated (see Chapter 9). This debate is returned to in more detail in Chapter 4 and in each of the chapters in Part 2 of the book.

Socio-cultural models

All the models so far discussed assume that mental disorders arise as a result of problems within the individual, be they genetic, biochemical or psychological. By contrast, the socio-cultural approach assumes that external, social factors contribute to their development. Socio-cultural factors include a wide range of influences, from the family to wider socio-economic factors, some of which were identified in the British Psychiatric Morbidity Survey (Jenkins et al. 1998). This revealed the highest rates of depression or anxiety to be among women, those living in urban settings, unemployed people, and those who were separated, divorced or widowed. Psychoses were more prevalent among urban than rural dwellers. Alcohol dependence was nearly twice as common among people who were unemployed than among those who were employed: drug dependence was five times greater among those who were unemployed than those in jobs. People who are members of ethnic minorities or in the lower socio-economic groups are also more likely to experience depression, non-specific distress, schizophrenia or substance abuse problems than those in other sectors of society (e.g. Hudson 2005). A number of, sometimes competing, theories to explain these differences have been proposed, each of which is discussed in more detail in Chapter 4.

Socio-economic status differences

- *Social drift*: this approach suggests that high levels of mental health problems among the lower socio-economic groups are the result of affected individuals developing a mental health problem, which renders them less economically viable. They may be unable to maintain a job or the levels of overtime required to maintain their standard of living, and drift down the socio-economic scale. That is, mental health problems precede a decline in socio-economic status.

- *Social stress*: this approach assumes that living in different socio-economic conditions results in differing levels of stress: the lower the socio-economic group, the higher the stress. That is, the stresses associated with social deprivation result in mental health problems.

- *Lack of resource model*: similar to the social stress model, this model assumes that those who are economically deprived have fewer resources to help them cope with any life demands they face. These resources may be economic, psychological, social or environmental. Poor mental health is thought to be a direct consequence of a lack of resources.

Gender differences

- *Willingness to express distress*: one theory is that gender differences in the prevalence of mental health problems are more apparent than real, and result from women's willingness to visit their doctor and complain of mental health problems. This theory has not been substantiated (Weich et al. 1998).

- *Role strain*: an alternative hypothesis suggests that women encounter more role strain and spillover between the demands of work and home than men. The resultant stress places them at increased risk for stress and mental health problems.

Minority status

- *Confound with social class*: this model suggests that the apparent relationship between minority status and mental health problems is spurious. It suggests that people in ethnic minorities largely occupy the lower socio-economic groups. That they also have higher levels of mental health problems is a result of this association, not of being a member of an ethnic minority *per se.*

- *The effects of prejudice*: this suggests a more direct link between ethnic minority status and mental health. Mental health problems may result from the additional stresses, including overt and covert prejudice, experienced by the members of minority ethnic groups.
- *Cultural transitions*: a further source of stress may be the tension experienced as individuals adopt or reject some of the norms of their own or other cultures. Both may result in feelings of alienation, rejection by members of differing cultures, and consequent mental health problems.

Social and cultural factors may also influence the type of problems people report, and how acceptable, or unacceptable, they are within a society. Some cultures positively affirm what might be considered hallucinations and signs of mental disturbance in others. People from different cultures may also report what we define as mental health problems in many different ways – and seek different treatments for them. Asian people, for example, often report mental distress framed as physical symptoms and their first line of treatment may involve herbs or other natural physical treatments. These issues are considered in more detail in Chapter 4.

Stop and think...

Most strategies for reducing the burden of mental health disorders have focused on treatment once they have developed. The importance of social and cultural factors points to another way of addressing the issue: to reduce the social, economic and cultural factors that may contribute to poor mental health. This could be done in a number of ways – anti-bullying campaigns in schools, providing cheap or free crèches so that young single mothers can access recreational facilities or have a break from child care, ensuring economic security for people in old age – that on the surface have little to do with mental health, but may actually have a significant impact on it.

So, if you had carte blanche, how would you change the society in which we live to maximize the mental health of the general population?

Systemic models

A more enclosed system that impacts on mental health is the family. Family system theorists consider the individuals within a family to form an interacting system. Each has a reciprocal influence on those around them. The behaviour of individuals within these systems, and the communication between them, can lead to individual members behaving in ways that seem 'abnormal'. Perhaps the most extreme form of family dysfunction occurs when a member of a family sexually abuses a child within it. Levels of sexual abuse are very high among women who seek psychological therapy for conditions as varied as depression, anxiety and anorexia (Jaffe et al. 2002).

One of the first models of family interactions in relation to mental health focused on people with schizophrenia. Brown and colleagues (e.g. Brown et al. 1972) were the first to identify a family characteristic, now termed high negative expressed emotion (NEE), in which individuals who were prone to episodes of schizophrenia fared particularly badly. Individuals in families who were particularly critical, hostile or over-involved had a higher rate of relapse than those who did not experience this environment. Reducing levels of NEE resulted in a dramatic reduction in relapse rates. A second, more complex, family system is thought by family therapists to contribute to the development of anorexia in young women (Minuchin 1974). These and other family models of pathology are considered in more detail in Chapter 5 and other chapters in Part 2 of the book.

Biopsychosocial models

Evidence reviewed so far in this chapter has shown that living in a stressful environment, however defined, does not inevitably lead to mental health disorders, nor does carrying the gene for a particular disorder. Both sets of factors place an individual at increased *risk* for the disorder. Whether or not this potential is realized is the result of an interaction between these, and other, factors. An individual who has some genetic risk for depression, for example, is more likely to develop the disorder if they live in a stressful environment than if they never encounter such conditions. Someone without genetic risk for the disorder is less likely to become depressed, but they are not invulnerable. If they encounter certain environmental conditions or adverse life-events, they may still become depressed. By contrast, some social environments may help an individual to develop resilience and to cope effectively with stress.

For most mental health problems, vulnerability to, or resilience against, mental health disorders is determined by a number of factors, some of which include:

- *biological factors*: genetic make-up, viral infections, injuries
- *psychological factors*: childhood trauma, maladaptive cognitive responses to environmental events
- *social/environmental factors*: socio-economic stress, the quality of personal relationships, the availability and quality of social support.

It is noteworthy that the boundaries between each of these dimensions of risk is somewhat fuzzy, and even this simple categorization fails to take account of the interaction between them. People in the lower socio-economic groups, for example, may be more prone to viral infections or injury. People with more or less adaptive coping styles, as a result of previous family experiences, may respond to potentially stressful events in differing ways. Nevertheless, they indicate the key risk dimensions involved in the aetiology of mental health problems.

Diathesis-stress model

These risk factors have been placed into a simple biopsychosocial model known as the diathesis-stress model. In it, diathesis refers to the biological vulnerability an individual carries: stress involves any event or condition that interacts with this vulnerability to influence risk for the expression of the disorder. The lower the individual's biological vulnerability for a particular disorder, the greater the stress needed to trigger that disorder: the higher their biological vulnerability, the less stress is needed. The nature of both the biological vulnerability and the type of stress that triggers the problems is likely to differ across disorders. In the chapters in Part 2 of the book, each of the various factors that contribute separately to risk of mental health problems is identified and discussed. Note that in most cases, these risk factors can be combined into this diathesis-stress/biopsychosocial model, even when this is not explicitly stated in the chapter.

Some commentators (e.g. Johnstone 2000) have argued that while the diathesis-stress model acknowledges the role of stress in the aetiology of mental health problems, it still adopts an essentially medical model of mental disorders, as it suggests that stress acts as a trigger to provoke an underlying biologically determined disease process. In other words, the role of stress is relatively minor, and the role of biological factors remains primary. It does not accept that mental health problems can result from the experience of stress or negative events alone, without there being a biological propensity to respond to stress in a way that leads to mental health problems. As such, it maintains the medicalization of what is an essentially psychological phenomenon. Despite these reservations, the diathesis-stress model remains the pre-eminent overarching model of the development of mental health problems.

1.5 Chapter summary

1 Defining 'abnormality' in relation to mental health disorders is difficult. Lilienfeld and Marino suggest it involves statistical rarity, maladaptive responses to particular circumstances, impairment and the need for treatment.

2 Diagnosis of mental health conditions, such as those within DSM classifications, largely follows the biological or disease/medical model of mental health established by Kraepelin in the late nineteenth century.

3 According to this model, accurate diagnosis is important to ensure consistent treatment and research in relation to mental health disorders.

4 Diagnosis is typically based on the presence of a number of symptoms, including hallucinations, poor sleep, and so on. This categorical approach leads to a dichotomous diagnosis process in which the individual either has or does not have a disorder.

5 Dimensional approaches state that the experiences of individuals with mental health disorders differ in degree from those of the 'normal' population but are not categorically different.

6 Psychotherapists generally find diagnostic labels to be unhelpful. Instead, they focus on the nature of the factors that contribute to and maintain the individual's problems. These, usually in the form of a treatment formulation, become the focus of therapy.

7 A number of factors may contribute to the development of mental health disorders: genetic and biological factors, socio-cultural and family factors, and individual psychological factors. No one approach is able to explain the development of any one disorder, and most result from a combination of factors: the bio-psychosocial approach.

1.6 For discussion

1 Should we limit the types of people with mental health disorders who are treated in the community? Should people such as psychopaths or so-called 'predatory' paedophiles thought to be at risk of reoffending be permitted to live or be treated outside hospital or prison?

2 What would you think if told an individual is 'schizophrenic'? How might this alter your interpretation of their behaviour or your responses to them?

3 Some severe psychiatric conditions such as Huntington's disease in which the individual develops increasing muscular spasticity and mental deterioration leading to death in middle age can be predicted by genetic testing. It cannot be prevented, but those who have the gene for the condition may choose not to have children and pass the gene on to them. Would you want to know as a young person whether you carry the gene?

4 If offered the choice of medication or psychological therapy for a mental health problem, which would you choose – and why?

1.7 Key terms

Aetiology explanations of the causes of disease.

Behaviour therapy form of therapy that targets behavioural change by changing the triggers or consequences of behaviour using operant or classical conditioning-based interventions.

Catharsis reliving past repressed emotions in order to come to terms with past conflicts.

Chromosome structures within a cell that contain genes.

Client a term often used to denote an individual in therapy. In contrast to words such as patient or subject, it is used to indicate the helping, non-hierarchical nature of the therapeutic relationship between therapist and individual.

Clinical supervision discussion and feedback on therapy by peers or experts intended to improve therapeutic formulation and treatment.

Delusion a strongly held inappropriate belief; usually a belief that is normally considered impossible.

Disorganized symptoms (of schizophrenia) include confused thinking and speech and behaviour that do not make sense.

DSM-IV-TR the *Diagnostic and Statistical Manual* (fourth edition with text revision: APA 2000) – US system of classification of mental health disorders.

Dyzygotic (DZ) twins non-identical twins.

Hallucination the experience of touch, visions or sounds in the absence of external stimuli.

Heritability coefficient the degree to which individual differences are due to genetic factors.

Hyperventilation short rapid breaths that lead to low levels of carbon dioxide in the blood and physical sensations including tingling in the arms, dizziness and feelings of an inability to breathe.

Hysterical disorder physical symptoms in the absence of physical pathology.

Lobotomy an early form of psychosurgery.

Monozygotic (MZ) twins identical twins, with identical genetic structure.

▶ Negative symptoms (of schizophrenia) include absence of activation, and include apathy, lack of motivation or poverty of speech.

Neurotransmitter chemical involved in maintaining neuronal activity; transmits information across the synaptic cleft.

Operant (Skinnerian) conditioning manipulation of behaviour through the use of reinforcement and punishment schedules.

Pharmacotherapy treatment with drugs.

Polygenic caused by multiple genes.

Positive symptoms (of schizophrenia) include hallucinations, delusions, disorganized speech or positive thought disorder.

Prevalence the frequency with which a particular condition is found within the population at any one time.

Primary care basic or general health care focused on the point at which a patient ideally first seeks assistance from the medical care system.

Psychoanalysis there are a number of different psychoanalytic therapies. Most share a number of therapeutic goals, including gaining insight into the nature of the original trauma and bringing troubling material to consciousness so the individual can cope with it without the use of ego defence mechanisms.

Psychomotor movements involving both mental and motor processes.

Psychotherapist a generic term for someone who provides some form of therapy. In this book, it does not denote any particular therapeutic orientation, and may include therapists as diverse as cognitive and psychoanalytic in practice.

Psychotic the presence of a mental health condition, such as schizophrenia, of which the main symptom is a loss of contact with reality.

Self-actualization described by the humanists as the experience of fulfilling one's potential for growth.

Spillover here, a failure to separate work and home life, such that each intrudes on the other.

Waxy flexibility a condition found in schizophrenia in which individuals maintain the posture in which they are placed for prolonged periods of time.

1.8 Further reading

Bentall, R. (2004) *Madness Explained: Psychosis and Human Nature.* Harmondsworth: Penguin.

Dallos, R. and Johnstone, L. (2006) *Formulation in Psychology and Psychotherapy.* London: Routledge.

Fernando, S. (2010) *Mental Health, Race and Culture.* New York: Palgrave Macmillan.

Johnstone, L. (2000) *Users and Abusers of Psychiatry: A Critical Look at Psychiatric Practice.* London: Routledge.

Page, A. and Stritzke, W. (2006) *Clinical Psychology for Trainees: Foundations of Science-informed Practice.* Cambridge: Cambridge University Press.

Schaler, J. (ed.) (2004) *Szasz under Fire.* Chicago: Open Court Publishers.

Stahl, S. (2008) *Stahl's Essential Psychopharmacology: Neuroscientific Basis and Practical Applications.* Cambridge: Cambridge University Press.

The psychological perspective

There have been four major schools of psychological therapy since the late nineteenth century:

- *Psychoanalytic*: views childhood trauma and the unconscious as the causes of problems in adulthood;
- *Behavioural*: considers psychopathology to arise from conditioning processes;
- *Cognitive or cognitive behavioural*: assumes that the critical element of psychopathology is inappropriate, dysfunctional, cognitions;
- *Humanistic*: considers psychopathology to be the consequence of deviation from the drive towards self-actualization.

To understand the rationale behind each therapy, it is necessary to understand the model of psychological disorder upon which it is based. The chapter therefore provides an overview of each approach's theory of psychological disorder as well as some of the strategies it uses to achieve change. New developments in cognitive and behavioural theory and interventions are also considered in some detail in the next chapter. In addition, the effectiveness of various therapeutic approaches are considered in the context of specific conditions in Part 2 of the book. For now, by the end of this chapter, you should have an understanding of:

- key psychological models of the aetiology of mental health disorders: psychoanalytic, behavioural, cognitive behavioural and humanistic
- some of the widely used interventions based on these models.

2.1 The psychoanalytic approach

Freud

Sigmund Freud (e.g. Freud 1900) was one of the first clinicians to explore the role of childhood factors and the unconscious in explaining problems of adulthood. His work, conducted in the late nineteenth and early twentieth centuries, was highly innovative and based on his formulation of the unconscious. These insights were largely derived from cases he saw in his practice in Vienna.

Freud considered personality to have three basic components: the id, ego and superego:

- The *id* is driven by the basic instincts of sex and aggression, which Freud considered the basic motivating forces of human behaviour. It operates under the pleasure principle. That is, it seeks to maximize immediate gratification. It is greedy, demanding and has no natural self-control.
- The *ego* is the realistic component of personality. It operates under what Freud termed the reality principle and also works to maximize gratification, but within the constraints of the real world.
- The *superego* contains the individual's morals and societal values. It acts as the conscience, creating feelings of guilt if social norms are violated.

These basic personality components are in a continuous struggle to control the individual. Sexual desire, for example, is rooted in the id. However, its immediate urge for sexual gratification is tempered by the superego's moralistic statements that such urges are a sin, and the ego's realistic consideration of the costs and benefits of various actions. The outcome of these competing processes is usually some form of socially acceptable sexual behaviour. However, should the id gain control, the likely outcome is rape or some other violent act.

Five stages of psychosexual development

According to Freud, the development of personality occurs through a five-stage sequence of psychosexual development. The first stage, known as the *oral stage*, is characterized by receiving gratification through oral means: sucking, crying or exploring objects with the mouth. The oral stage occurs between the ages of 18 and 24 months. At this time, children have only the id.

Accordingly, the stage is characterized by an inability to delay gratification, and selfish and demanding behaviour. Immediately following this is the *anal stage*, which continues until the child is between 42 and 48 months old. At this time, children achieve gratification through anal means. Freud argued that the process of toilet training is the first time the child becomes aware of their actions on other people, and learns to modify their behaviour to gain gratification from them. If the child satisfies parental demands, it receives praise and approval. If not, it experiences disapproval. Realistic expectation of these outcomes is the beginning of the ego development.

The third stage of psychosexual development is the *phallic stage*. This continues through to the age of about 5 or 6 years. In this stage, the superego begins to develop as a result of the child's experiences of sexual conflicts and the means by which they are resolved. According to Freud, boys in the phallic stage develop sexual desires focusing on their mother, driven by the urges of the id. These desires are known as the oedipal complex. By this stage, the ego is able to judge the realistic consequences of these actions and recognizes that they would meet the disapproval of their rival, their father. The boy also recognizes that if he were to enter into open rivalry with his father, he would be defeated. He begins to fear that his father will castrate him to prevent him from becoming a future rival for his mother – a phenomenon known as castration anxiety. The boy resolves this dilemma by identifying with his father. This permits him, at least symbolically, to make love to his mother as does his father. As part of this identification process, he begins to adopt the father's beliefs and values. He begins to develop a superego.

The young girl develops her superego in a similar way. Freud suggested that when a girl enters the phallic stage she begins to recognize that she is different from boys. She experiences penis envy: she feels incomplete or inadequate as a result of her lack of a penis. She also believes that if she makes love with her father she will 'possess' her father's penis, at least temporarily. In addition, if she is made pregnant, she may bring a penis into the world by giving birth to a boy. In this way, the girl's basic sense of inferiority leads her to develop sexual desires focusing on her father. These feelings are resolved by the girl identifying with her mother, allowing her to symbolically make love to her father when her mother does so, and leading her to adopt her mother's moral values: her superego.

The fourth stage of development is the *latency stage* which continues until puberty. During this stage, the individual channels their sexual and aggressive urges through age-appropriate interests and activities such as sports and hobbies. The final stage is the *genital stage*. This begins in puberty and continues throughout life. In it, the individual is driven by the two basic motivating forces: sex and aggression. Our bodies generate both sexual (libido) and aggressive energy. Healthy individuals discharge this energy through socially appropriate channels: sexual intercourse with age-appropriate adults, sports, career progression, and so on. Where people fail to find such outlets, energy builds until it can no longer be contained and is released in an uncontrolled fashion, guided by unconscious influences. To prevent the inappropriate discharge of these forces, the individual diverts or blocks them through a variety of unconscious mechanisms.

Defence mechanisms

According to Freud, mental health problems are the result of either ego anxieties or the defence mechanisms it sets up to prevent these anxieties becoming conscious. Ego anxieties frequently relate to troubling experiences experienced in early childhood. These can lead the individual to

Table 2.1 Some adult personality characteristics associated with a failure to progress through Freud's development stages	
Stage	**Associated problems**
Oral	Depression, narcissism, dependence
Anal	Obstinacy, obsessive-compulsive disorder, sadomasochism
Phallic	Gender identity problems, antisocial personality
Latent	Inadequate or excessive self-control
Genital	Identity diffusion

become fixated at a particular developmental stage, and to behave in ways appropriate to that stage during adulthood. Such behaviour forms an unconscious defence against anxiety caused by the experience and its memories. Its function is to prevent recognition of the hurt that was experienced at the time. Individuals may also regress to previous levels of psychosexual functioning through which they have successfully passed as a result of stresses in adulthood. The stage to which they regress is influenced by the severity of the stress, the similarity of the current stressor to problems experienced in previous stages, and the success with which each stage was passed through. Some of the repressed or fixated personality types in adulthood are summarized in Table 2.1.

A number of other defence mechanisms that do not involve regression may also be used to counter ego anxieties. The most basic Freudian defence mechanism is repression. In this, threatening material is unconsciously and actively blocked from awareness to prevent it from entering consciousness. Some other defence mechanisms are outlined in Table 2.2.

A classic case involving ego defence mechanisms was that of Little Hans. This young boy had an extreme fear of horses, which Freud suggested indicated a fear of his father: that is, castration anxiety. Hans's defence mechanism was to displace the fear of his father to more acceptable objects, horses, which were large and strong like his father, and acted as symbolic representations of him. Another condition which Freud identified as a defence mechanism was bed wetting, which he considered a symbolic form of masturbation. Its perpetrators expressed their underlying sexual urges by converting them to a more acceptable physical symptom.

Criticisms of Freudian theory

Freud broke new ground to develop a complex model of human development. His contribution to the development of theories of personality and psychopathology is without question. However, his theories have the weaknesses of any theory, particularly one so encompassing, developed before our present rigour of science and its empirical process were established. Even though a number of researchers (e.g. Dollard and Miller 1950) have developed experimental studies to assess Freud's theory, it is beset with such fundamental interpretive problems that whatever the results of these studies, they provide little evidence to support or disprove Freud's theories. Because processes such as id drives, ego defences and fixation are abstract and supposedly

Table 2.2 **Some Freudian defence mechanisms**

Defence	Definition	Example
Repression	Blocking threatening material from consciousness	An adult unable to recall being abused as a child
Denial	Preventing threatening material from entering consciousness	A parent who cannot accept the death of their child
Projection	Attributing one's own unacceptable impulse or action to another	Someone who denies their homosexuality, and considers homosexuals are constantly making sexual approaches
Displacement	Changing the target of an unacceptable impulse	'Kicking the cat' instead of whoever caused anger or upset
Reaction formation	Expressing the exact opposite of an unacceptable desire	A person who is considering ending a relationship, but continues to show strong affection for their partner
Sublimation	Expressing an unacceptable impulse in a symbolic manner	An individual with a strong drive for unattainable sexual relationships focuses their attention on achieving in their career or sport
Conversion	Expressing painful psychic material through symbolic physiological symptoms	A soldier who finds it unacceptable to shoot others, develops paralysis in his hands
Undoing	A repetitive action that symbolically atones for an unacceptable impulse or behaviour	Repeated washing of hands following an extramarital affair

operate at an unconscious level, there is no way of knowing for certain whether or not they are occurring. In addition, the theory provides few, if any, testable hypotheses. If an individual engages in a set of behaviours predicted by Freud's theory, it may be considered supported. However, if they do not, the theory is not challenged or falsified, as it could be hypothesized this was a consequence of the individual's defence mechanisms.

Some other criticisms of Freudian theory include the following:

- Freud's theories were based on interpretation of information gleaned from a relatively small and specific group of patients, in particular, middle-class Viennese women. The ability to generalize from these cases to the wider population is questionable.
- Freud's views on women were misogynistic and based on cultural attitudes of his time, rather than a true scientific perspective.
- Freud's theory changed over time, sometimes without clear rejection of previous versions. It is therefore difficult to know which theory should be tested.

Freud's contemporaries and descendants

Jung

Psychoanalysis now encompasses a diverse set of theories, all of which see childhood experiences or the unconscious as the driving forces of behaviour, but differ considerably from Freud's original theory. Carl Jung ([1912] 1956), for example, was seen by Freud as the 'Crown Prince' of psychoanalysis. However, his beliefs became less and less congruent with those of Freud, and he broke away to develop his own analytical psychology. Jung considered Freud's emphasis on sex as the major motivator of human behaviour to be simplistic and reductionist. By contrast, Jung emphasized psychological and spiritual influences on behaviour. He also disagreed with Freud's notion that personality and adult neurosis are established in early childhood. He suggested that people are motivated by future goals rather than by past events. While Jung believed that our unconscious was developed through individual experiences, he also considered part of it reflected universal themes and ideas. He considered this 'collective unconscious' to be biologically based and evident through symbols and myths common to all races and times – a sort of race memory that influences our reactions to the present world. Jung considered that the goal of personal development is to expand conscious awareness through the ego making contact with the unconscious. The ultimate end of this process is union between the conscious and the unconscious, although this is rarely completely achieved. In this, Jung was close to the humanistic school, considered later in the chapter.

Klein

A generation later, Melanie Klein (1927) focused on the social drives that underpin our psychological development. Freud originally used the word 'object' to denote anything from which an infant derives satiation. From a Freudian perspective, these were the results of the libidinal and aggressive drives. Klein, as part of a group of psychoanalysts (including D.W. Winnicott) who based their work on and developed object relations theory, suggested that human beings have an innate drive to form and maintain social relationships. In her analysis of the development of this drive, Klein focused on the psychological processes of young children, placing emphasis on the relationship between mother and child in the first few months of life. She considered psychic structures to evolve from these interactions rather than the biologically derived tensions and conflicts, anxieties and sexual impulses proposed by Freud.

According to Klein, the infant goes through two key pre-oedipal developmental stages. The first, known as the paranoid-schizoid position, is dominant in children from birth to around 4 to 6 months old, although it is never completely outgrown and older children and adults can operate in this mode at times. This stage is characterized as involving paranoid anxiety. The child experiences this as fear of external objects, but it is actually driven by their death instinct (or their fear of this instinct). It is a fear of imminent annihilation, and is dealt with through a number of defence mechanisms, including one known as *splitting*. Through this, the child identifies objects as either completely good or completely bad. There is no integration of the two. In doing so, the child prevents the good being destroyed by the bad, and the child identifies itself with the good objects. According to Klein, the mother is initially represented by the child as 'part-object' of the breast, and is experienced as either a 'good object' or a 'bad object'. She is good when the child's needs are met through feeding; bad when these needs are not met. The baby responds to the bad object with feelings of terror, insecurity and destructive rage.

The second developmental stage occurs roughly between 6 and 12 months. In this, phase, known as the depressive position, the infant learns to bridge the gap between 'good' and 'bad' objects, and between his or her own experiences of love and hate, which created them. In doing so, the child is able to view the world in a more holistic manner, and objects can be accepted as having both good and bad elements. The child begins to see his or her mother as a more realistic 'whole object' rather than the part-object of the breast, and to understand that good and bad can co-exist in the same person. However, this revelation leads to a deep sense of disappointment and anger that a loved person can be bad as well as good. There is a primitive sense of loss and separation now the possibility of complete fusion with the 'good mother' is no longer possible. There may also be a sense of guilt, as the child feels they may be responsible for the end of this relationship. In addition, fearing the loss of his or her object's love as a consequence of any destructive behaviour, they attempt to inhibit such behaviours. In doing so, the child develops an increasing tolerance for ambivalence, and learns to mediate between the need for a loved object and his or her own instincts that threatened to destroy the object. This prepares the way for stable object relations, first with the mother and then with other social objects. However, the developing child and adult still carry the potential to revert to the paranoid-schizoid position, particularly at times of stress or distress, and the process of splitting (or other more Freudian defence mechanisms). This is more likely to occur if the individual has been traumatized as a child, and may adversely influence adult relationships.

The practice of psychoanalysis

Despite the differences between the various psychoanalytic theories, they all share a number of therapeutic goals, including gaining insight into the nature of the original trauma and bringing troubling material to consciousness so the individual can cope with it without the use of ego defence mechanisms. By removing the need for the ego to engage its defence mechanisms, the symptoms may be 'cured'.

Freudian psychoanalysis

Freud experimented with a number of therapeutic techniques, including hypnosis and a form of suggestion in which he sat behind the patient, held their head in his hands, exerted mild pressure, and suggested that the troubling material would be 'released' when he released the physical pressure. He stopped using these methods as he came to believe that the patient–therapist relationship was critical to good psychotherapy. Instead, he used the process of free association. This involved the client speaking aloud whatever came to mind, with the therapist making no conscious effort to monitor or censor their speech. To facilitate the process, the client lay down so they were unable to see the therapist's face and could not be guided by any facial expressions resulting from their flow of thoughts.

Through free association, clients may remember traumatic or problematic childhood events. However, given the ego's use of defence mechanisms, such revelations are unlikely. Instead, the therapist is guided more by what the client does *not* say than what they do. Absences, where the client is unable to think of a word or finish a sentence, or abrupt changes in topic may indicate the proximity of sensitive issues. Errors, in which a client may mean to say one thing and actually say something different (the so-called 'Freudian slip') may also be indicative of sensitive issues that the therapist would then explore more deeply.

Another technique used by Freud involved the interpretation of dreams, which he considered 'the Royal Road to the unconscious'. An example can be found in Freud's (1900) interpretation of the dream of one woman which included images of flowers as table decorations for a party. When asked to freely associate to the elements in her dream, she associated *violet* with *violate*, a word carrying both sexual and aggressive connotations. Freud interpreted the flowers as symbols of fertility and the birthday as a symbol of an impending birth or pregnancy. Accordingly, her dreams symbolized her desire to become impregnated by her fiancé.

A third source of information about childhood experiences can be found through examination of the client's relationship with their therapist. Freud suggested that a client may develop strong positive or negative feelings towards their therapist, a process known as transference. Positive transference may result in the client becoming dependent on the therapist or even falling in love with them. Negative transference includes resentment and anger. According to Freud, these feelings reflect those held for significant others earlier in the client's life. If they fall in love with their therapist, for example, this may mean they have failed to resolve an earlier oedipal conflict. Freud used the transference process in two ways: first, as a diagnostic process, and second, for resolving earlier conflicts by 'working through' the transference process. Freud contended that once having achieved insight, the individual may still need to work through the issues raised by an understanding of the trauma. In a process known as catharsis, the individual is encouraged to expresses the emotions previously damped down by the defence mechanisms.

Contemporary psychoanalysis

Classical psychoanalysis was extremely lengthy. Freud preferred to see clients six times a week, and even 'mild' cases were seen for three sessions a week. In addition, because psychoanalysis used free association to bring insight into the clients' problems, and there may have been weeks or even months between sessions in which significant insights were attained, analysis took many months or even years. More recent versions of psychoanalysis tend to be shorter, typically lasting fewer than 25 sessions. They have three distinct phases: beginning, an active phase, and termination. Beginning involves assessment, developing a therapeutic alliance and preparing the client for therapy. In the active phase, the therapist determines the direction of therapy and the issues addressed within it. Strategies may involve the use of interpretation of current feelings in terms of past experiences, and the elicitation of emotions experienced at the time of any trauma. Issues of transference are deliberately minimized, for example, by discouraging client dependence. The end of therapy is a negotiated process, in which issues of loss and separation are considered and dealt with.

Most people who take part in psychoanalysis in Britain do so by seeking private therapy. Not surprisingly, most find it a useful experience:

> I found the process remarkably useful. No one to judge you, no one to comment – you don't even have to talk to anyone. It provides a space for me without pressure to explore issues that are important to me that I cannot speak – quite literally – to anyone else about. I feel my unhappiness stems from my poor relationship with my parents – and this has provided me with a means to explore this, and disentangle some of the issues that confuse me about this time.

2.2 Behavioural approaches

The roots of behaviour therapy lie in the theories of classical and operant conditioning developed in the early to mid-twentieth century by Pavlov ([1927] 1960) and Skinner (1953). Although differing considerably in their explanations of behaviour, both theories held that:

- behaviour is determined by external events
- past learning experiences drive present behaviour
- behavioural change can be achieved through direct manipulation of external events; there is no need to explore or change the individual's 'psyche' or 'inner world'
- the principles of learning are subject to scientific exploration and hold across all species: studies in rats inform our understanding of human behaviour.

Classical conditioning

Classical conditioning was initially explored by Pavlov's work on the salivatory response of dogs. During his experiments he noticed that, on occasion, his dogs would salivate *before* being given food, a response he termed 'psychic salivation'. Exploration of the process through which this occurred led to the discovery of what is now termed classical conditioning. Pavlov considered salivation to be a basic reflex to the presence of food that required no learning: an unconditioned response to an unconditioned stimulus. The novel element of Pavlov's work was that he noted that other salient stimuli present at the time of the elicitation of the unconditioned response subsequently come to elicit the same behaviours: in learning theory jargon, an initially neutral stimulus becomes a conditioned stimulus and elicits a conditioned response, identical to the unconditioned one. Learning the association between the neutral stimulus and unconditioned stimulus may take several pairings. Repeated presentation of the conditioned stimulus in the absence of the unconditioned stimulus will result in a gradual fading of response to it, a process known as extinction.

The link between these processes and emotional disorders was made when it became clear that conditioning experiences may influence emotional as well as behavioural responses to stimuli. Behavioural explanations of phobias, for example, assumed that they result from a conditioning experience in which the inappropriately feared object or situation was associated with the experience of fear or anxiety at some time in the past. The conditioned stimulus subsequently evokes a conditioned fear response. The conditioning process can be so powerful when acute fear is experienced, that it may require only one conditioning experience to result in a long-term fear response that is difficult to extinguish. Being in a car crash, for example, may result in a phobic reaction to being in a car, and subsequent avoidance of being in a car or driving. This response has three components: a *behavioural element* involving avoidance or escape from the feared object, a high state of *physiological arousal* evident through a variety of symptoms including physical tension, increased startle response, tremor or sweating, and the *emotion* of anxiety and fear.

The most famous early example of the conditioning of a phobic response was Watson and Rayner's (1920) conditioning of 'Little Albert'. Eleven-month-old Albert was a hospitalized child who had a fear of furry animals induced through the experimental association of loud noises at the same time as being given a rabbit to play with. Over time, he developed a conditioned fear (phobic reaction) to the presence of furry animals, a fear which generalized to similar-looking stimuli including balls of cotton, white fur and a Santa Claus mask. Sadly, although Albert was subsequently allowed to play with the toys in the absence of the loud noises, he was discharged from hospital with his phobia intact – an outcome now deemed ethically unacceptable.

Operant conditioning

In contrast to the reflexive behaviour associated with classical conditioning, operant conditioning attempts to explain behaviours that are voluntary and purposive. Skinner's basic premise was that behaviour that is rewarded (reinforced) will increase in frequency or be repeated; that which is not rewarded or is punished will decrease in frequency or not be repeated. His definition of a reinforcer was behavioural: that which is observed to increase the frequency or strength of a behaviour. He made no assumptions about internal mediating processes such as liking, pleasure or enjoyment.

Skinner distinguished between two types of reinforcer: *primary reinforcers*, such as food and water that have innate biological significance, and *conditioned reinforcers*, that have become associated with these primary reinforcers through a complex process of classical conditioning. In this way, reinforcers such as attention and social interaction, which are associated with the primary reinforcer of food and drink for young children, take on reinforcing properties in themselves.

Operant processes have been implicated in the development of a number of mental disorders. Lewinsohn et al. (1979), for example, considered depression to be the result of an individual being removed from a reward system they had previously occupied. Conversely, Seligman (1975) considered depression to arise from a failure to avoid negative stimuli within the environment. His theory stemmed from a series of studies in which animals received electric shocks they were either able or unable to avoid. Animals that could avoid the shocks seemed to experience no ill-effects. Those that could not, exhibited what Seligman termed learned helplessness. They were apathetic and, even when they were in conditions where they could avoid shocks, made no attempt to do so. This was seen as analogous to some elements of depression.

Combining classical and operant conditioning

The classical conditioning model of phobias so far considered is adequate in its description of the acquisition of anxiety and phobias. However, it is less able to explain why they are maintained over long periods, as repeated exposure to a feared object or situation in the absence of any negative consequences should lead to a reduction of anxiety through the process of extinction. Mowrer's (1947) two-factor theory combined both classical and operant process to provide an explanation of this phenomenon. He noted that once a phobic response is established through classical conditioning processes, the affected individual tends to avoid the feared stimulus. This has two consequences. First, it prevents the classical conditioning process of extinction, as the individual does not experience the conditioned stimulus under conditions of safety. Second, because avoidance itself produces feelings of relief (it is reinforcing), the avoidance response is strengthened by operant conditioning processes. In this way, anxiety is potentially maintained over long periods.

Behaviour therapy

Behaviour therapy assumes behaviour and emotions to be governed by the laws of learning: disorders arise as a consequence of specific learning experiences and can be treated using the same principles. The type of therapy it engendered differed fundamentally from psychoanalytic therapies:

- It is directive: the therapist actively treats the client using methods based on learning principles.
- The goal of therapy is behavioural or emotional change, not personality reconstruction.
- Behaviour therapy is generally shorter than other forms of therapy.
- Interventions are condition-specific: there is no common therapeutic goal such as 'insight' or catharsis.

Classical conditioning-based interventions

Classical conditioning-based interventions were primarily developed for the treatment of anxiety disorders including phobias. Techniques include systematic desensitization and flooding. The goal of both methods is to weaken and eliminate the conditioned fear response and to condition less aversive emotional associations to the previously feared object.

Systematic desensitization

Systematic desensitization involves repeatedly exposing the client to a series of stimuli, initially somewhat distant from, and then increasingly like, the feared stimulus, while in a state of relaxation. At the beginning of the intervention, the individual is taught to relax using standardized relaxation procedures. At the same time, they construct a hierarchy of stimuli that progressively resemble the feared object or situation.

Therapy proceeds through a series of stages. In each stage, the client first relaxes and is then exposed to a stimulus within the hierarchy, starting with the most distant stimulus from the feared object or situation. On each occasion, they remain in the presence of the stimulus until they feel fully relaxed. This process is repeated several times until the stimulus no longer elicits an anxiety response. They then progress along the hierarchy, repeating the same procedures until they are able to cope in the presence of their feared stimulus or situation. These procedures are thought to have a number of conditioning effects. First, they extinguish the fear response to the stimulus. Second, by being relaxed in the presence of the feared stimulus, a process of counter-conditioning is established in which a state of relaxation to the previously feared stimulus (see Box 2.1) is conditioned. Of note is that it can be difficult to set up a graded exposure programme using real stimuli. They may be difficult to obtain or control – such as snakes or driving in traffic. In such circumstances, the 'traditional' approach was to establish and go through an imaginal hierarchy. Now, technology allows us to produce a much more immersive experience, and the use of virtual reality allows the development of closely controlled and constructed hierarchies not previously thought possible. Chapter 8 considers the use of such a programme in the context of a car phobia.

Box 2.1 Ruth's spider phobia: an example of systematic desensitization

The image of an individual with a spider phobia is a person who, when they see a spider, becomes anxious and jittery, and usually asks for someone to remove it from their presence. But for Ruth, the problem was much greater. From Spring to Autumn her fear of spiders was so strong that she would not enter a room without someone first checking that there were no spiders in it. Similarly, she would not go into the hall or stairs of her house without a family member making checks. As a consequence, she remained restricted to one room in her house, unless there was someone in the house to check 'safety'. If she saw a spider, she hyperventilated, panicked, and would run as far away as possible from it.

Ruth entered a programme of systematic desensitization in the Spring. She was taught to relax using a programme of deep muscle relaxation. At the same time, she developed a hierarchy of stimuli to be used in a desensitization programme. She also determined her desired end-point of the programme, which was to be able to enter a room where there may be a spider without undue anxiety and to be able to kill any spiders she noticed in the room. The initial hierarchy she and her therapist constructed included the following stimuli:

1 a pencil-drawn line, resembling the leg of a spider
2 a pencil oval, resembling the body of a spider
3 a pencil-drawn sketch of a spider
4 a picture of an actual spider
5 a dead spider in a jar
6 a dead spider on a nearby table
7 a live spider in a jar
8 a live spider constrained by the therapist
9 a live, unconstrained spider.

Ruth worked through this hierarchy over a period of weekly meetings. On each occasion, she used the relaxation techniques and was exposed to the relevant stimulus within the hierarchy on several occasions. Each time, she remained in the presence of the stimulus until she was fully relaxed and calm. The stimulus was removed and then re-presented, and the procedure repeated, until there was good evidence that she was fully relaxed at that stage in the hierarchy and she felt confident to move to the next stage.

Once she was able to be relaxed in the presence of a live spider, Ruth began a second hierarchy:

1 walking into a room with a constrained spider in it;
2 walking into a room with the possibility of an unconstrained spider in it, remaining by the door;

3 walking into a room in which she knew there was a spider and killing it with a heavy object;

4 walking into a room with the possibility of an unconstrained spider in it, and being able to sit down in the room for several minutes.

Most people with a phobia of spiders would not require such a gradual or extended treatment programme. Nevertheless, this programme provides an example of the use of systematic desensitization.

Flooding

Systematic desensitization provides a gradual approach to the treatment of phobias and is user-friendly, but relatively slow. Flooding involves a diametrically opposite approach. In it, clients are exposed directly to their most feared stimulus and encouraged to remain with it until they no longer experience any fear, a process that may take an hour or more. The therapy is based on the principles of *habituation*. We cannot sustain a fear response for prolonged periods of time – physical exhaustion results in a diminution of a fear response even under circumstances that initially provoke high levels of fear. Accordingly, even though initial levels of anxiety or fear may be extremely high, if the client remains in the feared situation sufficiently long, they will experience a reduction in anxiety to normal levels. This low level of fear is then associated with the previously feared stimulus. Repeated flooding is usually necessary to fully extinguish some fear responses. Flooding can be an effective form of therapy (Wolpe 1982). However, many therapists prefer to use desensitization methods as they do not provoke the high levels of client distress associated with flooding. Nor do they run the risk of the recipient leaving before extinction of the fear is achieved, something that may actually add to their problems as avoidance of the feared stimulus is once more reinforced.

2.3 Cognitive approaches

While behavioural therapies achieved (and still do achieve) some notable successes, by the 1970s, conditioning theories of the acquisition of fear and other emotional responses were finding it increasingly difficult to account for emerging experimental and clinical findings (Davey 1997):

- Many people with a phobia were unable to identify any traumatic conditioning incident.
- Many common phobias were to relatively benign stimuli (such as spiders).
- Many common phobias were to stimuli rarely if ever directly encountered by most individuals (for example, snakes).
- By contrast, rates of phobias to many frequently encountered and potentially frightening stimuli (such as traffic) were relatively low.
- Phobias tend to 'run' in families.

Seligman (1970) provided one explanation of these findings. He suggested that some basic anxieties may be biologically 'hardwired'. This has survival advantages, in that avoidance of small, quick and possibly dangerous animals is likely to be of enormous benefit to individuals who live in a dangerous and wild environment. These instinctual reactions become problematic when we no longer live in these conditions, but because they are hardwired, we find it difficult to stop responding in this basic way.

While Seligman's theory gave some support to the behavioural model, other findings made it increasingly difficult to maintain purely behavioural models of fear acquisition. One of the most problematic findings stemmed from cases such as the individual whose initial fear of beetles generalized to a number of other stimuli including Volkswagen cars and the Beatles pop group (Carr 1974). While behavioural theory acknowledged the potential for the generalization of a fear response to stimuli that were similar to the phobic stimulus, this was based on the physical characteristics of the related stimuli. What was clear from cases such as this was that the associations between feared stimuli were of a semantic nature: the development of fear involved cognitive processes.

Social learning theory

At the same time as these problems in explaining clinical phenomena became evident, other theorists were beginning to explore the role of cognitive processes in directing behaviour. One influential theory to stem from this period was social learning theory (Bandura 1977). This suggested that we can learn fear responses without having direct experience of the feared object ourselves. Instead, fear can be acquired from observation of other people's responses, through a process known as vicarious learning. People with a fear of flying, for example, may develop this fear as a result of seeing air crashes on the television or hearing accounts of people describing their fear experienced during turbulence. Social learning theory also provided a cognitive explanation of why phobias run in families. Again, this involves learning fear from observation of other family members: children may learn a fear of spiders, for example, from observation of their parents' responses to them. Bandura also provided a cognitive explanation of the therapeutic mechanisms of systematic desensitization and flooding: reductions in anxiety were the result of the individual's increasing confidence – or self-efficacy as Bandura termed it – in their ability to cope with the presence of the feared object.

2.4 Emerging clinical models

Further pressure to integrate cognitive elements into behavioural interventions stemmed from the emerging cognitive therapies of Aaron Beck (1977) and Albert Ellis (1977). Both clinicians assumed that our cognitive response to events – not the events themselves – determines our mood, and that mental health problems are a consequence of 'faulty' or 'irrational' thinking. Emotional disorders result from *misinterpretations* of environmental events. These thoughts impact directly on our mood, our behaviour and our physiological state. Ellis referred to this process as the *A-B-C theory* of personality functioning, where:

- A refers to an activating event: something that triggers an emotional response
- C is the emotional or behavioural reaction to that event

- B refers to the intervening cognitive processing, the individual's beliefs about the event that always occur between A and C.

Beck referred to the thoughts that drive negative emotions as automatic negative assumptions. They come to mind automatically as the individual's first response to a particular situation and without logic or grounding in reality. Despite this, their very automaticity means they are unchallenged and taken as true. He identified two levels of cognitions:

- *Surface cognitions*: thoughts we are aware of – the automatic negative assumptions. We can access them and report them relatively easily. They influence emotions, behaviour and levels of physiological arousal.
- *Cognitive schema* (plural *schemata*): underlying our surface cognitions is a set of unconscious beliefs about ourselves and the world that influence our surface cognitions.

Beck hypothesized that our cognitive schemata develop in childhood. Some may affect an individual throughout their life. Beck suggested, for example, that people with an avoidant personality hold the fundamental belief that 'If people get close to me, they will discover the real me and would reject me – that would be intolerable.' As a consequence, they continually avoid others to prevent this catastrophe occurring. Other schemata, such as those underlying depression, may impact only at certain times.

To explain why people with some negative self-schemata are not in a permanent state of emotional distress or sadness, Beck suggested that some vulnerable individuals are able to override negative schemata for much of the time. However, when they encounter stressful circumstances in adulthood, in particular those that echo previous childhood experiences (divorce or separation, for example, reflecting earlier experiences of parental rejection), underlying negative schemata are activated, influence their surface cognitions, and lead to depression or other emotional disorders.

Evidence of the activation of underlying schemata at times of low mood can be found in experimental work reported by, for example, Miranda and Gross (1997). They studied the different reactions of people with and without a history of depression when asked to rate themselves on a series of self-descriptive adjectives either before or after listening to sad music designed to lower mood. They found no differences in self-ratings on measures taken before listening to the music. However, after listening to the sad music, participants who had previously experienced a period of depression endorsed more negative attributes than those who had not been depressed, a finding they interpreted as indicating the presence of underlying negative cognitive schemata that were activated by the induction of low mood (see Chapter 8 for further discussion of this issue).

Cognitive behavioural therapy

Acceptance of the role of cognitions in mental health disorders did not lead to the wholesale rejection of behavioural techniques. There was a therapeutic evolution rather than revolution, and behavioural and cognitive techniques were, and remain, used together under the rubric of cognitive or cognitive behavioural therapy (CBT). That said, the initial goal of CBT was primarily one of cognitive change, albeit through the use of both behavioural and cognitive techniques (but see Chapter 3 to see how this perspective may be changing in more recent advances in cognitive behaviour therapy). Early CBT had a number of elements:

- Its primary goal was to change cognitive distortions.
- It was usually short term – at least in comparison to psychoanalysis.
- It maintained a large behavioural component.
- Therapy focused on the here-and-now, although exploration of cognitive schemata may have required some investigation of past events.
- It was directive: the therapist was active in identifying cognitive errors and helping the client change them.
- It focused on skills (cognitive, behavioural) taught to the individual to help them cope better with their emotional problem. Meichenbaum (1985) referred to the therapist as 'educator'.

Beck, Ellis and other early cognitive therapists argued that cognitions did not follow the laws of learning. Ellis (1977) described faulty cognitions as 'magical', Beck (1977) described them as 'automatic'. This meant that they required a different type of intervention than those aimed at behavioural change, which did follow the laws of conditioning. This involved direct attempts to change both surface cognitions and more fundamental schemata through logical disputation: people with phobias could dispute the rationality of their fears, depressed people could dispute the reality of their negative expectations, and so on. In doing so, their fear or depression would dissipate.

Cognitive techniques

Perhaps the simplest method of directly changing cognitions is known as self-instruction training (Meichenbaum 1985). This involves interrupting the flow of negative 'stressogenic' thoughts by replacing them with pre-prepared realistic or 'coping' ones. These typically fall into one of two categories: reminders to use any stress-coping techniques the person has practised, and reminders that the individual can cope effectively with the situation ('You can cope with this . . . you have before . . . remember to relax . . .').

A more complex approach, known as cognitive challenge, involves identifying and challenging the reality of the negative assumptions an individual is making. In this, the person is taught to 'catch' their thoughts and identify the association between thoughts, emotions and behaviour. They then learn to treat their immediate negative cognitive response to particular situations as hypotheses or guesses, not reality; to challenge their veracity, and to replace them with more appropriate and less emotionally disturbing thoughts ('I'm feeling faint. I'm going to pass out and make a fool of myself' versus 'Well, I've felt this way before and nothing bad happened – It won't happen this time . . .'). This skill can be practised within the therapy session, before being used in the 'real world'.

Ways of identifying and changing negative assumptions can be taught through the Socratic method or *guided discovery* (Beck 1977). This involves the therapist helping the client to identify distorted patterns of thinking that are contributing to their problems and encouraging them to consider and evaluate different sources of information that provide evidence of the reality or unreality of the beliefs they hold. One technique developed specifically to help identify and challenge core beliefs is known as the *downward arrow technique* (Beck et al. 1979). When clients express what seem to be inappropriate thoughts or reactions to events, the downward arrow technique can be used to identify distortions in core beliefs that are contributing to their problems. Key questions include:

- What is your concern about . . . ?
- What would the implications be . . . ?
- What would the consequences be . . . ?
- What would the ultimate consequences be . . . ?

One example of their use is provided by this extract from a session with a problem drinker adapted from Beck et al. (1993):

Therapist:	You feel quite strongly that you need to be 'relaxed' by alcohol when you go to a party. What is your concern about being sober?
Client:	I wouldn't enjoy myself and I wouldn't be much fun to be with.
T:	What would be the implications of that?
C:	Well, people wouldn't talk to me.
T:	And what would be the consequence of that?
C:	I need to have people like me. My job depends on it. If I can't entertain people at a party, them I'm no good at my job . . .
T:	So, what happens if that is the case?
C:	Well, I guess I lose my job!
T:	So, you lose your job because you didn't get drunk at a party?
C:	Well, put like that, I think I may have not had it in the right perspective.

Here, the downward arrow technique has been used both to identify some of the client's core beliefs and to get them to reconsider the accuracy of those beliefs by showing how disproportionate they were.

Behavioural strategies

Behavioural interventions form an important element of many interventions. Two commonly used strategies in depression, for example, are behavioural activation and behavioural challenge. The first is usually targeted at people who are significantly depressed, and involves increasing levels of activity in a planned progressive manner: planning times to get out of bed, go to the shops, and so on. For those who are less depressed, it may involve engaging in more social or 'pleasant' activities. Behavioural challenge involves setting up behavioural experiments within the therapy session or as homework that directly test the cognitive beliefs that clients may hold, in the expectation that negative beliefs are disconfirmed and more positive ones affirmed. In the above case, for example, the individual may be encouraged to go to a party and try not to drink, to see whether or not this has the disastrous consequences they originally hypothesized. Success in these tasks is thought to bring about long-term cognitive, behavioural and emotional changes. One interesting behavioural challenge used by a colleague, Helen Barker, in the treatment of two people with schizophrenia involved simultaneously testing their assumptions about their unusual abilities. One felt that their thoughts were being 'broadcast' and heard by other people: the other believed that they could hear what other people were thinking. As a test of both their beliefs, both people were put in a room. One was asked to look at cards often used to test extrasensory perception (ESP), and asked to broadcast an image of each of the cards he looked at.

The other was asked to write down the images that he was 'receiving'. Of course, the received images bore no relationship to the images that were actually being 'broadcast': so both sets of beliefs were challenged by this particular behavioural experiment.

Relaxation techniques

Some emotional disorders, such as anxiety and pathological anger, have a large physiological component varying from high levels of physical tension to hyperventilation (see Chapter 3). Chronic stress may also be associated with high levels of physical tension, which may not be so noticeable but nevertheless result in chronic tiredness, poor sleep and an increased vulnerability to a variety of health problems. Relaxation provides a mechanism for moderating this drive.

Relaxation skills enable the individual to relax as much as is possible at times of both acute and chronic stress. This moderates the unpleasant symptoms experienced at such times as well as increasing actual or perceived control over the stress response – a valuable outcome in itself. The relaxation process most commonly taught is a derivative of Jacobson's deep muscle relaxation technique. This involves alternately tensing and relaxing muscle groups throughout the body in an ordered sequence. As the individual becomes more skilled, the emphasis of practice shifts towards relaxation without prior tension, or relaxing specific muscle groups while using others, in order to mimic the circumstances in which relaxation will be used in 'real life'. The order in which the muscles are relaxed varies, but a typical exercise may involve the following stages (the tensing procedure is described in parentheses):

- hands and forearms (making a fist)
- upper arms (touching fingers to shoulder)
- shoulders and lower neck (pulling up shoulders)
- back of neck (touching chin to chest)
- lips (pushing them together)
- forehead (frowning)
- abdomen/chest (holding deep breath)
- abdomen (tensing stomach muscles)
- legs and feet (push heel away, pull toes to point at head: not lifting leg).

Monitoring physical tension   Where high levels of tension are clearly associated with specific stimuli, an individual may quickly learn to use relaxation techniques to help them relax at such times. Where people are more chronically stressed and perhaps less aware of any excess tension, learning to relax effectively may involve a more structured approach. This may begin by the individual learning to monitor their levels of physical tension throughout the day. Initially, this provides an educative effect, helping them identify how tense they are during the day and what triggers their tension. As they move through the practice stage, monitoring may help identify further triggers and provide clues as to when the use of relaxation procedures may be particularly useful. This phase may entail the use of a 'Tension diary' in which the individual typically records their level of tension on some form of numerical scale (0 = no tension, 10 = very high levels of tension) at regular intervals through the day.

In vivo relaxation   After a period of monitoring tension and learning relaxation techniques, individuals can begin to integrate them into their daily lives. At this stage, relaxation involves the individual monitoring and reducing tension to appropriate levels while engaging in their everyday activities or at times of acute stress. Relaxation is best used initially at times of relatively low levels of excess tension. The consistent use of relaxation techniques at these times can prepare the person to cope with times of greater tension. An alternative strategy that many find useful involves relaxing at regular intervals (such as coffee breaks) throughout the day.

Stress inoculation training

The exact nature of any cognitive behavioural intervention will differ according to the present-ing problem and resources of the individual in therapy. A number of these differing approaches are considered in the chapters in Part 2 of the book. However, one simple approach combining the various therapy components was developed by Meichenbaum (1985) in his approach to treating general stress. He suggested that the various strands of CBT could be combined in a simple iterative process. He combined these strands in two ways. First, he suggested that when an individual is facing a stressor, they need to keep three processes under review: (1) check that their behaviour is appropriate to the circumstances; (2) maintain relaxation; and (3) give themselves appropriate self-talk. Second, he suggested that where a particular stressor can be anticipated, the opportunity should be taken to rehearse these actions before the event itself. Once in the situation, the planned strategies should be enacted. Finally, time should be given to review what occurred and the successes or failures to be learned from this after the stressor is over.

Experiencing cognitive behavioural therapy

Here are some views about the experience of CBT:

> I found it really helpful – but it was difficult. The therapist asked me to, like, question my thoughts. I found that really difficult. I couldn't really work out what I was thinking . . . let alone try to ques-tion them! But I remember one appointment when we talked through how I felt when I went on holiday, and I felt really sad at the beginning of the session. By the end I felt really good about myself! And I began to see how thinking about things differently could help me feel better. In the end I found this part of therapy really useful.

> I found the relaxation really good . . . I really enjoyed it. Yeah, it worked well – the rest wasn't easy. But I really valued the support of my therapist. I actually think that that was the most important thing I got out of therapy.

> I found it good to take a gradual approach to dealing with my panics. The therapist was very good as they listened to my concerns, and gave me advice about what to do to stop me panicking. I don't think I would have liked just talking – and telling her about my childhood, and so on – I can't see the point in that.

These comments reflect some of the problems that people face in CBT and the importance of the relationship between client and therapist, even in the relatively structured use of cognitive behavioural techniques.

Leichsenring, F., Salzer, S., Jaeger, U. et al. (2009) Short-term psychodynamic psychotherapy and cognitive-behavioral therapy in generalized anxiety disorder: a randomized, controlled trial. *American Journal of Psychiatry*, 166: 8755–81.

The authors note that although CBT is recognized as an effective treatment of generalized anxiety disorder, fewer studies have addressed the outcome of alternative therapies, including short-term psychodynamic psychotherapy. This study set out to rectify this deficit by comparing the effectiveness of CBT with short-term psychodynamic psychotherapy in the treatment of generalized anxiety disorder.

Method

Participants

Fifty-seven participants were adults with a primary diagnosis of generalized anxiety disorder, established using the Anxiety Disorders Interview Schedule – Revised. Exclusion criteria included any history of psychosis, neurological disorder or alchol dependence. Six dropped out of the study during treatment due to problems in the therapeutic relationship (n = 1), moving to another city (n = 5). Two dropped out at six-month follow-up, and received additional psychotherapy, one developed cancer. Most (81 per cent) participants were women, and their mean age was 42.5 years. Nearly half had received some form of psychotherapy in the past, and 72 per cent had some degree of **comorbidity** with other disorders.

The interventions

Participants were randomly assigned to one of two conditions comprising 30, hour-long, sessions of CBT or short-term psychodynamic therapy (STPD). The interventions were manualized (e.g. followed a set content each session). Cognitive behavioural therapy included relaxation training, problem solving, planning of recreational activities, and homework involving participants approaching feared situations. Short-term psychodynamic therapy provided a 'positive therapeutic alliance [to] provide a corrective emotional experience and allow the patient to approach feared situations'. Therapists encouraged participants to approach feared situations, 'consistent with Freud's recommendations for the treatment of phobia'. Participants completed an average of 29 sessions in both conditions. Sessions were audiotaped and randomly and independently assessed to ensure their content was appropriate to the condition.

Outcome measures

Participants were assessed at baseline, the end of treatment, and at six-month follow-up. Key outcomes were:

- The Hamilton Anxiety Rating Scale: HRS
- Penn State Worry Questionnaire: PSWQ
- State-Trait Anxiety Inventory: STAI
- Beck Anxiety Inventory: BAI

Results

The two groups did not differ at baseline on any clinical or demographic variable, or levels of drop-out during the study. Analysis involved repeated measures ANOVA, utilizing an **intention to treat** approach. Mean scores on key outcomes at each time are reported in Table 2.3.

Table 2.3			
	Baseline	End therapy	6-month
Hamilton Anxiety Rating scale			
CBT intervention	25.9	12.8	12.5*
STPD intervention	25.0	14.2	14.9*
Penn State Worry Questionnaire			
CBT intervention	63.5	49.9	50.3* +
STPD intervention	58.9	52.8	53.6*
State-Trait Anxiety-Trait			
CBT intervention	58.9	43.4	43.2* +
STPD intervention	55.7	47.2	47.8*
Beck Anxiety Inventory			
CBT intervention	24.6	9.8	10.1*
STPD intervention	17.8	8.9	9.3*

* significant main effect
⁺ significant treatment x time interaction

Discussion

The severity of the problems experienced by the participants in this trial were similar to those in other reported trials, as was the effectiveness of both interventions. The short-term psychotherapy fared well against the CBT, although the latter proved more effective in reducing levels of worry and, in the long run, trait anxiety. The authors also note that the trends in the numerical data favoured the CBT group and those measures where no statistical differences between the groups were found, allowing for the possibility that the small size of the sample did not allow such differences to become statistically significant. Larger studies are clearly needed. The one specific effect seems to be on levels of worry, which is a key target of CBT, and not psychoanalytic therapy. This may give this approach an advantage in this population.

2.5 Humanistic approaches

The humanistic school of psychology began in the 1950s in the USA. Its major figures include Carl Rogers (1961) and Abraham Maslow (1970). It developed largely as a reaction against both psychoanalysis and behaviourism, and formed a 'Third Force' countering both approaches. Humanists considered psychoanalysis to be too pessimistic as it emphasized the pathological, irrational, unconscious fragmentation of personality. Behaviourism was rejected because of its mechanistic approach to understanding the human condition. By contrast, humanistic psychologists wanted a psychology that focused on healthy, rational, higher motivations.

The approach has two common elements:

- Behaviour is understood in terms of the subjective experience of the individual: the *phenomenological* perspective. This accepts the subjective experience of the individual as a valid source of information about their values, motives and the meaning of their behaviour.
- Behaviour is not constrained by either past experiences or current circumstances. The individual has 'free will' and makes behavioural choices independent of past learning history or the unconscious influence of innate drives.

Models of the individual and neurosis

Rogers

Carl Rogers (1961) was one of the leading humanists. His theory of the individual has been termed a *self-theory*, in that it focused on the individual's self-concept and their subjective experience of the world. His basic premise was that all individuals have an innate drive to grow, develop and enhance their abilities in ways they choose: a process he called self-actualization. This 'actualizing tendency' stimulates creativity and leads us to seek new challenges and skills that motivate healthy growth. When the individual is in touch with their actualizing tendency, their behaviour is directed in ways that foster positive growth and happiness. When they are not, the result is sadness, anxiety or depression.

Rogers also noted that we live in subjective worlds of our own creation, formed by a process of perception: the *phenomenal field*. In many ways, this maps onto reality, but it may also be distorted and inaccurate. Nevertheless, our reaction to events, be they emotional or behavioural, is based on our perception of the world, not 'objective' reality. Within this framework, the most significant element is the sense of self, our understanding of 'who we are'. Rogers considered the self to be constantly in a process of forming and reforming. We experience it as unchanging only as a result of biases and selectivity in attending to those elements of our phenomenal field that are consistent with our prior experience. Our sense of self is influenced by past experiences, our present situation and expectations of the future. However, unlike the psychoanalysts, he argued that the past is only as important as the individual chooses to make it, through conscious choice. Free will allows us to break away from the past, and for our behaviour and emotions to be related more to the present, and perhaps the future.

Although the individual acknowledges their *actual self*, our actualizing tendency drives us towards another version of the self: the *ideal self*. This reflects who we would like to be: the goals and aspirations of our lives. Like the self, this is a changing and evolving concept. The degree to which the actual and ideal selves match each other has a profound effect on our emotions and behaviour. When the two are relatively similar (what Rogers termed congruent), we experience positive emotions. When the two are incongruent, we experience sadness and other negative emotions, and the actualizing process is inhibited.

For many, the beginnings of incongruence lie in childhood. Rogers argued that the way parental love and approval are given has a strong impact on the developing person. Subtle elements of parent–child interactions contribute to the development of pathology. One important process, known as *conditional positive regard*, occurs when parents simultaneously show their disapproval both of bad behaviour and of the child ('Your behaviour is bad, and I don't love you when you behave in this way'). Love and approval are granted only if the child behaves in a way that their parents want them to. As a result, children adopt their parents' 'conditions of worth'. That is, the child comes to associate their self-worth with their behaviour, and begins to adopt behaviours that are valued by their parents. The child begins to internalize the goals of his or her parents into its ideal self, and work towards achieving them rather than his or her own goals and aspirations. As a result, the child fails to progress towards self-actualization.

According to Rogers, three elements of the individual's interactions with others can facilitate their move towards self-actualization:

- *Unconditional positive regard*: acceptance and love that are not contingent upon the individual behaving in required manner: 'I do not approve of your behaviour . . . but I love you nonetheless'.
- *Genuineness*: an environment in which the individual is able to freely express their own sense of self, rather than playing a role or hiding behind a façade.
- *Empathy*: an environment in which the individual is involved with people who can understand the world from their viewpoint – who share their phenomenal field.

Maslow

Rogers's work and beliefs about the development of the individual largely stemmed from his therapeutic work, which is considered later in the chapter. Others, such as Abraham Maslow, contributed to humanistic theory but not to the development of therapy. Like Rogers, he believed that the individual strives throughout their life to achieve their human potential: to achieve *self-actualization*.

Maslow (1970) believed that we are motivated to fulfil a variety of needs, which are hierarchically structured, starting with basic biological imperatives such as obtaining warmth and food. Self-actualization, he argued, can be achieved only by obtaining the needs of the highest tier of the hierarchy, but the individual can progress up the hierarchy only if all the needs of each subordinate level are achieved. As a result, the individual is motivated to meet the needs within the different levels of the hierarchy and to progress upwards towards self-actualization. The hierarchy of needs described by Maslow had the following levels:

- *Physiological*: including food, air, sleep, sex, and so on.
- *Safety*: including both physical and psychological safety – stability, social order, and so on.

- *Love and belongingness*: giving and receiving acceptance and affection.
- *Esteem*: feelings of self-respect, competence, and receiving the regard of others.

Once the basic needs of biological and physical security are met, the individual can engage in behaviours that allow them to express their potential for growth and to use their capacities to the fullest. Maslow referred to the needs at this level as *meta-needs*: those which are based on a desire to grow. The hierarchy is not rigid, and may differ across individuals or time, but holds for most people, most of the time.

Maslow considered a number of experiences to be related to self-actualization. He termed the most profound and vibrant level of being a *peak experience*, a period of intense emotion when we really feel what it is to be alive. Other, longer-term experiences of heightened awareness can also exist. In what Maslow termed a *plateau experience*, the individual may feel a sustained heightened appreciation of life over months or even years. These two factors are related to self-actualization but are not synonymous with it. According to Maslow, it is possible to have both these experiences without integrating them into the process of self-actualization. Conversely, some individuals who live productive, self-actualized lives may never experience the shift of awareness associated with the peak or plateau experiences. Self-actualization results from a balance of needs being met and the individual achieving the 'full use' of their abilities, not just a transcendent episode.

Maslow considered self-actualizing to be something the individual actively works towards, but is achieved only by a small minority. It is not an inevitable outcome, and the individual may have to overcome obstacles or make choices that progress them towards self-actualization. A significant source of deviation from this process may be the culture the individual is situated within. Maslow contended that the Western culture places great emphasis on material sources of gratification, which satisfy physiological and safety needs, but not the higher ones of love, affection and esteem.

Humanistic therapy

There are several schools of humanistic therapy, with the *client-centred therapy* of Rogers being pre-eminent. Rogers considered pathology to be the result of a deviation from the self-actualizing process, usually as a consequence of experiencing conditional positive regard. Therapy involves the individual realigning with their own actualizing tendency.

Early in the history of Rogers's therapy, he described his approach as non-directive. The role of the therapist was to help the individual explore issues relevant to them and their development, with an equal relationship between therapist and client giving the client control over the issues explored. However, careful analysis of therapy transcripts by Truax (1966) indicated that rather than act as a neutral facilitator, the therapist (in this case Rogers himself) unconsciously reinforced statements that indicated progress on the client's part, and ignored those that were less positive. Acknowledging the impossibility of total neutrality by the therapist, Rogers abandoned the term non-directive, but still emphasized that therapy should focus on the development of the individual, not the interpretations or actions of the therapist. The name 'client-centred therapy' (later changed to person-centred) was deliberately chosen by Rogers to contrast with the medicalization and power structure implied by use of the term 'patient' by the psychoanalysts.

The goal of person-centred therapy is to provide an environment in which the individual can identify their own life goals and how they wish to determine them: to place them on the pathway to self-actualization. Rogers stated that therapy does not rely on techniques or doing things *to* the client. Rather, the quality of the interpersonal encounter is the most significant element in determining effectiveness. The goal of the therapist is to provide a setting in which the individual is not judged but is free to explore new ways of being. That is, therapy provides the conditions necessary for growth identified earlier. To achieve this, the therapist must have three characteristics:

- they are integrated and genuine in their relationship with the client
- they gain an empathic understanding of the client's perspective and communicate this to them
- they provide unconditional positive regard.

Being genuine means that the therapist shares feeling or gives feedback about how they feel as a consequence of what the client is telling them. Such feedback may be positive or negative, and shows that the therapist is human with human feelings. It may involve expressions of sadness or even anger in response to individual's stories. Empathy involves the therapist gaining an understanding of the individual's situation, problems, feelings and concerns, from *their* perspective and showing the client that they have achieved this level of understanding. The most frequent method by which this is achieved is through a process of reflecting back the therapist's understanding of the client's perspective. The final component of the therapeutic relationship is that the therapist is not judgemental, and does not repeat the past experiences of conditional positive regard.

Rogers suggested that these three therapist characteristics can facilitate a shift from the externally imposed standards of others to the identification and shift to the pathway towards self-actualization. This is thought to be achieved through a series of seven stages (Rogers 1961), in which the individual:

1 fails to acknowledge feelings, and considers personal relationships as dangerous
2 is able to describe their behaviour, but rarely their feelings, which are not 'owned'
3 can begin to describe their emotional reactions to past events, and recognize contradictions in their experience
4 develops an awareness of their current feelings, but finds it difficult to cope with them
5 begins to explore their inner life in a more meaningful and emotional way
6 is able to fully experience feelings while talking of past events
7 develops a basic trust in their own inner processes: feelings experienced with immediacy and intensity.

The therapist's actions facilitate each of these processes. Empathic feedback encourages and validates the exploration and expression of personal feelings and meanings of statements made in therapy. Acceptance and genuineness encourage the growth of trust in the self and increased risk-taking in the expression of previously withheld thoughts or emotions.

Experiencing person-centred therapy

Here are some reactions to this type of approach:

> I found it really quite disconcerting. All my therapist seemed to do was to repeat back to me things that I'd said to him. I wanted someone to suggest things and advise me what to do to help me cope with my problems. But all he seemed to do was to avoid this and say it was up to me!

> I really liked the space to sit and think – without someone on my back or things to deal with. Just thinking things through can help you change your perspective or think how to do things different. Just unloading some of the shit I'd had during the week really helped.

> I found it really useful – it gave me time to think and develop my plans for the future. Sometimes you need this sort of space, with someone you can trust and who does not sit in judgement on you – even if some of the things you say may not always put you in the best light.

These comments reflect some of the benefits that many people get from humanistic therapy. They also hint that different people may benefit from different types of therapeutic approach. The first person here, for example, may have benefited from a more structured form of therapy. Finally, they also draw attention to the non-specific benefits of therapy, which may just involve expressing negative emotions that cannot be expressed elsewhere.

2.6 How effective are the therapies?

The therapeutic approaches outlined in this chapter developed from different historical roots and at different times. Nevertheless, they are all still practised in one form or other, although the dominant method is now the cognitive behavioural approach. The reasons for this can be attributed to a number of factors, including the dominance of cognitive psychology within the broader discipline of psychology and the accessibility of the approach to both practitioner and client. However, the strongest argument for its use is the evidence of its effectiveness relative to the other therapeutic approaches.

Meta-analyses

As the number of studies of interventions in specific conditions proliferate, comparisons between the various approaches have increasingly become condition or therapy specific. However, several early meta-analyses drew together evidence of the relative effectiveness of each of the therapeutic approaches over a broad spectrum of disorders. These consistently showed cognitive behavioural approaches to be superior to both psychoanalytic and humanistic approaches. One of the most stringent meta-analyses was reported by Shapiro and Shapiro (1983), who identified 143 studies that compared different therapies both to one another and to a control condition. They found the following effect sizes: psychoanalytic therapy, 0.40; behavioural therapy, 1.06; CBT, 1.42. These compared with an effect size for placebo interventions of 0.71. These data both emphasized the relative strength of cognitive behavioural interventions and showed the analytic therapies to be marginally less effective than placebo. Smith et al. (1980) had previously found a mean effect size of 0.63 for client-centred therapy, suggesting a modest benefit. However, they also found that this did not differ markedly from that achieved by placebo treatment and was significantly less than that achieved by cognitive or behavioural treatments. More recently, Butler et al. (2006) synthesized data from 16 meta-analyses, and found large effect sizes for cognitive behavioural interventions in the treatment of depression, generalized anxiety disorder, panic disorder with or without agoraphobia, social phobia, post-traumatic stress disorder, childhood depression, schizophrenia and bulimia nervosa. They found moderate effect sizes for the treatment of marital distress, anger, childhood somatic disorders and chronic pain.

2.7 Chapter summary

1   Different psychoanalytic models of psychopathology place differing emphases on sexual and developmental issues. They are central to Freud's theory, but not those of Jung and Klein. All, however, place childhood experiences and trauma at the centre of later psychopathology.

2   Psychoanalytic therapy is aimed at gaining insight into the traumas that lay the foundations for future emotional problems. Insight may lead to catharsis, the expression of emotions previously withheld from consciousness by ego defence mechanisms.

3   Behavioural models of psychopathology have focused mainly on various types of anxiety. Phobias, for example, are considered a conditioned response to a particular stimulus, with fear maintained through operant conditioning processes.

4   Behavioural therapies are based on classical and operant conditioning paradigms. Key approaches involve flooding and systematic desensitization. These are thought to result in counter-conditioning or habituation of the fear response.

5   Cognitive understandings of psychopathology place cognitions as central to psychopathology. Therapists such as Beck have provided insight into the thought content associated with a variety of disorders.

6   Cognitive behavioural interventions involve changing inappropriate cognitions, which leads to changes in mood and behaviour.

7   Humanistic therapies aim to provide the individual with the emotional space to reorient them towards the path to self-actualization.

8   The key factor within humanistic therapy is the relationship between therapist and client, which removes conditions of worth imposed by parents and others, and allows the individual to move towards self-actualization.

9   Cognitive behavioural therapy has proven the most effective of the therapeutic approaches.

2.8 For discussion

1 Some clinical psychology training courses encourage their trainees to undertake a course of psychotherapy during their training. How might this be useful to their practice as clinicians? Should all clinicians receive some form of psychotherapy while practising?

2 One of the claims of the early behaviour therapists was that therapy could be delivered without the need of a therapist. Written and now computer-driven programmes could provide the skills and structure to treat mental health problems. Was this a realistic claim?

3 How accessible are the thoughts that influence mood, and how easy is it to change them?

4 What commonalities and differences are there between the various schools of therapy?

5 'It's not who you are, but what you do ...' Discuss this statement in the context of the treatment of mental health disorders.

2.9 Key terms

Classical conditioning the learned association between two co-occurring stimuli, such that a similar response is evoked by either.

Client a term often used to denote an individual in therapy. In contrast to words such as patient or subject, it is used to indicate the helping, non-hierarchical nature of the therapeutic relationship between therapist and individual.

Cognitive challenge the identification and disputation of maladaptive cognitions.

Cognitive schema a consistent set of beliefs that influence mood and behaviour.

Defence mechanism an unconscious mental act that prevents the individual from psychological harm.

Effect size provides a measure of the effect of an intervention; 0.2 is considered small, above 0.6 is a large effect, and between is moderate.

Ego according to Freud, the part of the personality that operates under the reality principle and works to maximize gratification within the constraints of the 'real world'.

Hyperventilation short rapid breaths that lead to low levels of carbon dioxide in the blood and physical sensations including tingling in the arms, dizziness and feelings of an inability to breathe.

Id according to Freud, the personality component driven by the basic instincts of sex and aggression.

Learned helplessness a belief that one has no control over events; results in a cessation of attempts at control.

Meta-analysis a statistical method of combining the data from several studies using similar measures that allows a more powerful analysis of the effect of the intervention than that provided by single, relatively small studies.

Placebo inactive treatments (either pharmacological or psychological) against which active treatment trials are often evaluated. These allow the assessment of the general effects of receiving some form of attention or 'treatment'. Differences in outcomes between placebo conditions and active interventions are considered to show the specific effects of the therapy against which it is compared.

Self-instruction training developed by Meichenbaum, involves the use of coping self-statements at times of stress.

Superego according to Freud, contains the individual's morals and societal values; the psychoanalytical equivalent of the conscience.

Transference the unconscious transfer of experience from one interpersonal context to another, i.e. the reliving of past interpersonal relationships in current situations, including therapies.

Vicarious learning learning the outcomes of behaviour or situations from observation of others.

2.10 Further reading

Grant, A., Townend, M. and Mill, J. (2008) *Assessment and Case Formulation in Cognitive Behavioural Therapy*. London: Sage.

Jacobs, M. (2004) *Psychodynamic Counselling in Action*. London: Sage.

Mearns, D. and Thorne, B. (2007) *Person-centred Counselling in Action*. London: Sage.

Rogers, C.R. (2003) *Client Centred Therapy: Its Current Practice, Implications and Therapy*. London: Constable.

Summers, R.F. and Barber, J.P. (2009) *Psychodynamic Therapy*. New York: Guilford Press.

Westbrook, D., Kennerly, H. and Kirk J. (2007) *An Introduction to Cognitive Behaviour Therapy: Skills and Applications*. London: Sage.

Chapter 3

New directions in cognitive therapy

Chapter contents

Cognitive behavioural therapy (CBT) is now the dominant therapeutic approach adopted by psychologists, and those involved in psychological therapy in professional health care settings – at least in industrialized countries. It is attractive to health care providers as there is a wealth of research showing its effectiveness in a wide range of problems and the relatively short time frames in which such changes can be achieved. At its most fundamental, CBT skills are also relatively easy to teach and implement (although skilled use of CBT remains a complex process, and therapist skill is a key determinant of the success or failure of therapy, e.g. Keijsers et al. 2000), and have been adopted by a range of professions and therapists. Accordingly, the approach has benefits for both health care providers and therapists. However, it is also undergoing a number of fundamental changes and challenges to its underpinning theory and the therapeutic approaches and methods used by its adherents. Since the pioneering work of Beck, Ellis and their contemporaries examined in the previous chapter, a number of theorists and clinicians have taken the basic tenets of cognitive therapy and developed them in various ways. Some cognitive models of psychopathology have combined factors such as cognitive content (as considered by Beck) with processes such as attention, long-term memory retrieval, and other constructs from more general information-processing models. Others have taken a more radical behaviourist stance and questioned both the central role of cognitions in psychopathology and developed interventions that do not attempt cognitive change. We consider both approaches in this chapter. By the end of this chapter, you should have an understanding of:

- The transtheoretical model
- The S-REF model and metacognitive therapy
- Relational frames theory and Acceptance and Commitment Therapy.

3.1 Is it necessary to change cognitions?

In an early critique of CBT, Beidel and Turner (1986) argued that there was little need for the 'cognitive' in cognitive behavioural therapy. They argued that rather than changes in cognitions being necessary to facilitate behavioural change, behavioural change may *itself* change cognitions and emotions: an anxious individual may feel more confident and less anxious after successfully confronting a fear, a depressed person may benefit emotionally from engaging in a pleasant activity, and so on. This being the case, they argued, the most direct therapeutic route is behavioural: cognitive change is an additional, and unnecessary, step within therapy. This view gained some support from a British cognitive therapist, Teasdale (e.g. 1993), who argued that changes in cognitions made within the therapy session were only short-term in nature. They led the individual to engage in behaviours that tested the old and new assumptions developed within the therapy session: the person with a phobia may approach their feared object with less expectation of being harmed; the depressed person may try out a new, more active, way of dealing with their problems with greater expectations of success. However, longer-term cognitive, emotional or behavioural change occurs only *after* these new assumptions are tested and confirmed. This model suggests that the role of cognitive interventions is essentially one of encouraging the individual to engage in some form of behavioural change. The logical outcome of both Beidel and Turner and Teasdale is that a behavioural intervention in which the client is directly encouraged to test their assumptions without any cognitive preparation should prove effective in engendering emotional change. Some 20 years after Beidel and Turner, this fundamental shift in orientation has formed a central tenet of the so-called third wave of cognitive behavioural therapies.

3.2 The third generation of CBT

Cognitive behaviour therapy has now been established since the mid-1970s and has its own history – often described in terms of 'waves' of theory and practice. The first wave, behaviour therapy, focused on identifying and changing contingencies between external contextual cues, emotions, and behaviour. The second wave, led by Beck and Ellis, shifted the focus of therapy to internal events – cognitions. The central tenet of this generation of therapies was that if we can identify aberrant cognitions and then challenge and change them through logic, we can reduce the emotional distress associated with them. Hayes et al. (2004) described this as a common-sense model of psychopathology. A number of theorists and clinicians have argued that the second-wave theories have a number of limitations, including an exclusive focus on the *content* of cognitions to the exclusion of other cognitive *processes* and the development of condition-specific theories. A third generation of theories and interventions has attempted to shift from these foci, sometimes in quite opposing ways, but also with a significant degree of commonality. These newer theories are often referred to as 'third wave' theories.

The first theory to be addressed in this chapter, the transtheoretical theory (Harvey et al. 2004), takes its name from its originators' contention that the degree of **co-morbidity** between the various mental health problems is so great that psychological theories of mental health problems need to focus on factors common to differing disorders rather than those that differentiate between them. They noted that any cognitive content may be specific to each of the different disorders (as suggested by Beck). However, they also stated that the psychological processes underlying these cognitions, including those related to attention and memory, will be the same. These underlying processes became the focus of their theoretical model. They stopped short, however, of developing a specific intervention based on their theoretical framework.

Other models have focused on both understanding the causes of mental health disorders, and treating them. The first to be considered in this chapter, the Self-Regulatory Executive Function (S-REF) model, was developed in the UK by Wells (2000). It is avowedly cognitive and has much in common with the transtheoretical approach. Like the transtheoretical approach, it focuses on processes such as attentional bias and memory retrieval, but also focuses on factors (including cognitive content) specific to different conditions. Indeed, Wells has developed a number of condition-specific theories (some of which are considered later in the book), each of which can be interpreted in the light of the S-REF model. He has also developed an intervention approach, known as metacognitive therapy, which can be applied to a number of conditions.

The third approach to be considered in the chapter is markedly different from either of these two models. Like the transtheoretical model, it provides a model of psychopathology that is relevant to a number of conditions. However, it adopts a radical behaviourist approach, with its theoretical base in relational frames theory. Despite this opposing view, its approach to therapy (known as Acceptance and Commitment Therapy; Hayes et al. 2004) has a surprising degree of overlap with that suggested by both the transtheoretical and the S-REF models.

3.3 The transtheoretical model

In one of the largest surveys of psychiatric co-morbidity so far conducted, Kessler et al. (1994) estimated that the average individual diagnosed with a mental health disorder would not have just one disorder: their symptoms would lead them to be diagnosed with an average of 2.1 disorders. Of course, just like the family with 2.4 children, such an individual would never actually exist; but the key issue here is that many people have co-existing disorders. Table 3.1 highlights the percentage of people with various diagnoses found to have at least one additional diagnosable disorder. Of note also, is that in the few intervention trials that have examined this issue (e.g. Tsao et al. 2002), improvements in one disorder seem to be matched by improvements in others that are not the focus of the intervention.

Together, these data led Harvey and colleagues to argue that these co-morbid conditions must be driven by similar processes, amenable to the same therapeutic interventions, and that

Table 3.1 The percentage of individuals diagnosed with various disorders that would be co-morbid for at least one additional disorder

Disorder	%
Eating disorders	70-80
Generalized anxiety disorder	80
Insomnia	52
Bipolar disorder	61
Schizophrenia	32

Source: Adapted from Harvey et al. (2004)

psychological models should attempt to determine factors common to them all, not those specific to each condition. This is not to say there are no differences in the factors that contribute to differing conditions. Indeed, Harvey at al. identify a number of cognitions (or concerns as they refer to them) that delineate *between* conditions: panic disorder is associated with concerns about bodily sensations, obsessive compulsive behaviour involves intrusive thoughts about responsibility of harm to others. However, their focus is on factors common to the various conditions. They draw on clinical and experimental cognitive studies to determine the processes of interest to them: (1) attention; (2) memory; (3) reasoning; (4) thought; and (5) behavioural processes.

- *Errors of attention* may maintain a disorder when an individual selectively attends to information that is consistent with their concerns or fails to attend to information that is *inconsistent* with their concerns and which would change their understanding of the situation or help them cope better with it. In addition, focusing on their own thoughts, feelings and actions may make the individual more likely to make self-attributions and take the blame for failure rather than looking for external factors. Finally, the automatic nature of attentional memories may lead some people to feel that their mind is not under their own control, leading to fears of 'madness'.

- *Errors of memory* may occur in the encoding or retrieval stages of memory. Encoding errors may occur as a result of our attentional bias. We tend to preferentially attend to stimuli pertinent to our survival. For this reason, people who experience severe life-threatening trauma tend to remember the threatening aspects of the situation. Our memory is also affected by our schema of the world. This guides our attention and thus the encoding process to certain aspects of our environment, resulting in encoding significantly biased information. One frequent bias in retrieval of memories occurs as a result of a phenomenon known as mood-dependent memory. This process results in recalling memories from the past that are consistent with our present mood. If, for example, we are feeling depressed or anxious, we are more likely to recall memories consistent with that mood, which may in turn exacerbate any depression of anxiety.

- A number of *reasoning errors* may also result in mood disorders. These errors map on to those identified by Beck and other second-wave theorists, and include errors of interpretive reasoning, expectancy reasoning, and a failure of hypothesis testing (biasing such tests to support rather than challenge negative beliefs).

- *Thought processes* involved in mood disorders include intrusive thoughts, worry and rumination. Worry is a chain of difficult-to-control thoughts and images which trigger negative mood states. Rumination is dysfunctional, redundant, repetitive and stereotypical thinking. It may repetitively focus an individual's attention on his or her negative feelings, and the nature and implications of these feelings. The higher the frequency of negative thoughts, the more impact such thoughts are likely to have on mood.

- A number of *behaviours* are also implicated in the initiation and continuation of emotional disorders. As noted in the previous chapter, escape from, or avoidance of, feared situations may serve to maintain long-term anxiety. Such avoidance may involve behavioural avoidance; it may involve the use of cognitive avoidance strategies such as distraction from distressing thoughts. Although this may reduce distress in the short term, in the longer term this may maintain anxiety, as the individual fails to habituate to worrying thoughts. Both cognitive and behavioural avoidance may mean that an individual fails to find evidence that their fears will not result in the harm they assume will occur.

3.4 The Self-Regulatory Executive Function (S-REF) model

Wells (2000) argued that the second-generation theories focused on the *content* of thoughts and ignored the *form* that such thinking takes and the mechanisms that give dysfunctional thoughts their power. His S-REF model was developed to remedy these deficiencies. The model focuses on both the content of cognitions and the processes associated with them across a range of mental health problems. In psychological jargon, the theory links schema theory (focusing on the content of thought) with information processing and self-regulation theory.

The model assumes three interacting levels of cognition:

- A stimulus-driven network of processing units, which guide routine responses to routine events around us.
- 'On-line' processing, involving the conscious focusing of attention, appraisals of events and control of actions and thoughts.
- Information about the individual stored in long-term memory.

According to Wells, low-level processing is largely automatic, and requires little active attention. By contrast, on-line processing requires attention and conscious awareness. In addition, the content and outcomes of this processing are influenced by self-knowledge derived from long-term memory. Wells identified two key 'modes' in which these various elements operate:

- *Object mode*: thoughts and perceptions are unevaluated and form an accurate perception of events. They are not subject to analysis and interpretation. Wells considers this to be our 'default setting'.
- *Metacognitive mode*: in this context, the individual is distanced from their thought and perceptions and actively evaluates them. They think about their thoughts, feelings and perceptions and in doing so may arrive at accurate, or frequently, inaccurate analyses of them. Some people, for example, may believe that they *have* to worry about issues that concern them ('Worrying helps me cope with my problems; if I don't worry, things will get out of control . . .')

and as a result may spend significant amounts of time worrying about even quite irrelevant things despite the discomfort they experience while doing so. That is, they choose to attend to their worries – in contrast to attending to other important things in their lives.

Wells refers to patterns of activation of the system as differing 'configurations', and refers to the configuration most closely linked to psychopathology as the S-REF configuration. This involves both an appraisal of a disjunction between an actual state and a desired state, and the development of plans to reduce or obviate this discrepancy. This may be a simple, short-term, process. Feeling hungry (and thus differing from the desired state of feeling comfortably full), for example, may trigger the plan and then action of eating a meal. Once the meal is eaten, the S-REF configuration ceases to exist, and the individual moves on to other issues. By contrast, many psychopathological conditions result from unsuccessful attempts to reduce this discrepancy, and/or continued inappropriate attempts at doing so. Phobic anxiety, for example, may be maintained over long periods of time as a result of the individual repeatedly following plans to avoid a feared situation. Here, the coping effort is successful in reducing the immediate discrepancy between feeling fearful and the desired state of not being fearful. However, continued use of avoidance as a coping strategy prevents the individual from learning that the feared situation will not actually result in harm. This explanation is similar to that of Mowrer (1947), discussed in the previous chapter. But Wells now explains the cognitive processes that underpin what Mowrer considered to be operantly driven behaviour.

According to Wells, S-REF processing is initiated either by some form of external threat or internally generated threat-related thoughts. In response to either of these, we develop plans to reduce the discrepancy between the actual and desired self. These coping plans are guided by a series of beliefs – or metacognitive knowledge as Wells refers to it. These plans are often unconscious and relatively automatic, although individuals may be able to verbalize them. Thus, an individual with generalized anxiety disorder may unconsciously scan their environment for threats, and be able to verbalize this as 'I must be vigilant so I won't be taken by surprise'; someone with depression may verbalize their plans as, 'I must be pessimistic, so I can avoid disappointment', and so on.

A second type of belief (you will already be familiar with) is also relevant. These are declarative beliefs about ourselves – 'I am worthless, vulnerable', and so on. Part of any plan (or metacognitive processing) may be to pay attention to such beliefs, making them salient at times of stress or distress. As a consequence, a spider phobic may pay attention to catastrophizing cognitions when faced with a spider and in S-REF configuration, but be more rational about the threat (or lack of threat) associated with spiders when not faced with a spider – and therefore not in S-REF configuration. Our emotional response to threat is also determined by metacognitive processes. Anxiety, for example, is linked to thoughts of *anticipated* failure in achieving one's goals (the spider phobic is only anxious when they are unsure whether they will be able to cope with the presence of a spider), depression is associated with *existing* failure in achieving goals, and so on (see also Lazarus 1991). Our emotional state may, in turn, bias the type of knowledge retrieved from long-term memory. Depression will lead to memories or thoughts consistent with low mood, and so on.

The example of the phobic response provides one example of the S-REF configuration. In this case, there is a clear time point at which the S-REF configuration becomes redundant, and the individual can shift into another, less stressful, configuration. But what maintains individuals in the S-REF configuration or allows an individual to shift away from the S-REF configuration in less clearly defined situations? Wells argued that in these situations, the S-REF configuration is maintained by internal processes – we check whether plans have been executed and the threat reduced, and maintain the S-REF configuration until this has been achieved. Accordingly, some S-REF-maintained behaviours continue until an internal monitor signals that they are no longer necessary. In cases where there is no external evidence of this (for example, obsessional washing to prevent contamination by germs), the individual may continue in S-REF configuration until it 'feels right' or they 'know' they can stop (i.e. after five washing rituals). The problem with the use of such criteria is that they require high levels of perceived security before the S-REF configuration can be left. Accordingly, the obsessive individual may check a situation or engage in safety rituals on many occasions – sometimes a disabling number of occasions – before they feel safe to stop doing so.

In summary, Wells argues that underlying most behavioural or emotional problems is a cognitive set, known as the S-REF configuration – arising in response to a perceived discrepancy between how we are and how we would like to be. This discrepancy may be the result of both external factors and internally generated dialogue. The S-REF configuration involves planning and executing plans to minimize or obviate this discrepancy. It may also involve accessing and attending to beliefs that may be negative and upsetting, and which trigger negative emotional states. Wells argues that individuals with psychological disorders lack problem-solving flexibility and become 'locked' in repeated activation of the same S-REF configuration as a consequence of a number of factors, including: (1) continued use of inappropriate coping strategies which fail to change our view of our self (e.g. as being better able to cope with a stressful situation) or the context in which we experience distress (e.g. as being less threatening); and (2) setting unrealistic goals, which result in failure and continued negative cognitive processing.

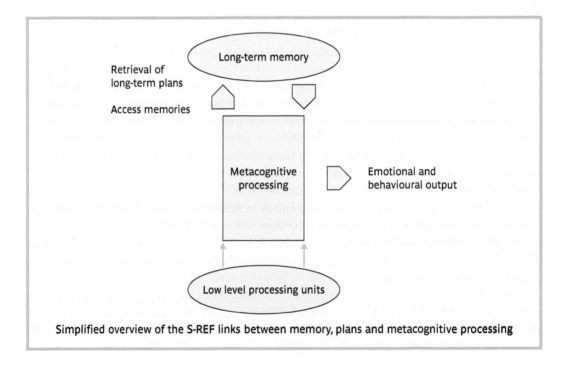

Simplified overview of the **S-REF** links between memory, plans and metacognitive processing

When do you believe beliefs?

Mrs Jones was a chronically depressed, severely obese, woman. She had married a man with severe multiple sclerosis who had since died. She had limited contact with a small group of friends – all of whom also had long-term mental health problems – and she saw her family rarely. This situation stemmed from her childhood, during which she was sexually abused by a family friend on several occasions. As a consequence of her abuse, she developed a number of beliefs as a child that continued into adulthood:

- *'I am a bad person'*: she believed this because she felt that of all the people that her abuser could have chosen, he had chosen her. She believed this indicated that he knew she was bad, and had therefore selected her from a number of other potential victims.
- *'My parents cannot love me'*: this stemmed from a number of perspectives. First, how could anyone love such a bad person as she was? In addition, she had been allowed so spend the night and weekends in the home of her abuser, while her family went out for the night or on weekend trips. This must indicate that they thought so little of her that they allowed her to spend time with someone they knew was abusing her.
- *'I am undeserving of love'*: a variant on her belief or being bad and unloved, and one that led her to avoid social relationships and to marry a man who was dependent on her, and who could not leave her whatever he thought of her. This (and some other beliefs not reported here) also justified her being obese, which she saw as a barrier to men developing personal and sexual relationships with her.

Therapy challenged some of these fundamental beliefs. She came to believe that her parents were unaware that she was being abused. She described, for example, how she behaved when she stayed with her abuser. She would smile and look happy when she was with her parents as she did not want them to know about the abuse or that she dreaded spending time in the house. She was also able to determine that the abuser's choice of her was based on convenience and the ability to manipulate her, rather than because she was inherently bad. As a result of this, Mrs Jones was able to argue coherently that she did not believe she was a bad person, that her parents did love her, and that she both deserved friendship and could establish friendships. She admitted to believing the logic behind these statements. But her mood did not improve despite making quite fundamental changes to her cognitive set, nor did her feelings about herself. Why should this be the case?

One key phenomenon that can be explained by this process is the frequently reported lack of association between intellectual and emotional beliefs. In this, the individual may state that he/she logically knows that belief is false but that they still 'feel' as if it is correct. A feeling of this kind may be metacognitive in nature.

Metacognitive therapy

The therapy developed by Wells based on the S-REF model is known as metacognitive therapy. Its aims are to do the following:

- teach individuals to develop more flexible coping strategies to use in stressful situations – to 'unlock' themselves from previous patterns of inappropriate coping responses
- gain new experiences of mastery and control over previously emotionally difficult circumstances
- change long-term memory, and beliefs about the self
- teach clients 'a higher metacognitive mode' which allows them to process information in ways that do not trigger high levels of S-REF activity.

In order to achieve these goals, therapy focuses on either changing the plans that lead to inappropriate coping responses or changing the individual's responses to any metacognitions or declaratory cognitions they may experience. The latter involves teaching the individual to tolerate and/or to become emotionally detached from any distressing cognitions or cognitions that relate to the feared or difficult situation rather than directly trying to change them. The individual can learn to become aware of distressing thoughts, but not be overwhelmed by them. Accordingly, key processes within metacognitive therapy include:

- changing inappropriate cognitive content (such as catastrophizing thoughts)
- changing the metacognitive beliefs (plans) that drive inappropriate coping responses
- learning to reduce attention to worries and other unwanted cognitive content – through the use of attentional control skills
- learning to adopt more realistic goals
- learning skills such as detached mindfulness that allow individuals to access potentially distressing thoughts without triggering high levels of S-REF activity and distress. This approach is discussed in more detail later in the chapter.

Wells argued that the primary factor involved in the maintenance of a number of disorders is the avoidance of feared situations or thoughts. An agoraphobic individual may avoid leaving the house or someone with obsessive-compulsive disorder may continue with their compulsive behaviour as a consequence of the fear they expect to experience should they change their behaviour. This prevents them learning that no harm will come to them should they stop these avoidance behaviours. A key goal of therapy is therefore to make the individual aware of their plans underlying this avoidance, to change them to ones that involve confronting previously feared situations, and to tolerate the distress that may result from such a confrontation. In other words, to confront rather than avoid previously avoided situations, and to learn to cope with any distress that this may trigger. In order to achieve this, Wells uses a psychoeducational approach, much as used by traditional cognitive therapists, to identify the beliefs, metacognitions and behaviours contributing to the individual's problems. In addition, Wells adopts two supportive strategies to help people achieve any changes they wish to make: mindfulness and active distraction. Both can be used to help people tolerate distressing thoughts that may arise while they are planning new ways of responding in difficult situations, or when they are actually coping with them.

Mindfulness and attentional control skills

Mindfulness has a central role in the teaching of the Buddha. According to Buddhist learning, mindfulness is necessary on the road to enlightenment and is achieved through the meditative process of focusing one's awareness on the present – not memories of the past or possible creations of the future. Through meditation, we can learn that 'thoughts are just thoughts' that may or may not be true; as, of course, do the cognitive therapists. However, we can also learn to ignore particular thoughts or to be aware of them without evoking an emotional reaction. Bishop et al. (2004) proposed a two-component model of mindfulness:

- *Self-regulation of attention*. Mindfulness involves being fully aware of our current experience – observing and attending to our changing thoughts, feelings and sensations as they occur. This allows us to be aware of these phenomena as they arise, but not to elaborate on them. Rather than getting caught up in ruminative thoughts, mindfulness involves a direct non-judgmental experience of events in the mind and body. This leads to a feeling of being very alert and 'alive'.

- *An orientation toward one's experiences in the present moment characterized by curiosity, openness and acceptance*. The lack of cognitive effort given to the elaboration on the meanings and associations of our various experiences allows us to focus more on our present experience. Rather than observing experience through the filter of our beliefs and assumptions, mindfulness involves a direct, unfiltered awareness of our experiences.

Clearly, mindfulness is not simple and requires significant effort to learn. Most programmes that teach mindfulness involve some form of meditation, often taught over sessions spread over many weeks or months. During meditation, participants learn to focus on a particular physical stimulus, such as a picture, or a sensory stimulus such as the sound of a repeated mantra, and to be aware of but not focused on unwanted intrusive sensations, thoughts or emotions. Participants also practise mindfulness during ordinary activities like walking, standing and eating. Wells and Matthews (1996) argued that mindfulness can be used to help people cope to be aware of and change their cognitions and metacognitions without being overwhelmed by them. They can also be used at times when potentially distressing thoughts come to mind. Rather than challenge such thoughts, practitioners of mindfulness are aware of them, but they only form a small, unattended part of their perceptual awareness. Other factors provide a stronger focus of their attention.

As well as a component of therapy, mindfulness can form a primary intervention in itself. The most frequently cited method of mindfulness training is the mindfulness-based stress reduction (MBSR) programme of Kabat-Zinn (e.g. 1990). The programme is conducted as an 8- to 10-week course for groups of up to 30 participants who meet weekly for around two hours for instruction and practice in mindfulness meditation skills, together with discussion of stress, coping and homework assignments. An all-day (7–8-hr) intensive mindfulness session usually is held around the sixth week. Several mindfulness meditation skills are taught. For example, the 'body scan' is a 45-minute exercise in which attention is directed sequentially to numerous areas of the body while the participant is lying down with eyes closed. Sensations in each area are carefully observed. In sitting meditation, participants are instructed to sit in a relaxed and wakeful posture with eyes closed and to direct attention to the sensations of breathing. Hatha yoga postures are used to teach mindfulness of bodily sensations during gentle movements and stretching. Participants also practise mindfulness during ordinary activities like walking, standing, and eating. Participants in MBSR are instructed to practise these skills outside group meetings for at least 45 minutes a day, six days a week. Audiotapes are used early in treatment, but participants are encouraged to practise without tapes after a few weeks. For all mindfulness exercises, participants are instructed to focus attention on the target of observation (e.g. breathing or walking), and to be aware of it in each moment. When emotions, sensations or cognitions arise, they are observed non-judgementally. When the participant notices that their mind has wandered into thoughts, memories or fantasies, the nature or content of them is briefly noted, if possible, and then attention is returned to the present moment. Thus, participants are instructed to notice their thoughts and feelings but not to become absorbed in their content. Even judgemental thoughts (e.g. 'This is a waste of time') are to be observed non-judgementally. Upon noticing such a thought, the participant might label it as a judgemental thought, or simply as 'thinking', and then return attention to the present moment. An important consequence of mindfulness practice is the realization that most sensations, thoughts and emotions fluctuate, or are transient, passing by 'like waves in the sea'.

Attention control skills

Attentional training is somewhat easier than mindfulness to master. Unlike mindfulness, it does not help participants to tolerate the experience of distressing thoughts. Rather, it gives the individual 'time out' from them. Because Wells argues that avoidance of worrisome thoughts is a core contributor to continued distress, he argues that distraction is not to be used at times of high distress – at such times mindfulness should be used to help the individual learn to tolerate their distressing thoughts. Rather, it can be used as to 'reset maladaptive thought processes' at times when the individual is not experiencing particularly high levels of distress. The process is first taught in a therapy session, and then used as homework. It involves initially fixating on a visual stimulus such as a mark on the wall and then focusing attention for several moments on each of a series of different sounds, such as the therapist's voice, tapping, the ticking of a clock. The individual is instructed to focus exclusively on only the sound. The patient then shifts their attention rapidly between the set of sounds, before listening simultaneously to all the sounds, trying to be aware of as many of them as possible. The whole sequence takes between 10 and 15 minutes to enact.

Metacognitive formulation and treatment approaches

Wells's approach to understanding mental health problems differs from that of second-wave therapists such as Beck in that it not only explores what Wells calls declarative beliefs (the main object of exploration by second-wave therapists), it also explores beliefs about beliefs – metacognitions. This moves the therapist from exploring the A-B-C pattern of antecedents, cognitions and emotional and behavioural responses outlined in the previous chapter (see Figure 3.1) to what Wells calls the A-M-C unit of analysis. Here, antecedents (A) lead to metacognitions (M), which direct attention to declarative beliefs, which both drive any emotional and behavioural consequences (C) (see Figure 3.2). In an example provided by Wells, a Beckian analysis in the case of a depressed individual would involve feelings of tiredness and disappointment triggering depressogenic thoughts such as 'I never get what I want', which in turn increase feelings of depression. The additional step added by Wells involves metacognitions. In this, the individual makes a conscious decision to access memories of previous failures and problems, as well as to ruminate about the situation in an attempt to try and sort it out. As a response to these metacognitions (or plans), the individual deliberately both retrieves negative memories that reinforce their negative beliefs, and chooses to dwell on them, significantly adding to their depressed feelings.

Changing inappropriate beliefs, behaviours and emotions involves what Wells calls the P-E-T-S protocol. In this, the individual *Prepares* for change, is *Exposed* to the feared situation and *Tests*

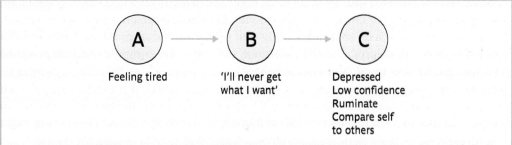

Figure 3.1 The Beckian analysis of depression, linking antecedents to cognitions, and cognitions to their emotional and behavioural consequences

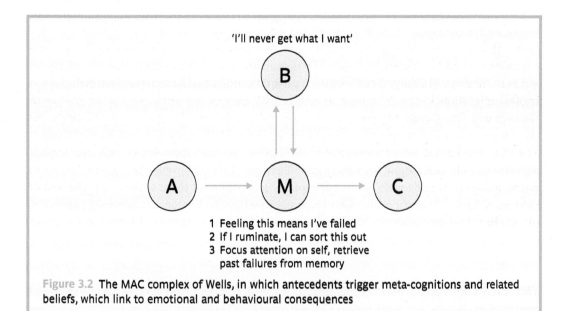

Figure 3.2 The MAC complex of Wells, in which antecedents trigger meta-cognitions and related beliefs, which link to emotional and behavioural consequences

new responses to it, and then Summarizes their responses to the situation as part of gaining an understanding of the factors contributing to the problem and developing further interventions.

- The *prepare stage* involves identifying problematic situations and the maladaptive responses used to cope with them, exploring the evidence supporting some of the potentially inappropriate cognitions the person experiences at such times, and teaching them about metacognitive therapy as a rationale for the therapeutic approach to be followed.

- The *expose/test* stages involve developing and implementing new plans for coping with difficult situations. These involve both adopting new behaviours and developing strategies for managing any fears the individual may experience while engaging in new behaviours. These strategies will include mindfulness, avoiding attending to memories of previous problems, and so on. The aim of this stage is help the individual discover that either engaging in previously feared behaviours or not engaging in previously used and inappropriate coping efforts such as avoidance or obsessive worry will not result in any feared negative consequences. Accordingly, a depressed person who avoids social situations will be encouraged to enter such situations, to focus their attention on engaging socially with people around them rather than memories of previous social 'failures'. Similarly, someone with obsessive-compulsive disorder will be encouraged to stop using cognitive or behavioural rituals such as repeating a mantra or repeated washing of hands when faced with situations that would previously trigger such responses. By contrast with second-wave therapy that would encourage the individual to evoke and challenge worrisome thoughts as they occur in such situations ('How logical is that my thoughts can actually cause someone physical harm? Well, there is no scientific evidence . . .'), mindfulness strategies may be used which allow the individual to experience such thoughts but not make them the focus of their attention.

- The *summarize* stage involves reflecting back on the previous stage, to determine its effectiveness and to develop further interventions designed to challenge previous inappropriate fears and coping strategies.

Wells, A., Welford, M., King, P. et al. (2010) A pilot randomized trial of metacognitive therapy vs applied relaxation in the treatment of adults with generalized anxiety disorder, *Behaviour Research and Therapy*, 48: 429–34.

The authors note that two treatments for GAD have so far been shown to be effective: Applied Relaxation (AR) and Cognitive Behavioural Therapy (CBT). However, the level of recovery across studies is variable with no overall superiority of either of these approaches. The aim of the present research is to find whether a metacognitive therapy approach is of more benefit than one of these interventions.

Design

This study comprised a pilot randomized controlled trial with follow-up. Twenty men and women were allocated to 8–12 sessions of metacognitive therapy (MCT) or applied relaxation (AR) and were assessed at pre-treatment, post-treatment and at 6- and 12-month follow-up. All participants were diagnosed with GAD using the SCID (see Chapter 1), were medication-free or had been on the same medication for at least three months, and had no previous experience of CBT.

Measures

These included the Trait-Anxiety Subscale of the State-Trait-Anxiety Inventory, the Penn State Worry Questionnaire, the Beck Anxiety Inventory, and the author's own Metacognitions Questionnaire, which is a 65-item measure of metacognitions. It has five subscales, but two were considered important to the present study, measuring metacognitions in relation to 'positive beliefs about worry' and 'negative beliefs about worry concerning uncontrollability and danger'.

Procedure

Following baseline assessment, participants took part in one of two interventions:

- MCT began with the development of a case formulation based on metacognitive therapy. Participants were 'socialized' into seeing how their problems were associated with beliefs about worry and their use of maladaptive coping strategies. This was followed by cognitive challenge and behavioural hypothesis testing to weaken beliefs about the uncontrollability of worry. Participants were also taught mindfulness in response to intrusive thoughts that normally acted as triggers for worry, and told not to try thought suppression. The next session continued challenging beliefs about uncontrollability by refining experiments: introducing, for example, attempts to lose control of worry to discover that this was not possible. Once participants were confident their worries were not uncontrollable, a similar process was used to help challenge their beliefs about the need to engage in worry as a coping strategy. Treatment did not involve challenging the content of worry or training in relaxation.

- AR involved presenting a generic formulation of the patient's problem of worry as a symptomatic response to stress and daily hassles. The therapist described how it was necessary to learn to detect the early warning signs of stress and apply a relaxation response that could reduce anxious bodily symptoms and worry. Treatment progressed through the stages of: progressive relaxation, release-only (no prior tension) relaxation, cue-controlled relaxation, differential relaxation (relaxing different parts of the body independently), rapid relaxation, and application training (using relaxation in the 'real world'). The intervention did not address or challenge the content of worry or consider beliefs about worry.

Results

In order to assess the relative effectiveness of the treatments, the authors conducted a series of ANCOVA. In these, they compared the differences between the two groups at each follow-up time, with the baseline measure of each variable as its covariate. The scale scores and significant between group differences are noted in Table 3.2. These show a significant and enduring benefit of MCT relative to that achieved by relaxation alone.

Discussion

The authors concluded that MCT was a highly effective treatment for GAD and more effective than AR. Levels of improvement and recovery following MCT were stable, and treatment was effectively delivered in 8–12 sessions of up to 60 minutes each, suggesting it is relatively economical to provide. Metacognitive therapy reduced symptoms of anxiety and worry and also key underlying metacognitions. The study was obviously very small, only including 20 people. In addition, a stronger comparison could perhaps have been made between a full 'second-wave' cognitive behavioural intervention involving worry exposure. Nevertheless, the results indicate a strong potential for metacognitive therapy to prove the most effective psychological treatment for GAD.

Table 3.2 **Mean scale scores and significant between-group differences at each time point**

Measure	Pre-		Post-		6 month		12 month	
	MCT	AR	MCT	AR	MCT	AR	MCT	AR
Penn State Worry	64.5	70.7	39.0	65.3***	40.7	60.2*	37.9	62.9**
Trait Anxiety	56.8	62.2	35.0	58.1***	36.7	54.2*	37.4	54.6*
Beck Anxiety Inventory	22.2	30.5	5.5	22.4*	8.1	24.5	7.8	19.2
Beck Depression Inventory	16.9	25.6	5.4	21.9**	5.7	17.4	5.3	16.4
Positive beliefs about worry	31.4	32.8	22.6	30.1**	22.3	30.9***	22.8	31.3**
Negative beliefs about worry	45.7	53.9	24.5	47.0***	27.2	47.0**	27.3	43.3*

*** $p < 0.001$.
** $p < 0.01$.
* $p < 0.05$.

3.5 Relational frames theory

In contrast to Wells, who considers pathology to be the outcome of cognitive process, relational frames theory considers cognitions to be relatively unimportant in the development of pathology. Interestingly though, despite its philosophical differences from the S-REF and its radical behavioural roots, relational frames theory concludes that the key to psychopathology is also the continued engagement in inappropriate behavioural responses to contextual cues within our environment.

Relational frame theory assumes that we naturally attend to, and act on, relationships between various elements of our environment. These relationships can be defined in three key ways:

- *Relational context*: we can identify the direct relationship between two elements within our environment – the brighter of two colours, the larger of two people, and so on.
- *Combinatorial entailment*: this involves logically combining relations. For example, if we learned that Stephen is larger than John, and John is larger than Mary, we also know that Stephen is larger than Mary.
- *Functional context*: this involves relating to *functions* of elements within our environment, not simply their physical relationships. For instance, using the above example, we may also consider that Stephen is better at carrying heavy objects than Mary.

Together, these three features of any context are referred to as its 'relational frame'. Hayes et al. (2004) argued we are able to abstract elements from one set of frames and can transfer them from one situation to another. They note, for example, that a child who is trapped inside a wooden box and experiences great fear may later experience the same fear when trapped in other contexts, such as relationships. Although the contexts are very different, the responses are similar because the relational frame is the same. According to Hayes et al., the developing child develops more and increasingly complex frames over time. These relational frames are brought to bear on new situations through analogies, stories, metaphors and rules. Recognition of a situation in terms of its relational frame triggers operantly conditioned responses to that context. According to Hayes, these relational frames are the dominant determinants of our behaviour and experience.

Critical to the development of psychopathology is Hayes's argument that because relational frames are verbally accessible (i.e. we are able to understand and describe them), they are also changeable. Accordingly, over time we may develop distorted concepts of relationships between elements within relational frames, and begin to respond to these distorted relational frames rather than the 'real' relational frames, at the same time as becoming less sensitive to the real outcomes of our behaviour. Hayes et al. refer to the process by which we interact with events on the basis of our 'verbally ascribed functions' rather than their 'direct functions' as involving cognitive fusion. We take our cognitively distorted view as being an accurate representation of a relational frame. In this way, worry about the future becomes worry about an *actual* future, rather than a *constructed* future. Similarly, the thought 'life is not worth living' is a conclusion about life and its quality, rather than a transitory, verbal evaluative process of the here and now.

One consequence of inappropriate relational framing is that individuals may begin to avoid contexts in which negative emotions and behaviours are triggered. This prevents us experiencing distress, but also prevents us having more positive experiences in these contexts. The individual with agoraphobia stays at home to avoid the anxiety attack that is sure to come if they go to the supermarket. The depressed person avoids a family reunion in response to the idea that people will avoid her. These contingencies can be considered in terms of rules: 'If I don't go out of the house then I won't feel panicky – which is good', 'I can avoid feeling miserable and bad about myself if I don't go to the party where people will avoid me', and so on. Hayes et al. contend that the consequence of cognitive fusion and experiential avoidance results in a state of psychological rigidity. In this, we engage in inappropriate coping attempts to minimize any distress we may experience. We may persevere doing things that are best stopped; and stop doing things when perseverance is the best option. These failed coping attempts become problems in themselves. So, by a different route, the S-REF and relational frames theory arrive at the same explanatory conclusion.

Acceptance and commitment therapy (ACT)

Based on relational frames theory ACT is a therapy approach *that uses acceptance and mindfulness processes and commitment and behaviour change processes to produce a greater psychological flexibility* (Hayes et al. 2004). ACT is rooted in radical behaviourism, as it assumes that psychological events (thoughts, emotions, behaviour) are the result of an interaction between the individual and the context in which they are in, that is both historically (e.g. prior learning histories) and situationally (current antecedents and consequences, verbal rules) defined. That is, they are the outcomes of both classical and operant conditioning processes. In addition, ACT does not consider thoughts or feelings to necessarily direct behaviour. Change can be achieved through changing contextual variables rather than attempts to change internal processes such as cognitions, emotions, sensations, and so on. Accordingly, ACT encourages clients to focus on living according to their own values rather than challenging any misconceptions about their situation.

The goals of ACT

In common with the S-REF model, ACT teaches the individual to be aware of ongoing private events (thoughts), but not to be driven by them: to be in touch with the present moment as fully as possible, and to either change or persist in behaviours in order to achieve valued goals. All ACT interventions aim to increase the individual's flexibility in responding to situations they face. This flexibility is established through a focus on five, related, core processes: acceptance, defusion, contact with the present moment, values and committed action.

- *Acceptance* involves allowing oneself to be aware of thoughts, feelings, and bodily sensations as they occur, but not to be driven by them. Instead, the aim is to experience non-judgemental awareness of these events and actively embrace the experience. Therapy emphasizes that attempts at inappropriate control are costly and stressful and frequently maintain the distress one is trying to control: 'control is the problem, not the solution'. Acceptance is taught through a variety of techniques, including mindfulness. Clients learn through graded exercises that it is possible to feel intense feelings or notice intense and bodily sensations without harm.

- *Cognitive defusion* involves teaching clients to see that thoughts are simply thoughts, feelings are simply feelings, memories are memories, and physical sensations are physical sensations. None of these private events are inherently damaging. Indeed, harm occurs when they are seen as harmful – bad experiences that need to be controlled and eliminated. Just as in the second wave of cognitive therapy, clients are taught that our thoughts form just one interpretation of events, and there are many others that may be equally appropriate to any situation. However, rather than attempt to identify incorrect thoughts and change them to a correct interpretation of events, clients are encouraged to accept their presence, and not to try to change or control them.

- *Contact with the present moment* comprises effective, open and undefended contact with the present moment. There are two features to this process. First, clients are trained to observe and notice what is present in the environment and in private experience (i.e. their thoughts and emotions). Second, they are taught to label and describe what is present, without excessive judgements or evaluation. Together these help establish a sense of 'self as a process of ongoing awareness' of events and experiences. Mindfulness is one technique through which this can be achieved.

- *Values* relates to the motivation for change. In order for a client to face feared psychological obstacles, they need a purpose for doing so. The aim of ACT is not simply to rid the person of their problems, but to help them build a more vital, purposeful life. This is a central element of ACT. Its goal is to enable the individual to progress towards valued life goals without being prevented from doing so by historical worries, emotions and other private events.

- *Committed action* relates to clients developing strategies for achieving desired goals. Once they have begun to understand how fusion and avoidance are preventing them from moving towards such goals, clients are encouraged to define goals in specific areas and to progress towards them. Progress, or lack of it, towards these goals becomes a key part of therapy.

In summary, the key goal of ACT is not to change private events, such as emotions, thoughts and physiological reactions, although these may be secondary outcomes of any intervention.

Rather, it is to enable the individual to work towards valued goals, which they define, and to prevent historically developed patterns of thoughts, emotions and other private events that occur in response to a variety of contexts the individual may encounter preventing such progress. It aims to do so by teaching clients to distance themselves from negative thoughts and emotions, to be able to note their presence but not be responsive to them, while actively engaging in positive behavioural change. Together, this means that ACT is not a condition-specific intervention. Rather, it is applicable to a wide range of conditions, from generalized anxiety disorder, through depression, to psychosis. And, incidentally, it has the same goals, if not therapeutic techniques, as Wells' metacognitive therapy.

The process of therapy

The previous section identified a number of key elements within the therapeutic process of ACT. Acceptance and commitment therapy is a complex intervention and is not conducted in a standardized manner. Interventions are often more complex than those developed by Wells from a similar perspective, and involve the use of metaphors, experiential exercises and behavioural tasks.

According to Strosahl et al. (2004), therapists have to achieve good levels of warmth and genuineness and to be able to speak to the client from an equal level, sharing their points of view and respecting their ability to move from unworkable to effective responses. In addition, the therapist should be able to actively model acceptance of challenging issues (e.g. what emerges within treatment) and a willingness to hold contradictory or difficult ideas. The therapist should not argue with, lecture, coerce or attempt to convince the client of anything. Instead, they help the client to get into contact with direct experience without attempting to rescue them from painful psychological content. Despite the need for flexibility, Strosahl et al. identified a number of broad strategies to help people make changes in each of the domains.

Developing acceptance/undermining attempts at experiential control:

- communicating that the client is not broken, but is using unworkable strategies
- helping the client make direct contact with the paradoxical effect of emotional control strategies, i.e. the more you try to avoid painful thoughts, the more they may be experienced, and avoidance of feared situations leads to continued fear
- encouraging clients to experiment with stopping struggling for emotional control and suggesting acceptance as an alternative
- using a graded and structured approach to acceptance as assignments, i.e. a form of systematic desensitization in which they learn acceptance of painful emotions (and other factors) in gradually more demanding situations.

Undermining cognitive fusion:

- helping the client to contact emotional, cognitive, behavioural or physical barriers to change and the impact these barriers have on their willingness to engage in new or previously avoided behaviours

- using various interventions to reveal that unwanted private experiences are not toxic and can be accepted without judgement.

Getting in contact with the present moment:

- modelling by the therapist of contact with and the expression of feelings, thoughts or sensations as they occur within the therapeutic relationship
- using exercises to expand the client's awareness of their experience as an ongoing process
- showing the client how to pull away from worries or ruminations and come back to the present moment
- identifying when the client is drifting into the past or future and teaching them how to come back to now.

Distinguishing the conceptualized self from self-as-context:

- helping the client distance themselves from their thoughts, learning that their thoughts are experiences they have, and are not the individual themselves. Strategies include 'thanking the mind for the thought', 'calling a thought a thought', and 'naming a thought'.

Defining valued directions:

- helping clients clarify valued life directions
- teaching clients to distinguish between values and goals.

Building patterns of committed action:

- helping clients identify value-based goals and build a concrete action plan
- encouraging clients to make and keep commitments in the presence of perceived barriers and to expect additional ones as a consequence of engaging in committed actions
- helping clients appreciate the qualities of committed action (e.g. vitality, sense of growth).

As you can see, ACT is a complex therapy involving the use of a variety of behavioural methods as well as of stories, metaphors and mental exercises to encourage change. As such, the approach cannot be fully considered within the present chapter. Interested readers may find the book edited by Strosahl et al. (2004) a useful further reader. However, the key aim of their approach is that the primary process of change is to engage in previously avoided behaviours or refrain from previous ineffective and problematic coping behaviours, to learn to cope or reduce the distress involved in doing this through the use, for example, of mindfulness, and thereby learn that the feared consequences will not occur. As such, despite many differences in philosophy and approach, both the cognitive approach of Wells and the behavioural approach of the ACT therapists have much in common.

3.6 Chapter summary

1   The transtheoretical model of Harvey et al. notes that many mental health problems co-occur, and that explanations for this should explore common processes across conditions rather than cognitive differences between conditions. These processes involve attention, memory, errors of reasoning, thought and behavioural processes. This approach has been explicitly adopted by a number of therapeutic approaches, including that of Wells.

2   Wells's Self-Regulatory Executive Function model notes three interacting levels of cognition: unconscious processing, processing that occurs at the time of emotional distress involving focusing attention, appraisal of events, and planning and executing behavioural responses, and information stored in memory.

3   According to Wells, emotional and behavioural problems occur as a result of a failure to adapt to stressful circumstances, and repeating ineffective plans (often involving avoidance and guided by metacognitive processes) which prevent the individual learning that a feared consequence will not occur should they confront the issue directly.

4   Therapy involves adopting new plans that directly confront feared contexts, and using strategies such as mindfulness to help individuals cope with the emotional consequences of these revised plans.

5   In common with the second wave of therapists, clients may also be encouraged to challenge inappropriate declarative beliefs. However, this is not central to the process of therapy.

6   Acceptance and commitment therapy comes from a radical behavioural perspective, and is based on relational frames theory. According to Hayes, people with mental health problems develop distorted 'relational frames', with inaccurate expectations of the outcomes of behaviour and the relationship between our behaviour and its outcomes. In turn, these distorted relational frames lead to inappropriate behaviour and emotional responses to events.

7   Hayes uses the term cognitive fusion to express the failure of people to treat their thoughts as interpretations of events or future possibilities – instead, thoughts are taken as truths, which lead to experiential avoidance and a state of psychological rigidity.

8   As with Wells, the therapeutic approach to reducing avoidance and psychological rigidity is to engage in previously avoided responses to difficult situations, and learn to cope with the emotions this process may arouse.

9   The core aspects of ACT are: acceptance, cognitive defusion, contact with the present moment, developing values supporting change and committed action. Although its aims are similar to Wells's metacognitive therapy, ACT involves a more complex use of metaphor, stories and mental exercises to encourage change. However, at its core, it involves engaging in previously difficult behaviours, and learning that doing so will not result in the feared outcomes.

3.7 For discussion

1 Consider the relationship between the behavioural therapies, the second-wave cognitive behavioural therapies, and the third-wave therapies described in this chapter. What commonalities are there, and how do they differ?

2 The second-wave cognitive therapies of Beck et al. consider changing cognitive content to be the primary agent of emotional change. In the light of the shift from this theoretical stance in the third-wave therapies, how important do you consider this process to be?

3 Is it realistic to expect to develop a single model for the development of mental health problems that cuts across all diagnoses?

4 Should therapists trained and competent in second-wave therapies train to be third-wave therapists?

3.8 Further reading

Harvey, A., Watkins, E., Mansell, W. et al. (2004) *Cognitive Behavioural Processes Across Psychological Disorders: A Transtheoretical Approach to Research and Treatment.* Oxford: Oxford University Press.

Hayes, S.C., Strosahl, K.D., Bunting, K. et al. (2004) What is acceptance and commitment therapy?, in S.C. Hayes and K.D. Strosahl (eds) *A Practical Guide to Acceptance and Commitment Therapy.* New York: Springer.

Hofmann, S.G. and Asmundson, G.J.G. (2008) Acceptance and mindfulness-based therapy: new wave or old hat? *Clinical Psychology Review*, 28: 1–16.

Kabat-Zinn, J. (1990) *The Full Catastrophe Living: Using the Wisdom of Your Body and Mind to Face Stress, Pain, and Illness.* New York: Delacorte.

Strosahl, K.D., Hayes, S.C., Wilson, K.G. and Gifford, E.V. (2004) An ACT primer: Core therapy processes, intervention strategies, and therapist competencies, in S.C. Hayes and K.D. Strosahl (eds) *A Practical Guide to Acceptance and Commitment Therapy.* New York: Springer.

Wells. A. (2000) *Emotional Disorders and Metacognition: Innovative Cognitive Therapy.* Chichester: Wiley.

Chapter 4

Biological explanations and treatments

Chapter contents

The basis of biological explanations and treatments of mental disorders is that behaviour and mood are regulated by brain systems. These allow us to perceive information, integrate that information with past memories and other salient factors, and then respond emotionally and behaviourally. Their disruption results in inappropriate perception, mood and behaviour. This may occur as a result of structural damage, or disruption of chemicals, known as neurotransmitters, responsible for activating different areas of the brain. By the end of the chapter, you should have an understanding of:

- Basic neuro-anatomy as it relates to mental health disorders
- The neurotransmitter systems and the key neurotransmitters that influence mood and behaviour
- The drug treatments that are used to alter neurotransmitter levels and, hence, mood and behaviour
- Three physical interventions used to treat mental health problems: electroconvulsive therapy (ECT), transcranial magnetic stimulation (TMS), and psychosurgery
- Some of the controversies and issues raised by each treatment method.

4.1 The behavioural anatomy of the brain

The brain is an intricately patterned complex of nerve cell bodies. It is divided into four anatomical areas: the hindbrain, midbrain, forebrain and cerebrum.

Hindbrain, midbrain and forebrain

The hindbrain contains the parts of the brain necessary for life: the *medulla oblongata*, which controls respiration, blood pressure and heartbeat; the *reticular formation*, which controls wakefulness and alertness; and the *pons* and *cerebellum*, which correlate muscular and positional information.

Above these lies the midbrain, which also contains part of the reticular system and both sensory and motor correlation centres which integrate reflex and automatic responses involving the visual and auditory systems and are involved in the integration of muscle movements.

Many of the key structures that influence mood and behaviour are situated in the forebrain. These include the following:

- *Thalamus*: links the basic functions of the hindbrain and midbrain with the higher centres of processing, the cerebral cortex. Regulates attention and contributes to memory functions. The portion that enters the limbic system is involved in the experience of emotions.
- *Hypothalamus*: regulates appetite, sexual arousal and thirst. Also appears to have some control over emotions.
- *Limbic system*: a series of structures including a linked group of brain areas known as the Circuit of Papez: hippocampus – fornix – mammillary bodies – thalamus – cingulated cortex–hippocampus. The hippocampus – fornix – mammillary bodies circuit is also involved in memory. The hippocampus is one site of interaction between the perceptual and memory systems. A further part of the system, known as the amygdala, links sensory information to emotionally relevant behaviours, particularly responses to fear and anger. It has been called the 'emotional computer' because of its role in coordinating the process that begins with the evaluation of sensory information for significance (such as threat) and then controls the resulting behavioural and autonomic responses.

- The *ventral tegmental area* (VTA) is an important nerve tract within the limbic system. Activation of the VTA sends messages to clusters of nerve cells in the nucleus accumbens and the frontal cortex. This linkage, known as the mesolimbic dopamine system, forms the brain's primary reward pathway.

Cerebrum

Above these three sets of structures lies the cerebrum. This is the part of the brain we are most familiar with, and is the most recently evolved part. It contains a number of structures:

- *Basal ganglia:* a dense mass of neurons at its core. It includes the corpus striatum responsible for complex motor coordination.
- *Cortex:* the convoluted outer layer of grey matter comprising nerve cell bodies and their synaptic connections. It is the most highly organized centre of the brain. Most cortical areas are involved to some degree in the mediation of any complex behaviour, although there are centres of functional control within it. It is divided into two functional hemispheres, linked by the *corpus callosum*, a series of interconnecting neural fibres, at its base. It is divided into four lobes: frontal, temporal, occipital and parietal (see Figures 4.1 and 4.2). As these are involved in the aetiology of a number of mental health and neurological disorders, the function of each will now be considered in more detail.

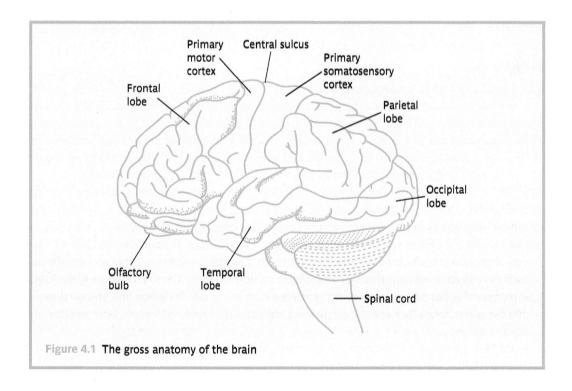

Figure 4.1 **The gross anatomy of the brain**

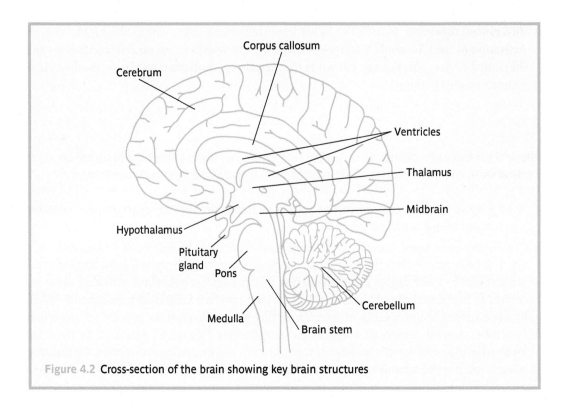

Figure 4.2 **Cross-section of the brain showing key brain structures**

Frontal lobes

The frontal lobes make up about one-third of the mass of the brain. The frontal cortex has an executive function, in that it coordinates a number of complex processes, including speech, motor coordination and behavioural planning. Loss of this executive function, as a consequence of damage, can result in a number of outcomes, including diminished anxiety and concern for the future, impulsiveness, lack of initiative and spontaneity, impairments in recent memory, loss of capacity to think in abstract terms, and an inability to plan and follow through a course of action or to take account of the outcome of actions. Individuals with frontal damage become inflexible and rigid. They have difficulty in shifting from one concept or task to another and changing from one established habit or behaviour to another. This can result in perseveration, where a particular behaviour is continued even in the face of clear instructions to change. The frontal lobes also seem to influence motivation levels. Damage to them can lead to a condition known as adynamia, evident through a complete or relative lack of verbal or overt behaviour. The prefrontal lobes are connected to the limbic system via the thalamus and motor system within the cortex. Links between the prefrontal cortex and the limbic system are activated during rewarding behaviours.

Temporal lobes

Although their functions are distributed, there are clear functional centres within the temporal lobes. The location of these centres differs according to handedness. In those who are right-handed, the main language centre is located in the left hemisphere, and visuo-spatial processing is located in the right hemisphere. In left-handed individuals, there is less localization within hemispheres. The temporal lobes are also intimately involved in the sense systems of smell and hearing. They are responsible for the integration of visual experience with those of the other senses to make meaningful wholes. Disruption within the temporal lobes, for example, as a consequence of temporal lobe epilepsy, can result in visual illusions or hallucinations. Olfactory (smell) hallucinations have also been reported, although less commonly. Reflecting the multi-faceted functioning of the temporal lobes, these illusions or hallucinations may be accompanied by strong emotions, in particular, fear. The temporal lobes have an important role in memory and contain systems which preserve the record of conscious experience. Damage to one of the temporal lobes results in relatively minor memory difficulties, some of which may be evident on psychometric testing, but may not cause problems to the individual. Damage to both can result in profound memory deficits. Finally, they have an intimate connection with the limbic system and link emotions to events and memories.

Occipital and parietal lobes

These lobes are primarily involved in the integration of sensory information. Their functions are distributed and there are no clear functional centres. The occipital lobe is primarily involved in visual perception. Links to the cortex permit interpretation of visual stimuli.

The synapse

Each of the millions of interconnecting nerves within the brain is known as a neuron. Activation of systems within the brain is the result of small electrical currents progressing along many different neurons. Critical to the flow of this current are the small gaps between neurons, known as synapses. Here, chemicals known as neurotransmitters are responsible for activation of the system.

Each neuron has a number of fine branches known as axons at its terminal. At the end of these is an area known as the presynaptic terminal which, in turn, is in close proximity to the postsynaptic terminal within the axon of another neuron. Between them is an enclosed area known as the synaptic cleft (see Figure 4.3). Neurotransmitter chemicals are stored within the axon in small pockets known as synaptic vesicles. Electrical stimulation of the nerve results in release of the vesicles' contents into the synaptic cleft. Once the transmitter has been released into the synaptic cleft, it moves across the gap between the two axons, where it is taken up by specialist cells within the postsynaptic membrane – the receptor cells. Once in the receiving neuron, chemicals known as second messengers are released and trigger the firing of the neuron, continuing the activity of the activated neurological system. If all the transmitter is not taken up by the postsynaptic receptor, further activation may be inhibited either by re-uptake of the unused molecules back into vesicles in the initiating neuron or by degradation by other chemicals, such as monoamine oxidase released into the synaptic cleft.

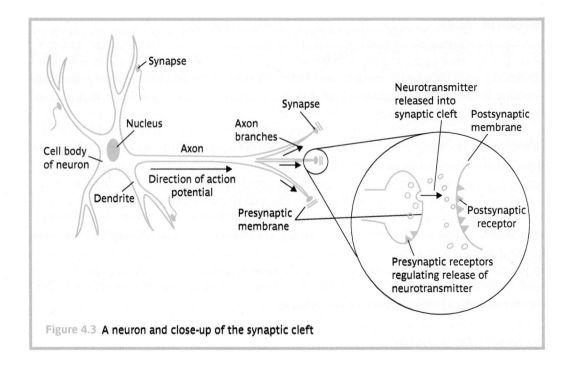

Figure 4.3 **A neuron and close-up of the synaptic cleft**

Neuronal activity itself is mediated by small electrical impulses that travel down the nerve axon towards the nerve ending. When a neuron is at rest, the outside of the cell wall is lined with sodium ions, and the inside wall is lined with potassium ions. When the neuron is stimulated by an incoming message at its receptor site, the sodium ions move from the outer side of the cell membrane to its inside. This starts a wave of electrochemical activity that continues down the length of the axon and results in it 'firing'. Immediately following this, the potassium ions shift from the inside to the outside of the neuron, returning it to its original resting state.

The neurotransmitters

A relatively small number of neurotransmitters have been implicated in the aetiology of the most common mental disorders. The effects of those considered in this chapter are summarized in Table 4.1, and are considered in more detail in the relevant chapters later in the book.

Serotonin

First identified in the 1950s, serotonin is an amino acid, and is synthesized from its precursor L-tryptophan. It is found in the striatum, mesolimbic system, forebrain, cortex, hippocampus, thalamus and hypothalamus. It is thought to be involved in moderating mood, with low levels leading to conditions including depression and obsessive-compulsive disorder.

Table 4.1 The key neurotransmitters, some of the drugs that affect them, and their role in key mental health disorders

Neurotransmitter	Primary disorder	Treatment*	Mode of action
Monoamine			
Serotonin	↓in depression	Tricyclics, SSRIs	Prevent re-uptake
Dopamine	↓in schizophrenia	Phenothiazines	Block receptor sites
		Reserpine	Block vesicular storage
Catecholamines			
Norepinephrine	↓in depression	MAOIs	Prevent degradation
		Tricyclics	Prevent re-uptake
Amino acids			
GABA	↓in anxiety	Benzodiazepines	Enhance GABA

* See pp. 87–93.

Norepinephrine

Norepinephrine is a second neurotransmitter involved in depression as well as a number of anxiety disorders. Among other areas, it is found in the hypothalamus, cerebellum and hippocampus. It belongs to a family of chemicals known as catecholamines.

Dopamine

Neurons mediated by dopamine are found in the mesolimbic system, in a brain area known as A10, with links to the thalamus, hippocampus, frontal cortex and the substantia nigra. Dopaminergic dysregulation has been associated with conditions as varied as schizophremia, autism and attentional deficit/hyperactivity disorders.

GABA

A group of drugs known as benzodiazepines were found to be an effective treatment of anxiety before their mode of action was understood. It is now known that they enhance the action of a neurotransmitter known as gamma-aminobutyric acid (GABA). This carries inhibitory messages: when it is received at the postsynaptic receptor site, it prevents the neuron from firing. Sites of GABA include the brain stem, cerebellum and limbic system.

The autonomic nervous system

Although most explanations of mental health problems focus on neurotransmitters and neuro-logical processes, another system, known as the autonomic nervous system, is also involved in some conditions, particularly those involving stress or anxiety. The autonomic nervous system links the brain to many of the body organs, including the heart, gut and smooth muscles. Its job is to control the activity of these organs in response to the various demands being placed on them, for example, by increasing heart rate, blood pressure and breathing rate during exercise. Overall control of the autonomic nervous system is provided by the hypothalamus. It receives blood-borne and nervous system inputs concerning the state of the body, such as oxygenation and acidity of the blood. In addition, it receives inputs from the cortex and limbic system regarding behavioural and emotional factors. Based on these various inputs, the hypothalamus either increases or decreases activity within the autonomic nervous system and the various organs it controls.

Autonomic processes

The autonomic nervous system comprises two subsystems, known as the sympathetic and para-sympathetic nervous systems. These arise in the medulla oblongata in the brain stem and travel down the spinal cord. At various points along the spinal cord, they link with other nerves connected to target organs such as the heart, arteries, skeletal muscles and colon. The *sympathetic system* is involved in arousal, and its activity within the brain and spinal cord is controlled by norepi-nephrine. High levels of norepinephrine result in increased arousal and activation of the target organs. The *parasympathetic system* is involved in calming or reducing arousal, and its activity is controlled by levels of the neurotransmitter acetylcholine. The two systems tend to work antagonistically and the level of physical activation of the individual at any one time is a function of the relative dominance of each system.

Endocrine responses

Neurotransmitters act quickly, but are unable to maintain activation for long. To enable a sustained response to stress, a second system is activated by the sympathetic nervous system. High levels of sympathetic nervous system activity cause part of the adrenal glands, known as the adrenal medulla, situated above the kidneys, to release hormonal counterparts of the neurotransmitter norepinephrine (and to a lesser extent epinephrine) into the bloodstream. These travel to the target organs, are taken up by receptors, and sustain the action initiated by the neurotransmitters.

When the emotion of stress is experienced, the sympathetic nervous system gains domi-nance, activates the body and prepares it to deal with physical damage. At its most dramatic, this response is known as the *fight–flight response*. At such times, sympathetic activity is clearly dominant, the heart beats more quickly and more powerfully, blood is shunted to the muscles and away from the gut (hence the experience of 'butterflies'), skeletal muscles tense in prepara-tion for action, and so on. The individual may shake, pace or want to engage in some form of physical activity. This ancient response is clearly advantageous at times when the causes of stress are acute and life-threatening: chronic activation in response to long-term stress or short-term activation at inappropriate times, such as while in a supermarket or bus queue, is more problematic.

4.2 Drug therapies

Activation of brain systems is dependent on the activity of individual neurons, which, in turn, are mediated by the amount of neurotransmitter available at the postsynaptic receptor site. Too much and the system is overactive; too little, and it is underactive. The goal of drug therapies is to ensure appropriate levels of key neurotransmitters. They do this by one of two actions:

- *Increasing the availability* of the neurotransmitter by preventing re-uptake at the synapse, preventing degradation within the synaptic cleft, or replacing low levels of a particular neurotransmitter with its pharmacological equivalent. Drugs that increase the action of a neurotransmitter are known as agonists.
- *Decreasing availability* of the neurotransmitter by depleting levels of the available transmitter or replacing the active transmitters with an inert chemical. Drugs that inhibit the action of a neurotransmitter are known as antagonists.

Drugs are usually administered by mouth or injection into muscles, and then enter the bloodstream. They enter the brain by permeation from the small blood vessels that pass through it. Designing drugs to influence brain activity has not proven easy. The brain is protected from infection and other blood-borne insults by the blood–brain barrier. In the rest of the body, drugs pass from the blood vessels to target sites through pores in the walls of the blood vessels. The blood vessels in the brain lack these pores, and drugs have to pass directly through the cells of the blood vessel wall. This mechanism means that only drugs using relatively small molecules can pass this barrier, and even then their perfusion will be less than in the rest of the body.

Treating depression

Drugs that increase norepinephrine: MAOIs

The first potent antidepressants to be developed were known as monoamine oxidase inhibitors (MAOIs). These prevent degradation of norepinephrine (and to a lesser extent, serotonin) by monoamine oxidase within the synaptic cleft and help sustain its action. As was the case of a number of early psychiatric treatments, the discovery of the antidepressant qualities of MAOIs was accidental. Their first use was in the treatment of tuberculosis, where they were found to improve mood in those treated. Since then, MAOIs have became a standard treatment for depression, with a success rate of about 50 per cent.

Despite this, MAOIs have to be used with some caution. As well as working in the brain, they prevent the production of monoamine oxidase in the liver and intestines, where it breaks down tyramine, a chemical that can result in potentially fatal and sudden increases in blood pressure if allowed to accumulate within the body. In order to prevent this, people who take MAOIs have to avoid foods such as cheeses, red wines, Marmite, bananas and some fish that contain tyramine. Eating these foodstuffs may trigger a sudden and potentially fatal rise in blood pressure. Some newer MAOIs, known as reversible selective MAOIs, have been developed that avoid these problems. However, as more recent research has suggested that serotonin is more important in the aetiology of depression than norepinephrine, treatment has mostly changed to drugs that affect serotonin levels: the tricyclics, selective serotonin re-uptake inhibitors (SSRIs), and serotonin and norepinephrine re-uptake inhibitors (SNRIs).

Drugs that increase serotonin: tricyclics, SSRIs and SNRIs

Three drug groups increase serotonin levels by inhibiting its re-uptake into the presynaptic terminal: the tricyclics (for example, imipramine, amitriptyline), SSRIs (for instance, fluoxetine, sertraline), and SNRIs (venlafaxine, milnacipran and duloxetine). Tricyclics and SNRIs also increase levels of norepinephrine.

The first tricyclic, imipramine, was used initially as a treatment for schizophrenia. It was unsuccessful in this, but did reduce levels of depression in many people. Between 60 and 65 per cent of those who take tricyclics do experience some improvement of symptoms (Hirschfeld 1999). Their effects can take ten or more days to become evident, probably as a result of an initial re-duction in the amount of serotonin produced at the presynaptic terminal in response to more being available within the synaptic cleft. Improvements in mood occur as the system adapts to the drug and begins to release normal amounts of serotonin again, with re-uptake prevention finally resulting in an increase in available serotonin. It is important to maintain a therapeutic regime for some months after changes in mood have been achieved: about 50 per cent of users will relapse within a year if tricyclic use is prematurely stopped (Montgomery et al. 1993).

Selective serotonin re-uptake inhibitors are a more recent pharmacological treatment. They increase serotonin levels without affecting norepinephrine levels, which may increase following treatment with tricyclics. Although they may not be more effective than tricyclics, this gives them fewer side-effects such as constipation and dry mouth and they are less dangerous in overdose. Rocca et al. (1997), for example, found that 56 per cent of people who took tricyclics reported an uncomfortably dry mouth, compared with 8 per cent treated with SSRIs. Tricyclics and SSRIs are the most commonly used pharmacological treatments of depression; MAOIs may have therapeutic effects on some individuals who do not respond to these drugs, but the potential risks associated with their use generally make these a second-line treatment. Of concern is evidence of a characteristic SSRI discontinuation syndrome (Tamam and Ozpoyraz 2002). It is usually mild, commences within one week of stopping treatment, resolves spontaneously within three weeks, and consists of a number of physical and psychological symptoms, of which the most frequent are dizziness, nausea, lethargy and headache. Restarting use of an SSRI leads to resolution within 48 hours. To minimize this risk, SSRIs, like other antidepressants, need to be withdrawn gradually. Because SNRIs work on both serotonin and norepinephrine levels, they appear to be more effective in the treatment of depression than are SSRIs. However, like tricyclics, they may have more severe side-effects and discontinuation symptoms (Sir et al. 2005; Stahl et al. 2005).

Side-effects such as a dry mouth may appear somewhat trivial, but they can have a significant impact on those taking these drugs, as one user pointed out:

> The worst thing about the drug was the dry mouth I got with it. And when I say 'dry mouth', I really mean it. My mouth and lips were dry all the time. I wanted to drink all the time, so I could refresh my mouth. But that didn't help much – so I ended up chewing gum all the time – and I hate gum! It may not sound much, but when you are already feeling down, it just adds to the bad feeling.

Another woman, who benefited from taking SSRIs, commented on a, perhaps, less obvious side-effect.

> Taking these drugs was great – I felt so much better on them. But one problem did arise. When I was depressed, the last thing I wanted to do was to have sex with my husband. Now, I can't wait . . . but the most frustrating thing is I can't climax! We have great fun, but it is so frustrating!

Emerging problems

The introduction of SSRIs was not without problems. Perhaps the most widely known controversy involved one of the first of this type of drug to be widely available – Prozac (otherwise known as fluoxetine). This was described by its makers as the first of a new generation of side-effect-free antidepressants. In addition, it rapidly gained a reputation as the only antidepressant that could not only help people who were depressed, but also improve the quality of life of people who were not. It seemed to increase confidence, sociability and to reduce shyness and social anxiety. As a result, it became widely prescribed in the USA, among both those who were depressed and those who needed the emotional lift that it provided.

This initial success was soon mitigated by a series of claims alleging that Prozac had far more side-effects than were initially reported by its makers, the most dramatic of which involved significant behavioural disinhibition that could result in either self-harm or violence towards others. Some of the links with violence were of a secondary nature. Lipinski et al. (1989), for example, reported significant levels of akathisia, a condition involving marked agitation and high levels of impulsiveness, in between 10 and 25 per cent of people who were prescribed Prozac. This may potentially be associated with suicide or aggression. Rothschild and Locke (1991) also reported the case histories of three people who felt suicidal and attempted suicide while being prescribed Prozac. Perhaps the most notorious association between Prozac and violence was the case of Joseph Wesbecker, who shot 20 people in his former workplace, eight of them fatally, before killing himself while he was taking Prozac (Geoffrey 1991). It is important to note that small case studies and sensationalist stories cannot be considered convincing evidence of a link between Prozac and dangerous behaviour, but they have increased the publicity surrounding prescription of the drug.

More empirical studies have indicated a smaller potential risk associated with Prozac than these initial studies may have indicated, and even these are open to alternative explanations. Jick et al. (1995), for example, identified over 170 000 people who had been prescribed one of ten antidepressants over a five-year period. They then compared suicide rates across the various types of antidepressant, reporting them as the 'rate of suicide per 10 000 person years'. The lowest rate of suicide, 4.7, was found among people taking Lofepramine (a tricyclic); the mean rate was 10.8 suicides per 10 000 years. The highest rate of suicide was found among those taking Prozac: 19.0 suicides per 10 000 years. In an explanation of this finding, the authors noted that many people taking Prozac were at particularly high risk of suicide as a result of factors other than their medication, including a history of feeling suicidal and poor outcome on other antidepressants. After accounting for these factors, the increased risk of suicide in those taking Prozac was less apparent, although suicide rates remained a little higher than the average.

More recently, Gunnell et al. (2005) reported the results of a meta-analysis of drug company data on suicide, suicidal thoughts and self-harm following treatment with a variety of SSRIs or a placebo. Their findings were based on data from over 40 000 individuals in 477 trials of drug effectiveness. Despite this large number of people, their findings were surprisingly equivocal, with evidence of both a protective and a risk-enhancing effect across a number of trials. The relative risk (compared with placebo) for suicide was 0.85, indicating a modestly reduced risk – but the 95 per cent confidence intervals ranged between 0.20 and 3.40, indicating a wide variety of outcomes across trials. A similar picture was found for self-harm and suicidal thoughts. They concluded on this evidence that 'more research is required', but that any very small increase in risk should be balanced against the effectivness of SSRIs in treating depression. Fergusson et al. (2005) found no evidence of any greater risk of suicide associated with SSRIs in comparison with tricyclics in a meta-analysis of the relevant trials. In addition, Yerevanian et al. (2004) found that suicide rates did not differ across SSRIs and tricyclics, and that suicide rates were higher following discontinuation of both SSRIs and tricyclics than during active treatment.

Treating anxiety

Drugs that enhance the action of GABA: the benzodiazepines

Although their mode of action is not fully understood, a group of drugs known as benzodiazepines was found in the 1960s to be an effective treatment of anxiety. Benzodiazepines appear to enhance the action of GABA, but do not bind to the same postsynaptic receptor sites. This class of drugs replaced the use of low doses of barbiturates, which made people drowsy, could prove fatal as they led to respiratory failure, and were highly addictive.

The first benzodiazepine was known as chlordiazepoxide (Librium). The best known, Valium, was marketed several years later. By the mid-1980s, benzodiazepines were the most widely prescribed psychotropic medication. However, their prescription has not been without cost. When their use is stopped, levels of anxiety frequently return to pre-morbid levels or above (Power et al. 1990). Sudden withdrawal of these drugs typically results in the rapid recurrence of previous symptoms combined with withdrawal symptoms, including sweating, shaking, nausea and vomiting. As a consequence of this, up to 80 per cent of people who stop taking benzodiazepines after a long period of use relapse and require further treatment. Many people have to be gradually withdrawn from the drugs over extended periods of time – often many months. In general, the shorter the half-life of a drug, the more sudden and severe any withdrawal symptoms (see Table 4.2).

Benzodiazepine use has also been associated with a number of undesirable side-effects, including drowsiness, memory loss, depression and aggressive behaviour including acute rage (Curran 1991). Long-term use may result in irreversible changes. Despite these concerns, benzodiazepines are still regularly prescribed, but now on a more short-term basis than previously. As well as impacting on sites within the brain such as the limbic system, they provide a relaxant effect as a result of their effect on GABA within the spinal cord.

Drugs that increase norepinephrine and serotonin

There is increasing evidence that some anxiety conditions, and in particular panic disorder, are mediated, at least in part, by norepinephrine. For these conditions, treatment with antidepressants

Table 4.2 **The half-life of various benzodiazepines**

Benzodiazepine	Time to peak blood level (in hours)	Half-life (in hours)
Alprazolam	1–2	9–20
Chlordiazepoxide	1–4	24–100
Clonazepam	1–4	19–60
Diazepam	1–2	30–200
Flurazepam	0.5–1	40–250
Lorazepam	2–4	8–24
Nitrazepam	0.5–7	15–48
Oxazepam	2–3	3–25
Prazepam	2.5–6	30–100
Temazepam	2.5	3–25

Source: adapted from Bezchlibuyle-Butler and Jeffries (2003)

has proven more effective than with traditional anxiolytics (Bakker et al. 1999). Treatment is usually with tricyclics rather than MAOIs, for safety reasons: although the primary effect of tricyclics is on serotonin, they also increase norepinephrine levels. Serotonin itself may also be involved in the aetiology of anxiety disorders such as panic and obsessive-compulsive disorder. As a result, these disorders are increasingly treated with both tricylics and SSRIs (Ballenger 2004).

Treating schizophrenia

Biological theorists have implicated dopamine in the aetiology of the positive symptoms of schizophrenia (see Chapters 2 and 7). Individuals with these symptoms do not show raised levels of dopamine but appear instead to have an excessive number of dopamine receptor sites on the postsynaptic terminal, making them over-reactive to normal levels of dopamine. The goal of therapy is usually therefore to reduce the number of receptor sites accessible to the dopamine by filling them with inert drugs that mimic dopamine's chemical composition. A less frequent intervention involves reducing the amount of available dopamine.

Drugs that reduce dopamine levels

The origin of the present pharmacological treatment of schizophrenia lies in the observations made in the 1940s by a French surgeon, Henri Laborit, that one of the drugs he used as an anti-histamine had a profound calming effect on his patients prior to surgery. The drug was called chlorpromazine. In the early 1950s, this was used experimentally with patients with psychotic symptoms, and rapidly became established as the primary treatment of schizophrenia.

Chlorpromazine belongs to a class of drugs variously known as phenothiazines, neuroleptics or major tranquillizers. They work by blocking the dopamine receptors in the postsynaptic receptor sites. Unfortunately, while successful in the short term, their use results in a proliferation of dopamine receptor sites (Strange 1992), adding further to the sensitivity of the postsynaptic receptors and resulting in the need for long-term treatment. They also have a number of significant side-effects. For these reasons, clinicians maintain people with schizophrenia on the lowest effective dose or gradually reduce and stop medication after a period of time in which the individual is functioning normally (see Chapter 7).

The phenothiazines' main side-effects occur as a result of their impact on the extrapyramidal areas of the brain, including the substantia nigra. These areas are involved in the control of motor activity and coordination. The most common extrapyramidal symptoms are Parkinsonian symptoms. These include stiffness in the arms and legs, facial expressions that are flat and dull, and tremors, particularly in the hands. These symptoms can usually be relieved by drugs that reverse the effects of phenothiazines or a reduction in the amount of drug prescribed. About 20 per cent of those who take phenothiazines for an extended time develop a second condition, known as tardive dyskinesia (APA 2000). Its primary symptoms include involuntary writhing or tic-like movements of the face or whole body. Facial movements include involuntary chewing, sucking and writhing of the tongue in and out of the mouth. Body movements include jerky, purposeless movements of the arms, legs and torso. Its severity varies between a single symptom and a severe whole body problem. These symptoms are difficult to treat and can be irreversible. If detected early, and treatment is stopped immediately, most symptoms will remit. However, many symptoms are similar to those found in schizophrenia and may not be observed – or even result in increased phenothiazine being prescribed. The longer an individual has taken phenothiazines, the less likely their symptoms are to remit, even after the cessation of therapy.

A second approach to the treatment of schizophrenia involves reducing the amount of dopamine available to be released into the synaptic cleft. The action of a drug known as reserpine is to inhibit the synthesis of dopamine. Once existing stores have been utilized, it can take up to two weeks for them to return to normal levels during treatment with reserpine.

Drugs that reduce NMDA levels

One additional form of drug has proven effective in the treatment of schizophrenia. Atypical neuroleptics were initially thought to have their action through their impact on NMDA receptors. Drugs such as phencyclidine (PCP, 'angel-dust') and ketamine are thought to increase activity in these receptors and cause symptoms similar to those of schizophrenia. Their activity seems to be blocked by the drugs clozapine and risperidone (Morimoto et al. 2002). These drugs may also reduce dopamine activity, possibly indirectly through their influence on serotonin levels, which control dopamine release at times of stress (Pehek et al. 2006).

These atypical neuroleptics are likely to prove a first-line treatment of schizophrenia in the future, as they may not only be more effective than phenothiazines but also cause significantly fewer extrapyramidal symptoms (Tandon and Fleischhacker 2005). Success rates with phenothiazines of about 65 per cent are typical: for the new drugs the success rate is about 85 per cent (Awad and Vorungati 1999). Unfortunately, the medication also carries some costs. Between 1 and 2 per cent of those who take the drug go on to develop agranulocytosis, a potentially fatal reduction in white blood cells, resulting in a need for all those prescribed these drugs to have regular blood tests so they can be withdrawn before this disorder becomes problematic.

Adherence to drug treatments

Any drug can achieve its potential only if it is taken regularly and at therapeutic levels. This is not always the case: up to 50 per cent of people prescribed psychotropic medication either do not take the recommended dose or do not take the drug at all (a figure, incidentally, that reflects a more general failure to adhere to recommended medication of all types within the general population). Bulloch and Patten (2009), for example, reported non-adherence rates in their survey of over 6000 people taking psychotrophic medication of: 34.6 per cent of people taking antipsychotics, 34.7 per cent of those taking sedative-hypnotics, 38.1 per cent for mood stabilizers (in the treatment of bipolar disorder) and 45.9 per cent for antidepressants. The most frequent reason for non-adherence was forgetting. More conscious decisions whether or not to take tablets are often based on a form of cost–benefit analysis, in which the benefits of taking medication, usually in terms of relief from symptoms, are weighed against the costs of taking it, usually the side-effects that accompany use of the drug. The more side-effects a drug has, the less likely those prescribed it are to adhere to its use, particularly where there are no immediate changes in symptoms when doses of a drug are taken or missed, as is the case for many psychiatric drugs. An example of this can be found in the findings of Demyttenaere et al. (1998), who found that 36 per cent of people prescribed the tricyclic amitriptyline failed to take their medication, compared with 6 per cent of those prescribed the SSRI fluoxetine. Level of depression was not predictive of drop-out. However, younger men who experienced severe side-effects were least likely to take the medication.

Not surprisingly, some side-effects are more problematic than others. Lingjaerde et al. (1987) listed a hierarchy of side-effects that people receiving phenothiazines considered most troublesome. In ascending order, these were sleepiness, increased fatiguability, weight gain, tension or 'inner unrest', and concentration difficulties. Extrapyramidal effects, which were the main concern of the prescribing psychiatrist, were rated as relatively unimportant. Other factors may also be involved. Day et al. (2005) found that a poor relationship with the prescriber, experience of coercion during admission and low insight predicted a negative attitude towards treatment. This finding is consistent with the findings of Myers and Branthwaite (1992), who found that adherence was greatest when clients and not the doctor chose the times when they took their drugs. Finally, Sirey et al. (2001) found high adherence to medication to be associated with lower perceived stigma of taking drugs, higher self-rated severity of illness, being aged over 60 years, and absence of 'personality pathology'. Finally, simply considering the medication you are taking to be necessary is a powerful factor in adherence (Jónsdóttir et al. 2008).

Adewuya, A.O., Owoeye, A.O., Erinfolami, A.R. et al. (2009) Prevalence and correlates of poor medication adherence amongst psychiatric outpatients in southwestern Nigeria, *General Hospital Psychiatry*, 31: 167–74.

The authors note that up to 50 per cent of psychiatric patients do not adhere fully to their prescribed medications. They also note that most studies exploring reasons for this phenomenon are limited by small sample size, focus particularly on people diagnosed with schizophrenia, and are carried out in western cultures. As beliefs about the nature of psychiatric conditions differ in Sub-Saharan Africa from those in the West (beliefs in spiritual causation, for example, are widely prevalent), reasons for adherence or non-adherence to medication are also likely to differ. The aim of this study was therefore to assess the rate of, and reasons for, non-adherence to medication among a variety of psychiatric outpatients in Nigeria.

Method

Participants

Participants were adult outpatients of the psychiatric services in Lagos, Nigeria, selected through random sampling of case files. Inclusion criteria included having a DSM psychiatric diagnosis and taking psychotropic medication for at least one year. Of 362 patients meeting the inclusion criteria, 16 refused to participate, leaving a sample size of 346.

Assessment

Assessment involved completion of questionnaires and clinician assessments. These included:

1 Sociodemographic details
   o Demographic information
   o Level of social support: 'good', 'fair' and 'poor'
2 'Illness-related' variables
   o *Psychiatric diagnosis*, duration, number of episodes, and number of hospitalizations
   o *Level of insight*: 'full, partial, or no insight'
   o *Brief Psychiatric Rating Scale* (BPRS) rated the presence and severity of psychopathology
   o *Mini Mental State Examination* (MMSE) assessed participants' level of cognitive functioning
   o *Global Assessment of Functioning* (GAF) rated health on a 100-point scale from 1 (sickest) to 100 (healthiest)
   o Participants reported the perceived *causes* of their condition, its *expected prognosis* and their *preferred method* of treatment. Causation was rated as predominantly psychosocial, spiritual or biological; perceived prognosis was graded as good, fair, poor, and preferred treatment was summarized as 'biological' or 'spiritual'.

3 Medication variables

- *Extrapyramidal and other side-effects*: assessed as either 'present' or 'absent' by the clinician
- *Attitude towards medication*: assessed with the 10-item Drug Attitude Inventory (DAI-10)
- *Stigma* associated with psychiatric illness was measured using the Internalized Stigma of Mental Illness (ISMI) scale
- *Adherence* was assessed by using the *Morisky Medication Adherence Questionnaire (MMAQ)*. The questionnaire differentiated between 'high/good', 'medium/fair' and 'low/poor' adherence.

All the questionnaires were translated into Yoruba, the predominant language of the region.

Findings

Of those interviewed, 342 provided complete datasets. These were mainly between 20 and 40 years and male (59 per cent). Nearly half (43 per cent) were unemployed. Nearly one-third had a diagnosis of schizophrenia. Forty-two per cent were diagnosed with depression/anxiety disorders. Most (59 per cent) showed no evidence of cognitive deficits on the MMSE, while 59 per cent showed full insight.

Table 4.3 **Percentage of participants prescribed different medications, in different categories of adherence, and with illness/treatment beliefs**

Variables	% of participants
Type of medication prescribed	
Antipsychotics	44.5
Mood stabilizers/antidepressants	18.1
Presence of extrapyramidal side-effects	19.9
Presence of other side-effects	28.1
Medication Adherence categories	
Good	22.2
Fair	29.8
Poor	48.0
Perceived cause of illness	
Predominantly psychosocial	29.5
Predominantly spiritual	53.2
Predominantly biological	17.3
Perceived best treatment method	
Predominantly spiritual	68.7
Predominantly biological	31.3

Associates of adherence

Many variables were correlated with levels of adherence, including work status, income, perceived social support, duration of illness and BPRS scores. To identify the independent contribution of each to the level of adherence, they were entered into a logistic regression. Those that remained significantly associated were working status, perceived level of social support, modified ISMI scores, and perceived causation of mental illness. The odds ratio and 95 per cent confidence intervals of the independently associated variables are reported in Table 4.4. This shows, for example, that employed individuals were more than three times more likely to report poor adherence than those who were unemployed, and those with high stigma scores were nearly five times more likely than those with low stigma scores to report poor adherence.

Table 4.4 Odds ratios (OR) and 95 per cent confidence intervals (CI) for the variables independently associated with poor medication adherence

	OR (95 per cent CI)
Working status	
Presently not employed	1 (reference)
Presently employed	3.42 (2.17 – 5.39)
Level of social support	
Good	1 (reference)
Fair	1.96 (1.15 – 3.35)
Poor	5.86 (2.87 – 12.17)
Modified ISMI scores	
0 – 6	1 (reference)
7 – 12	3.08 (1.83 – 5.22)
>12	4.70 (2.24 – 9.96)
Perceived causation	
Biological	1 (reference)
Psychological	2.55 (1.20 – 5.57)
Spiritual	3.74 (1.87 – 7.74)

Discussion

Forty-eight per cent of the sample reported poor medication adherence: higher than the 33–9 per cent generally reported in Western countries. To the authors' surprise, those in jobs were much less likely to be adherent than those without jobs – perhaps because side-effects were more problematic for those in work. Low levels of social support were also associated with low adherence. Whether this is a direct causal link is unclear. High levels of social support may encourage adherence; conversely, high levels of adherence may result in better symptom control and wider access to social support. Of particular interest was the association between poor adherence and self-stigma and a non-biological cause of psychiatric problems. Note that adherence was not associated with the extent to which individuals experienced side-effects of their medication, nor was insight which has been found to be associated with adherence in several Western studies.

While the study had many strengths, not the least of which were the relatively large sample size and coming from a non-Western country, it also had a number of limitations, including grouping all patients together whatever their diagnosis, and being cross-sectional. This makes the direction of association between variables difficult to infer, as noted above.

Stop and think...

Taking medication has both benefits and costs. We may experience a relief from symptoms, but at the same time experience a number of side-effects. Most of these are relatively innocuous – although they may have a significant impact on the individual. The dry mouth associated with some antidepressant medication, for example, sounds relatively trivial, but in reality is a significant and uncomfortable consequence. The side-effects of some other medication types may have a longer-term and more significant impact on health. Of note in this context is that these side-effects are frequently experienced immediately an individual starts taking medication – the benefits may take some time, often weeks, before becoming evident.

So, what would influence your adherence to medication? Would you accept significant side-effects in the hope of future gain – and if so, for how long? Many people have an 'against medication' bias. If you do, how severe would any mental health problem have to be before you decided to take medication?

4.3 Electroconvulsive therapy (ECT)

Electroconvulsive therapy is the brief discharge of an electric current through the brain with the aim of inducing a controlled epileptic convulsion to achieve an improvement in an abnormal mental state. Its origins lie in observations made in the 1930s that stunned pigs appeared particularly sedated and quiet in abattoirs, and justified by anecdotal evidence that people who had epilepsy rarely evidenced any form of psychosis and that their mood following epileptic seizures often improved.

Extrapolating from these observations, physicians attempted to induce epileptic fits in an attempt to treat mood disorders, initially using injections of camphor – a process that proved fatal in a number of cases. An alternative approach was pioneered by two Italian psychiatrists, Ugo Cerletti and Lucio Bini, who found that they could induce seizures by applying electrical currents to patients' heads, and began their treatment of schizophrenia. Cerletti later abandoned ECT and sought alternative treatments as a result of his concerns over the physical damage, including jaw dislocation and broken bones, and neurological effects such as memory loss that resulted from the seizures provoked by his treatment.

Until the 1950s, ECT involved placing electrodes on each temple and passing an electric current of between 65 and 140 volts through these 'paddles' for half a second or less. This provoked an epileptic fit lasting from half to several minutes. Initially, this was given 'straight'; that is, with the patient fully conscious. Vigorous convulsive muscle activity frequently led to bone fractures until the introduction of the muscle relaxants given prior to ECT. As awareness of this paralysis led to high levels of anxiety on the part of the recipient, this was soon accompanied by administration of an intravenous barbiturate to render them unconscious during the procedure, a process known as modified ECT. More recently, the electrodes have been placed over the non-dominant hemisphere only, a process known as unilateral ECT. This is thought to result in fewer side-effects. Although schedules of treatment vary, ECT is typically administered two or three times a week in courses ranging from 4 to 12 treatments. Less commonly, it is given fortnightly or monthly for six months or longer to prevent relapse, as continuation or maintenance ECT. Just how ECT achieves any benefits is unclear, although work by Ishihara and Sasa (1999) suggests that it may increase the sensitivity of postsynaptic neurons to serotonin in the hippocampus, increase levels of GABA and reduce levels of dopamine.

The use of ECT peaked and then began to decline substantially in the 1950s following the introduction of a range of psychotropic drug treatments. Nevertheless, its use is still recommended by many psychiatric authorities, including the English National Institute of Clinical Excellence (NICE 2008), who recommended its use in the treatment of depression that is resistant to pharmacological intervention or where there is a strong likelihood of suicide. By contrast, NICE did not find the evidence sufficiently compelling to recommend its use with a second patient group for whom ECT has been frequently prescribed – those with a diagnosis of schizophrenia (NICE 2008).

The ECT controversy

The use of ECT has not been without controversy, and the literature seems to be divided largely into those who enthuse over its use and those who vehemently oppose it. Measured debate is less frequent. Those against its use oppose it on moral grounds as well as question its effectiveness. Thomas Szasz (1971), for example, argued that electricity as a form of treatment 'requires the sacrifice of the patient as a person, [and] of the psychiatrist as a clinical thinker and moral agent'. This negative view is endorsed by a number of psychological organizations, including the British Psychological Society, which considers that the use of ECT should be prohibited in Britain. Even the psychiatric authorities that endorse its use have acknowledged the controversy. The US National Institutes of Health (NIH) Consensus Statement (1985) observed that ECT had been used inappropriately to treat disorders where there was no evidence of effectiveness and that many of these efforts proved harmful. It also noted that the use of ECT as a means of managing unruly patients, exemplified in the film *One Flew over the Cuckoo's Nest*, contributed to its perception as an abusive instrument of behavioural control for patients in mental institutions. The controversy around ECT revolves around the potential harm that may result from its treatment.

The short-term effects are associated with being given an anaesthetic and fitting. Adverse events are rare, but do occur. The NIH Consensus Statement suggested a rate of up to 4.5 deaths per 100 000 treatments, a risk comparable to the use of short-acting barbiturate anaesthetics in other conditions. They also noted that the risk of physical injury was much less than in the past, with a complication rate of 1 per 1300 to 1400 treatments. Problems included tooth damage, vertebral compression fractures, uncontrollable fitting, peripheral nerve palsy and skin burns. Some people also find ECT a terrifying experience, or regard it as an abusive invasion of personal autonomy. Some people experience a sense of shame because of the social stigma they associate with ECT (NIH 1985).

Effect on memory

Perhaps the most problematic outcome of ECT is its effect on memory. People who have had ECT typically experience an acute phase of confusion following treatment: it can take them five or ten minutes to remember who they are, where they are or what day it is. It also impairs the ability to learn and retain new information for a period of time following administration and may impact adversely on memories of events that occurred months or even years before treatment. Feliu et al. (2008), for example, found that nearly a month after receiving ECT, patients performed less well than before their treatment on objective measures of recognition memory, and short-term memory of both verbal and visual memory, despite improvements in mood. Similar findings have been found in tests of autobiographical memory. Lisanby et al. (2000) followed 55 people with major depression, randomly allocated to either unilateral or bilateral ECT. Prior to treatment, they obtained detailed autobiographical and impersonal memories and then tested recall of these memories immediately following the course of ECT and at two-month follow-up. A control group who did not have depression or ECT underwent the same testing procedures. All those who received ECT recalled fewer personal and impersonal memories, and in less detail, than controls on both testing occasions. By the second assessment, differences between the two groups who received ECT also emerged: those given bilateral ECT recalled less than those who had unilateral ECT.

Alternatives to ECT

Given the problems associated with ECT, a number of researchers have attempted to find alternative methods to achieve the same clinical results – without the unwanted side-effects. Transcranial magnetic stimulation (TMS) is one such approach. It involves passing a series of electrical pulses close to the brain. The coil is held on the scalp – no actual contact is necessary – and the magnetic field passes through the skull and into the brain. Small induced currents can then make brain areas below the coil more or less active, depending on the settings used. Transcranial magnetic stimulation can influence many brain functions, including movement, visual perception, memory, reaction time, speech and mood. The obvious effects of TMS last for very brief periods following stimulation. However, there is some evidence that the procedure may have longer-term effects on mood – and may prove an alternative approach to the use of ECT. In one relevant study, Schulze-Rauschenbach et al. (2005) compared TMS with unilateral ECT in the treatment of major depression. Treatment response was comparable: 46 per cent of people treated with ECT and 44 per cent of those treated with TMS group showed significant clinical improvements.

More encouragingly, while patients treated with ECT showed evidence of memory deficits, those treated with TMS showed no decrement and even improvements in memory. Quite how TMS impacts on mood is not clear. However, animal studies suggest it may result in increases in serotonin and a number of other neurotransmitters including dopamine (Kanno et al. 2003). Although there has been some interest in the use of TMS in other conditions such as anxiety or obsessive-compulsive disorder, it has yet to be shown to be effective (Pigot et al. 2008).

4.4 Psychosurgery

The modern practice of psychosurgery began in the 1930s, when two Portuguese neurologists, Egas Moniz and Almeida Lima, began severing connections to and from the frontal lobes in people with 'psychoneuroses'. By 1936, the procedure had been developed into what was termed a prefrontal leucotomy (sometimes referred to as a lobotomy). This operation was initially fairly crude, as the surgeon had to estimate where to lesion the brain without any form of neuro-imaging and did so freehand. However, it has gradually become more precise in its anatomical location and procedures. Between 1936 and 1961, over 10 000 people received this type of treatment in the UK. Of these, an estimated 20 per cent of people with schizophrenia and about 50 per cent of those with depression gained some degree of benefit (Malizia 2000). However, 4 per cent died as a result of surgery, 4 per cent developed a severe loss of motivation and up to 60 per cent developed 'troublesome' personality changes, while 15 per cent developed epilepsy. Despite these problems, this approach had many advocates, probably because there were no viable alternatives to this treatment for much of this time.

Rates of psychosurgery have fallen dramatically since effective pharmacological alternatives have become available. Now, only about 20 operations are conducted in the UK each year, and only for conditions that have proven unresponsive to a variety of alternative treatments. New, more specific, surgical procedures have also been developed, including the stereotactic subcaudate tractotomy and stereotactic cingulotomy. Stereotactic interventions involve a device called a stereotactic frame which is placed over the brain during operations and, in combination with neuro-imaging, allows highly accurate lesions to be conducted. Neurosurgeons now use a 'conservative' approach, creating small initial lesions, which can be added to with later operations should this be required.

Most lesions are created with heated electrodes, with the exception of the subcaudate tractotomy which involves placing radioactive rods in the target area, which destroy parts of the subcaudate brain area through a brief burst of radioactivity before becoming inert. It is usually used for the treatment of severe, intractable depression. Stereotactic cingulotomy is the most commonly used procedure for the anxiety disorders, including obsessive-compulsive disorder (see Chapter 7). The operation is conducted under general anaesthetic and involves placing electrodes into the cingulate bundle in each hemisphere. The tips of the electrodes are then heated to 85 degrees centigrade for about 100 seconds.

Availability of psychosurgery

Psychosurgery is banned by law in some countries, including Germany and some US states. To be given this form of treatment in the UK, an individual has to be resistant to all other attempts to treat the condition. In treating depression, for example, a candidate for surgery would typically have made more than two serious suicide attempts, have had an initial onset at least 18 years previously, and their present episode would have lasted seven years without a period of remission of at least six months. They would have received over 30 ECT treatments, unusually large doses of antidepressants, and be severely depressed on psychometric testing (Malizia and Bridges 1991). In England and Wales, a panel of three representatives appointed by the **Care Quality Commission** is required to assess that the person is providing full consent to the operation and that they are likely to benefit from it. In Scotland, this safeguard is evoked only if the person is detained for treatment against their wishes. No patient can be given psychosurgery without their consent.

Post-operative effects

Since the advent of the newer operations, mortality has dropped to one in a thousand cases, and post-operative epilepsy to between 1 and 5 per cent (Jenike 1998). In addition, there is no evidence of reduced intellectual function following surgery. Indeed, many people perform better on psychometric testing following surgery than before, perhaps because their depression is lifted and/or they are no longer taking antidepressant medication. Similarly, there is no evidence of significant 'personality changes' following neurosurgery, despite the potential for damage to the frontal lobe, which is considered by many to control functions considered fundamental to an individual's personality. The tests typically given in these studies do not test for subtle frontal lobe deficits, however, and Jenike (1998) acknowledged that the possibility of such damage cannot be excluded.

A number of people commit suicide following surgery. Whether this is a result of the surgical procedure or would have happened without this intervention is difficult to judge. It is possible that some people who view the operation as the treatment of last resort may commit suicide after disappointing results. Certainly, there is no evidence of this being a direct consequence of surgery. Jenike et al. (1991) found that four of a series of 33 individuals who underwent cingulotomy for the treatment of obsessive-compulsive disorder (OCD) committed suicide in the 13 years following the operation. All four experienced severe depression with prominent suicidal ruminations prior to surgery. The percentage of individuals to make a significant recovery following some form of psychosurgery is reported in Table 4.5.

Table 4.5 **Summary of published outcome data for neurosurgery**

Procedure	'Good' outcome (per cent)		
	Depression	OCD*	Anxiety
Stereotactic subcaudate tractotomy	53	44	43
Cingulotomy	34	56	50
Capsulotomy	60	93	
Stereotactic limbic leucotomy	55	67	27

* OCD obsessive-compulsive disorder.
Source: adapted from Jenike (1998).

How psychosurgery achieves these therapeutic gains is not fully understood. In OCD, it may sever the brain systems driving the behaviours (see Chapter 7). However, preliminary evidence suggests that people with OCD do not improve immediately following surgery. It may take several weeks or months before any benefits are observed. Jenike (1998) speculated that secondary nerve regeneration or metabolic alterations in brain areas other than those actually lesioned may be involved in any changes. What these may be, however, is unclear. This lack of understanding of what surgeons are actually doing provides critics of this approach with strong concerns about the nature and use of psychosurgery (www.antipsychiatry.org).

4.5 Chapter summary

1 The brain is divided into a number of anatomical areas, most of which are in some way related to functions that influence mood or behaviour.

2 Damage to most brain areas will result in deficits that may be evident as emotional or mental health problems.

3 Activity within the brain is mediated by neurotransmitters, which act at the neuronal synapse.

4 Neurotransmitters mediate the activity within brain systems that are responsible for mood and behaviour. The most important to mental health are serotonin, dopamine, GABA and norepinephrine.

5 Drug therapies affect the activity within brain systems by increasing or decreasing levels of neurotransmitters. Antidepressants increase the availability of serotonin (and to a lesser extent norepinephrine); anxiolytics increase levels of GABA; and neuroleptics decrease levels of dopamine.

6 ECT involves passing an electrical current through the temporal lobes of the brain to induce a seizure.

7 Treatment with ECT remains controversial; although it is now much safer than previously, it still evokes strong emotional arguments, among both those who support its use and those who oppose it. A number of medical authorities recommend its use in cases of depression that resist treatment using other methods.

8 ECT is linked to significant measurable memory problems that last a significant period of time. A new alternative, transcranial magnetic stimulation, may prove effective and have fewer such side-effects.

9 Psychosurgery is now used only in extreme cases of OCD or depression.

10 Psychosurgery achieves a moderate degree of clinical benefit in a population where previous, more conservative, treatments have failed, but carries with it a small but significant risk of subtle cognitive deficits.

11 How psychosurgery acts to relieve symptoms is not clear. It may interfere with activity within brain systems that mediate OCD or depression. However, the time frame in which changes occur following surgery indicates the possibility of other, as yet unknown, mechanisms.

4.6 For discussion

1. Is ECT a degrading and dehumanizing form of treatment, or a useful alternative to drug and psychotherapy treatments?

2. Drug treatment for schizophrenia carries both risks and benefits. What considerations should a doctor have when prescribing phenothiazine medication?

3. Would you consider having ECT or psychosurgery if others thought you might benefit from either treatment?

4. If offered a choice, would you opt for a medical or psychological treatment for a mental health condition that could be treated with either approach?

4.7 Key terms

Agonist drug that increases the action of a neurotransmitter.

Antagonist drug that inhibits the action of a neurotransmitter.

Electroconvulsive therapy (ECT) treatment involving passing a brief electric current through the temporal lobe(s) as a treatment for depression and schizophrenia.

Executive function neurological coordination of a number of complex processes, including speech, motor coordination and behavioural planning.

Extrapyramidal symptoms symptoms that result from low levels of dopamine in the extrapyramidal regions of the brain, often as a result of long-term phenothiazine use. Include Parkinsonism and tardive dyskinesia.

Half-life the time required for half the quantity of a drug to be metabolized or eliminated by normal biological processes.

Major tranquillizers see phenothiazines.

MAOI (monoamine oxidase inhibitor) a form of antidepressant, whose action is on the norepinephrine system.

Perseveration inability to shift from a cognitive set, resulting in inappropriate repetitive behaviour, including speech.

Phenothiazines major tranquillizers used to treat schizophrenia, of which the best known is chlorpromazine; their action is usually on the dopaminergic system.

Psychosis includes a number of mental health conditions, such as schizophrenia, each of which have the common symptom of a loss of contact with reality.

Psychotropic medication drugs used to treat mental health problems by their action on neurotransmitter levels.

SNRIs (serotonin/norepinephrine re-uptake inhibitors) antidepressants thought to inhibit neuronal uptake of serotonin, norepinephrine and dopamine in the central nervous system.

SSRIs (selective serotonin re-uptake inhibitors) a form of antidepressant, whose action is on the serotinergic system.

Tricyclic a form of antidepressant whose action is on the serotonin and norepinephrine systems.

4.8 Further reading

Bentall, R. (2009) *Doctoring the Mind*. London: Allen Lane.

Gibb, B. (2007) *A Rough Guide to the Brain*. London: Rough Guides.

Healy, D. (2008) *Psychiatric Drugs Explained*. Edinburgh: Churchill Livingstone.

Jenike, M.A. (1998) Neurosurgical treatment of obsessive-compulsive disorder, *British Medical Journal*, 163 (Suppl. 35): 75–90.

National Institute for Clinical Excellence (2008) *Guidance on the Use of Electroconvulsive Therapy*. London: NICE.

Stahl, S. (2008) *Stahl's Essential Psychopharmacology: Neuroscientific Basis and Practical Applications*. Cambridge: Cambridge University Press.

Beyond the individual

Chapter contents

Very few of us live isolated lives that do not involve interacting with other people or the wider society. These interactions impact on our mental well-being. Good relationships, for example, appear to be protective against mental health problems. Poor relationships or living in a stressful environment increase our risk for such problems. The first part of the chapter considers how family processes may contribute to mental health problems, and how these may be addressed in family therapy. It then considers a number of psychosocial factors that contribute to mental health problems, and how these may be addressed through some form of public health or economic initiative. Finally, the chapter considers how differing cultural factors may result in people from different cultures expressing distress in different ways, and how these may be addressed within therapy. By the end of the chapter, you should have an understanding of:

- Theories of family functioning and interventions that involve the whole family
- The impact of factors such as socio-economic class, gender and ethnicity on mental health
- How health promotion and public health programmes may improve the mental well-being of individuals and populations.
- How mental health problems may present and be treated across differing cultures

5.1 A systems approach

Family models of mental health disorders and their treatment are based on systems theory – and their related therapies are 'systemic therapies'. These view the family or other social groups as an interrelated set of individuals. The behaviour of each person within the system does not occur in isolation. Instead, behaviour follows a principle of circularity in which no one behaviour is seen as starting or being the outcome of events. The behaviour of X affects Y, whose behaviour reciprocally affects X, whose response to this affects Y, and so on. Behaviours form a continuous causal loop, with no beginning or end-point. Change within this continuous set of behaviours can be achieved by intervening at any point in the system.

The chapter considers two systemic therapies that have emerged from very different theoretical perspectives: structural family therapy and strategic family therapy. Other forms of family therapy are described in the following chapters as appropriate. Whichever systemic therapy a family engages in may appear complex and confusing. It may involve whole families and even extended families. There are frequently two or more therapists, one or more of whom may not be obvious to the family, but they will know of their presence. Often a team of therapists sits behind a one-way mirror and tracks the progress of therapy. They may discuss issues raised within the session, identify the nature of the interactions among family members and develop intervention strategies. They provide support to the therapist in the room with the family, who may be too involved in managing the process of therapy to notice all the complex interrelationships that occur. These observers may take an active role. They may communicate with the therapist in the room, either by telephone or by the therapist stepping out of the room for consultations with them, and share developing formulations about the nature of the problem. They may even tell the therapist to take a particular action or ask a specific question. The experience of family therapy is therefore very different from that of individual therapy, as is reflected in these participants' negative and positive responses to an initial therapy session:

> I found it unpleasant and uncomfortable. We didn't all want to be there, and when we did get there, it was not at all clear what was going on. I didn't feel it right that we were watched by people through a mirror. You can't see their reaction to what's going on . . . that is really uncomfortable. I didn't like it at all. I don't think we'll come back.

> It was weird, and not what I expected. The therapist was moving about talking to us all. He even got some of us to move around! Not what you expect. I thought they would be quiet and make us take it in turns to talk to them . . . not move around and interrupt and things . . . It was unnerving to know that people were watching through the mirror. But you couldn't see them, and I began to forget about them, especially when we were dealing with difficult things in the therapy session.

Structural family therapy

The structural school of family therapy was initially developed by Salvador Minuchin (1974), and is now a widely practised approach to the treatment of family dysfunction and individuals affected by this dysfunction. The core premise of this school of therapy is that families that operate well have a clear structure. When a family lacks such a structure, it fails to deal with any problems it faces from either internal or outside sources. This lack of structure may not be apparent to the family: they may not present complaining of family problems. More typically, one person from the family is seen as having mental health problems. According to Minuchin, this 'identified patient' is a symptom of a dysfunctional family, and the family as a whole would benefit from change.

According to Minuchin, families develop structures in order to carry out roles. One important family structure involves the rules that govern the way in which family members relate to each other. The father, for example, will relate to different people in different ways at different times: partner, father, disciplinarian, friend, and so on. The rules that regulate these various relationships differ. However, each is governed by overt and covert rules.

Minuchin also identified a series of elements that combine to determine each family's organization and style of interaction. Subsystems are small units within the family that share a common element: generation, gender, interest, and so on. One individual may be a member of several subsystems. Boundaries exist between subsystems and between the family and the outside world. According to Minuchin, clear boundaries are required to allow subsystems to carry out their specific functions and to develop autonomy and a sense of belonging. Problems arise when these boundaries are incorrectly established within families. Diffuse boundaries are highly permeable and information flows readily between subsystems. In such cases, family members are extremely close. Indeed, they may become too close, leading to a state of enmeshment in which individual members do not experience a state of autonomy or independence. Conversely, boundaries that are too rigid and which prevent information flow between subsystems result in a process of disengagement and emotional detachment between family members.

Subsystems are organized hierarchically. The parental subsystem is generally considered to be superordinate to others, such as sibling subsystems, and to have an executive function. It makes key family decisions. There may also be disruptions or temporary subsystems established, in the form of alliances. Here, members of different subsystems cooperate, typically on a short-term basis. Father and son may combine forces to influence the mother, and so on. These alliances, particularly if they are long term, are thought to disturb the family hierarchy and to be an indication of dysfunction.

Minuchin identified the characteristics of functional families as having clear boundaries, appropriate hierarchies, and sufficiently flexible alignments to adjust, change and foster individuals within them. Dysfunctional families have the opposite constellation of characteristics. According to Minuchin, when an individual presents with problems seen as requiring therapy, these 'symptoms' actually represent systemic problems. Minuchin's group associated particular diagnoses with specific types of family dynamics. The characteristic of 'anorexic families', for example, is being enmeshed, overprotective, rigid and conflict-avoidant, with unexpressed parental conflict (Minuchin et al. 1978; see formulation box, p. 111). According to Minuchin, the stresses associated with an adolescent's push for independence within such a family increase the risk of the parental conflict becoming overt. To avoid this, the adolescent develops anorexic behaviours to prevent total dissension within the family. These behaviours may hold the family together as it unites around the 'identified patient' and deflect attention away from parental conflict.

The goal of therapy is to identify where these dysfunctions lie and to change them: to establish a 'normal' family structure in which the parental subsystem has executive powers, the boundaries between and around generations are clear, and long-term alliances do not exist. Each family member should have age-appropriate independence while still feeling part of the family.

Structural family therapy is behavioural, directive and dynamic. The therapist is active within therapy sessions. They may move about, change the positions of family members to develop or disrupt alliances, interrupt particular allegiance patterns and align with different members of the family. Treatment of the family involves three elements:

- challenging the family's perception of reality
- providing alternative possibilities that make sense to them
- once the family has tried out new patterns of transactions, developing new relationships and structures that are self-sustaining.

The therapeutic process involves a series of stages:

1 *Joining with the family*: the therapist enters the system, joining or establishing rapport by accommodating to the family's culture, mood, style and language. The therapist may physically sit within the family and engage with them.

2 *Evaluating the family structure*: here, the therapist examines boundaries, hierarchies and alliances. This may be a very dynamic process. Individuals or subsystems are observed interacting using role play. The therapist may even set up conditions for these to be real interactions. Minuchin et al. (1978), for example, frequently held therapy sessions with the families of children with anorexia at lunchtime, when the family would be invited to have a meal together. These sessions could demonstrate, for example, the inability of parents to work together to encourage their child to eat, or a shifting pattern of coalitions between each parent and the child. This may lead to discussion among family members about the reasons for these various behaviours.

3 *Unbalancing the system*: during this phase, the therapist deliberately unbalances existing, dysfunctional, behavioural patterns in order to put the family into a state of disequilibrium. This process is highly directive and may involve the therapist aligning him or herself with different subsystems or alliances. An example of this process can be found in the case of a depressed woman who was pessimistic and hopeless at the start of a therapy session, but whose mood improved as she vented her feelings of frustration with her husband and her husband's family, who were critical and demanding of her. Rather than remain neutral, as would be the case in most one-to-one therapies, the therapist began to take sides with her husband, sympathizing with the problems he was having trying to keep everyone in the family happy, but also suggested that the two of them sat down and attempted to establish limits on the intrusiveness of his family on their relationship.

4 *Restructuring operations*: once the system has been unbalanced, attempts follow to establish a normative family structure. This may involve a series of strategies, including:

(a) *actualizing family transactional patterns*: developing more appropriate transactional patterns through strategies including role play, guided practice, and physical manipulation of individuals into appropriate subsystems (by, for example, sitting mother and father together and jointly interacting with members of other systems);

(b) *escalating stress*: blocking recurrent inappropriate transactional patterns, and developing conflict in order to encourage new alliances within more appropriate subsystems.

It is assumed that any changes are mutually reinforcing and that the family will continue to develop without the need for further intervention. Therapy may nevertheless continue at weekly intervals for several months. One advantage of this approach is that it presents a clear model of therapy. Targets and goals are clearly stated. The process of change and the strategies through which they can be achieved are well delineated. However, its simplicity may also be a disadvantage, and many new therapists attempt to restructure the family before they have sufficient grasp of family rules. The application of too rigid a blueprint of family functioning can have the effect of imposing the therapist's solution on the family, which may, of course, be incorrect.

Strategic family therapy

In contrast to the rigid structural model of the effective family developed by Minuchin, the approach adopted by Watzlawick et al. (1974) was less formal and more flexible. The focus of this approach was on the problem-solving strategies families used in response to pressures from within or without. They noted that when a family faces a problem, its members typically interact in repetitive ways and adopt previously used strategies to deal with the problem. If this is successful, the problem is resolved. When these strategies are unsuccessful, some families will adopt novel approaches in their attempts to resolve the problem. Others may continue to apply the same unsuccessful strategy to try to achieve change. Where this occurs, the attempts at problem resolution may themselves become the problem. An example of this process can be found in the man who responds to his wife's lack of engagement with him with upset and anger. In his anger, he attempts to persuade his wife to be more forthcoming in their relationship. However, in response to his anger, she becomes more withdrawn and avoidant, which results in him becoming more angry, her becoming more avoidant, and so on. Here, his anger, used in an attempt to change the original problem, has become part of the problem, not the solution – as has the woman's withdrawal. It is important to note that *both* repetitive responses actually exacerbate the problem – not just his anger or her lack of communication, which is what individual therapy may focus on.

The goal of therapy is to identify and change these repetitive and, ultimately, destructive, attempts at problem resolution. The family's tendency to look for a cause of the problems and to attribute them to one individual is minimized, as this is seen as contributing to, rather than helping, the problem. The strategic school placed significant emphasis on both verbal and non-verbal communication between family members. All behaviour was thought to act as a form of communication. One cannot fail to communicate: inaction provides a message just as much as action.

The goal of strategic therapy is to disrupt behavioural cycles that maintain the problem, and to introduce the conditions for more appropriate transactional patterns. Therapy follows a number of discrete stages:

1. Detailed exploration and definition of the difficulties to be resolved.
2. Developing a strategic plan of action to break up the sequences of interactions that are maintaining the problem.
3. Delivery of the strategic interventions – often involving homework between therapy sessions, the goal of which is to disrupt the problematic sequences.
4. Feedback on the outcome of these interventions.
5. Reappraisal of the therapeutic plan, including revision of homework or other interventions employed.

The style of the therapist is one of emotional distance from the family. To avoid confrontation, they may adopt a one-down approach rather than expert position. They also do not insist that the whole family attends therapy sessions: they will work with whoever attends. Therapy focuses on two key strategies of change: positive reframing and paradoxical interventions.

- *Positive reframing* involves placing a positive interpretation on the behaviours that are contributing to the problem. That is not as difficult as it may sound because, according to the strategic therapists, these behaviours are erroneous but genuine attempts at resolving a problem. In this way, a couple who are constantly antagonistic towards each other may be told that the good thing about their arguing is that it shows they both have sufficient commitment to the relationship to continue fighting in an attempt to make it work. The goal of reframing is to challenge the family's perception of the presenting problem and to encourage them to redefine and give a new meaning to it. Having redefined the problem, the family can no longer apply the same solutions, and new solutions and patterns of interaction become possible.
- *Paradoxical intervention* involves family members being asked to engage in tasks that are paradoxical or contrary to common sense. The arguing couple, for example, may be asked to *continue* arguing – perhaps linked to the positive reframe of 'because this shows your continuing care for each other'. By the use of paradox, the therapist creates a therapeutic bind by suggesting that there are good reasons why it is advisable *not* to change: while hoping to have the opposite effect. The paradox is intended to give the problem a new meaning so that those involved will be forced to decide on change or no change – itself a change within the system.

A number of paradoxical strategies have been identified. The above example is known as *symptom prescription*. A similar technique, known as *pretending*, involves a family member deliberately and consciously pretending to have a particular problem, with the family enacting their usual pattern around the presenting 'symptom'. Again, this is meant to disrupt the normal family interactions and facilitate behavioural change. The approach has a number of strengths, and the strategic group reported some impressive therapeutic gains (Watzlawick et al. 1974). However, the ethics of the approach have been strongly questioned, as the power lies with the therapist and the method of treatment is not clear to its recipient. The formulation box illustrates two differing formulations of one problem from both structural and strategic perspectives.

Formulation box

Jane's anorexia: an example of structural versus strategic therapy

Strategic and structural approaches view the problems that people have quite differently. Here are two formulations of the problems associated with anorexia.

A structural approach

Jane is an adolescent girl diagnosed with anorexia: the 'identified patient' indicative of structural problems within a family. The therapist has heard how the mother and father try to encourage her to eat, but have so far failed to do so. The therapist diagnosed the issue as one in which the family has failed to accommodate her transitional stage from adolescence. The parents are observed as powerless to persuade her to eat, and seem to put their differences aside and unite in their concern to get her to eat.

A structural view of this situation would be that the family is enmeshed: they are overly concerned about their daughter's behaviour and so close to her that they deprive her of her independence and decision-making autonomy. The power invested in the girl to control the family has inverted the power hierarchy within the family, and the parental system is weak: they cannot get her to eat.

The goal of therapy is to remedy these deficiencies, in particular, to strengthen the parental subsystem and restore the appropriate power hierarchy. One way in which this may be achieved is for the therapist to actively change the structure and to support the parents in their attempts to control the behaviour of their daughter.

A strategic approach

A different formulation of the problem may be gained by a strategic approach. One possible formulation is that as Jane entered adolescence she tried to gain more autonomy and independence. However, her parents were overprotective and controlling and did not accommodate to these changes. She therefore started to diet as an expression of control and autonomy. However, her dieting and loss of weight simply increased her parents' concern over her health and increased their desire to control her and ensure she ate 'properly'. Accordingly, they increased their attempts at controlling her eating. As a direct consequence, she rebelled and escalated her diet, which, in turn, increased her parents' concern and protective behaviour, which . . . The cycle continues. The pattern of interaction that is established is the main concern of the strategic therapist – not the initiating problem.

How effective is systemic therapy?

This chapter has described two very different approaches to working with families. However, there are many other approaches, some of which will be described in subsequent chapters.

Evaluation of the effectiveness of systemic interventions is therefore not a simple question. Nevertheless, it is clear that family therapy of one sort or another is an effective intervention for a number of problems. Meta-analyses, for example, have shown family interventions to be equally or more effective than individual interventions in conditions as diverse as adolescent substance abuse (Waldron and Turner, 2008), phobic disorders in children and adolescents (Silverman et al. 2008), bipolar disorder (Benyon et al. 2008), depression in both young people (Carr 2008) and adults (Henken et al. 2007), psychosis (Patterson and Leeuwenkamp 2008), and eating disorders (Keel and Haedt 2008).

5.2 Psychosocial explanations of mental health problems

Risk for mental health problems has been linked to a number of social and economic factors. The results of the British Psychiatric Morbidity Survey (Jenkins et al. 1998) provided evidence typical of the wider findings. The authors conducted diagnostic interviews on 10 000 people who were either living in their own home or were homeless and roofless. Among the former, they found relatively high rates of neurotic disorders (various types of depression or anxiety) among women, those living in urban settings, unemployed people, and separated, divorced or widowed individuals. Men were three times as likely as women to be dependent on alcohol, and twice as likely to be dependent on drugs. Unemployed people were twice as likely to abuse alcohol as employed people and five times more likely to be dependent on other types of drugs. Psychoses were more prevalent among urban than rural dwellers. The prevalence of neurotic disorders among hostel residents was 38 per cent; 60 per cent among night shelter residents, and among those sleeping rough, rates were 57 per cent. Rates of psychoses and alcohol and drug dependence were similarly high. Less dramatically, there is consistent evidence that mental health problems are more prevalent among the less well-off than among the better-off in most developed countries (e.g. Fryers et al. 2005).

Socio-economic status

Social causation versus social drift

Two hypotheses have been proposed to explain findings of higher rates of mental health disorders among people in the lower socio-economic groups than among the economically better-off. *Social causation models* suggest they result from higher levels of stress experienced by the less well-off: that is, low socio-economic status 'causes' mental health problems. The *social drift model* opposes this view. It suggests that mental health problems lead to a decline in socio-economic status. According to this model, when an individual develops a mental health disorder, they become less economically viable. They may be unable to maintain a job or the levels of overtime required to maintain their standard of living. They therefore drift down the socio-economic scale: that is, mental health problems 'cause' low socio-economic status.

The evidence generally favours the social causation hypothesis. Indeed, where there is social drift, this has been found to generally precede rather than follow episodes of depression and schizophrenia (Saraceno et al. 2005). These effects may even be intergenerational. Ritsher et al. (2001) followed a cohort of people whose parents had either experienced an episode of major depression or were depression-free. They hypothesized that if the social causation model held, the children of blue-collar parents were at increased risk of developing depression. If the social drift model held, having depressed parents placed participants at risk of a low socio-economic status. Their data supported the social causation hypotheses. The children of blue-collar workers were more than three times as likely to develop a major depressive disorder as those of white-collar workers. Parental depression did not predict the socio-economic status of their offspring. Nor was there any evidence of drift following the onset of depression.

These findings should not be surprising. The lower the individual is within the social structure, the greater the reported exposure to stressful life-events, hassles and problems, and the greater the emotional impact they have (e.g. Grzywacz et al. 2004). Not having a job also appears to have negative effects on mental health. Ferrie et al. (2001), for example, found that insecure re-employment and unemployment following redundancy were associated with significant increases in minor psychiatric problems and high use of family doctors.

Differential vulnerability

Not only do people in the lower socio-economic groups experience more stresses than the better off, they often have fewer resources to help them cope with them. Hobfoll's (1989) conservation of resources model proposed that both mental and physical health are determined by the amount of resources available to the individual. These may be economic, social (for example, family support), structural (such as housing), or psychological (for instance, coping skills, perceived control). A high level of resources is health protective. Low levels of resources place an individual at risk for mental health problems.

As well as more economic resources, people in higher socio-economic groups also appear to have more social and psychological resources known to be protective against mental health problems than the less well-off. Examples of this can be found in the research of Grzywacz et al. (2004), who found that high levels of education formed a buffer against stress and mediated, at least in part, the association between socio-economic status and mental health. Matthews et al. (2008) found an association between low levels of what they called 'reserve capacity' (a combination of optimism, self-esteem and social support), negative emotions and low socio-economic status. In addition, social support, which is highly protective against a number of mental health problems, is also generally less available to those in the lower socio-economic groups (Chaix et al. 2007).

Relativity issues

While social stress and lack of resources appear to be direct causes of many mental health problems, Wilkinson (1992) argued that *relative* lack of income may also contribute. He argued that the wider the wealth disparities within society, the lower the levels of social cohesion and social capital (feelings of social cohesion, solidarity and trust in one's neighbours) within society. Low social capital is associated with both individual distrust and dissatisfaction, and social factors such as high levels of crime. This, Wilkinson contended, is inherently stressful and results in high levels of mental health problems among those individuals who experience it. These hypotheses were supported by the findings of Phongsavan et al. (2006) in a large population study in Australia, who found that high levels of trust and feeling safe were consistently associated with low levels of psychological distress, even after adjusting for socio-demographic characteristics and health conditions.

Gender differences

A number of theories have attempted to explain consistent findings of higher levels of mental health problems among women than men. One argument suggested that these differences may be more apparent than real, and stem from women's willingness to report any psychological distress and men's relative unwillingness to do so. This theory has not been substantiated, however, and a number of well-conducted prevalence studies have consistently found gender differences in rates of mental health problems when random populations have been closely interviewed about the presence of psychiatric symptoms (e.g. Weich et al. 1998). Other theories have suggested similar mechanisms to those used to explain socio-economic differences in health: differential exposure and vulnerability to stressors.

Differential exposure

The differential stress hypothesis suggests that women encounter more stress in their lives than men, and as a result are more prone to mental health problems. What evidence there is suggests that women experience more hardship in their work and family roles than men (Rieker and Bird 2000). Even when working full-time, women tend to do more in the home than their partners. This process, known as work-home spillover, is now well recognized as contributing to high levels of stress in those who experience it (e.g. Kinnunen et al. 2006), although there is little evidence that it generally results in sufficient distress to warrant a diagnosis of a formal mental health disorder.

Women are also more subject to physical assault within the family, rape, and other traumatizing events than men. Although these events may be relatively uncommon, they may profoundly affect those involved and contribute to higher overall rates of anxiety or depression among women. Cloutier et al. (2002), for example, found that 19 per cent of their representative sample of women in North Carolina had been the subject of sexual assault at some time in their life. These women were two and a half times more likely to report 'poor mental health' than women who had not experienced this. A final source of stress among women may be poverty. Strickland (1992) suggested that 75 per cent of those living in poverty were mothers and children. Vulnerability to mental health problems as a result of low socio-economic status may therefore particularly impact on women.

Differential vulnerability

An alternative approach to this issue suggests that women may be more vulnerable to some types of stress than men. Elliott (2000), for example, suggested that women have a higher dependence on the support provided by social networks than men, and may be differentially affected by events that disrupt them. Related to this may be problems associated with the loss of attachment to the extended family, as children are more mobile and increasingly move from the family home as they mature. In addition, Simon (1995) suggested that women may react more strongly to work and family strains than men because of the importance that these roles have to their sense of worth.

Minority status

Minority status can be conferred by a number of factors: ethnicity, sexual choices, appearance, and so on. However, it is usually taken to mean obvious differences as a result of ethnicity.

Considering issues of ethnicity is not without its dangers. It encompasses a variety of issues: language, religion, experience of races and migration, culture, ancestry and forms of identity. Each of these may individually or together contribute to differences between the mental and physical health of different ethnic groups. It is dangerous to reify 'ethnicity' as a single factor which alone impacts on mental health. Any brief review of the relevant literature can therefore only scratch the surface of a complex literature and suggest some issues that may explain some differences in some mental health problems across some minority groups.

Differential exposure

One explanation for higher levels of mental health problems among social minorities is that they are exposed to more stress than the majority groups. One general stress to which many people in ethnic minorities are exposed is that associated with low socio-economic status. Indeed, some commentators have suggested that any distress resulting from being within an ethnic minority is entirely the result of occupying lower socio-economic groups, not being part of an ethnic minority *per se*. Sachs-Ericsson et al. (2005), for example, found that in their large US sample, more African-Americans reported high levels of depression than white people. However, this relationship was found to be mediated by a number of indices of socio-economic status. Other studies have found a more direct link between race, ethnicity and stress, not mediated by economic status (Williams 1999).

There are also a number of social stressors to which minority social groups are uniquely exposed. One obvious stressor is that of racial prejudice, and there are a number of research papers showing evidence of its negative emotional impact. In one such study, Noh et al. (2007) identified what they termed 'overt' and 'subtle' discrimination, and found that overt discrimination was particularly associated with low positive affect, while the experience of subtle discrimination was associated with high levels of depressive symptoms. A third source of stress experienced by ethnic minorities may be a consequence of tensions as individuals adopt or consciously reject some of the customs and values of other cultures, including those of the host culture. Both may result in feelings of alienation and rejection by members of the larger or one's own culture. In one study of this phenomenon, Lai (2004) studied Chinese immigrants to Canada, and found that the highest levels of depression were among those who established more cultural barriers against the new culture, and who had a higher level of identification with traditional Chinese cultural values.

Minority status is not just conferred by visible differences. Sexual minorities also experience prejudice that may impact on their mental health. Cole et al. (1996), for example, found that healthy gay men who concealed their sexual identity were more likely to experience poor mental and physical health than those who were able to express their sexuality.

5.3 Mental health promotion

As social and economic factors contribute to mental well-being, and only a minority of the one-in-four of us who develop mental health problems seek professional help (Jenkins et al. 1998), it may be beneficial to address factors within society that contribute to mental health problems. The World Health Organization (1996) acknowledged this need. It noted that health promotion involves a variety of complex interventions at differing levels, aimed not just at preventing ill-health, but also at promoting positive health. This perspective involves:

- having a holistic approach to health
- respecting diverse cultures and beliefs
- promoting positive health as well as preventing ill-health
- working at a structural (societal) not just individual level
- using participatory methods.

Removing the jargon, this means that public health services should work not just with individuals, but also at a societal level to bring about improvements in health. They should involve communities and attempt to improve health and quality of life, not just prevent disease. They can work at a legislative level, with communities, and groups and individuals within them. Initiatives can be conducted by a variety of people, some of whom would label themselves as workers in health promotion, many of whom would not. Some examples of the range of public health activities that can be conducted, in this case to minimize levels of alcohol-related problems, are outlined in Table 5.1. Here, interventions are aimed at the whole population of drinkers as well as those who drink to excess.

Table 5.1 Examples of differing levels of public health initiatives aimed at minimizing alcohol-related harm

Level of approach	Examples of practice
Whole population	
Central government	Establishing drink–drive laws High taxation on high percentage alcohol drinks Government guidelines on consumption limits
Local government	Local police policies on public houses and drink–driving Licensing of new pubs and drinking time limits
Media	Drink–drive campaigns Television programmes on the harmful effects of alcohol and promoting sensible drinking
Supermarkets/shops	Giving priority to low-alcohol drinks on the shelves
Population of drinkers	
Individual pubs/brewers	Establishing local minibus services to prevent drink–driving Provision of low alcohol beers Discouraging the obviously intoxicated from drinking alcohol (in the USA, a bartender can be sued for an incident – e.g. car accident – involving a drunk individual if they served them alcohol while visibly drunk)
Supermarkets/shops	Policing of drinking-age requirements for purchase of alcohol
Individual drinkers	
Health care/social services	Provision of detoxification services Therapy to prevent excess alcohol consumption Therapy to prevent relapse in people who have successfully stopped or reduced their excess drinking

Individual interventions

Despite the wide variety of potential interventions, most mental health initiatives have involved improving access to psychiatric and psychological care for groups with poor access to health care and who have high levels of mental health problems: the economically deprived, people without housing, and so on. Other interventions have been aimed at preventing relapse (Neto et al. 2008).

An approach of more relevance to *preventing* mental health problems involves providing relatively simple psychological interventions that are open to all: usually in the form of stress management classes. Brown et al. (2000) assessed one such programme. They ran eight free full- or half-day stress management workshops in a leisure centre following a publicity drive as part of the 'Healthy Birmingham 2000' programme. Their comparison groups comprised people who took part in a day-long programme focusing on healthy eating, alcohol awareness and physical exercise and a group of people on a waiting list for future workshops. The event proved very popular and attracted both people who had seen a health professional about stress-related problems and those who had not. The intervention also proved successful. Participants in the full-day workshops showed significantly greater reductions in stress and anxiety three months following the workshop than those in the comparison groups: an impressive result given the relative brevity of the intervention and the wide range of people attending.

The workplace can also provide a setting for learning stress management skills. Routsalainen et al's. (2008) meta-analysis reported data from over 2500 participants in 17 studies of occupational stress management interventions and found they resulted in 'small but probably relevant' (and statistically significant) reductions in stress, emotional exhaustion, anxiety, and burnout compared to no intervention. Oldenburg and Harris (1996) provide a cautionary note, however, when evaluating these statistics. They noted that stress management programmes typically attract only between 10 and 40 per cent of the workforce, and that many of those who attend have little to gain, while many anxious individuals do not attend them.

A second organization in which preventive interventions can be conducted is the school. The Promoting Alternative THinking Strategies programme (PATHS: Greenberg and Kusche, 1998), for example, taught pupils a number of cognitive strategies to help them regulate their emotions. This proved effective in improving social problem-solving, emotional understanding, self-report of conduct problems, teacher ratings of adaptive behaviour, and cognitive abilities related to social planning and impulsivity for up to two years following the intervention.

An interesting approach to reaching a wider audience was reported by van Straten et al. (2008). They provided training in stress management training and other psychological therapies on-line. In one study of their approach, participants in their treatment group were sent four, weekly, automated emails providing information on stress and relevant 'homework' for the following week. Participants sent back the results of their homework and received email feedback. Despite the simplicity of the intervention, participants in the intervention condition improved significantly more on measures of depression, anxiety and quality of life than those in the control condition.

Using the media

The mass media provides a means of accessing large populations at relatively low cost. Nevertheless, there is surprisingly little research examining the use of the media in the context of mental health, and evidence from other areas suggests that its impact is likely to be limited. An example of this approach was reported by Barker et al. (1993). They reported the outcome of a series of seven, 10-minute, programmes, covering a variety of mental health topics. An audience survey indicated that viewing the series led to attitudinal, but not behavioural, changes: probably as much as could be expected given the brevity with which each subject was dealt with. The effects of a more substantial television series, however, appear to have been no better. 'Pssst . . . the really useful guide to alcohol' (Bennett et al. 1991) aimed to encourage sensible drinking, particularly among younger drinkers, and involved both media personalities and experts providing information about what was meant by sensible drinking and models of sensible drinking. Rowan Atkinson, for example, provided humorous reminders of weekly sensible drinking limits, while one of the presenters gradually cut his consumption over the course of the series. Surveys conducted before and after the series suggested that it improved knowledge about sensible drinking among the general population, and resulted in a modest shift of stated intentions among moderate–high drinkers towards drinking less. Whether this translated into actual reductions in consumption is not known. The impact of a more explicitly 'mental health' programme, this time in South Africa, was reported by Wessels et al. (1999). They recorded over 3000 telephone calls asking for information on mental health issues following a television series which described and explained the signs and symptoms of a variety of mental health problems. Most calls related to depression and anxiety. Other programmes have had more limited goals, including attempts to reduce the stigma associated with mental health problems (Corrigan et al. 2007).

Economic interventions

So far, the preventive approaches discussed have focused on individuals. More radical approaches to mental health promotion go beyond the individual and consider how societal conditions impact on mental health. The link between poor mental health and socio-economic inequalities has led some commentators to suggest that the most compelling intervention strategies to reduce the prevalence of mental health problems are likely to be social, economic and political. Davey Smith et al. (1999), for example, argued for the implementation of 'affordable' basic income schemes as a means of ending poverty. These could take the form of a payment received by every person or household to provide a minimal income, with the amount paid based on age and family status. In addition, they suggested that all benefits to families with children which receive income support should be increased to avoid the next generation being disadvantaged from birth. They noted that a quarter of all children are born to mothers under the age of 25 years, and that the government should ensure that those under this age receive no fewer benefits than older individuals – as they did at the time of their paper. It is beyond the scope of this book to comment on the strengths and weaknesses of various economic systems. However, they have significant implications for mental health and should, therefore, form a legitimate area of influence for those involved in health promotion and public health.

Systemic interventions

Large-scale societal changes such as those considered above are clearly constrained by political factors. However, there are some enclosed communities such as the workplace or school where interventions designed to change the entire working or learning environment are more possible and may impact on the mental health of all those within them.

One of the few worksite interventions to report a systemic approach to reducing stress was reported by Maes et al. (1998). Their intervention drew upon studies that identified working conditions that can enhance both the well-being of workers and work production levels. These included individuals working within their capabilities, avoiding short and repetitive performance tasks, having some control over the organization of work, and having adequate social contact. With these factors in mind, they attempted, within the constraints of production, to change the nature of each worker's job in a number of large factories to bring it closer to the ideal. Although measures of 'stress' were not taken as part of the research programme, these changes resulted in an increase in the quality of work and lower absenteeism rates: both indicative of an increase in well-being at work.

In another context, the School Transitional Environment Project (STEP) (e.g. Felner et al. 1993) changed the school environment to make it less threatening to students during transitions from lower to higher schools. It aimed to reduce the complexity of the new school environment, to make teachers more supportive, and to create a 'stable support mechanism' through a consistent set of peers and classmates. This resulted in significantly lower levels of stress and anxiety, depression and delinquent behaviour than in schools where these changes were not instituted. It also proved more effective than a teaching programme focusing on coping and problem-solving skills on measures of adjustment to school change and academic performance.

5.4 Cross-cultural issues

The chapter has already noted that people from minority cultures may experience more mental health problems than the majority population. But there are other, perhaps more fundamental, differences in the experience of mental health and mental health problems across cultures. The next section of the book considers two sides of this phenomenon.

Presentation of problems

Not surprisingly, perhaps, many common conditions present in ways that reflect the culture in which they are situated. Members of the Inuit population, for example, may develop a condition known as *kayak angst* – a feeling of panic associated with being alone in a kayak in the Arctic wastes. This may be termed 'agoraphobia with panic disorder' in societies where there are lots of houses and busy streets, and no kayaks. Mental distress may also result from exaggeration of culturally specific normative behaviours or concerns. In Japan, where ritual and politeness are extremely important, a condition known as *taijin kyofusho* is an incapacitating fear of offending or harming others through one's own awkward social behaviour, glancing at their genital areas, or imagined physical defect.

Similar problems may also present quite differently in various parts of the world. One of the key differences across cultures is the greater or lesser emphasis placed on physical symptoms as either a metaphor for, or means of expressing, emotional distress. It is generally acknowledged that people from Eastern cultures tend to 'somatize' their distress, talking about it in terms of physical symptoms, while people from Western cultures talk more about psychological symptoms. An example of this type of expression can be found in the Korean word 'hwa-byung' which means 'fire illness' and can equally be epigastric pain or anger due to interpersonal conflict.

In South and East Asia, presentation of mental health problems through physical complaints is common. In an early report of this phenomenon, Kleinman (1977) reported the experiences of a group of Taiwanese people with 'depressive syndrome'. Eighty-eight per cent of them initially complained only of physical symptoms – and did not report any emotional or psychological problems when directly asked about them. Twenty-eight per cent rejected the idea that they were depressed even when they had experienced symptom relief following antidepressant medication. In a similar group of American patients, only 4 per cent presented complaining of physical symptoms. These cross-cultural differences remain. Hoge et al. (2006), for example, compared presentation of what DSM would term generalized anxiety disorder in people in Nepal and the USA, and found that the Nepalese people were more likely to report high levels of somatic symptoms such as dizziness and indigestion, while the Americans were more likely to report psychological symptoms including being scared or nervous.

In a study of this phenomenon in different ethnic groups within one country, in this case the UK, Bhatt et al. (1989) found that people from an Indian culture were more likely to attribute mental health problems to physical causes than were an indigenous English comparison group. Similarly, Gada (1982) found that depressed patients from an Indian background were more likely to report somatic symptoms and show evidence of hypochondriasis than were depressed indigenous British patients. Conversely, guilt feelings, obsessional and paranoid symptoms were significantly more frequent among the indigenous British patients. Later research by Commander et al. (2004) found no differences between the beliefs of indigenous British and South Asian people about the nature and cause of their anxiety or depression. This suggests that some of the findings reported here may be framed in time, and may change as cultural influences change.

Kleinman (1977) suggested that differing presentations reflect differing social beliefs, norms and attitudes towards mental health problems. He argued that people from cultures that stigmatize mental health problems or where treatments for such problems are usually somatic, are more likely to report physical rather than mental problems. An example of this was provided by Kirmayer et al. (2004), who reported a study of Vietnamese people who had emigrated to Canada. Many of them expressed emotional distress in terms of a condition they termed *uat u'c*. This was described in terms of having bodily aches, being cold and depleted of energy. However, further discussion with these individuals revealed that their symptoms resulted from a predicament that involved indignation over a social injustice that could not be denounced because of their status within the social hierarchy and a need to maintain social harmony. Similarly, Karasz (2005) examined conceptual models of depressive symptoms in South Asian and European immigrants to the USA. Participants were presented with a vignette describing depressive symptoms and then asked about their understanding of the symptoms presented. The Asian people identified the problem in the vignette in social and moral terms, and suggested treatment should involve self-help and non-professional help. The Europeans typically held one of two models. The first was similar to that of the Asians; the other emphasized biological explanations including 'hormonal imbalance' and 'neurological problem'.

More radical differences in beliefs about the nature of mental health problems have been found in a variety of non-Western countries, including those in Africa and Asia. In Malaysia, Razali (1995) found that 53 per cent of people with mental health problems attributed them to supernatural agents, such as witchcraft or possession by evil spirits. Interestingly, belief in supernatural causes of mental illness was not significantly associated with age, gender, level of education or occupation. A second example can be found in research from Zimbabwe, reported by Patel et al. (1995), who found that angered ancestral spirits, evil spirits and witchcraft were potent causes of mental health problems. Similar levels of belief in supernatural causes of mental health problems were found in Nigeria by Adebowale and Ogunlesi (1999), although they also found that 17 per cent of people attributed their mental health disorder to biological factors, and 23 per cent believed their condition was the result of psychosocial factors. The latter beliefs were more common among urban than among rural dwellers, suggesting that beliefs about the cause of mental health disorders may change as people become aware of alternative causal explanations. This change from traditional models of mental health problems to more Western understandings has been tracked over time in Kerala, southern India, where Halliburton (2005) reported a transition from explanations of mental health problems in terms of spirit possession to more Western understandings of 'depression' and 'tension' over time.

Fancher, T.L., Ton, H., Meyer, O.L. et al. (2009) Discussing depression with Vietnamese American patients, *Journal of Immigrant and Minority Health*, 12: 263–6.

Asian-American patients in the US mental health system have higher dropout rates, shorter duration of treatment, fewer positive outcomes and lower levels of satisfaction with care than their White-American counterparts. The authors considered these problems may reflect the way Asians with mental health problems present to health care providers, and that the latter do not have a good understanding of the experience of mental health problems in this cultural group. The present study aimed to improve this understanding. It comprised a series of interviews with Vietnamese community members to gain an understanding of their perspective on depression.

Method

Participants
Interviews were conducted with a total of eleven Vietnamese mental health experts, patients with depression, or their family members identified either by local mental health practitioners or through snowball sampling. Interviews were conducted in either Vietnamese or English.

Findings

Data analysis involved the use of grounded theory. In this, transcripts were read independently by research team members, and themes within the transcripts identified. These were discussed and agreed with other members of the research team. Once the themes were established, the transcripts were read and passages identified as fitting within each theme. Participants described experiences with depression and health care system using four themes: (1) stigma and face; (2) social functioning and the role of the family; (3) traditional healing and beliefs about medications; and (4) language and culture.

Stigma and face

Patients and families frequently denied signs and symptoms of mental illness to preserve their public appearance and save face for themselves and their family. They were concerned that other members of the Asian community would consider them to be a reflection of poor moral character, spiritual weakness or improper upbringing. These beliefs may be shaped by experiences in Vietnam where mental health problems were associated with institutionalization or imprisonment.

Social functioning and the role of the family

Participants emphasized the importance of including the family in medical care decision-making and in thinking about depression as a disruption of social group functioning rather than as an individual mental health problem. Mental health problems often led to intense family involvement in lieu of formal treatment, as a result of mistrust of the psychiatric services. There was also concern that seeking medical help would reflect inadequate family support. The struggle between the traditional and Western patterns of care creates stresses for the family and the individual with the mental health problem.

Traditional healing and beliefs about medications

Many Vietnamese Americans believe that mental illness stems from metaphysical imbalances. Accordingly, they frequently use traditional methods before seeking medical help. They also believe that Western medications work quickly and have many strong side-effects, but may be harmful to the body, and Vietnamese people tolerate less medication than Westerners. They were concerned that Western clinicians may not be aware of these facts.

Language and culture

Participants felt that non-Vietnamese health care professionals were unable to understand the nuances of their culture that include respect for authority, need for smooth relationships and traditional interdependent family relationships. Concerns about communication difficulties were common. Patients may also not want to question or show any disagreement with the high status health care providers.

Discussion

The research identified several barriers to effective mental health care for Asian Americans. Although the sample size was very small, the issues raised are likely to be common to many others. According to the authors, culturally informed care for Vietnamese patients should result from providers (i) minimizing stigma and helping patients find face-saving communication strategies, (ii) addressing social functioning and family roles, and (iii) where possible, actively engaging the family in the presence of the patient. In addition, Vietnamese patients value efforts to incorporate traditional beliefs into any treatment plan involving an explanation of depression as an imbalance in chemicals that affects both the brain and body. To optimize language concordance and cultural understanding, bilingual and bicultural staff should be essential members of the health care team.

5.5 Seeking help

Not surprisingly, the beliefs individuals hold about the cause of any problem will influence the type of help they seek. Razali and Najib (2000), for example, found that 69 per cent of Malay patients in their sample had sought help from traditional healers called a *Bomoh* before consulting a psychiatrist. Similar patterns of help seeking also occur in a number of African countries. Abiodun (1995) found the first point of contact for about one-third of patients attending a mental health service in Nigeria had been a traditional or religious healer. By contrast, Appiah-Poku et al. (2004) found that only 6 per cent of Ghanaian people using their local psychiatric services had seen a faith healer before coming to the service. Again, these data allow the possibility of shifting cultural understandings of the causes of mental health problems and the type of help that is sought. To put these data in some context, Elkins et al. (2005) found that 44 per cent of their sample of US psychiatric in-patients had tried to treat their condition by the use of herbal therapies before seeking professional help; 30 per cent had used spiritual healing.

Non-Western approaches to the treatment of mental health problems differ significantly from that familiar to most Westerners. Treatment by a *Bomoh*, for example, differs according to their diagnosis of the problem. If the condition appears to be caused by a spell, the *Bomoh* finds out the ingredients of the spells and removes or neutralizes them. If the problem is caused by ghosts or evil spirits, they try to drive out or defeat them. This involves going into a trance, carrying out exorcism, communicating with spirits and reciting special prayers or verses from the Koran. Traditional Chinese treatments may involve the use of herbs and diet therapy. Kleinman (1977) described the treatment one Chinese man had to treat his recurrent feelings of grief and loneliness following a number of bereavements, and depression following financial losses on the stock market. He attributed his symptoms to not having enough blood, and was treated with tonics to 'increase blood' and with symbolically 'hot' food to correct his underlying humoral imbalance. He was also considering treatment with acupuncture.

Stop and think...

Imagine waking up feeling miserable, sad and finding it difficult to face the day. How serious do these feelings need to be before you seek help? Do they have to last a week, a month, before you seek help? And who do you tell about your problems? Your doctor? Your friends? And when you *do* tell people, how much do you confide and how do you describe your problems?

Admitting both to yourself and others that you have a mental health problem is not always easy. But what factors influence when and how an individual decides to tell others about any emotional distress they are experiencing – and how much they tell? Culture is only one factor that determines when and how such problems are reported. What other factors will influence this process? Personality? The social context within which an individual lives? The strength of the support available to the individual?

5.6 Chapter summary

1 Both small and large social groups and other social factors impact on levels of mental health conditions.

2 Family models of mental health note the reciprocity between family members, and that mental health problems arise as a consequence of interactions between family members.

3 Structural family therapy adopts a model of a well-functioning family, based on the boundaries between units within the family. It uses behavioural strategies to shift dysfunctional families towards this model.

4 Strategic family therapy has no model of appropriate functioning. It uses two strategies of change: positive reframing and paradoxical manipulations.

5 Three major social variables impact on levels of mental health within the population: socio-economic position, gender and minority status.

6 Explanations for these differences include differences in levels of stress and coping resources and, perhaps, processes of social comparison.

7 Cultural factors may influence the causal explanations for mental health problems and the treatment individuals from differing cultures seek.

8 Proponents of radical health promotion suggest that health inequalities can best be addressed through economic and political changes.

9 Those involved in promoting mental health have typically done so using more circumscribed interventions including using the media and open access classes to teach stress coping skills. Some projects have also addressed working and school environments to make them less stressful.

5.7 For discussion

1 Virtually all conditions treated with family therapy can also be treated by one-to-one therapy. What are the advantages and disadvantages of each approach?

2 How effective is a white middle-class therapist likely to be when providing therapy for someone from a different social class and culture? How can they alter the approach they take with such an individual?

3 Consider how you could promote mental health within the wider population or specific groups, such as working mothers or students.

4 If mental health disorders result at least in part from social conditions, should psychologists be actively involved in attempts to influence public health policy and relevant government decisions?

5.8 Key term

Stress management a specialist cognitive behavioural intervention focusing on teaching people to cope with stress; includes the usual elements of this approach, including relaxation, self-instruction and cognitive challenge.

5.9 Further reading

Accortt, E.E., Freeman, M.P. and Allen, J.J. (2008) Women and major depressive disorder: clinical perspectives on causal pathways, *Journal of Women's Health*, 17: 1583–80.

Dallos, R. and Draper, R. (2005) *An Introduction to Family Therapy: Systemic Theory and Practice*. Buckingham: Open University Press.

Fernando, S. (2010) *Mental Health, Race and Culture*. Basingstoke: Palgrave Macmillan.

Wilkinson, R. and Pickett, K. (2009) *The Spirit Level: Why More Equal Societies Always Do Better*. London: Allen Lane.

PART 2

Specific issues

Part contents

Somatoform disorders

This chapter explores some of the psychological conditions in which the relationship between psychological and physical processes is most apparent. It explores four conditions which fall under the heading of somatoform disorders. At a quick glance, the first two, somatization and hypochondriasis, appear very similar as they both involve the reporting of inappropriately high levels of physical symptoms, and some clinicians have argued that they overlap in a number of ways. However, there are key differences between them. Somatization disorder involves the experience and reporting of recurrent and frequently changing physical symptoms, which cannot be explained by any known medical condition and may raise some concern. Hypochondriasis is excessive fear of illness and the belief that one has an undiagnosed physical disease. It may involve checking or seeking medical reassurance as a means of reducing fear.

The other two conditions are more easily distinguishable. The first, body dysmorphic disorder, involves an excessive dissatisfaction with one's body or particular body parts. Finally, the chapter examines one of the most intriguing psychosomatic conditions, conversion disorder, in which an individual may develop extreme and disabling physical symptoms, such as paralysis or blindness, with no apparent physical cause. By the end of the chapter, you should have an understanding of:

- The nature and aetiology of each condition from a number of theoretical perspectives
- The types of interventions used to treat each disorder
- The relative effectiveness of each of these interventions.

6.1 Somatization disorder

Somatization involves the experience and reporting of physical symptoms that cause distress but lack corresponding physical pathology and cannot be explained by physical examination or diagnostic techniques. DSM IV-TR identified the following diagnostic criteria for its diagnosis:

- A history of many physical complaints beginning before the age of 30 years which occur over a period of several years and result in treatment being sought or significant impairment, including:
  - four *pain* symptoms: a history of pain related to at least four different sites or functions (e.g. head, abdomen, menstruation, sexual intercourse)
  - two *gastrointestinal* symptoms: a history of at least two gastrointestinal symptoms other than pain (e.g. nausea, bloating, or intolerance of several foods)
  - one *sexual* symptom: a history of at least one sexual or reproductive symptom other than pain (e.g. sexual indifference, irregular menses, excessive menstrual bleeding)
  - one *pseudoneurological* symptom: a history of at least one symptom suggesting a neurological condition (e.g. impaired coordination or balance, difficulty swallowing or lump in throat, double vision).
- Either:
  - the symptoms cannot be fully explained by a known medical condition or the direct effects of a substance, or
  - when there is a related general medical condition, the physical complaints or resulting impairment are in excess of what would be expected.
- The symptoms are not intentionally feigned or produced.

Of note is the age at which symptoms typically start – well before the age of onset of most chronic diseases – and the wide variety of symptoms necessary for a diagnosis to be assigned.

Prevalence of somatization disorder

Most of us experience sensations or symptoms that are not related to an obvious illness at some time or other. Indeed, Hiller et al. (2006) reported that 82 per cent of their large population sample had experienced such symptoms in the previous week. Symptom reporting was highest among women, those aged over 45 years, with a lower educational level, lower household income, and from rural areas. The most common symptoms included various types of pain, food intolerance, and 'sexual indifference'. This background of symptom reporting makes if difficult to assess levels of somatization disorder – where the level of symptoms has become pathological. However, Creed and Barsky (2004) estimated that, at any one time, between 0.1 and 0.7 per cent of the general population would be given this diagnosis. Among people in medical wards, Fink et al. (2004) estimated its prevalence as 5.2 per cent, with a significant difference between the rates among men and women (3.8 and 7.5 per cent respectively). It is often accompanied by high levels of depression or anxiety (Henningsen et al. 2003).

Comparing rates of somatization disorder across countries and cultures is difficult, as people from some cultures are more likely to 'somatize', or report psychological symptoms in terms of physical states, than others (see the discussion in Chapter 5). Accordingly, care must be taken not to 'diagnose' somatization among people from cultures in which somatic symptoms are a frequent way of reporting of emotional distress, where some form of mood or anxiety disorder may be more appropriate.

Aetiology of somatization disorder

Childhood learning
Somatization may have its roots in early childhood experiences. There are several retrospective studies indicating that adults who report high levels of somatic symptoms are more likely to have witnessed illness in family members than is the norm. These include:

- excessive somatic complaints by parents
- excessive illness or complaints of illness from other family members
- excessive family complaints of pain.

In one study of this phenomenon, Craig et al. (2002) compared the (self-reported) history of three groups of women who were either chronic somatizers, had a long-term illness, or were healthy. Somatizing mothers were three times more likely than the other women to have witnessed a parent having a physical illness. The children of these somatizing mothers were, in turn, more likely to report health problems than were the children of the medically ill or healthy women, and had more consultations with family doctors. In a second study with the same women, Craig et al. (2004b) demonstrated the subtle way in which parents can focus on health-related issues. In their study, they observed the women playing with their 4–8-year-old children in a structured play setting. Somatizing mothers were emotionally flatter and gave their children less attention than the other mothers during both play tasks. However, they were *more* responsive to their child than the other mothers when they played with a medical box. Craig and colleagues suggested that childhood experience of illness is most likely to result in somatization if it is associated with a lack of parental care (Craig et al. 2002) or sexual abuse (Modestin et al. 2005). However, the role of severe trauma was questioned by Lackner et al. (2004), who found that low-level, long-term neglect may be a more important precursor than specific traumas. Integrating these various strands of evidence, Craig et al. (1993) suggested a two-stage process to the development of somatization disorder:

- lack of care or neglect increases risk of an emotional disorder such as anxiety or depression
- high levels of illness behaviour among parents predispose children to interpret their emotional symptoms as indicative of physical illness.

Psychoanalytic explanations

Classic Freudian explanations of physical symptoms focus on sudden, inexplicable presentations of physical symptoms – conversion disorder – and are considered later in the chapter. Some post-Freudian explanations of somatization are not dissimilar to the explanation considered in the previous section. According to Guthrie (1996), deficiencies in the early mother–child relationship leave the individual with an inability to use their imagination and language to describe and control stress and distress. This results in a limited fantasy life, difficulties in processing emotional experiences, and a susceptibility to somatic complaints. This leads to difficulties in developing appropriate relationships in adulthood. Any relationships the individual does develop are either chaotic or symbiotic. In the latter, they form a relationship with someone who adopts the role of carer – and they adopt the role of invalid. The physical symptoms they report therefore act both as a way of coping with intolerable emotional feelings and as a means of eliciting the care of their partner.

An alternative psychoanalytic understanding was proposed by Bucci (1997), who argued that as a child we establish representations of events or objects (such as people) across all modalities. These include memories of the event or object, their symbolic interpretations and related somatic, emotional, and even motoric associations. According to Bucci, somatization occurs when dissociation occurs within our emotional schema between the symbolic representation of objects and their associated somatic elements. As a consequence, the individual may experience significant emotional responses to particular individuals or situations, but not understand why these emotional responses occur or have the language to describe or resolve them. As an example of this process, an individual who was emotionally abused as a child by a parent may have experienced intense fear in the presence of that individual, but as they were totally dependent on them and could therefore not avoid them, the child could not develop appropriate links between feelings of fear, cognitive representations of fear, and behaviours typically associated with fear such as avoidance. In adulthood, interpersonal fear and discomfort would therefore be felt at a somatic level only – unconnected to thoughts that would help make sense of these feelings to the individual concerned. As a consequence, they would not develop appropriate strategies to resolve the problems causing their fear, and continue to experience the somatic experience over a sustained period of time. This would eventually be interpreted as an illness or set of symptoms with no obvious psychological cause.

A psychobiological model

The simplest biological model of somatization suggests that people with the disorder have a biological sensitivity to physiological activity within the body, which they report as 'symptoms'. The biological pathways through which this may occur are not clear – and not all evidence supports the notion of this hypersensitivity (e.g. Sherman et al. 2004). Nevertheless, Rief et al. (2004) speculated that dysregulation of amino acids and serotonin may contribute to somatization. They compared levels of various amino acids including tryptophan (a precursor to serotonin) in patients with somatization disorder, with and without depression, and normal controls and found that low levels of tryptophan were associated with high levels of somatization independently of the presence of depression. They took these data to suggest that the serotonergic system may be involved in a process of sensitization of neurons (including those in the muscles) that leads to a state of hyperalgesia, which forms the basis of chronic somatization.

In their perception-filter model (see Figure 6.1), Rief and Barsky (2005) hypothesized that all our body organs continually produce sensory information that is forwarded to higher cortical structures. The healthy nervous system learns to filter out this 'sensory noise', preventing over-stimulation of the upper cortical structures with irrelevant information: we experience higher levels of physical sensations if this filtering process is distorted. Rief and Barsky contend that a number of physical and psychological factors can increase or decrease both the need for the filter to operate and its effectiveness. Factors that increase the physical signals, and thereby increase the risk of experiencing unexplained symptoms, include high levels of sympathetic activity, stress, and neural sensitization. Factors that decrease the effectiveness of the filter include high levels of health anxiety, which may result in the individual interpreting any physical sensations in a catastrophizing manner. That is, they may misperceive body sensations as evidence of dangerous somatic processes. They may also selectively choose to attend to any sensations they experience. These beliefs and attentional processes may arise from the childhood experiences considered in the previous section.

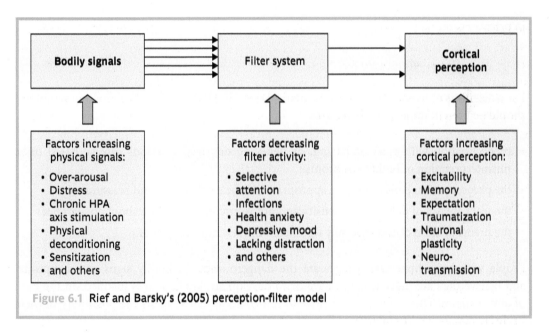

Figure 6.1 Rief and Barsky's (2005) perception-filter model

Treatment of somatization disorder

Pharmacological treatment

There are very few published pharmacological treatment trials for somatization disorder. However, one study has assessed the effectiveness of SSRIs, possibly linking back to the role of serotonin suggested by Rief and colleagues. Noyes et al. (1998) reported an uncontrolled trial in which 29 people with a variety of somatoform disorders were treated. Only seven had a diagnosis of somatization disorder. Of these, four evidenced moderate improvements, at least in the short term. So, there is preliminary evidence of a therapeutic benefit for SSRIs, but more trials are needed to confirm this.

Psychological interventions

There are also relatively few studies of the effectiveness of psychological interventions in the treatment of somatization disorder. The condition is often reported as difficult to treat. However, a number of studies have found some benefit following cognitive behavioural interventions. Lidbeck (2003) reported on the effectiveness of a programme involving a thorough physical examination, education about psychological and physiological stress designed to change the attribution of symptoms from being signs of illness to signs of stress, and relaxation training. In comparison with no treatment, this programme achieved reductions in cognitive worries and medication use both immediately following treatment and at six-month follow-up. A year later, participants in the intervention group maintained their improvements on measures of health worry, and also reported gains on measures of generalized anxiety and depression. Similar benefits were found up to 15 months after a similar intevention by Allen et al. (2006), while Martin et al. (2007) achieved benefits lasting up to six months following a single session of CBT in primary care.

6.2 Hypochondriasis

For a diagnosis of hypochondriasis to be made, DSM-IV-TR states that the following symptoms should be present for at least six months:

- preoccupation with fears of having, or believing one has, a serious disease based upon misinterpretation of bodily symptoms
- the preoccupation persists despite appropriate medical evaluation and reassurance
- the fears are not of delusional intensity and not restricted to concern about appearance
- the preoccupation causes clinically significant distress or impairment.

People with hypochondriasis exaggerate the dangerousness of bodily signs and symptoms, and believe they are more likely to have or to develop an illness than is justified on the basis of any evidence. They are highly sensitive to information that suggests the possibility of them having a disease, and frequently seek confirmation of their worries from a variety of sources. By contrast, they are highly resistant to reassurance: appropriate information, education and explanation typically fail to reduce any fears of disease (Rassin et al. 2008). Their fear seems limited to threats to health and is not found in other areas of life. Barsky et al. (2001), for example, found that hypochondriacal patients considered themselves at more risk of developing various diseases than a comparison group of patients from a primary care setting, but the two groups did not differ in their perceived risk of being involved in an accident or the subject of crime.

Prevalence of hypochondriasis

Rates of the disorder in the general population are relatively low. In a meta-analysis of data available at the time, Creed and Barsky (2004) suggested prevalence levels of between 0.03 and 2.8 per cent among the general population. Fink et al. (2004) estimated the prevalence of hypochondriasis among people admitted into general medical wards to be 3.5 per cent, with markedly different rates between men and women (1.5 and 6.0 per cent respectively).

Aetiology of hypochondriasis

Genetic factors

There seems to be a genetic predisposition to at least some elements of hypochondriasis. Gillespie et al. (2000), for example, examined the genetic risk for developing what they termed somatic distress. They gave measures of anxiety, depression, phobic anxiety and somatic distress to 3469 Australian twins aged 18 to 28 years, and found that 33 per cent of the variance in somatic distress appeared to be due to a gene action unrelated to depression or phobic anxiety. Accordingly, their data suggest a unique genetic contribution to the reporting of somatic distress, and that this is not simply a manifestation of a more general propensity to anxiety or depression. One responsible gene appears to be a serotonin transporter gene polymorphism (Veletza et al. 2009).

Psychosocial factors

Many of the risk factors for hypochondriasis overlap with those thought to increase risk for somatization disorder. Rates of physical and sexual abuse among people with hypochondriasis are higher than among comparison groups (e.g. Barsky et al. 1995), as are reports of inadequate or inattentive parenting (Bass and Murphy 1995). Other studies have reported high levels of childhood sickness (Craig et al. 1993) and parental overprotection and encouragement of sick-role behaviour (Parker and Lipscombe 1980). Noyes et al. (2003) found that hypochondriacal symptoms were positively correlated with all the insecure attachment styles they measured, especially the fearful style. These same symptoms were positively correlated with self-reported interpersonal problems and negatively correlated with patient ratings of satisfaction with, and reassurance from, medical care.

Psychoanalytic models

Hypochondriasis has received surprisingly little consideration within the psychoanalytic literature, which has focused on explanations for the cause of unexpected symptoms rather than worry about them. Indeed, Freud (1914) originally considered it to be an 'actual neurosis'. That is, unlike the defensive neuroses, he considered hypochondria to be a response to genuine symptoms – they were not generated by the unconscious as a result of some internal conflict. However, Freud (1914) subsequently developed a more psychoanalytic explanation for hypochondria, arguing that the libido could be divided into two dimensions. Object libido involves a love of external objects; ego libido involves love for oneself and one's body. It can also be called narcissism. According to Freud, challenges to the object libido result in neurotic anxiety; challenges to the ego libido result in hypochondria. One challenge may come from the individual himself. According to Freud, if an individual becomes absorbed by his ego libido, two things may happen. Their focus on external sources of love will diminish, and they will develop anxiety about their physical state. The individual focuses on their love of their body and physicality, but at the same time becomes anxious that they may lose the object of their love and attention. Thus, they focus on both the good things about their body, but also any threats to their health that may destroy the object of their love.

Interpersonal theory

Reflecting the overlap between the two disorders, the model of hypochondriasis proposed by Stuart and Noyes (1999) is similar to the model of somatization of Craig et al. That is, they consider it to involve seeking emotional care from professionals as well as family and friends, through the reporting of physical complaints or symptoms. According to Stuart and Noyes, this results from anxious and insecure parental attachments established early in life. As in the case of somatization, lack of parental care or an adverse early environment may cause a child to view others as unreliable caregivers. The one way of gaining attention these children may have is through complaints of physical symptoms, as their parents are unresponsive to complaints of psychological distress. Thus, a cycle of complaints about physical symptoms, reinforced by parental attention, is established. This then becomes the primary way of gaining adult attention and feelings of attachment. This has two outcomes. First, the child learns to use complaints of physical symptoms to gain attention and perhaps love. Second, the child fails to learn other ways of eliciting care and attention from their environment. As an adult, the still insecurely attached person may communicate his or her need for care through complaints of illness. Unfortunately, these attempts at seeking support are frequently ignored, and even viewed with some suspicion, which may reinforce the original fear of lack of attachment and supportive relationships.

Hypochondriasis as threat

The model developed by Warwick and Salkovskis (1990) focused on the immediate cognitive processes involved in hypochondriasis. They suggested that current life stresses or simply noticing bodily signs can activate previously latent cognitive schemata about health and disease – probably developed in childhood as a result of circumstances described above – that are faulty, unduly alarming, or pessimistic. This leads to a number of sequelae:

- *Selective attention to information supporting this schema:* an increased focus on internal physiological factors such as heart rate, gastric motility, and so on. People with hypochondriasis may also focus on observable bodily signs such as lumps, bumps and moles, and bodily products such as sputum, faeces, and so on.
- *Cognitive errors:* disconfirmatory information, such as medical reassurance (even when sought) is ignored, rumination about the consequences may occur – usually in some catastrophic form.
- *Physiological changes:* autonomic activity may increase due to the anxiety, resulting in change in bowel habits, sleeping, and so on. Each will confirm the health problem.
- *Behavioural responses:* these may involve safety behaviours such as repeated checking, taking unnecessary preventive medication, and so on. People with hypochondriasis may avoid

activities that trigger health rumination or seek family or medical reassurance that 'all is well'. Safety behaviours, like those in obsessive-compulsive disorder, maintain the problem, as the individual feels emotionally more secure following their execution and never learns that a failure to engage in them will not lead to disastrous outcomes.

This link with obsessive-compulsive disorder (see Chapter 8) is not coincidental. A number of commentators have linked hypochondriasis and obsessive compulsive disorder (see Fineberg et al. 2007). There are high levels of co-morbidity between the two conditions, they have some similarities in their presentation, and both respond to SSRIs (see below). However, there are also some important differences between the two conditions. First, people with hypochondriasis typically have less insight than those with obsessive-compulsive disorder and are more fixed in their beliefs. Second, the neural activity between the two conditions may differ. Rauch et al. (2002), for example, found that an emotional task activated the amygdala of people both with obsessive-compulsive disorder and hypochondriasis, but it only activated the ventrolateral brain regions of people with obsessive-compulsive disorder.

Threat plus symptom sensitivity

A variant of the threat model is one of threat combined with symptom sensitivity. That is, people with hypochondriasis are both more aware of any physical sensations they may have than most people, and are more likely to label these sensations as symptoms of some underlying medical condition (Marcus et al. 2007). In this process, benign bodily sensations are mistakenly attributed to a suspected serious disease. This focuses their attention on their symptoms, which increases their awareness of them, reinforcing the individual's suspicion that they are seriously ill. Evidence for this extension of the model is not strong. Barsky et al. (1995) found that people with hypochondriasis did not differ significantly from a 'normal' comparison group in their accurate awareness of heart beats. Within each sample, the only statistically significant association found was a moderate *negative* correlation between heart beat awareness and the severity of hypochondriasis. So, the results actively countered the threat plus symptom sensitivity model. This negative finding was echoed by Steptoe and Noll (1997) who found a negative correlation between hypochondriacal concerns and accuracy of perception of sweat gland activity.

Stop and think...

One of the jokes often said about medical students as they go through their training is that they experience every illness they encounter – or at least they think they do. Luckily, most of them recover from these non-existent illnesses before developing the next. But this reaction to health and health risk information may have implications for many more people. We are increasingly made aware of our health and the health risks associated with our behaviour, our genetic make-up, and the environment in which we live. Unfortunately, it seems that for some vulnerable people, just being made aware of potential health problems evokes high levels of health anxiety. So, while some may benefit from health advice, others simply become worried about their health. As well as creating a health-conscious society, are we also creating a health-anxious one?

Treatment of hypochondriasis

Psychological treatment

Psychological treatment for hypochondriasis can be difficult, particularly where individuals hold a strong belief in their having a physical disease. One way this has been addressed is through the use of a variety of CBT interventions, including:

- *Behavioural hypothesis testing:* this can involve working with a client to investigate the reality of their symptoms. If someone has a fear of a muscle-wasting disease, for example, they may predict they would become extremely weak if they engage in even light exercise. With some encouragement, this hypothesis can be tested – and hopefully found to be inaccurate.

- *Reducing checking and medical consultation:* in order to reduce safety behaviours in general, and use of medical support in particular, the client may reduce checking behaviour and medical consultations – or delay them. This is similar to the approach taken in obsessive-compulsive disorder and phobias: that is, exposure plus response prevention (see Chapter 7). They may also develop a realistic strategy for when to seek medical help.

- *Cognitive challenge:* this involves techniques to counter some of the catastrophic thoughts that an individual may have about their symptoms. Thus, fear that one has a serious heart problem may be based on the experience of chest discomfort, heart missing a beat, and breathlessness. These experiences may be contextualized and made less threatening by reframing:

  - 'Most heart beats change rhythm from minute to minute.'
  - 'It's normal to become breathless following exertion – especially if you are unfit.'
  - 'I've had these symptoms before, and although they made me worried, they did not lead to any problems.'

A number of studies have now shown cognitive behavioural interventions based on the Salkovskis model to be effective when compared with usual care. Barsky and Ahern (2004), for example, found benefits following a six-session CBT intervention including lower levels of hypochondriacal symptoms, beliefs and health-related anxiety at 6- and 12-month follow-up compared to a no treatment control group. Clark et al. (1998) compared their hypochondriasis treatment pro-gramme with a non-specific CBT intervention which targeted stress-related cognitions and emotions but not those specifically related to health concerns. Comparisons with a waiting list control group showed both treatments were more effective than no therapy. Initially, the inter-ventions had specific benefits: cognitive therapy for hypochondriasis was more effective than CBT stress management on measures of hypochondriasis, but not on measures of general mood disturbance. However, one year after treatment, both interventions appeared equally effective on all measures. A very different approach was adopted by Papageorgiou and Wells (1998), who examined the effectiveness of training people with hypochondriasis to distract away from their worrying thoughts. In a series of three case reports, this resulted in improvements both in mood and in illness-related thoughts and behaviours lasting at least six months following treatment. Sørensen et al. (2010) compared Salkovskis's CBT intervention augmented with the use of mindfulness and group therapy sessions with brief psychodynamic therapy and a waiting list control condition. By six-month follow-up, the augmented CBT intervention proved more effective than the psychodynamic one, which differed little from the control condition. By twelve-month follow up, these differences had reduced, but remained significant.

Pharmacological treatment

Until the late 1980s, the general consensus among clinicians was that pharmacotherapy would not benefit people who experienced hypochondriasis. However, the similarities between hypochondriasis and obsessive-compulsive disorder have led to the use of SSRIs in an attempt to treat it, with some success – although large trials of their effectiveness are still lacking. In one study, Fallon et al. (2008) reported a small placebo-controlled trial of fluoxetine and found significant benefits during the 24 weeks in which patients were receiving the drug. Unfortunately, they were not able to report outcomes following discontinuation of the drug. In a study comparing psychological and pharmacological treatments, Greeven et al. (2007) reported a greater response to cognitive behavioural intervention than medication. Using an intention to treat analysis, they found that after 16 weeks treatment, 45 per cent of people in the psychological group achieved significant reductions in symptoms, compared with 30 per cent of those treated with paroxetine (an SSRI) and 14 per cent given placebo. Of those to complete treatment, the equivalent percentages were 54, 38 and 12 per cent respectively.

Case formulation: hypochondriasis

Mrs T was a woman in her 60s. She lived with her son in a working-class area of Bristol. At the time she was seen by a clinical psychologist, she had been seen by the psychiatric services for many years complaining of various physical symptoms which had no obvious physical cause. These changed over the course of the years, but included a tingling down both sides of her body, dizziness, feeling weak, headache and episodic collapsing.

By the time she was referred to the psychology services, every General Practitioner in her local area had struck her off their list of patients, because she was visiting them once or twice every week complaining of various symptoms and requesting treatment. She had been given multiple diagnostic tests, none of which found any evidence of disease. The General Practitioners felt unable to treat her and had become increasingly frustrated and then frankly annoyed by her repeated visits. The situation had become so bad that the health board had organized for her medical care to provided by each General Practitioner on a three-month basis – something that they adhered to, albeit reluctantly. In addition to medical help, she had sought treatment from a variety of alternative practitioners including herbalists, chiropractors, reflexologists and shiatsu practitioners, none of whom had been of help. She denied any psychological element to her symptoms. She lived with her 40-year-old son, who spent much of his time out of the house or in his own room. She socialized with one or two long-term psychiatric patients she had met through her contact with the psychiatric services. She rarely left her house, and then only to go shopping in her local shops.

When first seen by a psychologist, she complained of long-standing physical symptoms, and was able to provide a diary of her symptoms, recorded on an hourly basis, over many months. She talked incessantly of her symptoms, and it was extremely difficult to divert from them. Investigation of relevant psychological issues proved difficult, as sessions were, at least initially, somewhat overwhelmed by her repeated descriptions of her physical symptoms. However, a time line of key issues did emerge.

Long-term antecedents

Mrs T came from a relatively poor, working-class family. She had three siblings and a history of illness within the family. Her father worked long hours and competition for parental attention was strong. She was unhappy at times, as she felt neglected and estranged from her parents, and did not socialize well with other children from the neighbourhood. There was little emotional warmth in the family. She was often sick as a child, and gained some attention within the family at these times. She left school with no qualifications, but did meet a man who she married and with whom she had a baby. Unfortunately, the marriage was unhappy and she described him as a little odd. She divorced him after a few years and brought up the child on her own. She stated that she had some physical health problems at the time of her marriage, and that they gradually got worse in the following years.

Short-term antecedents

Her son, who was in his 40s, did not marry and continued to live with her until the time she was seen by the psychiatric services. He was relatively happy, did not work and had minimal social relationships, but was keen to move out of the house and develop on his own. However, he was concerned about his mother's health and had continued to live at home in case she became acutely ill and he was unable to help her. He was very worried about his mother and would not forgive himself were anything to happen to her and he was not there to help. He coped with living at home by spending much of his time in his own room – to avoid her constant complaints of physical problems.

Formulation

Mrs T was brought up in a family of little emotional warmth, in which the emotional needs of the children were not recognized and certainly not responded to. One way in which she could gain some parental attention was through 'being ill'. It is possible that she learned to signal emotional distress through the reporting of physical symptoms. Her experience and reporting of such symptoms had varied across her life, with the distress associated with a poor marriage and subsequent divorce being obvious triggers. The latest cause of her symptoms was her worry that her son would leave home and she would be alone, with relatively little social contact. Her symptoms could therefore be seen as both her typical response to stress and a means of keeping her son close to home and as a source of companionship. The style of her attachment to him could be described as anxious attachment, as she feared that if he left home, he would also leave her. Her total focus on her symptoms increased her awareness of her bodily experiences, and increased their impact on her.

Intervention

Mrs T did not recognize that her symptoms might be associated with any psychological issues. She certainly did not recognize the formulation as relevant to her. Nevertheless, it was possible to negotiate some form of intervention. The ideal intervention might be:

- Help Mrs T and her son gain insight into the psychological factors contributing to her problems
- Teach her cognitive strategies to challenge her worries
- Teach her strategies such as mindfulness to help her tolerate her distress. Identify other ways of distracting from distress and worries
- Negotiate with her son a mutually agreeable plan in which he were to leave home, but maintain contact with his mother.

The actual intervention was in some ways more complex and involved more people:

- Regular and pre-arranged appointments with her doctor during which she could discuss her symptoms. It was acknowledged both by Mrs T and the doctors that they would not expect these to result in a 'cure' for her symptoms but this would help her limit her repeated, consistent and increasingly fractious appointments with her doctors.
- Regular meetings with a community mental health nurse, to discuss issues of a psychological nature and to gain support and help in her keeping to the plan.
- She was unwilling to practise strategies such as mindfulness. However, she agreed to leave the house more often and to engage in things to distract her from her worries – this included going out with one of her friends and attending a day hospital one or two days a week, joining in the activities there.
- Her son agreed to consider negotiating leaving home but only after he could see some improvement in his mother's health.

The intervention worked reasonably well, but was not without its problems. While she stuck to her agreement to limited access to her General Practitioners, for example, she began to attend her local hospital Accident and Emergency departments, at one time attending three hospitals in one week. We negotiated this issue by noting that her symptoms had lasted many years without becoming so serious that she had required medical treatment and that her visits to any doctor (including Accident and Emergency Departments) did not result in any effective treatment. Accordingly, delaying seeing a doctor by, say, a week would be unlikely to either result in a sudden deterioration of her health or stop her accessing an effective cure. She could see the logic of this argument, and agreed to try and reduce her visits to the hospitals. To help her cope with the consequent anxiety, she would try and talk with her friends on the phone about non-health-related issues or do other things to distract her from her worries. This proved an effective approach. Over the following six months, she showed significant improvements. Her mood lifted, she was more social, and went on day trips with friends. She focused less on her symptoms and did not let them dominate her life as much as before. She still experienced her symptoms, but was better able to cope with them. Her son continued to live at home, but life was better as (by mutual agreement in a joint session with the psychologist) Mrs T had agreed to talk less about her symptoms and he had agreed to be more social around the house and to spend more time with her. So, their relationship had improved and he no longer felt the need to leave home.

6.3 Body dysmorphic disorder

Many of us have some degree of dissatisfaction with our body. A survey of over 4000 people, in the magazine *Psychology Today* (http://cms.psychologytoday.com/articles/pto-19970201-000023.html), for example, found that 56 per cent of women reported being dissatisfied with their appearance. Major sources of dissatisfaction were the abdomen (71 per cent), body weight (66 per cent), hips (60 per cent), and muscle tone (58 per cent). Major concerns for men were their abdomen (63 per cent), weight (52 per cent), muscle tone (45 per cent) and chest size (38 per cent). Significantly less of us are so unhappy that this dissatisfaction reaches pathological proportions. Bohne et al. (2002), for example, found that while 74 per cent of American university students had body image concerns, only 29 per cent were preoccupied by them, and only 4 per cent met DSM-IV criteria for body dysmorphic disorder. Among the general population, prevalence rates are about 2.5 per cent in women and 2.2 per cent in men (Koran et al. 2008). Not surprisingly, perhaps, rates are higher among people seeking plastic surgery, where they are around 10 per cent (Aouizerate et al. 2003). Sadly for these people, surgery rarely improves their feelings about themselves.

Body dysmorphic disorder – sometimes referred to as dysmorphophobia – involves a preoccupation with an imagined defect in appearance. In addition, people with the disorder experience significant levels of negative thinking, self-criticism, anxiety and depression. DSM-IV-TR stated the following criteria must be met for its diagnosis:

- Preoccupation with an imagined defect in appearance. If a slight physical anomaly is present, the person's concern is markedly excessive.
- The preoccupation causes clinically significant distress or impairment in social, occupational or other areas of functioning.

Concerns can involve preoccupations with the face (such as scars, spots, acne, or the shape or size of the nose, mouth, etc.), the hair (fears of receding hairlines), or the size and shape of any other body part, including hips, buttocks, legs and hands. Men tend to be concerned about their body build, genitals and hair. Women focus on their hips, breasts and legs (Phillips et al. 2006a). Typical behaviours include:

- frequent checking of appearance in mirrors
- camouflaging the perceived defect with clothing, make-up or posture
- seeking surgery or other medical treatment
- attempts to convince other people of the deformity
- skin picking
- measuring the disliked body part
- excessive dieting or exercise
- avoiding social situations in which the perceived defect may be exposed
- feeling very anxious and self-conscious around other people because of the perceived defect.

Levels of distress can be such that many people with body dysmorphic disorder experience major depression, social phobia, and substance abuse (Sobanski and Schmidt 2000). Up to 80 per cent experience suicidal ideation at some time in their life, and around a quarter will attempt suicide (Phillips 2006). Less dramatically, the condition may prevent normal social, economic and sexual relationships. Didie et al. (2008), for example, found that 80 per cent of their sample of people with body dysmorphic disorder reported some degree of impairment in work: 39 per cent claimed not to have worked in the previous month as a result of their disorder. About 10 per cent of people with the disorder will also be given a diagnosis of anorexia (Philips 1996a). Rates of spontaneous remission are low (Phillips et al. 2008).

A number of clinicians have considered whether body dysmorphic disorder is significantly different to other diagnoses, and whether it can be subsumed within them.

- The American Psychiatric Association (2000) suggested that some people may believe so strongly that they have a physical deformity that their beliefs may be considered delusional, and the disorder be considered a psychotic disorder. By contrast, Phillips et al. (2006) adopted a dimensional view (see Chapter 2), arguing that people with extremely strong beliefs are no different from people with a 'non-delusional' disorder, except in the strength of their belief – and should therefore not be considered under a separate diagnosis.

- A second suggestion is that body dysmorphic disorder may be considered a variant of obsessive-compulsive disorder (Chosak et al. 2008). The preoccupations held by people with body dysmorphic disorder resemble obsessions, in that they are anxiety-producing, recurrent and difficult to control. Repeated checking or other procedures to reduce anxiety are also similar to obsessive-compulsive disorder. In addition, both psychological (exposure plus response prevention) and pharmacological (SSRI) treatments used to treat obsessive-compulsive disorder have also proven effective in treating body dysmorphic disorder. Finally, family members with body dysmorphic disorder are more likely to have a relative with obsessive-compulsive disorder than the general population. Despite these similarities, a number of important differences have been found between the two disorders (see Phillips et al. 2007). Compared to people with obsessive-compulsive disorder, those with body dysmorphic disorder experience poorer insight, higher co-morbidity with major depression, social phobia and psychotic disorders, and higher suicide attempt rates.

- A third approach has argued that body dysmorphic disorder is a form of eating disorder – or that body dysmorphic disorder and eating disorders lie on a continuum of disorders relating to body image distortion. Cororve and Gleaves (2001) identified the key driver of both body dysmorphic disorder and eating disorders as excessive concerns about physical appearance. Perhaps the most problematic issue for this model is that it assumes eating disorders are primarily driven by weight or appearance concerns. While this is generally true of bulimia, these may form only part of the clinical picture in anorexia.

Philips, K.A., Quinna, G. and Stout, R.L. (2008) Functional impairment in body dysmorphic disorder: a prospective, follow-up study, *Journal of Psychiatric Research*, 42: 701–7.

Previous studies have shown body dysmorphic disorder to be associated with significant social or occupational impairment, as well as decrements in mood and quality of life. However, it is not clear how consistent such impairments are over time. This study was first prospective study, involving a relatively large sample, of the course of body dysmorphic disorder over a period of 1 to 3 years. The authors hypothesized that: (i) psychosocial functioning would be poor and remain poor over time, (ii) few participants would 'functionally remit' over the study period, and (iii) high levels of symptoms (and in particular delusional beliefs) would predict poorer outcomes over time.

Method

The sample comprised 176 individuals who met the full criteria for body dysmorphic disorder. They were recruited from a variety of sources, including health professionals, advertisements, and the study website and brochures. Their mean age at intake was 32.5 years. Seventy-one per cent were female, 76 per cent were single.

Assessments

Participants were interviewed at intake and annually for up to three years. At each time, body dysmorphic disorder was diagnosed with the Structured Clinical Interview (SCID). Severity was assessed using the Yale-Brown Obsessive Compulsive Scale Modified for BDD (BDD-YBOCS). Delusional beliefs were assessed using the Brown Assessment of Beliefs Scale (BABS). Psychosocial functioning scores were obtained using the DSM-IV Axis V Global Assessment of Functioning Scale (GAF) measuring psychological, social, and occupational functioning, and the Social and Occupational Functioning Scale (SOFAS), a global measure of social and occupational functioning.

Findings

Levels of remission over time were very low. Over the entire course of the study only 5.7 and 10.6 per cent of the sample attained functional remission on the GAF and SOFAS respectively at any time, and many became worse again. The higher the level of symptoms, the worse the individual functioned (see Figure 6.2). In bivariate analyses, delusionality of BDD beliefs significantly predicted functioning on the GAF ($t = -6.84$, df = 191, $p < 0.0001$), and SOFAS ($t = -5.60$, df = 94, $p < 0.0001$). However, using multiple regression to control for BDD severity, delusionality no longer significantly predicted functioning on any measure.

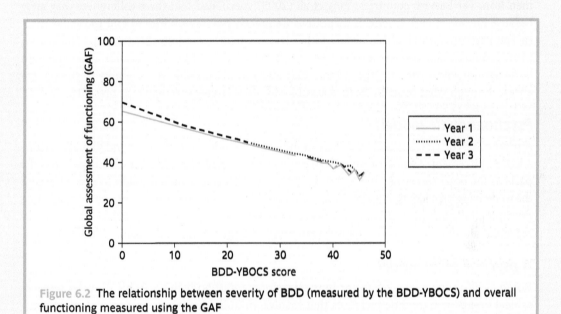

Figure 6.2 The relationship between severity of BDD (measured by the BDD-YBOCS) and overall functioning measured using the GAF

Discussion

The findings add to previous findings suggesting that people with BDD experience poor psycho-social functioning in all areas of their lives. The data also show that few people experience signficant reduction in symptoms, at least over the three years of the study. Unsurprisingly, per-haps, the higher the level of BDD, the greater the level of psychosocial disability. Finally, and against their hypotheses, while the degree of delusionality was predictive of poor functioning when analysed alone, after controlling for severity of BDD, it was no longer predictive. This may reflect findings in other studies that levels of delusionality are strongly associated with the severity of BDD (the absence in the report of the correlation between these variables requires some speculation that this was the case here).

Aetiology of body dysmorphic disorder

Socio-cultural factors

There has been little systematic research into the social and cultural factors associated with the development of body dysmorphic disorder. However, given the importance placed on physical appearance in society, it is not unreasonable to suspect that societal beliefs and attitudes have a role to play. There is certainly evidence that the media can influence our perceptions of what is healthy and attractive: attitudes that may differ across cultures. An example of this can be found in an increasing desire for muscularity among European and American males rarely reported by men from Far Eastern countries. Yang et al. (2005) speculated that these differences may arise because European and American magazines frequently portray undressed and muscular men. In Far Eastern countries, this occurs much less frequently. Despite these societal influences, most people do not become as obsessed or concerned about their appearance as people with body dysmorphic disorder. Other factors may give rise to a specific vulnerability to such influences, although what contributes to this vulnerability is largely speculative at present.

Psychoanalytic models

A psychoanalytic view suggests that body dysmorphic disorder arises from an individual's unconscious displacement of sexual or emotional conflict or feelings of guilt and poor self-image to specific parts of the body (Sobanski and Schmidt 2000). The displacement is thought to occur because the underlying problem is so threatening to the ego that it is unconsciously displaced into the more psychologically manageable issue of appearance. The body part of concern, such as the nose, may represent another, more emotionally threatening, body part, such as the penis (Phillips 1996a).

A psychological model

Rosen (1996) suggested a key factor in the development of body dysmorphic disorder involves critical events or traumatic incidents that involve an individual's appearance. The most common example is being teased about weight or size (Buhlmann et al. 2007), with many people with body dysmorphic disorder reporting repeated criticism about their appearance from members of their own family. More general vulnerability factors may involve being neglected as a child, leading to feelings of being unloved, insecure and rejected (Phillips 1991). Other trauma, such as sexual abuse or assault, may also be involved. Many people with body dysmorphic disorder also report having experienced a physical injury or illness. According to Rosen, these critical events activate dysfunctional assumptions about the normality of physical appearance and the implications of appearance for self-worth and acceptance. In one exploration of this phenomenon, Osman et al. (2004) conducted a semi-structured interview with people with body dysmorphic disorder and 'normal' controls. During the interview, the people with body dysmorphic disorder evidenced more spontaneously occurring negative appearance-related images than did control participants. These images were linked to early stressful memories.

Once established, the disorder may be maintained by selective attention to perceived physical problems or information that supports this belief. In addition, Rosen suggested that rehearsal of negative and distorted self-statements about physical appearance results in them becoming automatic and believable. Finally, the positive emotional responses associated with avoidance, checking and reassurance-seeking behaviours reinforce and maintain the condition. Buhlmann et al. (2006) provided experimental evidence of some of the cognitive distortions held by many people with body dysmorphic disorder. In their study, people with body dysmorphic disorder and a 'normal' control group completed two questionnaires accompanying facial photographs of people in various everyday situations. One questionnaire included self-referent scenarios ('Imagine that the bank teller is looking at you. What is his facial expression like?'); the other included other-referent scenarios ('Imagine that the bank teller is looking at a friend of yours . . .'). They were asked to identify the emotion evident in each face. Overall, people with body dysmorphic disorder had more difficulty identifying emotional expressions in self-referent scenarios than did the comparison group. They also misinterpreted more expressions as contemptuous and angry in self-referent scenarios than did controls.

Biological explanations

There have been relatively few studies of the biological underpinning of body dysmorphic disorder. The role of serotonin has been implicated in its aetiology as a result of its similarities with obsessive-compulsive disorder and its successful treatment with SSRIs (see below). Data from two case reports also provide some relevant evidence. Barr et al. (1992) noted a dramatic increase in symptoms after a woman was placed on a diet low in tryptophan (a serotonin precursor). Similarly, Craven and Rodin (1987) reported a significant worsening of symptoms following the chronic abuse of a drug known as cyproheptadine, which reduces the uptake of serotonin at the postsynaptic receptors and can be used to treat serotonin toxicity.

Treatment of body dysmorphic disorder

Psychological treatment

The most common psychological treatment for body dysmorphic disorder involves CBT. Exposure to avoided situations can include exposure to the sight of the individual's own body or showing their perceived defect in social situations. Often, exposure programmes follow hierarchies of increasingly difficult to cope with body parts or avoided situations. Prevention of checking or self-reassuring behaviours is used to counteract checking rituals. Finally, cognitive restructuring, in which dysfunctional thoughts are identified and then challenged, is a key component of any intervention.

In their systematic review of the relevant literature, Ipser et al. (2009) noted that very few adequately controlled trials of the treatment of body dysmorphic disorder had been conducted, although those that had suggested that exposure-based cognitive behavioural programmes were effective. In one study of this approach, Rosen et al. (1995) followed 54 people with body dysmorphic disorder during a baseline no-treatment phase and then group cognitive behavioural therapy comprising eight 2-hour sessions. Therapy involved modification of intrusive thoughts of body dissatisfaction and overvalued beliefs about physical appearance, exposure to avoided body image situations and elimination of body checking. Body dysmorphic disorder symptoms were 'eliminated' in 82 per cent of people in the intervention group immediately following the intervention and in 77 per cent at follow-up. This compared with a 7 per cent improvement reported during the baseline, no-treatment, phase.

Pharmacological treatment

In their review of the relevant three pharmacological trials, Ipser et al. (2009) concluded that treatment with SSRIs and tricyclics is generally successful. Data from the single placebo-controlled trial of fluoxetine (an SSRI: Phillips and Rasmussen 2004) suggested fluoxetine was more effective than placebo over a period of 12 weeks. Similar effects have also been found in randomized controlled trials evaluating fluoxetine and clomipramine (a tricyclic: Hollander et al. 1999), as well as a more recent small open trial of venlafaxine (an SNRI: Allen et al. 2008). Long-term follow-up data is lacking.

6.4 Conversion disorder

Long known as hysteria or hysterical conversion, the American Psychiatric Association now calls this condition conversion disorder. DSM-IV-TR provides the diagnostic criteria for this diagnosis:

- One or more symptoms or deficits affect voluntary motor or sensory function that suggest a neurological or other general medical condition.
- Psychological factors are judged to be associated with the symptom or deficit because the initiation or exacerbation of the symptom or deficit is preceded by conflicts or other stressors.
- The symptom or deficit is not intentionally produced or feigned.
- The symptom or deficit cannot, after appropriate investigation, be fully explained by a general medical condition, or by the direct effects of a substance, or as a culturally sanctioned behaviour or experience.

People with conversion disorder often present with striking neurological symptoms such as weakness, lack of coordination, paralysis, sensory disorders or memory loss, in the absence of any medical pathology. Less common symptoms include somatosensory disorders and skin changes. Many people appear unconcerned about their symptoms – a characteristic sometimes labelled *la belle indifférence*. Perkin (1989) estimated that up to 4 per cent of those attending neurology outpatient clinics in the United Kingdom have conversion disorders. Benbadis and Allen Hauser (2000) estimated that 10–20 per cent of patients referred for treatment of epilepsy in the USA had what they termed 'psychogenic non-epileptic seizures'. The prevalence of conversion disorders within the general population is harder to estimate. However, Favarelli et al. (1997) found a rate of 0.3 per cent among a relatively small population sample of 673 individuals. It also has high co-morbidity. Crimlisk and Ron (1999) estimated that up to 50 per cent of people with conversion disorder could be assigned a second diagnosis of depression: up to 16 per cent could be assigned a diagnosis of anxiety. The prognosis is not good. Crimlisk et al. (1998) followed 73 people with medically unexplained motor symptoms for six years. Only three people were given a medical diagnosis, indicating an initial misdiagnosis, in this time. Seventy-five per cent were diagnosed with a 'psychiatric disorder'; 45 per cent were diagnosed with a personality disorder. The presenting symptom was unchanged in 14 per cent, and had worsened in 38 per cent. Interestingly, Ahmad et al. (2008) found the rate of admissions to hospital with a diagnosis of medically unexplainable stroke symptoms varied according to the phase of the moon. Over a period of 13 years, admissions were higher during a full moon than at other times. They offered no explanation. On an equally bizarre note, Burneo et al. (2003) noted that a key diagnostic feature of the disorder was what they termed 'the teddy bear' sign: 87 per cent of the 903 cases they reported on brought a teddy bear to the diagnostic testing process.

The term hysteria originally derived from the Greek word for uterus. Initially, it was used to label a condition thought to occur as a result of the uterus literally wandering through the body, resulting in symptoms as varied as feelings of suffocation, dramatic fits, paralysis of the limbs, fainting spells, sudden inability to speak and inability to take in food. Treatment involved encouraging the womb back to its proper place through physical manipulation.

More recently, the condition came to prominence in the First World War, when many soldiers in the trenches developed a condition known as 'shell shock', of which the most prominent features were blindness, paralysis, contractures, aphonia, anaesthesias and profound amnesias. The initial interpretation of these symptoms was that they resulted from micro-haemorrhaging in the brain, as a consequence of the shock created by exploding shells – hence the term 'shell shock'. Subsequently, doctors noted that the majority of soldiers with the condition had not been close to any explosions, there was no evidence of any brain haemorrhages among those who had died and been subjected to autopsy, and the condition occured among recruits who had not yet been in battle. As a result of this, the condition became thought of as psychological rather than physical. Interestingly, social and cultural factors appear to have influenced both development and treatment of shell shock. Officers were less likely to develop these problems than enlisted men, but when they did they were more likely to be taken from the trenches and receive long-term treatment, even when their symptoms were relatively minor.

Aetiology of conversion disorder

Social processes

Social factors are involved in the development of conversion disorder, at least on some occasions. The condition has been described as contagious, in that the sight or knowledge of one person with unexplained symptoms may trigger similar symptoms in others, particularly in situations where many people are grouped together and placed under some form of stress. One such incident among US Army recruits occurred over a 12-hour period following evacuation of 1800 men from their barracks owing to a suspected toxic gas exposure – which turned out to be a false alarm (Struewing and Gray 1990). Despite the lack of toxin in the atmosphere, over two-thirds of the recruits developed at least one respiratory symptom, and 375 were evacuated by air ambulance for immediate medical investigation; 8 were kept in hospital. Two weeks after the incident, 55 per cent of a sample of this group reported developing at least one symptom, including cough, light-headedness, chest pain, shortness of breath, headache, sore throat or dizziness. Those who reported the most, or the most severe, problems reported high levels of physical stress, mental stress, and awareness of rumours of odours, gases and/or smoke.

Psychoanalytic explanations

Early psychoanalytic explanations of conversion disorder considered the condition to reflect anxiety aroused by unconscious conflict being converted into physical symptoms. Freud (Freud and Breuer 1984) thought that one ego defence mechanism against high levels of distress was to convert this distress from psychic to physical symptoms. Perhaps the most famous case he reported was that of Anna O, who was initially treated by Joseph Breuer. Anna O was a 21-year-old woman who became ill while nursing her terminally ill father. Her own illness began with a severe cough, and subsequently included paralysis of the extremities of the right side of her body, contractures, disturbances of vision, hearing and language, lapses of consciousness and hallucinations. Breuer noticed that when Anna told him the content of her daytime hallucinations, while under hypnosis, she became calm and tranquil. He considered this to be way of expressing the 'products' of her 'bad self': a process of emotional catharsis. Breuer further developed his understanding of her symptoms following a period of time when Anna O stopped drinking, and quenched her thirst by eating fruit and melons. At this time, she recounted in one of her sessions how she had been disgusted by the sight of a dog drinking out of a glass. Soon after this revelation she asked for a drink. Breuer took this to indicate that insight into the factors associated with the beginning of symptoms was a key issue in relieving them. This became a focus of later hypnotic sessions.

The twist in the story came from Freud's analysis of the situation. He noted that Anna specifically required Breuer to provide the therapy, and that when she was in a hypnotic state, she needed to feel his hands to ensure he was there. In addition, one of the symptoms she developed was believing that she was pregnant with his child. Freud took this as an indication that she was in love with Breuer – and that her hysterical symptoms were the result of these secret sexual desires. In fact, Freud considered conversion disorder to result from an unresolved Electra complex (see Chapter 2). In this, the young girl is sexually attracted to her father. If her parents' responses to this are harsh or disapproving, the girl's feelings are repressed. This leads to a preoccupation with sex, at the same time as an avoidance of it. If these sexual urges occur later in life, the defence mechanism evoked can involve conversion of the sexual impulses into physical symptoms.

Behavioural explanations

The behavioural explanation of conversion symptoms is that they are functional and under the control of the individual expressing them. They are functional in the sense that they lead to some sort of benefit or reinforcement – the obvious one in the case of the Anna O being the attention given to her by Breuer, while the men in the trenches potentially avoided being killed. In arguing this case, Miller (1999) suggested that it is very difficult to determine from an external standpoint what is motivated, controllable, voluntary behaviour and what is not. However, he argued that some notable cases of conversion disorder seem to be faked and under voluntary control – albeit it in a rather clumsy way.

One example of this was reported by Zimmerman and Grosz (1966), who asked a patient with hysterical blindness to identify which one of three visual stimuli was being presented to them. He performed this task at a level consistently below chance – a finding that may be considered unusual, because if he was unable to see, he should have performed at chance levels. Zimmerman and Grosz then presented the stimuli in a non-random order (left–centre–right: left–centre–right, etc.), and the person was informed of which stimulus had been presented on each trial following their attempt to identify it. This is a task for which one would expect a blind person to learn the sequence and perform at above-chance levels. The participant in their study did not. Finally, when he was allowed to overhear a comment by a confederate of the experimenter that 'the doctors reckon that the patient can see because he makes fewer correct responses by chance than a blind man would make' (1966: 259), his performance improved to chance levels. Miller speculated that this indicated the individual was dissimilating.

This argument can also be made from an anatomical perspective. Merskey (1995) noted, for example, that patients with hysterical aphonia (inability to speak) may be able to cough – yet both processes require the vocal cords to function normally. If an individual can cough, there are no anatomical reasons for them not being able to talk. Similarly, some patients with an inability to move their limbs may show evidence of tensing both the apparently affected muscles and those which prevent movement of the limb. Again, this suggests that some sort of voluntary processes are at work. Despite these cases, Miller (1999) acknowledged these findings do not necessarily mean that all people with these phenomena are faking.

Hysteria as a form of hypnosis

An opposing interpretation of conversion symptoms, proposed by Oakley (1999), suggests that they are evidence of some form of hypnotic processes at work. He noted a number of similarities between hysterical conversion and hypnosis:

- *Similarities in 'symptoms'*: many conditions that can be established in hypnosis are similar to frequently reported conversion symptoms: motor paralysis (inability to rise from a chair, move an arm, etc.), loss of touch or pain sensation, blindness, and the generation of pain sensations.
- *Lack of concern over symptoms*: both hypnotized individuals and many people with conversion disorder express a lack of concern over their strange symptoms.
- *Involuntariness*: the deficits or physical states that are associated with both conversion disorder and hypnosis involve a degree of involuntariness. People report that they would like to, for example, move their hand, but cannot. This has long been reported and is perhaps best phrased by someone from the nineteenth century (Paget 1873), who commented: 'They say "I cannot"; it looks like "I will not"; but it is "I cannot will" ' (cited in Oakley 1999).
- *Apparent malingering and display of 'implicit knowledge'*: both conditions can appear as if the individual is deliberately faking their symptoms. They may respond as if they do not have the deficit while still reporting it. People who are deaf as a result of hypnosis and conversion disorder, for example, have both been shown to alter their speech in response to external noise, implying some sort of knowledge of stimuli that they apparently cannot sense. The performance of the hysterically blind individual reported by Zimmerman and Grosz (1966) provides further evidence of this implicit knowledge. Miller suggests this could be evidence of faking. However, Oakley had a different explanation. He proposed that these examples could suggest that any mechanisms responsible for both hysterical and hypnotic blindness occur at a late stage in processing of visual material. Becoming aware of visual stimuli involves a series of processes before we become consciously aware of any stimulus: reception of information in the visual cortex, transmission of this information to the temporal and parietal lobes where the location and type of stimulus are determined, and then to the prefrontal cortex where this information is integrated with memories. All this occurs before we are aware of having

seen a stimulus. It is possible that processes/deficits associated with hypnosis or conversion disorder occur before we become consciously aware of the stimulus, but allow some form of apparently conscious response to stimuli.

Oakley suggested that if we accept that there are some commonalities between the conversion hysteria and hypnosis, there may also be common neurological processes. In one study of conversion disorder, Marshall et al. (1997) investigated the neural processes that occurred in a lady with conversion disorder when asked to move her paralysed left leg, using functional MRI scanning:

- *Preparing* to move her leg resulted in activation of her left premotor cortex and both cerebellar hemispheres – the same processes that occurred when she was preparing to move her non-paralysed right leg. The authors interpreted this as an indication of her 'genuine' preparation to move her left leg.
- When *trying* to move her leg, there was activation of the normal movement-related brain areas including the left dorsolateral prefrontal cortex and both cerebellar hemispheres. There was no activation of the right premotor areas or the right primary sensorimotor cortex necessary for movement. However, areas of the brain not usually involved in movement – the right cingulated cortex and right orbitofrontal cortex – *did* show activation. The authors proposed that this activation somehow inhibited movement of her left leg.

Marshall et al. suggested that the desire to move was evidenced by the activation of the movement-related areas of the brain. However, this activation was somehow overridden by other neurological activity: not 'I cannot' or 'I will not' but 'I cannot will'. These findings reflect similar processes found in people placed under hypnosis and who are given hypnotic commands mimicking the paralysis of conversion disorder (Halligan et al. 2000).

These neurological processes can be partially explained by cognitive models developed by, among others, Shallice (e.g. 1988). Shallice suggested that our decision-making involves a hierarchical cognitive system, controlled by a supervisory control system. The overarching control of responses to environmental events is provided by a central executive. At a lower level, mental functioning comprises a series of learned behavioural sequences. These are guided by action schema stored in long-term memory. They enable routine behaviours, and are relatively uncontrolled by the central executive. Action at this level is guided by processes which we are not aware of – they are unconscious. The executive becomes involved in active planning and decision-making only when the learned behavioural sequences are insufficient to cope with our responses: when there are no pre-existing action schemata. A major function of the executive is to exert attentional control: to focus attention on demanding tasks, and away from distracting stimuli. According to Shallice, any mental processing involving the central executive becomes part of our conscious awareness, and any actions that follow its activation are thought of as voluntary. Processing below this level (the learned behavioural sequences) is unconscious. These processes explain, for example, the commonly reported phenomenon of having driven a car for many miles, and yet having no real recollection of the journey. The process of driving can be relatively automatic and, if the driver focuses their attention on other things, may happen at an unconscious level and be filtered out from conscious awareness.

Oakley (1999) moved further than this to suggest that not all those elements being processed by the central executive come into consciousness. Indeed, one of the functions of the executive is to select from a range of processing which ones come into awareness: those that are relevant to current actions or concerns are selected, those less relevant remain unconscious. He also suggested that so-called negative hypnotic phenomena, such as analgesia, blindness and paralysis, may occur under hypnosis as a result of the executive system withholding sensory information from our awareness following suggestions from an external source. Because we are unaware of this selection, any failure to move or lack of sensation is thought of as involuntary. By contrast, action sequences may occur as a result of processing the executive does not allow into awareness; so an individual may make apparently 'involuntary' movements which they consider to have been out of their control. In this way, hypnotic phenomena are the result of selective awareness governed by the central executive. Oakley suggests that conversion symptoms may result from the same processes. In this case, the executive 'chooses' in some way to allow or disallow various information into awareness. This may be the result of a variety of unconscious 'internal dynamics and motivations in the interests of providing a solution to what may be an otherwise insoluble psychological problem' (1999: 260).

Stress as a precipitant to conversion disorders

Oakley's concept of conversion disorder as a consequence of individuals facing an otherwise insoluble problem hints at the role that stress may have as a precipitant to this disorder. Relatively few studies have examined this in any detail. However, what studies have been conducted confirm this hypothesis. Harris and colleagues (1996) found people with *globus pharyngis* (a persistent sensation of a lump in the throat) to have higher levels of anxiety and to have experienced more adverse life-events in the year preceding onset than controls with medical problems thought to have no psychosomatic content. Duncan and Oto (2008) reported high levels of trauma in their population of 'psychogenic nonepileptic attacks': 32.5 per cent reported sexual abuse, 26 per cent reported physical abuse, while 19 per cent reported a traumatic bereavement. Singh and Lee (1997) found that 72 per cent of a sample of people with conversion disorder reported serious concurrent stress. However, while stress may form a precipitant to the development of conversion disorders, this cannot be the only cause of the condition. Many other mental health problems are triggered by stress, and the levels of stress reported by people with conversion disorder do not seem to differ from those reported by people with other conditions, such as depression (Roelofs et al. 2005). What these other factors are is not yet clear.

Treatment of conversion disorder

Studies of interventions in conversion disorder are largely uncontrolled studies of cohorts of people with the disorder or case studies. At the time of writing, few randomized controlled trials – the gold standard of intervention research – had been conducted. This makes it difficult to ascribe any successes found in the published research to the specific intervention as any changes may be due to placebo effects or non-specific therapy effects. Such caution may be increased following the findings of Letonoff et al. (2002), who described three cases of psychogenic paraplegia, with symptoms including complete loss of motor control and sensation in the lower extremities and incontinence. Each individual 'ambulated out of the hospital without assistance', albeit up to several months following their diagnosis, with no other treatment than being told that their test results and medical examinations indicated no physical problems. Nevertheless, a number of case studies (e.g. Wald et al. 2004) have shown cognitive behavioural interventions, including imaginal exposure to trauma memories, to be of benefit. A different approach was taken by Ataoglu et al. (2003). They used a therapeutic technique called paradoxical intention, in which individuals are encouraged to maintain or even exacerbate their symptoms. They compared this approach with use of an anxiolytic, diazepam, in 30 patients diagnosed with pseudo-seizures. Of the 15 patients who completed paradoxical intention treatment, 14 showed some improvement; of the 15 treated with diazepam, 9 showed improvements at the end of six weeks of treatment.

One of the very few randomized trials of treatments of conversion disorder was reported by Moene et al. (2003). They assigned patients with motor conversion disorders with symptoms including paralysis, gait disturbance, coordination problems, aphonia, and pseudo-epileptic seizures either to a waiting list control or active treatment. Treatment involved 10 sessions of hypnosis focusing on suggestions of symptom reduction and age regression to enable emotional insight. The waiting list control group design did not allow long-term follow-up measures to be taken. However, at the end of therapy, patients in the intervention condition showed significantly more improvement on video-based measures of their disorder than those in the control group.

6.5 Chapter summary

1 Somatization disorder is characterized by the experience and reporting of physical symptoms that cause distress but lack corresponding physical pathology.

2 Up to 0.7 per cent of the general population could be diagnosed with somatization disorder.

3 Biological models of the disorder suggest it results from a sensitivity to physical sensations perhaps due to dysregulation in the serotonergic system. This may be added to by catastrophic interpretation of these sensations.

4 Psychological models suggest somatization results from modelling of somatic complaints by parents and gaining attention of parents by reporting physical problems. In time, individuals may come to express emotional distress through reporting physical symptoms.

5 There are relatively few reported treatment studies, although there is preliminary evidence that treatment with SSRIs or CBT may be of benefit.

6 The key symptom of hypochondriasis is a preoccupation with the fear of having a serious illness – in the absence of contrary medical evidence.

7 Warwick and Salkovskis considered hypochondriasis to be a response to immediate threat that triggers health concerns established earlier in life. These become the focus of attention and cause considerable distress.

8 The main treatment for hypochondriasis is generally cognitive behavioural, although there is some evidence that SSRIs may be effective.

9 Body dysmorphic disorder involves a preoccupation with an imagined defect in appearance, often with high levels of negative thinking, self-criticism, anxiety and depression.

10 Developmental psychological theories suggest that the condition is triggered by critical or traumatic incidents that involve an individual's appearance, and is maintained by selective attention to perceived physical limitations.

11 Low levels of serotonin may also be implicated in the disorder.

12 Treatment studies are rare and usually involve cognitive behavioural therapy.

13 Conversion disorder presents as a neurological or sensory disorder that is disabling but has no physical cause.

14 Aetiological explanations vary from it being a deliberate behaviour under the control of the affected individual to being a form of hypnosis. Both may be precipitated by stress, although why this should lead to conversion symptoms in particular is not understood.

15 Treatment studies are rare but suggest that cognitive behavioural and hypnotic treatments may be of some benefit.

6.6 For discussion

1 How may childhood factors translate into somatization disorders, and what factors may maintain them once established?

2 Why are somatization disorders hard to treat?

3 Are the somatization disorders distinct disorders or simply the end of a spectrum of health or appearance concern most of us experience at some time?

4 What factors may contribute specifically to the onset of a conversion disorder? Do these differ from those that trigger a variety of other mental health disorders? What other factors may contribute to the disorder?

6.7 Key terms

Aphonia inability to speak.

Hyperalgesia abnormally increased pain sensation – a lowered pain threshold.

6.8 Further reading

Aybek, S., Kanaan, R.A. and David, A.S. (2008) The neuropsychiatry of conversion disorder, *Current Opinion in Psychiatry*, 21: 275–80.

Brown, R.J. (2004) Psychological mechanisms of medically unexplained symptoms: an integrative conceptual model, *Psychological Bulletin*, 130: 793–812.

Marcus, D.K., Gurley, J.R., Marchi, M.M. and Bauer, C. (2007) Cognitive and perceptual variables in hypochondriasis and health anxiety: a systematic review, *Clinical Psychology Review*, 27: 127–39.

Phillips, K.A. (2005) *The Broken Mirror: Understanding and Treating Body Dysmorphic Disorder*. New York: Oxford University Press.

Rief, W. and Barsky, A.J. (2005) Psychobiological perspectives on somatoform disorders, *Psychoneuroendocrinology*, 30: 996–1002.

Witthöft, M. and Hiller, W. (2010) Psychological approaches to origins and treatments of somatoform disorders, *Annual Review of Clinical Psychology*, 6: 257–83.

The debate between Miller and Oakley (as well as several other interesting papers) is published in a special edition of the *Journal of Cognitive Neuropsychiatry* (1999, volume 4, part 3) and as a book called *Conversion Hysteria: Towards a Cognitive Neuropsychological Account*, published by Psychology Press Ltd.

The following websites also have information about somatoform disorders, their treatment, and people's experiences of them.

www.patient.co.uk/health/Somatization-and-Somatoform-Disorders.htm
www.thehypochondriac.com/
www.mentalhelp.net/poc/center_index.php?id=112

Schizophrenia

Chapter contents

Schizophrenia is one of the most controversial psychiatric diagnoses. Over time, debates have addressed whether a distinct state of schizophrenia actually exists, whether it results from genetic or environmental causes, and whether it should be treated using drug therapy, electro-convulsive therapy, or more social or psychological approaches. This chapter will address each of these issues. By the end of the chapter, you should have an understanding of:

- The nature of schizophrenia
- Alternative understandings of the 'symptoms' of schizophrenia
- The possible causal role of genetic factors, the family and psychosocial factors
- Neuronal and neurotransmitter models of the disorder
- Psychological models of the experiences of people diagnosed with schizophrenia
- Differing approaches to the treatment of schizophrenia and their effectiveness.

The condition now labelled schizophrenia was first described by Kraepelin ([1883] 1981) using the term *dementia praecox*. This label was chosen to indicate that it was a progressive and deteri-orating illness with no return to pre-morbid levels of functioning. Some years later, Bleuler (1908) identified four fundamental symptoms of what he termed the group of schizophrenias (literally, 'split mind'): ambivalence, disturbance of association, disturbance of mood and a preference for fantasy over reality.

7.1 The nature of schizophrenia

The exact nature of schizophrenia remains hotly disputed. However, the consensus view is that it comprises a number of related disorders characterized by fundamental distortions of thinking and perception. Disturbances in thought processes are usually the most obvious symptom of schizophrenia. Conversations may lack coherence, jumping from topic to topic and idea to idea in an apparently incoherent manner. People with schizophrenia may use neologisms or make bizarre associations between words. They may feel that someone is putting thoughts into their mind and lose track of their conversation or thoughts, perhaps not completing sentences. They may have deluded and sometimes bizarre beliefs about themselves or others. These may include *delusions of control* (being able to control others or being controlled by others), *delusions of grandeur* (believing they are rich, famous, talented) and *delusions of reference* (believing the behaviour of others is directly related to them: glances, looks, laughter, are all seen as being directed at the individual). People with schizophrenia may also experience hallucinations, the most frequent of which are auditory. Their content may vary from benign to persecutory. The emotions that such people experience are often described as *flattened*. That is, they experience a general lack of emotional responsiveness, although they may be prone to apparently inappropriate mood states such as anger or depression as a consequence of internal thoughts or hallucinations.

Personal experiences

The experiences of people with schizophrenia vary markedly, as does the degree to which any experiences interfere with their life. Many people experience delusions over long periods without any significant impact on their life; for others, the experience may be much more problematic. Two examples of this may be found in the experiences of Michael and David. Michael was a middle-aged man diagnosed with schizophrenia some years ago who was living a relatively normal life in a small flat in Cardiff. One of his delusional beliefs was that he is being attacked by lasers from an unknown, probably extraterrestrial, source:

> The lasers attack me. They aim for my head. I know when they are firing because I have pains when they hit me. They don't fire at me all the time. They come and go. I don't know what I have done to have them do this to me. But it's been going on for years. They usually hit me in the head, so I wear protection against it when they fire. I wrap metal foil over my head so it reflects the lasers away . . . that way they can't get to me . . . I think they are aliens that do this . . . The last time they fired at me was Sunday morning. They woke me up – the lasers – with my head really hurting. I couldn't get out of bed because of the pain. I had to wear protection and take my time to get going because of the pain . . . That was bad. Usually I can stop the lasers with the metal, but it can get through sometimes.
>
> [It is perhaps not coincidental that Michael had spent much of Saturday night drinking beer in a local pub.]

A more acute and devastating set of delusional beliefs resulted in David being admitted to hospital as he was running naked down the middle of a city road proclaiming that he was the son of God come to save us from our sins. At the time he was brought into casualty he was proclaiming:

> I am the messiah! I am David, David, the saviour . . . I will save you from the sins you have committed that commit you to the heat of the hell not heaven of the Lord my God. You cannot hold me . . . God is angry with you, the world, the whole round . . . the devil will take you for your sins of holding me here . . . the nine that follow will kill you for holding the son of God in your hall . . . I have come to save the world . . . you cannot hold me . . . By the writings of Methuselah and the prophets and God and Jesus I am here. God speaks to me! Not you! And he is angry at the wickedness of the world and the work of the people and the things they have done . . . the sins, things . . . wings of angels will come for me to take me away from this hall.

About 1 per cent of adults are diagnosed as having some form of schizophrenia (APA 2000). Prevalence rates appear stable across countries, cultures and over time, with onset typically occurring between the ages of 20 and 35 years. On average, women develop the condition three to four years later than men and show a second peak of onset around the menopause. It is an episodic condition with a poor prognosis. Of those people that have one episode, approximately half will experience a significant reduction in symptoms over the next five years. However, only a quarter are likely to maintain good social and vocational functioning, and only an eighth will meet the criteria for full recovery for two years or more (Robinson et al. 2004). Factors associated with a good prognosis include receiving appropriate treatment, an acute onset and short duration of the first episode, the presence of an identifiable stress trigger, a predominance of positive symptoms (see p. 160), good social support, no family history of schizophrenia, and having a job.

7.2 DSM diagnostic criteria for schizophrenia

For a diagnosis of schizophrenia to be made, DSM-IV-TR states that two or more of the following symptoms should be present for a significant period of time during a one-month period:

- delusions
- hallucinations
- disorganized speech: frequent derailment or incoherence
- grossly disorganized or catatonic behaviour
- negative symptoms: flattened mood, alogia or avolition.

Only one of these symptoms is required if the delusions are bizarre or the hallucinations comprise a voice keeping up a running commentary on the person's behaviour or thoughts, or involve two or more voices conversing with each other. A second criterion is that the symptoms result in significant impairment. Four sub-types of schizophrenia, in which differing symptoms predominate, have been identified:

- *Disorganized*: in this, disorganized speech and behaviour, and flat or inappropriate mood are the dominant features.
- *Paranoid*: the commonest type of schizophrenia, characterized by stable, paranoid delusions. Auditory hallucinations may support these delusional beliefs. Disturbances of mood and speech, and catatonic symptoms, are not prominent.
- *Catatonic*: characterized by marked psychomotor disturbances. The condition varies from extreme excitement to stupor and 'waxy flexibility' in which the individual can be placed in a position which they maintain for several hours. They may also evidence automatic obedience or a dreamlike state accompanied by vivid hallucinations. It is now rarely seen in industrial countries, though it remains common elsewhere.
- *Residual*: characterized by an absence of prominent delusions, hallucinations, disorganized speech, or grossly disorganized or catatonic behaviour. There is, however, continuing evidence of a disturbance, indicated by the presence of negative symptoms (see below) or two or more of the key symptoms in an attenuated form.

Table 7.1 **Some of the most frequent symptoms of acute schizophrenia**

Symptom	% of cases
Lack of insight	97
Auditory hallucinations	74
Ideas of reference	70
Flattened affect	66
Suspiciousness	66
Delusions of persecution	64
Thought alienation	52

Alternative view of the symptoms

A different way of thinking about schizophrenia to the DSM approach is to examine which symptoms cluster together, and to examine any underlying mechanisms that may contribute to these clusters. Factor analysis of the signs and symptoms of the various sub-types of schizophrenia has identified three clusters, known as disorganized, positive and negative symptoms (Liddle et al. 1994), each of which may have different psychological and biological causes:

- The disorganized cluster is characterized by disorganized speech, behaviour and flat or inappropriate mood (or 'thought disorder').
- The positive cluster includes hallucinations and delusions.
- The negative cluster denotes an absence of activation, and includes apathy, lack of motivation, or poverty of speech.

Deconstructing schizophrenia

The DSM-IV-TR criteria for a diagnosis of schizophrenia differ markedly from those of DSM-III, which differ from the alternative definitions of schizophrenia suggested by Liddle et al. (1994). This difficulty in establishing exactly what schizophrenia is presents clinicians and researchers with significant problems when developing aetiological models or treatment approaches. So great is this difficulty that many scientists and clinicians have begun to question whether schizophrenia exists in any form, let alone how it is defined by DSM.

A dimensional perspective

Associated with schizophrenia – in what are frequently referred to as the schizophrenic spectrum disorders – are a number of apparently more stable personality types, each of which contains some of the symptoms of schizophrenia, but at a less problematic or significant level. These include:

- *schizoid personality*: the individual does not enjoy close relationships, frequently chooses solitary activities, has little interest in having sexual experiences with another person, appears indifferent to the praise or criticism of others, and shows emotional coldness, detachment or flattened mood.
- *schizotypal personality*: the individual frequently experiences ideas of reference, has odd beliefs that influence behaviour and are inconsistent with sub-cultural norms, and unusual perceptual experiences, including bodily illusions. They may engage in odd thinking and speech, show suspiciousness or paranoid ideation, appear eccentric, lack close friends, and experience excessive social anxiety.

The existence of these personality types suggests that each of the symptoms of schizophrenia can vary across individuals and only achieve a significant level in some – opening the possibility of a dimensional view of schizophrenia rather than it being an all or nothing dichotomous condition as exemplified by DSM.

A further issue of relevance here is that the experiences of people diagnosed with schizophrenia, or disorders of the schizophrenic spectrum, are not exclusive to them. Many people who do not come to the attention of the psychiatric services also hear voices. What distinguishes between them and people who seek help for their 'problem' appears to be differences in their responses to the voices and their ability to cope with them. Positive coping strategies include setting limits to the time spent listening to voices, talking back to them, and listening selectively to more positive voices (Romme and Escher 2000).

Schizophrenia as multiple disorders

A further fundamental problem with the DSM model of schizophrenia is that the same diagnosis can be given to individuals who present with very different experiences and problems: only two, potentially quite different, symptoms need be present to achieve a diagnosis of schizophrenia. This contradicts the notion of a disorder that has one underlying mechanism: if this were the case, all people should present with the same cluster of symptoms. A related point is that different people with schizophrenia respond to different medications, including neuroleptics, lithium and benzodiazepines. Others fail to respond to any of these medications. Accordingly, the course and treatment of the condition vary considerably across individuals. As Bentall (1993: 227) noted, 'We are inevitably drawn to an important conclusion: "schizophrenia" appears to be a disease which has no particular symptoms, no particular course, and responds to no particular treatment.' On these grounds, he suggested that the diagnosis has no validity and that the concept of schizophrenia should be abandoned. Rather than attempting to explain multiple syndromes, future efforts should focus on explanations of particular behaviours or experiences: each of the various symptoms of 'schizophrenia' should be considered as a disorder in its own right, with differing underlying causes and treatments.

Having argued that attempts to link widely differing experiences under the rubric of 'schizophrenia' present significant problems, a number of the following sections of the chapter reflect a more traditional perspective, and review research based on DSM or similar definitions of schizophrenia. Some may argue that this type of research is doomed to failure as it is seeking to identify causal factors for a condition that does not exist. More positively, it may still indicate some of the factors that increase risk or provide effective treatment for some or all of the experiences now considered under the rubric of schizophrenia. As the research almost exclusively focuses on people with a diagnosis of schizophrenia, this term will be used throughout the sections, despite concerns about the validity of the concept.

7.3 Aetiology of schizophrenia

Genetic factors

Schizophrenia has been at the centre of a scientific debate concerning the role of nature and nurture in the development of mental health problems. Perhaps the dominant model of the aetiology of schizophrenia has been biological, driven by genetic factors. Evidence relating to genetic factors has therefore been closely scrutinized and has not been without controversy.

Early genetic studies indicated that the risk for schizophrenia among relatives of an identified 'case' correlated with the degree of shared genes. Table 7.2 summarizes the findings of some early family studies, although weak study designs may have resulted in an overestimation of the strength of the family linkages (Tsuang 2000). More methodologically sound studies (e.g. Kringlen 1993) have reported concordance rates for schizophrenia in MZ twins of between 30 and 40 per cent and between DZ twins of 10–15 per cent, suggesting a part-genetically mediated risk for schizophrenia. While this evidence shows that schizophrenia runs in families, it does not necessarily mean that it has a genetic causation. Those closest to the affected individual may share a similar environment, or be affected by their behaviour. Attempts to disentangle environmental from biological issues have led to a number of studies comparing the risk for schizophrenia among relatives or twins of adopted-away children.

Close examination of these studies reveals a far from clear set of evidence. The Danish Adoption Studies (Kety et al. 1975), for example, traced the biological relatives of 34 adopted children who later developed schizophrenia and those of 34 control cases with 'clean pedigrees', comparing the prevalence of schizophrenia among them. Interestingly, they found only one person diagnosed as having chronic schizophrenia among the relatives of either cases or controls.

Table 7.2 Risk for schizophrenia (definite and probable) of relatives of people diagnosed with schizophrenia

Relationship	Percentage shared genes	Risk (%)
General population	N.A.	1
Spouses of patients	N.A.	2
Third-degree relatives	12.5	
First-degree cousins		2
Second-degree relatives	25	
Uncles/aunts		2
Nieces/nephews		4
Grandchildren		5
Half-siblings		6
First-degree siblings	50	
Parents		6
Siblings		9
Children		13
Siblings with one schizophrenic parent		17
Dizygotic twin		17
Monozygotic twin	100	48
Children with two schizophrenic parents	100	46

Source: adapted from Tsuang (2000).

Only when they extended the diagnoses assigned to those within the schizophrenic spectrum, including borderline state, inadequate personality and uncertain schizophrenia, did differences between the groups arise. Using these diagnoses, they found nine affected relatives in the families of the cases and two among the controls. This, some critics (e.g. Roberts 2000) have argued, provided no evidence that schizophrenia *per se* is inherited. Roberts also noted that at least some of the diagnoses assigned were taken from hospital notes and not confirmed by the research team, and that at least one person's reported diagnosis changed from inadequate personality to borderline schizophrenia over the course of two reports by the same research team. Worse was to come: subsequent reading of this individual's notes showed an initial diagnosis of bipolar disorder (see Chapter 8: Rose et al. 1984).

A more recent study of genetics reported by Tienari et al. (2000) compared rates of schizophrenia in the adopted-away offspring of both mothers diagnosed with schizophrenia and those without the diagnosis. Risk for schizophrenia was four times greater among the children of the women diagnosed as having schizophrenia than among the children of the comparison mothers: a total incidence of 8.1 per cent versus 2.3 per cent. However, this was not entirely due to genetic factors. Using data from the same study, Wahlberg et al. (2000b) reported an interaction between genetic and environmental factors. Children of women diagnosed with schizophrenia who lived in households where there was good communication between the family members were not at increased risk of schizophrenia. By contrast, the children of women diagnosed as having schizophrenia who were placed in families with evidence of communication deviance were at greater risk of developing schizophrenia than children with 'normal' mothers who were placed in such households. That is, the development of schizophrenia seemed to depend on both genetic risk *and* communication deviance within the adoptive family. Importantly, any communication deviance seemed to predate the adoption, and was not a consequence of the child's behaviour.

Together, these and other data have generally been seen by biological theorists as supporting a model in which genetic factors influence risk for schizophrenia but do not form the single causal agent. They form a vulnerability factor rather than a causal factor. The search for the location of genes that increase risk of schizophrenia has also proven somewhat difficult. Perhaps the frustration of researchers is summed up by the title of a paper examining this phenomenon (Sanders et al. 2008): 'No significant association of 14 candidate genes with schizophrenia in a large European ancestry sample'. Nevertheless, some candidate genes involved in the development of schizophrenia are emerging, including the ERBB4 gene, responsible for dopamine regulation (Lu et al. 2010), and the 5-HTR2A gene (Tee et al. 2010) which is involved in serotonin regulation. When considering the role of genetics in schizophrenia, one final cautionary note should be borne in mind: 81 per cent of people diagnosed with schizophrenia have no known relative with the disorder (Shean 2004). Other factors are clearly implicated in the development of the disorder.

Biological mechanisms

The dopamine hypothesis

Much of the neurological research attempting to identify the causes of schizophrenia has been conducted on people who already are known to have the condition. This makes sense in some ways. But it provides significant problems for interpretation of many of the data. Johnstone (2000), for example, contended that any findings of neurological differences between people with schizophrenia and those without it may not indicate that these differences cause the condition. Rather, they may be explained by the effects of medication and/or the stress of experiencing vivid hallucinations or holding strong delusional beliefs.

Despite these provisos, a number of biological models of schizophrenia have been proposed. The first plausible theory involved the dopamine systems of the brain. Neurons mediated by dopamine are found in the limbic system, in a brain area known as A10, with links to the thalamus, hippocampus and frontal cortex, and the substantia nigra. The key feature of the dopamine hypothesis is that the experiences of people diagnosed with schizophrenia result from either an excess of dopamine, or from the receptors at neuronal synapses being supersensitive to normal amounts of dopamine. Evidence generally supports the latter, but either way this theory suggests that at least some of the experiences of schizophrenia may result from excess activity in those parts of the brain controlled by dopamine.

Evidence of increased dopamine activity comes from a number of converging types of study (Lieberman et al. 1990):

- Amphetamine use increases dopamine levels and can produce experiences that mimic the positive symptoms of schizophrenia. Small controlled doses of amphetamines can produce schizophrenic-like symptoms in at least some naïve subjects. These experiences may continue long after cessation of taking the drug. They do, however, mirror only one particular type of schizophrenia: paranoid schizophrenia.
- Some of the most effective drugs for treating both amphetamine psychosis and schizophrenia are the neuroleptic drugs known as phenothiazines, which block transmission of dopamine by preventing its uptake at the postsynaptic receptor site.
- Post-mortem evidence has shown a marked increase in dopamine receptor sites in people with schizophrenia in comparison with 'normal' controls, suggesting supersensitivity to dopamine. How much of this is a consequence of medication and how much the disease process is in dispute.

Other evidence is less supportive of the dopamine hypothesis (Duncan et al. 1999):

- No direct evidence of pathologic dopamine neuronal activity has been consistently demonstrated, such as increased levels of dopamine, its metabolites or its receptors, that are not the potential results of antipsychotic drug treatment.
- One of the most effective antipsychotic drugs, clozapine, appears to work by its impact on the serotonin and not dopamine systems. This suggests that other neurotransmitters may be involved in schizophrenia.
- A substantial proportion of people with schizophrenia do not respond to treatment with phenothiazines, suggesting that dopamine systems may not always be involved in its aetiology.
- Schizophrenic-like experiences are rarely induced in 'normal' individuals when they are administered drugs that increase dopaminergic activity.
- Neuroleptics are only partially effective in alleviating the negative symptoms of people diagnosed with schizophrenia.

In response to some of these findings, more complex models now implicate additional (rather than alternative) neurotransmitters including GABA, NMDA and serotonin in the aetiology of schizophrenia (e.g. Guo et al. 2009). However, an updated dopamine model considered in the next section can account for at least some of these challenges.

Neurological substrates

As well as errors in neurotransmitter levels, some studies suggest that negative, disorganized, and some positive symptoms may result from damage to the neural systems themselves (Basso et al. 1998). The most common findings of brain scans of people diagnosed with schizophrenia include enlarged cerebral ventricles and decreased cortical volume especially in the temporal and frontal lobes compared with normal scans. Post-mortem examinations have revealed reductions in neuron density and size in the limbic, temporal and frontal regions and that the connections between neurons are relatively disorganized. The various affected brain areas include systems that influence attention, memory and mood (limbic system), planning and coordination (frontal and prefrontal lobe), and acoustic and verbal memory (temporal lobes). Technologies such as functional Magnetic Resonance Imaging (fMRI) allow us to examine the relationship between these neural deficits and specific cognitive processes. Bleich-Cohen et al. (2009), for example, found reduced functional processing in the amygdale and prefrontal cortex to be associated with a lack of sensitivity to bizarre facial expressions presented on a computer screen.

The length of time a person experiences any problems before receiving drug treatment is a significant predictor of long-term outcome. Lieberman et al. (1990) took this to indicate that the neuronal degeneration is an irreversible progressive deterioration, resulting in both diminished cognitive abilities and an inability to recover them following treatment with antipsychotic medication. Such treatment may prevent further deterioration, but cannot recover lost function. A number of causes for this deterioration have been proposed:

Excess dopamine   In an extension of the dopamine hypothesis, Lieberman et al. (1990) suggested that the initial trigger to a first episode of schizophrenia may involve increased dopaminergic activity, which results in positive symptoms. However, continued excessive dopamine activity is neurotoxic and leads to degeneration of the neurons in the dopamine systems, paradoxically resulting in low levels of dopamine activity and, hence, negative symptoms. In a challenge to this model, Ho et al. (2005) contended that the hippocampus appears particularly sensitive to damage through a variety of chemical pathways. Accordingly, they argued that if high levels of dopamine were damaging neural systems, then the longer any episode of schizophrenia prior to medical treatment, the more damage to the hippocampus should occur – and as long as the measure was made prior to the initiation of treatment, this damage could be directly attributed to dopaminergic or other neurotoxic processes. To explore this issue, they examined the hippocampal volume of 105 individuals, following an average period of untreated symptoms of one year. They found no relationship between duration of symptoms and hippocampal volume, providing no support for the neurotoxic impact of dopamine.

One explanation for Ho's negative findings may be that any damage occurs rapidly at an early stage of the disorder. Evidence for this can be found in the work of Pantelis and colleagues who have found evidence of significant pathological changes at a very early stage in the development of schizophrenia. In one study by this group, Wood et al. (2005) compared hippocampal volumes of 79 male subjects at ultra-high-risk of schizophrenia with those of 49 healthy male volunteers. The high-risk participants had significantly smaller hippocampal volumes than the comparison group; a finding that provides at least tangential support for a dopamine-hippocampal damage association.

Viral infection   There is consistent evidence that children born in the winter months are more at risk of developing schizophrenia than those born in the summer. Why this should be the case is not clear. However, the best guess is that neural damage as a result of viral diseases, which are more prevalent during the winter, may be a causal factor. Epidemiological evidence to support this hypothesis can be found in the findings of Jones and Cannon (1998) who found that young children who had viral infections were five times more likely to develop schizophrenia than those who did not. More fundamental biological support was summarized by Meyer and Feldon (2009), who reviewed the evidence in animals that viral infection or inflammation can damage dopaminergic pathways in the mesolimbic and mesocortical cortex and GABA pathways in prefrontal and hippocampal structures in the developing brain. Together, these lead to problems of working memory, selective associative learning, and hypersensitivity to psychostimulant drugs. Thus, damage to dopamine pathways is again implicated in the possible development of neurological substrates associated with schizophrenia.

Pregnancy and delivery complications   Pregnancy and delivery complications may also cause subtle brain damage that increases risk for schizophrenia. In a meta-analysis of 11 studies reporting relevant data, Geddes et al. (1999) compared data on 700 children who went on to develop schizophrenia and 835 controls. A number of delivery complications were implicated by their data, including low birth weight, prematurity, requiring resuscitation or being placed in an incubator, lack of oxygen, and premature rupture of the membranes. As with the viral infections, these are thought to result in neuronal damage.

Maternal stress   A number of studies have also implicated maternal stress in the development of schizophrenia. Malaspina et al. (2008), for example, found that the children of women who were in their second month of pregnancy during the height of the Arab-Israeli war in June of 1967 were significantly more likely to develop schizophrenia over the following 21–33 years than those born at other times. The phenomenon was gender-specific, affecting females more than males. The cause of any relationship between maternal stress and subsequent disorders is far from clear. It could be mediated through hormonal changes at times of stress, changes in health behaviour such as smoking or alcohol use, delivery complications or some other mechanism.

Substance abuse

So far, the chapter has identified a number of factors that either increase risk of developing schizophrenia or explain the chronic degenerative changes associated with the condition. They have not considered what may actually trigger particular episodes. These triggers may be psychological (see below). However, one biochemical trigger may also be implicated. Amphetamines can cause transient psychotic experiences and precipitate relapse of an existing psychotic condition (Satel and Edell 1991). Evidence that cannabis consumption can also increase risk of schizophrenia may be found in a longitudinal study of nearly 45000 Swedish people reported by Andreasson et al. (1987). Those who used cannabis at the age of 18 were more likely to be admitted to hospital with schizophrenia over a 15-year follow-up period than those who did not. In addition, there was a dose–response relationship between the frequency of smoking cannabis and the risk of developing schizophrenia: the more cannabis smoked, the greater the risk of developing schizophrenia.

Reviewing this, and subsequent evidence, a meta-analysis by Henquet et al. (2005) found that young heavy cannabis users were at double the risk of non-users of developing schizophrenia. Evidence from work by Caspi et al. (2005), suggests that this risk may be largely specific to individuals with a particular genetic make-up (a functional polymorphism in the catechol-O-methyltransferase (COMT) gene). A potential biochemical route through which cannabis exerts this influence has also been determined. The active metabolite of cannabis (delta-9 tetrahydrocannabinol) raises levels of cerebral dopamine and might precipitate psychosis. People with the early experiences of schizophrenia may also take cannabis as a form of self-treatment to alleviate either negative experiences or depression (Peralta and Cuesta 1992), reversing the causal link.

Psychosocial factors

The highest population rates of schizophrenia are among those in the lower socio-economic groups. Werner et al. (2007), for example, calculated that individuals born into and/or living in low socio-economic area were more likely to be assigned a diagnosis of schizophrenia than those in higher socio-economic groups. One explanation for this finding is that the relatively high levels of stress associated with low socio-economic status may trigger the onset of schizophrenia in vulnerable individuals. This speculation is supported by findings that about one quarter of episodes of schizophrenia seem to be precipitated by some acute life stress, although a focus on examining the relationship between acute life events which occur relatively infrequently and the, often more problematic, daily hassles may have led to an underestimation of the association between more everyday stresses and onset or psychotic episodes (Phillips et al. 2007).

Long-term stresses also increase risk of initial onset of the condition. One long-term stressor may be the family in which the individual lives. One of the first theories to consider this issue identified the relationship between the child and their mother as a critical factor in schizophrenia. This psychoanalytic theory, developed by Fromm-Reichman (1948), suggested that schizophrenia is the outcome of being raised by a mother who appears warm and self-sacrificing, but is in reality self-centred, cold and domineering – the so-called *schizophrenogenic mother*. Fromm-Reichman suggested that the mixed signals that such a mother gives out confuse the child and make their world difficult to interpret, a process that eventually leads to chaotic behaviour and cognitions. A similar theory was proposed by Bateson et al. (1956). Their 'double-bind' theory suggested that some parents frequently deal with their children in contradictory and confusing ways. They may, for example, tell their children they love them in a tone of voice that implies the opposite, or ask them to do incompatible things: 'I think you should go out more often with your friends: please stay with me . . .'. Frequent exposure to these contradictory demands may confuse the person, and eventually prove so stressful that it results in the experience of schizophrenia. Both models have some logic, but they have little evidence in their support.

One family theory has proven more robust. A critical element in the family process seems to be the degree of family criticism that the individual experiences. According to this model, high levels of negative emotional expression, hostility or criticism may trigger a relapse in someone who has already had at least one episode of schizophrenia. The classic study of this phenomenon, now known as high negative expressed emotion (NEE), was conducted by Vaughn and Leff (1976) in a study of readmission rates of people with schizophrenia discharged from the Maudsley Hospital during the 1970s. Their findings were dramatic: those who were discharged to high NEE households were much more likely to relapse than those whose home was rated low in NEE, particularly when they experienced this family environment for 35 hours or more a week. These findings have been replicated in a number of countries and cultures (Miklowitz 2004).

The majority of studies have considered high NEE to be a trigger to relapse – not to a first episode. As such, the high NEE environment is often thought of as a consequence of the family coping with an individual within it whose behaviour may be at odds with family values and processes. High NEE lies within a circle of causality, being both a response to 'difficult' or inexplicable behaviour and a contributor to its development. In keeping with this family process, levels of NEE tend to be higher in families where odd behaviour is seen as wilful and under the control of the individual, and lower where any odd behaviour is attributable to an illness or an uncontrollable cause (Yang et al. 2004). Evidence that family processes may also trigger the initial onset of schizophrenia in vulnerable individuals can be found in the Wahlberg et al. (2000b) study described earlier in the chapter. Of note also, is that family processes may be moderated by a number of individual, cognitive, factors. Kéri and Kelemen (2009), for example, found that individuals with particularly poor attention and immediate memory experienced more 'unusual thoughts' while they were the subject of family criticism than those who had better attention and memory.

A psychobiological model

Combining the psychosocial and biological data suggests a possible stress-vulnerability model of schizophrenia involving three broad stages (Duncan et al. 1999):

- The first stage is one of disordered neuronal development resulting from genetic, natal or perinatal factors. These problems underlie subtle early cognitive, motor and social impairments. They provide a *vulnerability* for schizophrenia.
- These deficiencies may lead to the second stage, which occurs in adolescence and early adulthood. At this time, stressful but normal human experiences result in increases in dopamine activity. As a consequence of this neuronal disorganization, dopaminergic neuronal systems become sensitized to existing levels of dopamine and become more reactive to them, resulting in the positive symptoms of schizophrenia. The greater the stress experienced, the greater the risk of dysregulation and onset of schizophrenia.
- If prolonged or recurrent, high levels of dopamine can lead to the degeneration of neurons, leading to structural damage, and the onset of negative symptoms.

Accordingly, the dysregulation that underpins schizophrenia may be a consequence of both biological factors that increase vulnerability and may contribute to its chronicity, and stress factors that trigger or exacerbate the condition. Even this biopsychosocial model is too 'biological' for some critics (e.g. Johnstone 2000) who have argued that there are no compelling grounds to assume any biological underpinnings to either schizophrenia or its 'component' elements. They still do not feel the necessity to combine biological and psychological elements, arguing for a psychosocial rather than biopsychosocial model. One argument (although not completely watertight) against this totally psychological model stems from work with young children. There is increasing evidence that children who go on to develop schizophrenia have cognitive deficits including those related to executive function indicative of mild neural damage (e.g. Cannon et al. 2006). In addition, Poulton et al. (2000) found that 'quasi-psychotic phenomena' (including beliefs that people were reading their minds or spying on them) reported by young people were strong predictors of later psychosis.

Psychological models

Rather than attempt to identify factors that trigger 'episodes' of 'schizophrenia', psychological models of schizophrenia typically attempt to explain the processes that underlie each of the different experiences reported by people assigned the diagnosis.

Theory of mind

One of the most encompassing psychological models of schizophrenia was initially developed by Frith (e.g. Frith and Corcoran 1996). He proposed that our understanding of the social world around us depends on being able to interpret the causes of our own actions and the actions of other people. In social situations, we interpret others' verbal and non-verbal signals in order to try and understand what they are thinking, feeling, what they believe, what is real, and so on. In order to do so, theory of mind suggests we first of all need to understand our own cognitive processes – the way *we* interpret our world – and then need to translate this knowledge onto the actions of others. A failure in this process makes it difficult to understand the social signals during any interaction and to understand the full meaning of any conversation – to understand the world we inhabit.

Frith suggested that a key deficit of people with schizophrenia is that they do not have a fully intact theory of mind. They cannot fully understand their own cognitive processes: in particular, they can have difficulties in monitoring their own intentions – leading to feelings of passivity and being out of control of their own actions. Other phenomena associated with this problem include the belief that thoughts are being placed in an individual's mind by others, and auditory hallucinations. In addition, individuals with this problem cannot understand the minds of other people, and therefore find it difficult to interpret what other people are thinking or feeling. This may lead to delusions of paranoia and reference. Finally, because such individuals find it difficult to interpret their world, they may become withdrawn and isolated in order to avoid any distress or confusion such attempts may engender. The degree to which these problems exist may vary across individuals. According to Frith, some people with a diagnosis of schizophrenia may have a complete inability to represent other people's mental states. In this, they may be similar to autistic people. Others, including people with paranoid delusions, have some understanding that other people have minds and motivations, but make significant errors due to an inaccurate or poorly developed theory of mind.

This theory has significant implications for a variety of processes involved in the symptoms of schizophrenia. It also provides a number of experimentally testable hypotheses. Not surprisingly, therefore, a number of studies provide supportive evidence, while others are less supportive. Such studies have attempted to identify how well people diagnosed with schizophrenia can understand other people's mental states – often through the use of analogue studies. These can involve quite complex cognitive tasks. One of the simpler methodologies has involved exploration of the understanding of jokes which involve deception – and therefore require an intact theory of mind to understand. In one such study, Marjoram et al. (2005) presented 20 people diagnosed with schizophrenia and 20 controls with 63 single-image cartoons. Thirty-one of these were considered to be 'theory of mind cartoons', in that understanding the joke required an attribution of ignorance, false belief or deception to one of its characters and, therefore, an analysis of their mental state. The other jokes were more slapstick in nature and subsequently did not require theory of mind capabilities for their correct interpretation. People with a diagnosis of schizophrenia showed less understanding of both types of jokes than the control group – as has been found elsewhere. In addition, they showed significantly less understanding of the theory of mind jokes than the slapstick cartoons, suggesting impairment in their theory of mind. Craig et al. (2004b) used two tasks to measure theory of mind in people with paranoid delusions and healthy controls. The first assessed their ability to infer an individual's intentions based on hints within a short written passage; the second measured their ability to detect 'cognitive emotions' such as being embarrassed or pensive (which require inferences about other people's beliefs or intentions to fully understand) from photographs of faces showing only the eye region. People with a diagnosis of schizophrenia performed less well in both tasks.

In a more clinical study of this phenomenon, McCabe et al. (2004) analysed recordings of interactions between mental health professionals and people diagnosed with chronic schizophrenia during outpatient and cognitive behavioural therapy sessions. In these interactions, it was evident that some of the people recognized that they and the health professionals did not share their beliefs about particular issues. They were also able to attribute emotions and appropriate causes of emotions to other people. One participant stated that he did not tell people when he had 'funny' thoughts come into his head because he was aware that other people did not have such thoughts and he felt ashamed having them. The expression of shame – which is a socially determined emotion – showed an awareness both that other people were different and that they would consider his thoughts to be odd. Accordingly, this study found no evidence of a deficit in theory of mind in this particular sample of people.

Summarizing the available data, Brüne (2005) suggested that there is good empirical evidence that theory of mind is impaired in schizophrenia and that many psychotic symptoms, such as delusions of alien control and persecution, may best be understood as resulting from difficulties in monitoring one's own intentions and relating to other people's intentions. More cautiously, Brüne also noted that we still do not understand how any impairment fluctuates between acute and stable periods within the disorder or how it affects individual's use of language or social behaviour.

Hallucinations as a failure of attention

A number of explanations for hallucinations have been based on an early theory of attention and memory developed by Broadbent (1971). Early work suggested that people with schizophrenia were unable to filter out irrelevant and unwanted stimuli: they could not filter out, or decide, which were appropriate or inappropriate elements of their environment to attend to. As a consequence, they felt overwhelmed by sensory experiences and found it difficult to concentrate and respond to their environment appropriately. This approach was extended by Hemsley (e.g. 1996), who considered many of the symptoms of schizophrenia to result from two key failures of processing:

- an impairment of the rapid and automatic assessment of sensory input
- a breakdown in relationship between stored memories and current sensory input.

He suggested that we choose what to attend to within our sensory field as a consequence of our previous experience. We store in our memory what Hemsley referred to as 'regularities'; that is, information that determines our expectations or interpretations of any situation. This regulates our reactions in similar but novel situations. These processes occur rapidly and automatically and allow us to focus our attention on what is important within our environment, and what is not. As a result of these stored memories, we know what to attend to when we go into a shop to buy a pair of shoes, when we play football, and so on. According to Hemsley, these automatic processes do not occur in people with schizophrenia, and the individual is unable to focus their attention appropriately. They attend to everything within their environment, and become overwhelmed by sensory information. Three key problems arise from this sensory barrage:

- Hallucinations result from a failure to filter out redundant information and from giving all stimuli equal weight.
- One's own thoughts cannot be distinguished from external stimuli – and can be perceived as an external voice.
- Delusions occur when trying to impose meaning on a barrage of confusing internal and external stimuli.

This model explains the positive symptoms of schizophrenia. But Hemsley was also able to explain some of the negative symptoms. He suggested that symptoms such as social withdrawal, impoverished speech and flat affect may arise either as a consequence of, or as a coping strategy with, the sensory overload. Evidence for some of the key elements of the theory can be derived from a number of sources. One source of support stems from studies of people with speech hallucinations. There is consistent evidence that people with hallucinations have difficulty in identifying the spacial location of sounds, and are less accurate than controls in determining the meaning of words when said against a background of white noise – despite being highly confident of the meaning they attach to such sounds. In one investigation of this phenomenon, Hoffman et al. (1999) examined the performance of three groups of people during a variety of tasks. Those involved had either a history of hallucinations, a diagnosis of schizophrenia with no history of hallucinations, or were 'normal' controls. They took part in a masked speech tracking task with three levels of superimposed phonetic noise. Participants were asked to repeat the sentences they heard, as they heard them – to assess grammar-dependent verbal working memory. They also took part in a non-verbal tracking task to assess any differences in attention between the three groups. People with a history of hallucinations performed less well on the speech tracking task, but were not impaired on the non-verbal tracking task. The authors took this to indicate that hallucinated voices in schizophrenia arise from disrupted speech perception and verbal working memory systems rather than from non-language cognitive or attentional deficits. Rossell and Boundy (2005) subsequently found that people who hallucinated were particularly poor at distinguishing words with an affective meaning – leaving them susceptible to misinterpreting emotionally laden words in ordinary life.

In a study of the neurological processes that may contribute to this phenomenon, McGuire et al. (1996) used positron emission tomography to measure brain activity of people with a history of hallucinations, people with a diagnosis of schizophrenia with no such history, and 'normal' controls while they took part in a number of tasks. In the first condition, in which participants were asked to simply talk to themselves in their head, there were no differences in brain activity between the groups. However, when they were asked to imagine someone else talking in their head, people who had experienced hallucinations showed different brain activity from both other groups. This group showed reduced activation in the left middle temporal gyrus and the rostral supplementary motor area regions – which were strongly activated in both other groups. As this area is implicated in the monitoring of inner speech, they took this deficit to be a neurological substrate of the failure to identify the source of verbal information and for the hallucinations this group experienced.

A cognitive model of delusions

Perhaps the most common understanding of delusional beliefs is that they are qualitatively different from those held by 'ordinary people'. Berrios (1991), for example, argued that delusions are 'empty speech acts' that refer neither to the world nor to the self: they are not symbolic of anything. By contrast, clinicians such as Bentall (e.g. Bentall and Fernyhough 2008) have argued that delusions are at the extreme end of a continuum of types of thought that runs from 'ordinary thoughts' to those that are bizarre and impossible, but all of which are the end-product of similar cognitive processes. Cognitions, including delusions, are seen as an interpretation of events, maybe even rational attempts to make sense of anomalous circumstances. While the thought content may be out of the ordinary, the psychological processes underpinning it are not.

In the model of persecutory beliefs developed by this group (Bentall et al. 2001) drew on the humanistic concepts of the actual and ideal self. They suggested that many people with schizophrenia have a poor self-image and experience significant discrepancies between their actual- and ideal-self, that is, how they see themselves and how they would like to be. These discrepancies may be maintained by attentional and attributional biases, in particular, by considering negative events or outcomes of their behaviour to be the result of personal deficiencies. An awareness of the discrepancy between ideal- and actual-self may result in depression. Persecutory beliefs may occur as the result of a struggle to minimize the discrepancy. According to Bentall and colleagues, when discrepancies between actual- and ideal-self are activated by negative life-events or other triggers, the individual tries to minimize this discrepancy by shifting this attribution onto others, as a form of psychological defence: 'I think I am OK, even though others don't.' It may be less distressing for the individual to think that others think poorly of him or her than to accept their own feelings of inadequacy. Bentall and colleagues further suggest that the natural history of schizophrenia within the family can be explained by this model, as attributional styles may be learned from other family members, and parental criticism may precipitate relapse by triggering actual–ideal self-discrepancies. Developmental processes that may contribute to this attributional style implicate insecure attachment in childhood which continues into adulthood, combined with low self-esteem and difficulty in trusting others. Repeated experiences of victimization are likely to exacerbate negative self-esteem while provoking an externalizing explanatory style in which negative events are assumed to be caused by powers external to the self. Evidence for this model is outlined in the Research box 7.

Bentall, R.O., Rowse, G., Shyrane, N. et al. (2009) The cognitive and affective structure of paranoid delusions: a transdiagnostic investigation of patients with schizophrenia spectrum disorders and depression, *Archives of General Psychiatry*, 66: 236–47.

The authors contend that research into psychotic disorders has been hampered by the wide range of abnormalities that can contribute to them, and a lack of theoretical or empirical framework identifying which abnormalities typically co-exist. The absence of such a framework means that it is not possible to identify biological or psychosocial factors that contribute to the development of specific types of psychotic disorder, which would allow us to discriminate between them.

To remedy this deficit, the authors attempted to identify factors associated with the development of paranoid disorder. They measured a number of psychological constructs including: (i) deficits in theory of mind, (ii) impaired cognitive performance, (iii) a pessimistic thinking style, and (iv) a tendency to make inflated estimates about threat value of future events, and assessed how closely each was associated with a diagnosis of paranoid delusions.

Method

Participants

Participants were 237 individuals ranging from 20 to 94 years old, with a range of diagnoses including schizophrenia, schizoaffective disorder and major depression with psychotic features, all of whom were experiencing or had experienced paranoid delusions. A sample of 'healthy' adults was also recruited. Individuals with evidence of negative signs or overt thought disorder were excluded from the study.

Outcome measures

Questionnaires measured the following:

- Frequency of paranoid beliefs
- Estimate of the likelihood of future neutral, pleasant, and threatening events
- Anxiety and depression
- Self-esteem
- Attributional Style: attributions for six positive and negative events on dimensions of internality/externality, stability over time and globality.

In addition, two cognitive tasks were also presented.

- The 'Beads in a Jar task' (a conditional reasoning task) was used to measure the tendency to jump to conclusions. In this, participants were presented with two jars: one containing 85 per cent white beads and 15 per cent black beads, and one filled with the opposite ratio. The participant was then presented with a series of pictures of increasing numbers of beans and was asked to make a decision about which jar was the source of the beads as soon as they were 'as certain as possible' which jar this was. It is impossible to be absolutely sure which jar the beans came from. The earlier participants are willing to come to a judgement, the more impulsive they are.

- 'Theory of mind stories' were used to measure understanding of intentional deception. In these, stories were read to participants alongside a set of cartoon pictures depicting events in the story. At set points, questions were asked tapping theory of mind, memory and inference skills. The theory of mind questions asked participants what they thought a character in the story was thinking (first order inference) and what they thought a character in the story thought another character was thinking (second order inference). Together, these allowed the researcher to assess the ability to understand deception.

Intellectual functioning and memory were assessed using the Wechsler Abbreviated Scale of Intelligence.

Statistical analysis

Analysis involved the use of structural equation models with latent variables. Their analysis entailed specifying a number of theoretically plausible models *a priori* and then comparing the fit of these models to the observed data.

Results

The best fit equation identified three overarching cognitive and psychological processes to be associated with paranoid delusions: (i) the presence of persecutory beliefs and anticipation of threat to the self; (ii) a depressive or pessimistic thinking style, involving low self-esteem, high levels of depression and anxiety, and assumptions that the causes of negative events would be pervasive and persistent; and (iii) 'general intellectual performance' (or executive functioning), comprising the ability to understand the mental states of other people, and to formulate hypotheses on the basis of sequentially presented information. This was negatively associated with paranoid beliefs. The significance of the fit of this model was: chi^2 (296) = 131.69, $p = 0.01$; comparative fit index = 0.95; Tucker-Lewis Index = 0.96; root-mean-square error of approximation = 0.04.

Discussion

One important difference between the present and previous studies is that the researchers investigated psychological factors in relation to the specific symptom of paranoia and not positive schizophrenia symptoms in general. As such, they generated a model of paranoia not psychosis. Comparison with previous studies examining associates of psychosis are of limited value. The study had some interesting findings, many of which did at least partially replicate findings in individuals broadly diagnosed as psychotic. The study also had some limitations, the most important perhaps being its cross-sectional nature. It is not possible on the basis of a cross-sectional study to infer direct causal relationships between the latent variables and symptoms of paranoia. This requires longitudinal studies.

A trauma model of hallucinations

Romme and Escher (2000) began their exploration of the nature of hallucinations by considering them to be a normal response to traumatic events, particularly bereavement and sexual or physical assault. They considered that their function is to draw attention to emotional traumas that need resolving and to provide a defence against the emotional upset associated with them by placing them into the third person. This may be considered a form of dissociation similar to that involved in the processing of traumatic memories discussed in Chapter 9. The goal of therapy should therefore be to help people develop strategies to understand the meaning of the voices, not to rid them of their voices. This approach has received little empirical attention. However, one key element of their model is that many people hear voices. What distinguishes those who become 'patients' and those that do not is that non-patients perceive their voices as predominantly positive, are not alarmed by them, and feel in control of the experience.

Despite the lack of scientific data in support of their model, Romme and Escher have had a significant impact on the normalization of the experiences of people with schizophrenia and supporting people who hear voices. The 'hearing voices network' (http://www.voicesforum.org.uk/index.htm), inspired by their work and supported by them, provides support to people with this type of experience. It started in Holland in 1987, and is now worldwide. The aims of the network are:

- to raise awareness of voice hearing, visions, tactile sensations and other sensory experiences
- to give people who have these experiences an opportunity to talk freely about this together
- to support anyone with these experiences seeking to understand, learn and grow from them.

Support is provided through self-help groups, training sessions for health workers and the general public, an Internet discussion site and a telephone helpline.

7.4 Treatment of schizophrenia

Antipsychotic medication

Most people diagnosed with schizophrenia receive some form of medication, although dosages may be reduced or even discontinued during periods of remission. Chlorpromazine, haloperidol and clozapine are three of the most commonly used drugs (see Chapter 4 for a review of their mode of action and effectiveness). Their most striking effect is one of sedation. They also have a direct effect on hallucinations and delusions, although their effectiveness varies markedly between individuals. Chlorpromazine and haloperidol seem to affect only the positive symptoms of schizophrenia: clozapine, an atypical neuroleptic, is more successful in treating both positive and negative symptoms, and is often effective when other treatments fail (Essali et al. 2009).

Antipsychotic medication has been so successful in treating people with schizophrenia that their typical hospital stay during an acute episode has declined to less than 13 days, when formerly it was months, years, even a lifetime. Appropriate medication also lies at the heart of the relatively good levels of relapse (10 per cent in the first year) reported earlier in the chapter. Nevertheless, they appear to delay relapse rather than prevent it.

The use of antipsychotic drugs is not without problems. They have a variety of side-effects that frequently lead those receiving them to minimize or stop their use. Side-effects of chlorpromazine, for example, include a dryness of mouth and throat, drowsiness, visual disturbances, weight gain or loss, skin sensitivity to sunlight, constipation and depression. More problematic, however, are what are known as extrapyramidal symptoms. These include the symptoms of Parkinsonism and tardive dyskinesia (see Chapter 3), which have been estimated to affect over a quarter of individuals who receive medium- to long-term neuroleptic treatment. Treatment by clozapine or other atypical neuroleptics does not carry this risk, but those who receive it may be at risk of a condition known as agranulocytosis, which results in significant impairment of the immune system and can result in death. In addition, although psychomotor symptoms may not occur, people on clozapine experience more drowsiness, hypersalivation or temperature increase, than those given conventional neuroleptics. Despite this, clozapine is the preferred medication (Essali et al. 2009).

Adherence to antipsychotic drug regimes can be as low as 25 per cent among people living in the community (Donohue et al. 2001). This does not seem to be associated with socio-demographic variables, severity of the disorder, or even the extent to which people experience extrapyramidal symptoms. Instead, low adherence seems to be related to attitudes towards medication, expectations of drug effectiveness, available social support, and the quality of the therapeutic alliance. Poor memory may contribute to accidental adherence.

Strategies to maximize adherence include education, developing a high quality therapeutic alliance, and the use of memory aids for those with a poor memory. Depot injections may also be of benefit, as these have a relatively long active therapeutic life, and involve the client in less day-to-day decisions about taking oral medication. One relatively new strategy is known as motivational interviewing (Miller and Rollnick 2002). This approach encourages the client to choose whether or not to take their medication as a result of a careful exploration of the costs and benefits of doing so. This gives a degree of control to the client, maintains or improves the therapeutic alliance as the therapist is not seen as coercive, allows any misunderstandings about medication to be identified and corrected, and seems to be more effective in encouraging drug use than direct attempts at persuasion (Coffey 1999). In one exploration of this approach, Kemp et al. (1998) compared motivational interviewing designed to increase adherence to medication with routine care following relapse. The group which received the motivational approach showed higher levels of adherence to the drug regimen and lower readmission rates over an 18-month period. This positive finding compares well against even quite sophisticated education programmes involving several sessions, which have not proven so effective (e.g. Byerly et al. 2005).

Minimizing drug usage: early signs

The psychological and physical consequences of long-term drug treatment of schizophrenia have led clinicians to seek innovative methods by which medication usage can be minimized. One approach, involving 'early signs', is based on findings that many people with schizophrenia and their families can detect subtle changes in behaviour and mood that precede a relapse (see Box 7.1). The 'early signs' approach assumes that while a person is well, they receive less medication or are withdrawn from medication completely. When they experience changes that indicate risk of relapse, these should trigger the individual to seek help (following a prearranged care plan) and to receive intensive drug and/or psychological therapy to prevent relapse and maintain their recovery (Birchwood et al. 2000).

Box 7.1 Early signs of relapse

Birchwood and colleagues (2000) asked clients to tick off a checklist of 'early signs' which they experience at different times within a process of relapse. Others ask them to identify them through discussion. Here are some of the early signs reported by Sean using this approach, roughly in the order in which they occur at times up to several months before any obvious 'relapse':

Sean

- sleeping later in the morning
- reduced contact with people – staying in
- loss of interest in music
- anxiety
- smoking and drinking more
- paranoia – think I'm being poisoned
- depression
- erratic eating
- stop shaving
- litter around the house – don't clean up, live in a mess
- fear
- mental exhaustion – peripheral hallucinations, flashes of light and dark.

This approach can be effective. Gaebel et al. (2002) compared outcomes in 363 people with schizophrenia who received either intermittent (early signs intervention) or continuous medication following either a psychotic episode. People treated using the early signs approach used less medication over a two-year period than those in the continuous medication condition. There were no differences in effectiveness between the treatments on measures of psychopathology, social adjustment and subjective well-being. Despite this success, some have questioned the effectiveness of this approach. Gaebel and Riesbeck (2007), for example, found that the early signs identified by many individuals were not predictive of relapse.

Electroconvulsive therapy

Electroconvulsive therapy (ECT: see Chapter 3) has been a front-line treatment of schizophrenia in the past, and has achieved some success. A meta-analysis by Tharyan (2002) concluded that about half those treated with ECT showed short-term improvements in general functioning when compared with those given placebo. This effect, however, did not last. Moreover, ECT is less effective than antipsychotic drug treatment. Combining antipsychotic drugs and ECT is of benefit only in the short term, and only one out of every five to six people appears to benefit. For these reasons, ECT in the treatment of schizophrenia has largely been curtailed, and the NICE guidelines for the treatment of schizophrenia did not recommend its use (NICE 2009).

Psychological approaches

Psychoanalytic approaches

One of the first psychosocial treatments of schizophrenia was developed by Harry Stack Sullivan in the early part of the twentieth century. Sullivan (1953) considered schizophrenia to involve difficulties in living arising from problems in personal and social relationships, and that 'personality warps' were the lasting residue of earlier unsatisfactory personal experiences. His treatment approach involved examination of the individual's life history and the historical roots and current ramifications of their maladaptive interpersonal patterns, evident in their relationship with their doctor and in daily life. Characteristic difficulties were thought to include a basic mistrust of others, and a marked ambivalence in relationships, with swings between a longing for, and a terror of, close relationships. Resolution of this conflict through the psychotherapeutic process was thought to result in improvements in psychosis, and maturation of the patient and their non-psychotic personality. While Sullivan's interventions were important, as they encouraged the psychological treatment of people with schizophrenia, the approach has been found to be less effective than supportive therapy, and is no longer carried out.

Family interventions

The recognition that high NEE was contributing to relapse in schizophrenia resulted in a number of studies of family interventions targeted at its reduction. In one of the earliest of these, Leff and Vaughn (1985) randomly assigned people with schizophrenia who had at least 35 hours per week face-to-face contact with family members in a high NEE household to a family intervention or usual care condition. The intervention included a psycho-educational programme that focused on methods of reducing NEE within the household, family support and the opportunity for family therapy. The programme was highly successful. Nine months after the end of therapy, 8 per cent of the people in the treatment group had relapsed, in contrast to 50 per cent of those in the comparison group. By two-year follow-up, 40 per cent of the treatment group and 78 per cent of the control group had relapsed.

A similar therapeutic approach was adopted by Falloon et al. (1982). Their intervention included education about the role of family stress in triggering episodes of schizophrenia and working with the family to develop family problem-solving skills. Their results were equally impressive. At nine-month follow-up, 5 per cent of the people in families receiving treatment had relapsed, in contrast to 44 per cent of those receiving standard medical treatment. By two-year follow-up, relapse rates were 16 per cent and 83 per cent respectively. On the basis of this and other related evidence, Pharoah et al. (2000) concluded that family interventions reduce risk of relapse by about half in comparison with standard medical care. They also noted that family interventions decreased the frequency of admissions to hospital, time spent in hospital, and improved compliance with medication regimens.

Cognitive behavioural therapy

Two forms of CBT are increasingly being used with people with a diagnosis of schizophrenia. The first, stress management, involves working with individuals to help them cope with the stress leading to or associated with psychotic experiences. The second, known as belief modification, involves attempts to change the nature of delusional beliefs the individual may hold.

Stress management   Stress management approaches involve a detailed evaluation of the problems and experiences an individual is having, their triggers and consequences, and developing strategies to help cope with them. These include cognitive techniques such as distraction from intrusive thoughts or cognitive challenge, increasing or decreasing social activity as a means of distraction from intrusive thoughts or low mood, and using relaxation techniques (see Chapter 2).

This approach has proven successful in preventing or delaying individuals at high risk of developing schizophrenia moving into a first episode (Salokangas and McGlashan 2008). McGorry et al. (2002), for example, randomized such individuals into what they termed an intervention, involving supportive psychotherapy focusing on social, work or family issues or low-dose risperidone therapy combined with CBT. Each intervention lasted for six months. By the end of treatment, 36 per cent of the people who received supportive psychotherapy progressed to first-episode psychosis compared with 10 per cent in the specific CBT-risperidone group. Short-term gains were also found following a purely cognitive intervention by Morrison et al. (2006), but by three-year follow-up the intervention proved no more successful than usual care.

Other studies have evaluated interventions intended to promote recovery following an acute episode of schizophrenia. In one such study, Tarrier et al. (e.g. 2000) randomly assigned individuals to either drug therapy alone, or in combination with stress management or supportive counselling. The stress management intervention involved 20 sessions in ten weeks, followed by four booster sessions over the following year. By the end of the first phase of treatment, those who received this intervention evidenced a greater improvement than those in the supportive counselling group, while people who received only drug therapy showed a slight deterioration. One-third of the people who received stress management achieved a 50 per cent reduction in psychotic experiences; only 15 per cent of the supportive counselling group achieved this level of benefit: 15 per cent of the stress management group and 7 per cent of the supportive counselling condition were free of all positive symptoms. None of those in the drug therapy group achieved this criterion. One year later, there remained significant differences between the three groups, favouring those in the stress management condition. By two-year follow-up, those who received only drug therapy had significantly more problems than those in the psychological treatment groups. However, both psychological interventions proved equally effective.

Belief modification   Belief modification involves the use of verbal challenge and behavioural hypothesis testing to counter delusional beliefs and/or hallucinations. Verbal challenge encourages the individual to view a delusional belief as just one of several possibilities. The person is not told that the belief is wrong, but is asked to consider an alternative view provided by the therapist. New possibilities may then be tested in the 'real world' as appropriate. A similar process is used to challenge hallucinations, focusing on the patient's beliefs about their power, identity and purpose. Behavioural hypothesis testing involves challenging any thoughts in a more direct, behavioural, way (see also discussion of these issues in Chapter 2).

Reflecting the novelty of this approach, the number of studies to evaluate this type of intervention is relatively small. Nevertheless, from their meta-analysis of four randomized controlled trials, Jones et al. (2000) concluded that these interventions reduced both the frequency and the impact of hallucinations. In addition, while they had a limited impact on measures of conviction in delusional beliefs, they reduced the amount of distress associated with them. Overall, people who were taught ways of challenging their delusional beliefs or hallucinations were half as likely to relapse as those who were not.

Since then, Trower et al. (2004) followed a group of 38 individuals with command hallucinations who were randomly allocated to usual care or a cognitive intervention. The results were impressive. At both six- and twelve-month follow-up, those in the cognitive intervention group reported significantly less compliance with the commands, as well as less belief in their power superiority. A more multifaceted intervention was reported by Drury et al. (2000). This involved both individual and group cognitive therapy in which participants learned to cope with delusions and hallucinations. In addition, they took part in a six-month-long family psycho-education programme and an activity programme including life-skills groups. The effects of this intervention were compared with those of an activity programme involving participants in sports, leisure and social groups. The short- and mid-term impacts of the intervention were impressive. Those in the active therapeutic programme recovered more quickly following the relapse that brought them into therapy. By nine-month follow-up, 56 per cent of the control group still had moderate or severe problems, in comparison to 5 per cent of the intervention group. By five-year follow-up, however, there was no evidence of any differences between the two groups on measures of relapse rates or levels of positive symptoms. To achieve longer-term benefits, it may be necessary to introduce a second, perhaps less extensive, 'booster' intervention.

Case formulation

John was a 23-year-old man who lived with three other people in a rented flat in a suburb of Birmingham. He had experienced problems in childhood as a consequence of both his parents' violence to each other and their neglect of their children. He had been moved from the family home, and away from his siblings, to a foster home as a consequence of these problems. He was quite happy in the foster home and school, and gained a number of A levels. However, after leaving home to go to college, he began a history of significant drug and alcohol use, and dropped out of college in his first year. Since then, he had had a number of short-term casual jobs, but nothing long term. He continued to be a heavy user of drugs including marijuana, amphetamine and cocaine over a period of years. To sustain his drug use, he had engaged in petty crime and occasionally dealt drugs. He was known to the local police force, who had detained him on a number of occasions, although he had not been to prison. He was well known to the local probation officers.

John was admitted into a local hospital following the onset of an acute psychotic episode, which appeared to follow a break-up with a girlfriend of several weeks previously. His flatmates had noticed that his behaviour had become increasingly strange and withdrawn over a period of several weeks. He was telling them that he was hearing voices indicating that the police were after him and that they had put out a contract for him to be killed because of his history of crime and the way he had treated his girlfriend. He could hear the voices because they were being transmitted through the police radio system, which he was able to detect through radio receivers in his brain. He had locked himself in his room, closed the curtains, and was not eating. He felt frightened and believed that if he left the house, he would be found by the police, and either taken to prison or killed. In order to calm himself down he was using significant amounts of marijuana and alcohol. His flatmates' concern was such that they had contacted their family doctor, who had visited John in his flat. Under the guise of doing some tests to check out the reality of the changes to his brain and to try and sort them out, the doctor had persuaded John to be admitted to a local psychiatric hospital on a voluntary basis.

Once in hospital he was assessed by a psychiatrist, and placed on anti-psychotic medication. After a few weeks, although he felt calm and safe in hospital, he still appeared depressed and believed that the police were 'after him'. He was therefore referred to a clinical psychologist in the hope that they could change his paranoid beliefs.

Formulation

John was a vulnerable individual as a consequence of his damaged upbringing, difficulties in engaging with others, and the stresses associated with relationships and use of non-prescription drugs. The incident appears to have been triggered by his breaking up a relationship with a woman he had been seeing for several months. He had not treated her well during the relationship and the break-up had been quite uncaring and disrespectful to her. According to Bentall (2001), this may have evoked memories of his childhood and the pain he experienced at this time, making him feel guilty for his behaviour and like his parents, for whom he received little respect or love. He differed significantly from an ideal self of being caring and cared for. This guilt led to ruminations and worry about how he had behaved, its implications for him, and the belief that he was a bad person. Exacerbated by the use of drugs, he had externalized these feelings of guilt and self-deprecation onto the police.

Intervention

The first stage of therapy involved a period of John and therapist simply talking about his experiences, in a process of gaining trust and gaining empathy. Evidence has shown this to be particularly important in the process of treating psychosis – too quick or too challenging, and the client is highly likely to disengage from therapy. After several sessions, during which the therapist identified and acknowledged (but not agreed with) several distorted beliefs and delusions, he began to gently probe their reality. One way in which this began was to simply question whether or not John agreed with any of the negative beliefs about himself that he believed the police to hold. This led to discussion of a number of negative beliefs about himself, his past, and disappointment at his life situation that he felt – without directly challenging his belief that the voices he heard were those of the police radio. Following this discussion (over a number of therapy sessions), the therapist began to gently question the foundations of some of John's beliefs: why would the police want to kill him for very minor offences? Would they do this with other people? Had they shown evidence of this attitude when he had previously been involved with the police? As a consequence of these discussion, John was able to question the likelihood of some of his beliefs being true, and became less disturbed by them. This allowed the therapist to move to a different approach: more direct challenges to his beliefs through the use of behavioural hypothesis testing. One belief John held was that the police were watching him and would pick him up if he left the safety of the hospital ward. This was tested by encouraging John to walk out of the ward, first in the hospital grounds and then to local shops. He did so, with a degree of anxiety, but succeeded in doing so, and began to question further the strength of his paranoid beliefs, as they had not come true.

Over a period of several weeks of intensive therapy (meeting with his therapist twice a week), John was able to question and counter much of his paranoid ideation and delusions. This process was no doubt aided by his no longer taking non-prescription drugs and the use of anti-psychotics. However, the positive outcome of these various processes were that John was able to leave hospital with the support of a social worker and community mental health team, and engage in longer-term processes of reducing his drug and alcohol use, dealing with unresolved issues from his childhood, and developing better relationships with friends and partners. But that is another story . . .

7.5 Chapter summary

1 Schizophrenia is one of the most disabling mental health disorders.

2 DSM identifies four types of schizophrenia: disorganized, paranoid, catatonic and residual.

3 An alternative classification system identifies two clusters of symptoms. Positive symptoms include hallucinations, delusions and thought disorder, and negative symptoms are those related to a general lack of motivation.

4 Concerns over the nature of schizophrenia have led some to argue that the concept can no longer be considered valid. Instead, they have argued that the various experiences of people diagnosed as having schizophrenia would be better considered as separate and unrelated factors.

5 There is no exclusive 'cause' of schizophrenia, although a number of factors have been implicated, including genetics and social and family stress.

6 The biological bases for schizophrenia include disruption of the dopamine system and neuronal degeneration, partly as a consequence of perinatal factors, partly due to excess dopamine.

7 Psychological models adopt a dimensional view of the disorder and attempt to understand the psychological processes that contribute to the experiences of people diagnosed with schizophrenia rather than to identify triggers to a 'condition' in which the individual differs categorically from the norm.

8 Theory of mind explanations of schizophrenia attribute the condition to an inability to monitor and understand one's own thought processes and those of others.

9 Cognitive explanations of delusions suggest they may form an attributional process, to help people cope with negative self-evaluations.

10 Cognitive models of hallucinations consider them to result from failures in attentional and filtering processes.

11 Treatment is largely with phenothiazines such as chlorpromazine and newer drugs including clozapine. These seem to delay rather than prevent the onset of further problems.

12 The high level of side-effects associated with these drugs has led to a number of innovative strategies to minimize their use, including the relapse prevention strategy known as 'early signs'.

13 Drug therapy may be significantly augmented by family therapy, particularly for those who live in a high NEE environment, which has been shown to profoundly alter the course of schizophrenia.

14 Newer cognitive techniques may also be of benefit.

7.6 For discussion

1 Is the diagnosis of schizophrenia a valid one?
2 Should people with schizophrenia receive genetic or family counselling when planning a family?
3 Should family or cognitive therapy form the first-line treatment for schizophrenia, with drug therapy used only if this is unsuccessful?

7.7 Key terms

Agranulocytosis condition in which the bone marrow fails to produce enough white blood cells called neutrophils. Leaves the individual prone to infection.

Alogia poverty of speech; literally, 'no words'.

Avolition lack of volition, or voluntary motivation.

Catatonic behaviour behaviour found in one form of schizophrenia; includes posturing, or 'waxy flexibility', mutism and stupor.

Community Mental Health Team a multidisciplinary team providing mental health care within the community. Usually includes psychiatrists, community psychiatric nurses, psychologists and other therapists.

Depot injections injection of a slow-release drug that will provide a therapeutic dose for days or weeks.

Flattened mood lack of emotional response, either positive or negative, to events.

Ideas of reference the, inappropriate, belief that objects, events or people are of personal significance. For example, a person may think that a television programme he is watching is all about him. May reach sufficient intensity to constitute delusions.

Incidence the frequency with which new cases of a condition arise within the population.

Neologism making up new words.

Neuroleptics a broad class of drugs used to treat psychotic condition such as schizophrenia; otherwise known as major tranquillizers or phenothiazines.

Psycho-educational programme a treatment usually combining elements of education about a problem or means of coping with it with cognitive behavioural strategies of change.

Ventricles one of a system of four communicating cavities within the brain that are continuous with the central canal of the spinal cord.

7.8 Further reading

Bentall. R.P., Rowse. G., Shryane. N. et al. (2009) The cognitive and affective structure of paranoid delusions: a transdiagnostic investigation of patients with schizophrenia spectrum disorders and depression, *Archives of General Psychiatry*, 66: 236–47.

Brekke, J.S., Hoe, M. and Green, M.F. (2009) Neurocognitive change, functional change and service intensity during community-based psychosocial rehabilitation for schizophrenia, *Psychological Medicine*, 39: 1637–47.

Haddock, G., Barrowclough, C., Shaw, J.J. et al. (2009) Cognitive-behavioural therapy v. social activity therapy for people with psychosis and a history of violence: randomised controlled trial, *British Journal of Psychiatry*, 194: 152–7.

National Institute for Clinical Excellence (2002) *Schizophrenia: Core Interventions in the Treatment and Management of Schizophrenia in Primary and Secondary Care – Clinical Guideline 1*. London: NICE.

The following websites also have information about the condition, its treatment, and people's experiences of it:

www.schizophrenia.com/
www.patient.co.uk/health/Schizophrenia.htm
www.world-schizophrenia.org/

Anxiety disorders

Chapter contents

Anxiety is a useful emotion. Without it, we are likely to be reckless and engage in activities that could lead to harm or even death. However, when levels of anxiety become inappropriately high, they stop being a proportionate response to the threats within the environment and become problematic to the individual experiencing them. The anxiety disorders lie at the extreme end of the distribution of anxiety within the population, and fall under the DSM category of neurotic and stress-related disorders. This chapter will focus on four diagnoses within this group: simple phobias, generalized anxiety disorder, panic disorder and obsessive-compulsive disorder. Each represents a differing response to either diffuse or specific causes of anxiety. By the end of the chapter, you should have an understanding of:

- The nature and aetiology of each condition from a number of theoretical perspectives
- The types of interventions used to treat each disorder
- The relative effectiveness of each of these interventions.

8.1 Simple phobias

A simple phobia is an unrealistic fear of a specific stimulus. DSM-IV-TR states the following criteria for this diagnosis to be met:

- Marked and persistent fear that is excessive or unreasonable, cued by the presence or anticipation of a specific object or situation.
- Exposure to the phobic stimulus almost invariably provokes an immediate anxiety response, which may take the form of a panic attack.
- The person recognizes that the fear is excessive or unreasonable.
- The phobic situation is avoided or endured with intense anxiety or distress.
- The avoidance, anxious anticipation or distress in the feared situation(s) interferes significantly with the person's normal routine or they experience distress about having the phobia.
- In individuals under age 18 years, the duration is at least 6 months.

The DSM further notes that phobic responses can occur in response to a variety of types of stimuli, including animals, natural environmental factors (heights, water), blood-injection-injury, specific situations (aeroplanes, lifts), and 'other' situations including fear of vomiting, contracting an illness, and so on. More complex disorders, such as a phobic fear of social situations and agoraphobia receive separate diagnoses. Agoraphobia is linked to panic disorder, and will be discussed later in the chapter.

In the US, about 9 per cent the population are likely to experience a phobia of some kind at some time in their life, with the highest prevalence among young, female, low income, or Hispanic and Asian individuals – although among Chinese people living in China, the prevalence of phobias is much lower (Lee et al. 2006). The most prevalent fear is that of snakes, affecting about 25 per cent of the population. Between 90 and 95 per cent of people with an animal phobia are women – other phobias, such as blood-injury phobia, are less gender-specific. Age of onset tends to follow a particular pattern, with phobias relating to animals, blood-injury, dentists and natural environments beginning in childhood, while others such as claustrophobia and agoraphobia typically start in adolescence and early adulthood (Öst 1987).

Some common and not so common phobias are:

Mysophobia	Fear of germs or contamination
Claustrophobia	Fear of enclosed spaces
Trypanophobia	Fear of injections
Monophobia	Fear of being alone
Helminthophobia	Fear of (parasitic) worms
Taphephobia	Fear of being buried alive
Triskaidekaphobia	Fear of the number 13
Ailurophobia	Fear of cats
Aviophobia	Fear of flying
Arachnophobia	Fear of spiders

Phobias such as a fear of snakes or spiders seem universal. The nature and prevalence of other phobias, however, appear to be influenced by cultural factors. Agoraphobia, for example, is much more common in the USA and Europe than in other areas of the world (Kleinman 1988). A very specific social phobia common in Japan but almost non-existent in the West is known as *taijin kyofusho*. This involves an incapacitating fear of offending or harming others through one's own awkward social behaviour, glancing at their genital areas or imagined physical defect (Kirmayer 1991). The focus of this phobia is on the harm to others, not on embarrassment to self as in social phobias in the West. As such, it appears to be a pathological exaggeration of the modesty and sensitive regard for others that, at lower levels, are considered proper in Japan.

Aetiology of phobias

Psychoanalytic models

According to Freud (1906), phobias act as a defence against the anxiety experienced when impulses formed by the id are repressed – resulting in a displacement of the repressed feelings onto the object or situation with which it is symbolically associated. These become phobic stimuli and the individual is able to avoid dealing with their repressed conflicts by avoiding them. These conflicts often involve childhood trauma or conflict. The most famous case of a phobia discussed by Freud is that of Little Hans. Hans was a 5-year-old boy who was afraid of horses, and avoided leaving the house for fear of being bitten by one. He also developed a specific fear of the blinkers and muzzles on horses' faces. Freud considered his fears to relate to the Oedipus complex (see Chapter 2), and that he was having sexual fantasies about his mother and feared his father's retaliation. He therefore displaced the fear of his father onto horses who reminded him of his father. A more prosaic explanation for these fears may have been his witnessing an incident in which a horse fell down in the street in front of him. Another psycho-dynamic interpretation, in which the feared object or behaviour is seen as symbolic of other fears or issues (agoraphobia as a response to feeling trapped within a marriage) may be less sexually charged than Freud's interpretation but of relevance to more modern psychodynamic therapists (Barber and Luborsky 1991).

Behavioural models

Early behavioural models of phobias considered them to result from conditioning experiences, in which the inappropriately feared object or situation was associated with the experience of fear at some time in the past. The conditioning process can be so powerful when acute fear is experienced, that this association need happen only once to result in a long-term fear response that is difficult to extinguish. Being in a car crash, for example, may result in a phobic reaction to being in a car, and subsequent avoidance of being in a car or driving. This response has three components:

- a *behavioural* element involving avoidance or escape from the feared object
- high levels of *physiological arousal* evident through a variety of symptoms including physical tension, increased startle response, tremor or sweating and driven by the sympathetic nervous system
- the *emotion* of anxiety and fear.

The most famous early example of the conditioning of a phobic response was Watson and Raynor's (1920) conditioning of 'Little Albert', discussed in Chapter 2.

The classical conditioning model of phobias is adequate in its description of the process of acquisition of anxiety and phobias. However, it is less able to explain why they are maintained over long periods, as repeated exposure to the feared object or situation in the absence of any negative consequences should lead to a reduction of anxiety through the process of extinction. Mowrer's (1947) two-factor theory combined both classical and operant processes to provide an explanation of this phenomenon. He noted that once a phobic response is established through classical conditioning processes, the affected individual tends to avoid the feared stimulus. This has two consequences. First, it prevents the classical conditioning process of extinction, as the individual does not experience the conditioned stimulus under conditions of safety. Second, because avoidance itself produces feelings of relief (i.e. it is reinforcing), the avoidance response is strengthened by operant conditioning processes. In this way, anxiety is potentially maintained over long periods.

By the 1970s, conditioning theories of the acquisition of fear and other emotional responses were finding it increasingly difficult to account for emerging experimental and clinical findings (e.g. Davey 1997):

- Many people with a phobia were unable to identify any traumatic conditioning incident. This seemed particularly true of some animal phobias and fear of heights and water. Murray and Foote (1979), for example, found that less than 10 per cent of snake phobics had been attacked or bitten by a snake. By contrast, over 90 per cent of people reporting a dental phobia had at least one painful episode at a dentist (Davey 1989).
- Many people exposed to trauma do not develop a phobia. Only about 16 per cent of people who attend hospital following a serious road traffic accident, for example, develop a phobia or fear of travelling by car (Mayou et al. 2001).
- Many common phobias are to relatively benign stimuli (e.g. spiders).
- Many common phobias are to stimuli rarely if ever encountered by most individuals (e.g. snakes).
- By contrast, rates of phobias to many frequently encountered and potentially frightening stimuli (e.g. traffic, knives, guns) are relatively low.
- Phobias tend to 'run' in families.

A cognitive behavioural model

In response to these concerns, more recent models of the aetiology of phobias have retained the conditioning processes of the early models but added a number of other processes. The most important of these is the addition of cognitive variables as mediators of both the acquisition of a phobias and their potential time course (Davey 1997).

Factors that may influence the *acquisition* of phobias include:

- The degree of familiarity with the feared stimulus. The more trauma-free associations an individual has had with a particular stimulus, the less likely they are to develop a phobia if that stimulus subsequently becomes associated with high levels of fear: a process known as latent inhibition. Conversely, the more negative emotions are associated with a particular stimulus prior to a traumatic event, the more likely an individual is to develop a phobia.

- Information from other people or observation of someone else expressing high levels of fear in the context of a particular stimulus. The latter process is known as vicarious learning and provides one explanation for the high prevalence of the same phobias in some families (Bandura 1982).

Factors that influence the *maintenance* of phobias, include:

- Socially or verbally transmitted information about the feared stimulus. Unfortunately, it seems easier to increase fear by telling people that a trigger event was more horrific than it appeared at the time than to reduce fear through reassurance that it was less horrific.
- Rehearsal and overestimation of the possible adverse outcomes that may occur should the individual encounter the feared stimulus. The more this occurs, the stronger the fear reaction during 'live' encounters with the feared stimulus.

Biological/evolutionary model

A second influential theory used to account for the non-random distribution of phobias is known as preparedness theory. Seligman (1971) proposed that some phobias or fears are more easily acquired as a result of their evolutionary usefulness than others. He contended that at some time in our evolutionary history it was beneficial to have a fear of potentially dangerous stimuli such as snakes, small animals, and so on – stimuli he termed 'phylogenetically relevant cues'. As a result, we may be hardwired, or biologically prepared, to react fearfully to stimuli that were once threatening to prehistoric man. Note that Seligman did not suggest we have an inborn fear of snakes, spiders, and so on. Rather he suggested that we acquire fear to such stimuli more easily following some form of conditioning experience than we do to others. The theory has four key predictions (Merckelbach and de Jong 1999):

- The most prevalent phobias should be to stimuli that were potentially dangerous in a pre-technological age: this does seem to be the case (Merckelbach and de Jong 1999).
- Fear of these stimuli is easily acquired (and more easily than other phobias): again, this may the case. Marks (1977), for example, gave an example of a woman who was looking at a picture of a snake at the time she was involved in a car accident. She become phobic to snakes, but not to cars.
- Because of their biological significance, they are non-cognitive.
- They resist extinction: experimental work by Öhman and colleagues (e.g. Öhman 1986) found that once a conditioned response to phylogenetically relevant stimuli was established in the laboratory, it took longer to extinguish than other conditioned phobias.

Accordingly, although not all the evidence is strongly supportive of the model (see Merckelbach and de Jong 1999), the consensus seems to be that some evolutionary/genetic processes may be involved in the acquisition of phobias.

Genetic factors

The core of the preparedness model is that there is some genetic predisposition to a phobic response to certain stimuli. What evidence there is suggests some degree of heritability of phobias.

Skre et al. (2000), for example, found that the measures of agoraphobia, social phobia and animal phobias were more strongly correlated in 23 MZ twins than in 38 DZ twins. They calculated a genetic heritability of 0.47 for common phobic fear of small animals and of 0.30 for agoraphobic fear. However, there was no evidence of heritability for the fear of 'nature phenomena' and situational fear. These findings support a modest genetic contribution to at least some phobias and a predisposition to a fear of small animals in particular. The exact location of any genetic loci has yet to be established (Smoller et al. 2008).

Biological mechanisms

The expression of any genetic risk of developing phobias may be through high levels of autonomic reactivity. A central element of the phobic response is a high level of physiological arousal, triggered by hypothalamic activity and mediated by the sympathetic nervous system (see Chapter 3). This response is driven by the neurotransmitter and hormone norepinephrine, and to a lesser extent, epinephrine. When the emotion of anxiety is experienced, these both activate the body and prepare it to deal with physical damage. At its most dramatic, this response is known as the fight–flight response. At such times, the heart beats quickly and powerfully, blood is shunted to the muscles and away from the gut (hence the experience of 'butterflies'), skeletal muscles tense and blood pressure rises. These and other processes prepare the body for rapid and dramatic action. This may be apparent through running away from a feared situation, or shaking, breathlessness, sweating and dizziness. These symptoms can be so extreme that it can lead to fear of having a heart attack. The one exception to this occurs in people who have a phobia concerning blood-injury or injection. When they encounter these stimuli they typically experience an initial acceleration then reduction in heart rate and blood pressure, a parasympathetic response. As a consequence they experience nausea, dizziness and may faint. Up to 70 per cent of such individuals report having fainted at some time (Öst and Hellström 1997).

The predominant model of phobias relates to autonomic arousal. Little has been considered in terms of neurotransmitter processing such as GABA and serotonergic mechanisms – perhaps because their short-term, and specific, activity during a phobic response is difficult to measure. However, as these appear to be involved in other anxiety conditions, they may also be involved in simple phobias, but strong evidence is lacking.

Treatment of phobias

Behavioural treatments

The premise underpinning behavioural treatments of phobias was outlined in Chapter 2. Both involve exposure to the feared stimulus either directly (flooding) or in a series of hierarchical stages (systematic desensitization). These approaches may be augmented by teaching people skills such as relaxation or cognitive strategies to counter negative expectations and fear of catastrophic outcomes. However, the effects of these additions have been mixed – with both treatment gains and losses – indicating that the core of any treatment involves direct exposure to the feared stimulus and staying with it until any fear is extinguished (Wolitzky-Taylor et al. 2008).

Systematic desensitization and flooding have long been considered the primary interventions to treat phobias, and recent research has involved attempts at fine-tuning the approach and making it cost-effective. One strand of research has focused on the effects of single-session exposure to the feared stimulus. These sessions may be fairly lengthy – sometimes over three hours. In one study of its effectiveness, Hellstrom et al. (1996) reported outcomes of a group treatment of people with a spider phobia. They were randomly assigned into one of two conditions: small groups of 3–4 people and larger groups of 7–8 people. They each received one three-hour session in which the principles of the treatment – based on flooding – were explained to participants. They watched as the therapist was exposed to the spiders and coped with their fear. They were then encouraged to handle four spiders and shown how to cope with this experience. Immediately after treatment, 82 per cent of people in the small groups had made clinically significant improvements, compared to 70 per cent of those in the large groups. By one-year follow-up, the equivalent percentages were 95 and 75 per cent respectively. By 2006, a total of 21 studies had reported this or similar one-session treatment programmes. Even so, in their review of these studies, Zlomke and Davis (2008) were somewhat cautious in their conclusions, stating that the one-session approach is 'probably efficacious' as the quality of many of the studies was not sufficiently robust to allow clear conclusions to be determined.

A second strand of research has focused on minimizing contact between client and therapist in programmes of systematic desensitization. The effects of this 'self-directed exposure' have varied from being as effective as therapist-led exposure to significantly worse. Öst, Salkovskis and Hellström (1991), for example, compared the effectiveness of a single three-hour therapist-led session with that of a self-exposure programme involving use of a therapy manual given to participants. The single session group did far better than the client-determined therapy, with success rates of 71 per cent in the therapist-led therapy and 6 per cent in the self-directed exposure group. By contrast, Schneider et al. (2005) found a self-exposure programme delivered via the internet to be significantly more effective than a stress management programme without the element of exposure.

A third strand of therapy has involved the use of virtual reality. In one study of this approach, Walshe et al. (2003) treated car phobics using a virtual reality exposure programme involving up to 12 one-hour sessions. The participants improved significantly on measures of travel distress, avoidance and maladaptive driving strategies. This approach is clearly more expensive and complex than the treatment for spider phobia described above. However, where exposure to a controlled or safe 'live' exposure may be difficult to establish, it can be of benefit (Garcia-Palacios et al. 2007).

Pharmacological treatments

According to Hayward and Wardle (1996), most clinicians consider pharmacological treatment of phobias to be of little benefit. As a consequence, many major reviews of the pharmacological treatment of anxiety (e.g. Nutt 2005) do not even address the pharmacological treatment of specific phobias.

8.2 Generalized anxiety disorder

DSM-IV-TR defines generalized anxiety disorder (GAD) as excessive or ongoing anxiety and worry, occurring on more days than not, over a period of at least six months. In addition:

- The person finds it difficult to control the worry.
- The anxiety and worry are regularly associated with three or more of the following:

- restlessness or feeling keyed up or on edge
- being easily fatigued
- difficulty concentrating or mind going blank
- irritability
- muscle tension
- sleep disturbance.
- The anxiety, worry or physical symptoms cause significant distress or impairment.

The worries reported by people with GAD usually involve relatively minor, everyday, matters. Nevertheless, they find both their worries difficult to control and the extent to which they worry distressing. Between 1 and 5 per cent of the population will be experiencing GAD at any one time (Lim et al. 2005). Rates are highest among women, middle-aged people, people living alone, and of low income. GAD usually begins in childhood or adolescence. Once established, it tends to be a chronic disorder: up to 80 per cent of people diagnosed with GAD report having been worried or anxious all their lives (Butler et al. 1991). It has high levels of co-morbidity with mood and somatoform disorders (Conway et al. 2006).

Aetiology of GAD

Genetic factors

The influence of genetic factors on the risk of developing GAD appears to be modest. Hettema et al. (2001b), for example, obtained a lifetime history of GAD through interviews with 3100 twin pairs. Concordance rates between the pairs were relatively low, leading them to estimate the heritability of GAD to be about 15–20 per cent across both sexes. Links have been made between GAD and polymorphisms of the RGS2 gene, which may also be implicated in bipolar disorder (Koenen et al. 2009).

Biological mechanisms

GAD appears to be associated with overactivation of a brain system involving the septohippocampal system (linking the septum, amygdala, hippocampus and fornix) and the Papez circuit (otherwise known as the circuit of emotion: linking the mammillary bodies, thamalus, cingulate gyrus and hippocampus, pre-frontal cortex, amygdala and septum). Gray (1983) called this the behavioural inhibition system (BIS), because activation of these brain circuits is thought to interrupt ongoing behaviour, and redirect attention to signs of threat or danger. According to Gray, the BIS receives information about the environment from the sensory cortex. It then checks this against predictions it makes about future changes. When a mismatch occurs, the system is activated and the individual experiences the emotion of anxiety. In GAD, the criteria for such discrepancies may be 'set' too low, resulting in the individual constantly responding to perceived mismatches and the system being chronically activated. This system appears to be mediated by GABA, norepinephrine and serotonin, and is linked to the sympathetic nervous system via the amygdala and hypothalamus (Evans et al. 2009).

Paradoxically, people with GAD have a lower sympathetic response to *acute* stress than average, perhaps as a consequence of its chronic activation. This is probably a result of receptivity of norepinephrine at the postsynaptic site becoming less sensitive over time (Spiegel and Barlow 2000).

Psychoanalytic explanations

Freud distinguished two routes to general anxiety in adulthood, both of which have their roots in childhood: too rigorous punishment and overprotection. He suggested that both 'neurotic' and 'moral' anxiety begin when the child is repeatedly punished for, or prevented from, expressing their id impulses. This leads them to believe that such impulses are dangerous and have to be controlled. In adulthood, when parental control is no longer available, the individual fears that their id impulses will not be controllable and they may take actions they do not want to. By contrast, a child protected from threats and frustrations will not develop defence mechanisms adequate to dealing with the demands of adult life. As a consequence, relatively small threats result in feelings of high levels of anxiety.

Evidence relating to these explanations is mixed. Chorpita and Barlow (1998), for example, found over-protectiveness, excessive punishment and critical comments as a child to be associated with high levels of anxiety in adulthood. By contrast, Raskin et al. (1982) found no relationship between excessive discipline or parental protection and the development of GAD.

Humanistic explanations

A further explanation of any link between parental control and the development of GAD is provided by the humanists. Humanists consider GAD to occur when individuals fail to accept themselves for who they are. As a consequence, they experience extreme anxiety and are unable to fulfil their potential as a human being. According to Rogers (1961), this negation of self arises from childhood experiences of excessive discipline. If the individual is subject to criticism and harsh standards as a child, they adopt the standards of those around them, in order to receive conditional positive regard for doing so. They subjugate their own beliefs and desires and try to meet these externally imposed standards by repeatedly denying or distorting their true thoughts and experiences. Despite such efforts, threatening self-judgements can break through and cause intense anxiety. While theoretically elegant, this theory has not been subject to empirical testing, and the importance of these processes is largely unknown.

Socio-cultural factors

Social stress influences the prevalence of GAD. Its prevalence is relatively high among people in low socio-economic groups, ethnic minorities, urban populations, people living in countries subject to war and political oppression, or those experiencing chronic work stress (e.g. Melchior et al. 2007). As the demands of everyday living become more complex, so too does the proportion of the population experiencing GAD. Prevalence levels in the USA, for example, rose from 2.5 per cent in 1975 to 4 per cent by the early 1990s (Regier et al. 1998).

Surprisingly few studies have considered longer-term antecedents to GAD – and these have found little evidence of a particular role of childhood trauma. Bulik et al. (1999), for example, investigated retrospective reports of child sexual abuse in women who had experienced major depression, GAD, bulimia nervosa, panic disorder, or alcohol or drug dependence. Although many of the women reported experiencing childhood sexual abuse, this was not uniquely predictive of any diagnosis. Wilhelm et al. (2004) found an association between separation anxiety as an adult and GAD, raising the possibility that childhood fears of separation and poor attachment may contribute to longer-term problems of GAD. By contrast, Waters et al. (2008) found no evidence of any impact of parental style on children's levels of anxiety; rather, any differences appeared to lie within the children themselves. They compared the interpretations of a number of ambiguous situations in three groups of children: (i) children of anxious parents, (ii) children of non-anxious parents, and (iii) children with some form of anxiety disorder. Of note, was that the children of anxious and non-anxious parents did not differ in their perceptions of threat, control, or emotional reaction to these situations. By contrast, children with an anxiety disorder experienced more threat, less control, and more negative emotional responses than either other group.

Cognitive behavioural explanations

The fundamental behavioural model of the acquisition and maintenance of anxiety is that of Mowrer (1947). His two-factor model stated that fear of specific stimuli is acquired through classical conditioning, and maintained by operant conditioning While this remains a viable model of the acquisition and maintenance of specific fears, the model cannot easily explain the diffuse anxiety associated with GAD, and more cognitive models have been developed to account for this phenomenon. According to Beck (1997), people who experience high levels of generalized anxiety initially interpret a relatively small number of situations as dangerous and threatening. Over time, they apply these assumptions to more and more situations and develop an increasingly generalized anxiety. Beck identified a number of cognitive schemata that underpin this anxiety, including 'a situation or a person is unsafe until proven safe', and 'it is always best to assume the worst'. As a consequence of such thoughts, the individual becomes alert to the possibilities of danger and threat throughout their everyday life, and responds with the emotion of anxiety. The process may also work in reverse. Beck noted a form of reasoning he called emotional reasoning, which suggests that if we feel an emotion such as anxiety in certain situations, this leads us to have cognitions that support this anxiety: 'If I am feeling anxious, there must be something to be anxious about here.' Thus, the individual may enter a cycle of negative emotions driving negative cognitions, which in turn drive negative emotions, and so on.

An alternative cognitive model of GAD was developed by Wells (1995), who proposed that the core feature of GAD was excess worry. He identified two types of worry experienced by people with GAD:

- *Type 1 worries* are the typical worries that most of us experience, albeit at an amplified level: worries related to work, social, health and other issues.
- *Type 2 worry*, or 'meta-worry', involves the negative appraisal of one's own worries: 'Worrying will drive me mad . . .', 'I worry about my worries taking me over . . .'.

Type 1 worries are relatively common in population samples. Type 2 worries are common in samples of people with GAD. Wells (1995) therefore suggested that individuals with GAD are defined by high levels of Type 2 worries. These worries, while unpleasant, also form a coping response to reduce distress: 'Worrying helps me cope with my problems . . .' (see discussion of the S-REF in Chapter 3). As a result, the individual may be motivated to continue worrying, despite their discomfort while so doing. At the same time, they may hold increasingly negative views about their worrying. They may believe it is uncontrollable and that it has negative effects on their psychological, social, and physical functioning. However, these beliefs co-exist with the more positive beliefs about worry, and the individual may vacillate between trying to avoid worrying and active worry. This combination of processes led Dugas et al. (2005) to suggest that the central elements of GAD are an intolerance of uncertainty, positive beliefs about worry, poor problem orientation, and cognitive avoidance. The latter strategy may be prove ineffective, as attempts at suppression of intrusive thoughts typically make them more frequent and salient (e.g. Muris et al. 1998).

Claire provides an example of the worries and meta-worries that people with GAD experience:

> It's a family joke, but it's true . . . one day we set of from home to shop in Nottingham – a journey of about an hour and a half . . . and from the minute we got in the car I was worried about where we were going to park, what the traffic would be like when we got there, and so on. I just worried the whole trip and drove my family mad. It sounds funny, but it's true!
>
> I worry about everything and nothing. I worry if the kids are late back at night. They know I worry, so they really try to be back on time. I've given them a mobile phone so they can ring me if there are any problems or if they are going to be late . . . and they do because they know I'll be in a right state when they get home if they don't. I worry about the food – I won't eat it if it's over the recommended date even though my husband assures me that that's OK and we're not going to get any disease. You name it, I'm sure I've worried about it. It does get me down . . . I can see me worrying myself into an early grave . . . But I can't stop worrying. My husband says 'Just get on with things, try not to worry.' But I can't. I sit and knit or watch the television in the evening trying not to worry about things, but once something's on my mind it's really difficult to stop – however hard I tell myself to. I worry about my health – the slightest thing, and I'm off to the doctor. I know I'm going to worry about things when we have stopped talking. Sometimes it really feels as if I'm going mad. It does get me down, because every day I cannot relax and just get on with things like most people. Mind you, I think many people worry too little . . . just cruise through life without a care in the world . . . that can't be right either . . .
>
> What sounds even more mad is that I worry about NOT worrying. What if the worrying I do does stop bad things happening? I know it doesn't really, but I could never forgive myself if something happened to the children and I had just been getting on with things and didn't have their safety in mind. I could never forgive myself. What sort of a person would that make me – not caring for them when they were in danger?

Treatment of generalized anxiety disorder

Cognitive behavioural treatment

Behavioural treatments of GAD initially involved exposure to feared situations combined with response prevention – much as in the treatment of phobias (see Chapter 2 and below). In this, the individual is exposed to their feared situations, frequently in a graded manner starting with the least feared. On each occasion, they remain near the feared object until they are no longer anxious: that is, they are prevented from using their escape response. This was thought to extinguish the fear response as the individual learned the lack of association between the stimulus and its expected negative consequences.

Unfortunately, while effective in the treatment of some other anxiety disorders, these methods proved of little value in the treatment of GAD as the situations that threatened people with GAD were so diffuse. Cognitive behavioural interventions did not prove effective in the treatment of GAD until they incorporated three key strategies:

- cognitive restructuring of anxiety-provoking thoughts
- relaxation training
- worry exposure assignments.

Cognitive restructuring involves identifying the cognitions leading to anxiety and challenging any inappropriate assumptions. Strategies may be rehearsed in the therapy session before being used in the situation in which the client feels anxious. Relaxation training involves a structured programme of learning to physically relax and to slow and control breathing at times of anxiety. Worry exposure follows an exposure and response prevention approach. Many people with GAD attempt to mentally block or distract from negative or catastrophic thoughts. As a result, they fail to extinguish the associated anxiety, and continue to be worried by the thoughts in the long term. Worry exposure involves the individual focusing on their frightening or catastrophic thoughts or images for increasing periods of time, eventually up to between 25 and 50 minutes. Anxiety typically rises then falls, as the images are held and the individual habituates to them.

This approach has proven relatively effective. One meta-analysis involving eight studies (Hunot et al. 2007) reported that 46 per cent of patients who received CBT made a clinically significant improvement. This compared to only 14 per cent in the treatment as usual comparison groups. Similar gains were achieved on measures of worry symptoms and overall quality of life. A cognitive approach incorporating mindfulness and acceptance-based strategies has achieved outcomes matching those of the best second-wave CBT interventions (Roemer et al. 2008), albeit in a trial involving a very small number of participants. A small trial evaluating meta-cognitive therapy has also been reported (Wells and King 2006), achieving a recovery rate at 12 months of 75 per cent. A second, albeit still relatively small, study of metacognitive therapy conducted by the same group (Wells et al. 2010) is reported in Research box 3 (see pp. 70–2). This study found metacognitive therapy to be more effective than applied relaxation, for up to one-year follow-up. The potential for these third-wave interventions still needs to be verified in larger, randomized controlled trials. Nevertheless, they have the potential to become the psychological treatment of choice for GAD.

Psychoanalytic therapy

One study has examined the effectiveness of psychoanalytical therapy in the treatment of GAD, comparing it with a cognitive intervention (Durham et al. 1994). Psychoanalytical therapy involved the exploration and understanding of the individual's problems within the context of their current relationship, their developmental context, and in terms of the transference and resistance within the therapeutic relationship. The cognitive behavioural approach followed that described above. Levels of contact were similar across both interventions. Cognitive behavioural therapy proved significantly more effective than psychoanalytical therapy, both immediately following therapy and at six-month follow-up. By this time, 76 per cent of those receiving CBT were 'better' or 'very considerably' improved; 42 per cent of those in psychoanalytic therapy achieved the same levels of success. Using a more conservative criterion of 'return to normal functioning', the results were less supportive of analytic therapy: 20 per cent of those receiving psychoanalytic therapy achieved this criterion in comparison with 66 per cent of those in the cognitive therapy condition. Drop-out from therapy was much lower in the cognitive therapy group than in the analytic therapy condition: 10 versus 24 per cent respectively.

Pharmacological therapy

Benzodiazepines have frequently been used in the treatment of GAD, achieving an overall success rate of about 35 per cent (Davidson 2001). A further 40 per cent of people show moderate improvement but still have some symptoms. However, benzodiazepines bring a number of drawbacks, particularly when used in the long term, including impaired cognitive performance, lethargy, drug tolerance and dependence, depression, and relapse upon withdrawal, and are no longer considered the drug treatment of choice (Davidson 2001). For this reason, although the effectiveness of benzodiazepines is generally similar to that of antidepressants (Mitte et al. 2005), the latter are usually the drug of choice. Both tricyclics and SSRIs appear equally effective, although the lower number of side-effects associated with SSRIs, and the greater levels of adherence to them, make them the pharmacological treatment of choice (Rocca et al. 1997).

Combining psychological and drug therapy may be of some benefit, although the additional benefits occur after the cessation of drug therapy. Barlow et al. (2000), for example, found significant gains on a measure of global improvement in 41 per cent of their study participants who received imipramine (a tricyclic) plus CBT 6 months after discontinuation of the drug. The same figure for those in the CBT alone group was 32 per cent, while only 20 per cent of those in the imipramine-alone group still evidenced significant gains.

8.3 Panic disorder

A panic attack is a period of intense fear or discomfort that reaches a peak within ten minutes, and is associated with at least four symptoms including breathlessness, palpitations, dizziness or trembling, nausea, and tingling sensations in the arms and fingers. As noted earlier, this may be a severe element of a phobic response. It may also be given a separate diagnosis in DSM of panic disorder (APA 2000). According to DSM-IV-TR, to be given this diagnosis, the individual will report recurrent unexpected panic attacks, at least one of which has been followed by at least one month of one or more of the following:

- persistent concern about having further attacks
- worry about the implications of the attack or its consequences (e.g. having a heart attack, 'going crazy')
- a significant change in behaviour related to the attacks.

A common feature of a panic attack is known as hyperventilation, which involves rapid short inhalations and exhalations. As a consequence, carbon dioxide is rapidly exhaled and not absorbed into the bloodstream, while oxygen is over-absorbed, leading to the symptoms described above. As the breathing response is triggered by high levels of carbon dioxide within the circulation, the physiological trigger to breathe does not occur, resulting in feelings of shortness of breath, which encourage further over-breathing. It is at times such as this that the eponymous 'brown bag' can come in useful. Placing one over the mouth and nose ensures that the person re-breathes the carbon dioxide they are exhaling, increasing its absorption from the lungs into the blood, stabilizing the breathing pattern and stopping the symptoms.

Charles Darwin provided one of the first descriptions of a panic attack when he described one of his own. He was not unusual, and the prevalence of panic attacks may be increasing. The prevalence of US citizens to report having had at least one panic attack rose between 1980 and 1995 from 5.3 to 12.7 per cent (Goodwin 2003). However, the number of people achieving the diagnostic criteria for panic disorder is much less. Batelaan et al. (2006) for example, estimated that about 2 per cent of the general population will develop repeated panic attacks, diagnosable as panic disorder. The condition is universal and consistent across geographical and cultural boundaries, although triggers to panic may vary across cultures. In the Arctic, a fear of being alone, known as *kayak angst*, and a Chinese anxiety syndrome involving the fear of penile retraction into the body resulting in death known as *koro*, show striking similarities to panic disorder.

Aetiology of panic disorder

Genetic factors

Evidence that panic disorder has a genetic component can be found in studies such as that by Kendler et al. (1993) who found concordance rates of 24 per cent between MZ twins, and 11 per cent between DZ twins. These and other data placed within a meta-analysis by Hettema et al. (2001a) indicated that panic disorder has a heritability coefficient of 0.40. Specific genes related to panic disorder are now being identified. Kim et al. (2009), for example, have found a gene variant (rs4570625 polymorphism) that controls the production of serotonin in the brain to be implicated.

Biological mechanisms

As with simple phobias, the central element of the panic response is a high level of physiological arousal, triggered by hypothalamic activity and mediated by the sympathetic nervous system. This response is driven by the neurotransmitter and hormone norepinephrine, and to a lesser extent epinephrine. Two further biochemical systems also seem implicated in the development of panic disorder. The effectiveness of tricyclics and SSRIs in treating the disorder as well as emerging genetic evidence has implicated the role of serotonin in the disorder. This has now been supported by neurological evidence of reduced production and post-synaptic binding along serotinergic pathways in the raphe, orbitofrontal cortex, temporal cortex and amygdala (Nash et al. 2008). The success of modern benzodiazepines in treating the condition has also implicated a role of GABA. The amygdala is involved in the generation of fear and its activity is largely controlled by GABA: low levels of GABA lead to high levels of fear (Goddard et al. 2001).

GABA receptors also control activity within the hypothalamus, and hence the sympathetic nervous system.

Social factors

As with GAD, high levels of social stress increase risk for panic disorder. The highest rates of panic disorder are among those who are widowed, divorced or separated, live in cities, with limited education. They may also have experienced early parental loss and physical or sexual abuse (Ballenger 2000). Not surprisingly, childhood anxiety, which may be related to poor attachment with parents, also predicts panic disorder in adulthood (Biederman et al. 2005). However, Battaglia et al. (2009) suggested the link between childhood separation anxiety and adult panic disorder may be largely the result of common genetic factors rather than childhood separation anxiety being a cause of adult panic disorder.

Psychological explanations

Psychoanalytic and humanistic theories do not discriminate between panic disorder and GAD, and the models outlined in the section of GAD hold for both disorders. Both explanations also receive limited empirical support, as people with panic disorder frequently recall their parents being overly concerned and protective of them as a child (Silove et al. 1991). Mowrer's (1947) model of fear acquisition and maintenance can provide only a partial explanation of panic disorder, as it assumes high levels of conditioned anxiety to be triggered by the presence of a feared stimulus. It has difficulties in explaining high levels of anxiety in the absence of an obvious stimulus: a defining characteristic of panic disorder.

More recent aetiological models have considered how cognitions can lead to episodes of panic in the absence of any obvious trigger. The most influential of these cognitive models is that of Clark (1986), which identified three triggers to panic attacks:

- fear-related cognitions related to a particular stimulus or situation
- high levels of physiological arousal associated with different emotional states
- other events that may result in a physical disturbances.

According to Clark, each of these factors triggers the central cognitive element of panic disorder, which is the catastrophic misinterpretation of bodily sensations. The misinterpreted sensations are mainly those involved in the normal anxiety response (including high heart rate, sweating, shaking). Other triggers include arousal associated with other strong emotions such as anger, raised heart rate as a result of caffeine ingestion, and so on.

Catastrophic misinterpretation involves believing these sensations to be more dangerous than they really are; believing they are signs of serious physical or mental health problems. These thoughts lead to activation of the fight–flight response, resulting in an increase in physiological arousal, which is again interpreted in a catastrophic fashion ('Yes, my heart really is pounding: I really am heading for a heart attack'). These anxiety-laden cognitions further increase arousal and its associated bodily sensations, which lead to further levels of anxiety: a vicious circle which culminates in a panic attack (see Figure 8.1).

Once an individual has developed a tendency to interpret bodily sensations catastrophically, two further processes contribute to the maintenance of panic disorder. First, because they are

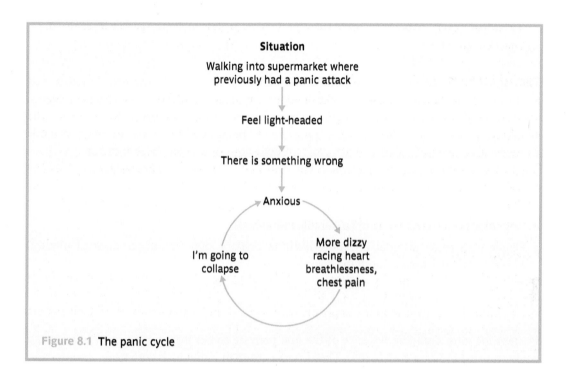

Figure 8.1 The panic cycle

frightened of certain sensations, they become hypervigilant and repeatedly scan their body checking for them. These are taken as further evidence of the presence of a serious physical or mental disorder. Second, safety behaviours, usually involving not entering a feared situation, or leaving it at the onset of symptoms, tend to maintain the individual's negative interpretations. Such avoidance prevents the individual from learning that the symptoms they have experienced are not as dangerous as they consider, and prevents the extinction process.

The case of Sue provides an example of these processes:

When did it begin? I remember my first panic – who wouldn't? It was in the car park in Tesco's. I remember feeling a bit faint. I thought I was going to pass out. I thought I would look such a fool if I did. Stupid to pass out in a car park. And everyone would look at me . . . Now I know it was a panic attack. But when it happened I didn't have a clue what was going on. I felt bad for no reason . . . I didn't think I was going to die or anything like that, but I was frightened I would collapse and end up in hospital. I think I could have got over it OK, but the next time I went shopping, I began to think about things again. I wondered whether there was anything about Tesco's or shopping that might bring it on again. Perhaps I had pushed myself too hard . . . I was in a bit of a rush when it happened – I don't know. They weren't very sensible thoughts, really. But I suppose they began to wind me up. Anyway, the next time I went shopping . . . yes, I had another attack. That was it really, I just thought, 'I'm not going there again.' So I started to shop in other places, but I began to worry that the same thing would happen, and then I had another panic, and that just confirmed my worries.

In the end, it got easier to stay at home out of the way than to go out. I quite like it at home. I feel safe, and I watch TV without any hassle. My friends come and see me, so it's not as if I don't have a life. I was never one for going out much. If I go out, then I worry before I set off, and while I am out.

> I often have a panic, so it's just not worth going out. I can get to the local shop if I go with my husband. And I can go in the car with him – as long as I don't have to get out. But I don't like to go far . . .

The example of Sue fits Clark's (1986) model of the development of panic disorder. She also hinted at a further factor that can contribute to the development of the disorder or its associated problems: a process known as secondary gain. Being restricted to the house was quite pleasant for Sue. She gained sympathy from her husband and quite enjoyed being at home. These secondary rewards contributed to the maintenance of her avoidant behaviour once it had been initiated.

Clark's model has been experimentally tested in a number of ways. These have examined key elements of the theory, including:

- Cognitions can trigger panic in vulnerable individuals.
- People with panic disorder are more likely to panic if they experience unusual physical symptoms than people without the disorder.
- If people with panic disorder experience unusual symptoms and are given an appropriate explanation, they will experience less panic than those not given such an explanation.

Perhaps the most dramatic evidence of the first premise comes from what is now a rather old study reported by Clark et al. (1988). They asked a group of individuals with panic disorder and 'normal' controls to read out loud a series of word pairs. Some of these pairings included combinations of body sensations and catastrophic feelings or thoughts typically made by individuals while panicking: 'breathless – suffocate', and so on. Each group was asked to rate their anxiety before and after reading the cards and to rate any changes in any panic symptoms. The manipulation proved unexpectedly powerful. Ten out of the twelve people with panic disorder, but no controls, had a panic attack while reading the cards.

Investigation of the second and third elements of the theory has frequently involved use of an experimental paradigm known as respiratory challenge. In this, participants take a breath of air with higher than usual levels of carbon dioxide (various studies use between a 5 and 50 per cent carbon dioxide mixture). This induces feelings similar to those that occur during hyperventilation: shortness of breath, light-headedness, tingling in arms and legs, and so on. There is consistent evidence that following this procedure, people with panic disorder are significantly more likely to panic than are people with obsessive-compulsive disorder, GAD, or depression (Telch et al. 2003).

This panic may be moderated if individuals are given a non-catastrophic explanation for any symptoms they experience. In one study of this effect, Rapee et al. (1986) gave different information about the sensations likely to be experienced as a result of a single inhalation of 50 per cent carbon dioxide and 50 per cent oxygen to people with panic disorder. Half their participants were given a detailed explanation of all the possible sensations they could experience, and told they resulted from inhalation of the gas. The others were given no explanation of what to expect. As expected, participants in the detailed explanation group reported less catastrophic cognitions and less anxiety than those in the naïve condition. Of note also is that if people with panic disorder are simply told (incorrectly) that their heart rate is increasing in response to a psychological task, they experience more panic symptoms than do individuals who do not have panic disorder (Story and Craske 2008).

Stop and think...

We often talk about risk factors for various disorders, but rarely if ever think about *protective* factors. We know some: men benefit from being married (the advantage is less for women), women benefit from having a wider support system. But what factors may be protective, in both the long and the short term, against the anxiety disorders so far discussed in this chapter?

Treatment of panic disorder

Cognitive behavioural interventions

Some of the most successful treatment programmes for panic disorder have been based on Clark's aetiological model. Clark et al. (1994), for example, developed a two-phase treatment approach. The first phase involved teaching clients the cognitive model of panic. The second involved three elements:

- relaxation to reduce physiological arousal at the time of stress
- cognitive procedures to change panicogenic cognitions
- behavioural procedures in order to control panic symptoms.

Relaxation involves learning to physically relax and to slow and control breathing. These techniques can be applied before potential panic attacks, for example, when approaching a situation where a panic attack has occurred previously, and during them. Cognitive procedures include self-instruction and cognitive challenge (see Chapter 3). The goal of the behavioural procedures is to teach the individual, through direct experience, that the outcome they fear at times of panic will not actually happen. Increasingly, therapists instigate the symptoms of panic within the therapy session and practise its control through the use of cognitive and relaxation techniques. Symptoms may be generated by a variety of procedures, including reading words linking bodily sensations and catastrophic outcomes, and hyperventilating. These behavioural experiments can show how thoughts and behaviours influence symptoms previously considered the result of unknown factors and allow rehearsal of cognitive and relaxation panic control strategies. Once control over symptoms has been achieved within the therapy sessions, these skills can be used in real-life situations. This may be done in a graduated process, starting with relatively easy circumstances and moving on to more difficult ones.

By the end of therapy, over 80 per cent of individuals are typically panic-free, in contrast to about 12 per cent of those in no-treatment control groups. Clark et al. (1994), for example, reported outcomes following this approach, relaxation alone, a tricyclic (imipramine), and a waiting list control period. Participants in the CBT group took part in 12 sessions over three months, followed by up to three booster sessions over the following three months. Imipramine was withdrawn after six months. At one-year follow-up, all three treatments proved more effective than no treatment. However, CBT was the most successful at this time, with 85 per cent of individuals being panic-free, in contrast to 60 per cent of those who received imipramine or who were taught relaxation. Of note is that 40 per cent of those receiving imipramine and 26 per cent of those receiving relaxation sought an alternative therapy in the year following the intervention. Only 5 per cent of the CBT group did so.

This form of intervention may also be provided over the internet. Schneider et al. (2005), for example, gave people with panic disorder access to one of two web-based self-help programmes, combined with brief back-up telephone contact with a clinician. One programme involved a CBT programme similar to that of Clark and colleagues, with specific planned exposure to feared situations. The second group experienced a briefer CBT intervention and did not have a planned exposure programme. By the end of therapy, both groups evidenced significant benefits on a variety of measures, and did not differ in the level of improvement achieved. However, by one-month follow-up, those who participated in the planned exposure programme showed more consistent gains.

Salkovskis, P.M., Hackmann, A., Wells, A. et al. (2007) Belief disconfirmation versus habituation approaches to situational exposure in panic disorder with agoraphobia: a pilot study, *Behaviour Research and Therapy*, 45: 877–85.

Introduction

Clark proposes that panic attacks are a result of catastrophic misinterpretations of bodily sensations. Safety-seeking behaviours are motivated by catastrophic misinterpretations and prevent belief change and clinical recovery. Accordingly, situational exposure will be most beneficial when it helps the person to disconfirm any catastrophic misinterpretations they may hold. Although this disconfirmation may occur incidentally in the course of exposure interventions, the most effective treatments will be those that provide participants with an explanation of the role of catastrophizing and avoidance, and a rationale for not engaging in their safety-seeking behaviours. The present study tested this hypothesis. It compared an exposure programme alone or combined with a cognitive component explaining the way cognitive beliefs contribute to panic and designed as a direct means of disconfirming previous held panicogenic beliefs. The researchers expected the second approach to be most successful.

Participants

Sixteen participants had a DSM diagnosis of panic disorder with moderate or severe agoraphobic avoidance, were unable to complete the penultimate step of a standardized behavioural walk test (see below), experienced catastrophic thoughts during panic attacks, and engaged in safety-seeking behaviours to prevent feared catastrophes.

Method

All patients completed the Beck Depression Inventory (BDI), Beck Anxiety Inventory (BAI), a measure of panic frequency, and a modified Chambless Agoraphobic Cognitions Questionnaire

(CACQ). They also undertook a standardized Behavioural Walk (BW), involving completion of a standardized 30-minutes walk through a busy town centre with ratings of anxiety at key points.

Participants were randomized to receive either habituation-based exposure therapy (HBET) or a CBT programme designed to disconfirm catastrophic thoughts and prevent safety-seeking behaviours (CBT).

The intervention

The exposure programme comprised one 15-minute *in vivo* exposure away from their house, allowing participants to maintain safety behaviours. Participants then received two further sessions lasting between 1.5 and 2.5 hours. In these, they were encouraged to enter and remain in feared situations until they no longer felt anxious. They were told they needed to remain in feared situations for long planned periods to allow habituation of anxiety and confidence building. Participants then constructed a hierarchy of situations they avoided, and were encouraged to enter and stay in each situation, working up the hierarchy, until they no longer felt anxious.

The CBT programme involved the same components. However, the intervention explained how catastrophic misinterpretations were involved in panic, how these were maintained by safety-seeking behaviours, and how not engaging in safety-seeking behaviours would allow disconfirmation of any catastrophic misinterpretations and make avoidance unnecessary. Participants were specifically told to not engage in avoidance behaviours, and so learn that their feared catastrophes would not occur.

Results

CBT was significantly more effective than the exposure programme, achieving change on all key variables not found in the latter.

Table 8.1 Mean change scores between baseline and end of therapy according to intervention type

	BAI	Agoraphobic avoidance	Panic frequency	Agoraphobic cognitions frequency	Agoraphobic cognitions belief	BW: peak anxiety
CBT						
Pre-post treatment	−28***	−6.9***	−2.4***	−17.2***	−489+++	−52***
Exposure programme						
Pre-post treatment	+1	−3.0	−0.2	−3.3	−57	−3

*** $p < 0.001$ between CBT and Exposure Programme.

Discussion

The study identified the advantages of a programme explicitly providing a clear rationale and targeting the cessation of avoidance behaviours. The number of participants was small ($n = 16$) and although they had high levels of agoraphobic anxiety, they had no other co-morbidities. Accordingly, the results of this study must be viewed with some caution, and larger studies (in more representative populations) need to be conducted. Finally, it should be noted that both the rationale for the interventions and the instructions concerning the use of safety behaviours differed between the conditions. Further research should be used to identify which of these may be necessary to achieve the maximum effectiveness of any intervention.

Pharmacological and combined interventions

Both benzodiazepines and SSRIs have proven effective in the treatment of panic disorder, at least in the short term. SSRIs, for example, have reduced the frequency of panic attacks to zero in 36–86 per cent of people treated using them (Kasper and Resinger 2001). In addition, at least one study has shown drug therapy to be more effective than CBT within this time frame. Bakker et al. (1999) compared the efficacy of an SSRI (paroxetine), a tricyclic (clomipramine) and CBT in the treatment of panic disorder. Paroxetine proved more effective than CBT over the 12-week intervention period. Subsequently, van Apeldoorn et al. (2008) reported a combination of cognitive therapy and SSRI to be superior to either treatment given alone. While these outcomes are notable, it is important to note that the therapeutic gains reported were achieved while participants were receiving their medication. The problem with drug treatments is often one of relapse once they are stopped. Relapse rates as high as 50 and 60 per cent have been reported following withdrawal of benzodiazepines and of between 20 and 50 per cent following withdrawal of tricyclics and SSRIs (Spiegel et al. 1994). Evidence for this drop-off effect can be found in a study reported by Barlow et al. (2000) who found outcomes of treatment with CBT to be superior to those following either imipramine or a combined drug and CBT intervention six months after the end of all treatments. Combining behavioural or CBT with benzodiazepines appears to have no additional benefit (Watanabe et al. 2009).

8.4 Obsessive-compulsive disorder (OCD)

Obsessive-compulsive disorder is a chronic and disabling condition. It typically involves intrusive thoughts that some form of harm will occur if the individual does not perform certain acts or rituals. This results in high levels of anxiety which are usually reduced by performing the required acts or rituals, known as safety behaviours. DSM-IV-TR defines obsessions and compulsions in the following ways:

Obsessions

- Recurrent and persistent thoughts, impulses or images that are intrusive and inappropriate and cause marked anxiety or distress.

- In addition:
  - these are not simply excessive worries about real-life problems
  - the person attempts to ignore or suppress them with some other thought or action
  - the person recognizes they are a product of his or her own mind.

Compulsions

- Repetitive behaviours (for example, hand washing, checking) or mental acts (such as praying, repeating words silently) that the person feels driven to perform in response to an obsession or according to rules that must be applied rigidly.
- They are intended to prevent or reduce distress, or prevent some dreaded event or situation. They are not connected in a realistic way with what they are designed to neutralize or prevent, or are clearly excessive.

To be assigned a diagnosis of obsessive-compulsive disorder, compulsions must cause marked distress, last at least one hour a day, or significantly interfere with the person's normal routine functioning. Rachman (2003) identified some of the more common obsessions as concerning:

- *aggressive actions*: thoughts of harming or harm coming to family or children
- *sexual acts*: fear of inappropriate acts or gestures ('I will molest a young child'), images of sex with inappropriate partners
- *blasphemous acts*: a fear of making sacrilegious gestures in a holy place, pollution of prayers with impure thoughts.

He also identified some of the safety behaviours in which people with obsessive-compulsive disorder often engage to counter particular concerns, some of which are summarized in Table 8.2.

Table 8.2 Frequent concerns and safety behaviours reported by people with obsessive-compulsive disorder

Concern	Safety behaviour
Concern with cleanliness (dirt, germs, contamination)	Excessive and ritualized bathing, washing, cleaning
Concern about body secretions (saliva, urine, stool)	Rituals to remove contact with body secretions, avoid touching, etc.
Sexual obsessions (forbidden urges or aggressive sexual actions)	Ritualized and rigid sexual relationships
Obsessive fears (harming self or others)	Repeated checking of doors, stoves, fire alarms, locks and emergency brakes; when driving, retracing route for fear of having run over someone
Concern with exactness (symmetry, order)	Ritualized arranging and rearranging
Obsessions with health (something terrible will happen and lead to death)	Repeating rituals (checking and rechecking vital signs, rigid dietary intake, constantly checking for new information about health, death and dying)

An example of the nature of obsessive-compulsive disorder and its associated problems is provided by Stephen. He was a factory worker frightened of catching AIDS from 'contamination' in his work area as a consequence of someone he believed to be HIV positive having touched a nearby workbench – some months previously. To avoid this, he engaged in a number of protective behaviours, including turning on taps using his elbows, waiting by doors so that someone else would open them and using disposable towels to avoid the possibility of contamination. He washed his hands frequently through the day to make sure no stray contamination affected him. On each occasion he washed his hands until his skin was raw and bleeding. If he touched an area he 'knew' to be contaminated, he became extremely anxious and had to wash his hands repeatedly until he could reassure himself that he was not contaminated and reduce his anxiety. He described his situation as follows:

> I am frightened to touch anything M has been in contact with – well I won't touch it. I know he had venereal disease and he could have AIDS, and you know how it can spread . . . and you cannot, like, avoid it. It's invisible – and I can't take the risk of coming into contact with it. I was really angry when he came into where I work. It's one thing avoiding things when I could kick doors open, but when I knew he had touched my workbench, I was horrified . . . because I didn't want me and my family to get the disease, and I didn't know how to avoid it. I washed and scrubbed it down with disinfectant and rubbed my hands raw – but you can never guarantee that things are entirely clean. So, I start each day by cleaning my work area, hands, and arms for security . . . to protect me and my family from the dirt that this man has spread . . . Once that's done, I can relax . . . I've got eczema on my hands because of the washing and they get really sore but it's worth it. It stops me worrying about things – and that's a lot worse. If I worry I think about getting AIDS and dying and my family dying. I just can't stop until I've got things sorted.
>
> From the minute I come into work, I get really anxious. I get anxious on the way to work, because I have to face the risk of catching venereal disease . . . it feels such a relief when I have finished washing, even though my hands are sore. I wash before I go home, and I take my clothes off before going into the house when I get back from work. I put them in the washer and wash them straight away – my wife can't touch them . . . I have a shower before I do anything else and wash myself thoroughly. I would never forgive myself if I brought the disease into the house . . . I leave my shoes outside.
>
> I don't care if other people use my work bench – unless they work with M. I don't worry for them – that's for them to look out for. But if they don't get a disease it doesn't reassure me, because I know that these things are hidden . . . just because they don't seem to have the disease doesn't mean they don't have it. If they know M, then I have to redo the washing, because I worry that they may be contaminated.

Aetiology of obsessive-compulsive disorder

Genetic factors

Evidence of a genetic risk for OCD is mixed. Carey and Gottesman (1981) reported an 87 per cent concordance between MZ twins and a 47 per cent concordance for DZ twins, implying a part genetic explanation for risk of the disorder. By contrast, Andrews et al. (1990) found no evidence of higher concordance in MZ than in DZ twins. Similarly, Black et al. (1992) found 2.5 per cent of their large sample of relatives of people with OCD had the disorder: a figure not dissimilar to the 2.3 per cent prevalence among their control group and population norms. Biological studies have met a similar impasse: Samuels (2009) recently concluded that despite several candidate genes being investigated, specific genes causing OCD have not been identified.

Biological mechanisms

Biological theorists (e.g. Christian et al. 2008) have identified two interconnected brain systems that are implicated in obsessive-compulsive disorder. The first is a loop connecting the orbito-frontal area, where sexual, violent and other primitive impulses normally arise, to the thalamic region, where the individual engages in more cognitive and perhaps behavioural responses as a result of this activation. A second loop connects the orbito-frontal region to the thalamic region, but via the corpus striatus. The striatal region is thought to control the degree of activity within the systems. It tends to filter out high levels of activity within the orbito-frontal area so that the thalamus does not over-respond to these initial impulses. In OCD, it may fail to correct over-activity in the orbito-frontal–thalamic loop, so the individual over-responds to environmental stimuli, and is unable to prevent their cognitive and behavioural responses to them. The first system appears to be mediated by the excitatory neurotransmitter glutamic acid. The second system appears to be mediated by a number of neurotransmitters including serotonin, dopamine and GABA.

Psychoanalytic explanations

Freud (1922) considered OCD to result from the individual's fear of their id impulses and their use of ego defence mechanisms to reduce this anxiety. This 'battle' between the two opposing forces is not played out in the unconscious. Instead, it involves explicit and dramatic thoughts and actions. The id impulses are typically evident through obsessive thoughts, while the compulsions are the result of ego defences. Two ego defence mechanisms are particularly common in obsessive-compulsive disorder: undoing and reaction formation. Undoing involves overt behaviours designed to counter the feared outcome: washing to avoid contamination, and so on. Reaction formation involves the adoption of behaviours diametrically opposed to the unacceptable impulses. The compulsively clean individual, for example, may experience strong 'inappropriate' sexual compulsions that are countered by their cleanliness and orderliness.

The origins of OCD lie in difficulties associated with the anal phase of development. Freud suggested that children in this stage gain gratification through their bowel movements. If their parents prohibit or curb this pleasure through, for example, over-zealous potty training, this may result in a state of anger and aggressive id impulses expressed through soiling or other destructive behaviour. If the parents respond to this with further pressure, and if they embarrass the child in attempts to encourage toilet training, the child may feel shame and guilt as a consequence of their behaviour. So, the pleasure of the id begins to compete with the control of the ego. If this continues, the child may become fixated in this stage and develop an obsessive personality. Traumas experienced in adulthood may result in a regression to this stage if the passage through it is incomplete.

Not all psychodynamic theories are in agreement with Freud, although all agree that the disorder represents competition between aggressive impulses and attempts at controlling them.

Kleinian analysts suggest that as a consequence of stress some individuals may lose the ability to see both good and bad in the same object. Rather, they consider it to be either good *or* bad: there is a *splitting* of good and bad with no shades of feelings in between. Obsessive-compulsive disorders arise where the individual protects themselves against these 'bad' thoughts that would make them a 'bad' person through the use of obsessional behaviours.

Behavioural explanations

The behavioural model of obsessive-compulsive disorder is based on the two-process model of Mowrer (1947): fear of specific stimuli is acquired through classical conditioning and maintained by operant processes. What differentiates OCD from phobic or panic disorders is that anxiety arises in conditions from which the individual cannot easily escape. As a result, reductions of distress are achieved by engaging in covert or overt ritual or obsessive behaviours designed to reduce the anxiety associated with the particular stimulus. These form escape or avoidant behaviours, and reduce anxiety in the short term. However, they maintain longer-term anxiety and avoidant behaviour, as the affected individual fails to learn that no harm will occur in their absence. The individual also attempts to prevent initial contact with a feared stimulus.

Cognitive explanations

Salkovskis's cognitive model (Salkovskis and Kirk 1997) is a development of the behavioural models of OCD. He suggested that obsessions are intrusive cognitions which the individual interprets as indicating they may be responsible for harm to themselves or others unless they take some form of action to prevent this. This belief leads to a state of fear or distress which the individual tries to reduce by: (i) trying to suppress these thoughts, and (ii) taking actions intended to reduce their responsibility for any negative outcomes: safety behaviours. This may also be accompanied by a high level of expectation that an unwanted event will occur – and is more likely than if other people were responsible: 'I know that if I don't wash my hands I will spread contamination – if you don't wash your hands, this is less likely.'

Unfortunately, attempts at suppression of intrusive thoughts can, paradoxically, make them more frequent and salient. Salkovskis and Kirk (1997), for example, reported a series of single-case studies in which people with OCD used a diary to record the frequency of intrusive thoughts during alternate days in which they either attempted to suppress their thoughts or not. They found a clear difference in the number of intrusive thoughts during each phase of the study: during 'suppression' days, levels of intrusive thoughts were about double the rate reported on non-suppression days. This inability to choose not to think about particular thoughts leads to other safety behaviours, including:

- *Compulsive behaviour*: such as excessive washing to remove the threat of contamination, ritual or repeated checking.
- *Neutralization*: a cognitive equivalent of compulsive behaviour. This can involve thinking a thought to counter the original thought. Thoughts related to evil or harm may be countered by repeating phrases such as 'Jesus cares for me' several times.
- *Avoiding situations*: related to the obsessional thoughts.
- *Seeking reassurance*: repeatedly asking for reassurance that the feared outcome will not happen.

- *Diluting or sharing responsibility*: asking others to take some responsibility for an action, or reassurance that the individual is not fully responsible for potential harm to others.

Engaging in these strategies may reduce anxiety in the short term, as the individual feels relief once they have occurred. Unfortunately, they maintain long-term anxiety, because the individual never experiences the expected harm not occurring in their absence. They therefore cannot learn or gain confidence that not using them will not result in harm,

In his metacognitive, S-REF model (see Chapter 2), Wells (2000) argued that OCD is driven by the individual's beliefs about the nature of their beliefs. According to Wells, people with OCD often blur the boundaries between thoughts and reality. They may believe, for example, that having a thought about an event will make that event happen ('If I think of the devil, the devil will appear') or that thinking about an event in the past must mean that it actually happened ('If I think I have abused her, I probably have'). The metacognitive model identified three domains of fusion beliefs:

- *Thought-event fusion*: the belief that having a thought means an event has happened, will happen, or will make an event happen.
- *Thought-action fusion*: the belief that thoughts will lead to the uncontrollable engagement in unwanted actions.
- *The thought-object fusion*: the belief that thoughts, feelings and memories can be transferred into objects and/or 'caught' from objects.

These types of beliefs, combined with the meta-belief that behavioural or cognitive rituals may prevent harm arising from any potentially damaging thought fusion, lead to OCD. In a study comparing the Salkovskis and Wells models, Myers and Wells (2005) examined the relationship between responsibility, metacognitions, thought fusion, and various measures of OCD in a non-clinical sample. Their results indicated a clear association between levels of obsessive-compulsive symptoms and cognitions related to perceived responsibility (the Salkovskis model). However, in their multivariate analysis, after controlling for metacognitive beliefs, the relationship between responsibility and obsessive-compulsive traits was no longer statistically significant. From these data they argued that the metacognitive model was a better explanation of obsessive-compulsive symptoms than the responsibility model.

Treatment of obsessive-compulsive disorder

Behavioural and cognitive behavioural approaches

Behavioural treatment of OCD typically involves exposure and response prevention. In this, the individual is exposed to their feared stimulus, frequently in a graded manner, and then helped to prevent avoidance through their use of escape rituals: 'contaminating' hands and not washing them, and so on. This is thought to extinguish the fear response as the individual learns the lack of association between the occurrence of harm-related thoughts and any expected negative consequences. Relaxation may also be taught to help people cope with the high levels of physio-logical arousal associated with the fear response.

Many clinical studies using this approach achieved moderate success, although complete remission was achieved by less than half of those who engaged in such programmes (Salkovskis and Kirk 1997). Behavioural treatments were also difficult to apply to people who ruminated or who had no ritualistic behaviour, and treatment refusals and drop-outs were relatively common. Accordingly, as models of the disorder have evolved, so have the treatment programmes, which now focus increasingly on the cognitive factors that maintain the disorder.

The cognitive approach still involves exposure to a feared stimulus and response prevention. However, these procedures are augmented by a number of cognitive strategies, including:

- challenging inappropriate thoughts
- mind experiments
- behavioural hypothesis testing.

Mind experiments allow the individual to test the validity of their expectations, particularly focusing on the threat associated with their thoughts. Someone who is frightened that their thoughts may kill someone, for example, may be encouraged to test the reality of this assumption by a mind experiment in which the therapist and then client test out this assumption by thinking the feared thoughts – hopefully with no negative effects!

Although cognitive behavioural interventions are consistently better than no intervention or treatment as usual (Gava et al. 2007), comparisons between behavioural and cognitive approaches have failed to consistently identify either one as the superior approach (Siev and Chambless 2007) – indeed, one study found a cognitive intervention to be less effective than a behavioural one. McLean et al. (2001) compared the effectiveness of a purely behavioural intervention (exposure and response prevention) and a cognitive intervention involving challenging cognitions thought to underpin the disorder, with a particular focus on inflated responsibility, overestimation of threat, and intolerance of uncertainty. By the end of therapy, 16 and 38 per cent of participants in the cognitive and behavioural groups respectively had made 'significant' recoveries. At three-month follow-up, the figures were 13 and 45 per cent respectively. Unfortunately, the method of cognitive therapy used in the study may not have been optimal. In the behavioural programme, participants were exposed to their feared stimuli on several occasions and remained with them without responding with safety behaviours until their anxiety had significantly diminished, facilitating the extinction of their anxiety response. In the cognitive intervention, participants were similarly exposed to the feared stimuli, but only to practise their cognitive skills. They did not remain with the feared stimulus until their fear had diminished. Participants may have left the presence of the feared stimulus while still highly anxious. This procedure may therefore have maintained or even exacerbated their initial levels of anxiety and obsessional behaviour. The relative failure of the cognitive approach may therefore be of no surprise. No difference in effectiveness between cognitive and behavioural therapy was reported by Cottraux et al. (2001) when cognitive therapy involved challenging assumptions underlying the obsessional behaviour, but did not use exposure and response prevention methods. Finally, Van Oppen et al. (1995) found cognitive therapy combined with exposure and response prevention to be superior to behaviour therapy. It seems that 'pure' cognitive interventions without exposure/response prevention are less effective than exposure/response prevention alone. However, a combination of both approaches may be most effective.

Pharmacological interventions

Until the advent of SSRIs, the pharmacological treatment of choice for obsessive-compulsive disorder was clomipramine, a tricyclic. This has been shown to be effective in the treatment of obsessive-compulsive disorder independent of any effect on mood. The Clomipramine Collaborative Study Group (1991), for example, reported an average 40 per cent reduction in symptoms, in comparison with 5 per cent achieved by placebo. Where the effectiveness of clomipramine and SSRIs has been directly assessed, both treatments seem to be equally effective, and to have similar levels of side-effects (Bandelow 2008). Unfortunately, many people relapse after discontinuing treatment, and it may take many months before a maximum response is achieved. Pato et al. (1988), for example, reported that 16 out of 18 people treated with clomipramine relapsed within seven weeks of not taking the drug, despite some of them having been on the drug for over a year.

In the strongest comparative study of the efficacy of drugs and exposure plus response prevention, Foa et al. (2005) compared the effects of clomipramine with an exposure and response prevention, a combination of both, and a pill placebo. By the end of therapy, all the active treatments proved superior to the placebo intervention. The least effective intervention was the clomipramine. The most effective intervention was exposure plus response prevention – which had no additional benefit from being combined with clomipramine.

Case formulation

Mr R was a 38-year-old gentleman referred to the Lancashire Clinical Psychology Services with a diagnosis of obsessional compulsive disorder. At the time of referral, he lived alone after the end of a long-term relationship. He lived in flat, in which he was restricted to the use of three rooms as he felt unable to use other rooms which he considered to be contaminated. He held down a job as a teacher, but found it increasingly difficult to do so, as his obsessive-compulsive disorder was becoming increasingly difficult to hide and/or control. His fears related to what he considered to be symbols related to death or existential nothingness. These included a wide range of stimuli, including the numbers 6, 9, 7 (or any combination of these), blank walls (symbolizing 'nothingness'), and people he associated with religions of various types. He attempted to avoid such stimuli by, for example, avoiding looking at car registration plates, not using supermarket aisles with the key numbers, avoiding purchases which included the key numbers, and avoiding looking at a particular white wall in the entrance to the school. If he encountered any of these stimuli, he engaged in brief safety behaviours, which were wide-ranging, and involved, for example, repetition of safe numbers, thinking of alternative 'safe' people, and so on. Most safety behaviours were relatively brief and easy to engage in, although the high frequency with which they were elicited nevertheless made them extremely problematic. He could, for example, encounter a key number several times during any one lesson – and have to engage in brief safety behaviours on each occasion. Others were more disruptive – he delayed purchasing food or items he would want to keep for a long time to dates without key numbers, and would leave purchases unused if the bill total included a key number. If he noted a car registration number including a key number before making any purchase he would circle the shop three times in his car, before parking.

Long-term antecedents

Mr R was an anxious child, and tended to be a worrier, although there was no particular focus to his worries. His mother, to whom he was very close, tended to be obsessive, worrying and fussing about a variety of things. He remained very close to his parents, eating most days with them and staying overnight in their house quite frequently. As an adult, he had left school and attended a local university. He established a number of friendships, although these were based around a pub and drinking culture. He enjoyed drinking, but restricted this to one or two days a week, and did not use it as a coping strategy to help him cope with his anxiety. He had had two long-term relationships, but both had eventually collapsed, partly due to his dissatisfaction with the relationship, partly because of his somewhat rigid lifestyle. Although not dominated by obsessive or compulsive behaviour, he nevertheless led an extremely ordered and rigid lifestyle.

Short-term antecedents

His disappointment with these relationships led him to seek counselling. During this process, he was hypnotized and encouraged to read books exploring the existential meaning of life. During one period of hypnosis he reported being terrified by an image of death and existential 'nothingness'. He was unable, or unwilling, to provide any detail on this experience, but it was clearly terrifying and triggered his present problems. He developed a strong fear of death and 'detachment from life' or 'existential nothingness', and sought to avoid symbols or other factors associated with these thoughts. Key triggers to thoughts of death or nothingness included key numbers, religious icons and individuals, and certain books. The latter were easy to avoid; the first two were more problematic.

Formulation

The acute fear Mr R experienced while hypnotized triggered a strong conditioned fear to a wide variety of symbolic objects – all of which represented death, separation of the self from others, and existential 'nothingness'. He experienced, in Wells' terms, thought-event fusion, in that he feared that the experience of having a thought linked to death or existential nothingness implied that he would experience either death or its associated 'nothingness' while alive. His fear failed to habituate as he consistently engaged in safety behaviours in response to these thoughts, and never allowed himself to experience that his fears were unfounded.

Intervention

Despite the wide-ranging and, to him, terrifying, nature of his concerns, Mr R was aware that his safety behaviours were irrational and inappropriate. He had good psychological insight, and was happy to follow a psychological treatment approach. In view of the frequency and number of triggers to his compulsive behaviour, this meant that a number of target obsessions/triggers were selected as therapeutic targets rather than trying to change his response to them all simultaneously. Accordingly, he developed a hierarchy of triggers to his fearful thoughts. Easy triggers to work on included: a wall in his house which was adjacent to the next house in which a Muslim lived, a wall he passed as he entered and left his school. More difficult triggers included specific individuals who were associated in some way with his fears, including work colleagues and a previous girlfriend. The most difficult triggers were those involving numbers, with the highest difficulty associated with purchasing food or long-term purchases from aisles 6 or 9 or with prices including these numbers. Each week, Mr R elected to cut out the safety behaviour, associated with one or two key triggers. In the sessions between these homework tasks, he developed cognitive challenges that he could use to challenge any fears he experienced if necessary and planned and rehearsed his response to each trigger. Due to the regularity with which he encountered many triggers, he did not deliberately seek them out trigger situations, but learned to respond without safety behaviours in a somewhat *ad hoc* manner. Less frequent behaviours over which he had significant control and had consistently avoided, such as purchasing food at certain prices or using aisles in the supermarket were more planned. Over a period of several months, he achieved significant gains – albeit with some weeks in which progress was better than others – and was discharged after ten treatment sessions.

8.5 Chapter summary

1 Simple phobias are an unrealistic fear of a specific stimulus: DSM identifies four types: animals, natural environmental factors, blood-injection-injury, and other situations.

2 Psychoanalytic models suggest that phobias result from anxiety impulses when id impulses are repressed.

3 Behavioural models consider them to stem from negative conditioning experiences.

4 Cognitive behavioural models consider the condition to arise from a variety of potential causes, including conditioning and vicarious learning, and to be moderated by factors including previous experience of the feared stimulus and the use of coping strategies.

5 Seligman argued that the potential to develop some phobias may be hardwired into our brains – preparedness theory.

6 Phobias involve high levels of autonomic system arousal. As yet, there is little evidence of more general neurotransmitter dysregulation in the condition.

▶ 7 Behavioural or cognitive behavioural treatments appear to be the most effective treatment for the condition.

8 Generalized anxiety disorder (GAD) is an excessive, long-term, diffuse and inappropriate anxiety.

9 Levels of GAD vary according to the social and economic stress across the population and time.

10 It is partly genetically mediated via the septohippocampal system and Papez circuit, in the Behavioural Inhibition System. Activity of this system is dependent on levels of norepinephrine, serotonin and GABA.

11 Psychoanalytic explanations consider GAD to arise from excess punishment or protection during childhood. These lead to distorted id impulses or inadequate defence mechanisms.

12 Humanists consider GAD to be the result of deviation from the pathway to self-actualization as a result of conditions of worth imposed by others distorting the idealized self, and then the actual self.

13 Cognitive models of GAD emphasize the role of worry and meta-worry in maintaining anxiety.

14 Pharmacological treatment may be equally or more effective than psychological therapies in the short term. Cognitive therapies are most effective in the long term.

15 Panic disorder occurs when an individual experiences repeated unexpected panic attacks.

16 It has a modest genetic heritability, and is mediated by high levels of norepinephrine and low levels of GABA.

17 Cognitive models provide an explanation of panic in the absence of obvious triggers: people with the condition experience catastrophic cognitions in response to internal, usually physiological, stimuli.

18 Cognitive behavioural interventions appear to be the most effective treatment for the disorder.

19 Obsessive-compulsive behaviour is the result of anxiety-triggers the individual is unable to avoid.

20 Psychoanalytic theories and cognitive theories agree that compulsions form part of a repertoire of safety behaviours the individual uses to reduce the threat associated with the anxiety. They disagree about their nature and causes.

21 The symptoms of OCD appear to result from lowered serotonin levels and raised dopamine levels, affecting the functioning of areas of the frontal cortex and basal ganglia.

22 Cognitive behavioural therapy combining exposure/response prevention and cognitive restructuring may prove the most effective treatment for obsessive-compulsive disorder, although many people do not benefit from this or pharmacological therapy.

23 Relapse following the cessation of pharmacological therapy is common.

24 Psychosurgery may be the treatment of last resort for obsessive-compulsive disorder.

8.6 For discussion

1   Which strategies may increase or decrease levels of worry in GAD?
2   Which factors would indicate either psychological or pharmacological approaches being the treatment choice in people with an anxiety condition?
3   How important are cognitive processes in the development of anxiety disorders?
4   Should the various anxiety disorders be seen as differing presentations of similar, related disorders, or are they, in fact, unrelated disorders?

8.7 Key term

Waiting list control used in randomized controlled trial; provides a group whose treatment is delayed, so comparisons can be made between treatment and no-treatment conditions without withholding treatment from some people.

8.8 Further reading

Butler, G., Fennell, M. and Hackmann, A. (2008) *Cognitive Behavioral Therapy for Anxiety Disorders.* New York: Guildford.

Fairfax, H. (2008) The use of mindfulness in obsessive compulsive disorder: suggestions for its application and integration in existing treatment, *Clinical Psychology and Psychotherapy*, 15: 53–9.

Field, A.P. (2006) Is conditioning a useful framework for understanding the development and treatment of phobias? *Clinical Psychology Review*, 26: 857–75.

Moulding, R. and Kyrios, M. (2006) Anxiety disorders and control related beliefs: the exemplar of Obsessive-Compulsive Disorder (OCD), *Clinical Psychology Review*, 26: 573–83.

Wells, A. (2007) *Cognitive Therapy of Anxiety Disorders: A Practical Guide.* Chichester: WileyBlackwell.

The following internet sites also have a range of information about anxiety and the experience of living with the condition:

www.anxiety.net/
www.anxietyguru.net/
www.patient.co.uk/showdoc/27000122/

Mood disorders

Mood disorders are those in which depression is a significant symptom. What determines the differing diagnostic categories are the causes of depression and conditions with which it co-exists. Major depression is a condition in which the individual experiences a significant degree of impairment as a result of depression. Seasonal affective disorder is a seasonal condition, occurring only in winter. Finally, bipolar disorder is a condition in which the individual fluctuates between periods of profound depression and manic behaviour. The chapter also considers the causes of suicide (not all of which are associated with depression) and treatment of people who have unsuccessfully attempted suicide. By the end of the chapter, you should have an understanding of:

- The nature and aetiology of depression, seasonal affective disorder and bipolar disorder from a number of theoretical perspectives
- The causes of suicidal behaviour
- The types of interventions used to treat each disorder
- The relative effectiveness of each of these interventions.

9.1 Major depression

DSM-IV-TR defines a major depressive episode as the presence of at least five of the following for at least two weeks:

- depressed mood
- markedly diminished interest or pleasure in almost all activities
- significant weight loss or gain, or increase in or loss of appetite
- physical agitation
- fatigue or loss of energy
- feelings of worthlessness or excessive guilt
- reduced ability to think, concentrate or indecisiveness
- significant distress or impairment.

People who are depressed are characterized by emotional, motivational, physiological and cognitive problems. They feel low and gain no pleasure from their usual activities. They are frequently unmotivated to take voluntary action, often spending considerable time in bed or withdrawing quietly from the company of others. They may be markedly slow in their activities or speech. They generally hold negative views about themselves and marked pessimism about the present and future. They may feel out of control and unable to change their situation. Some, but by no means all, will experience suicidal thoughts or actions. Depressed people often report confused or slow thoughts, and difficulties in retaining information or solving problems.

About 5 per cent of the European population will be clinically depressed at any one time (Paykel et al. 2005). Women are twice as likely as men to report depression: lifetime prevalence rates for women are 26 per cent compared with 12 per cent for men (Keller et al. 1984). About a quarter of depressive episodes last less than one month. Between 25 and 30 per cent of people remain depressed one year after onset, while nearly a quarter are depressed for up to two years. The typical age of onset of a first episode of depression is between the ages of 24 and 29. Treatment of depressive disorders utilizes significant health resources, accounting for 16 per cent of primary care consultations in one Canadian state (Block et al. 2009).

Aetiology of major depression

Genetic factors

Although there have been some negative findings, there is an increasing consensus that genetic factors influence risk for major depression. McGuffin et al. (1996), for example, found that MZ twins had a concordance rate of 46 per cent, while the equivalent in DZ was 20 per cent. Genes thought to be associated with depression include those involved in the synthesis of serotonin from tryptophan and the transmission of serotonin at the synapse (Surtees et al. 2006) as well as norepinephrine metabolism (Uher et al. 2009). Interestingly, as well as influencing risk for disease, genes may also influence the effectiveness of medication such as SSRIs used to treat depression (Tsai et al. 2009).

Biological mechanisms

Both norepinephrine and serotonin have been implicated in the aetiology of depression (see Chapter 4). It was initially thought that low levels of either neurotransmitter impacted on mood. This simple model is now being challenged by recent data. It seems that mood is the result of an interaction between both serotonin and norepinephrine systems. It may even be the result of interactions between these and other neurotransmitters. Rampello et al. (2000), for example, argued that mood is a consequence of an imbalance between several neurotransmitters, including serotonin, norepinephrine, dopamine and acetylcholine. It is possible that serotonin provides overall control of a variety of brain systems, and that low serotonin levels disrupt activity within these systems which results in depression. The major brain area involved in depression is the limbic system.

Socio-cultural factors

A number of social stresses have been shown to increase risk for depression. Prevalence rates of depression are relatively high among the poor, ethnic minorities and those with poor social or marital support (Jenkins et al. 1998). Many people experience a combination of factors that make them particularly prone to depression. A classic study by Brown and Harris (1978), for example, found that working-class women who had three or more young children, lacked a close confidante, had no outside employment, and whose father had died while they were young, were more prone to depression than those with the opposite constellation of circumstances. More recently, Andersen et al. (2009) revealed the magnitude of the risks associated with economic factors. They found that people without a job were over eleven times more likely to develop major depressive disorder than those with a job. The risk of people with a low income being depressed was nearly 10 times the risk of those with a high income. Many people in minority ethnic groups may have to cope with adverse economic circumstances. In addition, they may have to contend with issues of prejudice and integration with the majority population that can cause significant stress (Clarke 2000). More acute life stresses, such as divorce or separation, may also trigger episodes of depression. Adverse life events that occurred in the past may also increase vulnerability to depression. Child abuse and neglect are strongly predictive of depression later in life (DeMarco 2000). Elder abuse is a significant risk factor for depression among older people although good social support can moderate its effects (Dong et al. 2009) as it can in other situations (Paykel 1994).

Explanations of why more women report depression than men vary. Initially dismissed as a reporting bias, there is now good evidence that there are real gender differences in the prevalence of depression (Weich et al. 1998). Social explanations of these phenomena suggest that women experience more responsibilities and lower quality of life than men. Women tend to have lower-status jobs and have more spillover between work and home (Bird and Rieker 1999). That is, when they finish work they are more likely than men to take on domestic roles and continue working. A more psychological explanation was provided by Holen-Hoeksema (1990) who argued that when men experience circumstances that may lead to depression, they are more able to distract from any negative thoughts than women, who are more likely to focus on issues and their possible causes, increasing the salience of potentially depressing cognitions. Among the elderly, illness may also contribute the onset of depression. Tsai et al. (2005), for example, found that respiratory disease, poor cognitive function, poor social support network, dissatisfaction with their living situation, perception of poor health status, and perceived income inadequacy were significant predictors of depressive symptoms in their sample of Taiwanese older adults.

Psychodynamic explanations

Freud ([1917] 1957) considered depression to be similar to grieving. During grieving, the individual regresses to the oral stage of development as a defence mechanism against overwhelming distress. This involves complete dependence on the loved one, as a consequence of which they merge their identity with them and symbolically regain the lost relationship. In addition, through a process known as introjection, they direct their feelings for the loved one into themselves. These feelings may include anger as a result of unresolved conflicts. This reaction is generally short-lived, but can become pathological if the individual continues to introject their feelings in the long term, leading to self-hatred and depression.

Freud suggested that 'normal' depression results from an imagined or symbolic loss. Events are seen as somehow removing the love or esteem of important individuals, and the depressed person introjects their negative feelings towards the individual they consider to be rejecting them. Those most prone to depression are people who fail to effectively progress though the oral stage of development, because they are either gratified too much or too little at the time. Such people remain dependent on others for love and approval through their lives, and are susceptible to events that trigger anxieties or experiences of loss.

Behavioural explanations

Behavioural theories of depression focus on operant conditioning processes. Lewinsohn et al. (1979), for example, suggested that depression is the result of a low rate of positive social reinforcement. This leads to low mood and reductions in behaviour intended to gain social rewards. The individual withdraws from social contacts, an action that may actually result in short-term increases in social contact as they gain sympathy or attention as a result of their behaviour. This may establish a further reinforcement schedule, known as secondary gain, in which the individual is rewarded for their depressive behaviours. This phase, however, is usually followed by a reduction in attention (reducing the frequency of rewards available from the environment) and lowering of mood.

Learned helplessness

The shift from behavioural to cognitive models of depression is exemplified by changes made to Seligman's (1975) learned helplessness model of depression. Seligman initially considered that depression resulted from the individual learning they were unable to control their physical or social environment. The term 'learned helplessness' stemmed from animal experiments in which animals were typically placed in an area from which they could escape, for example, by jumping over a low barrier. Following a mild electric shock, the animals quickly learned to jump over the barrier to avoid it. However, when they were prevented from doing so by being placed in a harness, they eventually stopped trying to avoid the shock even when the possibility of escape was open to them. They had learned that they could not avoid the shock, and expressed their helplessness by inertia and not trying to change the situation. A number of studies used differing procedures to induce learned helplessness both in animals and humans. Those that went through these procedures evidenced 'symptoms' similar to clinically depressed individuals, including lack of motivation, passivity and disrupted learning.

Cognitive explanations

Seligman's behavioural model of depression was revised in the late 1970s by Abramson et al. (1978), partly in response to the developing paradigm of cognitive psychology. The revised learned helplessness theory suggested that depression – or more accurately, hopelessness – was the result of three key attributional processes in response to both positive and negative events:

- *internal/external*: did the outcome arise as a result of the person or the situation?
- *stable/unstable*: will the result happen every time, or is it changeable or random?
- *global/specific*: does the outcome occur in all situations, or only in specific instances?

According to the revised model, individuals prone to depression tend to view negative events or outcomes as internal, stable, and having global causes ('It's my fault, it will always go wrong . . . and this is just typical of my life'). By contrast, positive outcomes are attributed to external, unstable, specific causes: 'Things went well, but no thanks to me. It was luck and won't happen again.' That is, they have a negative attributional style. Abela and Seligman (2000) stated that these attributions will result in depression only if they produce a sense of hopelessness, that is, a belief that the individual has no response available to them that will alter their situation coupled with an expectation that desirable outcomes will not occur. Longitudinal evidence that particular attributions contribute to the development of depression comes from studies such as that reported by Abramson et al. (2002) who found that students with a negative attributional style were seven times more likely to become clinically depressed over a two-year follow-up period than those with a more positive style. This risk was further magnified among those students who tended to ruminate about their negative thoughts. Similar findings, but over a much shorter time period, were reported by Kwon and Laurenceau (2002) who found that students' attributional styles were not predictive of the number of daily hassles they reported in a diary study conducted over a ten-week period. However, a negative attributional style predicted greater depressive symptom reactivity in response to those hassles.

Matching these changes in the learned helplessness model, behavioural explanations of depression have largely been superseded by cognitive ones, the best known of which is that of Beck (1997). Beck argued that depression results from inaccurate cognitive responses to events that affect us. In depression, the immediate responses to such events are what Beck termed automatic negative thoughts. These seem immediate and valid, and are often accepted as true. However, they systematically misinterpret events in ways that lead to depression. Errors that typify such thinking include overgeneralization, selective abstraction and dichotomous thinking (see Table 9.1). They influence what Beck referred to as the *cognitive triad*: beliefs about our self, events or other people that affect us and our future.

According to Beck, our conscious thoughts are distorted by underlying depressogenic schemata (schema in the singular). These are unconscious underlying beliefs about ourselves and the world that influence conscious thought and are established during childhood. Negative events in childhood, such as parental rejection, for example, establish negative cognitive

Table 9.1 **Some examples of Beck's depressogenic thinking errors**

Absolutistic thinking	Thinking in 'all-or-nothing' terms: 'If I don't succeed in this task, I am an absolute failure. I am either the best teacher, or I am nothing ...'
Overgeneralization	Drawing a general (negative) conclusion on the basis of a single incident: 'That's it – I always fail at this sort of thing ... I can't do it!'
Personalization	Interpreting events as personal affronts or obstacles: 'Why do they always pick on ME ... even when I'm not to blame?'
Arbitrary inference	Drawing a conclusion without sufficient evidence to support it: 'They don't like me ... I could tell from the moment we met ...'
Selective abstraction	Focusing on an insignificant detail taken out of context: 'I thought my lecture went well. But that student who left early may have been unhappy with it. Perhaps the others were as well but didn't show it ...'

schemata about the self and the world. For most of the time, these beliefs are not particularly salient, or else the individual would be chronically depressed. However, when we encounter stressful circumstances in adulthood, and particularly those that echo previous childhood experiences (divorce or separation, for example, reflecting earlier experiences of parental rejection), underlying negative schemata are activated, influence our surface cognitions, and lead to depression (see Figure 9.1).

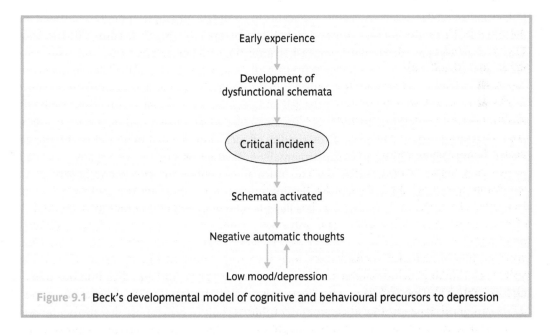

Figure 9.1 **Beck's developmental model of cognitive and behavioural precursors to depression**

There is good evidence that some negative schemata are more accessible at times of low mood than at other times. Others may remain salient throughout the life course (see discussion of schemata models of personality disorder in Chapter 12). However, Meichenbaum (1985) challenged the notion that schemata are irrevocably established during childhood, and may change as a consequence of events over the life course. Determining which explanation is right has proven extremely difficult. Clinical practice has shown that some negative schemata beginning in childhood endure over long periods, and can be difficult to change. However, this does not necessarily reflect a childhood critical period. An alternative explanation may be that childhood beliefs are maintained because nothing happens to make the individual question their initial assumption. Indeed, their own behaviour may result in these beliefs being reinforced. A girl who does not believe that her parents love her, for example, may react against them and cause them to treat her more severely or rigidly than would otherwise have been the case, providing support for the initial belief. Over time, this belief and its associated behaviours may spill over to other relationships, resulting in relationship problems that continue for many years. Here, the schemata laid down in childhood are maintained in adulthood not because of a critical period, but because the woman's behaviour as an adult continued to elicit responses that reinforced her childhood beliefs.

There is a strong reciprocity between mood and cognition: negative cognitions lower mood, and low mood increases the salience of negative cognitions. Depressive thoughts, for example, can be triggered in non-depressed subjects following mood induction techniques in which they read aloud a series of adjectives describing negative mood states. Boury et al. (2001) found a significant correlation among the number of negative automatic thoughts, number of core beliefs, and the severity and duration of depression. However, there has been some debate as to whether cognitive distortions contribute to the *initiation* of episodes of depression or simply follow its onset. Although relatively little research has examined this issue, what data there is suggests that at least some cognitive factors influence risk of depression. In one study of this process, Abela and D'Alessandro (2002) asked university applicants to complete measures of depressed mood and dysfunctional attitudes between one and eight weeks before receiving their admissions decision. This measure was preceded by a priming task (completion of a questionnaire focusing on negative life events) designed to activate latent depressogenic schemata. Two months later, following the decision to accept or reject them from entry into the university, participants completed measures of depressed mood, negative views of the self and negative views of the future. Consistent with Beck's theory, dysfunctional attitudes at baseline predicted negative mood immediately following a negative decision. Evidence of the rigidity of such thinking can be found in the work of Deveney and Delvin (2006) who experimentally evoked either positive or negative moods in people with major depressive disorder and 'normal' controls. Following mood induction, the control group evidenced less cognitive flexibility when the trigger evoked positive emotional change, while the depressed group was less flexible following induction of negative mood.

Treatment of major depression

Biological interventions

Antidepressants There are now three types of antidepressant in general use that impact on serotonin levels: tricylics, SSRIs and SNRIs (see Chapter 4). A third group of antidepressants, known as monoamine oxidase inhibitors (MAOIs) proved reasonably effective, achieving clinically significant changes in about 50 per cent of the people prescribed them. However, the dangers associated with their use (see Chapter 4) mean they are used less as other drugs become available.

SSRIs have little therapeutic advantage over tricyclics, but have fewer side-effects and are tolerated better. Rocca et al. (1997), for example, reported 56 per cent of people treated with tricylics complained of a dry mouth compared with 8 per cent treated with SSRIs. The percentages to report constipation were 39 and 8 per cent respectively. Anderson (1998) reported that 14 per cent of people taking tricyclics discontinued their use due to adverse side-effects in comparison to 9 per cent of those receiving SSRIs. Gillman (2007) suggested that some SNRIs do not have sufficient biochemical impact on the noradrenergic system to effectively influence mood, so their impact is likely to be no greater than that of SSRIs, an argument consistent with the findings of a randomized controlled trial reported by Shelton et al. (2006) who found no clinical differences between an SSRI and SNRI. Interestingly, Herrera-Guzmán et al. (2009) found that although an SNRI proved no more effective in treating depression than an SSRI, it *was* more effective in a very specific symptom area, achieving greater improvements in episodic and working memory.

St John's wort   A more 'natural' remedy involves using extracts of the plant *Hypericum perforatum*, more popularly known as St John's wort. Its mode of action is little understood, but it does seem to benefit those receiving it. Linde and Mulrow (2002), for example, identified 14 trials that compared preparations of hypericum against placebo or antidepressant medication. The percentage of people to clinically improve following treatment with hypericum preparations and placebo were 56 per cent and 25 per cent respectively. Comparisons with antidepressants revealed few differences in benefit, with clinical gains in 50 per cent of those treated with hypericum compared with 52 per cent with standard antidepressant treatments. Of those treated with a combination of hypericum and antidepressant, 68 per cent evidenced clinically significant improvements. St John's wort seemed to be more acceptable to those prescribed it than standard pharmacological medication, with drop-out rates due to side-effects averaging 2 per cent among those prescribed hypericum in contrast to 7 per cent of those receiving standard antidepressants.

St John's wort does have some side-effects, including gastrointestinal discomfort, fatigue, dry mouth, dizziness, skin rash and hypersensitivity to sunlight. It may also interfere with the effectiveness of indinavir, a protease inhibitor used in the treatment of AIDS; cyclosporin, an immunosuppressive drug used to protect patients from organ rejection after heart transplantation; and warfarin, an anticoagulant. As a result, its use has to be limited in some cases.

Electroconvulsive therapy

The success of antidepressants in treating depression, and concern over its acceptability as a first-line treatment (see Chapter 4), have meant that ECT is increasingly used as a second-line treatment for 'treatment-resistant cases': those individuals who do not respond to pharmacological, and perhaps psychological, treatments. At this point, ECT does appear to have some benefit, and given the lack of response to other treatments, any gains at this point may be considered a success (McCall 2001).

Perhaps more controversial has been the question whether ECT should be continued over an extended period of time to maintain initial improvements in mood. Gagné et al. (2000) explored this issue by comparing outcomes over a three-year period in a group of people initially treated with ECT and then maintained on antidepressants or antidepressants plus ECT.

ECT was initially delivered once-weekly, and then gradually decreased to once-monthly. Their findings appeared to support the use of maintenance ECT: 7 per cent of those receiving ECT plus antidepressant compared with 48 per cent of those receiving only antidepressants relapsed over this time. However, the authors noted that participants in the combined intervention spent more time with their doctor than those only receiving medication. In addition, participants who did not attend ECT clinics were vigorously followed up and encouraged to attend, potentially resulting in more immediate remedial action should they have begun to relapse than would be given to those treated only with antidepressants. Both may have contributed to the better outcome in this group.

Psychological interventions

Cognitive therapy The seminal cognitive treatment of depression was developed by Beck (1977). Despite its name, cognitive therapy has its historical roots in the behavioural treatment of depression, and still maintained a strong behavioural element (see also discussion of cognitive therapy in Chapter 2). It typically involves a number of strategies, including:

- *an education phase* in which the individual learns the relationships between cognitions, emotions and behaviour
- *behavioural activation* and *pleasant event scheduling* to increase physiological arousal and engagement in functional, social, and other rewarding activities
- *cognitive rehearsal* to prepare participants to cope with behavioural hypothesis testing or other situations that have previously been problematic
- *behavioural hypothesis testing* in which the individual deliberately tests the validity of their negative assumptions, in the hope of disproving them.

Despite the emphasis on cognitive causes of depression, treatment may first involve increasing engagement in physical activities. For those who are profoundly depressed, this may involve planning times to get out of bed, go to the shops, and so on. For those who are less depressed, it may involve engaging in social or 'pleasant' activities. Cognitive factors are usually addressed only after the client has experienced some improvement in energy or mood. At this time, they are taught to identify 'faulty thinking' that leads to low mood and to use cognitive challenge to counter it. In addition, the client is typically given homework to do between sessions, usually involving some form of behavioural hypothesis testing or practice in the use of new coping skills. Hypothesis testing involves direct, behavioural challenges of negative cognitions. Someone who is not sure they will be able to cope with a particular situation, for example, may be encouraged to enter the situation and try to cope with it. Such tasks should be selected with care. The therapist, at least, should be confident the client will be able to cope with the situation, as failure will reinforce negative expectations: the very thing the task was set up to disprove.

By the mid-1980s, there was a general consensus that cognitive therapy was at least as effective as antidepressant therapy in the treatment of both moderate and severe depression. This consensus was broken following publication of the results of the most influential treatment trial so far conducted. The National Institute of Mental Health (NIMH) Treatment of Depression Collaborative Research Program (Elkin et al. 1989) was a particularly important trial as it was

the first to compare two psychological treatments, cognitive therapy and interpersonal psychotherapy (IPT), with both a tricylic and a placebo drug intervention. By the end of the 16-week
treatment phase, all the active interventions appeared to be equally effective. Fifty-five per cent
of those in the IPT condition were clinically 'improved', in comparison with 57 per cent in the
active drug intervention, 51 per cent in the cognitive therapy group and 29 per cent in the
placebo group. For those who were severely depressed, cognitive therapy proved significantly
less effective than pharmacotherapy.

This latter finding caused significant debate and discussion, not least because its results led
both the American Psychiatric Association and the US Agency of Health Care Policy and
Research to recommend against the use of cognitive therapy for more severe cases of depression. However, the results have been questioned from a number of perspectives. Psychiatrists
were puzzled by findings that the effectiveness of the placebo was much greater than is typically
found. Psychologists were surprised that the cognitive intervention proved less effective than in
earlier studies; so much so, that Jacobson and Hollon (1996) suggested that it had been implemented by insufficiently skilled therapists at some sites. Subsequent data have also challenged
this short-term finding. DeRubeis et al. (1999), for example, compared the short-term outcomes of antidepressant medication and cognitive therapy in people with severe depression in
sub-groups of four major randomized trials. In contrast to the NIMH study, both cognitive
therapy and pharmacotherapy fared equally well.

The long-term results of the NIMH study were more favourable to the psychological interventions (Shea et al. 1992) – and here may lie their advantage over pharmacological therapy.
Relapse rates following discontinuation of drug therapy are often much higher than those
following cognitive therapy, even when the initial treatment is successful. Hollon et al. (2005),
for example, compared outcomes in three groups of patients over a period of one year. The first
group comprised people who had been successfully treated with cognitive therapy, which was
then discontinued. The second group comprised individuals successfully treated with medication, which was also discontinued. The final group comprised a group of people successfully
treated with medication, which was then withdrawn and replaced with a placebo. Relapse rates
in the following year were 31 per cent following cessation of cognitive therapy, 76 per cent
of those who received neither medication nor placebo, and 47 per cent among those who continued on placebo.

In an attempt to improve the still significant relapse rate following the cessation of CBT,
Teasdale et al. (2000) implemented a programme of mindfulness (see Chapter 3) to try to teach
participants coping skills to help them avoid relapse. This proved successful, and the approach
has been repeated by a number of investigators (see Research box 9). Unfortunately, although
Coelho et al. (2007) concluded from their meta-analysis of these studies that mindfulness is likely
to reduce relapse rates for patients with three or more previous depressive episodes, they also
warned that the designs of the relevant studies prevented these findings being unambigously
attributable to mindfulness.

Research box 9

Kuyken W., Byford S., Taylor R.S. et al. (2008) Mindfulness-based cognitive therapy to prevent relapse in recurrent depression, *Journal of Consulting and Clinical Psychology*, 76: 966–78.

Teasdale and colleagues reported a halving of relapse rates relative to usual care following the use of mindfulness-based cognitive therapy (MBCT) with patients not receiving antidepressant medication. The present study aimed to determine whether (i) the intervention was of value to patients receiving antidepressant medication, (ii) it allowed patients to reduce or discontinue their medication, (iii) it proved effective when therapy was conducted by therapists not in its originating group, and (iv) it was more effective than another active treatment.

Participants

Participants were 123 patients with a history of three or more previous episodes of depression, prescribed antidepressant medication, and in full or partial remission.

Method

Participants were randomly allocated to either antidepressant treatment (usual care) or a group, two-hour per session, 8-week-long, mindfulness-based cognitive therapy (MBCT) programme as described in Chapter 3, with the addition that it also included support in reducing or discontinuing their medication. Therapy sessions were videotaped to allow checks on therapist competence, treatment adherence, and to facilitate supervision sessions. Participants were supported in reducing their medication by a local primary care doctor.

Outcome measures

Measures were taken at the time of treatment allocation, and then a further four times at three monthly intervals. Outcome measures included:

- Depression module of the SCID (see Chapter 1) to measure relapse/recurrence.
- Rating of the severity of relapse on 1–100 scale rated by participants.
- Residual symptoms were measured using an observer-rated interview (Hamilton Rating Scale for Depression: HRSD) and the Beck Depression Inventory (BDI).
- Quality of life was measured using the World Health Organization Quality of Life (WHOQOL) measure.

Results

Figure 9.2 shows the cumulative relapse rates, based on SCID diagnostic interviews, over the time period of the study. By the end of the follow-up period, 47 per cent of the MBCT group had relapsed, compared to 60 per cent of the antidepressant medication group. This difference achieved statistical significance ($p = 0.05$) when the analysis included all patients in the trial, and was marginally significant ($p = 0.07$) when the analysis included only those participants who adhered fully to the study protocol.

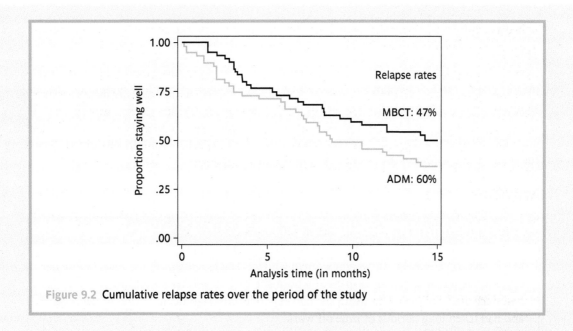

Figure 9.2 Cumulative relapse rates over the period of the study

Seventy-five per cent of the patients in the MBCT arm of the trial discontinued their medication. However, there were no differences in outcome between those who did and did not discontinue their medication. In addition, participants in the MBCT group evidenced greater gains than those in the medication condition on the WHOQOL physical ($p = 0.05$), social ($p = 0.003$) and (marginally) psychological ($p = 0.06$) domains, and residual symptoms measured by the HRSD ($p = 0.04$) and BDI ($p = 0.04$).

Table 9.2 Mean scores on key secondary measures 1 and 15 months after the intervention

	1 month		15 months	
	MBCT	Medication	MBCT	Medication
Quality of Life (WHOQOL-BREF)				
Physical	24.08	22.86	23.97	22.93
Psychological	18.88	17.46	18.61	17.36
Social	10.09	9.07	10.10	9.66
Residual symptoms				
HRSD	5.83	7.75	7.05	8.69
BDI	13.12	17.47	12.61	17.02

Discussion

This was the first study to compare MBCT against another active treatment. Its conclusions were relatively positive. In people with recurrent depression, it produced modest gains on measures of relapse, and clear gains on measures of quality of life and residual symptoms, despite significantly less use of medication in the MBCT group. In addition, rates of adherence to MBCT were comparable to those in previous trials (85 per cent) suggesting the high levels of acceptability of this approach. Nevertheless, during recruitment to the study, the time commitment and group aspect of the intervention were noted as reasons to decline participation.

Case formulation

Mrs V was an extremely overweight woman who worked as a nurse. Some years before her referral, she had married an ex-patient whom she had nursed with multiple sclerosis. He had since died. Following his death she had experienced a significant period of depression and had taken long periods of time off work.

Long-term antecedents

Mrs V was an only child. She had been brought up in a small village some miles from Gloucester. Unfortunately, she was sexually abused by a close friend of the family for a period of 2 to 3 years from around the age of 6 years. She felt disgust at the abuser's behaviour, but also blamed herself for much of what happened. She believed she deserved to be abused as (i) she was a bad person, because of all the people that he could have abused, he chose her and that must indicate that he saw something bad in her, (ii) her parents did not love her, because they did nothing to prevent the occurrences, and (iii) God did not love her. These beliefs were strengthened by incidents, for example, in which her parents occasionally left her with the abuser while they went away on weekend trips.

Despite her low self-esteem and disgust, Mrs V had performed well at school and went on to train as a nurse, working in a local hospital. She had, however, a poor social life and her relationship with her parents was poor. She did not have any boyfriends, and did not try to make herself attractive to men. She became significantly overweight, partly because she gained some pleasure from eating and partly because it made her unattractive to men.

Shorter-term antecedents

Mrs V met her husband-to-be while he was an in-patient. At the time he was severely disabled by multiple sclerosis, and had a poor prognosis. On his discharge they established a relationship, and after some months began to live with each other, and married soon after. Due to his physical infirmity, they did not have sexual relationships. In fact, she rapidly became his carer, eventually helping him to eat and drink as well as other basic biological functions. From her perspective, he provided company, he could not leave her however unattractive she was or poor their relationship, and was unthreatening sexually. He provided a safe focus for her love, in that she was quite literally in control of their relationship. His death was therefore not only the loss of a loved one, but the loss of a feeling of safety in the world. She was unable to gain support from her parents, whom she considered did not care for her, and the negative beliefs she held about herself came to the fore. By the time she was seen by a psychologist, she was withdrawn, disengaged from the world, spending most of her time in her house with her dog.

Formulation and intervention

Mrs V had chronic low self-esteem because of events that had occurred in her childhood, and her failure to challenge the basis of those beliefs. She felt unloved and did not love herself. She was frightened of sexual relationships, but nevertheless desired 'safe' relationships with men. The one, safe, relationship with an adult she had achieved was not strong, but had protected her against her negative self-beliefs and self-disgust. The absence of this relationship and the lack of any supportive relationships, combined with a re-activation of her negative beliefs about herself resulted in significant distress and depression.

Intervention

The great challenge to Mrs V was to confront her negative beliefs about self, established in her childhood and re-evoked following the death of her husband. These beliefs were both depressogenic and cut her off from the potential support of her family at times of difficulty. These issues were considered in therapy using the Socratic dialogue approach. One issue discussed in this context was Mrs V's belief that her parents knew she was being abused by her abuser, and chose to let this happen. The therapist and Mrs V examined the evidence related to this belief. One key issue was that Mrs V spent occasional nights with the abuser. She took this as a clear sign that her parents both knew what was happening and condoned it. However, close questioning on this issue reminded Mrs V that she did not want her parents to worry about her or the abuser to tell her parents what was occurring, so when she went to stay with this individual she had pretended to be looking forward to the time and smiled and laughed while her parents were there. As a consequence, they could not have been aware of her concerns and distress. Through similar questioning, she began to believe that she was chosen not because of who she was, but because of her availability, that her parents were unaware of what was occurring, and was less strong in her beliefs that she was a bad person and that (as a consequence) God did not love her. These changes did not immediately transform Mrs V into a happy and carefree person. Nevertheless, she was able to establish warmer and more loving relationships with her mother, and began to develop stronger acquaintanceships and then friendships with people she knew, including one man with whom she developed a strong, if asexual, relationship. Her mood lifted and she was able to return to work. She remained a vulnerable individual, but was coping well with life.

9.2 Suicide

Only about half of those who commit suicide have an identified mental health problem, the most common being depression, substance-related disorders and schizophrenia. About 15 per cent of people with each disorder kill themselves (Meltzer 1998). Surprisingly, perhaps, suicide is more strongly associated with moderate than severe depression, as those who are severely depressed may lack the volition to act on their feelings. Indeed, some people kill themselves as their depression begins to lift as they are still hopeless but have increasing levels of impulsivity and motivation. According to Bronisch and Wittchen (1994), 56 per cent of their sample of people with a diagnosis of depression reported thinking about death, 37 per cent reported a wish to die and 69 per cent had suicidal ideas. However, these thoughts were not exclusive to depressed individuals: 8 per cent of a comparison group who had never been assigned a psychiatric diagnosis reported having suicidal ideas, and 2 per cent had made a suicide attempt. Suicide by people with schizophrenia is more often a result of demoralization than the result of hallucinations or delusions.

Aetiology of suicide

Socio-cultural factors

Suicide rates vary across countries. Russia, for example, has an annual rate as high as 40 per 100 000 people, while Greece has a rate of 4 per 100 000 (World Health Organization: www.who.int). Suicide rates are relatively low among those who are married or co-habiting, and higher among divorcees and social groups under particular pressure. Shahmanesh et al. (2009), for example, reported that 19 per cent of sex workers in Goa had made at least one suicide attempt in the three months prior to their survey. This was linked to partner violence, violence from others, entrapment and worsening mental health. Social deprivation combined with high access to alcohol contribute to the relatively high levels among social groups such as American Indian and Alaskan natives (Centers for Disease Control: www.cdc.gov/ncipc/wisqars).

Men are more likely than women to commit suicide (in a ratio of around 5:1), and young men are at particularly high risk. In 2000, UK rates were 11.7 suicides per 100 000 men and 3.3 per 100 000 women (World Health Organization: www.who.int) – a substantial difference. Suicide is particularly prevalent among young people, and is the third leading cause of death among Americans aged between 15 and 24 years (Anderson and Smith 2003). Young people may commit suicide as a consequence of abuse, bullying, exam stress and other problems combined with catastrophic thinking, poor coping strategies and low levels of social support. Gay, lesbian or bisexual people are also at particular risk of suicide, with rates nearly two and a half times higher than in their heterosexual counterparts (King et al. 2008). This may be particularly evident among younger people. Remafedi et al. (1998) found that 28 per cent of homosexual or bisexual males but only 4 per cent of heterosexual male adolescents had considered or attempted suicide. For females, the corresponding figures were 21 and 15 per cent. Among older people, suicide may occur as a consequence of increasing disability: 44 per cent of one sample of elderly people apparently committed suicide to prevent being placed in a nursing home (Loebel et al. 1991). Suicide among those who have recently been bereaved is also frequent.

A recent phenomenon has been the development of suicide pacts made through the internet, often between people who did not previously know each other. However, this is not a new phenomenon. Although suicide pacts account for less than 1 per cent of the total number of suicides in the UK (Brown and Barraclough 1997), one pact occurs, on average, every month (Rajagopal 2004). In contrast to the internet pacts, the relationship between individuals in these is typically exclusive, isolated from others, and the immediate trigger is frequently a threat to the continuation of the relationship, such as the impending death of one member. Both people involved typically employ the same method.

A more theoretical social model of suicide was developed by Durkheim ([1897] 1951) who identified three types of suicide: anomic, altruistic and egoistic. According to Durkheim, *anomic suicide* occurs when the social structure in which an individual lives fails to provide sufficient support for them, and they lose a sense of belonging – a state known as anomie. High levels of anomie occur at times of both societal and personal change, including economic stress, immigration and social unrest. *Altruistic suicide* occurs when an individual deliberately sacrifices themself for the well-being of others or the community. Perhaps the clearest example of this can be found among suicide bombers who Grimland et al. (2006) argued are not suicidal in a despairing or negative sense, but see their behaviour as a glorious martyrdom, an act of war, bolstered by cultural and religious beliefs (and a period of indoctrination and preparation). Finally, *egoistic suicide* occurs among those not governed by the norms of society, who are outsiders or loners in a more permanent state of alienation than those who commit anomic suicide.

Psychoanalytic explanations

According to Freud ([1920] 1990), suicide represents a repressed wish to kill a lost love object, and is an act of revenge. Hendin (1992) identified a number of other psychoanalytic processes that may lead to suicide, including ideas of effecting a rebirth or reunion with a lost object as well as self-punishment and atonement.

Cognitive explanations

The psychological characteristics of individuals who attempt suicide often involve feelings of hopelessness (Stewart et al. 2005), worthlessness, guilt, despair, depressive delusional symptoms, inner restlessness and agitation (Wolfersdorf 1995). Individuals at risk are also likely to have pre-morbid characteristics including high levels of impulsivity, irritability, hostility and a tendency to aggression, as well as a history of alcohol or drug abuse (Dumais et al. 2005). People with low intelligence (Gunnell et al. 2005) and deficits in memory and problem-solving skills (Schotte and Clum 1987) are also over-represented among those committing suicide, perhaps reflecting a limited ability to solve problems while going through an acute life crisis or suffering from mental health problems.

A more elaborate cognitive model of suicide was developed by Rudd (2000), based on Beck's model of emotional disorders and his own clinical experience. According to Rudd, the components of the underlying cognitive triad are the self as worthless, unloved, incompetent and helpless, others as rejecting, abusing, judgemental, and the future as hopeless. In contrast to depression, where sadness predominates, the suicidal individual may experience a range of emotions including sadness, guilt and anger. Thoughts may focus on revenge, but this will not lead directly to suicidal behaviour. Thoughts and emotions associated with suicide occur at the same time as high levels of physiological arousal and agitation: the profoundly depressed non-aroused individual will not have the motivation to attempt suicide. Risk of suicide varies over time, with periods of acute risk interspersed with lower levels of risk. High levels of risk occur when multiple risk factors converge. These may include situational stress, activation of negative schemata, emotional confusion and deficient coping skills.

Treatment of attempted suicide

People who attempt suicide and have a mental health problem may benefit from treatment of this disorder regardless of its influence on their mood or behaviour. They may also benefit more directly from addressing factors that contributed to their suicide attempt. One way through which this can be achieved is by developing strategies to cope more effectively with the problems they face. The key elements of this approach include:

- both client and therapist gaining a good understanding of the nature of the problems
- identifying in what ways the situation could be improved: the desired goals (such as better relationship with partner)
- identifying strategies by which these goals can be attained (for example, talking more, going out together, and so on).

This approach can be used with individuals as well as couples and even families. Therapy sessions may be frequent in the early stages of therapy, and then more widely spaced as the individual begins to cope better with their problems. Therapy may also involve relatively few sessions: partly because this may be the only form of therapy acceptable to those who attempt suicide, partly to facilitate early client independence (Hawton 1997).

Evaluations of the effectiveness of this approach have generally supported its use. Indeed, in a meta-analysis of psychosocial interventions following suicide attempts, Van der Sande et al. (1997) found problem-focused and cognitive behavioural interventions to be the only interventions to prove effective in this group. In one study of these approaches, Salkovskis et al. (1990) compared a brief, five-session cognitive behavioural and problem-solving approach with routine outpatient care. In the six months following the intervention, 25 per cent of those in the active intervention group made at least one further suicide attempt, in comparison with 50 per cent of those who did not receive the intervention. More recently, Brown and Barraclough (1997) found that people who participated in a ten-session cognitive therapy intervention were 50 per cent less likely to re-attempt suicide than participants in a usual care group over an 18-month follow-up period: 24 per cent of the cognitive therapy group and 42 per cent of the usual care group made at least one subsequent suicide attempt over this period.

A second strand of research has focused on working with the family left behind by people who commit suicide. For these individuals, there is evidence of some benefit for family therapy or bereavement groups, but the evidence is limited and not strong (McDaid et al. 2009).

Stop and think...

Assisted suicide is a highly contentious issue, with strong advocates both for and against. In a 2009 article, Edwards debated the value of the UK government establishing Suicide Centres across the country in which people would be helped to commit suicide if they were approaching the end of life. His arguments in support included: (i) respect for the autonomy of the individual to make decisions consistent with their values and beliefs, and (ii) an acknowledgement that it is reasonable to make personal choices that reduce the experience of suffering. His arguments against were: (i) it is inappropriate to support an autonomous action if that action prevents the possibility of future autonomous desires (e.g. the finality of suicide prevents one changing one's mind), (ii) it crosses the sanctity of human life, and (iii) it could provide a mechanism for 'state-approved' deaths. More pragmatic questions include, who would assist in the suicides, and would certain individuals be pressured to accepting suicide? So, should the state support some individuals in ending their lives, and if so what type of individual? Or should no one be allowed to commit suicide?

Edwards, S.D. (2009) An argument in support of suicide centers, *Health Care Analyis*, May 7.

9.3 Seasonal affective disorder (SAD)

Seasonal affective disorder (SAD) was recognized as a distinct disorder by Rosenthal and colleagues only in the mid-1980s (Rosenthal et al. 1984). DSM-IV-TR considers it to have the following characteristics:

- a regular temporal relationship between the onset of an episode of depression and a particular time of year
- full remissions occur at regular times of the year
- two major depressive episodes that meet these criteria have occurred in the previous two years
- any seasonal depressive episodes outnumber the number of nonseasonal episodes of depression.

The characteristics of SAD appear to be quite different from major depression, and include increased appetite, weight and duration of sleep, as well as other depressive symptoms including sadness, decreased activity, anxiety, work problems, decreased libido, and day-time tiredness (Magnusson and Partonen 2005). The depression is seldom severe enough to require absence from work. Winter episodes typically begin in November and last about five months. Age of onset is typically between the ages of 20 and 30 years. It may prove a chronically recurring problem: up to 42 per cent of patients have recurring episodes for up to 11 years following initial onset, some of which may occur in winter and some of which may become non-seasonal (Thompson et al. 1995). The prevalence of SAD varies between less than 1 per cent and more than 10 per cent depending on the country in which rates are measured. In the northern hemisphere, prevalence rates are higher in northern countries, and lower in southern countries (Magnusson and Partonen 2005). Symptoms get worse if people move from south to north and improve if they move in the opposite direction (Rosenthal et al. 1984). The opposite pattern occurs in the southern hemisphere.

Those whose symptoms are so severe that they receive a diagnosis of SAD may be a subset of a larger group of people who experience a variety of negative symptoms over the winter. Less dramatic seasonal changes in activity and weight levels occur within the general population. Terman (1988), for example, reported that 50 per cent of the general population reported lowered energy levels, 47 per cent reported increased weight, while 31 per cent reported decreased social activity in the winter months. Twenty-five per cent reported that these changes were sufficiently marked to signify a personal problem.

Aetiology of seasonal affective disorder

Explanations of SAD are almost uniquely biological.

Genetic factors

There is now increasing evidence of genetic processes in the aetiology of SAD. In one population study, Madden et al. (1996) examined the prevalence of SAD in MZ and DZ twins, concluding that about 29 per cent of the variance in the risk for developing SAD was attributable to genetic factors. Interestingly, given the apparent different aetiology between non-seasonal depression and SAD (see below), biological studies have implicated genes related to serotonergic transmission (Sher 2001) as well as those that influence circadian rhythms (Kripke et al. 2009; Partonen et al. 2007).

Circadian hypothesis

According to the circadian hypotheses, the key to SAD is a hormone known as melatonin. Release of melatonin from the pineal gland in the base of the brain is triggered by darkness, and it is found mainly in the midbrain and hypothalamus. It controls sleep and eating. In mammals that are living wild, the release of melatonin as the nights get longer reduces their activity, slows them down and prepares them for winter rest or hibernation. Early melatonin models thought that SAD resulted from an excess production or responsiveness to melatonin. However, evidence of differences in levels of melatonin in people with and without SAD have not proven conclusive. As a consequence, Lewy et al. (1998) suggested that rather than the *level* of melatonin being the determinant of mood, it is the times at which it is secreted that are important. In their circadian hypothesis, they suggested that 'normal' depression can result from poor sleep resulting from disruption of the circadian wake–sleep cycle. In the case of SAD, changes in the times of dawn and dusk in the transition from summer to winter affect the time that melatonin is released, shifting the circadian rhythm of sleep, and taking it out of alignment with other biological rhythms. The goal of therapy is to rephase the wake–sleep cycle to that of the summer. According to Lewy and colleagues, this may be achieved through exposure to light early in the morning, which helps maintain the summer wake–sleep cycle and delays the secretion of melatonin until later in the day. This, combined with earlier times of sleep in the evening, should prove an effective treatment for SAD. Their own work supported this hypothesis, with findings that light therapy in the morning was more effective than if it was provided in the evening: an effect that seems to hold as long as the individual maintains their summertime waking and sleeping times (Lewy et al. 1998). Countering this hypothesis, however, are data from, for example, Terman et al. (2001) who have found bright light treatment in the morning and evening to be equally effective allowing the possibility that there may be two sub-groups of SAD: one with a general melatonin disorder, and one with a distorted circadian rhythm.

Serotonin hypothesis

A final hypothesis suggests that at least some of the mechanisms underlying SAD may not be particular to this syndrome, and may be those that underpin other forms of depression. A number of factors tie serotonin to the aetiology of SAD. Serotonin is involved in the control of appetite and sleep, and is a precursor to melatonin. Serotonin levels vary seasonally, and reducing serotonin levels by removal of a precursor to serotonin known as tryptophan from the diet results in depressive symptoms during the summer in people who typically develop winter SAD (Neumeister et al. 1997). Further evidence of a role for serotonin has come from treatment trials involving SSRIs. Both sertraline and fluoxetine have proven moderately effective in the treatment of SAD. However, these are generally not as effective as light therapy (Partonen and Lonnqvist 1998) or may work best with people who have not responded to light therapy (Pjerk et al. 2004), suggesting that while serotonin levels may be implicated in SAD, they do not provide the entire picture.

Treatment of seasonal affective disorder

The recognized treatment of SAD is known as 'bright light' treatment which lowers levels of melatonin. In this, the individual is typically exposed to high levels of artificial light, varying from 2500 lux for a period of 2 hours to 10 000 lux for half an hour each day over a period of between one and three weeks. For comparison, light in the house typically measures 100 lux or less. Outside lux levels may vary between 2000 lux or less on a rainy winter day and 10 000 lux in direct sunshine. Exposure is increasingly done in the morning to help shift individuals into an appropriate melatonin day–night rhythm.

These interventions can be effective. Sumaya et al. (2001) reported a trial in which participants were subject to three conditions in a random order: (i) a therapeutic dose of 10 000 lux for 30 minutes daily for one week: (ii) a non-therapeutic dose of 300 lux over the same time period (placebo): (iii) and a no-treatment period. After light treatment, 50 per cent of those receiving the active treatment no longer met the criteria for depression. Levels of depression did not change following either the placebo or no-treatment phases. Building on this success, more recent studies have tried to find the optimal wavelength of the light to improve mood. In one such study, Strong et al. (2009) compared the effects of short wavelength light (blue light) against dim red LED lights. The blue light proved the more effective of the two. Despite these successes, not all studies have proven light therapy to be effective. Wileman et al. (2001) randomly allocated people with SAD to either an active (four weeks of 10 000 lux exposure) or what they considered to be a placebo (four weeks of 300 lux) condition. Immediately following treatment, 30 per cent of those in the active treatment and 33 per cent of those in the placebo treatment were no longer depressed; 63 per cent of those in the active group and 57 per cent of the placebo group showed 'significant' improvements. The authors took this to indicate either a high level of placebo response among people with SAD, or that the threshold for light therapy was lower than initially thought.

Although light therapy remains the pre-eminent treatment for SAD, some people prefer to take medication. SSRI medication results in greater improvements than those achieved by placebo (Pjerk et al. 2005) and achieves significant gains among people who have benefited little from light therapy (Pjerk et al. 2004). A further candidate treatment involves the use of nor-adrenaline reuptake inhibitors (NARI) which have been shown to have a similar benefit to SSRIs (Pjerk et al. 2009).

9.4 Bipolar disorder

People with bipolar disorder experience both depression and periods of mania. According to DSM-IV-TR, mania involves at least three of the following:

- inflated self-esteem or grandiosity
- decreased need for sleep
- more talkativeness than usual or pressure to keep talking
- flight of ideas or the experience that thoughts are racing
- distractibility
- increased activity or psychomotor agitation
- excessive engagement in high-risk activities.

Manic individuals move rapidly, talk rapidly and loudly, and their conversation is often filled with jokes and attempts at cleverness. Flamboyance is common. Judgement is often poor, and individuals may engage in risky and other behaviours that they regret when less manic. They may also become extremely frustrated by the actions of others, whom they see as preventing them achieving their great plans. Of note is that while many people appear extremely happy while in a manic episode, this may not always be the case. The experience of Christina, who had experienced significant mood swings for many years, illustrates this issue. When she was in a manic phase, she typically wore livid coloured clothes, used bright and excessive make-up, and was generally hyperactive, gregarious and had difficulty in concentrating on one thing at a time. She looked like she was having fun. Talking to her about her experiences gave a different impression:

> I know it looks like I'm having fun, being happy and all that. But it's not how I feel. I feel driven by things, it's like there's something in me driving me, making me do things wild. Like the make-up, it's all over my face, and I don't like it but I do it. I feel really down sometimes while I'm acting all manic. It's not like I choose to though, it's like it's happening despite how I feel – it's not happy. I really don't like it. And I don't like people around thinking I'm happy too . . . it's really weird.

DSM-IV-TR described two types of bipolar disorder:

- *Bipolar disorder I*: individuals typically experience alternating episodes of depression and mania, each lasting weeks or months. Some individuals may experience several episodes of either mania or depression, separated by periods of 'normality', in sequence. Some people may swing between depression and mania in one day.

- *Bipolar disorder II*: depressive episodes predominate. The individual may swing between episodes of hypomania (an increase in activity over the normal, but not as excessive as mania) and severe depression. In addition, they will not have experienced an episode of mania.

Between 1 and 2 per cent of the adult population will experience bipolar disorder at any one time, with disorder I being the more prevalent (Bebbington and Ramana 1995). While the overall prevalence among men and women does not differ, women seem to have more depressive and fewer manic episodes than men and to cycle between these episodes more frequently (APA 2000). The first episode of bipolar disorder usually occurs between the ages of 20 and 30 years. Over half of those who have an initial episode of major depression and at least 80 per cent of those who have an initial episode of mania will have one or more recurrences (APA 1994), and over 50 per cent will experience this within the first year of the disorder (Yatham et al. 2009). Each episode may last days, weeks or, in some cases, years. The seriousness of the disorder tends to increase over time, although after about ten years there may be a marked diminution in severity.

As with major depression, the prevalence of the condition differs according to social and cultural circumstances. Grant et al. (2005) found an overall prevalence within the US population of 2 per cent. However, the prevalence was highest among Native Americans, young adults, people who were living alone following separation or bereavement, and those in lower socio-economic groups. Prevalence rates were lowest among Asian and Hispanic people.

Aetiology of bipolar disorder

Genetic factors

An early review of the genetics of bipolar disorder by Allen (1976) reported overall concordance rates for MZ twins of 72 per cent, while concordance rates for DZ twins averaged 14 per cent. More recently, these estimates have been reduced to 40 per cent and between 5 and 10 per cent respectively (Craddock and Jones 1999). Attempts to identify the locus of the genes that contribute to risk for the disorder have suggested that it may lie on chromosomes 4, 6, 12, 13, 15, 18 and 22 (Berretini 2000), although Craddock and Sklar (2009) noted that there still remains insufficient evidence to confirm a specific gene involvement in the development of the disorder.

Biological mechanisms

Given the role of serotonin and norepinephrine in depression, it would seem logical to assume that they also play a role in mania. However, the biological model that has emerged is not as simple as may have been expected. Data on norepinephrine are consistent with a simple model of mood disorders. High levels of norepinephrine are associated with elevated mood and mania; low levels result in depressed mood. No such relationship has been found for serotonin levels. Indeed, mania has been associated with low levels of serotonin (Mahmood and Silverstone 2001) – just as in depression. This finding is perhaps relevant to psychological studies that suggest manic behaviour may be somehow 'masking' depressed mood. Data such as these led some researchers to suggest a *permissive theory of bipolar disorder*, in which low serotonin levels somehow permit the activity of norepinephrine to determine mood. Low serotonin combined with low norepinephrine results in depression; combined with high norepinephrine, it results in mania.

A second model of bipolar disorders moves from consideration of neurotransmitters to the electrical conduction of whole neurons. Two processes involved in nerve transmission may be implicated: disturbances in activity of second messengers known as *phosphoinositides*, that instigate the firing of nerves including those involved in moderating mood, and altered sodium and potassium activity in the same neurons (see Chapter 3). In mania, second messenger activity or sodium and potassium transport across the cell membrane may be excessive and result in overactivity of the neuron system; in depression, there may be low activity in the neurons (Lenox et al. 1998).

A third factor that may contribute to bipolar disorder involves actual damage to the neurons. Sassi et al. (2005) found evidence of neuronal abnormalities in the prefrontal cortex of young people with bipolar disorder – similar to those found in adults with the disorder. Because this was found in both groups, they concluded that this damage was unlikely to represent long-term degenerative processes, and was more likely to reflect an underdevelopment of dendritic connections and synaptic connections. By contrast, Nugent et al. (2006) found evidence of neuronal damage in adults in parts of the brain, including the amygdala and hippocampus. These structures within the limbic system contribute to control over emotions and emotional behaviour. They suggested that repeated stress and elevated glucocorticoid secretion may have contributed to neuronal damage, and dysfunctional processing of these brain areas. The damage to these and other neurons appears to lead to marked cognitive decrements in individuals with bipolar disorder including deficits in executive functioning and verbal memory (Sobczak et al. 2002).

Psychoanalytic explanations

Psychoanalysts view mania as an extreme defence mechanism to counter unpleasant emotional states or unacceptable impulses. Katan (1953), for example, suggested that as periods of mania frequently follow states of depression, the conflict in mania may be of a similar nature to that in depression. People who pass from depression into mania maintain their preoccupation with a real or imagined loss. In the manic state, this anxiety is externalized. Aggressive drive is directed outwards, and the individual reacts to external objects in the same manner as introjection directs anger inwards in depression.

Cognitive models

The cognitive model of unipolar depression has been adapted to explain bipolar problems by two research groups. Newman et al. (2002) suggested that schemata can act in a 'bidirectional' manner in people with bipolar disorder. A schema related to being loved, for example, may have two poles – 'I am totally unlovable' versus 'Everybody loves me.' Depending on mood and any relevant life-events, both positive and negative, either one of these poles may be activated. A second cognitive model (Lam et al. 2003) suggested two key beliefs underpin the condition:

- The ability to achieve goals – 'If I try hard enough, I should be able to excel at anything I attempt.'
- A lack of dependence on others – 'I do not need the approval of other people to be happy.'

According to Lam, success in achieving goals leads to euphoria, and a positive feedback loop in which vulnerable individuals continue to try to achieve different goals in an attempt to maintain or enhance the positive emotional state they have achieved through their success. In order to do so, their behaviour becomes increasingly goal-driven and the views of others are disregarded. Failure to achieve their goals results in low mood and a downward cycle of behaviour. Countering this model were the findings of Scott et al. (2000) who found people with bipolar disorder (while neither depressed nor manic) reported higher levels of interpersonal dependence and stronger needs for social approval than controls. Of course, it is possible that these needs differ at times of depression or mania.

As in psychoanalytic models, the third cognitive model of Winters and Neale (1985) suggested mania is a defence reaction against depression, arguing that a combination of low self-esteem and unrealistic standards of success may drive both depressive and manic episodes. According to Winters and Neale, when individuals with this constellation of cognitive schemata experience an adverse event, they experience either the emotions of depression and cognitions related to low self-esteem, or a defensive reaction against them, in which they adopt the *manic disguise* through which they report normal self-esteem levels. Why such individuals adopt differing strategies at different times is unclear. However, it may be a result of the acceptability of each response to those around the affected individual. Where the expression of negative emotions is unacceptable, they may adopt a manic coping style, which may be rewarded by continued or even increased social contact with important others. Despite this social reinforcement, however, the individual may eventually be unable to continue with these behaviours, and their depression may 'break through'. They then swing into a depressive episode.

In one of the few experimental tests of the manic defence hypothesis, Lyon et al. (1999) compared the attributions made by people with bipolar disorder who were either manic or depressed and 'normal' controls, in response to hypothetical positive and negative events. Both groups of people with bipolar disorder attributed personal responsibility for more negative events and for fewer positive events than those in the control group. By contrast, when asked to endorse a number of positive and negative attributes as descriptors or 'self', both controls and people with mania endorsed largely positive items. Those in the depressed group endorsed mostly negative items. On a subsequent memory test of these words, however, people who were both manic and depressed recalled more negative words than the normal controls. Lyon and colleagues took this pattern of results to indicate that while people with mania explicitly made positive attributions about themselves, underlying this was a set of negative beliefs about self: the manic defence.

Treatment of bipolar disorder

Lithium therapy

Standard antidepressants are typically not used in the treatment of bipolar disorder, as they may provoke rapid mood swings rather than stabilize mood (Keck et al. 2007). Instead, lithium bicarbonate is the main treatment of choice to minimize mood swings. Lithium typically achieves this within 5 to 14 days in about 60 per cent of cases, and has to be taken continually to minimize risk of the onset of depression or mania. Suppes et al. (1991) reported relapse rates 28 times higher among individuals who stopped taking lithium when not experiencing symptoms than those who continued its use. How it achieves these therapeutic gains is unclear. It may act on all three processes that appear to influence mood: increasing serotonin activity, regulating the activity of second messengers, and/or correcting sodium and potassium activity within the neuron (e.g. Huang et al. 2007).

Despite its therapeutic potential, the effectiveness of lithium in clinical practice has been less than was hoped for, possibly because of poor adherence to recommended treatment regimes. Between 18 and 53 per cent of those receiving treatment do not adhere to the recommended regime (Guscott and Taylor 1994). Reasons for this include side-effects of weight gain, problems with coordination and tremor, excessive thirst and memory disturbances. Psychological factors include a dislike of medication controlling mood, feeling well and seeing no need for medication, and missing the highs of hypomania. In addition, many users complain of a 'damping down' of all emotions all the time, which they find problematic. A further caution is that the window between ineffective and toxic doses of lithium is narrow. Too high a dose will result in lithium intoxication, the consequences of which include nausea, vomiting, tremors, kidney dysfunction and, potentially, death. Accordingly, levels of lithium have to be regularly monitored by blood testing, a further disincentive to adherence.

A final aspect of research into the effectiveness of lithium has revealed how a surprisingly large number of psychosocial factors moderate its effectiveness. Kleindienst et al. (2005) found that high social status, good family support, and adherence to taking the medication each contributed independently and positively to the effectiveness of lithium therapy. By contrast, living in a high expressed emotion environment (see Chapter 6), neurotic personality traits, and stressors including unemployment and other adverse life-events, contributed to a poor response to lithium.

Cognitive behavioural approaches

The biological model of bipolar disorder has been dominant for some years, and it is only recently that attempts to change the course of the disorder using cognitive behavioural methods have been attempted. The main psychotherapeutic approach has involved the use of psycho-educational programmes to prepare people to cope with relapse. In one evaluation of this approach, Scott et al. (2001) randomly allocated people with bipolar disorder into treatment with lithium either alone or in combination with cognitive therapy. The cognitive therapy involved three elements:

- an educational phase to prepare people for the cognitive approach
- a focus on cognitive behavioural methods of symptom management including establishing regular activity patterns and time management, as well as challenging dysfunctional thoughts
- anti-relapse techniques involving developing strategies for managing medication, coping strategies to deal with stress, or seeking help at times of the onset of signs of relapse.

Each intervention lasted six months. By this time, those in the combined intervention showed more improvements on measures of general functioning and depression than those in the drug treatment group. The data on relapse were equally impressive. Those who received the combined intervention were 60 per cent less likely to relapse than those in the drug-only condition. Lam et al. (2003) found that cognitive therapy plus drug therapy also proved more effective than drug therapy alone. Over a one-year follow-up, those who received the additional intervention experienced fewer relapses and hospitalizations, with relapse rates of 44 per cent in the cognitive therapy group and 75 per cent in the drug-only group. Subsequent analysis showed a reduction of effect over time, with smaller (but still significant) gains maintained to three-year follow-up (Lam et al. 2005). A further approach to working with individuals has involved the use of mindfulness, which has been shown to reduce anxiety and residual depressive symptoms between acute episodes over a short period (Williams et al. 2008). More studies are required to determine its impact on relapse rates.

A second therapeutic approach has involved working with families – justified by reports such as Kleindienst et al. (2005) – who showed the role of family dynamics in relapse. Miklowitz et al. (2003) reported an intervention designed to improve communication, problem-solving and coping strategies training within the family, comparing this with standard care and a brief two-session family intervention. At two-year follow-up, those receiving the family therapy experienced fewer relapses than the standard care group (71 per cent versus 47 per cent). The benefits were greater for those living in a high expressed emotion environment. Rea et al. (2003) compared family and individual psycho-educational interventions and found that the family intervention was superior in the long term. Relapse rates were 60 per cent among those who received the individual intervention and 28 per cent of those who received the family intervention.

9.5 Chapter summary

1 Major depression involves significant psychological impairment lasting at least two weeks. About one-third of the people who become depressed will remain depressed one year later.

2 Genetic factors contribute to the risk of depression.

3 Serotonin dysregulation may result in depression as a result of a loss of control over a number of brain systems, including those mediated by norepinephrine and dopamine.

4 Socio-cultural explanations of depression focus on differences in stress and coping across social groups.

5 Psychodynamic explanations consider depression to result from the symbolic loss of love or esteem, and internalization of negative feelings towards the responsible person.

6 Behavioural theories suggest that depression is the result of a lack of social reinforcement.

7 Cognitive theories consider negative automatic thoughts and dysfunctional schemata to be causal.

8 Both pharmacological and cognitive interventions appear to be equally effective in the short-term treatment of depression. Cognitive interventions may be more effective in the long term. Mindfulness may provide an effective treatment for people with recurrent depression.

9 St John's wort may prove an effective natural therapy.

10 ECT may be effective for some 'treatment-resistant cases', but 'maintenance ECT' remains controversial.

▶ 11 While individuals with serious mental health problems may be at increased risk of suicide, so are individuals without such disorders.

12 In adults, the primary trigger to a suicide attempt is interpersonal problems.

13 Freud considered suicide to be an attempt at revenge on a hated individual.

14 Cognitive explanations suggest that poor problem-solving skills and feelings of being worthless and rejected combined with situational stress, emotional confusion and high levels of physiological arousal place an individual at risk of committing suicide.

15 Interventions that increase problem-solving skills appear to reduce the risk of suicide.

16 SAD appears to result from disordered melatonin and circadian rhythms.

17 Bright light therapy appears to be the most effective treatment for SAD.

18 Bipolar disorder is the result of neural mechanisms involved in the transmission of information along the neuronal axis.

19 Cognitive models provide a psychological explanation for the development of bipolar disorder.

20 The primary treatment of the disorder involves lithium medication, although cognitive behavioural and family interventions also appear to be of significant benefit.

9.6 For discussion

1 Jacobson and Hollon (1996) argued that the short-term findings of the NIMH depression study were flawed as a result of the inexpert implementation of cognitive therapy. Given the spread, and possible dilution, of therapist skills away from centres of excellence, is this an argument for the use of pharmacological therapies in preference to the psychotherapies?

2 Consider why the relapse rate among people with depression treated with antidepressants is significantly higher than that among people treated with cognitive therapy.

3 Is SADness in winter a common phenomenon? If so, why?

9.7 Key terms

Glucocorticoid a corticosteroid. Has anti-inflammatory and immunosuppressive effect.

Interpersonal psychotherapy a form of therapy focusing exclusively on changing interpersonal problems that contribute to mental health problems.

9.8 Further reading

Clark, D., Beck, A. and Alford, B. (1999) *Scientific Foundations of Cognitive Theory and Therapy of Depression*. New York: Wiley.

DeRubeis, R.J., Gelfand, L.A., Tang, T.Z. et al. (1999) Medications versus cognitive behavior therapy for severely depressed outpatients: mega-analysis of four randomized comparisons, *American Journal of Psychiatry*, 156: 1007–13.

Hofmann, S.G., Sawyer, A.T., Witt, A.A. and Oh, D. (2010) The effect of mindfulness-based therapy on anxiety and depression: a meta-analytic review, *Journal of Consulting and Clinical Psychology*, 78: 169–83.

Lyon, H.M., Startup, M. and Bentall, R.P. (1999) Social cognition and the manic defense: attributions, selective attention, and self-schema in bipolar affective disorder, *Journal of Abnormal Psychology*, 108: 273–82.

Power, M.J. (2005) Psychological approaches to bipolar disorders: a theoretical critique, *Clinical Psychology Review*, 25: 1101–22.

Sohn, C.H. and Lam, R.W. (2005) Update on the biology of seasonal affective disorder, *CNS Spectrum*, 10: 635–46.

Wells, D. (2008) *Metacognitive Therapy for Anxiety and Depression*. London: Guilford Press.

The following websites also have information about depression, its treatment, and people's experiences of it:

www.depression.com/
www.bipolaraware.co.uk/
www.mdf.org.uk/
www.sada.org.uk/
www.depressionalliance.org/

Trauma-related conditions

Chapter contents

This chapter focuses on three types of problems that may occur as a result of significant trauma experienced by the individual either as an adult or child. The first, post-traumatic stress disorder (PTSD), is widely acknowledged as a natural response to being involved in or seeing highly traumatic events. The other two conditions explored in the chapter are rather more controversial. Indeed, their very existence has been called into question. The chapter explores evidence relating to two apparent responses to childhood trauma: hidden and recovered memories, and dissociative identity disorder (DID), previously known as multiple personality. By the end of the chapter, you should have an understanding of:

- The nature and treatment of post-traumatic stress disorder
- The controversy surrounding 'recovered memories'
- The controversy surrounding dissociative identity disorder
- Treatment approaches used in DID.

10.1 Post-traumatic stress disorder (PTSD)

The DSM-IV-TR criteria for a diagnosis of PTSD are that the individual has experienced or witnessed an event that involved actual or threatened death or serious injury, or a threat to the physical integrity of self or others, and that their immediate response involved intense fear, helplessness or horror. In the longer term, the individual must have experienced three clusters of symptoms for one month or more:

- *Intrusive memories*: The trauma is re-experienced through intrusive thoughts, flashbacks or nightmares. Such review may be deliberate as the individual ruminates about the traumatic event. Images may also spring unbidden to mind, in the form of flashbacks. These images often feel as real as the event, but may be fragmentary or partial. Emotions associated with the trauma may be relived with similar intensity to those felt at the time. Images are often described as if being in a film of the incident. Initially, the person may feel they are actually 'in' the film: as they recover, they feel they are watching the film as an outside observer. That is, they begin, almost literally, to feel more detached from the trauma.
- *Avoidance*: This may involve mental defence mechanisms including being unable to recall aspects of the trauma, emotional numbness, or detachment from others, as well as physically avoiding reminders of the trauma.
- *Arousal*: Persistent feelings of over-arousal that may be evidenced by irritability, being easily startled or hypervigilant, suffering insomnia, or having difficulty concentrating.

The triggers of PTSD vary widely, and include war experiences, childhood sexual and physical abuse, adult rape, and natural and technological disasters. Perhaps the most frequent cause of PTSD is road traffic accidents: about 20 per cent of those involved develop some degree of PTSD (Ehlers et al. 1998). About 1 per cent of men and 2 per cent of women in the general population will have PTSD at any one time (e.g. Perkonigg et al. 2000). Prevalence rates among groups that regularly encounter traumatic events are much higher. Bennett et al. (2004), for example, found a prevalence rate of 22 per cent among emergency ambulance personnel, rates among combat veterans from Vietnam are as high as 30 per cent for men and 27 per cent for women (Kulka et al. 1990), while rates of PTSD among child soldiers in Africa approach 60 per cent (Ovuga et al. 2008). PTSD often begins within a few weeks of the precipitating event, but can be triggered by further trauma or life-events as diverse as trauma anniversaries, inter-personal losses, or changes in health status some time after the originating event. Of the three key symptoms, re-experiencing appears to decrease most rapidly. People in whom hyperarousal is the dominant symptom appear to have the worst prognosis (Schell et al. 2004). According to Freedy et al. (1992), an adult's risk for distress will increase as the number of the following 'risk' factors increases:

- female gender
- aged 40 to 60 years old
- little previous experience or training relevant to coping with disaster
- low socio-economic status

- for women, the presence of a spouse at the time of the trauma, especially if he is significantly distressed
- psychiatric history
- severe exposure to the disaster, especially injury, life threat and extreme loss
- living in a highly disrupted or traumatized community
- secondary stress

Here is the story of Ron, which shows how both the situation and the reaction of the people around him can contribute to the development of PTSD.

At the time this happened, I was working in a small hut on an industrial estate. They had been building some more units and had a crane on a lorry to lift things around the site. This was right next to our office. You couldn't see it, because there were no windows on that side of the hut, but you knew it was there . . . I don't know why, but on the day of the accident they were using the crane without stabilizing it by putting the legs onto the ground. The upshot of this was that the crane toppled over and fell onto the building I was in. The first we were aware of things was a lot of shouting and mechanical noises we now know were it toppling. Then there was a great crash and the arm of the crane smashed through the building. I was in there with my mate. Amazingly, neither of us were actually hit by the thing. But we were both trapped by debris from the building. I think I was knocked out for a while because I cannot remember in detail what happened, but it could only have been for a minute or two. I wasn't hurt too badly, but I was trapped. The worst part of it all, was just having to wait to get out. I was frightened that the gas pipes were fractured and the image of dying in a fire went through my mind. I hate being unable to move and all sorts of things went through my head about what would happen to me while I couldn't move. I felt really frightened until I could hear people coming to dig us out, and they lifted the heavy stuff off me and I could move . . .

Once I was out, I went to the sick bay and was sent home. I told them I was OK, just 'cos I wanted to get home and get out of it. I was driven home and spent the rest of the day like a zombie. I just phased out. I didn't want to talk about it. Kept myself to myself. I slept OK. I hate missing work so I went in the next day. My mates took me to look at the hut, and they were saying how lucky we were to get out alive. Everyone I met said the same thing! I know they were being friendly, but that made things worse, and I began to think about things more and more. I felt shaky and sick . . . In the end, I had to go home.

The nightmares began a couple of days later. I dreamt that I was in the building – this time I was watching the crane fall even though I didn't in real life and felt trapped as it hit. Each dream was terrifying and I woke up sweating and breathing hard. I could dream two or three times a night. I had to get up and watch TV, have a cup of tea and a fag to help me calm down after them . . . I couldn't go back to sleep. I took about eight or nine weeks off work because of all this. I was just too knackered to work.

I was also pretty uptight during this time. I'm usually very easy going. But I ran into problems with the wife because I was so difficult to live with . . . The dreams gradually got better and I forced myself to go back to work. I had a few panic attacks when I went back to start with because I was working in a temporary building which had no windows, so I panicked at the thought of things that were happening outside. The new office has large windows, and that's OK for me now.

9/11 and PTSD

Following the destruction of the World Trade Center buildings by Al Qaeda on 9 September 2001 a number of studies examined the psychological impact of this very public traumatic event. Galea et al. (2003) conducted psychiatric telephone surveys one, four and six months after the event throughout the population of New York. The prevalence of 'probable PTSD' directly related to the attacks declined from 7.5 per cent one month after the event to 0.6 per cent five months later. Symptoms were highest among people who were directly affected by the attacks – but a significant number of people not directly affected also met criteria for a diagnosis. Predictors of PTSD symptoms included worries about future terrorist attacks, reduced self-confidence and feelings of personal control, guilt/shame and helplessness/anger, and low levels of social support (e.g. Simeon et al. 2005). More frequent viewing of television images was associated with a higher risk for PTSD and depression (Ahern et al. 2002). People who both watched the events on television and knew someone involved in them were at particularly high risk of PTSD and depression. One key image that seemed to influence rates of PTSD was that of people 'falling or jumping' from the building. The prevalence of PTSD among individuals who repeatedly saw this image was 17.4 per cent: 6.2 per cent of viewers who did not see this image developed PTSD.

The attack also increased risk for a number of mental health problems, including agoraphobia, separation anxiety and PTSD among children in New York (Hoven et al. 2005). Direct exposure to events, exposure of a family member, and a prior history of trauma increased the risk of problems. As with adults, exposure to events through the television contributed to risk for PTSD. Lengua et al. (2005) found that 8 per cent of the children in their sample of children in Seattle, who had only seen events on the television, met criteria 'consistent with PTSD'. As in the Hoven study, girls experienced more emotional problems than boys.

Aetiology of PTSD

Biological factors

The brain systems involved in PTSD are thought to be those involved in processing emotions and memory, in particular, the amygdala and hippocampus. The hippocampus is responsible for storing and retrieving the memories. It is linked to the amygdala, the area of the brain particularly associated with the formation of conditioned fear responses. Both the hippocampus and the amygdala are activated either in establishing memories of the event and its associated emotions, or in recalling them.

Two stress hormones are implicated in establishing traumatic memories: norepinephrine and cortisol. Increases in these hormones generally enhance memory, although the levels that may occur at times of traumatic stress may actually be toxic to brain tissue and result in neuronal death, damaging the memory systems. The hippocampus, for example, may experience damage following severe trauma, leading to reductions in its size which do not recover following treatment or resolution of the trauma (Bonne et al. 2008). This may result in problems in working memory (Shaw et al. 2009) and an exaggerated conditioned fear response (Bonne et al. 2008). Norepinephrine release has been found to produce high states of arousal and fear, and intense visual flashbacks in some, but by no means all, cases (Leskin et al. 1998). Brewin (2001) speculated that flashbacks may occur when information is transferred from the amygdala to the hippocampus. The sympathetic nervous system (see Chapter 3), controlled by the hypothalamus and levels of norepinephrine, is responsible for the high levels of physiological arousal associated with the condition. Genetic factors may influence dopamine and norepinephrine reactivity in response to trauma, and hence risk of PTSD (Mustapić et al. 2007; Voisey et al. 2009).

Conditioning models

The conditioning model of PTSD (Foa and Kozak 1986) is based on Mowrer's (1947) two-factor theory. That is, it considers PTSD to be a classically conditioned emotional response. According to Foa and Kozak, associations are stored in neural networks (see Chapter 2), linking emotions, cognitions and perceptual memories. As such, re-exposure to similar contexts or stimuli evokes memories of the event and the conditioned fear response. Avoidance of reminders of the trauma not only prevents distress, but also prevents habituation of the fear response to stimuli associated with the event (Mowrer 1947). As a result, occasional and accidental encounters with relevant stimuli result in flashbacks and other cued memories. Chemtob et al. (1988) proposed a similar model to that of Foa, but suggested that memories of the incident are maintained within a neural network which is permanently activated (as opposed to being activated by environmental and emotional cues) and causes the individual to function in 'survival mode', resulting in the hyperarousal symptoms of PTSD.

A schema model of PTSD

The first schema model of PTSD, developed by Horowitz (1986), was strongly influenced by psychoanalytic theory. He proposed that PTSD occurs when the individual is involved in events that are so horrific they cannot be reconciled with their view (schema) of the world. The belief that one may die in an incident, for example, may shatter previous beliefs of invulnerability. The individual feels unsafe and vulnerable. To avoid this ego-damaging discrepancy, defence mechanisms of numbing or denial are evoked. However, these compete with a second innate drive, known as the completion tendency. This requires the individual to integrate memories of trauma into existing world models or schemata: either to make sense of the memories according to currently held beliefs about the world or to change those beliefs.

The completion tendency maintains trauma-related information in active memory in an attempt to process it. Defence mechanisms try to stop these memories entering consciousness. The symptoms the individual experiences are the result of fluctuating strengths of these competing processes. When the completion tendency breaks through the defence mechanisms, memories intrude into consciousness in the form of flashbacks, nightmares and unwanted thoughts or emotional memories. When defence mechanisms are effective, the individual experiences periods of numbness or denial. Once trauma-related information is integrated into general belief systems, the symptoms cease.

Stein, J.A., Nyamathi, A. and Zane, J.I. (2009) Situational, psychosocial, and physical health-related correlates of HIV/AIDS risk behaviors in homeless men, *American Journal of Men's Health*, 3, 25–35.

PTSD can have a significant impact on behaviour, including behaviour that potentially places an individual at significant health risk. This study explored examined factors that contributed to the development of PTSD and the relationship between PTSD and risk behaviour in a group of homeless men, living in the Skid Row area of Los Angeles. The study used the biopsycho-social model to determine factors that contribute to poor mental and physical health and related emotional and behavioural states. It examined the impact of four factors (poor social support, quality of housing, duration of homelessness and ethnicity) on emotional health (PTSD, distress) and physical health, and their joint influence on injection drug use (IDU), risky sexual behaviour and health care utilization.

Method

Participants were 664 men homeless men taking part in a study evaluating the impact of an intervention to encourage completion of a hepatitis vaccination programme. Recruitment involved responding to posters and/or talks given in homeless shelters throughout the Skid Row area. People were eligible for the study if they were aged 18–65 years, willing to undergo hepatitis antibody testing, take part in the vaccination programme, and had no history of hepatitis vaccination. Their average age was 42 years. Seventy-one per cent were African-American, 14 per cent white, and 13 per cent Hispanic. The data reported in this study were from the baseline measures.

Questionnaires completed included:

- *Social support*: the social support scale of the RAND Medical Outcomes Study SF-36 questionnaire.
- *Severity of homelessness*: the number of periods of homelessness and total years of homelessness.
- *Poor quality housing*: defined as sleeping place in the last 30 days including an abandoned building, car or the street.
- *Post-traumatic stress disorder (PTSD)*: the PTSD Symptoms Checklist.
- *Health status*: included self-assessed health, bodily pain in the past six months, and the 10-item SF-36 physical functioning scale.
- *Emotional distress*: the Mental Health Index (MHI) subscale from the SF-36, assessing mood in the previous four weeks.
- *Injection drug use (IDU)*: risk behaviour in the past 6 months indicated by yes/no responses to injection of various drugs, needle-sharing and having a sex partner who injects drugs.
- *Sexual risk behaviour*: the average number of times per week they had sex without a condom.
- *Health care utilization*: whether they were currently accessing health care and had visited a clinic or private doctor in the past 6 months.

Results

Following bivariate analysis (correlations), path analysis using the EQS structural equation programme was used to determine the relationship between these variables.

Highlights within the correlation table were the following findings:

- Higher social support was associated with being younger, better health, less emotional distress, less IDU and better housing quality.
- Chronic homelessness was associated with PTSD, poor health, emotional distress, IDU, sexual risk behaviour and being white.
- PTSD was associated with poor health, emotional distress, IDU, sexual risk behaviour, more use of health care services and being white.
- Emotional distress was associated with greater IDU and poor housing quality, and was most prevalent among the white participants.

The final predictive structural equation model is presented in Figure 10.1, after non-significant paths and covariances were deleted.

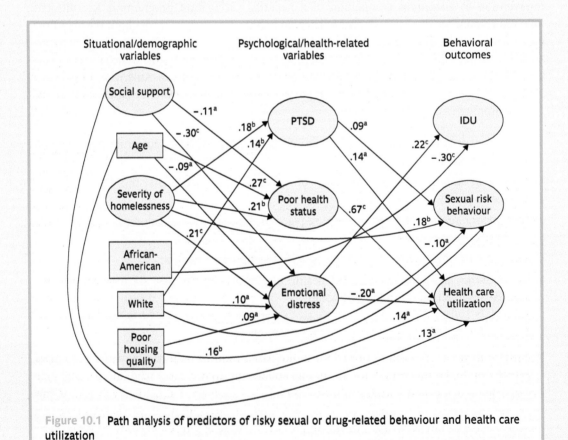

Figure 10.1 **Path analysis of predictors of risky sexual or drug-related behaviour and health care utilization**

This shows that key predictors of PTSD were the severity of homelessness and being white. PTSD, in turn, was predictive of both health care utilization and risky sexual behaviour. By contrast, more general distress was linked to poor housing, being white, severity of homelessness, age and poor social support, and was linked to risky drug behaviour and (negatively) to health care utilization. There were no links between sexual and drug behaviour.

Discussion

This was a cross-sectional study, so direct cause and effect between the various variables cannot be unequivocally determined. To achieve this would require longitudinal analysis (as presumably the authors intend to do later in the study). Despite the over-riding importance of homelessness on risky behaviours, PTSD and emotional distress were linked to risky sexual and drug-related behaviour respectively. Despite these meaningful findings, many of the findings raise questions. Why, for example, is being white associated with emotional distress and PTSD, while being black is not? Does this reflect differences in why these groups tend to become homeless? Why do people with PTSD engage in one risky behaviour (unprotected sex), but not others such as using UDI; and why is the opposite constellation found for people with psychological distress? Much more research is needed to disentangle the findings of this study.

A process model of PTSD

Brewin (2001) added a second level of information processing to the model proposed by Horowitz. According to Brewin, the individual can both deliberately choose to address their traumatic memories, and memories may also come to consciousness without deliberate recall. These processes involve two differing memory systems:

- *Verbally accessible memories (VAMs)*: this system involves memories of the incident that can be deliberately accessed. They tend to be fragmented, based on normal recall processes, and therefore can be changed as the person processes information about the traumatic incident. They may, for example, become less traumatic as the individual reframes the incident as being less threatening than they initially thought; they may become more traumatic if they later consider the event to have been more personally threatening.

- *Situationally accessible memories (SAMs)*: these memories cannot be deliberately accessed, but come to consciousness in response to cues that remind the individual of the incident – including activation of the VAM system. They may also occur when the brain is not actively processing information – most commonly at night in the form of nightmares. They feel as if they are 'in the event' and cannot be deliberately changed.

According to Brewin, resolution of PTSD requires both sets of memories to enter the normal memory system. By this time, they are still accessible but do not carry the high levels of emotional content associated with both VAMs and SAMs. Resolution of VAMs involves deliberate recall and reframing of information. This leads to an integration of the VAMs with their pre-existing beliefs and models of the world, and restores a sense of safety and control over both self and the world. Activation of the SAMs is also required, and the SAMs gradually change over time and become less emotion-laden and frightening. Changes in SAM representations may occur through the integration of new, non-threatening information or, more frequently, through the creation of new SAMs. As SAMs may be triggered through conscious processing of VAMs, this process may occur naturally. Both these processes are similar to the completion tendency described by Horowitz. Thus, the model includes elements of the schema theory of Horowitz, as PTSD resolves when memories of the event are integrated within pre-existing memory structures and elements of Foa's fear network in terms of the representation of memories.

Empirical investigation of these processes can be difficult. However, Brewin and colleagues have been able to find differences in the types of memories people provide from VAMs and SAMs. In two studies, Hellawell and Brewin (2002, 2004) asked people to recall and write a narrative of the trauma that led to their PTSD and then to identify which parts of the narrative were based on flashback memories (SAMs) and which were based on 'ordinary' memory (VAMs). In the first study, they found that narrative involving flashback memory was associated with higher levels of autonomic and behavioural arousal (as observed by a researcher) than writing based on ordinary memories. In the second study, they found that writing based on flashback memories was more detailed, made more mentions of death, fear, helplessness and horror. It was also more likely to be written in the present tense than memory sections written from ordinary memory. By contrast, sections written from ordinary memory tended to mention more 'secondary' emotions such as guilt and anger, which may have been experienced following the incident rather than at the time of its occurrence.

Brewin suggested that the hippocampus is the neural centre involved in processing VAMs. The amygdala may be involved in processing the more emotionally laden SAMs. Brewin, like Horowitz, suggested that emotional processing results from a drive towards resolution of conflict between previously held schemata and new information. The activation of SAMs provides the detailed information needed to allow cognitive readjustment to the trauma. Once integration has been achieved, the symptoms of PTSD will resolve.

A psychosocial model

Rather than focus on the immediate cognitive processes involved in PTSD, Joseph et al. (1995) explored a wider set of factors that influence the development and course of the disorder. These included:

- *Event stimuli*: iconic representations of the event held in immediate memory.
- *Event cognitions*: memories that provide the basis for re-experiencing phenomena or intrusive memories – Brewin's SAMs.
- *Appraisals and reappraisals*: the individual's thoughts about the incident – Brewin's VAMs. These involve interpretation of information relevant to the incident, drawing on past representations and experiences. They may take the form of automatic schemata linked to strong emotional states triggered by stimuli associated with the trauma or more considered attempts to think through and perhaps reappraise the meaning of the event. Key appraisals that influence the outcome are those related to guilt, control and self-blame.
- *Coping attempts*: flashbacks and emotional memories of the event may result in coping attempts intended to minimize emotional distress. These usually take the form of avoidance of reminders, memories or similar emotions and activities associated with the event. They may also involve attempts at inhibiting unwanted memories.

- *Personality*: this will influence the type of cognitions and emotions experienced at the time of a traumatic incident, the appraisals made in response to it, and subsequent coping strategies. Accordingly, personality has a significant impact on whether or not the individual develops PTSD and its course.
- *Social support*: an important moderator of the response to trauma: perhaps because talking to other people helps the individual assign new meanings to the event and provides support for the expression of negative emotions.

According to Joseph et al. (1995), traumatic events result in immediate cognitions that give rise to extreme emotional arousal. This arousal interferes with the processing of these cognitions. As a consequence, they are held in specific memory networks as outlined by Horowitz. These form the basis of the re-experiencing phenomena, and are influenced by the nature of the trauma, the core assumptions and beliefs an individual has about the world, elements of the situation which presented the most threat, and the personality of the individual. In other words, the nature of the post-traumatic symptoms will reflect both the nature of the trauma to which an individual was exposed, and the nature of the individual.

Subsequent reappraisal of the situation, envisaging more or less threatening outcomes, may also influence outcome. If an individual reflects on events, and thinks that they were less threatening than they appeared at the time, they may experience fewer symptoms and their PTSD will have a shorter duration than if they do not reduce, or even increase, the level of threat experienced. Attributions of failing to take control of an event ('I could have done something to stop it – and I didn't') are linked to the emotions of shame and guilt, and increase risk for PTSD. Andrews et al. (2000), for example, found shame and anger to be key predictors of levels of trauma one month after experiencing a violent crime, and shame to be predictive of symptoms six months following the incident. Similar findings have been reported following sexual abuse (Feiring et al. 2002) and being stalked (Kamphuis et al. 2003). Together with feelings of loss of core beliefs and values, distrust, alienation from others and a sense of being permanently damaged, these responses have been termed the 'experience of mental death', which Ebert and Dyck (2004) labelled the core feature of PTSD.

The appraisals an individual makes may also influence their coping strategies. Strong feelings of guilt may be associated with intrusive thoughts and images. Shame may evoke attempts at avoidance and denial – which may result in a paradoxical increase in symptoms. Beliefs that an individual is unable to cope with strong emotions may also lead to avoidance of potentially stressful situations and prevent the individual from learning that they can, indeed, cope with such emotions. Good social support will generally lessen the symptoms of PTSD, partly perhaps, because this supports rehearsal and positive reappraisal of event-related cognitions (Joseph et al. 1996). In one study of this phenomenon, Andrews et al. (2003) measured levels of available positive support and negative responses from other people in both male and female victims of violent crime. Men reported significantly fewer negative responses from family and friends, which contributed to lower levels of PTSD symptoms six months after the event.

Finally, appraisals and coping efforts may be influenced by trait, personality, variables. Two personality constructs appear associated with the development of PTSD are neuroticism (Bennett et al. 2001) and alexithymia (Fukunishi et al. 1996). Neuroticism may increase risk because it is indicative of a propensity to appraise events as negative and threatening, and to dwell on such events. Alexithymia involves a paucity of emotional experience and awareness, with an associated poverty of imagination and a tendency to focus upon the tangible and mundane (especially perhaps the physical symptoms of emotional responses). This may inhibit the processing of emotional experiences into general schemata and place the individual at risk for recurrent memories of the frightening event.

Stop and think...

The outcomes of traumatic events, or even the experience of PTSD, are not all negative. Calhoun and Tedeschi (1999) identified a more positive outcome, they termed post-traumatic growth. These changes include improved relationships, new possibilities for one's life, a greater appreciation for life, a greater sense of personal strength and spiritual development. People who experience post-traumatic growth frequently report an increased sense of their own capacities to survive and cope with whatever life throws at them. They also may find themselves becoming more comfortable with intimacy and having a greater sense of compassion for others who experience life difficulties. A commonly reported change is that people begin to value the smaller things in life more and also to consider important changes in the religious, spiritual and existential beliefs they may hold. They may also change their life goals in the light of their traumatic experience.

Most psychological research and interventions in relation to traumatic issues focus on pathology. Perhaps both should focus more on understanding and facilitating positive growth . . .

Treatment of post-traumatic stress disorder

Preventing PTSD by psychological debriefing

Psychological debriefing is a single-session interview conducted immediately following a traumatic event intended to help those involved cope with their emotional responses to the trauma and prevent the development of PTSD. It involves encouraging the individual to talk through the event and their emotional reactions to it in a detailed and systematic manner. It is thought to aid integration of incident memories into the general memory system. Debriefing is now regularly offered following traumatic incidents, despite increasing questions about its effectiveness. Rose et al. (2002), for example, concluded from their meta-analysis of four well-conducted randomized controlled trials that debriefing may not only be ineffective in preventing PTSD, it can actually increase risk for the disorder. None of the studies they reviewed found a reduced risk for PTSD in the three to four months following the incident. The two studies that reported longer-term findings found that those who received debriefing had nearly twice the risk of developing PTSD than those who did not receive the intervention. That is, debriefing seems to inhibit long-term recovery from psychological trauma. A number of explanations have been proposed for these findings, although each remains speculative:

- 'Secondary traumatization' may occur as a result of further imaginal exposure to a traumatic incident within a short time of the event.

- Debriefing may 'medicalize' normal distress, and increase the expectancy of developing psychological symptoms in those who would otherwise not have done so.
- Debriefing may prevent the potentially protective responses of denial and distancing that may occur in the immediate aftermath of a traumatic incident.

Although psychodynamic approaches have been used to some benefit with people with PTSD (Marmar 1991), the most frequently used interventions in the treatment of PTSD are based on cognitive behavioural principles.

Exposure techniques

The principles underpinning exposure methods in the treatment of PTSD are that the individual will ultimately benefit from exposure to memories of the event and their associated emotions. The conditioning model suggests that distress lessens as the individual's emotional response to these memories habituates over time. A more cognitive explanation is that exposure leads to reconciliation between memories and the meaning of the traumatic event and pre-existing world schemata. Only by accessing and processing these memories will resolution occur.

Trauma-focused CBT may lead to an initial exacerbation of distress as upsetting images, previously avoided where possible, are deliberately recalled. To minimize this distress and to prevent drop-out from therapy, Leskin et al. (1998) recommended a graded exposure process in which the individual initially talks about particular elements of the traumatic event at a level of detail they choose over several occasions until they no longer respond with a stress response. Any new, and potentially more distressing, memories are avoided at this time, and become the focus of the next levels of intervention. Reactivation of memories by this procedure involves describing the experience in detail, focusing on what happened, the thoughts and emotions experienced at the time, and any memories that the incident triggered. This approach may be augmented by a variety of cognitive behavioural techniques, including relaxation training and cognitive restructuring. Relaxation may help the individual control their arousal at the time of recalling the event or at other times in the day when they are feeling tense or on edge. Cognitive restructuring may help them address any distorted cognitions they had in response to the event and make those thoughts less threatening ('I'm going to die! . . . It felt like I was going to die, but actually that was more my panic than reality . . .'). Wells and Sembi (2004) focused on teaching people to minimize the rumination that can be a particularly distressing element of PTSD by using active distraction techniques.

A number of studies have shown trauma-focused therapy to be superior to no treatment and alternative active interventions including supportive counselling and relaxation therapy without exposure (Bisson et al. 2007). In one such study, Foa et al. (1991) randomly allocated female rape victims to either a waiting list control condition, self-instruction training, supportive counselling or an exposure programme. Participants in each of the active interventions evidenced greater gains than those in the waiting list condition. Immediately following the intervention period, participants in the self-instruction training condition fared best. By three-month follow-up, however, those in the exposure programme reported significantly fewer intrusive memories and less arousal than participants in the other conditions. Similar results were reported by Marks et al. (1996) in a comparison of relaxation, exposure alone, cognitive restructuring alone, and exposure plus cognitive restructuring. By the end of the intervention phase, all the other treatments proved superior to relaxation, with no differences in effectiveness between them. By three- and six-month follow-up, the exposure programme proved superior. It seems that self-instruction and other cognitive techniques may help participants cope with the anxiety and other emotions evoked in the early stages of exposure programmes, while exposure to traumatic memories is critical to long-term benefit. The optimal treatment seems to involve a combination of self-instruction training or other cognitive strategies in the early stages of therapy combined with gradual exposure to traumatic memories.

Treating people with PTSD may not require large amounts of specialist training. Gillespie et al. (2002) taught health care staff with minimal background in cognitive behavioural therapy how to provide an exposure-based intervention for PTSD in response to a large bomb which exploded in the small Northern Irish town of Omagh in 1998. Staff received a two-day workshop plus telephone contact with an expert in the treatment of PTSD and therapy supervision. The effectiveness of their intervention was similar to those reported in previous studies involving expert therapists.

Eye movement desensitization and reprocessing (EMDR)

The most recent, and controversial, treatment of PTSD, known as EMDR, was discovered by chance by Shapiro (1995). She noticed that while walking in the woods her disturbing thoughts began to disappear, and when recalled were less upsetting than previously. She associated this change with her eyes spontaneously moving rapidly backwards and forwards in an upward diagonal. Since then, the procedure has been developed into a standardized intervention and subject to a number of clinical trials in the treatment of PTSD.

Treatment typically involves recall of target memories by the client as visual images along with a negative cognition that goes with the image, framed in the present tense ('I am terrified'). The client next rates the strength of emotion evoked by this process. They are then asked to track the therapist's finger as it is moved increasingly quickly back and forth across their line of vision. After 24 such movements, the client is instructed to 'Blank it out' or 'Let it go', and asked to rate their level of emotion. This procedure is repeated until the client experiences minimal distress to the presence of the image and negative cognition. If no changes occur, the direction of eye movements is changed.

EMDR incorporates exposure to elements of the trauma stimulus. An important question is therefore whether the addition of the eye movements enhances the effect of exposure. This does not seem to be the case. Bisson and Andrew (2007) used meta-analysis to examine the effectiveness of EMDR in the treatment of PTSD in comparison with no treatment, non-specific treatment and the exposure methods described above. While their analyses indicated a benefit for EMDR when compared with no treatment or non-specific treatments, its benefits were similar to those resulting from exposure approaches.

Pharmacological interventions

A variety of drug types have been used in the treatment of PTSD to some effect, including antidepressant MAOIs, SSRIs and tricyclics (see Chapter 4). Ipser et al. (2006), for example, conducted a meta-analysis on studies of antidepressants in the treatment of PTSD, finding that SSRIs achieved significantly greater improvements than placebo on measures of functioning and the core PTSD symptoms of intrusion and avoidance.

Case formulation

Mr F was a prison officer in a small town in the west of England. At six feet four inches, he was a big strong man, fond of playing rugby for a local team and drinking with his mates. He was happily married with two young children. He had no history of mental health problems, and looking at him one would imagine him as an archetypal 'good coper'. However, his history of PTSD showed that even 'good copers' may develop significant mental health problems.

Long-term antecedents

As is often the case with PTSD, there were very few long-term antecedents for Mr F's development of PTSD. He had no history of mental health problems and was happily married with his wider family also around for support. He was happy at work, and had no work or home-related problems.

Short-term antecedents

The trigger to Mr F's PTSD was a simple event. He was walking a group of prisoners down a flight of steps in an isolated stairwell, when he slipped and fell. Against prison regulations (as a result of his shift being short-staffed), he was on his own in the stairwell with no fellow prison officers. As a consequence, the prisoners took the opportunity to knock him to the ground, and began to beat and kick him around the body and head. The force of his beating was such that he was briefly knocked unconscious. The last thought he remembers before losing consciousness was that he was going to die. He was taken to the prison wing, before being sent home to recover from his injuries.

Over the next few months he experienced a significant number of flashbacks to the incident, feeling the force of the blows to him and experiencing the fear of dying. Many occurred at night, while in bed. Every flashback was terrifying, and in the hour following them he had to get out of bed and try and watch television or read a book to help him calm down. He regularly had two or more flashbacks per night. As a consequence he became increasingly exhausted. In addition, he spent much of the day mulling over the causes and consequence of the attack. He would spend many hours ('A day may disappear') looking out of a house window dwelling on the attack. He believed that both the prisoners were to blame – as they had, he believed, tried to kill him – as well as his fellow prison officers who had allowed the incident to occur. The prison service was unsympathetic to his condition, writing frequent letters asking when he would return to see the prison occupational health physician, threatening to reduce his pay, and so on. He began to believe that these letters were a deliberate form of harrassment.

As a result of these various processes his mood became increasingly depressed. He was able to engage with his wife and son for brief periods in the day – helping prepare breakfast, for example – but found these periods increasingly difficult to manage and he became increasingly isolated even within the family home. He also isolated himself from the home, spending hours away in peaceful places – including local graveyards – dwelling on the events and their consequences. He was unable to go into any area where he believed there would be prison officers or ex-prisoners, as he was unsure how he would be able to cope with the sight of them, expecting to be extremely frightened, but also angry and possibly expressing his anger. In a relatively small town, this severely limited where he was able to go.

Formulation

Mr F had a significant post-traumatic response. The critical factor in its development was his belief that he was going to die as a result of his beating. He continued to hold this belief, believing that it was only the somewhat late intervention by his colleagues that prevented him dying in the incident. This continued catastrophic belief helped maintain his anxieties. His response to the incident was typical, if rather stronger than, most responses in PTSD. He experienced the three key symptoms of PTSD: flashbacks when his mind was unoccupied, pre-occupation and rumination on the originating incident, and heightened arousal. His depression stemmed from the nature of his beliefs, including the belief that some prisoners wanted him dead and that the institution for whom he worked and his work colleagues cared little for his well-being. These beliefs were maintained by his avoidance of colleagues who *did* try to visit him at home following the incident: visits which tailed off over time as they were apparently unwanted. In addition, his rumination constantly focused on his negative beliefs about the incident and how close to death he had been, and his anger towards the prison service. Accordingly, although he chronically ruminated about the incident, he had failed to normalize or reappraise it into something less threatening, both of which may have reduced the frequency and severity of his flashbacks. The time spent dwelling on these negative thoughts combined with exhaustion due to lack of sleep and his dislocation from his family and friends led to depression, and a vicious cycle of rumination, flashbacks, avoidance of positive aspects of life, low mood, rumination . . . and so on.

Intervention

Mr F had severe PTSD and depression (a relatively common co-morbidity). The usual treatment for PTSD involves either exposure or EMDR. Some individuals prefer the latter particularly as if they find it difficult to focus on the distressing issues for a prolonged time or to verbalize their thoughts. However, Mr F was unwilling to utilize either approach. In addition, his belief that he could have died in the incident was unshakeable. Accordingly, initially, he and his therapist took another approach. Instead of focusing on the PTSD symptoms, they focused on reducing his rumination, his depression and avoidance of feared situations. One strategy for this was to plan things to do in the day that broke him out of his ruminations, and began to normalize his day. His daily plans, for example, involved sitting with his family watching television, walking the dog with his wife, and going out for drives or (when they occurred) watching rugby matches with his brother. The aim was to reduce the time he spent ruminating, and provide a number of rewarding/enjoyable experiences each day. In addition, he began a graded exposure to places in the town that he had begun to avoid for fear of meeting ex-cons or colleagues. In preparing for this, he rehearsed how he would respond to seeing such individuals – using relaxation and breathing techniques he was taught, and using self-instruction to calm himself. He also used the relaxation and breathing exercises to help him calm down following any flashbacks he had, particularly at night. This approach took several weeks before he began to feel less depressed and more able to go into town. He also experienced several setbacks when he received letters from the prison service, which he now considered to be a form of harassment. Once he began to feel less depressed and more engaged with his family (including his brother), therapy began to focus on reducing the trauma-related symptoms. As he was already ruminating frequently on the trauma (and he had successfully reduced the time spent ruminating) therapy involved EMDR rather than an exposure programme. This was gradually introduced as his tolerance to the images increased. In addition, he engaged in cognitive therapy, reappraising the role of his colleagues more positively (some had, for example, visited him at home after the incident – so they had shown concern for him). In addition, while he continued to believe that the prisoners who attacked him had wanted him dead, he was able to defuse some of these thought, entertaining the idea that they perhaps wanted to hurt rather than kill him, and that the attack was not personal but one which any officer might have experienced if the occasion presented. Depersonalizing the attack was important as it reduced his feelings of threat and shame ('I was so hated by the prisoners that they wanted to kill me') that had been triggered by the attack. Recovery occurred, but not quickly, and despite normalizing his life away from the prison, Mr F was unable to work at the prison.

10.2 Recovered memory

Since the late 1980s, a number of clinicians have argued that many adults who were traumatized as children had repressed all memories of these events, and that these memories could be recovered only in the course of psychological therapy. In a seminal text, Bass and Davis (1988) argued that such repression is not unusual, and advised therapists to accept their 'recovered memories' of sexual abuse, and to suspend disbelief even if they found some parts of their history doubtful. Memories have been recovered in considerable detail up to 40 years after the alleged trauma. Individuals may describe partial or complete memory loss for periods of months or years while they are growing up. Surveys have found that between 20 and 60 per cent of women in or having completed therapy have reported periods of forgetting some or all of the abuse they have experienced (e.g. Loftus and Ketcham 1994). Individuals identified as abusers, often parents or other family members, frequently deny the episodes and claim that they have been wrongfully accused: that is, that the recovered memories of abuse are false memories. False or true, the impact these accusations can have on families is often profound.

Explanations of recovered memory

The recovered memory phenomenon has engendered considerable controversy and debate. Three differing explanations for this phenomenon have been proposed.

Accurate accounts

Recovered memories are accurate accounts of previously forgotten events, and should be accepted as such even in the absence of corroborative evidence. Explanations of why these memories are forgotten focus on unconscious mechanisms that prevent the laying down of easily retrievable memories at the time of any traumatic incident and problems of recall. The first involves a process known as dissociation. This is an altered state of consciousness in which ordinary perceptual and cognitive functioning is impaired: events feel unreal and distant from the individual. Dissociation may occur during the traumatic experience and act as a defence that prevents the individual from experiencing the full emotional impact of what is happening. Retrieval of associated memories is poor, as little if any ordinary conscious processing took place at encoding. What memories there are may be fragmented, but vivid and intense. Hunter (1997) described three forms of dissociation that have been reported by child abuse victims: (1) out-of-body experiences in which events were seen as happening to someone else who looked like the victim; (2) conscious attempts to 'blank out' memories of the assaults during or after they had happened; and (3) the creation of an imaginary world to which the respondent could escape and feel safe during or after the abuse. Failure to recall events is thought to be the result of denial and long-term dissociation that prevent the retrieval of information once in memory stores.

Illusions

Recovered memories are illusions: false memories resulting from the therapy process itself (Zola 1998). Such memories are 'implanted' by therapists who have decided that the patient is an abuse victim and who use therapeutic techniques to persuade the client to remember these 'forgotten' episodes of abuse in order to 'recover'. The likelihood of suggestive influences leading to memory errors is increased by the perceived authority and trustworthiness of the therapist, and their repetition and plausibility. Perhaps the least plausible of these accounts is the recovery of memories of alien abduction (McNally 2003), although memories of long-term ritual and satanic abuse involving gang rape and ritual (child) murders have proven equally untenable (e.g. Noblitt and Perskin 2000).

Normal forgetting

Recovered memories are not 'special', but are the result of normal forgetting (e.g. Loftus and Ketcham 1994). This explanation may be particularly relevant to single traumatic episodes, but has more difficulty in accounting for the forgetting of repeated traumatic episodes.

Evidence of recovered memory

Protagonists on each side of the debate have interpreted research findings both to support their case and question those who disagree with them. The debate has drawn on research related to normal memory processes as well as more clinical issues.

Age at time of incident

Recovered memories are sometimes described from before the age of 2, and often in significant detail (Loftus and Ketcham 1994). Morton et al. (1995), for example, reported that 26 per cent of allegations involved abuse that began when the claimant was aged between 0 and 2 years old. This, argue opponents of recovered memory, makes such memories unlikely to be accurate. Most people are unable to recollect experiences from the first two to three years of their lives, as the cortical areas that eventually become the sites for permanent memory storage are undergoing a process of maturation at this time that makes them unable to process and store information needed for long-term recall (Bauer 2006).

Evidence of emotionally intense memory distortion

Some clinicians (e.g. Terr 1991) have argued that trauma-related memories are not subject to the normal processes of memory decay and distortion over time, and are therefore more accurate than 'normal' long-term memories. Empirical evidence suggests this may not be the case. Neisser and Harsch (1992), for example, asked students one day after the *Challenger* disaster, in which a space shuttle burst into flames on lift-off, to describe their personal memories of the event. Two years later, when asked to redescribe their memories, the accounts of one-third of the students differed substantially from their initial memories. Of note was that there was little relationship between the accuracy of recalled 'facts' and students' confidence in their ability to recall them. The *Challenger* disaster may not have been sufficiently traumatic for those not directly involved to result in unchangeable memory traces. Whether more salient emotional events can evoke differing memory processes is unclear, although a number of case studies in which long-term emotional memories show discrepancies with actual events suggest not (Loftus and Davis 2006). Of course, this argument may challenge the accuracy of recall of events, but not statements as to whether or not particular incidents actually happened.

Corroboration

Gaining corroborative evidence of child sexual abuse is clearly problematic, and the majority of research focusing on false memories relies on uncorroborated evidence (Loftus and Davis 2006). Nevertheless, Feldman-Summers and Pope (1994) found some degree of corroborative evidence in 47 per cent of the cases they examined, including the abuser acknowledging some or all of the remembered abuse or someone else reporting abuse by the same perpetrator. Similar levels of corroboration, 41 per cent, were reported in an unrelated survey of British clinical psychologists (see Brewin and Andrews 1998).

Conditions of recall

Clearly, if recovered memory is a therapy-generated phenomenon, the majority of memories should reappear during therapy. This does not always appear to be the case. Feldman-Summers and Pope (1994) found that while over half such memories were recovered in the context of therapy, 44 per cent of their respondents stated that recovery had been triggered exclusively in other contexts. By contrast, Goodyear-Smith et al. (1997) reported summary data from several papers indicating that in over 80 per cent of cases of sexual abuse, memories had emerged while complainants were undergoing psychotherapy. Of note, is that memories that occur outside therapy are usually triggered by events that remind the individual of the abuse, are of single incidents, and the memories are instantly recalled in full (Brenneis 2000). By contrast, memories stemming from therapy tend to be fragmented, vague and lacking detail. In addition, the majority of incidents recalled in this way (multiple events beginning in early childhood, involving bodily penetration by male family members), are rarely reported among verified recovered memory cases (Brenneis 2000). Of note also in this context are the findings of Geraerts et al. (2009) who identified two different sub-groups of people who recover memories in different contexts. Those who recalled memories within therapy were found on psychological testing to evidence a heightened susceptibility to the construction of false memories and no tendency to underestimate their prior remembering. By contrast, those who spontaneously recall such events appeared highly susceptible to forgetting prior incidences of remembering, but showed no susceptibility to suggestion. They took this to indicate that spontaneous memories were more likely to be reliable than those which emerged from therapy.

Attempts to forget

A key factor in the repressed memory debate is the assumption that those who remember childhood trauma as an adult have used unconscious coping mechanisms to 'forget' their trauma. If this is the case, then one would assume that a significant percentage of people who undergo other traumas as a child would engage in similar coping strategies and have similar problems of recall. Evidence of accurate recall in adults who experienced being kidnapped, the Holocaust and parental murder as children suggests this does not typically occur (see Zola 1998).

Proponents of the repressed memory hypothesis counter these data by suggesting that sexual abuse is different from other trauma and that it has specific and unique consequences for coping. They argue that because abuse is usually carried out by parents or significant others rather than strangers and occurs in isolation rather than with companions, the effects are unique. One proponent of this argument, Freyd (1996), argued that sexual abuse of children is more than a trauma, it is a betrayal, and that 'betrayal trauma' is more prone to repression than other types of trauma. According to her model, sexual abuse by a trusted caretaker will be more likely to be repressed than sexual abuse by a stranger. Evidence in support of this hypothesis was reported by Pope and Feldman-Summers (1992) who surveyed a representative population of US psychologists. Seventy-nine people reported having been abused at some time: 32 reported forgetting this abuse for a period of time. Of this group, 56 per cent reported that it involved sexual abuse by a relative, while only 37 per cent reported that it involved sexual abuse by a non-relative. While other surveys (e.g. Schultz et al. 2003) have reported similar findings, this result has not always been replicated, including in a sample of adults with documented abuse as children (Goodman et al. 2003).

Evidence of the creation of false traumatic memories

Those who argue against the concept of recovered memory suggest that such memories result from therapists planting suggestions of childhood abuse in people to whom this has not happened. There are many examples of this process occurring outside therapy. Piaget (1954), for example, was able to recall being kidnapped as a 2-year-old in some detail. This, despite the event never having occurred: it was a childhood story told to him by his nurse. A more experimental example of the phenomenon is provided by Loftus and Coan (1998), who asked adults about childhood events, one of which had never occurred, in the presence of other family members, who 'reminded' them of the event during the interview. Subsequently, 6 of the 24 participants in the study 'remembered' the false episode as real and provided additional details about it. Using a similar method, Hyman et al. (1995) asked college students about various childhood events that had never happened, including spending a night in hospital for treatment of an ear infection. At the end of the first interview, in which no participants 'recalled' the false events, they were encouraged to try to remember more information about them before a subsequent interview. During this interview, a quarter of the participants remembered detailed information about this false event.

The therapeutic process

Loftus and Davis (2006) highlighted the number of processes that may combine to allow or even encourage the construction of false memories within therapy often in the absence of deliberate or malicious bias by either therapist or client:

- *A priori expectations of abuse*: many clients and therapists may have *a priori* assumptions that abuse has occurred, even in the absence of direct evidence. Confirmatory bias may lead both to search for evidence or interpret information in the light of these expectations.
- *Motivated cognition*: many, if not most, people enter therapy with the hope of finding a 'cause' for their problems. They are therefore motivated to explore potential routes to their distress. If a therapist is also so motivated, then evidence may be sought to identify abuse. Therapists may even suggest the possibility of abuse and search for evidence of it.
- *Identify maintenance*: once a client has begun to admit the possibility of abuse, they may take on the identity of an abused person (which may provide validation of their distress) and look for evidence supporting this new identity.
- *Therapeutic techniques*: such as hypnosis, regression, guided imagery and dream interpretation all permit and may facilitate the development of false memories.
- *Repeated attempts at recall*: even in the absence of specific therapeutic techniques repeated attempts at recall increase the number of both true and false memories recalled.
- *Abuse-related images and misattribution as memories*: repeated discussion of abuse may evoke images of abuse, which become increasingly prone to being attributed as memories.

Retraction

Although the percentage of people to do so is unknown, many people who recall traumatic memories eventually retract and claim that the events never actually occurred: that they are a consequence of within-therapy processes (e.g. Laney and Loftus 2005). Here, for example, is the testimony of Clare, who retracted her claims of sexual abuse by a family member. Her story here focuses on the power that her therapist had over her, how he shaped her 'memories', and how she came to recognize his negative influence over her:

> Looking back, it's difficult to see how things could have got this far, and been so destructive. How could a relationship with a therapist become the only – the total – focus of my life for three years? How could I have sold my soul, my very self, to another human being? How could I have fallen

under the spell of a man who, it turns out, had problems in his own life; a man so inadequate himself that he needed me and others to be 'sick' in order for him to be powerful and strong? I trusted this man with my life – my soul. I shared everything with him – my dreams, the desires of my life. I confessed my sins to him. He was my partner, mother, father, sister, best friend, and teacher. My role model. He was everything to me. Whatever he said, I agreed with. How could he be wrong? My life became so linked with his life, my ability to think for myself disappeared. I thought what he wanted me to think. I believed what he wanted me to believe. I became what he wanted me to become.

Overview of the evidence

While some commentators (e.g. Loftus and Davis 2006) are extremely sceptical about the nature of recalled memories, Brewin and Andrews (1998) took a more cautious and conciliatory view, and suggested the present state of the evidence is as follows:

- The age at which the majority of events are said to have occurred extends beyond the period of the infant amnesia.
- Corroboration occurs with reasonable frequency given the nature of the alleged incidents.
- The content of most recovered memories concerns a variety of events known to occur with reasonable frequency, and is not limited to child sexual abuse.
- Well-trained therapists not using inappropriate techniques have reported clients recovering memories.
- The context of recall is not limited to the therapist's office.

On this basis, Brewin and Andrews suggested that the evidence is not sufficient to rule out the possibility that recovered memory may genuinely occur, at least in some cases, and that each case should be taken on its own merit. Nevertheless, because there is serious doubt over the accuracy of at least some recovered memories, a number of professional bodies have developed guidelines about how clinicians should respond to reports of 'recovered memory'. Those of the Australian Psychological Society (www.psychosociety.com.au) are typical:

- 'Memories' that are reported either spontaneously or following the use of special procedures in therapy may be accurate, inaccurate, fabricated or a mixture of these.
- The level of belief in memories does not necessarily relate to the accuracy of the memory.
- The available scientific and clinical evidence does not allow accurate, inaccurate or fabricated memories to be distinguished in the absence of independent corroboration.

Psychologists/therapists should:

- be alert to the ways they can shape the memories reported by clients through the expectations they convey, the comments they make, the questions they ask, and the responses they give to clients;

- be aware that clients are susceptible to subtle suggestions and reinforcements, whether intended or unintended;
- be empathic and supportive of the reports of clients, while ensuring they do not jump to conclusions about the truth or falsity of their recollections;
- inform any client who recovers a memory of abuse that it may be an accurate memory of an actual event, may be an altered or distorted memory of an actual event, or may be a false memory of an event that did not happen.

10.3 Dissociative identity disorder (DID)

A defining characteristic of individuals with a diagnosis of DID is that they behave as if they possess two or more distinct identities or personalities, known as 'alters'. In contrast to the past, where people with DID (or multiple personality as it was previously known) reported relatively few alter personalities, the average number of alters now reported is about 15, and some individuals exhibit more than 100. According to DSM-IV-TR, the diagnostic criteria for DID are:

- the presence of two or more distinct identities or personality states, each with its own relatively enduring pattern of perceiving, relating to and thinking about the environment and self;
- at least two of these identities or personality states recurrently take control of the person's behaviour;
- an inability to recall important personal information that is too extensive to be explained by ordinary forgetfulness;
- the disturbance is not due to the direct physiological effects, substance abuse or a general medical condition.

The number of alters depends on a number of factors, such as the severity and time period of the abuse. Each alter has a job within the system. Most alters protect the host personality from memories of the trauma. It is common for each alter to guard a particular memory. Some alters are aware of other alters; others do not know of their existence. Most alters do not see themselves in the physical body they are in: children see themselves as 4 feet tall, women see themselves as girls, and so on. They may be of different nationalities and races. Some may speak different languages. Alters may have different facial expressions and different mannerisms. There are many different kinds of alters and all systems are different, but here are some of the more common types of alter described by someone living with a partner who experienced DID (www.mpdfriends.homestead.com):

- *Host*: this person can either be the original birth child, or can be an alter that is the main personality presented to the outside world.
- *Original birth child*: this person may be awake and functioning, or said to be asleep. This person is sometimes referred to as the core personality.
- *Child alters*: child alters (or 'littles' as they are affectionately known) can range from the age of an infant upwards. These are the alters that took much of the abuse, and often carry a large

number of memories. They display behaviour that is appropriate for their age. Often they carry much pain, both physical and emotional.

- *Teens*: most systems have teen alters. These alters were often the ones who went to school, and were out for those years.

- *Gatekeepers*: some systems have a gatekeeper, who directs and has control of the body. They may also control the length of time an alter is in body. They do not often come out themselves, but just seem happy to observe and direct the others.

- *Internal self helpers*: these internal self helpers keep the alters safe. They usually know all the alters and the details of the abuse the alters endured. They are very helpful in therapy, and help the therapist understand why a particular alter feels the way they do, or decide the action of a particular alter. They also decide what information is passed to other alters and to the host.

- *Protectors*: protectors protect (!) the system from outside threats. They can usually talk hard, or fight, or do whatever is necessary to keep the system safe. They often use anger as a defence. They are especially protective of the child alters.

Switches between alters often result from some sort of stress or upset, which causes another alter, usually a protector alter, to emerge. Stresses can include comments by others, seeing the abuser, an unexpected touch, arguments and aggression – even having sex. Sel (1997) suggested that the individual has an ecosystem of alters who compete with each other to gain control over the output channels. The alter that most successfully maintains an emotional equilibrium is most likely to be best adapted. When the individual moves to a different context, different cognitive schemata may be more adaptive and the dominant alter will switch.

Aetiology of DID

The nature and, indeed, existence of 'true' DID, have been as hotly debated as the existence of recovered memories, and the arguments are very similar (see, for example, Piper and Merskey 2004). Such is the level of debate that even some studies of this disorder remain neutral about its nature and aetiology. Elzinga et al. stated, for example, that they adopted a 'pragmatic stance . . . without making a priori claims about the nature of so-called "identities"' (2003: 237). Some contend that its existence is self-evident, and that there are too many people experiencing these symptoms to deny the reality of the problem. Others reject the concept, arguing that the symptoms are invented by the individuals reporting them, or even implanted in their consciousness by over-zealous therapists. The two dominant theories of DID are that it is either the result of childhood trauma (e.g. Gleaves 1996) or a socially constructed system created by the affected individual and shaped by the therapist (e.g. Spanos 1994).

Childhood trauma

There are relatively few studies of DID – perhaps because of the low prevalence of the condition. However, what evidence there is suggests that it is associated with childhood trauma. Boon and Draijer (1993), for example, reported that 94 per cent of the series of people diagnosed with DID in their sample reported a history of childhood physical and/or sexual abuse. Proponents of the childhood trauma model (e.g. Gleaves 1996) suggest that the experience of severe trauma during childhood produces a mental 'splitting' or dissociation as part of a defensive reaction. The abused child learns to dissociate, or enter a self-induced hypnotic state, placing the memory of the abuse in the subconscious as a means of coping with the trauma. These dissociated parts of the individual 'split' into alter personalities that, in adulthood, manifest themselves to help the individual cope with stressful situations and express resentments or other feelings that are unacceptable to the primary personality. This model fits well with the model of hypnosis in psychosomatic disorders outlined in Chapter 6.

Taking a similar approach, Putnam (1997) proposed a developmental model of these phenomena. He suggested that traumatic environments prevent children from completing the developmental task of consolidating an integrated sense of self from what he termed the 'discrete behavioural states' – involving cognitive and emotional functioning – which predominate in infancy. He suggested that normal caregiving environments facilitate integration of these differing states into a single integrated whole. Trauma actively inhibits this integration. Instead, the child develops a series of separate states that are adaptive to their parental behaviours.

Socio-cognitive model

By contrast, socio-cognitive theorists (e.g. Lilienfield et al. 1999; Piper and Mersky 2004) have argued that DID is a set of beliefs and behaviours constructed by the individual in response to personal stress, therapist pressure and societal legitimization of the construct of 'multiple personality'. They suggest that DID has become a legitimate way for many people to understand and express their failures and frustrations, as well as a tactic for the manipulation of others. According to this account, individuals diagnosed as having DID learn to portray themselves as possessing multiple selves and to reorganize and elaborate on their personal biography to make it consistent with their understanding of what it means to be a 'multiple'. That is, they actively construct their various selves. They argued that psychotherapists have contributed to the development of this disorder by encouraging clients to construe themselves in this way and by providing official legitimation for the different identities their patients enact.

The battleground of DID

A number of issues have been identified as the 'battleground' of evidence in relation to DID:

DID and child abuse Findings that people with DID report extremely high rates of repeated and frequent childhood sexual or physical abuse have led some theorists (e.g. Kluft 1996) to suggest that dissociation as a result of repeated sexual abuse is a defining characteristic of DID. In response to this, Piper and Mersky (2004) noted that many cases were entirely uncorroborated, relying on patient accounts, or when evidence was claimed, this was generally weak. In addition, Spanos (1994) argued that the apparently high level of association between child sexual abuse and the phenomenon of DID may be spurious and the result of therapist and client beliefs about the nature of the phenomenon. He suggested that:

- Child sexual abuse is relatively common in the USA, and rates are particularly high among those who seek psychiatric help. High rates among people who develop DID may therefore be indicative of these high background rates rather than risk for DID.

- Because some clinicians consider a history of sexual abuse to be a possible sign of DID, they may be more likely to expose abused than non-abused patients to hypnotic interviews and other procedures that result in 'multiplicity'.

- Some patients with DID do not remember being abused until their multiplicity is discovered in the course of therapy. Any recovered memories should be treated with some caution.

- Therapists may disbelieve DID patients who claim not to have been abused and may probe repeatedly in an attempt to unearth such memories. When patients believe they may be fantasizing, their uncertainty may be presented to them as evidence that they are unwilling to face the fact of their abuse (Bliss 1986).

- Many patients with DID report not just sexual abuse but also that this was ritualistic and long-term. These histories are usually identified following a series of leading questions under hypnotic suggestion, and none have been found to be substantiated.

- Some of the data related to abuse are not in accordance with data on memory recall and typical patterns of abuse. Ross et al. (1991) reported on the age of earliest sexual abuse reported by their patient group. Over a quarter reported being abused before the age of 3 years, and 10 per cent reported being abused before the age of 1 year. These ages are much younger than is typical in cases of sexual abuse and prior to the establishment of neural substrates that permit long-term recall (see p. 263).

Problems of prevalence   The prevalence of DID has changed over time, increasing substantially since the 1980s. Foote et al. (2006), for example, found that 29 per cent of admissions to one US inner city psychiatric hospital were diagnosed with DID. A number of authors (e.g. Piper and Mersky 2004) have argued that if DID were a naturally occurring state, this degree of change would not occur, and that it represents an increase in the social construction of the condition by therapists and clients. They noted that among 'investigators who are sympathetic to DID', diagnostic rates are extremely high. Modestin's (1992) survey of Swiss psychiatrists, for example, suggested that about 1 per cent of cases within their psychiatric system were diagnosed as having DID. In addition, while 90 per cent of the psychiatrists he surveyed had not seen a case of DID, three reported seeing more than 20 people with the disorder: 66 per cent of the cases were reported by less than 0.1 per cent of the psychiatrists surveyed. He suggested that these clinicians may have either misidentified symptoms as evidence of DID or encouraged their clients to construct various manifestations of the disorder.

Defenders of DID (e.g. Kluft 1996) have responded to this argument by suggesting that it is not surprising there were differences in observation rates among differing clinicians. According to Kluft, this may have resulted from different referral rates, an unwillingness among some clinicians to give a diagnosis of DID, and a reluctance among the same clinicians to ask the questions that would lead to this diagnosis being assigned. He also suggested that the increase in reported prevalence may be a function of previous misdiagnoses as a result of it being a relatively new diagnostic category, increased awareness of the prevalence and problems of child abuse, and increased interest in dissociative states. A further critique of the incidence issue is provided by Piper and Mersky who noted that while there has been a massive rise in the reported prevalence of DID, there has been no corresponding rise in reported levels of child abuse. In addition, Kihlstrom (2005) noted that prospective studies of traumatized children have revealed no convincing cases of DID.

Teaching multiplicity   The most critical attack on clinicians who diagnose DID is that they lead their patients either covertly or overtly to report the presence of alters. Spanos (1994) noted that proponents of DID have described a large body of symptoms that indicate the possible presence of the disorder, including depression, periods of missing time, headaches and impaired concentration, and justify probing to confirm a diagnosis. Merskey (1992) suggested that highly leading and suggestive procedures are frequently used, to the point that some therapists insisted to doubting patients that they were multiples and supplied them with the names of their alters.

The generation of alters often occurs in the privacy of the consultation following use of hypnotic techniques. Spanos (1994) argued that the use of persuasive techniques or suggestion while under hypnosis may itself result in some individuals reporting alters and subsequently behaving as if they were 'multiples'. The role of hypnosis in generating alters was challenged by Gleaves (1996), who noted that the percentage of patients diagnosed with DID following hypnosis varied between 4 and 27 per cent across studies and that some studies have shown no differences in prevalence dependent on the type of treatment given in therapy (including hypnosis).

Finding evidence of suggestion in clinical sessions is difficult, as their content is rarely made public. However, Spanos was able to review the transcripts of the interview of a suspected murderer, Ken Bianchi, who was found to have DID by Schwarz (1981) and who confessed to a murder perpetrated by an alter named Steve. Spanos argued that the instructions given to Bianchi led him to report having an alter, as they repeatedly informed him that there was another individual within, who could be addressed. When Spanos et al. (1985) used this procedure with naïve participants under hypnosis in an experimental study, most participants enacted the symptoms of DID by adopting a different name, referred to their primary personality in the third person, and displayed amnesia for their alter personalities after termination of the hypnotic interview. The participants maintained their role successfully in a second session by exhibiting marked and consistent differences between their primary and secondary personalities on a variety of psychological tests.

Gleaves (1996) responded to findings such as this by arguing that while they raise interesting questions about the capacities and workings of the human mind, they do not indicate that DID is necessarily created within the therapy session. According to Gleaves, these analogue studies produced phenomena that were only superficially similar to DID. Participants did not experience any of the established features of DID – such as episodes of time loss, depersonalization or derealization or hearing voices – in any of these studies. According to Gleaves, just because some people can replicate some of the symptoms of DID does not invalidate the concept: a person may replicate depression, anxiety and so on, without challenging the reality of the condition.

Further evidence countering the role of the therapist in developing a diagnosis of DID can be found from studies showing significant evidence of DID pathology prior to any therapist contact. Gleaves (1996) also reported evidence of symptoms including journals in differing handwriting or memories of dissociative experiences going back to childhood. Some of this evidence could be verified by family members and friends. By contrast, Piper and Merskey (2004) noted that relatives of people with DID have usually not seen evidence of multiple identities before treatment.

Motivation, legitimation and DID   Spanos (1994) argued that people may seek or collude with a diagnosis of DID as a means of gaining the support of their therapist and others. He suggested that the idea of being a multiple may provide some people with a viable and face-saving way to account for personal problems as well as a dramatic means of gaining concern and attention from significant others. Spanos suggested that people who are diagnosed with DID are often unhappy and insecure people with a strong investment in gaining the interest and approval of their therapist. By contrast, therapists are highly valued by their clients and their suggestions are treated seriously. This combination of therapists 'on the look-out' for signs of DID and clients wanting to create a good impression with their, valued, therapist may result in a gradual shaping of responses to fit those of DID. Spanos (1994) did not claim that people with DID are necessarily faking their multiplicity. Rather, they have come to adopt a view of themselves that is congruent with the view conveyed to them by their therapist, to adopt and believe in their presentation as someone with multiple alters.

The wider social environment may also be supportive of their diagnosis. Spanos argued that support for DID has almost taken on the characteristics of a social movement. People with DID and therapists participate regularly in workshops and conferences, and both those affected and their therapists frequently have access to national newsletters that provide ongoing legitimisation for the multiple-self enactments. All this may reinforce the presentation of self as someone with multiple alters. Gleaves (1996) contended that this is not always the case, and that therapy is not always easy for patients with DID. Many people with the symptoms of DID experience hostile reactions from professionals and public alike. Many are told they are lying or faking, or even that their therapist is crazy.

Gleaves noted that some protagonists have suggested that some people with DID are seeking attention. By contrast, he contended that many are actually secretive about their condition and conceal their disorder for fear of being labelled crazy and typically have an avoidant style that inhibits disclosure of their abuse histories (Kluft 1994). This speculation was supported by Fink and Golinkoff (1990), who found that people with DID evidenced relatively low levels of histrionic behaviours and emotional lability, and were more intellectualized, obsessive and introvert than a comparison group of people without the disorder. However, while this may indicate a general unwillingness to portray themselves to the general public as DID sufferers, it does not counter the argument that expression of multiple personalities develops over time as a result of therapist–client interactions.

Experimental evidence   A key issue in the medical explanation of DID is that memories remain 'locked' within certain alters and do not leak out into other states. Thus some alters, at least, are protected against memories of traumatic events – and in adulthood, memories of events that occur are thought to remain within the memory system of the alter that experiences them, and not spread into other memory systems. This phenomenon could provide a test of the DID diagnosis, as it allows experimental testing with clear hypotheses: memories should not pass between alters. In one study of this issue, Elzinga et al. (2003) assessed both implicit and explicit memory performance in 12 people with DID. They presented participants with 96 words, half of which had a threatening or sexual connotation, half of which were neutral. Participants were instructed after each presentation to either remember or forget the presented word, as forgetting them would aid their recall of the other words in a subsequent memory test. They then completed an interference task, following which they were instructed to change state. All participants reported they achieved this change, and the new state (alter) reported that they had no conscious recall of the words they had previously been exposed to. They then took part in an implicit memory test in which 48 words were flashed 'briefly' on a computer screen followed by a mask of letters for one second. They were then asked to guess what word had been presented. Following a second interference task, participants were then presented with the stems of the previously presented words and asked to complete them. Finally, participants were asked to switch back to their original state and this sequence of testing was repeated. Their findings indicated a significant reduction of explicit memory between states. Participants were more likely to recall words they had been asked to recall when in the same state than when in a different state from the state in which they were presented with the words. However, the second alter still remembered significant numbers of words. Levels of recall of emotional to-be-remembered words, for example, were 36 per cent in the same state and 21 per cent in the second state. In addition, there was no evidence of any differences across states on their measure of implicit memory. These data show some transfer of information between states, and counter the argument of a compartmentalized memory, with each memory system specific to different personalities. Similar findings by Huntjens et al. (2006) led them to conclude that the problems reported by people with DID did not reflect actual memory retrieval inability – but were better characterized as a meta-memory disorder, in that they held inaccurate beliefs about their own memory functioning.

Treatment of DID

Not surprisingly, protagonists for and against the concept of DID have differing ideas about its treatment. Spanos, for example, contended that the goal of treatment is to help clients accept that their alter identities are real personalities rather than self-generated fantasies. By contrast, Gleaves contended that the opposite is true. He argued that the central goal of treatment should be to help the individual understand that the alters are in fact self-generated, not to convince them that they are real people. He argued that therapists working with people with DID should emphasize the fundamental nature of the disorder as a difficulty in integrating various aspects of the personality rather than a profusion of personalities (Fraser 1992).

For most therapists, the ultimate goal of therapy is to integrate the various alters into one cohesive personality, a process known as fusion. In this state, the person is aware of all their behaviours and thoughts and accepts them as their own. Oke and Kanigsberg (1991) used a combination of play, guided imagery, life skills teaching, projective techniques and group therapy to help bring awareness and understanding of other selves, and through this eventually achieve cohesion between all alters. Unfortunately, the effectiveness of this and similar types of intervention (e.g. Kellett 2005), remains limited to descriptions of interventions with no outcome data, or case reports, which by their very nature tend to be positive (few therapists like to broadcast their failures widely, and most journals are biased against publishing 'negative results'). Their efficacy or otherwise has yet to be fully investigated.

A fundamental cautionary note about such efforts has come from people with DID. Many sub-personalities reject integration as a therapeutic goal, as they see integration as a form of death (Spiegel 1999). In support of this stance, Rossel (1998) argued that in a disintegrating postmodern world, it is of little benefit to attempt to achieve integration. Instead, the individual should be open to the experience of shifting between alters, which should be construed as a positive and comfortable experience, not a negative, destructive one.

10.4 Chapter summary

1 PTSD has three central symptoms: (1) intrusive memories; (2) attempts at avoidance of these memories; and (3) high levels of arousal.

2 The neurological substrates of PTSD are the amygdala and hippocampus that together mediate fear and memory, and link the two together. High arousal is mediated by the sympathetic nervous system.

3 The conditioning model of PTSD provides a partial explanation of the phenomenon, but cognitive models such as that of Brewin provide a more in-depth understanding.

4 Clinical incident debriefing is often provided at traumatic incidents. Evidence is mounting that this may actually inhibit long-term recovery from psychological trauma.

5 Exposure methods may prove the best intervention for PTSD, particularly when combined with strategies to help clients cope with any emotional distress triggered by the therapeutic process.

6 EMDR appears to be of benefit, but no more than exposure methods.

7 Since the 1980s, an increasing number of people have begun to report recovered memories of trauma, usually sexual trauma, experienced in childhood.

8 Three explanations have been proposed to account for this phenomenon: (1) the memories are real and have been hidden as a result of a number of unconscious self-protective mechanisms; (2) they are the result of therapists shaping clients' apparent recall of past events that did not in reality occur; and (3) they are incidents forgotten as a result of normal forgetting processes.

9 Arguments about which of these explanations are correct have focused on a number of issues: the age at the time of the incident, distortions in memory over time, mixed levels of corroboration of events, and experimental evocation of false memories.

10 Brewin and others have suggested that while some memories may be false, others may be truly repressed and recovered. Each case should be considered on its own merits.

11 The clinical model suggests that DID is a response to repeated childhood sexual trauma involving severe dissociation at the time of the trauma, resulting in the development of 'alters' or alternative personalities.

12 The socio-cognitive model suggests this is a response to therapist and social pressure to behave in a way that suggests multiple personalities.

13 Debate about which of these models is the better has focused on differing explanations of the prevalence of the disorder, whether therapists can 'teach multiplicity', social and therapist pressures to present with DID, and the relationship between childhood abuse and DID.

14 While some cases of DID may be created by the process of therapy, others may represent a 'real' clinical condition. Each case should be considered on its own merits.

10.5 For discussion

1 How should we treat people following a major trauma?
2 Which factors may contribute to the development of PTSD?
3 Is there such a thing as 'recovered memory'?
4 What are the causes of DID?

10.6 Key term

Alexithymia a paucity of emotional experience and awareness, with an associated poverty of imagination and a tendency to focus upon the tangible and mundane.

10.7 Further reading

Brewin, C.R. and Holmes, E.A. (2003) Psychological theories of posttraumatic stress disorder, *Clinical Psychology Review*, 23: 339–76.
Brewin, C.R., Lanius, R.A., Novac, A. et al. (2009) Reformulating PTSD for DSM-V: Life after Criterion A, *Journal of Traumatic Stress*, 22: 366–73.
Colangelo, J.J. (2009) The recovered memory controversy: a representative case study, *Journal of Child Sexual Abuse*, 18: 103–21.
Loftus, E.F. and Davis, D. (2006) Recovered memories, *Annual Review of Clinical Psychology*, 2: 469–98.
Gillig, P.M. (2009) Dissociative identity disorder: a controversial diagnosis, *Psychiatry*, 6: 24–9.
Kihlstrom, J.F. (2005) Dissociative disorders, *Annual Review of Clinical Psychology*, 1: 227–53.

The following websites also have information about the conditions described in this chapter, their treatment and people's experiences of them. It also provides a number of sources on both sides of the argument for recovered memories.

PTSD

www.patient.co.uk/showdoc/27000223/
www.ptsduk.co.uk/

DID

www.dissociation.com/
www.dissociation-world.org.uk/

Recovered memories

www.religioustolerance.org/rmt.htm
www.brown.edu/Departments/Taubman_Center/Recovmem/index.html
recoveredmemorytherapy.blogspot.com/
www.bfms.org.uk/

Sexual disorders

Chapter contents

There are two categories of sexual disorders: *sexual dysfunctions*, which involve a problem in sexual response, and *paraphilias*, which involve repeated and intense sexual urges, behaviour or fantasies in response to objects or situations that society deems inappropriate. This chapter examines both types of problems. It considers problems that some people experience during the sexual act, focusing on the male problem of failing to achieve an erection and its female 'equivalent', known as vaginismus, and considers how these may be treated. It then describes the aetiology and treatment of paedophilia and transvestism. Finally, the chapter considers the problems faced when an individual questions their very sexual identity and wishes to change it: gender identity disorder. By the end of the chapter, you should have an understanding of:

- The nature and aetiology of erectile dysfunction, vaginismus, paedophilia, transvestism and gender identity disorder
- The types of interventions used to treat each disorder, and their relative effectiveness.

11.1 Sexual dysfunctions

The sexual dysfunctions are those that involve a problem with the sexual response. They include disorders of desire, such as an aversion to sexual activity and low sexual drive, problems of orgasm including premature ejaculation in men and a failure to achieve orgasm in both men and women. Here, two conditions are considered: erectile dysfunction in men, and a condition known as vaginismus in women. Both problems markedly interfere with, or may prevent, the sexual act. Both are treatable using relatively simple behavioural and pharmacological interventions.

11.2 Erectile dysfunction

A DSM-IV-TR diagnosis of erectile failure requires persistent or recurrent inability to gain or maintain an adequate erection until completion of sexual activity, which results in marked distress or interpersonal difficulties. It is a fairly common disorder, particularly among older men, although younger men are not immune. Laumann et al. (1999) reported a 7 per cent prevalence among men aged 18–29. The prevalence rate was 9 per cent for men aged 30–39, 11 per cent for those aged 40–49 and 18 per cent for those aged 50–59. Some of the causes of erectile dysfunction are physical, including high blood pressure, and the long-term effects of drugs such as alcohol, heroin, marijuana and cigarettes. However, Masters and Johnson (1970) found a relevant physical condition in only 7 out of 213 men they assessed; the most common causes of the problem are psychological. These may be immediate or remote:

- *immediate*: performance anxiety, lack of adequate stimulation, relationship conflicts, lack of partner intimacy, poor partner communication
- *remote*: childhood sexual trauma, unresolved partner or parental attachments, sexual identity or orientation issues.

Aetiology of erectile dysfunction

Psychodynamic explanations

According to Janssen (1985), erectile failure results from an oedipal conflict constellation involving fear of castration or incest, uncertainties in sexual identity, incestuous object choices, latent homosexual tendencies and fear of aggressive-phallic impulses. These may develop as a result of factors that inhibit appropriate passage through the oedipal stage of psychosexual development (see Chapter 2). In a case example, Janssen described one man who reported that as a child his mother had turned to him to discuss matters relating to her relationship with his father. When his father became aware of this, he became angry and abused his mother. The client feared that he too would become the focus of his father's wrath and experienced a conflict in wanting to defend his mother, but to avoid confrontation with his father. This prevented his successful resolution of the oedipal conflict. In adulthood, the fear of his aggressive father prevented him developing appropriate emotional and sexual relationships with women. Treatment involved dealing with his relationship with his father, not any explicit sexual function.

Cognitive explanations

In a more cognitive explanation, Bancroft (1999) argued that anxiety adversely affects sexual performance as a result of cognitive and perceptual factors. He suggested that men's sexual excitement depends on a delicate balance between excitatory and inhibitory mechanisms. Two key inhibitory processes are performance anxiety and fear of negative outcomes. Both may lead to a process coined by Masters and Johnson as *spectating* in which the individual becomes so concerned by the adequacy of their performance or the consequences of potential failure that they distract from sexually arousing cues, and lose their erection. Evidence in support of Bancroft's model can be found in a number of laboratory studies which have shown performance demand to increase sexual arousal in most men, but to have the opposite effect on those with erectile dysfunction. In addition, the presence of non-sexual stimuli is more disruptive to men with the disorder than those without (Cranston-Cuebas and Barlow 1990).

Many men set themselves inappropriately high levels of performance to which they aspire. Zilbergeld (1992), for example, noted that men frequently buy into the fantasy that their performance is the 'cornerstone' of every sexual experience and that a firm erection is the key element of every sexual encounter: views not necessarily subscribed to by their female partners. According to Zilbergeld, a failure to achieve this ideal results in fears of dysfunction, loss of masculinity, and declining interest in their partner.

Treatment of erectile dysfunction

Anxiety reduction and desensitization

The classic treatment programme for erectile failure, known as *sensate focusing*, was developed by Masters and Johnson (1970). It involves a structured approach, designed to take the stress out of the sexual act. It begins with the couple learning to touch each other in pleasurable ways, but with a mandate not to touch each other's genitals. Their goal is to enjoy the intimacy of touch, not to give or receive sexual pleasure. Once couples are comfortable with non-genital sensate focusing, they are directed to gradually make genital contact and to give and receive pleasure doing so. At this time, they are still mandated not to attempt intercourse, nor for the male to try to achieve or maintain an erection (although this typically occurs). Finally, when the couple are comfortable with this level of intimacy, they may progress to full intercourse. This is a frequently applied intervention; although there are relatively few studies of its effectiveness, it is generally considered to be highly effective (Hawton et al. 1986).

Cognitive techniques

There are relatively few formal assessments of cognitive interventions in the treatment of erectile failure, although Goldman and Carroll (1990) reported the outcomes of a number of workshops in which participants were given appropriate sexual information and inappropriate cognitive concerns were challenged. Participants showed significant changes in knowledge and attitudes towards sex, and reported increased sexual frequency and satisfaction in the short term; no long-term data were reported.

Interpersonal interventions

Hawton et al. (1992) reported that the most important predictor of outcome following a pro-gramme of sensate focusing and graduated stimulation techniques was the couples' ratings of marital communication before treatment. Three domains are the main foci of interpersonal interventions (Rosen 2001):

- status and dominance issues
- intimacy and trust
- loss of sexual attraction.

Each of these may be more or less salient in the lifetime of a sexual relationship. Status and domin-ance issues may be salient when one partner loses a job or achieves promotion; intimacy or trust issues may be salient following an affair, while loss of sexual attraction may follow weight gain or some other physical or psychological changes. Following an intervention addressing these factors, Hawton and colleagues reported that 70 per cent of couples reported a positive outcome.

Medical approaches

Perhaps the best-known pharmacological treatment for erectile failure is sildenal, more popu-larly known as Viagra. This works on the smooth muscle of the penis. It is an inhibitor of the enzyme phosphodiesterase type 5 (PDE5) which normally breaks down cyclic guanosine mono-phosphate (cGMP), a chemical that brings about smooth muscle relaxation, and maintains the erectile response. It is generally effective in treating erectile dysfunction, whatever the cause. Goldstein et al. (1998), for example, reported that 70 per cent of men treated with Viagra re-ported improvements in the quality and frequency of erections; 70 per cent of attempts at inter-course were successful, in comparison with 22 per cent of attempts by those treated with placebo. PDE5 is predominantly found in the penis. However, it is also found in other areas of the body. As a consequence, about 16 per cent of users experience headaches, 10 per cent experience facial flushing, with other effects such as gastrointestinal upset and alterations in colour vision being somewhat rarer. One of the more dramatic side-effects was thought to be the onset of a heart attack, but this is now thought to be a result of exercise, not the drug (Holmes 2000). One of the benefits of Viagra is that it enhances the sexual response rather than initiates it. Erection there-fore follows sexual stimulation, and does not immediately follow taking the drug, as is the case in some alternatives. Erection may also be achieved by vacuum pumps, direct injection of drugs into the penis and the use of prostheses. Each method has achieved some success, and many continue to be used, but less so in the light of the development of Viagra and similar drugs (Ralph and McNicholas 2000).

11.3 Vaginismus

Vaginismus is the recurrent or persistent involuntary spasm of the musculature of the outer third of the vagina that prevents sexual intercourse. It can cause considerable distress or inter-personal difficulties. It is thought to be one of the most common of the female psychosexual dysfunctions, although its exact prevalence rate among the general population is unknown. About 20 per cent of women experience occasional pain during intercourse, but less than 1 per cent are thought to have vaginismus (Heiman and LoPiccolo 1988).

Aetiology of vaginismus

Psychoanalytic explanations

Classic psychoanalytic theory considers vaginismus to result from unresolved psychosexual conflicts in early childhood. Women with the condition have been characterized as fixated or regressed to the pre-oedipal or oedipal stages. According to Abraham (1956), in less severe cases, women are not able to transfer their libidinal energy from their father to their husband/partner. In more severe cases, women remain fixated on their mothers, and have a poor prognosis.

Behavioural explanations

According to behavioural theory, vaginismus is a phobic reaction to actual or imagined negative experiences related to penetration. Fear or anxiety concerning penetration results in high levels of sympathetic nervous system activity, one of the results of which is involuntary vaginal muscle spasm. These fears may, in part, arise from ignorance of sexual issues. Three other factors may increase the fear reaction (Ward and Ogden 1994). First, a mother who is frightened of intercourse may pass a fear of pain to her daughter. Second, the experience of sex may be painful for the affected woman, and memories of pain trigger the symptoms: nearly three-quarters of women with vaginismus in Ward and Ogden's sample reported this type of fear. The third issue involves a fear of punishment related to sexual guilt. Ward and Ogden found that many women with vaginismus experienced sexual guilt, stemming from a belief that 'sex is wrong', which led to a fear of punishment for engaging in sexual acts. Childhood sexual trauma and a background of religious orthodoxy may also contribute to the conditioning of fear or guilt in relation to intercourse.

Treatment of vaginismus

Psychological approaches

One way of reducing anxiety associated with the sexual act is through the use of sensate focus techniques, with a gradual progression to genital touching. However, the most common treatment of vaginismus involves systematic desensitization together with the use of graded dilators. This may be conducted in combination with education, homework assignments and cognitive or relaxation therapy. In this procedure, the woman, and in some cases a physician, inserts dilators of gradually increasing size into the vagina until the woman is relaxed and the involuntary spasm is not triggered by the entry of an object into the vagina. When she is able to accommodate a fairly large dilator, the woman may be encouraged to keep it in place for several hours every night. This type of approach has proven very effective. Masters and Johnson (1970), who pioneered this approach, reported complete success with no relapse in the treatment of 29 women with this condition.

11.4 The paraphilias

Defining which of the various forms of sexual activity is 'normal' and 'abnormal' is not unproblematic. However, a number of sexual behaviours are generally considered to be 'abnormal'. These are referred to as the paraphilias, which include behaviours that are legal, such as fetishism and transvestism, and some that are illegal, in particular, paedophilia (see Table 11.1).

Table 11.1 **Some of the more prevalent paraphilias**	
Fetishism	Recurrent intense sexual urges, sexually arousing fantasies or behaviours that involve the use of non-living objects, often to the exclusion of all other stimuli; common fetishes are to women's underwear, boots and shoes
Exhibitionism	Recurrent urges to expose the genitals to another person of the opposite sex – often while having sexually arousing fantasies
Voyeurism	Recurrent and intense urges to secretly observe unsuspecting people as they undress or have intercourse
Sadomasochism	Sexual stimulation through the act of being humiliated, beaten, bound or otherwise made to suffer, or being the one to inflict such acts
Frotteurism	Repeated and intense sexual urges to touch and rub against non-consenting others

Many people who engage in paraphilic behaviour do not experience distress as a result, nor do they seek help to change the nature of their sexual interest. As a consequence, people who engage in unusual sexual behaviour may be considered as at the edge of the distribution of sexual interests rather than disordered. With this in mind, DSM-III stated that any paraphilic behaviour had to result in distress on the part of the individual before a diagnosis of a 'disorder' be assigned. However, following strong criticism of this *laissez-faire* approach, DSM-IV stated that paedophilia was to be considered a disorder regardless of the perpetrator's emotional reaction to their behaviour. In its latest version, DSM-IV-TR states that exhibitionism, frotteurism, sexual sadism and voyeurism are also now to be considered 'disorders' if the person acts on their desires, even though their behaviour may not cause them any distress or 'impaired functioning'. Relatively few people receive a diagnosis of paraphilia, but the number of specialist websites and other services suggests that these behaviours are more prevalent than this would suggest.

Aetiological explanations have tried to identify common pathways to all the paraphilias. Accordingly, while the next sections consider the aetiology and treatment of paedophilia and transvestism in some detail, the general process by which these conditions develop could be applied to all the paraphilias.

11.5 Paedophilia

Sexual relationships between adults and children are not new. Across the ancient world, there are clear examples of what would now be referred to as paedophilic relationships, particularly involving young boys. In Greece such relationships were seen as contributing to the boy's education; in Rome, the relationship may have been more focused on the pleasure of the man.

Reflecting this, perhaps, such relationships were not permitted with free-born boys in later Roman times. In other countries also, there were clear examples of such practices: for example, among the warrior Samurai in Japan and other warrior groups in Africa. In the West, the subsequent rise of Christianity placed an emphasis on heterosexual relationships within marriage, and medieval legislation prohibited against homosexual and incestuous relationships. However, in most European countries there was no minimum age for marriage – suitability being judged on the basis of reaching physical maturity: and even this requirement was often neglected. The most influential legal text of the seventeenth century in England, written by Sir Edward Coke, noted that the marriage of girls of less than 12 years of age was frequent and normal. During the Renaissance (approximating to the fourteenth to seventeenth centuries), although homosexuality was still officially illegal, there was a liberalization, and a return to the acceptance of man–boy relationships, at least among some social groups: evident through the work of European artists such as Michelangelo, Parmigianino, and the poet and dramatist Christopher Marlow. Against this background, many were reluctant to admit to problems of child sexual abuse in contexts such as the family. Pioneering work by physicians such as Ambroise Tardieu in the mid-nineteenth century, for example, which described the prevalence of a variety of child abuse, including battered child syndrome and infanticide as well as incest, was largely ignored by his fellow physicians. More important, at least in the UK, was the work of the journalist and social reformer William Stead who wrote a series of articles decrying the conditions of child prostitution in London, which aroused great public outcry and led feminist groups to become involved in the issue. The pressure from feminist and other philanthropic groups in the US and the UK pushed the age of consent to sexual relations upwards, such that at the beginning of the twentieth century a survey of 50 countries by Hirschfield found that the age of consent was 12 in fifteen countries, 13 in seven, 14 in five, 15 in four, and 16 in five. Since then, the age of consent has increased in many countries, rising from 14 to 16 years as late as 2008 in Canada.

Attitudes towards paedophilia across the world have also shifted markedly from the *laissez-faire* mood of say, the Renaissance period or even the late nineteenth century. Since the beginning of the twentieth century, attitudes toward paedophile behaviour have become markedly stronger and more negative – with the exception perhaps of the more sexually accepting 1960s – and have been described by some as a moral panic. However, such mores are by no means universal. An infamous case was brought against seven men living on the Pitcairn islands in 2004, for example, claiming they had engaged in paedophile behaviours, finding six guilty of repeatedly over many years raping girls as young as 12 or 13. What brought the attention of the world to this case was the strong support given to the perpetrators by the society in which the events had occurred, the earlier collusion of many of the victims of the abuse, and the revelation that such behaviour had occurred over several generations of men. In a male-dominated society, this type of behaviour had apparently become an acceptable norm. Together, these various data show that what we term paedophilia is a socially constructed act, the definition of which is time and culturally dependent.

Modern diagnostic criteria

DSM-IV-TR defined paedophilia as 'recurrent intense sexual urges and sexually arousing fantasies involving sexual activity with a prepubescent child or children' and that the person has acted on these urges, or the sexual urges or fantasies cause marked distress or interpersonal difficulty. In addition, the perpetrator has to be at least 16 years old and at least 5 years older than the child or children involved. Note the emphasis on the victim's sexual maturity, not age. Legal definitions lay clear boundaries as to the age at which consenting couples may have intercourse. Violation of these limits will result in an individual being termed a sex offender, but not a paedophile unless the other child is pre-pubescent.

Paedophilic behaviours vary. Some paedophiles may look at and not touch a child. Others may want to touch or undress them. When sexual activity occurs, it often involves oral sex or touching the genitals of the child. In most cases, except incest, there is no penetration. Where sex is penetrative, it is usually with older children and may involve threats or force. More typically, however, paedophilic individuals depend on persuasion, guile and 'friendship' (Murray 2000). Paedophiles who are attracted to females usually prefer 8–10-year-olds, while those attracted to boys prefer slightly older children (APA 1994). Most are relatives, friends or neighbours of the child. Prevalence levels of paedophilia are extremely difficult to determine. Most surveys report the prevalence of people who have been sexually abused rather than the prevalence of perpetrators. Barbaree and Seto (1997), for example, calculated that at least 7 per cent of US females and 3 per cent of males have experienced some form of childhood sexual abuse, although some surveys suggest even higher prevalence rates.

Aetiology of paedophilia

Theories of the aetiology of paedophilia are rather limited and focus more on social and psychological factors than on biological ones. These split into long-term background factors and proximal factors that form more immediate triggers to such behaviour.

Long-term risk factors

Many child sex offenders report that their early parent–child relationships were disruptive and/or that they have experienced childhood sexual abuse: up to 67 per cent of respondents in one survey (Hanson and Slater 1988). Similarly, in a matched comparison between male paedophile and 'healthy' individuals, Cohen et al. (2002) found that 60 per cent of paedophiles reported experiencing adult sexual advances as a child. This compared with 4 per cent of the comparison group. These data are extremely difficult to validate. Many people who engage in paedophilic behaviour have a vested interest in reporting such events as a way of minimizing their own responsibility for their actions or gaining the sympathy of others. Attempts at validation by asking the alleged perpetrators are equally likely to result in misreporting. In an attempt to minimize these problems, Dhawan and Marshall (1996) used detailed interviews and questionnaire methods to try to corroborate or challenge any misreporting. They concluded that 50 per cent of imprisoned paedophiles had been sexually abused as children. What this, of course, does not explain is why such episodes predict later sexual offences. A number of authors have speculated why this may be the case, with various suggestions that the abused child is trying to gain a new identity by becoming the abuser, they are engaged in an imprinted sexual arousal pattern established by early abuse, or that early abuse leads to hypersexual behaviour (see, for example, Cohen et al. 2002a; Cohen et al. 2002b).

Behavioural theories (e.g. Barbaree 1990) suggest that child offenders develop a strong sexual attraction to children following pairings of sexual arousal and images of children. These associations typically occur in early adolescence, and may initially be accidental. However, they may be strengthened by masturbation to images of children and the use of pornography. In a partial test of this model, Barbaree and Marshall (1989) measured the sexual response to pictures of female children and mature women among men who had either sexually abused children not in their family, committed incest, or claimed to have no sexual interest in children. Their findings were somewhat surprising. Less than half of the non-familial offenders and only 28 per cent of those who had committed incest were more sexually stimulated by pictures of young women than those of mature women. In addition, 15 per cent of men who reported no sexual interest in children were more sexually aroused by pictures of children than of mature women. While the conditioning model may hold for some individuals, it does not hold for all.

These data indicate that sexual interest is not the only factor that influences the sexual choices of paedophiles. Another important factor may be a failure to develop satisfying psychological and sexual relationships with adults. Many paedophiles report high levels of loneliness, perhaps arising from inadequate attachment styles developed as children (Ward et al. 1996). As a result, some seek out intimacy with children, with whom they find it easier to instigate both physical and non-physical relationships, and who are easier to control. However, this is certainly not the case for all paedophiles, emphasizing that the route to paraphilias differs widely between individuals. Nevertheless, Finkelhor's (1984) 'preconditions theory' of paedophilia identified these factors as key to the condition. He suggested that paedophilia is the result of four factors:

- the belief that sex with children is emotionally satisfying;
- the belief that sex with children is sexually satisfying;
- an inability to meet sexual needs in a more socially appropriate manner;
- disinhibited behaviour at times of stress.

Pithers (1990) provided a useful description of the process of disinhibition at times of low mood. He noted that the desire to engage in paedophile behaviour is frequently triggered by low mood as a result of stress or conflict. As a result, individuals seek some way of decreasing these negative feelings, and allow themselves to enter a high-risk situation. This may appear the result of seemingly irrelevant decisions that place them in increasing proximity to potential victims. Once in this situation, they are overwhelmed by the potentially powerfully rewarding feelings associated with paedophile acts. They focus on these rather than the long-term negative outcomes to the situation, and as a result engage in some form of paedophile behaviour. Once the immediate 'rush' has receded, they may once more experience remorse, but feel out of control of their behaviour, a negative mood state that may trigger the cycle again.

These factors are added to by cognitive distortions that support sexual acts with children. Common cognitive distortions are that children are as interested in sex as adults, that they seek out sex with adults, and that they enjoy and benefit from the experience. Some of these may be truly believed by the individual. Others may be deliberate falsification, to minimize negative reactions from others. Implicit tests of attitudes are, perhaps, particularly revealing in this context. In one study, using the implicit association test, Mihailides et al. (2004) found that child sex offenders were more likely to implicitly endorse 'children as sexual beings', 'uncontrollability of sexuality' and 'sexual entitlement-bias' beliefs than other types of offender and non-offenders. Paedophiles also frequently have a repertoire of beliefs/justifications used in their defence within the justice system, including denial ('Is it wrong to give a child a hug?'), minimization ('It only happened once'), justification ('I am a boy lover, not a child molester'), fabrication (activities were research for a scholarly project), and attack (usually character attacks on the child, prosecutors, or police) (Lanning 2001).

Putting these various strands together, Ward and Siegert's (2002) pathways model identified a number of pathways to paedophile behaviour, including:

- *intimacy deficits*: the individual possesses normal 'sexual scripts' (i.e. they know and can conform to the rules of appropriate sexual acts), and only offend at certain times such as when a partner is unavailable or during a period of sustained loneliness.
- *deviant sexual scripts*: the individual has 'subtle' distortions in their sexual scripts and dysfunctional schema about the nature of relationships. Paedophiles in this category prefer adult sexual partners. However, they fear intimacy and rejection from adults, and equate sexual relationships with emotionally intimate relationships. They therefore experience their emotional needs as sexual needs, and seek sexual relationships obsessively, particularly when they feel lonely. Sex with children may occur simply because 'they are in the right place at the right time' (Gannon et al. 2004).
- *antisocial cognitions*: men in this pathway hold strong anti-social beliefs and do not feel the need to conform to societal norms. They may enjoy inappropriate sexual activity as an exciting statement of their antisocial attitudes.
- *multiple pathway dysfunction*: these individuals may be considered 'classic' paedophiles. They choose children as their preferred sexual partners. They are characterized by intimacy and social skills deficits, engage in sexual acts as a means of emotional regulation, and have cognitive distortions supportive of paedophile acts. They usually consider children as sexual beings who have the capacity to make their own decisions about when, where and with whom to have sex.

Case formulation

Mr J was a 30-year-old man, admitted to hospital as a result of a period of severe depression. Prior to his depression he had been a teacher in a school in the north of England. Although there was no evidence that he had engaged in paedophile acts with any children, his name was found on a distribution list for child pornography kept by a paedophile ring. His house was raided and paedophile materials were found in it. He was therefore charged by the police, and found guilty of using child pornography. The school at which he worked was notified of this outcome and he was immediately dismissed from his job. He was married at the time that this occurred, but was immediately asked to leave the marital home and his wife began divorce proceedings. He moved to London, where he could be 'lost among the crowd' and had some family contacts. There he became profoundly depressed, and was admitted to hospital where he entered into therapy for his depression.

Long-term antecedents

Mr J was homosexual, and had experienced a sexual preference for males since he became sexually aware. During his adolescence he had no sexual relationships with either boys or girls. However, while masturbating, his imagery focused on young adolescent boys. As he grew older and left home to go to university, he found both his homosexuality and sexual interest in young boys shaming and inappropriate. He therefore did not seek sex with young men, but did have a number of age-appropriate homosexual relationships prior to his marriage, but these had generally ended disastrously. As a consequence, in an attempt to conform to both his and his parents' perceived norms, he began to date women towards the end of his university studies and was able to establish a long-term relationship with a woman with a low sex drive. He later married this woman. They lived together from the time he was at university to the time he was identified as a paedophile. His marriage had been functional and pleasant, but not sexually satisfying. During this time, he had regularly used child pornography (with a particular interest in young adolescent boys) unknown to his wife. He taught physical education (and mathematics) at school so clearly had the possibility of seeing young boys with little or no clothing. He denied ever having abused this possibility, and no complaints had been made against him at school. Of course, the truth of his claims is difficult to determine, as however motivated he was to change, there is little benefit to admitting behaviours that could be both embarrassing and put him at risk of legal action.

Formulation

Mr J did not fit the 'classic' profile of a paedophile. He was able to develop age-appropriate social (and to a more limited extent sexual) relationships both with men and women. He was not 'driven' to paedophilia as a consequence of an inability to engage with age-appropriate individuals. In addition, he did not condone his behaviour, and considered his sexual interest to be inappropriate and felt ashamed by it. He thought that while he claimed to have had no physical contact with young boys, even using photographs in this way was exploitative and morally unacceptable. His depression was a consequence of the loss of his job and his marriage, the probability that he would never find work again, and the shame he felt as his behaviour had been made public. His interest in young boys was maintained by masturbation to their images.

Intervention

Mr J was motivated to engage in therapy because he found his sexual interests inappropriate and shaming. He began a programme of masturbatory reorientation. In this, he began to masturbate to images of young children to achieve sexual excitement, before shifting the focus of his images to those of more mature boys or young-looking men. He found the image of one young-looking male Hollywood star (who will remain nameless!) particularly exciting. This programme worked very well, and over time he found that he could become sexually excited by the images of age-appropriate men.

Despite these gains and the claims he made about only using child pornography to provoke sexual excitement, his behaviour followed the pattern suggested by Pithers (1990) on at least one occasion. At this time he was feeling depressed, and decided to go for a walk, which drew him 'accidentally' to a shopping area frequented by local schoolchildren, and 'he happened to pass by a [public] toilet' when a young boy walked into it. At this point, he was excited by the thought of seeing the young child expose himself, and followed him into the toilet. There, he watched him use the urinal. The child was unaware of his presence, and there was no social or physical contact with him. Nevertheless, this reinforced the need to set up a relapse prevention programme, in which he drew up a list of alternative behaviours to do when he felt depressed or the need for sexual excitement. The alternative behaviours he engaged in were fairly limited, and included calling his family on the telephone or visiting them, and focusing on chores or tasks about the house. The one thing that he determined not to do was to leave the house at such times as this inevitably would lead to his 'accidentally' walking into high-risk areas. In addition, when leaving the house at all times he walked routes that did not pass schools or other places where young people might congregate, to reduce the likelihood of temptation. Despite this setback, both interventions appeared to progress well after this point, and Mr J was able to avoid putting himself at risk of offending for several months. He was eventually discharged, although with regular follow-up appointments in an attempt to monitor and prevent future problems.

Treatment of paedophilia

Social constraints

One way in which society has dealt with issues of paedophilia has been to try to control – not treat – the actions of paedophiles. A number of laws have been instituted to facilitate this process in the UK, including:

- *The Sex Offenders Act 1997*: lists all people convicted of acts 'of a sexual nature involving an abuse of power, where the victim is unable to give informed or true consent'. It covers a range of offences, including rape, incest, child abuse and indecent assault. Offenders have to register with the police and notify them of any changes in their name and address. People who do not register can be imprisoned or receive a £5000 fine. People stay on the register for differing times, depending on the nature of their conviction. People who receive a non-custodial sentence or caution stay on the list for five years: those given sentences of 30 months or over stay on indefinitely.
- *Crime Sentence Act 1997*: allows for sex offenders who are convicted of a second serious sex offence to be automatically given a life sentence.
- *Crime and Disorder Act 1998*: gives police particular powers against sex offenders, allowing them to apply for a 'Sex Offenders Order' for any offender who can reasonably be considered a public risk. Courts can impose conditions on offenders, such as banning them from places where children are likely to come together, such as parks and schools.

Stop and think...

In some states in the USA, a law unofficially called Megan's Law provides information about the presence of a child sex offender in the neighbourhood. This may involve the individual involved telling his neighbours that he is a paedophile and leaving a notice in their window with this information on. This does not happen in the UK at present, although schools or youth clubs can be made aware of the presence of a convicted offender by the police. Where names have been publicized, for example, through a series of photographs in the *News of the World* newspaper, the high publicity given to these issues apparently led to a number of attacks on people suspected of being paedophiles. In one instance, in South Wales, the house of a doctor who worked with children – a paediatrician – was mistakenly attacked. Clearly, there are a number of issues raised by these facts:

● How do we ensure that the risk of paedophiles accessing and assaulting children is minimized?

● How to we counter the need to ensure the safety of children with the physical safety and rights of people who may or may not have committed paedophile acts?

Where do *you* stand on these issues?

Treatment programmes

As sexual activity with young persons is against the law, treatment is usually initiated in a prison or a secure forensic facility. Even here, engagement in treatment programmes is not compulsory, and only about 25 per cent of those offered treatment choose to engage in treatment programmes.

Physical treatments

Physical treatments suppress sexual urges and behaviour, but do not change the object of sexual desire. Two surgical procedures, castration and neurosurgery, are no longer considered ethically acceptable. However, chemical approaches involving administration of drugs that block the production or action of androgens, hormones that influence the male sexual response, remain in use. These have achieved modest results. Berlin and Meinecke (1981), for example, followed 20 men treated with androgen-blocking drugs; 3 repeated their offences while taking medication, but relapse rates were high following cessation of therapy. A major problem for anti-androgen treatments is that between 30 and 100 per cent of the people prescribed these drugs do not take them (Barbaree and Seto 1997). Many of those who stop taking them presumably do so because they want to re-offend, as they do not change any of the beliefs or attitudes that drive deviant sexual behaviours. In addition, the drugs have a number of side-effects, including weight gain and reducing the size of testes, which may discourage their use. Finally, these treatments are effective only in individuals with abnormally high testosterone levels. Most paedophiles do not have these levels of testosterone, so would not benefit from the treatment even if they were fully compliant with the therapy. Summarizing the research on another biochemical treatment, luteinizing hormone-releasing hormone (LHRH) agonists (which prevent luteinizing hormone being released in the pituitary gland to stimulate the production of testosterone), Briken et al. (2003) identified four case reports, seven uncontrolled studies and only one study comparing LNRH agonists with an androgen antagonist. Thus the total sample of patients treated (often in an uncontrolled study) was 118, and all outcomes were self-report. With these cautions in mind, they concluded that the LNRH was an effective form of treatment. Of course, treatment does not come without its problems, which as well as sexual dysfunction include loss of body hair, hot flushes, mood swings, breast growth and weight gain.

Behaviour therapy

Both aversion therapy and masturbatory reconditioning methods have been used in the treatment of paedophilia. In aversion therapy, an inappropriate sexual stimulus is paired with an aversive event such as mild electric shock or strong aversive odour. This process is thought to condition a negative emotional state to the presence of the sexual stimulus. Most studies show some reduction of arousal to stimuli of young children. However, this may not result in reductions in offences. Rice et al. (1991), for example, followed 136 non-familial child molesters, 50 of whom received aversion therapy, following their discharge from a maximum security prison. Over a period of about six years, 31 per cent were convicted of a new offence. Recidivism rates were no lower among those who received aversion therapy than those who did not.

Masturbatory reconditioning involves the individual initiating a sexual response through the use of their favoured sexual images. Once they have achieved an erection, they switch to more appropriate images, such as a naked woman or man. They continue to masturbate to orgasm, when they concentrate deeply on this image. This approach may be combined with a graded series of 'normal' images, from less to more typical of the desired sexual focus. This approach has a number of advantages over aversion therapy. First, it is less ethically challenging and more acceptable to potential recipients. Second, it does not involve laboratory equipment and can be practised between therapy sessions. There is little empirical evidence of its effects and it is considered to be relatively ineffective and is now little used (Fagan et al. 2002).

Relapse prevention

Relapse prevention involves teaching the individual to do the following:

- identify situations in which they are at high risk of offending behaviour
- get out of the risky situation
- consider lapses as something to be learned from
- identify factors that led to relapse and plan how these could be avoided in the future.

The relapse prevention programme described by Marques et al. (2000) is typical of its type and the largest study so far conducted, involving over 700 participants. It involved an intensive in-patient programme conducted in a secure forensic hospital and a one-year support programme following discharge. Participants were given sexual education and taught general coping skills such as relaxation, stress and anger management, as well as social skills. More specific interventions included identifying the behaviours that preceded offending behaviour and addressing how these may be interrupted. It also dealt with issues of responsibility and minimization. Over a five-year follow-up, this intervention had a known re-offence rate of 10.8 per cent in contrast to the 13 per cent rate among those who did not receive the intervention – a modest difference. The programme was most successful with offenders who had male victims, and less successful with those who had female victims, although why is not clear. Unfortunately, by its eight-year follow-up assessment (see Research box 11: Marques et al. 2005), there were no differences in outcome between those people who took part in the programme and those that did not. While this is the largest reported study, other studies have reported more positive results. A recent meta-analysis collapsed across 69 studies with a total sample size of 22 181 sex offenders (Lösel and Schmucker, 2005) found a 6 per cent reduction in sexual recidivism with treatment.

Marques, J.K., Wiederanders, M., Day, D.M. et al. (2005). Effects of a relapse prevention program on sexual recidivism: results from California's Sex Offender Treatment and Evaluation Project (SOTEP), *Sexual Abuse: A Journal of Research and Treatment*, 17: 79–107.

This paper is the final report of the effectiveness of a year-long relapse prevention programme run as part of California's sex offender programme for offenders who volunteered for treatment in a small (50-bed) Unit at Atascadero State Hospital during the final two years of their prison term between the years 1985–1995.

Participants

The study sample comprised 704 offenders. Of these, 50 per cent were child molesters with female victims, 20 per cent had male victims, 8 per cent had both, and 22 per cent were rapists with adult victims. Most were white, with a lower percentage of African American and Hispanic men. Twenty-two per cent had previous arrests for sexual crimes.

Method

In-treatment measures

Relapse prevention group members were assessed on a battery of assessments. Here, they report known re-offending.

Outcome measures

Outcome measures were data from FBI and California Department of Justice measures of criminal activity, reports on parole violations, and returns to prison. Arrest reports and investigation reports were used to rate the type of offence, and various levels of offence severity. Offences were rated as 'hands on' (e.g. child molestation) or 'hands off' (possession of child pornography), and 'high-risk' (e.g. being in presence of minors). Only the first two were considered offences and used to determine outcome. However, offences were included if the crimes were considered 'possible' even if charges were dropped. The maximum time of follow-up was 12 years: the average follow-up time for each group is reported in Table 11.2.

Procedure

Participants were randomly allocated into one of three groups:

- The *intervention group* (*n* = 259) were involved in an intensive two-year treatment programme. Its core treatment comprised a relapse prevention group which met for three 90-minute sessions each week throughout the programme. In it, participants' cognitive-behavioural 'offence chain' was constructed and used to identify risk factors and patterns the relapse prevention programme had to address. They worked on accepting responsibility for offences, modifying cognitive distortions, and learned how to respond differently to urges to engage in inappropriate sexual behaviour. In addition, they attended groups on sex education, human sexuality, relaxation training, stress and anger management and social skills. Those with significant alcohol and drug histories took part in a related treatment programme. The first year of the programme was conducted in hospital, the second while participants were free in the community.
- A *volunteer control group* (*n* = 225) comprised sexual offenders who volunteered to take part in the research, but were allocated to a 'usual care' (e.g. no specific sexual behaviour programme).
- A *non-volunteer control group* (*n* = 220) comprised inmates who qualified for the project but chose not to participate.

Findings

A number of participants were removed from the programme due to severe behavioural problems in the Unit, although this was kept to a minimum. Others withdrew themselves from treatment at various stages. The results of the intervention group were therefore split into those who withdrew prior to treatment, those who received a substantial element of the programme but dropped out before one year of the programme, and those who received more than the first year of the programme.

Table 11.2 Re-offence levels according to treatment of all participants (first three columns) and child molesters (final column)

	N	Years at risk	% re-offend	Child molester
Relapse prevention				
• *All*	259	8.3	22	22
• *Withdrew prior to treatment*	55	7.9	20	N/A
• *< 1 year*	14	8.4	35	N/A
• *> 1 year*	190	8.4	21.6	N/A
Volunteer control	225	8.4	20	17
Non-volunteer control	220	8.3	19.1	20.6

As can be seen in Table 11.2, differences between the outcomes were not significantly different, except for the rates of re-offending among those who dropped out in the first year of the programme, who had significantly higher levels of re-offending than any other group. The data reported in Table 11.2 were not adjusted for baseline differences between the groups. More participants in the relapse prevention group were considered to be at high risk of re-offending. However, adjusting for this did not change the lack of significance between group differences. Analyses stratified for level of risk at baseline revealed an apparently lower recidivism rate in the relapse prevention group (39.5 per cent versus 43 per cent in the volunteer control and 46.2 in the non-volunteer group) but this was not statistically significant.

Discussion

The results show no benefit of attending the relapse prevention programme. Why should this be the case, particularly in the light of other published, and more positive findings? The authors speculated that this may have been one result of keeping participants in the relapse prevention programme in a single enclosed unit within a hospital. This may have encouraged them to openly discuss crimes and sexual deviance, perhaps swapping stories and ideas without the knowledge of hospital staff. This would not have been possible in a prison setting in which other study participants remained. A second issue may have been the interventions response to termination of treatment. Participants remained in the programme unless they presented severe management problems. Lack of motivation or engagement was not a reason for exclusion. The non-completion rate of 18 per cent is much lower than in other studies (where half the participants may be excluded) which report better outcomes. It may be that these differences in outcomes reflect the type of individual maintained within therapy. Inclusion of unmotivated individuals may have impacted negatively on the motivation and progress of other members of the group.

11.6 Transvestic fetishism

DSM-IV-TR defined transvestic fetishism as:

- recurrent, intense, sexually arousing fantasies, sexual urges or behaviours involving cross-dressing over a period of at least six months in a heterosexual male
- these fantasies, sexual urges or behaviours cause clinically significant distress or impairment in social, occupational or other important areas of functioning.

Boys who grow up to engage in transvestite behaviour do not engage in 'feminine' behaviours before puberty, nor do they cross-dress. Similarly, men who are transvestites are unremarkably masculine in their adult hobbies and career choices. Transvestites usually begin cross-dressing at puberty, and rarely later than mid-adolescence. This typically results in sexual excitement, although many people report that they dress in this way because they like the feel of the clothes and that there is no sexual motivation to their behaviour. Some adolescents wear female clothes occasionally; others compulsively wear them under their masculine clothes. Attempts at passing off as a woman are rare in adolescence. However, cross-dressing is frequently accompanied by fantasies of being female, and these fantasies may form the nucleus of sexual fantasies. The prevalence of transvestism within the general population is rarely measured. However, Langstrom and Zucker (2005) found a prevalence rate of 3 per cent among men in a Swedish population sample. There is little evidence of an analogous form of the disorder in women.

In a survey of over 1000 adult transvestite men, Docter and Prince (1997) reported that 40 per cent of their sample experienced sexual excitement and orgasm 'always' or 'often' when they cross-dressed. Only 9 per cent of the sample said they never experienced this. Cross-dressing frequently elicits less and less sexual excitement as the individual grows older and may eventually have no discernible sexual association. However, the desire to cross-dress may remain the same or even grow stronger, and may be accompanied by feelings of comfort and well-being. Lack of opportunity to cross-dress can result in a lowering of mood and marked irritability. As a result, many transvestites continue to wear women's undergarments beneath their normal male clothes.

Among Docter and Prince's (1997) respondents, 87 per cent reported being exclusively heterosexual; 83 per cent were either married at the time of the survey or had been married; 32 per cent of their wives knew they cross-dressed before marriage; 28 per cent were completely accepting of the behaviour once they became aware of it, while 19 per cent were 'completely antagonistic'. It is common for transvestite men to stop cross-dressing in the early months or years of relationships with a new partner, although many revert to cross-dressing in time. Many enjoy 'normal' heterosexual intercourse. Others need props such as wearing feminine attire to achieve sexual pleasure.

As social reaction can be very negative to transvestic behaviour, cross-dressing usually takes place in arenas where such behaviour is acceptable, including the home and transvestite clubs or organizations. Nevertheless, Docter and Prince (1997) reported that 71 per cent of their sample had cross-dressed in public: 10 per cent had ridden on a bus or train while cross-dressed, 28 per cent had eaten in restaurants, 26 per cent used the ladies' toilet and 22 per cent had tried on feminine clothing in stores. When asked their preferred gender identity, 11 per cent preferred their masculine self, 28 per cent preferred their feminine self and 60 per cent preferred each equally.

Some people experience guilt and shame as a result of their feelings and behaviour. Such individuals may make repeated, frequently unsuccessful, efforts to overcome their perceived anomaly. They may rid their wardrobe of feminine clothes, before acquiring new ones in the following weeks and months. This cycle may occur repeatedly in younger people who later become more accepting of their feelings. In Docter and Prince's sample, 70 per cent reported having purged their wardrobe on at least one occasion, and 45 per cent reported seeking counselling as a result of their feelings.

Aetiology of transvestic fetishism

Biological factors

There are surprisingly few studies of a biological cause of transvestism – and most are case studies rather than formal scientific studies. One such case, reported by Riley (2002), involved a 72-year-old man who was treated with a drug known as selegiline, an MAOI (see Chapter 4) which, among other actions, increases serotonin and dopamine activity. Following this treatment, the man developed a frequent impulse to wear women's clothing – despite never having had this desire previously. The drug was withdrawn, and his urge to wear women's clothing stopped. This remains one of the very few studies of biological mechanisms.

Parental relationships

Various, often contradictory, family theories of transvestism have been proposed. Newcomb (1985) found that transvestite men were more likely than other heterosexual men to characterize their parents as less sex-typed and more sex-reversed in terms of dependence and affiliation. This suggested some form of modelling process may be involved. However, men who become transvestites tend to adopt typical masculine roles as a young child, countering this type of theory. A second theory has suggested that the principal maternal influence in transvestism is one of hostility and anger towards males. Zucker and Bradley (1995) noted evidence that boys who develop transvestism have higher separation rates from their mothers than is the norm, suggesting this reflected their mothers' aggressive attitudes towards men, and that transvestites are avoiding this hostility by dressing as women.

Behavioural models   One school of thought suggests that transvestism results from being cross-dressed during childhood, particularly by mothers or other female figures, as a form of punishment – a process known as 'petticoat punishment'. A number of case examples have been published (Stoller 1968), although it is not clear why an adult should choose to adopt a behaviour used to punish them as a child as a sexual fetish. Stoller argued that this may represent a form of mastery over the punishment. However, a number of clinicians have claimed that incidences of forced cross-dressing are rare, and that it is usually the child who initiates such behaviour. More conventional reinforcement models (Crawford et al. 1993) suggest that if a child is exposed to women's clothing and enjoys the feel of them or masturbates while wearing them, this may establish a reinforcement process that results in the continuation of this behaviour.

Psychoanalytic models   Ovesey and Person (1973) suggested that the psychoanalytic processes that lead to transvestism occur after an individual has consolidated their sense of maleness. Their mother is typically warm and supportive, their father distant and threatening, even verbally or physically abusive. As a result, the mother turns towards her son for gratification not forthcoming from her marriage. She is seductive towards the boy, but at the same time encourages his cross-dressing either overtly or covertly. In doing so, she is thought to be gratifying herself sexually, but repressing her real (sexual) interest by denying his masculinity. The child is gratified by her intimacy, but also feels guilty. He assumes that his mother wishes to dress him as a girl in order to placate his father. The intimacy of his mother and the perceived rivalry of his father prevent a successful resolution of the oedipal complex (see Chapter 2).

After childhood, the individual seeks to preserve the mother as a dependence object, and is attracted to women like his mother who will accept or even encourage cross-dressing. Adult transvestites resort to cross-dressing under periods of stress and wear female underclothing as a protective device. Female clothes provide protection in three ways:

- they symbolize the mother and perpetuate dependence and continued need for her protection
- they symbolize auto-castration, a token submission to male competitors, which wards of their retaliation
- they disguise masculinity to disarm rivals.

The clothes conceal the penis, the symbol of masculine power, and deny hostile intent. They allow the individual to avoid detection by their rivals, which not only allays anxiety, but even confers on the individual an inflated sense of masculinity. Ovesey and Person (1973: 69) went so far to suggest that 'the transvestite is Superman in drag!'

Treatment of transvestic fetishism

Transvestism is not a condition that requires treatment. Nevertheless, people whose behaviour is affecting their relationships or who find their behaviour unacceptable may seek treatment. Marital problems often lead to attempts at behavioural change and the initiation of therapy. Wives often have negative feelings towards their husband's behaviour even when they know about it early in their relationship (Bullough and Weinberg 1988).

Treatment usually focuses on the sexual elements of transvestite behaviour, and includes aversion therapy and modification of sexual fantasy. Some aversion programmes have proven moderately successful. Marks et al. (1970) reported that two-thirds of participants in electrical aversion therapy improved with treatment, up to a follow-up period of two years. This compared with one-quarter of a control group who did not receive the intervention. A second approach to the treatment of transvestism involves masturbatory retraining. Here, the individual masturbates using his preferred sexual object, including female props worn either by the individual or his partner, before reverting to images of more 'normal' sex objects immediately before and at orgasm. Again, a number of case descriptions and uncontrolled studies have shown this method to have been used with good effect (Laws and Marshall 1991). More recently, Chiang et al. (1999) reported significant changes following a cognitive behavioural programme instituted following the individual developing 'severe moral anxiety' (p. 299). The individual involved did not respond to psychodynamic therapy, but a combination of supportive and cognitive therapy proved of some value, at least in the short term.

11.7 Gender identity disorder

In contrast to transvestism, where men dress as women, but accept their male identity, individuals with gender identity disorder (GID) believe themselves to have been born the wrong sex. DSM-IV-TR defines the disorder as:

- a strong and persistent cross-gender identification
- persistent discomfort with one's sex, or a sense of inappropriateness in the gender role of that sex
- clinically significant distress or impairment in social, occupational or other important areas of functioning.

In adolescents and adults, gender identity disorder is manifested by a preoccupation with the belief that they are born 'the wrong sex' and a desire for the removal of primary and secondary sex characteristics. Many people with this disorder opt for surgery to change their body to what they consider to be their appropriate sex. They become transsexuals. Others do not take such a radical step, but dress and try to pass themselves of as a member of their desired sex. People with GID are often sexually attracted to people of the same sex, which they interpret as conventional heterosexual preference. There are no prevalence data of the condition within the general population. However, what little evidence there is suggests that people with gender identity disorder are highly likely to experience clinically significant distress at some period in their life (Hepp et al. 2005).

Most adults with GID report a history of consistent cross-gender behaviour in childhood. Boys may reject the rough-and-tumble play and prefer the company of girls. They frequently dress in women's clothing and insist they will grow up to be a girl. Some claim their penis and testes are disgusting and hope they will somehow change into female genitalia as they grow older. Girls may reject urinating in the sitting position, and assert that they do not want to grow breasts or menstruate. They may reject typical girls' clothing. Green and Blanchard (1995) reported that these behaviours and attitudes are usually detected before the age of 3 years. These characteristics are not static, however, and many children adopt more gender-appropriate behaviours and identities over time. Wallien and Cohen-Kettenis (2008), for example, followed a cohort of 77 children referred to a clinic as a result of gender dysphoria. At 10 years follow-up, 43 per cent of their sample were no longer gender dysphoric. Of note was that the stronger the cross-gender behaviour, the more likely the child to remain gender dysphoric. Some adults may also spontaneously change their gender identity (Marks et al. 2000), although such occurrences are rare.

Findings that most individuals experience significant reductions in distress if they change sex through hormonal and surgical means, have led some to argue that GID is not a mental health disorder. Rather, any mental distress experienced is an understandable outcome of a physical disorder – having gender-inappropriate genitalia and body type. According to this argument (see, for example, Winters and Karasic 2009), DSM-IV and certainly DSM-V should no longer include GID as a psychiatric diagnosis.

Aetiology of gender identity disorder

Genetic factors

One of the very few studies of the genetic processes in GID, reported by Coolidge et al. (2002), found 2 per cent of their sample of over 300 MZ and DZ twins showed some evidence of gender identity disorder symptomatology based on self-report measures. Applying statistical modelling to their data, they found that 62 per cent of the variance in reported symptoms could be attributed to biological factors; 38 per cent was attributable to environmental factors. These data led the investigators to suggest that the causes of GID were primarily biological – not psychological.

Biological factors

Although most commentators, and the genetic data, suggest that GID is primarily the result of biological processes, what these are is far from clear. Studies of sex hormonal disturbance in adulthood are surprisingly difficult to conduct, because many people with GID take hormones of the opposite sex either as part of a treatment programme or by purchasing them on the black market. Despite these interpretive difficulties, what evidence there is does not support a hormonal explanation. Summarizing the evidence, Gladue (1985) reported few, if any, hormonal differences between men with GID, male heterosexuals and male homosexuals. Similarly negative results have been found in women. Meyer-Bahlung (1979) found some women with GID had elevated levels of male hormones, but most did not.

A variant of the hormonal explanation is that abnormal levels of prenatal hormones may influence behaviour, and possibly gender identity. This may affect both sexes. The female children of women who have taken precursors to male hormones during pregnancy to prevent uterine bleeding tend to express high levels of tomboyish behaviour in preschool years (Ehrhardt and Money 1967). Boys whose mothers have taken female hormones while pregnant tend to be less boyish than their peers and to engage less in rough-and-tumble play (Yalom et al. 1973). However, there is no evidence that either group of children dislike their gender.

Although a number of studies have failed to find any differences between the brains of people with and without gender identity disorder, some studies have found evidence to suggest a neurological substrate to this disorder. Zhou et al. (1995) conducted autopsies on the brains of six people who had changed their sex from male to female. They found an area of the brain, known as the bed nucleus of stria terminalis (BST), within the hypothalamus to be much smaller than is typically found in men. Indeed, the size of the BST matched that typically found in women, which is usually about half the size of that found in men. In a further investigation of this phenomenon, Kruijver et al. (2000) examined the number of somatostatin-expressing neurons in the BST. They found the same pattern of neurological findings. The number of these neurons in the BSTs of male-to-female transsexuals was similar to those in the females' BST, while the number of these neurons of a female-to-male transsexual was in the male range. What this difference actually means is not clearly understood, although the BST is known to regulate sexual activity in male rats. It is possible, therefore, that this may contribute in some way to GID.

Several research groups have measured differences between people with and without GID on more general neuropsychological tasks including those, such as rotation, visualization and verbalization tasks, whose performance typically differs between the sexes. Haraldsen et al. (2003), for example, found that untreated people with GID performed on cognitive tests in ways that were predicted by their biological sex, not their gender identity – suggesting few neurological differences between people with GID and those without such issues. By contrast, Schöning et al. (2010) found differences in areas of brain activation between untreated men with and without GID during spatial rotation tasks, suggesting that there *are* neurological differences between the two groups. Interestingly, at least one study in which performance on cognitive and other tasks has been assessed during hormone therapy for GID has shown the extent to which the brain is susceptible to hormonal treatment. Van Goozen et al. (1995) found that among women transforming to men, administration of androgens was associated with significant increases in aggressiveness, sexual arousability and spatial ability, and reduced scores on verbal fluency tasks. For the male-to-female group, the opposite constellation of outcomes was observed: anger and aggression proneness, sexual arousability and visuo-spatial ability decreased, while verbal fluency improved. Unfortunately, several more recent studies including that of Schöning et al. (2009) have failed to find this pattern of results.

Psychoanalytic explanations

Psychoanalytic explanations suggest that male transsexuals have an ambiguous core gender identity. According to Ovesey and Person (1973), male transsexualism originates from extreme separation anxiety early in life before the individual has fully established his own sexual identity. To alleviate this anxiety, the individual resorts to fantasy of symbiotic fusion with the mother. In this way, mother and child become one and the danger of separation is nullified. In the transsexual's mind, he literally becomes the mother, and to sustain this fantasy attempts to revert his core identity from male to female.

To explain the desire for the removal of the penis, Ovesey and Person (1973) noted that the transsexual does not experience castration anxiety, as do most boys. Instead, they experience anxiety that continues until they *are* castrated. The penis is clear evidence that they have failed to psychically fuse with the mother. For the same reason, they reject the act of homosexuality, as this would also acknowledge them as male. They prefer to reject any sexual experience, and generally have little or no experience of sex, even masturbation. In sum, the motivation for security takes priority over motivation for sexuality, as a result of fear of early maternal abandonment.

Early life conditioning

Perhaps the most widely accepted psychosocial theory of GID is that of early life conditioning. Parents of people with gender identity disorder frequently report that they encouraged and gave attention to their child when he or she cross-dressed. This appears to be particularly relevant in boys, where they may be taught how to wear make-up and other feminine behaviours (Green 1987). More subtle factors may also be at play. Girls who exhibit high levels of tomboy behaviour tend to have parents who do the same, and to choose their father as their favourite parent. This allows the possibility of learning such behaviours from their parents and being rewarded for expressing them (Zucker et al. 1994).

Conditioning experiences may also explain why more children than adults are identified as having gender identity disorder. Early life experiences are dominated by family. However, as an individual grows up, they are subject to influences of a wider range of people: peers, school teachers, and so on. It is possible that such exposure results in differing reinforcement processes in which the individual is punished for behaving in 'inappropriate' ways. The competing strengths of each reinforcement system may determine whether or not the individual does or does not behave in gender-discrepant ways. While this approach can explain the development of non-gender-typical behaviours, it has more difficulty in explaining the extremely strongly held beliefs about their gender that such people hold, and their resistance to any form of psychological therapy.

Treatment of gender identity disorder

Psychological therapies

Most people with gender identity disorder are resistant to psychotherapy. As a result, there are no clinical trials reporting attempts to change gender identity. However, a number of case reports indicate that behaviour and attitudes can be changed should the individual wish, or even when they do not seek help. Meyer-Bahlburg (2002) argued that young people often experience ostracism from peers and even other family members and other social difficulties, which can lead to them dropping out of school and experiencing significant emotional problems. They argued that therapy was therefore justified 'to speed up the fading of the cross-gender identity which will typically happen in any case' (p. 361). Meyer-Bahlburg worked with parents of eleven young people to modify key factors known to be associated with the persistence of gender identity disorder. Therapy was conducted through the parents, who attended sessions in the absence of the young person. These involved developing strategies to, for example, increase time spent between father and son, and decrease time with mother; distraction from cross-gender behaviour rather than prohibition, increased attention to gender-typical behaviour, identifying suitable male peers for play dates, and as the boy gains peer-relational skills, joining male social groups such as the scouts or sports teams. They report a number of successful case histories.

Physical treatment

Many people with gender identity disorder request sex reassignment surgery. This involves a complex, staged process. For male-to-female transitions, treatment starts at least a year before surgery (see Box 11.1). First, the individual starts taking the female hormone oestrogen that results in a number of physical changes, including the development of breasts and a softening of the skin. Fat may shift from the shoulders to the hips in feminine fashion.

Box 11.1 Problems of gender identity disorder

Access to sex change surgery in Britain is limited. At times of inadequate resources for health care, this type of surgery is given a low priority, and many people with gender identity disorder can find it extremely difficult, if not impossible, to obtain this treatment from the National Health Service. Many people who choose to have surgery do so by paying privately for it, through specialist private companies such as TRANSFORM, who provide an assessment of the individual's suitability for gender reassignment, hormone therapy, support for a year while they await surgery and try to live as someone of the opposite sex, and then surgery and post-surgery support.

Simon was a 30-year-old man just beginning this process. He had been to the initial assessment and accepted as a possible 'case', and had begun hormone therapy at the time of the interview in which he described what led him to seek gender reassignment and the frustrations he had experienced on the way:

I am so angry. I know I have the wrong body, and no one can convince me that I am wrong. As long as I can remember, I have felt this way. I wanted breasts, to be a girl, to have a period – to get rid of my penis. I envy them so much . . . I have tried to go along with things, not to be as I am. It's really pretty frightening admitting it and having to go the whole way like I want to. But it's what I want . . .

I married someone just to try and conform. I love her as well. Not in a physical way, though. We don't have sex . . . she isn't really a sexual person so that's all right. That's why

I began to see her. She isn't very attractive, but she's a good person, so it feels good that she's with someone like me, where sex isn't a big deal. It doesn't feel right, but we are good friends and we get on well. I tried to keep things a secret. I have – had – a place in my wardrobe where I keep women's clothing. I put it on when she is at work. It feels so natural and fantastic. It's the only time I felt I was really me, and how I wanted to be. I had a wig, make-up and stuff so I could really feel like a woman. It was secret, but she came home when I was wearing it one day, and so I had to explain some of how I feel and what I want. She knows I want to change my sex. We're going to live together until I do, even though my body is going to change with the hormones. But she wants to live with me despite it. I don't know what will happen and how we'll feel in time, though ... I wear the clothing and the wig at home all the time now, now she knows. She's OK about it ... I'm not a 'trannie' [transvestite] though, because I want more – just dressing up isn't enough. They are just men playing at being women. I want and have always wanted to be a proper woman.

It has been so frustrating getting so far. I went for an interview at Charing Cross Hospital and they agreed to put me on their programme, but the local health people wouldn't pay for it, even though I had letters from my GP and a psychiatrist saying I needed it. So I had to go to TRANSFORM. I went to see them and they agreed to give me an assessment by a psychologist, and he agreed to put me on the programme. And that was great ... but I had no money, so I couldn't do it straight away. I felt so low at the time ... very depressed. I really needed it, but no one would let me get on with things. I was pretty close to suicidal ... I thought things would never change ... and I couldn't tell my wife why I was so low ... I'm still on antidepressants now ... I think they're the only thing keeping me going ... I still don't know how I'm going to pay for surgery ... I would sell the house but that's not fair on my wife, so I'm happy I'm on the hormones and beginning to see changes, but I can't see how I will go the whole way ... but I won't be happy unless I do, because emotionally it all feels so right.

Once initiated, hormones are taken indefinitely. This itself appears to bring benefit. Eighty per cent of those treated with hormones report less gender dysphoria and improvements in quality of life (Murad et al. 2009). At the same time, the person will undergo electrolysis to rid them of masculine hair patterns. They are also trained to raise the timbre of their voice. At this early stage, some people may also have cosmetic surgery to alter facial features such as their chin or larynx to make them appear more feminine. Most of these changes are reversible. More enduring changes are usually held back for at least a year during which the individual is required to live as a woman. Only if this 'trial period' is completed successfully will the final surgery be conducted. This involves amputation of the penis and construction of an artificial vagina. This will permit normal sexual intercourse.

For female–male reassignment a similar process is followed. Hormone therapy changes body shape, redistributing fat, as well as deepening the voice. However, surgery is more arduous and the end results are less successful. The penis that can be constructed is generally small and not capable of a normal erection. Accordingly, sexual intercourse is not possible without the use of artificial supports. Surgery may also include bilateral mastectomy and hysterectomy.

The social and psychological outcomes of surgery are generally good. Weyers et al. (2009), for example, reported that transsexual women compared favourably with the general population on measures of both physical and mental quality of life. In addition, they reported high levels of satisfaction with their self-image as women. They were less satisfied with their sexual functioning, which while they can achieve and enjoy intercourse, was less satisfying than the comparison group. This dissatisfaction with physical limitations was echoed in the findings of Kuhn et al. (2008), who found low levels of regret and emotional difficulties in transsexual men and women, but that they did report more physical and role limitations than a comparison group. Y.L.S. Smith et al. (2001) followed a cohort of adolescents, who either did or did not receive sex reassignment surgery, for a period of four years. By this time, none of those who received surgery regretted their choice and they considered themselves to be functioning psychologically and socially 'quite well'. Those who did not receive surgery generally did less well, although they showed modest improvements on measures as diverse as gender dysphoria and body dissatisfaction. These gains, however, were of a different order of magnitude to those made in the group treated with surgery. Positive outcomes in uncontrolled studies have been reported in domains such as cosmetic appearance, sexual functioning, self-esteem, body image, family life, social relationships, psychological status and satisfaction. The small number of serious postoperative incidents includes requests for reversal, hospitalization and suicide. New problems may also emerge following reassignment surgery. Some individuals may need to come to terms with painful loss, including jobs, families, partners, children and friends, as a result of their gender change. Many people are forced to move away from a familiar environment and, despite being confident in their gender role, may have difficulties with social adaptation and acceptance by others.

11.8 Chapter summary

1 There are two broad categories of sexual disorder: disorders of response (including erectile dysfunction and vaginismus) and disorders of desire, the paraphilias.

2 Erectile dysfunction can be the result of physical factors, but is frequently the result of psychological ones. Common factors include anxiety, often as a result of distorted beliefs about sexual performance, and 'spectating'.

3 Vaginismus is also triggered by anxiety.

4 Treatment using sensate focus and graded exposure methods is effective in both disorders.

5 Paraphilias are generally considered to be the result of conditioning processes in childhood, although specific paraphilias may have multiple casual factors.

6 Paedophilia may result from conditioning processes, poor adult attachment and sexual relationships, an emotional congruence with children, and processes such as justifying cognitions that support the behaviour.

7 Many people imprisoned as a result of paedophile behaviour do not enter treatment programmes. For those that do, cognitive behavioural programmes that address the cognitions

▶ supporting the behaviour and develop strategies for dealing with high-risk situations appear the most effective treatment. Masturbatory reconditioning may also alter the object of sexual pleasure. Hormonal therapies may be effective as long as the drug is taken, but compliance is low and relapse, once the drug is stopped, is high.

8 Transvestic fetishism is not a 'disorder' that requires treatment, but some people choose to seek treatment due to social and marital pressures.

9 Transvestism is usually considered to be the consequence of conditioning processes, and treatment involves reconditioning using masturbatory retraining techniques. Aversive approaches are rarely used for ethical reasons.

10 Gender identity disorder occurs when an individual feels that they are the incorrect gender and wishes to change it.

11 Gender identity disorder is poorly understood. No evidence of biological determinants has been found, and psychological models struggle to provide adequate explanations of the condition.

12 People with gender identity disorder are generally resistant to psychological therapy and most eventually seek surgery and hormonal treatments, following which most enjoy a better quality of life.

11.9 For discussion

1 Is transvestism a true sexual 'disorder'?

2 Given the difficulties of treating people who engage in paedophilic behaviour, should those people remain in hospital or some other institution to protect society from them? If they are released into society, should the public be made aware of where they live?

3 Consider the argument that applying behaviour modification principles to make a young person's behaviour more gender-appropriate is simply reinforcing cultural stereotypes, is unethical and is against the best wishes of the child, who should be free to express his or her own sexuality and behave in a way that they choose.

4 Could enforced celibacy as an adult increase risk for paedophilia? If so, how?

11.10 Key term

Dysphoric unhappy, but not sufficiently so to warrant a diagnosis of depression.

11.11 Further reading

Blanchard, R. (2009) The DSM diagnostic criteria for transvestic fetishism. *Archives of Sexual Behavior*, 39: 363–72.

Marshall, W.L., Marshall, L.E., Serran, G.A. et al. (2008) Sexual offender treatment: a positive approach, *Psychiatric Clinics of North America*, 31: 681–96.

Möller, B., Schreier, H., Li, A. et al. (2009) Gender identity disorder in children and adolescents, *Current Problems in Pediatric Adolescent Health Care*, 39: 117–43.

Murray, J.B. (2000) Psychological profile of pedophiles and child molesters, *Journal of Psychology*, 134: 211–24.

Ward, T., Polasheck, D. and Beech, A.R. (2005) *Theories of Sexual Offending*. Chichester: WileyBlackwell.

The following websites also have information about the conditions described in this chapter, their treatment, and people's experiences of them. Some also link to the sites on both sides of the paedophile argument.

Paedophilia

www.nambla.org/
www.attractedtochildren.org/
www.mapsexoffenders.com
www.mako.org.au/home.html

Transvestism

www.beaumontsociety.org.uk/index.html
www.tvdreams.co.uk/

Gender identity disorder

www.genderpsychology.org/
www.avitale.com/

Personality disorders

Chapter contents

Personality disorders affect an individual for much of their life. A number of these disorders have been identified, some of which, such as the schizoid or schizotypal disorders, have some of the features of other, more disabling, conditions – but not to such a degree that a formal diagnosis can be assigned. Others, including borderline personality or psychopathy, differ markedly from any other DSM diagnoses. The chapter begins with a discussion of the validity of the concept of personality disorders as distinct 'disorders', before considering a general theory explaining their development. The chapter then considers each of three clusters of personality disorders, with a particular focus on two conditions that have received the most attention from psychologists: borderline personality disorder and the associated diagnoses of antisocial behaviour and psychopathy. By the end of the chapter, you should have an understanding of:

- Issues related to all personality disorders
- Challenges to the diagnostic category of personality disorder
- A general theory of personality disorders
- The type A, B and C personality disorder clusters, with particular focus on:
  - borderline personality and its treatment
  - the aetiology and treatment of antisocial behaviour and psychopathy.

12.1 Introduction

Personality disorders are also known as axis 2 disorders within DSM (see Chapter 1), in that they are considered stable long-term conditions. DSM-IV-TR defined such disorders as an enduring pattern of inner experience and behaviour that deviates markedly from the expectations of the individual's culture in at least two of the following: cognition, mood, interpersonal functioning or impulse control. The pattern is inflexible and pervasive across a range of personal or social situations and is long lasting. Its onset can be traced back to adolescence or early childhood. It is usually, but not always, associated with significant distress or impairment. DSM-IV-TR identified ten personality disorders in three clusters, although the overlap between some disorders is so great that it can be difficult to distinguish one from another, raising concerns about the reliability and validity of such diagnoses:

- Cluster A: *'Odd or eccentric'* – paranoid, schizoid and schizotypal
- Cluster B: *'Flamboyant or dramatic'* – antisocial, histrionic, narcissistic, borderline
- Cluster C: *'Fearful or anxious'* – avoidant, dependent, obsessive-compulsive.

Personality disorders are often accompanied by other disorders of mood. Depending on the study, between 24 and 74 per cent of people diagnosed with a personality disorder also have major depression, and between 4 and 20 per cent have bipolar depression. Co-morbidity with anxiety disorders is also very common (Grant et al. 2005). Antisocial and narcissistic disorders are generally thought to be more prevalent in men, and histrionic and borderline disorders more prevalent among women (APA 2000).

By definition, personality disorders are relatively stable over time. However, they may be more mutable than first thought, and a number of studies have shown significant changes over time in the experiences of people diagnosed with them. In one of the longest follow-ups yet conducted, Paris and Zweig-Frank (2001) reported the 27-year outcomes of a cohort of individuals diagnosed with borderline personality disorder. By this time, only 5 out of 64 individuals in the cohort met the criteria for the diagnosis. A more fine-grained analysis was reported by Shea et al. (2008), who followed a cohort of men and women with the same diagnosis for a period of six years, with yearly assessments. Encouragingly, they found gradual and consistent year-on-year improvement – with the exception of some of older study participants, in their late 30s and early 40s, who showed a worsening of functioning over time. Another challenge to the concept of the DSM personality disorders has been their somewhat arbitrary definitions. Widiger et al. (1987), for example, reported that 55 per cent of people diagnosed as having borderline personality using DSM-III criteria could also have been diagnosed as having schizotypal disorder. Similarly, Morey (1988) found that 33 per cent of people diagnosed with schizotypal disorder also met the diagnostic criteria for having narcissistic personality disorder, while 59 per cent met the criteria for avoidant personality disorder and paranoid personality disorder. The change to DSM-IV and DSM-IV-TR and the development of structured clinical interviews are said to have improved levels of diagnostic agreement, which now match those of the major diagnostic categories of depression, anxiety, schizophrenia, and so on. Nevertheless, some problems remain. There is, for example, considerable overlap between the diagnostic criteria for the anxious personality types and axis 1 diagnoses such as social phobia, depression and generalized anxiety disorder, making differential diagnoses difficult to achieve at times. Indeed, Ralevski et al. (2005) suggested that avoidant personality disorder and social phobia are 'alternative conceptualizations of the same disorder'. In addition, while Zanarini et al. (2002) reported high levels of inter-rater reliability in the diagnosis of borderline personality disorder using an interview schedule based on DSM-IV, test–retest reliability was not so strong. In this, one-third of their symptom dimensions achieved excellent levels of reliability (based on Cohen's kappa statistic), but two-thirds were only in the fair-good range.

A dimensional approach

The concept of personality disorders may be also be challenged at a more fundamental level. Personality disorders may be considered as distinct 'disorders' – this is certainly the model taken by DSM. However, a number of commentators (e.g. Trull 2005) have argued that people with these traits should not be assigned a categorical diagnosis identifying them as 'disordered' or mentally ill. They may better be considered as being at the extreme of the distribution of personality characteristics rather than categorically different from the norm (see Chapter 1). Here is a hypothetical profile, suggested by the five-factor model of personality (Costa and McRae 1995), for antisocial personality disorder which received empirical support in a cohort of adolescents studied by Lynam et al. (2005):

- *Low neuroticism*: lack of appropriate concern for potential problems in health or social adjustment; emotional blandness.
- *Low extraversion*: social isolation, interpersonal detachment and lack of support networks; flattened affect; lack of joy and zest for life; reluctance to assert self or assume leadership roles, even when qualified; social inhibition and shyness.
- *Low openness*: difficulty adapting to social or personal change; low tolerance or understanding of different points of view or lifestyles; emotional blandness and inability to understand and verbalize own feelings; alexithymia; constricted range of interests; insensitivity to art and beauty; excessive conformity to authority.
- *Low agreeableness*: cynicism and paranoid thinking; inability to trust even friends or family; quarrelsomeness; ready to pick fights; exploitive and manipulative; lying; rude and inconsiderate manner alienates friends, limits social support; lack of respect for social conventions can lead to trouble with the law; inflated and grandiose sense of self; arrogance.
- *Low conscientiousness*: underachievement: not fulfilling intellectual or artistic potential; poor academic performance relative to ability; disregard of rules and responsibilities can lead to trouble with the law; unable to discipline self (such as stick to diet or exercise plan) even when required for medical reasons; personal and occupational aimlessness.

Not only can the dimensional view be argued on theoretical and philosophical grounds, it also may be better at predicting outcome than the DSM categorical approach. Ullrich et al. (2001), for example, found that scores on personality tests were better able to predict subsequent offending behaviour than categorical diagnoses of antisocial personality disorder. In addition, a number of other studies, including Zanarini et al. (2002), have reported higher levels of diagnostic agreement using the dimensional approach than the more traditional diagnostic criteria.

A cognitive model of personality disorders

Although there are ten personality disorders (or personality types), Beck et al. (1990) attempted to develop a single, unitary, explanatory model for the development of them all. In doing so, they adopted an evolutionary perspective. They suggested that key neuro-cognitive responses, including those affecting perception, mood and behaviour, are genetically pre-programmed and that these responses may be adaptive in some evolutionary times, but less adaptive in others. Competitive behaviour, for example, may be of benefit at times of scarcity but not at times of social cohesion and mutual cooperation.

According to Beck and colleagues, what we term personality disorders are the inappropriate expression of these pre-programmed responses. They suggested that it is not the behaviour *per se* that is problematic, but the individual's lack of adaptability and responsiveness to the environment. Most of us learn to adapt our behaviour as a result of life experiences, particularly those in childhood. For some people, however, childhood experiences may maintain or reinforce inappropriate pre-programmed responses. The naturally shy child, for example, whose parents' responses are to be overprotective, may not experience any other way of dealing with the world. As a result, they may fail to develop alternative coping skills and come to believe that the only way to survive in the adult world is to be dependent and subservient. Adult personality is the combined result of these pre-programmed responses and childhood experiences. Rigid cognitive schemata develop over time, each of which governs behaviour. Beliefs of 'being bad', for example, will lead to self-punishment; beliefs of 'not being worthy of love' will result in the avoidance of closeness, and so on.

As in his model of depression, Beck considered the core schema that drive personality disorders to be the cognitive triad concerning the self, others and the future. Instead of being episodically activated as in the case of depression, however, these underlying schemata are chronically activated in people with personality disorders. Placing these schema as the central driving factor in all personality disorders provides an explanation for an apparently diverse set of attributes and behaviours. The content of the schemata may vary, as a result of different child and adult experiences (and perhaps the pre-programmed neuro-cognitive responses), but the underlying structures are the same. Some of the key beliefs for the different personality 'types' include:

- Avoidant personality
  - *self*: socially inept and incompetent
  - *others*: potentially critical, uninterested and demeaning
  - *beliefs*: the self as worthless and unlovable: 'If people get close to me, they will discover the real me and reject me – that would be intolerable.'

- Dependent personality
  - *self*: needy, weak, helpless and incompetent
  - *others*: need a strong 'caretaker' in an idealized way; can function well in their presence, but not without them
  - *beliefs*: 'I need other people – specifically a strong person – in order to survive.'

- Schizoid personality disorder
  - *self*: self-sufficient and a loner
  - *others*: intrusive; closeness provides an opportunity for others to fence the individual in
  - *beliefs*: 'I am basically alone'; 'I can do things better when I am unencumbered by other people.'

According to Young and Lindemann (1992), the schema most involved in personality disorders are those that relate to the need for security, autonomy, desirability, self-expression, gratification and self-control. Once formed, they become self-fulfilling, and are maintained through three different processes: schema maintenance, schema avoidance and schema compensation. *Schema maintenance* involves resistance to information or evidence that would disconfirm the schema through cognitive distortions and self-defeating behavioural patterns. *Avoidance* involves avoiding situations that may test or provide information counter to the schema. Finally, *schema compensation* involves overcompensating for a negative schema by acting in the direction opposite to the schema's content. This may reinforce the initial schema, as the outcome of such actions may not be positive. A shy woman, who believes herself unattractive to men, yet acts flirtatiously, for example, may find herself in situations in which she feels unsafe, or hurt by men drawn to her flirtatiousness who reject her when they find her withdrawn and quiet, thus supporting her schema of being unattractive. Although a great deal of successful clinical work has been based on the schema model, until recently there have been few experimental studies of the phenomenon. However, what studies have been conducted support the schema models developed by both Beck and Young (e.g. Wenzel et al. 2007; Arntz et al. 2005).

12.2 Cluster A diagnoses

According to DSM-IV-TR, paranoid disorder involves a pervasive distrust and suspiciousness of others such that their motives are interpreted as malevolent. It begins in early adulthood. To be assigned a diagnosis, four of the following need to be present. The individual:

- suspects, without sufficient basis, that others are exploiting, harming or deceiving them
- is preoccupied with unjustified doubts about the loyalty or trustworthiness of friends or associates
- is reluctant to confide in others because of unwarranted fear that the information will be used maliciously against them
- reads hidden demeaning or threatening meanings into benign remarks or events
- persistently bears grudges and slights
- sees attacks on their character or reputation that are not apparent to others and is quick to react angrily or to counterattack
- has recurrent suspicions, without justification, regarding fidelity of spouse or sexual partner.

Schizoid disorder presents as a pervasive pattern of detachment from social relationships and a restricted range of expression of emotions in interpersonal settings, beginning in early adulthood. Four of the following have to be present for a diagnosis to be assigned. The individual:

- neither desires nor enjoys close relationships, including being part of a family
- almost always chooses solitary activities
- has little, if any, interest in having sexual experiences with another person
- takes pleasure in few, if any, activities
- lacks close friends or confidants other than first-degree relatives
- appears indifferent to the praise or criticism of others
- shows emotional coldness, detachment or flattened affectivity.

Finally, schizotypal personality disorder is defined as a pervasive pattern of social and interpersonal deficits marked by acute discomfort with, and reduced capacity for, close relationships. In addition, individuals may experience cognitive or perceptual distortions and show eccentricities of behaviour. A diagnosis requires the presence of five or more of the following:

- ideas of reference (excluding delusions of reference)
- odd beliefs or magical thinking that influence behaviour and are inconsistent with subcultural norms
- unusual perceptual experiences, including bodily illusions
- odd thinking and speech (e.g. vague, circumstantial, metaphorical, over-elaborate or stereotyped)
- suspiciousness or paranoid ideation
- inappropriate or restricted affect
- behaviour or appearance that is odd, eccentric or peculiar
- lack of close friends or confidants other than first-degree relatives
- excessive social anxiety that does not diminish with familiarity and tends to be associated with paranoid fears rather than negative judgements about self.

The prevalence of these various disorders within the general community varies, according to different studies, between 0 and 4.5 per cent for paranoid personality disorder, 0 and 4.1 per cent for schizoid personality disorder, and 0 and 5.1 per cent for schizotypal personality disorder (Torgersen et al. 2001). Each of these disorders involves some of the manifestations of schizophrenia. As such, they fit into a range of conditions known as the schizophrenia spectrum disorders – a linkage stemming from early observations of the relatives of people identified with schizophrenia, among whom there were relatively high rates of cluster A personality disorder (Nigg and Goldsmith 1994). Interestingly, though, few people diagnosed with these personality disorders go on to be diagnosed as having schizophrenia.

Perhaps not surprisingly, given the linkage with schizophrenia, factors associated with the development of schizophrenia, including prenatal exposure to famine, influenza and even cold temperatures, have also been considered in the development of these disorders (see Parnas et al. 2005). There is clear genetic component to the personality type. Genetic studies have identified high concordance rates for each of the disorders between MZ twins (see Parnas et al. 2005). In addition, one of several longitudinal studies, the Copenhagen High-Risk genetic risk study (Parnas et al. 1995), followed the offspring of women with a diagnosis of schizophrenia and those of a 'normal' comparison group of children from the age of 15 to 42 years. Twenty-one per cent of the children of schizophrenic mothers were assigned a cluster A personality diagnosis, compared with 5 per cent of the children in the comparison group. Of particular note is that among the children of the women diagnosed with schizophrenia, those exposed to a particularly stressful environment in childhood were most likely to be subsequently diagnosed with schizophrenia. Those who were exposed to a moderately stressful environment were more likely to be assigned a diagnosis of personality disorder, suggesting a gradient of risk based on both genetic factors and the degree of exposure to stress – a finding in keeping with the diathesis-stress model. Data such as these have led genetic theorists such as Meehl (e.g. 1990) to suggest that the core personality disorder is genetically mediated, while risk for schizophrenia involves further genetic influences and high environmental stress factors.

Treatment studies of cluster A disorders are relatively rare – perhaps because people who could be assigned these diagnoses rarely seek treatment, and when they do, this may be related to associated problems such as depression. With this in mind, Parnas et al. (2005) noted that antipsychotic medication may be of some benefit, but that adequate controlled trials of any psychotherapy or alternative medical treatments were lacking.

12.3 Cluster B diagnoses

Borderline personality disorder

DSM-IV-TR defines borderline personality disorder as a pervasive pattern of instability of interpersonal relationships, self-image and affect, and marked impulsivity. It begins in early childhood and its key characteristics include five of the following:

- frantic efforts to avoid real or imagined abandonment
- a pattern of unstable and intense personal relationships characterized by alternating between idealization and devaluation
- identity disturbance: markedly and persistently unstable self-image
- impulsivity in at least two areas that are potentially self-damaging (such as substance abuse, reckless driving)
- recurrent suicidal behaviour or self-mutilating behaviour; may involve repeated threats or gestures
- chronic feelings of emptiness
- inappropriate intense anger or difficulty in controlling anger
- transient stress-related paranoid ideation or severe dissociative symptoms.

About 2 per cent of the US population is thought to have this cluster of traits, and about 75 per cent of these are thought to be women (APA 2000). It typically begins in adolescence and continues through adulthood. Thoughts of suicide and suicide attempts are common: up to 10 per cent of people with this disorder eventually commit suicide (e.g. Zanarini et al. 2005). Self-harm – in particular cutting of arms, legs or torso, burning or other mutilatory acts – is also common. This is usually in response to experiencing strong negative emotions such as anger or anxiety, attempts to block painful memories or as a cry for help. These behaviours may also be used in a manipulative manner, to control relationships or the behaviour of others around them. People with the disorder often have intense, over-involved relationships, and have a deep fear of being rejected. This may result in them becoming panicky at the thought of being isolated, and they may engage in self-destructive behaviour to try to maintain relationships that are disintegrating ('If you leave, I will hurt myself . . .'). As with other personality disorders, it is not as immutable as was once thought. Zanarini et al. (2005), for example, found that only three-quarters of a cohort of people initially given this diagnosis warranted the diagnosis some six years later. In addition, only 6 per cent of those people who improved experienced a 'relapse'.

Aetiology of borderline personality disorder

Biological factors

There have been relatively few studies of the family/genetic influences on borderline personality disorders. However, a number are now emerging. Distel et al. (2008a), for example, studied a total of 3644 twins aged between 18 and 86 years across the Netherlands, Belgium, and Australia. They estimated 42 per cent of the variation in borderline personality features was attributable to genetic factors, with similar levels of heritability across all three countries. These findings compare with the 35 per cent variance of traits explained by genetic factors in a Norwegian cohort (Torgersen et al. 2008). Any genetic process is still far from clear, however, and likely to be polygenic. Distel et al. (2008b), for example, are even now considering 'candidate' genes for the condition, while work by Tadić et al. (2008) suggests the possibility that the condition may involve interactions between genes controlling both dopaminergic and noradrenergic systems.

Other studies have investigated neural and neurochemical mediators of the condition. In one such study, Tebartz van Elst et al. (2003) found that the hippocampi of people with borderline personality disorder were 20 per cent smaller than those of a 'normal' comparison group, while their amygdalas were 24 per cent smaller. There is also evidence of damaged or poorly functioning frontal cortices (De la Fuente et al. 1997), which may be related to the dysregulation of serotonin within this brain area (New et al. 2004). This may contribute to a lack of inhibition in the regulation of aggression. Reports of the effectiveness of antipsychotic medication in the treatment of at least some cases of borderline personality disorder (e.g. Rocca et al. 2002) suggest that low levels of dopamine may also be implicated in its presentation – a finding consistent with the findings of Tadić et al. above. A very different view on possible biological mechanisms in borderline personality stems from work on a hormone and neurotransmitter called oxytocin. This is perhaps best known for its role in birth and breastfeeding. However, there is also increasing evidence that within brain structures including the amygdale, hypothalamus, oxytocin is involved in empathy and social bonding. Not only may oxytocin encourage socially positive behaviour, it may enhance encoding and conceptual recognition of positive social stimuli over social-threat stimuli (Guastella et al. 2008).

Socio-cultural factors

Risk for personality disorder is increased by a number of social factors. People with borderline personality are more likely than the general population to have been neglected by their parents, to have had multiple caregivers and to have experienced parental divorce, death or significant childhood trauma such as sexual abuse or incest. In one study of this phenomenon, Bandelow et al. (2005) found that people with borderline personality disorder reported much higher levels of traumatic childhood experiences such as sexual abuse, violence, separation from parents, childhood illness and other factors than a matched, 'normal' comparison group.

Psychological processes

Psychological processes translate the social factors considered above into individual experiences. One significant outcome may be poor attachment and bonding with parents – both of which may contribute to the development of borderline personality disorder (Nickell et al. 2002). Of interest in relation to these findings are those of Zweig-Frank and Paris (2002) who followed a cohort of people diagnosed with borderline personality disorder for 27 years and found that while reports of parenting quality and childhood abuse or trauma did not predict the long-term outcome of the condition, a measure of parental bonding did. From a psychoanalytic view-point, object relations theorists (e.g. Kernberg 1985) suggest that as a result of negative child-hood experiences, the individual develops a weak ego and needs constant reassuring. They frequently engage in a defence mechanism known as *splitting*, dichotomizing objects into 'all good' or 'all bad' objects, and fail to integrate the positive and negative aspects of self or other people into a whole (Klein 1927; see also Chapter 2 in this volume). This inability to make sense of contradictory elements of self or others causes extreme difficulty in regulating emotions as the world is constantly viewed as either 'perfect' or 'disastrous'.

Cognitive theorists (e.g. Young and Lindemann 1992) argue that negative childhood experiences translate into maladaptive schemata about self-identity and relationships with others. These include beliefs that 'I am bad', leading to self-punishment; 'No one will ever love me', leading to avoidance of closeness; and 'I cannot cope on my own', leading to over-dependence. Self-harm may be maintained by operant processes: successful control of other people's behaviour by threats of self-harm reinforces its use as a means of coping.

Strong negative emotions experienced as a consequence of catastrophic or other negative beliefs may also lead to episodes of self-harm. Many people with borderline personality feel numbness or dissociation immediately before or while they harm themselves. Self-harm may therefore provide a means of escape from unbearable emotions, and may not be accompanied with feelings of physical pain. Other people, who feel confused and out of control, may find any pain they experience a form of self-validation of their own status and self-identity (see Table 12.1). According to the cognitive model, the use of self-harm to avoid emotional pain or to manipulate others is indicative of high levels of interpersonal anxiety, low self-esteem and a lack of alternative coping strategies to deal with personal stress.

Cognitive processing deficits may also underpin some of the traits of borderline personality. Sala et al. (2008), for example, noted that hippocampal and frontal cortex deficiencies may be related to poor memory control. To investigate this phenomenon, they exploring the capacity of people with borderline personality to first learn and then to inhibit memories of various word pairs, and found both processes to be impaired. They took this to indicate that people with border-line personality disorder may be less able than others to inhibit the emergence of unwanted memories and dissociative symptoms. In another cognitive deficit model of the condition, Wupperman et al. (2008) correlated measures of mindfulness with core features of borderline personality disorder including interpersonal problem-solving abilities, and impulsive and passive emotion-regulation strategies in a sample of young adults. They found that deficits in mindfulness were linked to difficulties in attention, awareness and discrimination between 'internal and external experience', factors that they saw as central to the disorder. Finally, Dyck et al. (2009) reported that people with borderline personality disorder experienced difficulty in the immediate discrimination of both neutral and negative emotional expressions – again, factors likely to result in the underlying difficulties in social interaction central to the disorder.

Table 12.1 **Example of an episode of self-harm and the development of alternative coping strategies**

What happened before self-harm?	Two hours before meal with parents. They were stuck, not talking to each other. I felt stuck in the middle: couldn't eat
Feelings leading up to the self-destructive act	Numbness
Associated thoughts	I feel nothing. I am nothing
Self-destructive behaviour	Cut thighs with a razor blade
Feelings	No one feeling; pain on cutting
Associated thoughts	At least I feel pain: I can feel something
Consequences	More marks on thighs
	Blood on clothes
	Feel ashamed
	Hate self
Alternative to cutting	Go to bed and sleep or listen to loud music
	Tense my muscles really hard
	Melt ice cubes in my hand

Source: Davidson (2000)

Treatment of borderline personality disorder

Psychological approaches

Treatment of people with borderline personality is not easy, and there are relatively few controlled trials examining the effects of therapy. Roth and Fonagy (1998) tried to establish some overall goals of therapy and guidelines for who may benefit from it most. They suggested the following:

- Psychotherapy is more likely to be effective for less severe personality disorders.
- In individuals under the age of 30 years, the greatest risk comes from suicide. Prevention of this, rather than 'cure', may form a legitimate therapeutic target.
- Individuals with good social support, chronic depression, who are psychologically minded and with low impulsivity, are most likely to benefit from 'talking therapies'.

- People who have high levels of impulsivity are most likely to benefit from a 'limit-setting' group or a therapist who is supportive of their attempts to struggle with uncontrollable impulses.
- Commitment and enthusiasm of the therapist may be of special significance, and finding the 'right' therapist for the 'right' patient is particularly important.

Because of the complex facets of the disorder, including the threat of self-harm, therapy with people with personality disorder is necessarily complex and the approaches used should be governed by the individual's ability to cope with particular therapeutic issues. It may be useful for some people to stay in hospital during the early stages of therapy, as they may find therapy sessions so stressful they either drop out or harm themselves in some way. The hospital can provide a safe environment, where their behaviour can be observed and controlled, and both therapist and client have the security of knowing that any impulsive self-harming behaviour will be seen and dealt with should it occur.

Cognitive therapy   The core of cognitive therapy is the identification and modification of cognitive schema that drive inappropriate behaviours, using an approach known as schema therapy (Young 1999) or cognitive analytic therapy (Ryle and Kerr 2002). These approaches may combine with a number of other strategies, including developing problem-focused plans to cope with urges to self-harm, mood disturbances and suicidal feelings, improving relationships, and so on. The issues addressed in therapy and the strategies used are dependent on the most pressing and problematic behaviour at the time (Davidson 2000).

One of the most important therapeutic aims is to minimize risk of self-harm. This involves identifying the antecedents to episodes of self-harm, the thoughts and feelings that accompany them, and their consequences (see Table 12.1). Each of these forms a potential point of intervention. Alternatives to self-harm often involve a high intensity action, such as listening to loud music, or painful, but not damaging, behaviours such as squeezing a ball until the muscles ache. Where there is risk that an episode of self-harm will escalate into a serious attempt at suicide, specific strategies may be used to minimize this risk, including problem solving and identifying reasons for living (see Chapter 8).

Evidence of the effectiveness of these approaches is still gradually accumulating. Blum et al. (2008) compared outcomes of a cognitive behavioural programme similar to schema therapy with 'treatment as usual'. In addition to working with individuals, they included what they termed a systems approach, involving a two-hour session to which family members or other significant individuals were invited. During this session, these people were taught about the nature of the problems their relative was experiencing and patients were encouraged to share their experiences of the treatment programme. In the year following the intervention, participants in the cognitive behavioural intervention experienced greater improvements on measures of impulsivity, negative affect and global functioning. They were no better on measures of the frequency of self-harm or suicide attempts, which are generally considered key outcomes of any intervention. However, they did make fewer visits to hospital emergency departments. Giesen-Bloo et al. (2006) compared two interventions, each of which was conducted over a three-year period: schema therapy and psychodynamically based transference-focused psychotherapy. They found that more people remained in the schema therapy over this time (presumably indicating the degree to which they felt they were gaining some benefit from attending). In addition,

participants in the schema therapy intervention were most likely to recover, to have better improvement scores, and to report better overall quality of life.

Dialectical behaviour therapy   A second key therapeutic approach to the treatment of borderline personality disorder involves a form of therapy called dialectical behaviour therapy (DBT: Linehan et al. 1993). This can be considered a third-wave approach (see Chapter 3) as it has a strong behavioural component (and many similarities to ACT) and does not focus on cognitive change as a key contributor to change. The therapy involves the client in working individually with a therapist and in therapy groups. As with schema therapy, self-injurious and suicidal behaviours are key targets. Therapy involves teaching four sets of skills: interpersonal effectiveness, core mindfulness, emotion regulation and distress tolerance, which draw strongly on mindfulness, distraction and acceptance skills. A few studies have shown DBT to be an effective intervention. In one of the early randomized controlled trials of its effectiveness, Van den Bosch et al. (2005) evaluated treatment outcomes, comparing one year of DBT versus usual care, and found lower levels of parasuicidal and impulsive behaviours, sustained for six months after the completion of treatment. In a comparison between a similar programme and non-behavioural psychotherapy, Linehan et al. (2006) found one-year follow-up outcomes were again supportive of DBT: participants receiving DBT were half as likely to make a suicide attempt and required less hospitalization for suicide ideation than those in the psychotherapy intervention. In addition, they were less likely to drop out of treatment and to be admitted to hospital. More recently, Clarkin et al. (2007) compared the effectiveness of DBT with transference-focused psychotherapy and found the transference-focused therapy to be the more effective of two. Both interventions achieved good results, with significant gains on measures of suicidality, depression, anxiety, global functioning and social adjustment. However, the psychotherapy achieved reductions in anger not found with DBT.

Case formulation

Ms H was a 26-year-old single woman. She presented with a history of self-harm including cutting her wrists and arms, overdosing on prescription medication, and stabbing herself in the abdomen. On more than one occasion these, and other harming behaviours, were intended to end her life. She had previously been seen by a clinical psychologist, but had dropped out of therapy after only a few sessions, and had not taken the opportunity for further therapy offered following hospital admissions following episodes of self-harm. She had few acquaintances, and no close friends, living on her own in a bedsit in a large town. She was unemployed at the time she was seen by a clinical psychologist.

Long-term antecedents

Ms H reported being sexually abused by her father as a young girl. This was originally denied by her family. Her mother initially did not acknowledge the reality of her claims of abuse. However, once this was acknowledged (after several months of abuse), her mother left the relationship bringing Ms H up alone (or in the company of a succession of uncaring and

occasionally verbally and physically abusive 'boyfriends') from the age of 11 years. The relationship between Ms H and her mother was not good, and although she lived with her mother until the age of 19 years, she felt unloved and uncared for. She was often ignored, and at best tolerated; not loved or respected. However, she learned to keep a 'good face' on her experiences and hide any distress she may have felt. When she did express any distress she felt from her mother or her mother's boyfriends' behaviour, they only way she could gain attention was through engaging in extremes of behaviour. She learned that self-harming behaviour such as cutting would actually lead to her having some attention, although it was also related to subsequent conflict and her being forced to leave home. Episodes of low mood, related to her poor self-esteem, memories of abuse and difficulties in relationships would also form triggers to episodes of self-harm such as overdosing, with an intent if not to die, at least to provide a time out from the distress she was experiencing. She had a succession of short-term relationships with a number of men, each of which was typified as stormy. She was claustrophobically needy, demanding her boyfriends' full attention and becoming upset and threatening self-harm if they were away too long. These typically ended in a dramatic argument followed by her self-harming in some way. She was offered psychiatric treatment following two of these episodes, but chose not to take this up. However, on a third episode she agreed to see a psychiatric nurse before being referred to a clinical psychologist. However, she had only attended two sessions, saying she did not feel able to relate to the therapist.

Formulation

As a consequence of her early history, Ms H had low self-esteem and a strong sense of shame. She had not learned to tolerate or express negative emotions in a meaningful and appropriate way. Indeed, she had learned to express any negative emotion in a histrionic and overly expressive manner. When things were stressful in her life (for example, relationships failing), she felt extremely vulnerable and anxious and experienced high levels of negative affect. She had not learned to manage these emotions appropriately, and frequently did so by becoming overly reliant on support from anyone willing to provide it (usually her boyfriends), or, when this support was not available, she resorted to self-harm as a means of expressing distress, trying to manage this distress, and manipulating others ('Stay with me or I will really hurt myself'). She found therapy challenging and distressing because it addressed issues she was unable to cope with effectively. She therefore dropped out or refused to engage in it.

Intervention

The intervention with Ms H lasted many months, and involved both individual and group sessions. The first aim of treatment was to reduce her likelihood of self-harming. This involved identifying factors likely to precipitate self-harming, in order to understand and possibly avoid them happening, and learning skills including mindfulness and distraction techniques such as squeezing a ball in her hand to the point of pain to help her control her strong emotions in a more positive manner. In addition, she was taught interpersonal

skills (including appropriate assertiveness and talking to people about her emotions) in order to learn to express any emotional distress in a more appropriate and acceptable manner. While these reduced the risk of self-harm, they did not entirely prevent some incidents. Nevertheless, Ms H reduced her self-harm significantly. Once she was better able to monitor and manage her negative emotions, the therapist examined some of the inappropriate beliefs related to her shame and low self-esteem ('It was my fault I was sexually abused'; 'My parents did not love me, so I am unworthy of love', etc.) using the Socratic approach of cognitive behaviour therapy. This was conducted carefully and slowly, and because the distress this process may evoke could potentially trigger self-harm, there was some debate between her therapist and the ward nursing team about whether Ms H should stay in hospital at this time. However, she and her therapist made a joint decision that she would not come into hospital, but that the therapist could be contacted at agreed times (not 'randomly' as this may increase dependency on the therapist) should contact be necessary. Ms H found this process stressful, but was able to confront some of her beliefs and she became less shamed and her episodes of low mood became less frequent. She was also able to develop appropriate (non-dependent) relationships with some members of the group sessions she attended. These became a source of long-term support and reinforced changes in her approach to others – in particular learning to become less dependent and demanding. Over a period of many months, Ms H became more independent and confident. She remained fragile, but was able to cope with difficult emotions without consistently harming herself (although this did not stop completely), and was able to use a number of coping mechanisms should this occur. She was able to develop supportive relationships with a number of people (all of whom themselves had a history of mental health problems). She was discharged after around one year of gradually decreasingly frequent sessions with her therapist and therapy group. However, she was given regular follow-up sessions every 3–4 months for some time longer to support her in her changes and, in particular, if she were to begin to experience more significant problems in the future.

Pharmacological treatment

There have been relatively few controlled trials of the effectiveness of drug therapy in borderline personality. Most studies have been relatively small, and evidence of any effectiveness is 'weak' (Paris 2008). Rinne et al. (2002), for example, found that treatment with the SSRI, fluvoxamine, proved successful in reducing rapid mood shifts, but not impulsivity and aggression in women with a diagnosis of borderline personality. Roepke et al. (2008) found an atypical antipsychotic, quetiapine, achieved modest gains on measures of depression but not impulsivity in the 12 of 15 people who took the drug for an eight-week period. Linehan et al. (2008) assessed whether treatment with another atypical antipsychotic, olanzapine, improved the outcome of individuals already receiving dialectical behaviour therapy. In a study of 24 women who either received placebo or active treatment, irritability and aggression scores tended to decrease more quickly for the olanzapine group than for the placebo group. However, self-inflicted injury tended to decrease more for the placebo group than for the olanzapine group.

Mackay, N. and Barrowclough, C. (2005) Accident and emergency staff's perceptions of deliberate self-harm: attributions, emotions and willingness to help, *British Journal of Clinical Psychology*, 44: 255–67.

Deliberate self-harm accounts for 150 000 visits each year to British Accident and Emergency (A&E) Departments. When there, these individuals often receive an unsympathetic response. They are not popular with health service staff, who often feel that people presenting with other problems are more worthy of care. Most studies of this phenomenon have involved surveys of staff attitudes and patient satisfaction with their care. Mackay and Barrowclough moved this research on by examining the phenomenon using psychological theory and an experimental approach. They tested Weiner's (1986) theory that people are likely to withhold help if they consider an individual's problems to be controllable by the individual and arise from factors within them. If the need for help is attributed to uncontrollable factors, this leads to sympathy and pity, which in turn lead to offers of help. Conversely, if the need for help is attributable to controllable factors, this leads to negative emotions such as anger and then denial of help. This theory was tested on A&E staff.

Method

Participants

Participants were qualified nursing staff and junior doctors in four A&E departments in the north-west of England. Of 180 questionnaires sent out, 80 (49 per cent) were returned, with no difference in response rates between professions. The final group comprised 33 per cent men, 66 per cent nursing staff, and 34 per cent doctors.

Design and materials

The study adopted a 2 × 2 design, in which participants were asked to rate their responses to a number of scenarios in which the researchers varied the controllability of the reasons for an incident of self-harm (controllable – financial debts versus uncontrollable – death of a close friend) and the frequency of attending A&E (unstable – first attendance versus stable – sixth attendance). For each scenario, participants completed a number of scales:

- The *Attributional Style Questionnaire* (Peterson et al. 1982) measuring four types of attributions about the self-harm: its controllability, stability of cause, stability of outcome and internality.
- A revised version of the *Emotional Response Rating Scale* (Weiner 1980) measuring four emotional responses (irritation, sympathy, anger, frustration) to the patient.
- A revised version of the *optimism/pessimism scale* (Moores and Grant 1976) measuring the extent to which staff thought their own response and any follow-up would have a positive impact on the patients self-harming in the future.

- The *Helping Behaviour Scale* asked three questions about participant's willingness to prioritize the person, to offer extra time and support, and the likelihood of them initiating a referral to the psychiatric service.

Findings

Regardless of their job, male staff reported less sympathy, greater irritation and frustration, less personal optimism and less willingness to help than female staff. Similarly, doctors expressed more irritation, less personal optimism and less helping behaviour than the nurses.

Table 12.2 Mean scores on key variables across gender and profession

	Male	Female	Doctor	Nurse
Irritation	2.97	2.13*	2.93	2.14*
Sympathy	4.24	4.97*	4.43	4.88
Pity	3.28	3.81	3.57	3.73
Frustration	3.90	2.95**	3.70	3.03
Optimism: personal	3.10	3.93*	2.97	4.02**
Optimism: follow-up	5	5	5	5
Helping	14.04	16.17**	14.07	16.19**

Table 12.3 Correlations between key variables

	Irritation	Frustration	Sympathy	Pity	Helping
Controllability	.37**	.33**	−.40**	−.07	−.37**
Stability of cause	−.03	.08	.05	.00	−.16
Stability of outcome	.05	.20	−.02	.10	.06
Personal optimism	−.06	−.08	.25	−.09	.38**
Other optimism	−.09	−.8	.11	.07	.36**
Internality	.13	.17	−.26	−.10	−.08
Helping	−.55**	−.40**	.25	.06	1.00

As predicted, there were significant associations between the attributional dimensions and emotional responses (see Table 12.3). Low ratings of controllability of the self-harm were associated with greater sympathy. High ratings of controllability were associated with greater irritation and frustration. In turn, a significant negative correlation was found between both irritation and frustration and helping behaviour. A significant positive association was found between sympathy and helping. Finally, there were significant positive associations between optimism and helping behaviour.

Discussion

The relatively low response rate means that the results of this study may not be representative of the wider population of health professionals. In addition, the implication of these results for individual behaviour is not clear. There are many studies which show marked disparities between reported attitudes and behaviour. Nevertheless, these results do suggest that many A&E staff hold negative beliefs about people who self-harm, that these vary according to the perceived cause of the behaviour, and that the negative emotional reactions triggered by these beliefs impact on health care workers' willingness to help.

Antisocial personality and psychopathy

The terms antisocial personality and psychopathy are often used interchangeably. Indeed, the DSM-IV-TR category of antisocial personality disorder was intended to combine diagnoses of antisocial personality and psychopathy, which DSM-III did not. Critics of DSM-IV-TR have argued that it has not succeeded in this attempt, and that the two conditions are not synonymous. They have different characteristics and long-term outcomes. According to Hare et al. (2000), DSM-IV-TR still describes an individual who is criminally antisocial. By contrast, psychopathy refers to an individual who not only has these characteristics, but also experiences a poverty of both positive and negative emotions, and is motivated by thrill-seeking as much as by any other gain. Antisocial behaviour tends to reduce with age; psychopathic behaviour does not.

DSM-IV-TR defines antisocial personality as a pervasive pattern of disregard for, and violation of, the rights of others occurring from the age of 15 years. Its core characteristics include:

- repeatedly performing acts that could lead to arrest
- repeated lying, use of aliases, or conning others for personal profit or pleasure
- impulsivity or failure to plan ahead
- reckless disregard for the safety of self or others
- consistent irresponsibility: repeated failure to sustain work or honour financial obligations
- lack of remorse for others.

Without specific DSM diagnostic criteria, those who distinguish between antisocial behaviour and psychopathy generally use Hare's (1991) Psychopathy Checklist (PCL) to diagnose psychopathy. This identifies two sets of factors associated with psychopathy: emotional detachment and an antisocial lifestyle. Emotional detachment involves a lack of capacity to process emotional information, and a consequent lack of understanding and disregard for the emotions of others. It is Hare's defining characteristic of psychopathy. Using the PCL to diagnose psychopathology, Hare found that up to 80 per cent of criminals could be categorized as having antisocial personality disorder: only 20 per cent met the criteria for psychopathy (Hare et al. 2000), a finding supporting his argument of clinical differences between the two conditions.

Aetiology of antisocial personality and psychopathy

The apparent confusion between antisocial personality and psychopathy has meant that the relevant literature often confuses the two concepts. Some studies of antisocial personality include within them what Hare and others would consider to be psychopathy. Other studies specifically focus on psychopathy as defined by Hare. As psychopathy is linked to an 'antisocial lifestyle', it is perhaps not surprising that many of the factors that predispose to antisocial behaviour are also associated with psychopathy. What distinguishes psychopathy from the antisocial personality are distinct neurological factors that are uniquely associated with the emotional detachment and limited range or depth of emotions central to the condition. Accordingly, this section first considers factors that increase risk for antisocial behaviour or personality, before considering the neurological factors that contribute uniquely to the development of psychopathy.

Genetic factors

Genetic studies of families have found it difficult to discriminate between genes for problem drinking, criminality and antisocial behaviour, all of which seem to be closely related. Nevertheless, two early adoptee studies implicated genetic factors in the aetiology of antisocial behaviour. Crowe (1974) reported that adopted-away children of women prisoners with antisocial personality disorder had higher rates of antisocial personality than control adoptees without this family history. Similarly, Cadoret (1982) found that rates of antisocial behaviour were higher among adopted adolescent females with a biological relative who engaged in antisocial behaviour than a matched group of adolescents without this family history. Risk for engaging in antisocial behaviour was further increased if the environment of the adoptive family was 'adverse', indicating an interaction between social and genetic factors in the development of antisocial behaviour. Two recent studies add to the evidence of this interplay between genetic and environmental influences. In one US study, Legrand et al. (2008) found that antisocial behaviour was substantially influenced by genetic factors in urban environments, By contrast, environmental factors were more influential in rural environments. The apparent lack of influence of the urban environment may reflect the lack of variation – and universally challenging nature – of many urban environments. In a study adding strength to Hare's distinction between antisocial personality and psychopathy, Larsson et al. (2007) found that psychopathic behaviour was largely driven by genetic factors, while the impact of genetic factors on antisocial behaviour was significantly moderated by environmental factors.

Biological mechanisms

One gene that appears to be implicated in moderating risk for antisocial personality affects serotonin metabolism within the body (Lyons-Ruth et al. 2007). Not surprisingly, therefore, there is increasing evidence that high levels of impulsivity, and perhaps aggression, irritability and sensation seeking are associated with low levels of serotonin (Oades et al. 2008), although the issue is far from clear-cut. Dolan et al. (2002), for example, found that impulsivity appeared to be related to both frontal lobe (executive) and serotonin function. By contrast, while aggression was correlated inversely with frontal (executive) and temporal lobe (memory) function, it was not related to serotonin levels. Low levels of sympathetic activity (noradrenalin) at times of stress may also be implicated in antisocial behaviour (Raine et al. 1998), perhaps because they predispose the individual to fearlessness and thrill seeking as a means of increasing arousal levels.

Neurological mechanisms in psychopathy

Converging evidence suggests that the deficits in emotional processing associated with psychopathy are linked to damage to the limbic system inhibiting the processing of emotional information. Laakso et al. (2001), for example, used brain imaging techniques to gain accurate data on the brain anatomy of 18 habitually violent psychopathic offenders. They found a strong negative association between the size of the hippocampus and scores on the PCL, suggesting that damage in this area, which is involved in the acquisition of conditioned fear, may explain the lack of fear associated with psychopathic behaviour.

These data are added to by the findings of Kiehl et al. (2001) who used brain imaging to study activity within the limbic system in response to an 'affective memory task'. In it, three groups of participants (criminal psychopaths, criminal non-psychopaths and 'normal' controls) were asked to rehearse and remember lists of either neutral words or words describing negative emotions, and to identify these words in a subsequent recognition task. Psychopaths had significantly less activity within their limbic systems and greater activation of the frontal lobes while processing negative emotional words than the other groups, suggesting that the psychopaths and non-psychopaths used quite different brain systems to process emotional information. Birbaumer et al. (2005) extended this work to examine neurological processes while participants received painful pressure following presentation of various stimuli. The presentation of these stimuli before the pain meant that 'normal' participants learned to expect pain, reported some anxiety about these expectations, and developed a conditioned 'pain' response to these stimuli – evident through increased sweat gland activity when presented with the stimuli. During the acquisition phase of the study, they showed enhanced differential activation in the limbic–prefrontal circuit (amygdala, orbitofrontal cortex, insula and anterior cingulate). By contrast, psychopaths displayed no significant activity in this circuit, no conditioned 'pain' response and reported no anxiety.

Socio-cultural factors

Social factors clearly influence the probability of an individual engaging in antisocial behaviour and being diagnosed with antisocial personality. Henry et al. (2001), for example, found that lack of emotional closeness within the family and poor parenting at the age of 12 years was predictive of both violence and delinquency at the age of 17 years. Perhaps the longest longitudinal study of this phenomenon is the Cambridge Study in Delinquent Development (Farrington 2000). This was able to identify childhood factors that were predictive of antisocial personality and adult convictions up to the age of 40 years. The most important childhood predictors were similar to those of Henry et al.: a convicted parent, large family size, low intelligence or school attainment, a young mother and disrupted family. Family factors may also contribute to the lack of emotion associated with psychopathy. It has been suggested that the sustained experience of negative emotional events during childhood results in the individual learning to 'switch off' their emotions in response both to negative events that occur to them and to their behaviours that affect others. While family influences are clearly important, external influences may also impact on the individual. Henry et al. (2001) found that having violent peers was predictive of later violent and nonviolent delinquency. Similarly, Eamon and Mulder (2005) found that impoverished neighbourhood and school environments, exposure to deviant peer pressure, and parenting practices involving physical punishment and excessive monitoring of behaviour (perhaps as a consequence rather than cause of their antisocial behaviour) were related to anti-social behaviour among Latino adolescents in the USA. In an attempt to quantify the degree to which family and peer factors contribute to antisocial behaviour, Eddy and Chamberlain (2000) followed a group of offenders over a two-year period. Family management skills and deviant peer association accounted for 32 per cent of the variance in antisocial behaviour over this period. Borduin (1999) summarized the non-family antecedents of antisocial behaviour as:

- *peer relations*: high involvement with deviant peers, poor social skills, low involvement with pro-social peers
- *school factors*: poor academic performance, drop-out and low commitment to education
- *neighbourhood and community*: criminal sub-culture, low organizational participation among residents, low social support and high mobility.

The prevalence of antisocial behaviour is increasing over time in many countries, virtually doubling over a period of 15 years in the USA to about 3.6 per cent of the general population. There are also marked differences in its prevalence across countries, ranging from about 0.14 per cent in Taiwan to over 3 per cent in countries such as New Zealand. These various findings led Paris (1996) to speculate that Asian cultures are protective against antisocial personality as a result of their family structure, which is typically highly cohesive and has clear limits on acceptable behaviour – the opposite constellation of characteristics to those implicated in the development of antisocial behaviour.

Cognitive models

Children within family systems that increase risk of antisocial behaviour do not have clear limits set to their behaviour. As a result, they frequently fail to internalize the controls on their behaviour that other children adopt. These types of environment may also foster beliefs about the individual and the world that support antisocial behaviour. Lopez and Emmer (2002), for example, found that adolescents who engaged in crime believed aggression to be an effective and appropriate response to threat. Liau et al. (1998) and Sukhodolsky and Ruchkin (2004) found that specific beliefs led to specific behaviours: beliefs concerning overt antisocial behaviour ('People need to be roughed up once in a while') were associated with overt but not covert anti-social behaviour. Conversely, beliefs related to covert behaviour ('If someone is careless enough to lose a wallet, they deserve to have it stolen') led to covert but not overt antisocial behaviour. Sukhodolsky and Ruchkin found that aggressive acts were significantly associated with high levels of anger and beliefs that physical aggression is an appropriate course of action in conflicts. Non-aggressive antisocial behavior was associated with approval of deviancy, but not with anger or beliefs legitimizing aggression. Similar scripts may underpin adult behaviour of psychopaths. Beck et al. (1990), for example, identified their core beliefs as 'people are there to be taken', and the strategy derived from this to be one of attack. Other core beliefs included:

- Force or cunning is the best way to get things done.
- We live in a jungle and the strong person is the one who survives.
- People will get at me if I don't get them first.

- I have been unfairly treated and am entitled to get my fair share by whatever means I can.
- If people can't take care of themselves, that's their problem.

As well as these belief structures, there may be more fundamental differences in cognitive processing between psychopaths and average individuals. The previous section considered how psychopaths process emotional information. However, Sadeh and Verona (2008) found other cognitive differences between psychopaths and average individuals. In an experimental study, they found that participants who scored highly on traits indicating primary psychopathy (low anxiety, dominance, callousness) were more focused and less distracted by task-irrelevant stimuli than those without these characteristics. This suggests that such individuals had reduced attentional capacity, and had to focus more on tasks and less on peripheral issues. They also found that some characteristics of what they termed secondary psychopathy (social alienation, cynicism) were associated with poor working memory. Overall, they took this to indicate that psychopaths have a number of cognitive impairments, and that different aspects of psychopathy are associated with different aspects of cognitive function.

Treatment of antisocial personality

Psychological interventions

Interventions to reduce antisocial behaviour have focused almost exclusively on young people within the criminal system – fortuitously perhaps, as attempts at change in older people may prove more difficult (Davidson et al. 2008). As such, they may be better considered as programmes designed to change criminal behaviour than antisocial personality *per se*. The consensus of these studies is that the classic 'boot camp' or incarceration does not work. More effective interventions appear to be those targeting the family. Borduin (1999), for example, described a multi-systemic, family-based approach, the goal of which was to provide participants with the skills to help them cope with family and other problems. Family interventions aimed to improve parenting skills, encourage parents to support their child, and reduce levels of parental stress within the household. Parents were encouraged to develop strategies to monitor and reward progress at school, and to establish homework routines. Peer-oriented interventions were designed to increase affiliation with pro-social peers through participation in youth group meetings, organized athletics and after-school activities. Sanctions were applied following associations with deviant peers. Cognitive behavioural interventions focused on teaching social and problem-solving skills. Interventions generally lasted up to five months, with initial sessions occurring as frequently as once a day, tailing off to weekly as therapy progressed.

This approach has achieved significant success rates. Henggeler et al. (1992), for example, compared it with monitoring and general counselling in a group of 'serious juvenile offenders', most of whom had committed some form of violent crime. Immediately following the intervention, participants in the multi-systemic intervention had improved their family and peer relationships more than those in the comparison condition. By one-year follow-up, they had also been arrested less frequently and had spent less time in prison: an effect that held up to the two-year follow-up. In a four-year follow-up of a similar trial by the same group, Borduin et al. (1995) reported a halving of the known recidivism rate among those who received the intervention compared with a control group (21 versus 47 per cent) four years after the intervention.

One problem faced by this type of intervention is that many parents do not engage with any therapy. With this in mind, Nock and Kazdin (2005) examined how a brief intervention could enhance parent participation in this type of intervention. They used a technique they called participation enhancement intervention, which involved giving parents information about the importance of attendance and adherence, eliciting motivational statements about attending and adhering to treatment, and helping parents to identify and develop plans for overcoming problems that may occur over the period of treatment. The total time of the intervention was between 4 and 45 minutes and formed part of the first three therapy sessions. It also proved effective. Parents who received the intervention reported higher levels of treatment motivation, attended more treatment sessions, and engaged more in the treatment than those in a control group.

A different approach to the treatment of antisocial behaviour does not involve the identification of particular individuals with particular problems. Instead, preventive programmes may target all 'at risk' individuals. The best place to run such programmes may be within the normal day-to-day running of schools. An example of this approach is the 'good behaviour game', a widely used classroom management approach in the USA that rewards children for engaging in appropriate on-task behaviour during teaching. In it, the class is divided into two teams and a point is awarded to each team for any inappropriate behaviour involving one of its members. The team with the fewest points at the end of each day wins a group reward. If both teams keep their points below a preset level, they share the reward. The intervention therefore both reinforces and establishes group pressure and norms supporting appropriate behaviour. In one study of the effectiveness of this approach, Petras et al. (2008) compared rates of antisocial, violent and criminal behaviour in young men aged between 19 and 21 years who had attended schools in poor to lower middle-class areas of the US which had either implemented the programme or were in control areas. Those who had shown signs of early problems at baseline – the key target group of the programme – were significantly less likely to engage in any of these outcomes if they attended the schools in which the programme had been implemented.

Pharmacological interventions

A number of pharmacological interventions have been used to treat individuals who present with delinquent or antisocial behaviour. Some have proven effective, particularly in the treatment of aggression. Lithium or other treatments for bipolar disorder, for example, has been shown to reduce the number of impulsive aggressive episodes. Hollander et al. (2003), for example, found greater reductions than those achieved by placebo on measures of irritability, verbal assault and assault against objects with a drug known as Divalproex. SSRIs have also been suggested as a means of controlling impulsive aggression, but there are as yet no large controlled trials of their efficacy (Tcheremissine and Lieving 2006), and one small study of 26 participants found no benefit in their use (Lee et al. 2008). How these interventions would compare with psychological programmes in which individuals are taught to control their anger is not known.

Treatment of psychopathy

Psychopathic individuals do not seek treatment, and most interventions occur within prison or other custodial settings. As a result of their lack of motivation to change, psychopathy has often been considered an untreatable condition, although there have been some voices of dissent from this somewhat negative viewpoint. Of interest are three review papers of the treatment of psycho-pathy published within two years of each other and reviewing essentially the same literature. Salekin (2002) conducted a meta-analysis on data from 42 treatment studies, and concluded that while ECT and therapeutic communities were relatively ineffective interventions, good results could be achieved following psychoanalytic and cognitive therapy. Evaluating much the same literature, Reid and Gacono (2000) were more pessimistic in their conclusions and could find no evidence of consistent therapeutic gain following any form of treatment. Similarly, Wong and Hare (2002) concluded that, of the 74 empirical studies they could identify, only two were adequately conducted, and that the evidence was so weak that it remained unclear whether any intervention could be effective.

Measuring the effectiveness of programmes to treat psychopathy is problematic. A defining characteristic of psychopathic individuals is that they tell lies and are manipulative. Self-report measures should therefore be treated with considerable caution. Even behavioural measures cannot be relied on. The results of a study by Seto and Barbaree (1999) illustrate the problem. Their study examined the impact of a relapse prevention programme for sexual offenders similar to those described in Chapter 11. Participants included a range of people, not just psychopathic individuals. Their report focused on the relationship between apparent progress made within therapy as a function of in-session behaviour, homework quality, and therapist ratings of motivation and 'progress', and the frequency of reoffending following treatment. Among non-psychopathic individuals, greater within-therapy improvements were predictive of lower levels of offences following discharge from prison. By contrast, there was a *positive* association between apparent progress in therapy and the frequency of offences committed by the psychopathic individuals who took part in the programme. It seems that these people were able to learn the responses that the therapists considered indicative of progress and were able to simulate them. Those that were best at this simulation were also the most likely to re-offend. Therapy did nothing to change the underlying motivation of their behaviour.

Stop and think...

At present, few psychiatrists treat psychopaths. Most consider psychopathy an untreatable condition – as the evidence reviewed here suggests. But new UK legislation not only requires psychiatrists and other health professionals to treat psychopaths . . . it will also give them the right and responsibility to treat them within some sort of secure setting if they believe that the individual will (at some unspecified time in the future) behave in a way that puts others at risk – whether or not they have ever done so in the past. Of course, this then makes the psychiatrist legally responsible should they choose not to place that person in a place of care and some 'inappropriate' behaviour were to occur.

So, psychiatrists and others may be placed in a situation where they are having to treat a condition that cannot be treated . . . and/or place people in some secure place – also unspecified – in case they commit some form of offence.

Does this seem unreasonable? Or should society, acting through health professionals, be able to control the actions of potentially 'dangerous' individuals?

Psychoanalysis

A number of early studies of the treatment of psychopathic individuals involved psychoanalytic methods (Salekin 2002). These were virtually all case studies, and none compared the intervention with any other form of treatment or changes within a control group. Case histories are generally considered with some caution, as clinicians typically report their treatment successes, not their failures, so they represent a biased sample of cases. The successes reported in these studies may therefore not indicate the likely success rates among an unselected group of individuals, and do not provide strong evidence for the effectiveness of psychoanalysis in this population.

Therapeutic communities

Therapeutic communities were first developed under the leadership of Maxwell Jones in the UK in the late 1940s. These provided an intensive 24-hour-a-day intervention to change psycho-pathic behaviour. Those within them were made responsible for the physical and emotional care of others within the community. The group itself established acceptable and unacceptable behaviours. Members were required to accept the authority of the group, and to submit to its sanctions if they disobeyed the rules. Communities were loosely based on Rogerian principles (see Chapter 2), and tried to inculcate high levels of honesty, sincerity and empathy.

One of the best evaluations of the effectiveness of this approach was reported by Rice et al. (1992) – although the community it assessed was significantly more authoritarian than the UK model. They focused on a therapeutic community situated within a maximum security prison in the USA. The programme was led by those within it, and comprised 80 hours of intensive group therapy each week, intended to help participants develop empathy and responsibility for their peers. Those who responded well led therapeutic groups and became involved in adminis-tering the programme. All participants were involved in decisions about who was released or transferred from the programme.

Participants had little contact with professional staff. Nor did they have much opportunity for diversion: access to television or even informal social encounters were severely limited. Participation in the programme was compulsory: disruptive behaviour, for example, resulted in entry into a sub-programme in which the individual discussed their reasons for not wanting to be in the programme, but they were ultimately expected to resume participation. The authors noted that some of these programme characteristics would now not be ethically acceptable, but that the programme was well regarded at the time it took place in the 1960s and 1970s.

The programme accepted both psychopaths and non-psychopaths, who were followed up for an average of ten years after discharge. Analyses compared the outcomes on psychopathic individuals, non-psychopathic participants and a matched control group who did not enter the community. Their results were similar to those reported by Seto and Barbaree (1999). Non-psychopathic individuals were less likely to offend following discharge than those in the control group. By contrast, psychopathic individuals who participated in the programme were more likely to engage in violent crime following discharge than those in the control group, with known recidivism rates of 78 versus 55 per cent respectively. The therapeutic community approach may actually have taught psychopathic individuals how to manipulate others more effectively – an unexpected and unwanted result.

Cognitive interventions

Cognitive behavioural interventions may not be immune from this paradoxical outcome. Hare et al. (2000) examined the outcome of a number of short-term, prison-based, cognitive behavioural programmes including anger management and social skills training. Their data revealed that the interventions had little effect on re-offence rates of most psychopathic individuals. However, among offenders with particularly high levels of psychopathy, re-offence rates rose following treatment. Again, it seems that these courses taught these people how to be 'better psychopaths'.

Despite these negative results, a number of research groups have considered how the goals and strategies of cognitive behavioural therapy could be adapted to treat psychopathic individuals. Beck et al. (1990) attempted to define the realistic goals of such interventions. They noted that the individual will continue to act primarily out of self-interest, and that the goal of therapy should therefore be to help them act in ways that are functional and adaptive within these limits. Cognitive challenge, which lies at the heart of the intervention, may therefore not only address core schemata such as 'I am always right', or 'Other people should see things my way', but also question whether antisocial behaviour is in the individual's own interest. Participants in therapy may, for example, be encouraged to question whether behaving in a way that assumes 'other people should see things my way' causes interpersonal friction which interferes with their own goals, and to change their behaviour if this is the case. This approach allows client and therapist to work together towards agreed goals.

Wong and Hare (2002) developed a substantial cognitive behavioural approach to the treatment of psychopathy, involving interventions at both an institutional (prison) and individual level. Their intervention was problem-focused and addressed issues specific to psychopathic individuals. Key elements of the programme included the following:

- *Support of pro-social attitudes and behaviour*: many psychopathic individuals within an institution seek out others with similar views who will reinforce their own beliefs. To minimize the risk of this happening, Wong and Hare (2002) suggest that a 'pro-social milieu' is established within the institution. This may be achieved by high-status individuals within the programme modelling positive attitudes and encouraging them in others, and encouraging group reinforcement of pro-social behaviours. Note that the results of Rice et al. (1992) suggest that this may not be easy to establish.

- *Changing dysfunctional behaviours – aggression, manipulation, intimidation*: strategies to achieve change include self-instruction training (Meichenbaum 1985: see Chapter 2 in this volume) to prevent overreacting to situations in which the individual feels inappropriately threatened or angry, and interpersonal skills training where these are lacking and contributing to the use of intimidation or other dysfunctional behaviours. These may be taught through role play and reinforcement of appropriate behaviour.

- *Learning to take responsibility for one's actions*: the intervention here involves a detailed analysis of the factors that lead up to offences, and identifying where the individual made choices that ultimately lead to offending. This also forms the core of relapse prevention training (see Chapters 10 and 13), as information here both encourages the individual to take responsibility for the actions that led to offending behaviour and to identify strategies to avoid them in the future.

The programme also examined strategies for minimizing substance misuse and helping participants gain work skills or develop leisure activities to help avoid boredom once discharged, as this may trigger antisocial behaviour. Finally, the programme addressed the social network into which the individual is discharged following their stay in prison. Attempts to maintain or re-establish links with supportive family or other means of social support were recommended, although family contacts may be conducted with some caution, as relationships with family members are frequently poor. Evidence of the effectiveness of these therapeutic approaches has yet to be reported.

12.4 Cluster C diagnoses

Cluster C diagnoses subsume what may be termed neurotic disorders. According to DSM-IV-TR, avoidant personality is characterized by social inhibition, feelings of inadequacy and hypersensitivity to negative evaluation. It begins in early adulthood and the individual has at least four of the following features. People with avoidant personality:

- avoid occupational activities that involve significant interpersonal contact, because of fears of criticism, disapproval, or rejection
- are unwilling to get involved with people unless certain of being liked
- show restraint within intimate relationships because of the fear of being shamed or ridiculed
- are preoccupied with being criticized or rejected in social situations
- are inhibited in new interpersonal situations because of feelings of inadequacy
- view themselves as socially inept, personally unappealing or inferior to others
- are unusually reluctant to take personal risks or to engage in any new activities because they may prove embarrassing.

A person with a dependent personality has the following characteristics. They do the following:

- have difficulty making everyday decisions without an excessive amount of advice and reassurance from others
- need others to assume responsibility for most major areas of his or her life
- have difficulty expressing disagreement with others because of fear of loss of support or approval
- have difficulty initiating projects or doing things on his or her own (because of a lack of self-confidence in judgement or abilities rather than a lack of motivation or energy)
- go to excessive lengths to obtain nurturance and support from others, to the point of volunteering to do things that are unpleasant
- feel uncomfortable or helpless when alone
- urgently seek another relationship as a source of care and support when a close relationship ends
- are unrealistically preoccupied with fears of being left to take care of himself or herself.

Finally, the characteristics of the obsessive-compulsive personality are that the individual:

- is preoccupied with details, rules, lists, order, organization or schedules to the extent that the major point of the activity is lost
- shows perfectionism that interferes with task completion (e.g. is unable to complete a project because his or her overly strict standards are not met)
- is excessively devoted to work and productivity to the exclusion of leisure activities and friendships
- is over-conscientious, and inflexible about matters of morality, ethics or values
- is unable to discard worn-out or worthless objects even when they have no sentimental value
- is reluctant to delegate tasks or to work with others unless they submit to exactly his or her way of doing things
- adopts a miserly spending style towards both self and others; money is viewed as something to be hoarded for future catastrophes
- shows rigidity and stubbornness.

The prevalence of cluster C disorders in the general population varies from between 1 and 8 per cent depending on the disorder and study (Tyrer 2002). The linkage between the conditions is not as strong as that within the cluster A group, and a number of factor analyses have found little or no overlap between the characteristics of obsessive-compulsive personality disorder and the others (e.g. Costa and McCrea 1992). There is, however, considerable overlap between the diagnostic criteria for the anxious personality types and axis 1 diagnoses such as social phobia, depression and generalized anxiety disorder, making differential diagnoses difficult to achieve at times. So close are these diagnoses that Ralevski et al. (2005) suggested that avoidant personality disorder and social phobia are 'alternative conceptualizations of the same disorder'. Certainly, these personality types place individuals at significant risk of developing axis 1 (see Chapter 1) diagnoses of anxiety or depression. When people with these personality types go on to develop axis 1 disorders, they typically experience more severe problems than individuals without such a background (e.g. Boone et al. 1999).

There are relatively few studies exploring the origins of cluster C personality disorders. However, Reichborn-Kjennerud et al. (2007) found that heritability ranged between 27 and 35 per cent across the disorders. In addition, work by Torgersen et al. (2000) indicated both genetic and biological pathways to the disorders based on their genetic study. They modelled the role of genetic and environmental factors in the development of a variety of personality disorders and found a significant genetic contribution to the development of dependent, avoidant and obsessive-compulsive disorders. Their analyses excluded a role for a familial environment in cases of avoidant and obsessive-compulsive disorders, but a mixture of both genetic and environmental factors contributed to the development of dependent personality. By contrast, Parker et al. (1999) found associations between retrospective ratings of parents as uncaring, over-controlling or abusive to be associated with anxious, cluster C, personality types. How much this reflected reality, and how much cognitive distortion cannot be determined. Similarly, Nordahl and Stiles

(1997) found that patients diagnosed with obsessive-compulsive personality disorder reported lower levels of paternal care and higher levels of paternal overprotection than a 'normal' control group. By contrast, avoidant, dependent and cluster A personality disorders were not associated with abnormal parental bonding.

There are also very few studies of treatment research related to the cluster C disorders. There is some evidence of a short-term benefit of treatment by MAOIs (Deltito and Stam 1989) and SSRIs (Fahlen 1995), although placebo-controlled, definitive studies are still lacking. Studies of the effectiveness of psychological therapies have involved sub-analyses of people with both personality disorders and axis 1 disorders in larger treatment trials or uncontrolled trials of CBT. Using the former approach, Tyrer et al. (1993) compared the impact of tricyclic antidepressants and CBT in patients with anxiety and depressive disorders, including some with cluster C personality type. Over a two-year follow-up period, tricyclics proved the most effective intervention in this group. Gude and Vaglum (2001) found some benefit over a one-year follow-up following brief treatment using schema-focused therapy, which attempted to change the core beliefs underpinning the personality, but there was no control group against which to measure progress. Subsequently, Svartberg et al. (2004) compared the effectiveness of two active therapies (short-term dynamic psychotherapy and cognitive therapy) in the treatment of a variety of cluster C disorders. Two years after treatment, 54 per cent of the people who received short-term dynamic psychotherapy and 42 per cent of those who received cognitive therapy showed clinically significant improvements. Finally, Emmelkamp et al. (2006) compared brief dynamic therapy and cognitive behavioural therapy in the treatment of people diagnosed with avoidant personality disorder and a waiting list control. Those in the cognitive behavioural therapy fared best. There is also evidence cluster C diagnoses may influence the outcomes of treatment of other conditions. Hansen et al. (2007), for example, found that individuals with type C personality benefited more than individuals of differing personalities from a cognitive behavioural treatment of obsessive compulsive disorder.

12.5 Chapter summary

1 DSM identifies ten types of personality disorder in three clusters: A – odd or eccentric; B – flamboyant or dramatic; and C – fearful or anxious.

2 These may be better considered as extremes on a continuum of personality factors rather than distinct 'diagnoses'.

3 Beck's evolutionary model of personality disorders suggests they are the inappropriate maladaptive pre-programmed responses to environmental events, that result from an interaction between genetic and childhood factors.

4 Cluster A diagnoses are also known as the schizophrenia spectrum disorders, and include paranoid, schizoid and schizotypal disorders.

5 Meehl suggested that the core personality disorder is genetically mediated, while risk for schizophrenia involves further genetic influences and high environmental stress factors.

6 Borderline personality disorder belongs to the cluster B group. Its core elements are an intense fear of abandonment, difficulties in coping with strong emotions, and the use of self-harm as means of coping with strong emotions.

7 The origins of the disorder seem largely linked to experiences of childhood rejections and trauma that translate into strong negative self-schemata and dissociation as a means of coping with distress.

8 Borderline personality disorder is difficult to treat, although significant therapeutic gains have been made using cognitive behavioural techniques. The effectiveness of a method known as emotional awareness training has yet to be fully evaluated. The disorder seems resistant to pharmacological therapy.

9 Although DSM tried to combine psychopathy and antisocial behaviour under one diagnostic umbrella, critics such as Hare have argued that they are different conditions. The DSM diagnostic criteria describe someone who is criminally antisocial. Psychopathic individuals experience a poverty of emotions as well as engage in antisocial behaviour.

10 Antisocial behaviour seems primarily to be the result of adverse social circumstances.

11 Psychopathic individuals also have neurological deficits within the limbic system that inhibit emotional processing.

12 Family or systemic interventions appear to be effective in the treatment of antisocial behaviour.

13 Finding effective treatments of psychopathic behaviour has proven more difficult. Standard interventions may actually increase psychopathic behaviour. Beck and Wong have been developing cognitive therapeutic interventions that may prove more effective – although there is no data yet concerning their effectiveness.

14 Cluster C diagnoses include those of avoidant, dependent and obsessive-compulsive personalities.

15 These personalities appear to be the product of both genetic and family factors – although the role of family may be less than that of genetics according to Torgersen and colleagues.

16 Although there are few studies of the effectiveness of interventions for cluster C personalities, cognitive therapy and psychodynamic therapy both appear to be of benefit.

12.6 For discussion

1 Are the 'personality disorders' categorically different from the personalities of 'normal' people?

2 Should families whose dynamics increase the risk of their children developing personality (or other) disorders be routinely offered some form of therapeutic support?

3 Should psychopaths be treated or punished for their behaviour?

12.7 Further reading

Davidson, K. (2007) *Cognitive Therapy for Personality Disorders: A Guide for Clinicians*. Oxford: Butterworth-Heinemann.

Livesley W.J. (2005) Principles and strategies for treating personality disorder, *Canadian Journal of Psychiatry*, 50: 442–50.

Loeber, R., Burke, J. and Pardini, D.A. (2009) Perspectives on oppositional defiant disorder, conduct disorder, and psychopathic features, *Journal of Child Psychology and Psychiatry*, 50: 133–42.

Siever, L.J. and Weinstein, L.N. (2009) The neurobiology of personality disorders: implications for psychoanalysis, *Journal of the American Psychoanalytic Association*, 57: 361–98.

Trull, T.J. (2005) Dimensional models of personality disorder: coverage and cutoffs, *Journal of Personality Disorders*, 19: 262–82.

The following websites also have information about BPD and psychopathy, their treatment, and people's experiences of them.

www.cassiopaea.com/cassiopaea/psychopath.htm
www.hare.org/
www.bpdworld.org/
www.bpdfamily.com/index2.htm
www.personalitydisorder.org.uk/

Chapter 13

Eating disorders

Chapter contents

Most of us have 'gone on a diet' at some time in our lives or wished to change our shape. Many of us succeed, at least in the short term, although we often experience a gradual increase in weight as we get older. For some, the imperative to diet or change shape may be more extreme than the norm – and be diagnosed as an eating disorder. Two eating disorders are considered in this chapter: anorexia nervosa and bulimia nervosa. By the end of the chapter, you should have an understanding of:

- The nature of anorexia and bulimia
- The various aetiological explanations of both disorders, including genetic, social, familial and cognitive factors
- The nature and effectiveness of interventions conducted with people who have eating disorders.

Although both disorders present in quite different ways, they have a number of elements in common, and many people with anorexia may shift into bulimic eating patterns at some time. Both involve prioritizing weight control. There are also significant differences between the conditions. People with bulimia, for example, are rarely underweight and they value being sexually attractive, unlike most people with anorexia. The chapter first describes the two conditions. Then, it discusses the aetiological factors that the conditions have in common and those on which they differ. It finally considers the treatment of the two conditions.

13.1 Anorexia nervosa

First identified in the late nineteenth century, anorexia nervosa involves behaviours intended to keep the individual as thin as possible. Indeed, the defining characteristic of anorexia is being significantly underweight. DSM-IV-TR suggested a weight-based cut-off point for a diagnosis of anorexia as being 15 per cent below the normal weight for age and height. Weight loss and control are generally achieved using one of two methods: the classic, type 1, pattern of self-imposed starvation, and the type 2 pattern of binging and purging through vomiting or the use of laxatives. Where anorexia is discussed in this chapter it usually refers to the first of these two types.

The DSM-IV-TR criteria for a diagnosis of anorexia are:

- a refusal to maintain body weight above a minimally normal weight for age and height
- intense fear of gaining weight, even though underweight
- disturbed body perception, undue influence of weight or shape on self-evaluation, or the denial of the seriousness of current low weight
- cessation of menstruation if this has already begun.

Between 80 and 90 per cent of those who develop anorexia nervosa are female, with the typical age of onset being between 14 and 18 years old (Pike 1998). Across the world, between 0.5 and 2 per cent of women are likely to develop anorexia in their lifetime (e.g. Preti et al. 2009; Wade et al. 2006). For most people with anorexia, weight control is a long-term issue. Loewe et al. (2001), for example, found that 21 years after their initial admission, just over half of a cohort of women identified as anorexic were 'fully recovered', 21 per cent were 'partially recovered' and 10 per cent still met the full diagnostic criteria for anorexia. Few had sought help or any form of treatment, and 16 per cent had died of causes related to anorexia.

Many people with anorexia go on to develop eating habits typical of bulimia nervosa (e.g. Eddy et al. 2008): that is, maintenance of normal weight while still having abnormal eating and vomiting patterns, leading some (e.g. Fairburn 1997, 1998) to argue that both conditions share significant common elements. This is discussed later in the chapter. In contrast to many mental health disorders, the prevalence of anorexia is highest among women in the higher socio-economic groups, and among those who achieve high academic achievement. People with anorexia tend to score low on measures of assertiveness and self-esteem, and high in self-directed hostility (Williams et al. 1993). They also typically measure highly on measures of perfectionism (Halmi et al. 2000).

Despite their avoidance of eating, most people with anorexia are preoccupied with thoughts of food. They may spend much of their time thinking about food, preparing it for themselves or others, or watching others eat. They may report dreaming about food, experience hunger pains and retain an appetite for food. High levels of exercise or other behaviours that consume calories are common weight-loss strategies. Most, but not all, people with anorexia have a distorted body image, considerably overestimating their body proportions, and have a low opinion of their body shape (Hrabosky et al. 2009). Psychological problems, including mild depression, obsessive-compulsive disorder and anxiety, are common among people with anorexia.

The control and reduction in weight associated with anorexia can result in a number of health consequences. The most immediate is the absence of menstruation (or amenorrhoea). Less obvious problems include anaemia, increased tooth cavities and gum infections, high blood pressure, reduced bone mineral density, low blood pressure, rough and cracked skin, and dry and brittle hair. Health problems may move to crisis in the form of metabolic and electrolyte imbalances that can be life-threatening. Across studies, between zero and 21 per cent of people with anorexia die as a consequence of their problems (e.g. Birmingham et al. 2005), with the most common causes of death being starvation and suicide. The brain may also show evidence of changes at times of severe starvation, with reductions in brain volume and increases in the amount of cerebrospinal fluid. Thankfully, Wagner et al. (2006) found these changes to be reversible in people recovered for over one year.

13.2 Bulimia nervosa

The DSM-IV-TR (2000) criteria for bulimia are:

- recurrent episodes of binge eating
- recurrent inappropriate compensatory behaviour, such as vomiting after eating, in order to prevent weight gain
- compensatory behaviours occur, on average, at least twice a week for three months
- undue influence of weight or shape on self-evaluation.

Many people with bulimia feel unattractive, have a fear of becoming fat, and consider themselves to be heavier than they actually are (Striegel-Moore et al. 2004). Their attempts to avoid being overweight are more chaotic than in anorexia, and periods of controlled eating are frequently interrupted by repeated, relatively short episodes of uncontrollable eating. These are followed by behaviours designed to counteract the consequences of bingeing. The amount of food consumed in binges can be vast: up to and beyond 5000 calories at any one time. Food is not eaten for pleasure; indeed, it is usually eaten secretly, rapidly and barely tasted. Episodes are usually preceded by periods of considerable physical and psychological tension, and eating serves to reduce this tension. While bingeing, the individual may feel out of control, and episodes are typically followed by feelings of guilt, self-blame and depression. The weight of people with bulimia usually remains within the normal range, although it may fluctuate considerably over time. Between 80 and 90 per cent of people with bulimia vomit after eating in an attempt to control their weight, one-third abuse laxatives, while others may exercise excessively (Anderson and Maloney 2001). Compensatory behaviours reduce discomfort and feelings of anxiety, self-disgust or lack of control associated with bingeing. Ironically, however, they frequently fail to prevent the calorific intake from much of the ingested food. Bulimia involves some risk to health. Repeated vomiting and laxative abuse can lead to problems including abdominal pain, digestive problems, dehydration, damage to the stomach lining and to the back of the teeth, where regurgitated acid can do permanent damage to the tooth enamel. The most serious outcome can be an electrolyte imbalance leading to renal damage and potentially fatal cardiac arrhythmias.

Between 1 and 3 per cent of women will develop bulimia in their lifetime (Preti et al. 2009; Wade et al. 2006), and although the majority will no longer be bulimic five years after diagnosis, nearly a half will revert back to bulimic behaviours at some point (Grilo et al. 2007). Among young women, rates are particularly high. Up to 50 per cent of female students surveyed by Schwitzer et al. (2001) reported periodic binges; 6 per cent had tried vomiting; and 8 per cent

Table 13.1 Differences between 'classic' anorexia nervosa and bulimia nervosa

Restrictive anorexia	Bulimia nervosa
Body weight significantly below age/height norms	Weight varies: underweight, overweight, close to age/height norms
Less likely to experience intense hunger	More likely to experience intense hunger
Less likely to have been overweight in the past	More likely to have been overweight in the past
More likely to be sexually immature and inexperienced	More likely to be sexually active
Considers behaviour as reasonable and 'normal'	Considers behaviour as abnormal
Less likely to abuse drugs or alcohol	More likely to abuse drugs or alcohol
Less likely to engage in deliberate self-harm	More likely to engage in deliberate self-harm
Tendency to deny family conflict	Acknowledges family conflict
Age of onset between 14 and 18 years	Age of onset between 15 and 21 years
Relatively independent	Seeks the approval of others; wants to be attractive to others
Weight loss is not driven by a wish to look 'feminine'	Accepts social concepts of 'femininity' and wishes to adhere to them
High self-control	Impulsive and emotional instability

had used laxatives on at least one occasion. Few, however, engaged in these behaviours sufficiently frequently for them to be considered a disorder (see Table 13.1).

Aetiology of anorexia and bulimia

Genetic factors

Genetic factors may contribute to risk for both anorexia and bulimia. Klump et al. (2001), for example, estimated 74 per cent of the variance in anorexic behaviours to be attributable to genetic factors, following a twin study in which they found 50 per cent of MZ twins and no DZ twins to be concordant for anorexia. Similarly, Kendler et al. (1991) found the rate of concordance for bulimia between MZ twins to be higher than that between DZ twins, although the concordance rates for both groups were relatively low: 23 and 9 per cent respectively. In addition to genetic risk for eating disorders, Keel et al. (2005) found evidence of shared genetic risk for both eating and anxiety disorders in a large-scale twin study involving nearly 700 twins. Genetic studies have now moved from family studies, indicating potential genetic processes, to examination of actual genes. Key genes identified as being involved in eating disorders appear to control serotonin metabolism, with particular attention given to various alleles of the serotonin 5-HT(2A) receptor gene (e.g. Monteleone and Maj 2008) – although other variants have also been studied. The dopamine receptor genes D2/D3 and DRD4 also seem to be implicated (e.g. Bachner-Melman et al. 2007).

Biochemical mechanisms

The main brain area involved in the regulation of appetite is the hypothalamus, although other brain areas and factors in the gut also influence hunger and satiety. The lateral hypothalamus produces hunger when stimulated; surgical damage results in dramatic reductions in food intake and weight loss. Activation of the ventromedial hypothalamus triggers feelings of satiation and reduces hunger: for this reason it has been called the satiety centre. Activity within the hypothalamus is largely mediated by two neurotransmitters: dopamine and serotonin, which initiate, maintain and then inhibit eating.

Dopamine   At the onset of or when anticipating eating, dopamine activity increases in both the lateral hypothalamus and the mesolimbic dopamine system – the primary reward system (see Chapter 4). Thus, the early stages of eating are both triggered and maintained by a direct effect on hunger and a feeling of pleasure. As eating continues, the dopaminergic activity is replaced by serotinergic activity, which reduces appetite and inhibits eating. Jimerson et al. (1992) suggested that people prone to binge eating may experience low levels of dopamine release (or be insensitive to the dopamine that is released) when they start eating. This may lead to binge eating as they attempt to achieve previous levels of satisfaction/reward from eating. Such speculation is supported by findings of low levels of HVA (a metabolite of dopamine) in the cerebrospinal fluid of people with bulimia (Kaye and Weltzin 1991). Paradoxically, perhaps, people with anorexia may also have a diminished capacity to experience pleasure or reward as a consequence of low levels of dopamine in the mesolimbic system but feel less motivated to eat rather than overeating as some form of compensation (Wagner et al. 2007). This may be re-established when they recover.

Serotonin   Animal studies have shown that when serotonin is released into either the ventromedial or lateral hypothalamus, animals stop eating and may starve despite the presence of food. Thus, high levels of serotonin lead to feelings of satiation and lower levels of eating – as well as improve mood. Low levels of serotonin result in excess eating and obesity – and low mood. This is not simply the result of serotonin's influence on the hypothalamus – areas such as the limbic system are also involved.

One explanation for the eating binges associated with bulimia has been that dieting reduces levels of tryptophan, a precursor to serotonin, leading to low mood and cravings for food high in tryptophan – carbohydrates such as chocolate, cakes and chips (Kaye et al. 1988). Eating these restores serotonin and mood levels to normal. In support of this hypothesis, Kaye et al. (1988) found that women with bulimia typically stopped bingeing if their levels of tryptophan increased significantly following an eating binge: those whose tryptophan remained relatively low continued bingeing. In a related study, Goldbloom et al. (1990) found that following release into the synaptic cleft, bulimics' serotonin was more quickly reabsorbed by the initiating axon than that of normal controls, resulting in a reduced *availability* of serotonin at the receptor cells. In response to these findings, Jimerson et al. (1992) suggested that periodic binge eating may cause sudden increases in serotonin levels within the brain. This causes the receptors to become less sensitive to serotonin when released. This low sensitivity to serotonin means that the individual may become less responsive to normal levels of serotonin, requiring them to take in larger amounts of tryptophan to convert to serotonin in order to maintain emotional equilibrium.

Despite some supportive data, neither theory has always been supported by empirical evidence. Weltzin et al. (1995), for example, found no evidence of reduced levels of tryptophan prior to binge eating episodes in women with bulimia, and Jansen et al. (1989) found that levels of tryptophan in the foods typically eaten in a binge were actually quite low in tryptophan and were not a particularly effective means of increasing tryptophan levels. Behavioural studies also provide limited support for the hypothesis. Steiger et al. (2005) used hand-held computers to obtain repeated 'online' measurements of eating behaviours and mood in 21 women with bulimia. As expected, their mood was typically depressed before binge episodes. However, following bingeing, their mood deteriorated further.

Some studies (e.g. Kaye et al. 1988) have shown people with anorexia to have lower levels of serotonin metabolites in their cerebrospinal fluid than controls. Kaye (2008) has argued that this is a consequence of anorexia rather than a cause. Indeed, Kaye (2008), argued that anorexia may be the result of too *high* levels of serotonin rather than too low levels. He suggested that these high levels of serotonin may leave the individual feeling nervous and jittery, feelings that are may be reduced by reducing food intake, and thereby reducing tryptophan, and then serotonin levels. Unfortunately, even Kaye's own work has not always supported this hypothesis, as he (Kaye et al. 2005) found lower levels of serotonergic activity during periods of both starving *and* recovery among people with anorexia than among 'normal' controls. Brain areas involved include the frontal, cingulated, temporal and parietal cortical regions – which are involved in anxiety, behavioural control and body image. Together, these data suggest that while serotonin dysregulation may be involved in both bulimia and anorexia, its exact role in either disorder is yet to be fully understood.

Socio-cultural factors

'Thin is attractive.' People with both anorexia and bulimia place a prime importance on shape and weight, probably because of a more general cultural emphasis placed on physical appearance within Western society. Images of femininity and female attractiveness have shifted since the 1960s to a slimmer, less 'hour-glass' shape. The classic 'figure' portrayed in *Playboy* magazine, for example, slimmed during the 1990s, with smaller hips, waist and bust measurements (Rubinstein and Caballero 2000). Not surprisingly, the prevalence of low body weight and eating disorders is particularly high among those groups where physical attractiveness or performance is placed at a premium, such as models, dancers and athletes. As social groups develop positive attitudes towards thinness, levels of eating disorders rise within them. In the USA, for example, as a high value on thinness has shifted from white upperclass women to those in the lower socio-economic groups and other ethnic groups, so has the prevalence of dieting and eating disorders (Striegal-Moore and Smolak 2000).

Judgements based on weight are not only aesthetic; attributions of a variety of personal attributes can be based on the appearance of the individual. Food, eating and weight are seen by many as moral issues, and body shape can be a major criterion of self- and other-evaluation (Wardle and Marsland 1990); many people hold prejudicial views against overweight individuals.

Over half the families in which an individual develops an eating disorder are likely to place a strong emphasis on weight and shape (Haworth-Hoeppner 2000). They are also likely to come from families with high levels of negative affect and discord and have mothers who are perfectionist (Pike et al. 2008; Woodside et al. 2002). Successful dieting may be one way of gaining acceptance from parents with high aspirations, particularly where the child has not 'succeeded' in other life domains. Not eating may make an individual important within the family, and give them some degree of control over other family members ('I'll eat if you . . .'). It may also provide a means of punishing them ('I'm not eating because you . . .'). A second consequence of anorexia is that it can lead the individual to be treated as a child, and allow them to avoid the responsibilities they would otherwise have to face; again, this may be most influential in families where there is a high emphasis on achievement.

A completely different model of anorexia is afforded by some family therapists, in which the person with anorexia is viewed as a symptom of a dysfunctional family. Minuchin et al. (1978) defined the characteristic of 'anorexic families' as being enmeshed, overprotective, rigid and conflict-avoidant. That is, there is conflict between parents which is controlled and hidden. According to Minuchin et al., adolescence is a stressful time for such families, as the adolescent's push for their independence within the family increases the risk of the parental conflict being exposed. The development of anorexia prevents total dissension within the family, and may even hold it together as the family unites around the 'identified patient'. The presentation of the young person as weak and in need of family support ensures that they become the focus of family attention and deflects it away from parental conflict. Evidence for this theory is mainly based on the clinical experience of the Minuchin group of family therapists.

A final socio-cultural model suggests that both anorexia and bulimia may occur as a result of sexual abuse (Oppenheimer et al. 1985). According to this model, abuse results in the adolescent girl having strong negative attitudes towards her femininity, resulting in a rejection of the typical feminine shape and attempts to avoid it. This is most likely to occur around puberty. The evidence for this is not strong. Even though rates of sexual abuse are relatively high among people with eating disorders (e.g. Rayworth et al. 2004), it is not a defining characteristic, as they are no higher than those among people with mood, anxiety and other psychological disorders.

Psychological explanations

Weight-related schemata   Social factors translate into behaviour through cognitive processes. Despite the many differences in presenting problems, Fairburn's (1998) cognitive model proposed a similar cognitive disturbance in both anorexia and bulimia: a set of distorted beliefs and attitudes towards body shape and weight. Thinness and weight loss are prioritized, perhaps because of the high status given to looking thin and attractive, and the individual works to avoid weight gain and becoming fat. The underlying schemata involve judging one's self-worth on the basis of achieving a low body weight and being thin – so-called weight-related self-schemata.

Once weight-related schemata are established, they distort the way the individual perceives and interprets their experiences. Other people are evaluated not on the basis of personal qualities, but in terms of being thinner or fatter than the individual. All activities are assessed in terms of weight control, and any situation that leads to self-evaluation also results in an intensified focus on weight and shape. Any weight fluctuation has a profound effect on thoughts and feelings. For some people, their concerns and prioritizing control over their weight reflect a wider lack of self-esteem, a vulnerability to cultural messages about body weight (Stein and Corte 2003), and the desire to gain control over one aspect of their life. They hope to feel better about themselves if they are thinner – a process that leads them to be perpetually dissatisfied with their appearance and to be continually working to lose weight. Depression that may result from anorexic behaviour may intensify feelings of low self-esteem and increase dependence on controlling weight as a means of maintaining self-worth.

Both anorexia and bulimia may reflect different ways of coping with the same underlying cognitions. According to Fairburn (1997), people with anorexia are more able to sustain long-term control over their eating than those with bulimia, who are more chaotic and less consistent. He suggested that because of their restrictive dietary habits, individuals with both bulimia and anorexia are under significant psychological and physiological pressure to binge eat. To cope with these demands, both groups set a series of rules to govern their eating: when they should eat, what they can and cannot eat, and so on. These rules are typically perfectionist and difficult to achieve. Despite this, people with anorexia have sufficient self-control to be able to follow the rules they have set. By contrast, individuals with bulimia may on occasion fail to do so. This type of analysis is supported by personality studies (e.g. Cassin and von Ranson 2005) that have found both anorexia and bulimia to be consistently characterized by perfectionism, obsessive-compulsiveness, neuroticism, negative emotionality, and harm avoidance. However, anorexia is typically associated with traits of high constraint and persistence, while people with bulimia are more impulsive and sensation-seeking.

Once an individual with bulimia starts to eat, Fairburn suggests that they typically engage in dichotomous thinking ('I've eaten, so that's the end of my diet. What's the point of even trying to diet?') and a binge occurs. Binge eating also tends to improve low mood, and is thus in itself reinforcing (but see Steiger et al. 2005, discussed above). This is due to several effects, including drowsiness that follows eating large quantities of food and, in those who vomit, the feeling of relief and release of tension. These initial positive feelings are typically followed by feelings of disgust and shame at overeating, which results in a determined effort to follow the dietary rules set, which places the individual at risk of bingeing, and so the cycle continues (see Figure 13.1).

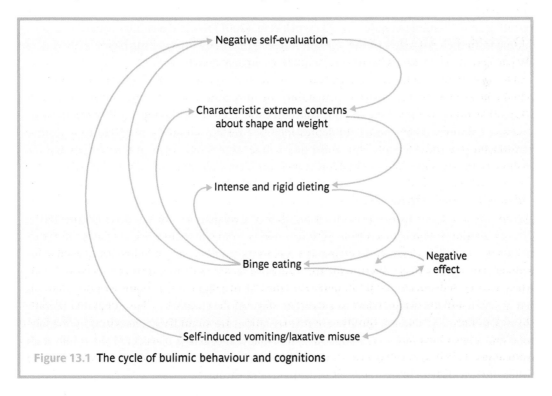

Figure 13.1 The cycle of bulimic behaviour and cognitions

Initial attempts at weight loss may be triggered by a variety of factors, including critical comments about weight or appearance, teasing, or role confusion at the time of transition from child to woman. As well as cognitive processes, dietary changes may also be maintained by a number of reinforcement processes. Positive reinforcement may initially be experienced in the form of compliments on looking slim. As these comments turn to concern, they may still provide positive reinforcement as the individual gains attention from their family. One specific form of feedback may be particularly important: the daily or weekly reinforcement of the bathroom scales. These provide unequivocal feedback on performance. For people with low self-esteem, weight loss may provide one element of control and success in their life. Weight loss becomes equated with self-esteem and self-worth, perhaps more so than any other factor in life. Anorexic behaviours may also be driven by negative reinforcement processes. People with anorexia experience an intense fear of gaining weight. Avoidance of this fear, by restrictive eating, provides relief from such fears.

Distorted body image　A second cognitive model, involving a distorted body image, applies only to people with anorexia. This suggests that such people feel 'fat' even when their weight is actually clinically subnormal (Bruch 1982). Summarizing a plethora of research studies, Gupta and Johnson (2000) suggested that many people with anorexia considerably overestimate their body proportions, have a low opinion of their body shape, and consider themselves to be unattractive. By contrast, Slade and Brodie (1994) suggested that many of these reports represent an *emotional* reaction to their body shape rather than a perceptual experience. They suggested that those who experience an eating disorder are uncertain about their body size and shape, and only when they are compelled to make a judgement about these issues do they err on the side of reporting an overestimated body size. Skrzypek et al. (2001) reached a similar conclusion, concluding from their summary of the relevant research that body image disturbance is not due to any perceptual deficit, but is based on 'cognitive-evaluative dissatisfaction'.

The restricted food intake achieved by people with anorexia may have biological effects unrelated to body size or shape that serves to perpetuate any cognitive distortions. Starvation affects a number of cognitive processes, resulting in poor concentration, concrete thinking, rigidity, withdrawal, obsessive-compulsive behaviour and depression. As a result, starvation may lead to a positive feedback loop in which people with anorexia become increasingly rigid in their beliefs and are unable to consider other ways of looking at their problem (Whittal and Zaretsky 1996).

Psychoanalytic explanations

Classic psychoanalytic theory provides a number of explanations for anorexia (Zerbe 2001). One explanation is that it stems from an unconscious confusion between eating and the sexual instinct. Some women may avoid eating as a means of, symbolically, avoiding sex. Another interpretation suggests that women with anorexia have fantasies of oral impregnation, and confuse fatness with pregnancy. Starvation reduces the risk of pregnancy. Yet another explanation is that anorexia reflects a regression to an earlier stage of development. The individual literally 'shrinks' in size. This, and the cessation of menstruation, are an unconscious rejection of adulthood and a wish to revert to a childhood state. Finally, anorexia is considered the result of an arrested psychosexual development. If the child is fixated in the oral stage, sexual anxieties and obsessions are likely to be expressed as disturbances of eating.

Integrating psychoanalytical and cognitive processes, Bruch (1982) saw anorexia as the result of disturbed mother–child interactions that lead to ego deficiencies including a poor sense of autonomy and control, manifest through disordered eating patterns. According to Bruch (1982), some mothers fail to attend appropriately to their young child's needs, perhaps as a result of prioritizing their own needs over those of the child or misunderstanding their behaviour. They may, for example, provide food and intimacy at times that suit them rather than the child, or misinterpret the child's emotions or needs. As a result, the child may grow up confused and unaware of their own internal needs, not knowing for themselves when they are hungry or full, and unable to identify their own emotions. As a consequence of their confusion, they turn to external guides such as their parents, and appear to be 'model children'. However, they fail to develop genuine self-reliance and the experience of being in control of their behaviour, needs and impulses. They feel as if they do not own their own bodies. Adolescence increases their innate need to establish autonomy, but they feel unable to achieve this. To overcome their sense of helplessness, they seek excessive control over their body size and shape and eating habits. A number of studies have provided some support for Bruch's assertions. Steiner et al. (1991), for example, reported that many parents of young girls with anorexia tended to have fed them as a baby on their schedule rather than that of child. Fukunishi (1997) reported that many people with bulimia mistake emotions such as anxiety or upset as signs of hunger and respond to them by eating. Finally, Walters and Kendler (1995) reported that people with eating disorders tend to rely excessively on the opinions of others, and worry about how other people view them (see Box 13.1).

Box 13.1 Bulimia and anorexia

Here are two accounts of people with bulimia and anorexia. Despite both being concerned with eating-related disorders, the two discourses are completely different. The account of the person with bulimia centres on the drive to eat and the guilt and discomfort associated with it. That of the person with anorexia focuses on wider issues, in particular, issues of revenge and control. The pathways to each disorder differ across people, so although these may be considered 'typical' accounts in some ways, the accounts of other people with the same disorder may differ markedly.

Bulimia

I think it's easier not to drink or take drugs than to eat normally. You can either take them or not. If you don't want to – you just avoid them. But eating is so different. You have to eat . . . and once you – well, I – start, it's so difficult to stop. I want to be slim and look good. And I like my food. So I say to myself OK. Today you will not eat till 6 o'clock and you will eat a healthy meal. So I start the day with good intentions.

But then I live for food. I can avoid eating at lunchtime – it's almost easy with people around me. But as the day goes on, I want food!! I don't feel hungry. But what happens when

I get home, I just want to eat. It's on my mind, and I know there's food in the fridge – lovely ice cream . . . chocolate. God, I love chocolate! Why can't I like something healthy and low calorie?! I sit and watch the TV, but I'm thinking of food. I am now! Anyway, some nights I can get by, cook myself something reasonable – nights when I'm busy or interested in what's on TV or something. But other nights, I just go straight to the fridge and have a snack. Unfortunately, it's never a small one – what does that do to you? A couple of biscuits just doesn't work for me. So, I tend to snack on something big and calorific. Even that would be OK if I could stop there. But I tend to think, 'I've blown it now . . . I've begun to eat, so what's the point of stopping now?' Once I've blown away my good intentions, then I just give in to eating I suppose. So I eat and eat. I don't stop when I am full. I eat till I am bursting. I feel uncomfortable, and I know I'm bound to put on weight. I feel really guilty – another day when I haven't kept my good intentions. So, I make myself sick. I'm good at it. It's not difficult now. Then I feel better. At least I can relax and know that I won't put on weight. It feels such a relief. But I also know that I shouldn't have had to do it, so I feel guilty and vow that tomorrow I will control my eating and not need to do it. But, of course, tomorrow never comes . . .

Anorexia

My anorexia kicked in at age 13. I battled food issues for years before that. Mum was always on a diet – and I was often hooked into being her dieting partner, and sometimes competitor. Both our food struggles – I see now – only diverted our and the family's attention from the emotional turmoil permeating our household. I became the convenient whipping post of my parents' outbursts of anger, insecurities . . . I was hit a lot and verbally abused. At age 13, my parents cracked down and tried to totally control my life – friends, boyfriends – everything. That control pushed me over the edge . . . Dieting became an obsession for me. I dropped two stone in a month! The hunger was still there. Some days, all I thought about was food. But I was determined to conquer it. I strove for complete control – perhaps the only control I had. I felt repulsed if I ate – I had let myself down, lost control. I wanted to look good, to fit the ideal of womanhood. But a large part of the drive was revenge! I loved to see my parents' reactions to me starving. Dieting was no longer good, something to do with my mother . . . it was a weapon. Turning her own behaviour on her. They were partly angry because they could not control this part of me, and partly fear and worry. But I had control. They ranted, they shouted, and tried to get me to eat. But I wouldn't – not for them. I began to lose contact with my feelings. I wanted to starve to be in control, to prove I could do it, but also because I deserved to . . . because I hated myself.

Attachment theory suggests that some of these behaviours may be interpreted in terms of insecure attachment with a mother figure, leading to insecurity and anxiety at times of independence (Troisi et al. 2005). Ward et al. (2001) went further, and suggested that the mothers of adolescent girls with anorexia may transmit their anxious attachment patterns with their own mother to their daughters.

Interventions in anorexia

Given the multiple routes to anorexia, the optimal emphasis of treatment may vary considerably across individuals. Potential interventions include cognitive behavioural therapy, family therapy, insight-oriented psychotherapy, with each being complementary rather than competitive interventions. Interventions can be considered in two stages: first, initial treatment, usually in hospital, focusing on weight gain; and second, longer-term outpatient treatment focusing on sustained cognitive and behavioural change.

Promoting weight gain

In-patient care may be necessary where an individual's weight is seriously compromised: that is, less than 75 per cent of 'normal' for an individual's height and age. Interventions in hospital usually focus on providing extrinsic rewards for weight gain. This operant-based process involves gaining pre-specified rewards for pre-specified gains in weight, the most valued of which may be discharge from hospital on achieving a target weight. This avoids the danger of rewarding food intake, which may be subsequently vomited up and is therefore ineffective.

Some years ago, the nature of these rewards included access to a telephone or television. These are now considered to be basic rights, and removal of them would infringe such rights. Accordingly, the 'rewards' for eating are now typically defined by the individual and are more than the basic elements available to all in-patients. They may include increased social privileges, access to visitors, and exercise privileges. Calorific intake is gradually increased over time: too high an initial calorie intake may result in refusal to consume the calories. Nurses may also educate the individual about anorexia and provide more informal support and encouragement. Critical here is the reassurance that weight gains made at this time will not be translated into becoming overweight in the longer term. In a recent study of this approach, from a research group in Milan, Gentile et al. (2008) reported that of 99 individuals, 18 prematurely interrupted their treatment and 75 continued intensive inpatient treatment until they achieved their required weight. Thirty-two people with severe malnutrition were fed through a nasogastric tube until their weight increased and 'they started to cooperate with treatment'. The issue of whether people should in essence be 'force fed' is a very live issue in anorexia, and is particularly associated with the risk to health of continued non-eating as well as having other psychological co-morbidities (Carney et al. 2008).

Stop and think...

Before reading the next section, consider the implications of a failure to achieve any weight gain – or continued weight loss – during the first phase of treatment.

Most people with anorexia are intelligent and capable individuals. They choose to stop or minimize their eating. Do health professionals or others have the right to force them to eat, to prevent them engaging in what is their choice of behaviour? If someone is actively wishing not to have nutrition, should we force them to have food or put intravenous drips into their arm to improve their nutritional status? Or should we hope that they will eventually eat if their health becomes seriously compromised? It can be frightening to watch someone literally starving themself to death. But do we have the right to force them to eat or receive nutrition through drips in the knowledge that this will be distressing to the individual . . . and once it stops, the person is likely to continue to starve themself?

This debate has focused, in particular, on the competence or otherwise of people with anorexia to make what are truly life and death decisions. Some clinicians (e.g. Russon and Alison 1998) have argued that the majority of people with anorexia are mentally competent to make decisions about whether or not to eat. As a result, they suggest that it is inappropriate to treat them against their wishes, even if this leads to their death. Others (e.g. Treasure 2001), while accepting that force-feeding is inhumane and unacceptable, have pointed out that both it and other active treatments can be legally used with people with anorexia *in extremis*, as they are not mentally competent to make decisions that may result in their death.

Treasure (2001) identified four general principles that define whether an individual is competent under the law to make therapeutic choices or to refuse treatment.

They must be able to do the following:

- take in and retain information relevant to their decision and understand the likely consequences of having or not having the treatment
- believe the information
- weigh the information in the balance as part of the process of arriving at a decision
- recognize they have a health problem and take action to remedy their condition.

According to Treasure, individuals with anorexia do not conform to these criteria and are therefore deemed, under law, incompetent to make medical decisions that may endanger their life. Accordingly, doctors have the right to treat the individual without their consent. This argument is in accord with legal precedents (Dyer 1997) that have stated that compulsory treatment of people with anorexia, including force-feeding, is both legal and may be necessary on occasion.

Cognitive behavioural approaches

The second phase of treatment involves interventions aimed at achieving and maintaining long-term behavioural change. Perhaps the most widely used cognitive behavioural approach was developed by Garner and Bemis (1985). This was divided into a number of phases, the first of which was intended to establish a working alliance with the individual. Garner and Bemis stated that at this time, it is critical that the individual's core beliefs are not directly challenged, as this is likely to result in a withdrawal from therapy. Instead, the therapist needs to align with the individual, recognize how their weight-control strategies are intended to fulfil important functions for them, and appreciate that these strategies have been partly successful. This may be linked to questioning whether they have achieved everything the individual intended, and evaluating the emotional and physical costs of extreme dieting. The first few sessions may be spent developing a list of the advantages and costs of their anorexic behaviour. There may also be exploration of the deeper schemata underlying this behaviour. Homework assignments may be used to gather data on how events influence thoughts and feelings, and to provide opportunities to practise different ways of interpreting weight- and eating-related events. Only once a working alliance has been achieved and the individual is motivated to at least consider change, can cognitive therapy begin.

Cognitive interventions may have multiple targets, including modifying inappropriate cognitions and developing autonomy. Emphasis may be placed on challenging perceptual/attitudinal distortions. While these may never change to perceptions of being thin, an awareness of distortions and an acceptance that they have some degree of exaggeration may help change the individual's willingness to eat. Autonomy may be encouraged by challenging negative cognitions and encouraging the individual to trust their own intuitions and feelings. Cognitive challenges encourage the individual to consider the high emotional cost of their behaviour, and help them to explore some of the more entrenched schemata that underpin this behaviour, such as the belief that body weight or shape can serve as the sole criterion for self-worth and that complete control of one's body is necessary. Participants in therapy may also be taught problem-solving techniques to help them deal with any crises that might occur more effectively.

Studies of cognitive behavioural interventions have shown mixed efficacy, Treasure et al. (1995), for example, compared the effectiveness of a cognitive and combined cognitive/psycho-analytic therapy. By the end of the one-year intervention, both therapies proved equally effective, with 63 per cent of participants having achieved a 'good' or 'intermediate' recovery. Pike et al. (2003) found cognitive behavioural therapy to be more effective than nutritional counselling in reducing relapse rates in people recovering from anorexia. The combined percentage of people to drop out of therapy and/or relapse over a one-year period was 22 per cent of those in the cognitive therapy condition and 73 per cent in the nutritional counselling condition. By contrast, the finding of McIntosh et al. (2005) suggested that cognitive behavioural therapy may not always prove more effective than some alternatives. They compared the effectiveness of cognitive behavioural therapy, interpersonal therapy and non-specific supportive clinical management. The latter was thought to be the baseline against which these active therapies were measured. However, it proved the most effective approach, with 56 per cent of the people in this condition showing significant improvement, compared with 32 per cent in the cognitive behavioural intervention, and 10 per cent of those in the interpersonal therapy. The authors were surprised by these findings, and speculated that the cognitive behavioural therapy may have failed as the cognitive rigidity of the people with anorexia may have made it difficult to achieve cognitive, and hence behavioural, change. A further apparent failure of cognitive behavioural therapy (Gowers et al. 2007) is described in Research box 13. More positively, Carter et al. (2009) found a year-long cognitive behavioural intervention to be more effective than usual care in preventing relapse in participants who had already achieved a criterion weight. By the end of the year, 64 per cent of the comparison group had relapsed, while only 35 per cent of the intervention condition had.

Family therapy approaches

A number of different family therapies have been used to treat anorexia, although all seek to change the power structure within the family by empowering parents, preventing alliances that cross generations, and reducing tensions and problems between parents. Note that this approach contrasts markedly with the cognitive behavioural interventions described above which encourage autonomy and personal control over eating.

Structural family therapy   One of the first family approaches to treating anorexia was reported by Minuchin et al. (1978; see Chapter 5). They reported an 85 per cent success rate, although this has been viewed with some caution as it was based on a series of case reports with relatively young and 'intact' families rather than data from controlled trials. More recently, Russell et al.

(1987) followed a similar therapeutic approach which focused on the underlying stresses within the family. The approach had three tasks. The first involved engaging the family in the therapy process. They termed the second part the refeeding phase. In this, the family was observed eating together to identify relationships, communication of support, and rules about food and eating. At this time, the 'identified patient' and their siblings were encouraged to align, in order to reinforce appropriate boundaries within the family. The final stage involved changes in the family system, including return of control over eating to parents, working to support cooperation between parents, and stopping alignments or collusion between one or other parent and the person with the eating disorder.

Russell et al. (1987) compared the effectiveness of this approach with that of individual supportive therapy in the treatment of people with both anorexia and bulimia. Their findings were somewhat disappointing. Although many of the people with anorexia achieved significant weight gain, most participants achieved only modest gains on more general measures of outcome. At one-year follow-up, 23 per cent of the participants were rated as having a 'good' outcome, 16 per cent had a 'moderate' outcome and 61 per cent had a 'poor' outcome. Family therapy proved more effective than individual therapy on measures of weight, menstrual functioning and psychosocial adjustment for participants whose problems began before the age of 19 years and where the duration of problems was less than three years. Individual therapy proved marginally more effective than family therapy for older participants.

Behavioural family therapy   Behavioural family therapy (Robin et al. 1995) combines systemic and behavioural therapy approaches. The goals of therapy begin with restoration of weight. Strategies to achieve this include changing eating habits and cognitive therapy to minimize body image distortions, fear of fatness, and feelings of ineffectiveness. Family interaction patterns such as conflict avoidance, enmeshment and over-protectiveness are also targeted. Therapy follows three phases. First, control over eating is taken away from the individual and given to the parents, to restore the family hierarchy. Parents are taught and encouraged to implement a behavioural weight-gain programme for their child, including making meals, regulating exercise and establishing consequences for following or not following the plan. Once weight gain has been achieved, therapy moves to the second stage. This combines three elements:

- cognitive restructuring of distorted body image and unrealistic food beliefs
- working with the family to alter enmeshment, coalitions and inappropriate family hierarchies (see Chapter 5)
- gradually giving control over eating to the person with the eating disorder.

Finally, the family may be taught problem-solving and communication skills. Robin et al. (1995) evaluated the effectiveness of their approach, comparing it with supportive individual therapy, in a group of female adolescents aged between 12 and 19 years. At one-year follow-up, both forms of treatment had positive effects, although there were no between-group differences. Subsequently, Eisler et al. (2007) compared 'conjoint family therapy' with 'separated family therapy'. Both used the behavioural principles outlined above. However, in the conjoint therapy, the therapists worked with the whole family together, while in the separated family intervention they worked with adolescent girls and their parents separately. Both interventions proved effective over a one-year-long period of treatment, achieving significant gains on measures of symptomatology such as bulimic symptoms, as well as on nutritional status and mood. However, among families where there was significant maternal criticism towards the adolescent, the separated family intervention proved most effective. At five-year follow-up there remained little difference between the groups, with 75 per cent of their study population having no eating disorder at this time. These data are in accord with the findings of Perkins et al. (2005) who found that adolescent girls who did want not involve their parents in their treatment for bulimia considered their mothers to be more blaming and to hold a more negative attitude towards them than those who wanted them to be involved.

Psychoanalytic therapy

A number of case studies and uncontrolled studies have shown psychoanalytic approaches to the treatment of anorexia to be effective with adolescents with relatively minor problems. However, studies of the effectiveness of this approach compared with others are limited. Dare et al. (2001) provided one such comparison. Their psychoanalytic intervention was relatively time-limited, averaging 24 sessions over a one-year period. In it, the therapist took a non-directive stance, gave no advice about eating or other problems of symptom management. Instead, he or she addressed the conscious and unconscious meanings of the symptom (that is, not eating) in terms of the individual's history, the effects of the symptom and its influence on their current relationships, and the manifestations of these influences in their relationship with the therapist. Dare et al. compared the effectiveness of this approach with family therapy similar to that provided by Russell et al. (1987), an individually based intervention with elements of both analytic and cognitive approaches, and a low-contact support condition in which participants received no systematic therapeutic approach. Participants in the study had a relatively poor prognosis. They had a late age of onset, a long duration of problems, and had not improved with other therapies. Nevertheless, by the end of the year-long interventions, about one-third of the women in the active interventions no longer met the criteria for a diagnosis of anorexia. Only 5 per cent of those in the control group had shown such improvements. No one intervention proved more effective than the others.

Pharmacological interventions

Given the role of dopamine and serotonin in eating disorders, it should not be surprising that drugs involving these neurotransmitters have been used in the treatment of anorexia. Kaye et al. (2001b) reported an intervention in which women with anorexia were treated with either fluoxetine or placebo control. Of those on fluoxetine, 63 per cent achieved a 'good' response as a result of gains in 'appropriate weight maintenance', obsessionality, 'core eating disorder symptoms' and mood. Only 16 per cent of those in the placebo group achieved comparable gains. However, this positive finding may be rather optimistic, as Attia and Schroeder (2005) reviewed the evidence from all the controlled studies of the treatment of anorexia using antidepressants and neuroleptics then available, and found little evidence of benefit. However, treatment with SSRIs may prove effective in the treatment of depression that may coexist with anorexia, there is no evidence of consistent changes in 'core' anorexic symptoms (Ferguson et al. 1999). Interestingly, anti-psychotic medication may provide more, or at least comparable, benefits. Mondraty et al.

(2005) found that anorexic individuals treated with an atypical antipsychotic (see Chapter 3) reported fewer ruminations than those treated with a phenothiazine. In addition, Bissada et al. (2008) reported that treatment with the atypical anti-psychotic Olanzapine, which includes weight gain among its side-effects, resulted in greater weight gain than a placebo intervention over a 10-week treatment period.

Gowers, S.G., Clark, A., Roberts, C. et al. (2007) Clinical effectiveness of treatments for anorexia nervosa in adolescents, *British Journal of Psychiatry*, 191: 427–35.

Most treatment studies examine the effectiveness of any intervention on highly selected participants and use highly trained, frequently highly specialist, and carefully assessed clinicians. By contrast, this study evaluated the effectiveness of three treatment programmes provided on an unselected sample of young people with anorexia provided by 'normal' therapists working within the British National Health Service.

Method

Child and Adolescent Health services in one geographical area within the UK identified young people with probably anorexia and invited them to meet the researchers. Those who agreed were interviewed by a clinician (often in the presence of a parent), who confirmed their diagnosis and obtained their consent to be randomly allocated to one of three conditions:

In-patient treatment: 6 weeks, in which participants received individual supportive therapy plus either cognitive or family therapy. In addition, participants were expected to gain up to a kilogram of weight per week, using a behavioural system similar to that described in the chapter.

Specialized out-patient treatment: a motivational interview followed by 12 sessions of individual cognitive behavioural therapy plus parental feedback, parental counselling (4–8 sessions), dietary therapy (4 sessions), and regular feedback on weight, mood, and so on. The treatment programme followed a standard manual.

Treatment as usual: involved a multidisciplinary family therapy-based approach, with varying dietetic and medical support. This was not structured or prescribed by the research team.

Measures included:

- an interview to assess the clinical diagnosis based on DSM-IV
- *Morgan-Russell Average Outcome Scale* (MRAOS): completed by a clinician, measuring nutritional status, mental state, sexual adjustment and menstruation. This was then graded as good, intermediate and poor (see results)
- *Eating Disorder Inventory* (EDI): measuring 12 domains of eating cognitions, behaviours and social functioning

● *Mood and Feelings Questionnaire (MFQ)*: rated depression

Results

A total of 167 young people diagnosed with anorexia were randomized to one of the three study arms. Their mean age was 14 years and 11 months, 92 per cent were female, and their mean duration of problems was 13 months.

Adherence to treatment varied between groups: 49 per cent for in-patient treatment, 75 for specialist treatment, and 69 per cent for the usual care group. However, the research team were able to track between 92–8 per cent of all participants at one-year and 73–96 per cent at two-year follow-up, depending on the measure in question.

One-year outcome: using an intention to treat analysis, they found no differences between the groups on any measure. However, those who completed the out-patient interventions fared significantly better than those who dropped out. Twenty-one per cent were deemed to have achieved a 'good' outcome on the MRAOS (full remission, weight above 85 per cent of age norm, return of menstruation, bingeing/purging one or fewer times a month), 18 per cent achieved an intermediate outcome (weight within normal range, no return of menstruation, residual concerns about weight and shape, bingeing/purging more than once a month), and 46 per cent had a poor outcome (still being treated as in-patient or weight below 85 per cent of age norm). Unfortunately, many participants did not adhere to the assigned treatment programme, and even switched between out- and in-patient care. So, these intention to treat analyses were somewhat contaminated by drop-out and change of condition. However, the outcomes of those fully adherent with each intervention are described in Table 13.2.

Table 13.2 Percentage of fully adherent participants to achieve differing levels of recovery at one- and two-year follow-up (note: no statistical analysis of this data was reported)

		Year 1			Year 2		
	n	Good	Intermediate	Poor	Good	Intermediate	Poor
General out-patient	38/55	21	57	21	39	32	26
Specialist out-patient	41/55	19	37	44	27	53	17
In-patient	28/57	10	32	53	21	32	39

Two-year outcome: overall, 33 per cent were considered to have achieved a 'good' outcome, 30 per cent an intermediate outcome, and 30 per cent a poor outcome. However, there were no differences between the groups on any of their outcome measures. Other scores are reported in Table 13.3.

Table 13.3 Mean scores on key outcome measures taken at baseline, and one- and two- year follow-up

	Specialized out-patient	General out-patient	In-patient
Body Mass Index			
Baseline	15.3	15.5	15.3
1 year	17.9	18.3	17.5
2 year	18.7	19.4	18.7
EDI total			
Baseline	86.5	88.5	89.6
1 year	57.6	69.4	60.6
2 year	52.5	61.0	40.3
MFQ			
Baseline	14.7	16.1	32.6
1 year	16.7	17.7	18.2
2 year	15.1	20.2	15.8

Discussion

This study found that over the period of two years, many participants achieved significant change, although a larger proportion gained no benefit from any kind of treatment. Overall, the three treatments fared equally well when analysed using the intention to treat approach. These findings did not support their hypothesis that the specialist treatment would achieve greater benefit than the general treatment.

The study shows that in the general hurly burly of the provision of a psychiatric service, no one approach appeared to be more effective than any other. What it does not show is why this could be the case. The specialist out-patient programme comprised CBT, while the non-generalist approach favoured family therapy – so do the results mean the two approaches are of equal benefit? This may be the case, but given the lack of control over this intervention, it is not clear what treatment the participants actually received. Nevertheless, this lack of specificity in the effectiveness of particular therapies also resonates with the findings of McIntosh et al. (2005) who found supportive clinical management to be as effective, if not more effective, than formal psychological therapies.

Interventions in bulimia

Cognitive behavioural therapy

In contrast to interventions in anorexia, those in bulimia are more structured, and have a better prognosis (Anderson and Maloney 2001). One of the pioneers of cognitive behavioural interventions in bulimia developed a three-stage approach (Fairburn 1998). The initial stage has two aims: first, to provide a rationale for the treatment, and second, to replace binge eating with a pattern of more regular eating. Eating is restricted to three planned meals a day, plus two or three planned snacks, none of which is followed by vomiting or other compensatory behaviours. This is not usually accompanied by weight gain. Indeed, reductions in the frequency of binge eating often result in weight loss. Distracting activities, such as having a bath or contacting friends, can be used to minimize the risk of bingeing. Once regular meals are established, the desire to vomit may reduce naturally. However, where this remains problematic, continued use of these inhibitory behaviours for an hour or so after eating may be necessary. Laxative and diuretic use should also be stopped at this time, with a phased withdrawal programme established for those who are unable to do so immediately. Knowledge that these strategies do not prevent food absorption aids this process. Towards the end of this phase, therapy sessions may involve both the client and key friends or relatives, with the intention of establishing an environment that will support behavioural change.

The second stage involves the using of both behavioural and cognitive procedures to counter concerns about shape and weight, and other cognitive distortions. Behavioural interventions may involve eating previously avoided types of food and, where necessary, increasing energy intake. This may be achieved by working up a hierarchy from relatively acceptable foods to those that initially invoke high levels of anxiety or desires to binge or purge. At the same time, clients are encouraged to identify negative assumptions about their shape and weight, and to find evidence in support or against them using cognitive challenge techniques. Fairburn (2008) noted that many clients have a limited repertoire of such thoughts, triggered by a range of different circumstances. By repeatedly examining these thoughts and the circumstances that trigger them, their potency and automacity gradually decline. Further behavioural hypothesis testing may involve a gradual introduction of previously avoided and feared behaviours, including exposing body shape through wearing tight clothing, undressing at swimming baths, or even no longer undressing in the dark. The third stage involves maintenance of progress achieved in the first two stages and consideration of strategies to prevent relapse once therapy is terminated.

This, or similar approaches, is usually considered the treatment of choice for bulimia, although relatively few trials have been conducted (Wilson et al. 2007). Wilson (1996), for example, reported that an average of 55 per cent of participants in cognitive behavioural therapy programmes no longer purged at the end of therapy, and those who continued to purge did so much less: an average of an 86 per cent reduction in purging. Long-term follow-up data are also encouraging. Fairburn et al. (1995) reported that 63 per cent of their sample had not relapsed at an average of nearly six-year follow-up. Comparisons of behavioural therapy and cognitive behavioural therapy suggest that both are equally effective in reducing binge-purging immediately following treatment. However, cognitive behavioural therapy is superior in reducing the 'core psychopathology' of distorted weight and shape and in maintaining long-term changes

(Fairburn 1997). Disappointingly, this form of intervention did not prove effective when translated into a guided self-help programme conducted in primary care using family doctors as 'therapists' (Walsh et al. 2004). Le Grange et al. (2007) reported outcomes of a family therapy intervention involving 20 sessions in which parents are first empowered to disrupt binge eating and control behaviours (including restrained eating, purging), to 'externalise and separate the disordered behaviours from the affected adolescent in order to promote parental action and decrease adolescent resistance to their assistance' (p. 1051), and then hand back control over these behaviours to the adolescent. By the end of treatment, 39 per cent of participants were no longer binge-purging, compared to 18 per cent in the comparison group who received supportive psychotherapy. Schmidt et al. (2007) reported a direct comparison of a cognitive behavioural and family therapy intervention, finding that although the cognitive behavioural intervention proved superior at 6-month follow-up, there were no between group differences at one-year follow-up.

Interpersonal psychotherapy

One other psychological approach appears to be particularly effective in the treatment of bulimia. Interpersonal psychotherapy (IPT) focuses exclusively on strategies for improving interpersonal relationships to the exclusion of any other therapeutic issues. Fairburn et al. (1993) found it to be less effective than cognitive therapy in the short term. However, by one-year follow-up, the differences between the two conditions were not significant, as a result of continuing improvements among those who received IPT. Remission rates at this time were 46 per cent for IPT and 39 per cent for cognitive behavioural therapy. The authors speculated that these gains in the IPT condition resulted from an improvement in self-worth and relationships, which made weight and shape much less important to the individual. As the effects of IPT are more indirect than cognitive methods, they took longer to become apparent. A second comparison of the two approaches was reported by Agras et al. (2000). They found a similar outcome. Cogntive therapy proved more effective than IPT at the end of a 20-week intervention, with 29 per cent versus 6 per cent fully recovered. However, by one-year follow-up, although the cognitive therapy still appeared more successful, the differences between the groups were no longer significant (40 versus 27 per cent).

Case formulation

Ms F was a 23-year-old single woman. Her weight appeared normal (and according to her Body Mass Index was within the upper range of average for her height and age). She worked as a secretary for a local firm and lived with her parents. At school, she felt some awareness of and negativity towards her own physique – she considered herself to weigh a little heavier than ideal, but was not unduly worried by her appearance. However, she became more concerned over this when she and her long-term boyfriend split up, and he told her that he thought she was fat and this made her unattractive. She had had few previous boyfriends and found it difficult to develop such relationships as a consequence of shyness and low self-esteem. As a result, she had no history of more complimentary comments from boyfriends, and losing weight to become more attractive became a major goal in her life. She began to link having a boyfriend with losing weight, and withdrew from situations where she could potentially meet another boyfriend until she looked more attractive.

She initially tried to diet, but found it difficult to do this consistently and did not lose weight. So, she began to experiment with other ways of losing weight. She tried the use of laxatives, and found that she initially lost weight following their use, but then regained the weight over the next few days. She felt that she needed to take more extreme action and visited a website where she learned how to vomit effectively. She did not change her eating pattern (and may even have increased her food consumption), and still took meals with the family, even going out with them to a restaurant and eating a full meal with pudding. However, over the next month she began to visibly lose weight. This pleased her, but worried her family who considered her to be at an appropriate weight already, and were puzzled by her weight loss despite apparently eating normally. They also noted her absences from the room and trips to the toilet immediately following meals. After some detective work, her family recognized the reason for her weight loss, and confronted her about it. As a result of this, she agreed to stop the purging. However, she found this difficult to do, and continued to eat and purge albeit at a lower frequency than before. Further confrontations with her family led her to seek help from specialist clinic.

Formulation

The formulation here is quite simple. She was engaging in purging behaviours in a drive to reduce her weight, make her (in her view) more attractive to men, and to bolster her self-esteem which was increasingly dependent on her losing weight. Any intervention needed to reduce her bulimic behaviour, shift her self-esteem from being weight-dependent, and to increase her self-esteem and confidence in general.

Intervention

Following the Fairburn model, the first stage of the intervention involved planning a regular eating programme – eating three meals a day, but avoiding large meals or bingeing. The aim was to eat the required number of calories to maintain her weight, and no more. The planned meals and calorie intake provided some reassurance to Ms F that she would not put on weight even if she did not purge. To help her cope with the anxieties that would inevitably follow eating without purging, she planned things to do following each meal, to distract away from bingeing. She wanted her family to be involved in helping her, so at home this involved such things as going for walks or playing card games with her parents in the half to one hour following meals. This approach proved successful, and she quickly reduced the degree to which she was eating and purging.

The second phase of the intervention involved modifying her dysfunctional beliefs about her body shape. This involved cognitive work, including discussion of societal understandings of attractiveness, questioning the validity of the previous boyfriend's statement about her weight and the reliance on thinness as a requirement within a relationship. At a wider level, she also explored her expectations of relationships and through this exploration to be less absolutist about them: to be willing to enter relationships with no expectation of longevity or success and to enjoy the relationship for what it was 'in the moment' and not to feel she had to compromise herself in doing so. On a behavioural level, she explored meeting new partners through going out dancing with friends and joining a dating agency. This led to her meeting a number of men, all of whom found her attractive, reinforcing her improved self-confidence and lack of dependence on weight control as a means of facilitating relationships.

Pharmacological interventions

Overall, antidepressant medications for bulimia decrease binge frequency by an average of 56 per cent, compared with an average decrease of 11 per cent following treatment with placebo (Jimerson et al. 1992). However, many people treated with antidepressants drop out of treatment due to drug side-effects. In addition, a significant relapse rate of between 30 and 45 per cent is typical in patients between four and six months following cessation of medication. Bacaltchuk and Hay (2003) summarized the data then available (19 trials of various antidepressants) and found that people prescribed such medication were up to 75 per cent more likely to experience a significant reduction in symptoms than those in placebo conditions. Many people, however, dropped out of therapy due to unacceptable side-effects. Three of five studies that have compared cognitive behavioural and pharmacological interventions found no differences in their effectiveness (Bacaltchuk et al. 1999). Two found cognitive behavioural interventions to be superior. Overall, long-term remission rates were 20 per cent for antidepressants and 39 per cent for cognitive approaches. In addition, drop-out rates were higher among those receiving antidepressants than among those receiving cognitive therapy: 40 versus 18 per cent. In one of the studies reported in this analysis, Agras et al. (1994) randomly allocated women with bulimia into a number of conditions, including a short-term course of antidepressants, cognitive behavioural therapy or a combined treatment. At four-month follow-up, both cognitive behavioural therapy and the combined treatment were superior to medication alone on measures of binge eating and purging. These advantages were maintained up to one-year follow-up. At this time, 18 per cent of those receiving antidepressant treatment were free of binge eating and purging, in comparison with 78 per cent of those receiving the combined treatment. The one exception to these findings of the superiority of psychological therapy was reported by Walsh et al. (2004) in their study of the treatment of bulimia using guided self-help in primary care. In this context, treatment with an SSRI (fluoxetine) proved more effective than psychological therapy. Fluoxetine may also prove a useful intervention among people who do not respond to cognitive behavioural interventions (Walsh et al. 2000).

13.3 Chapter summary

1   Anorexia is defined by the desire to achieve a body weight significantly below normal. This can be achieved in two ways: self-imposed starvation, or bingeing and purging.

2   Anorexia has a relatively poor prognosis, with long-term mortality rates of up to 16 per cent and complete 'recovery' in just over half the cases.

3   Bulimia has a better prognosis, with most people achieving something like normal eating patterns.

4   Cognitive models suggest that both conditions are driven by cognitions which prioritize control over eating and weight control. The behaviour of people with each condition varies as a result of their abilities to control their responses to hunger. People who engage in type 1 anorexic behaviour are able to control their hunger; those who are bulimic occasionally give in to urges to eat and compensate by purging.

5   Psychoanalytic models of anorexia suggest that it forms a rejection of sexual instincts and risk of pregnancy.

6   Bruch contested that anorexia arose out of chaotic parent–child interactions that leave the child confused about their own emotional and physical needs. They turn to their parents to provide feedback on their own feelings. At the time of adolescence, they seek but fail to achieve autonomy from their parents. As a response, they seek excessive control over their size and shape.

7   Socio-cultural models emphasize the role of social pressures in shaping young women's striving for thinness and the perfect body.

8   Family models suggest anorexia results from aberrant family dynamics. Minuchin, for example, suggested that the person with anorexia serves to maintain family cohesion as the family focuses on them and their needs, and ignores the dysfunctional relationship between their parents.

9   There appears to be a genetic risk for anorexia, possibly mediated through disorders of serotonin metabolism.

10 Interventions in anorexia usually involve two stages: first, weight gain to safe levels, and second, longer-term interventions involving cognitive behavioural therapy, family therapy, psychotherapy or drug therapy. The best intervention for each individual may depend on the specific factors that led to their problems, with each of the psychological approaches being of benefit to some. The long-term prognosis, however, is not good.

11 Cognitive behavioural interventions are acknowledged as the treatment of choice in bulimia, with most people making significant long-term gains. However, in some contexts, pharmacological therapy using SSRIs may be advantageous.

13.4 For discussion

1 Should we actively treat people with anorexia who are close to dying as a result of their restrained eating, or should we respect their desire not to eat whatever the consequences?

2 Anorexia is perhaps one of the most difficult psychological conditions to treat. Given the success of cognitive behavioural techniques in other conditions, why should this not be the case in anorexia?

3 Bulimic behaviour could be considered a highly functional way of controlling weight. If this is the case, should it be treated only where the affected individual is distressed by their way of controlling their weight?

13.5 Further reading

Carney, T., Crim, D., Wakefield, A. et al. (2006) Reflections on coercion in the treatment of severe anorexia nervosa, *Israeli Journal of Psychiatry and Related Sciences*, 43: 269–65. (Available free via pubmed).

Fairburn, C. (2008) *Cognitive Behavior Therapy and Eating Disorders.* New York: Guilford Press.

Fisher, C.A., Hetrick, S.E., and Rushford, N. (2010) Family therapy for anorexia nervosa, *Cochrane Database of Systematic Reviews*, 4: CD004780.

Grange, D. and Lock, J. (2005) The dearth of psychological treatment studies for anorexia nervosa, *International Journal of Eating Disorders*, 37: 79–91.

Slade, P. and Brodie, D. (1994) Body-image distortion and eating disorder: a reconceptualization based on the recent literature, *European Eating Disorders Review*, 2: 32–46.

The following websites also have information about anorexia and bulimia, their treatment, and people's experiences of them. The anorexia web addresses include a link to the controversial pro anorexia site.

www.thesite.org/healthandwellbeing/mentalhealth/eatingdisorders/compulsiveeating
www.anorexiabulimiacare.co.uk/
www.bulimiaguide.org/
hubpages.com/hub/Pro-Anorexia
anaregzig.blogspot.com/
www.anad.org/

14

Developmental disorders

Chapter contents

This chapter looks at three disorders within the diagnostic category of pervasive developmental difficulties. It describes three conditions in which difficulties in childhood are predictive of subsequent adult problems. It considers the problems associated with a variety of disorders grouped under the broad category of learning difficulties. It then discusses the aetiology and treatment of more specific conditions: autism and attention-deficit/hyperactivity disorder (ADHD). By the end of the chapter, you should have an understanding of:

● Definitions and some of the causes of learning difficulties

● Aspects of the social and psychological care of people with learning difficulties

● The biological and psychological bases of autism

● The MMR vaccination and autism controversy

● Treatment of autism and autistic behaviours

● Factors that contribute to ADHD

● Biological and psychological treatments of ADHD.

14.1 Learning difficulties

Learning difficulties is a broad term that encompasses a variety of conditions whose defining characteristic is a significant impairment of intellectual functioning. The terms used to describe people with this condition differ across the world and in time. In the UK, they have in the past been referred to as 'handicapped', 'subnormal' or 'retarded'. Now, all people with intellectual deficits, however profound, are referred to as having learning difficulties. The reasons for these changing terms are not trivial: they reflect attempts to minimize prejudice towards this group of people. In the USA, people with mild learning difficulties are referred to as having learning difficulties, those with more profound deficits are still referred to as having mental retardation.

The first criterion for a diagnosis of having a learning disability is that its onset is before the age of 18 years, to exclude the affects of trauma or other neurological illness later in life. In addition, the individual needs to score significantly below the norm on intelligence tests. The usual cut-off score for this diagnosis is between 70 and 75 on the standard IQ test: two standard deviations below the population mean of 100. About 3 per cent of the population fall into this category. Within this category are a number of subcategories.

- IQ 50/55–70 *Mild learning difficulties*: includes about 85 per cent of people with learning difficulties. As children, they may be superficially indistinguishable from children with normal IQs, although their school performance shows they have clear learning difficulties. As adults, they are likely to be able to hold down unskilled jobs, although they may need help with social and financial issues.

- IQ 35/40–50/55 *Moderate learning difficulties*: includes about 10 per cent of people with learning difficulties. Within this group of people, learning difficulties are often combined with other neurological deficits, including problems with motor skills such as walking, holding implements, and so on. People in this group usually live independently within families or in group homes. Many have obvious brain damage and other pathologies.

- IQ 20/25–35/40 *Severe learning difficulties*: usually associated with genetically mediated physical abnormalities and limited sensorimotor control. Most people with severe learning difficulties live in institutions and require constant aid and supervision. As adults, they are typically lethargic and lack motivation. They may, nevertheless, communicate at a simple and concrete level.

- IQ < 20/25 *Profound learning difficulties*: profound mental and physical problems mean that people with this degree of difficulty require total supervision and nursing care all their lives. They cannot communicate using language and cannot get around on their own.

Severe learning difficulties are more common among males than females. Mild learning difficulties are most common among males and those from economically deprived or adverse family backgrounds (Roeleveld et al. 1997). As the medical care of people with learning difficulties improves, the prevalence of older people with learning difficulties within society is increasing, at the same time as there are reductions in childhood prevalence resulting from increased prenatal screening and better child health care.

Aetiology of learning difficulties

Only about 25 per cent of cases of learning difficulty have an identified cause. These include:

- *genetic conditions*: including Down syndrome and Fragile X syndrome
- *infectious diseases*: including rubella, parental syphilis and encephalitis
- *environmental hazards*: including lead paint and exhaust fumes in leaded petrol
- *antenatal events*: including parental infections (including rubella) and endocrine disorders such as hypothyroidism
- *perinatal trauma*: including asphyxia during birth.

For many people, there is no known biological cause. This is unsurprising, as IQ, like all other natural phenomena, follows a normal distribution within the population, with the exception of the so-called 'hump' within the lower end of the distribution that occurs as a consequence of biological causes (see Figure 14.1). This does not mean that poor performance on IQ tests is totally biologically determined. Environmental factors, including quality of parental care, education and the social environment, can markedly influence IQ scores, academic performance and the development of adaptive skills, particularly for people with mild–moderate learning difficulties. Birch et al. (1970), for example, identified all children born with learning difficulties in Aberdeen between the years 1951 and 1955. Some 20 years later, they collected information from health and social services, and conducted interviews with the parents and the individuals themselves. Mild learning difficulties were significantly more prevalent in families from the lower socio-economic groups and families classed as unstable, defined by high levels of multiple carers, abuse and child neglect. No such relationship was found for more severe learning difficulties, which may be more biologically determined.

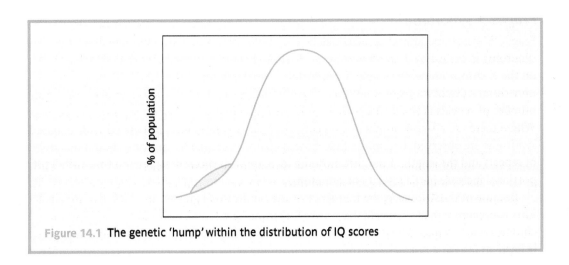

Figure 14.1 **The genetic 'hump' within the distribution of IQ scores**

Down syndrome

People affected by Down syndrome are short and stocky in stature, and have typical facial characteristics, including upward-slanting eyes, sparse, fine straight hair and a large furrowed tongue which protrudes as the result of a small mouth. They may also have a number of other less obvious characteristics, including serious heart malformations. All people with this condition have some degree of learning difficulty. Autopsy reveals brain tissue very similar to that found in Alzheimer's disease.

Down syndrome is found in about 1 of 500–600 live births and has been detected in about 3 per cent of foetuses that spontaneously abort before 20 weeks' gestation. It occurs sporadically. People with the disorder are generally the children of parents without it, precluding an obvious genetic linkage. Because the risk of having a child with Down syndrome increases with the age of the mother, rising significantly in women giving birth over the age of 32 years, it was originally thought to be the result of an 'unfavourable' interaction between mother and foetus during pregnancy. However, it is now known to result from a chromosomal abnormality. People with Down syndrome have three, instead of two, chromosomes-21, leading to the more technical name of the disorder, trisomy-21.

This is the result of a process that occurs during the first few cell divisions that occur prior to fertilization. In trisomy-21, as the female egg cells duplicate, they fail to do so properly and some sex cells receive two chromosomes-21; some receive none. If these eggs are fertilized by a normal sperm, the resultant cells contain either three or one chromosome-21. The latter is not a viable combination and the developing cells are aborted. However, in the case of trisomy-21, the embryo and then the foetus remain viable and survive. The age-related risk is thought to be the result of some kind of metabolic or physical damage accumulated by the egg cells while lying in the ovaries for decades before ovulating. Although Down syndrome is considered to be untreatable, some aspects of the syndrome may respond to medical treatment. Van Trotsenburg et al. (2005), for example, found that treatment with thyroxine from immediately following birth may reduce the level of both motor and mental developmental delay during early childhood.

Fragile X syndrome

Fragile X syndrome affects approximately 1 in 1000 male and 1 in 2500 female births. This syndrome is caused by a defect within the FMR-1 (Fragile X mental retardation) gene located on the X chromosome. In Fragile X syndrome, a small region of the gene undergoes repeated, unnecessary duplications of a number of amino acids that result in a longer gene. When the number of repeats is small (fewer than 200) the individual often has no signs of the disorder. Where there are a larger number of repeats, the learning difficulties associated with Fragile X syndrome are observed. In families that show evidence of Fragile X syndrome, both the number of repeats and the length of the chromosome increase with succeeding generations, with a proportional increase in the severity of symptoms.

Because of the X-linkage, the frequency of the syndrome is greater in males than in females. This is because females typically have two X chromosomes, and males have one X and one Y chromosome. A female who inherits a chromosome carrying the Fragile X gene from either parent is likely to inherit a normal X chromosome from the other parent. This masks the presence of the Fragile X gene in a female. However, she may carry the gene and be capable of passing it on to her children. By contrast, because a male has only one X chromosome, if he inherits an affected X chromosome, he will inevitably inherit the condition. This simple genetic model does not always hold, however: about 20 per cent of males who carry mutated forms of FMR-1 are either unaffected or only mildly affected. In addition, a single copy of the Fragile X gene can be sufficient to cause the syndrome in some females. Why this happens is not understood.

Social interventions in learning difficulties

The lives of people with learning difficulties have been affected by socio-political factors as well as psychological and social interventions. One ideological movement, known as *normalization* (Wolfensberger 1972), has been particularly influential. This began in the 1960s in response to the poor institutional conditions in which many people with learning difficulties then lived. The movement called for people with learning difficulties to live a life as close to normal living conditions as possible, to have normal rhythms to their lives, and the means to establish and maintain behaviour as close to their cultural norms as possible. Under the rubric of *social role valorization* (Wolfensberger 1983), the movement subsequently called for the creation, support and defence of valued social roles for people with learning difficulties. These have led to five key aims of any service provided for people with learning difficulties:

- *Community presence*: people with learning difficulties live in the community, in normal houses, not institutions. To avoid 'pockets' of disability, housing is distributed through the community.
- *Choice*: people have the choices of accommodation, care and day-to-day routine, available to the 'normal' population.
- *Competence*: the competences of people with learning difficulties are acknowledged and maximized.
- *Respect*: people with learning difficulties are afforded the respect due to all other people within the population.
- *Participation*: people with learning difficulties have equal rights of participation in society, including access to work, leisure facilities, political activities and sexual relationships, as the rest of the population.

In the spirit of this integrated approach, children with learning difficulties are increasingly being taught in mainstream classes, and most adults with learning difficulties live in the community following the closure of large institutions. However, these changes fall short of the goals of normalization, and there is still work to do. Nearly two-thirds of British adults with learning difficulties, for example, continue to live with their family of birth – a significantly higher proportion than among the 'normal' population.

Schooling

Government policy within most Western countries is that all children should be educated in ordinary schools, although in the UK at least, education authorities are left with substantial discretion, and many 'special schools' still operate. However, the number of children taught in them is gradually reducing: only 1 per cent of all British 5–15-year-olds were enrolled in special schools in 1998 (Emerson et al. 2001). This political and social policy is supported by the empirical evidence: educating children with learning difficulties in mainstream schools with additional support seems to be at least as effective as placing them in segregated 'special' schools. Buckley et al. (2007), for example, found gains in communication skills (including expressive language and literacy skills) among children with Down syndrome schooled in mainstream classrooms not found in those taught in specialist units.

Preparing for adulthood

The transition from school to adult life requires planning, as many people require some sort of social support in adulthood. Children leaving school are assessed and a care plan is drawn up, setting out how services will meet their continuing needs. Individual circumstances differ, but this process includes consideration of the following:

- future daytime activities: including possible further education, supported employment and attendance at day services
- living arrangements: choices may include remaining in the family home or moving to more independent living
- leisure opportunities
- physical health care needs.

Occupation and employment

Support in adulthood is usually provided through some form of day care or employment. In the UK, this has involved attendance at adult training centres. In them, the individual takes part in a number of 'productive' activities, including simple contract work for which they receive a token 'wage', simple skills training, sports and arts and craft activities. These centres also provide day care for people with severe or complex disabilities.

More recently, significant effort has been given to placing people with learning difficulties into real working environments. One of the best models of this approach, known as the *supported employment model*, originated in the USA. It assumes that almost anyone can be employed if given sufficient support. It is colloquially known as a 'place, train and maintain' model, because the process involves identifying a job suitable to the individual, training them to do the job effectively, and then supporting them in the job, with decreasing levels of support as appropriate. This can be effective in increasing integration into the workplace, particularly where co-workers are prepared and receive appropriate training, although it can also be very challenging for those involved (Wistow and Schneider 2003).

Living away from institutions

Most adults with learning disabilities continue to live in their family of origin. Others may live independently in rented accommodation. A number of other options are available, each providing differing levels of support, including the following:

- *Registered care homes*: have up to 20 residents, though between 3 and 6 is more typical; 24-hours-a-day support is provided. All personal care and meals are provided.
- *Shared housing*: usually for groups of three or four people; levels of support vary from staff visiting once or twice a week to 24-hours-a-day support. Residents may do their own shopping, cooking, budgeting and housework, with some support from staff.
- *Cluster of flats or bedsitters*: self-contained units, usually on a single site but occasionally dispersed across a neighbourhood. Support staff are available, but residents are more independent than in other settings.

Psychological interventions in learning difficulties

Psychological interventions for people with learning difficulties usually have one of two goals: either to teach people the skills necessary to maximize their abilities or to reduce inappropriate behaviours. Both approaches are frequently based on the principles of operant conditioning, in which behaviour is shaped by a series of rewards and, less frequently, punishments. The remaining part of this section focuses on three interventions relevant to people with learning difficulties, starting with a programme aimed at preschool children. More programmes, developed for people with a combination of autism and learning difficulties, are described in the next section of the chapter.

Teaching skills

Most children with learning disabilities live in their family home. Preschool programmes provide opportunities for teaching age-dependent skills necessary for when the child starts to attend school. One of the most widely used systems through which this is provided is known as Portage.

First established in the town of Portage, USA, this home-visiting service is now used in countries as far apart as India, Japan, as well as the USA, and is widely accessible in the UK (Russell 2007). The teaching process first involves assessment of the child's abilities. Therapists and parents then work together to develop a training programme addressing six domains: infant stimulation, social development, communication speech and language, self-help, cognitive development and motor development. Once the programme is designed, the parent works with the child on a planned programme of skills training, with weekly visits by health professionals providing support and assessment of progress. Parental interventions are facilitated by the provision of cards describing in detail how to teach 580 behaviours. Each card has a behavioural description of a skill (such as 'Mary will place 6 pieces in puzzle with verbal prompt'), suggested teaching materials and the type of reinforcement to be used in its development. Despite its widespread use, there are relatively few formal evaluations of the approach. However, what evidence there is suggests it works. A Vietnamese study by Shin et al. (2009), for example, reported gains on measures of adaptive behaviours, personal care and motor skills relative to a group of children not receiving the intervention, although they did not show any relative improvement on measures of communication and social skills.

Psychological methods can also be used to facilitate skills acquisition in adults. One frequently used approach involves the use of self-instruction training (Meichenbaum 1985:

see Chapter 2) to either facilitate skills acquisition or lower anxiety levels associated with behaviours requiring sequencing or social skills. In these, the client is first talked through appropriate behaviours by the therapist using very specific and clear instructions, and then uses their own internal dialogue to do the same. This approach has been shown to be effective, even in treating an individual engaging in inappropriate sexual activity ('Think about prison. Walk away.') (Willner 2005). However, outcomes are limited. Corrigan (1991), for example, reported outcomes of studies of the effects of this type of training to improve the social skills of people with learning difficulties, psychosis and offenders. People with learning difficulties gained significantly from the intervention. They performed best on measures of skill during role play and maintenance of skills over time. They were, however, less successful in transferring these skills to situations beyond the training setting.

Coping with challenging behaviour

Between 10 and 15 per cent of people with learning difficulties engage in challenging behaviours, that is, behaviours that transgress social rules, and usually involve aggression either towards themselves or others, destructive behaviours, or place the individual or others at risk of harm (e.g. Lowe et al. 2007). These may persist over long periods of time, and are now considered to be operantly conditioned behaviours, through which people with restricted abilities try to achieve some degree of control over their environment and the people around them: for example, by attracting attention or getting someone to stop an unwanted action. Because each of the challenging behaviours differs in its causes, nature and the type of intervention required, the effects of any intervention are not easily measured using the randomized controlled trials used to study interventions in many other conditions. Indeed, Hassiotis and Hall (2008) found only four studies with more than four participants to include in their review of the area, and insufficient data to allow a meta-analysis. Nevertheless, a number of broad principles for reducing the frequency and severity of challenging behaviour have been developed. Emerson (1998), for example, identified the following three key intervention approaches, none of which involves punishing the individual.

Enrich the environment Reinforcement theory suggests that the rate of behaviours maintained by positive reinforcement should reduce as the background level of reinforcement increases. Enriching environments by increasing social interaction or providing more things to engage and interest the individual should therefore reduce challenging behaviours. In one study of this approach, Golding et al. (2005) found an improvement in the challenging behaviours shown by a group of six men with mild to moderate learning difficulties when moved from an institution to a more enriched environment in a specialized community-based home. Following relocation, they found a significant increase in participants' domestic activity skills, a decrease in the occurrence of problem behaviours and an increase in engagement and staff contact.

Reduce exposure to the triggers to challenging behaviour One simple way in which challenging behaviour can be prevented is to minimize or obviate its triggers. Touchette et al. (1985), for example, identified that one woman's outbursts were associated with her attendance at pre-vocational and community living classes. Rescheduling them resulted in an almost total cessation in the frequency of aggressive behaviour.

Teach or support alternative behaviours   Most challenging behaviour is considered to be functional, that is, it occurs in order to achieve a particular outcome. A key intervention, therefore, involves teaching people how to gain their desired outcome without engaging in challenging behaviour. To be effective, the new behaviour has to achieve exactly the same outcome as the original behaviour and be a more 'efficient' way of achieving this goal. An example of this approach was reported by Steege et al. (1990), who taught two young children with severe multiple disabilities to press a micro-switch to activate a tape-recording of a request for a break from self-care activities, a process that led to marked reductions in self-injurious behaviour previously used to stop such activities.

Treating emotional problems

Psychological interventions to help people with learning difficulties are perhaps less frequently used than those addressing behavioural problems. Nevertheless, Nagel and Leiper (1999) found that 35 per cent of their sample of clinical psychologists in the UK reported using CBT 'frequently' or 'very frequently'. Slightly less (31 per cent) used humanistic approaches, while 17 per cent reported using psychodynamic approaches with equal frequency. There are no randomized controlled trials of the effectiveness of any psychological interventions intended to reduce emotional distress among individuals with learning difficulties. However, studies that have been reported suggest that although the approach may need some simplification, CBT can be as effective as in adults without learning difficulties (Willner 2005) in the treatment of anxiety, anger and depression.

Case formulation

Mr R was a 27-year-old man with an IQ of around 55. As a child he lived at home, but his parents were unable to cope with his behaviour and were themselves ill, so he moved into a residential home in his early teens. His behaviour in the home was generally unremarkable, and he developed good relationships with most of the staff and residents in the home. However, he also experienced frequent and, at times, frightening episodes of anger and aggression towards his fellow residents and staff in the home. These were characterized at different times by screaming, shouting, banging his head, biting, becoming abusive and physically threatening. As he was a large man, these actions were very intimidating to the residents of the home. As a result of these episodes, Mr R had been admitted to a local hospital for treatment on a number of occasions – each time following an aggressive outburst, and each time with the intention of preventing further episodes of this type of behaviour. Over the years, he had received a number of medications (including major tranquillizers such as haloperidol), he had been taught basic anger management skills such as relaxation, and had been on behavioural programmes that rewarded appropriate behaviour with, for example, social contact with staff, and punished inappropriate behaviours by punishment, such as being ignored by staff. These interventions had worked for short periods over the years, but their effects then faded, and his outbursts continued.

One reason for this episodic ebb and flow of his outbursts was that most of the interventions to reduce them had taken place in hospital, away from the residential home in which he lived. Accordingly, they influenced his behaviour while in hospital, but their effects did not generalize beyond this context. With this in mind, the staff in the home and a clinical psychologist attempted to develop an intervention to reduce his outbursts actually in the home.

Functional analysis

In contrast to self-management approaches, which require the individual concerned to deliberately change their behaviour, functional analysis aims to identify (and then change) external, environmental, factors that contribute to either triggering or maintaining target behaviours. This process involves a period of naturalistic observation of the target behaviour, identifying when, where and why it occurs and factors that contribute to it being maintained. This process is known as functional, or A-B-C, analysis in which A is the antecedent, B is the behaviour and C is the consequence of the behaviour. In the case of Mr R, this process involved a psychology assistant spending time in the residential home observing Mr R through the day and keeping a diary of these issues. As key behaviours became evident – such as biting or shouting – the frequency of these specific events was recorded. In order to ensure a full understanding of the A-B-C process, the assistant worked at different times of the day to capture the full time frame in which such incidents could occur. In addition to this diary keeping, staff in the home were asked their views about the causes and factors that maintained Mr R's behaviour and how they responded to it.

Formulation

The observation revealed a number of triggers to Mr R's behaviour. These included: jokes about him or teasing by members of staff or other residents and times at which Mr R was frustrated by waiting for things to happen: to be given food, money, staff attention, and so on. Conversations with staff members revealed that staff in the home responded very differently to Mr R's behaviour. Some tried to argue with him when he became angry, threatening sanctions, while others took a completely opposite approach of ignoring his outbursts. Some staff were consistent in their response: others responded differently depending on the context in which the behaviour occurred. Observation of incidents in the home suggested that his behaviour was worse and continued for longer if his outbursts were responded to with remonstrations or threats by staff or residents.

Intervention

Once the psychology team had completed their functional analysis and had an understanding of the causes and maintaining factors of Mr R's outbursts, they met with the home staff to develop a response to them. They planned a series of changes including: (i) avoiding triggers to the outbursts by ensuring that Mr R did not have to wait long for food, money, etc., stopping any teasing, providing regular attention to him at appropriate times, and (ii) responding to any outbursts in a consistent manner – keeping a quiet and calm voice while talking to him, keeping a reasonable distance from him, and avoiding any appearance of confrontation. The staff team met at weekly intervals to share any problems they were experiencing or to suggest strategies they had found useful (within the overall behavioural programme). The assistant psychologist also continued to monitor the key target behaviours and to report back to these meetings how the intervention was progressing. Finally, and importantly, Mr R was given an explanation of the programme and why staff may be responding to him differently than before. The programme proved effective. Over a period of one month, there was a substantial drop in the frequency of Mr R's outbursts. The inception of the programme resulted in a dramatic fall in the number of outbursts from two to three a day to two in the first week. This number fell to zero in the second week, and only one incident occurred in the third week. The programme could therefore be considered a success. The key to maintaining its success, of course, is that the staff continue their behavioural changes – and any new staff in the home learn to adopt their response style.

14.2 Autism

Autism was first identified in 1943, and was differentiated from schizophrenia only in 1971. For a DSM diagnosis of autism to be made, a total of at least six symptoms must be present, with at least two from the first section and at least one from each of the second and third sections, with onset prior to age 3 years.

1 Impairment in social interaction:
- impairment in the use of non-verbal behaviours, such as eye-to-eye gaze, facial expression and gestures, to regulate social interaction
- failure to develop peer relationships
- lack of spontaneous seeking to share enjoyment, interests or achievements with other people
- lack of social or emotional reciprocity.
2 Abnormalities in communication:
- delay in, or total lack of, the development of spoken language
- in individuals with adequate speech, marked impairment in the ability to initiate or sustain a conversation
- stereotyped and repetitive use of language or idiosyncratic language
- lack of spontaneous make-believe play or social imitative play.

3 Restricted, repetitive and stereotyped patterns of behaviour, interests and activities:
- inflexible adherence to specific, non-functional routines or rituals
- stereotyped and repetitive motor mannerisms
- persistent preoccupation with parts of objects.

In its severest form, autism occurs in about 7 individuals per 10,000 population. There is, in addition, a wider spectrum of milder problems, affecting 20 children per 10,000 (Williams et al. 2006). The abilities and difficulties of people with autism vary considerably. Some people with the disorder are able to take an active part in society, with no deficits apparent to the casual observer, although they may have significant problems in establishing and maintaining relationships. About 80 per cent of children with autism score less than 70 on intelligence tests, placing them in the learning disabilities range. These deficits are quite specific, and relate to abstract thought, symbolism and sequential logic. Some people may have isolated skills that reflect great talent, including prodigious mathematical or memory skills, in a condition known as 'idiot savant'.

Core limitations of autism

The core limitations associated with autism are social isolation, communication deficits and obsessive-compulsive or ritual behaviours.

Social isolation

Many children with autism act as if people have no special characteristics that distinguish them from inanimate objects. As babies, they do not respond to their mothers when being touched or fed, and may reject attempts at cuddling by arching their back. By the age of 2 or 3, they may form a weak emotional bond with their parents. Few will initiate play with other children, and they are usually unresponsive to attempts by other children to engage them in play. Attempts at achieving eye contact are usually met with avoidance or movement away, and carry no social message (Mottronb et al. 2005). By contrast, children with autism may develop strong bonds with inanimate objects, and carry them around with them if possible.

Communication deficits

About 50 per cent of children with autism never learn to speak. Those that do have a number of common abnormalities. One frequent speech characteristic is known as *echolalia*: the repetition of words or phrases spoken to the child immediately, hours or even days earlier. This is now thought to be an attempt at communication, and may be associated with an event or stimulus. Repetition of the phrase, 'Do you want a sweet?', for example, may indicate a learned association between the phrase and being given a sweet. A second common characteristic is known as *pronoun reversal*. In this, children refer to themselves in the third person. This may be associated with echolalia and reflect how they have heard others speak about them (e.g. 'How are you, Mary?' – 'She's here . . .'). This is highly resistant to change, even after substantial training programmes.

Obsessive-compulsive and ritualistic acts

Children with autism rarely engage in symbolic play. More frequently, they engage in repetitive, stereotypic and seemingly meaningless behaviour. These include ritualistic hand movements, such as flicking fingers across their face, or repetitive body movements, including rocking or walking on tip-toe. They may become upset if prevented from doing these behaviours or when minor elements of their daily routine are changed. Their play often has an obsessive flavour to it, lining up toys or constructing complex patterns with household objects.

Growing up

The prognosis of children with autism is mixed. Those with learning difficulties often make a poor adjustment to adulthood, and most need some level of supervised care. By contrast, those without learning difficulties frequently go on to achieve an independent life, gain employment and live independently. Some go on to make significant contributions in their lives. However, most continue to have significantly impaired social relationships and little understanding of social and emotional aspects of life. For a powerful description of the feelings and development of a 'high functioning autistic' (her phrase), it may be useful to go to a chapter by Temple Grandin, a professor at Colorado State University (available at www.autism.org/temple/inside. html). Here are some of her fascinating insights into her own condition, starting with her childhood frustration at not being able to speak:

> Not being able to speak was utter frustration. If adults spoke directly to me I could understand everything they said, but I could not get my words out. It was like a big stutter . . . My speech therapist knew how to intrude into my world. She would hold me by my chin and made me look in her eyes and say 'ball'. At age 3, 'ball' came out 'bah', said with great stress. If the therapist pushed too hard I threw a tantrum, and if she did not intrude far enough no progress was made. My mother and teachers wondered why I screamed. Screaming was the only way I could communicate . . .
>
> I wanted to feel the good feeling of being hugged, but when people hugged me the stimuli washed over me like a tidal wave . . . I pulled away to avoid the all engulfing tidal wave of stimulation. The stiffening up and flinching were like a wild animal pulling away. At age 18 I built a squeezing machine. This device is completely lined with foam rubber, and the user has complete control over the duration and amount of pressure applied. The machine provides comforting pressure to large areas of the body. It took me a long time to learn to accept the feeling of being held and not try to pull away from it . . . I almost never feel aggressive after using it. In order to learn to relate to people better, I first had to learn how to receive comfort from the soothing pressure of the squeeze machine . . .
>
> Shortly after my first menstrual period, the anxiety attacks started. The feeling was like a constant feeling of stage fright all the time. The 'nerves' were almost like hypersensitivity rather than anxiety. It was like my brain was running at 200 miles an hour . . . The 'nerves' were worse in the late afternoon and early evening. They subsided late at night and early in the morning. There are two . . . ways to fight the nerves: fixate on an intense activity, or withdraw and try to minimize outside stimulation. Fixating on one thing had a calming effect. I used to write three articles in one night. While I was typing furiously I felt calmer. I was the most nervous when I had nothing to do.

Aetiology of autism

Genetic factors

Genetic studies of autism are difficult to conduct as the condition is so rare. Nevertheless, what evidence there is suggests a significant genetic component to the risk for autism. McBride et al. (1996), for example, reported that the siblings of people with the disorder are about 75 times more likely to develop the disorder than those without an affected sibling. Further data have been reported in twin studies, where concordance rates of between 60 and 91 per cent for MZ and 20 per cent for DZ twins have been reported (e.g. Bailey et al. 1995). The recurrence rate in siblings of affected children is approximately 2 per cent to 8 per cent, much higher than the prevalence rate in the general population but much lower than in single-gene diseases (Muhle et al. 2004). Any genetic model is, therefore, likely to be polygenic. According to Muhle et al. (2004), candidate genes include those that influence serotonin and GABA processes as well as oxytocin (a hormone and neurotransmitter associated with, among other things, emotional bonding).

Biological mechanisms

The opioid theory

It has proven difficult to find a biochemical model of autism. Perhaps the most widely advocated theory, the opioid theory, suggests that the condition is the result of an early overload of the central nervous system by opioids. This is based on findings that certain behaviours found in autism, including stereotyped behaviour, can be artificially induced in animals following injection with opioid agonists. The excess opioids are thought to be the result of incompletely digested dietary gluten and/or casein found in barley, rye, oats and milk products (Reichelt et al. 1991). These result from a lack of chemicals known as peptidases within the gut which break down natural opioids found in these foodstuffs into innocuous metabolites. Unfortunately, what biological studies have been conducted have not always supported this theory. Neither Hunter et al. (2003) or Dettmer et al. (2007), for example, found any evidence of these opioid peptides in the urine of children with autism. A number of studies have used drugs or dietary restrictions to inhibit uptake of opioids from the gut as a treatment of autism. These have met with limited success (see p. 375). However, treatment studies may provide only a tangential test of the opioid theory, as it is not clear whether any neurological changes resulting from this excess of opioids are reversible.

MMR and autism   In the later 1990s, Wakefield et al. (1998) examined 12 children referred to hospital with a normal developmental history followed by an apparently sudden loss of cognitive skills accompanied by a number of abdominal symptoms. Symptom onset was reported to have followed the Measles, Mumps and Rubella (MMR) vaccination in eight of the children; nine were diagnosed as having autism. Each of these nine children was found to suffer from an inflammation of the bowel wall, known as lymphoid hyperplasia. Wakefield et al. suggested that this may have resulted in a failure to break down dietary gluten and/or casein and, hence, triggered the onset of autism. This finding, and the subsequent public fears of MMR, sparked a widespread controversy and significant reductions in the uptake of the MMR vaccination.

A number of subsequent reports have both supported and challenged Wakefield's conclusions. The same research group (Uhlmann et al. 2001) compared 91 patients with lymphoid hyperplasia and 70 controls without the condition. Of those with lymphoid hyperplasia, 75 were found to have the measles virus in their gut; only 5 of the control group had the virus. They concluded that this was evidence of a plausible link between measles, MMR and lymphoid hyperplasia – with its potential link to the onset of autism. Since then a number of findings which challenge the MMR–autism link have been reported. Taylor et al. (1999), for example, examined trends in births and any subsequent registration of children with special needs and disabilities since 1979 in the UK. They noted a gradual increase in the numbers of children with autism since this time, but no sudden increase coinciding with the introduction of the MMR vaccine, nor any evidence of a cluster of children with developmental regression occurring within two to four months of MMR vaccination. In an even more clear-cut study, Honda et al. (2005) reviewed the rates of autism diagnosed in the Kohuku area of Yokohama between 1988 and 2002. During this time, rates of MMR fell dramatically (for reasons not related to the autism scare) and no MMR vaccines were administered from 1993 onwards. Nevertheless, rates of autism rose throughout this period with the greatest increase beginning in the cohort of children born in 1993 – after the MMR vaccination was no longer given. These, and other data, led Demicheli et al. (2005) in their review of the evidence to suggest that exposure to MMR was unlikely to be associated with Crohn's disease, ulcerative colitis, autism or mumps.

So, why did so many people become convinced that MMR had caused their child to develop autism? Perhaps the answer lies in the coincidence of timing between the MMR and the developmental history of autism. About 600,000 children receive the MMR vaccine in any year, mostly at the time that autism first becomes evident. It is possible that among these children, the identification of a small number of cases of autism will coincide with vaccination. This apparent association could have been exaggerated by the highly selective way in which children were identified and assessed in the Wakefield et al. (1998) study. In addition, it is possible that the link between receiving the MMR vaccine and the onset of symptoms made by parents may be inaccurate. It is usually difficult to identify the time of onset of symptoms of autism, and most people search for a 'cause' of such problems. If parents were to attribute their child's problems to the vaccination, this may result in unconscious memory biases and inappropriate linkages of behaviour with the timing of the MMR vaccination.

An emerging, and possibly stronger, candidate for some of the problems associated with autism is the dysregulation of serotonin both before and after birth. Reviewing the evidence, Whitaker-Azmitia (2005) suggested that in the early stages of development, when the blood–brain barrier is not yet fully formed, high levels of serotonin in the blood can enter the brain of genetically vulnerable foetuses and damage serotonin terminals during development. The loss of serotonergic nerve fibres persists throughout subsequent development and contributes to the symptoms of autism. Exactly where in the brain any damage may occur is still not fully investigated, but animal studies suggest that the amygdala, a brain region involved in fear-responding, and the hypothalamus, a brain region involved in social memory and bonding, may be particularly vulnerable to damage. The anterior cingulated area of the brain, which is involved in face recognition, social, cognitive and affective functions relevant to autism, may also be particularly damaged. Dysregulation of serotonin may continue into adulthood among people with autism (Chugani 2004).

Psychodynamic explanations

Early psychological theories of autism focused on psychodynamic processes. Autism was seen as a form of escape from environments that lacked warmth and care. Bettelheim (1967), for example, suggested that children who develop autism have rejecting parents and are able to perceive their negative feelings. The infants learn that their actions have little or no impact on their parents' emotions or behaviour. They come to believe they have no power to influence the world, and so choose not to enter it. Instead, they build an 'empty fortress' of autism against this pain and disappointment. Unfortunately, from Bettelheim's perspective, there is no evidence that the parents of children who develop autism differ from those of children who develop normally. Cox et al. (1975), for example, found that the parents of children with autism and those of children with problems in understanding speech did not differ in terms of emotional demonstrativeness, responsiveness to their children or sociability.

A biopsychosocial model

A similar explanation is found in the psychobiological theory of Koegel et al. (2001). They suggested that children who develop autism lack motivation to engage with other people and, as a result, withdraw from social interactions. This may begin early in life as a result of neurological dysfunction. However, it can be exacerbated by carers' efforts to 'help' affected children by doing things for them regardless of their behaviour. Whatever the child does, they receive the same response from their environment. As a result of this, and because social interactions and communication are inherently difficult, they revert to early forms of communication such as crying or tantrums to get their needs met and avoid social interactions.

Treatment of autism

Pharmacological approaches

A number of psychoactive drugs have been used to treat the symptoms of autism. Perhaps the most commonly used drugs are neuroleptics, which block the effects of dopamine (see Chapter 3). Campbell et al. (1988), for example, found haloperidol to be more effective than placebo in decreasing levels of stereotyped behaviour and withdrawal. In addition, it enhanced the effects of behavioural techniques used in developing the use of language, perhaps because it allowed the children to focus more on the learning process than previously. Similarly, the Research Units on Pediatric Psychopharmacology Autism Network (2005) reported significant benefits from the use of risperidone in the treatment of severe tantrums, aggression and/or self-injurious behaviour in a small group of adolescents with autism. To avoid the long-term adverse effects of neuroleptics, including tardive dyskinesia and Parkinsonism (see Chapter 4), the drugs may be used at relatively low dosage and episodically (five days on, two days off) and still be effective.

Tricyclics and SSRIs have also proven effective in reducing repetitive behaviours and aggression, and have shown consistent benefits on measures of global functioning, although some studies also report increased activation and agitation (Kolevzon et al. 2006). Kolevzon et al. also concluded that research methodologies employed in most trials were not strong, and further definitive trials were still needed.

Opiate antagonists, such as naltrexone (see also Chapter 16), have been used with only modest effect. Perhaps the most consistent effect of naltrexone is a reduction in activity levels (Parikh et al. 2008). It did not aid a behavioural programme conducted by Campbell et al. (1993), nor did it reduce self-injurious behaviour in a study reported by Willemsen-Swinkels et al. (1995). Indeed, in this study, treatment with naltrexone actually increased levels of stereotypic behaviour.

An alternative biological approach has been to reduce levels of dietary casein and gluten in order to reduce the extent to which opiates continue to be absorbed from the gut. Evidence of the effectiveness of this approach is not yet convincing. Millward et al. (2004) noted that there was little evidence of the effectiveness of this approach, and those studies which have found positive results have not been methodologically strong. Knivsberg et al. (1998), for example, reported on the outcomes in a group of 20 children who either received or did not receive this restricted diet for a period of one year. They reported significant success, with improvements in the treated group relative to those who did not receive the diet on a combined measure of behaviour and communication. However, the relatively small number of children in the trial, together with a lack of statistical analyses and measures of the diet given to the children, makes these results somewhat preliminary, and there is little data to make any judgement about the effectiveness of this type of intervention (Millward et al. 2004).

Behavioural approaches

Many programmes to change behaviours associated with autism have involved direct reinforcement of behaviours such as speech or pro-social behaviours. In these, the therapist/trainer typically provides a cue, usually a question or command, to evoke a specific response. This may be physically prompted if necessary, and performance of the behaviour is reinforced by a tangible reward such as a sweet: 'Look at me' – move head to face therapist if necessary – reward with sweet. In some programmes, inappropriate behaviours such as self-injury may be followed by an aversive response, including mild electric shocks or exposure to the smell of ammonia (Koegel et al. 2001). Other, more ethically acceptable, programmes have implemented non-aversive procedures even in response to challenging behaviour. Gena et al. (2005) used both live and video models of appropriate behaviour and rewards for appropriate changes to both instigate and reward appropriate behavioural change. This type of approach has resulted in reductions in self-injury, aggressive behaviour and echolalia, and gains on measures of eye contact, vocalizations and toileting.

One of the key researchers in this area is Ivar Lovaas, who developed a highly intensive operant programme for children. In his initial study (Lovaas 1987), therapy continued for much of the children's waking hours both at home and in school, for a period of two years. Children were rewarded for being less aggressive and more socially appropriate: talking, playing with other children, and so on. They were also punished, on occasion, for engaging in challenging behaviour. They were taught with their peers, not in special groups. This intensive intervention was compared with a similar treatment maintained for only ten hours a week. The differences between the two groups were dramatic. By the end of the two-year programme, the average IQ of the intervention group was 83 points, compared with 55 in the less intense intervention; 12 of the 19 children in the intensive intervention group had IQs at or above the norm, compared with 2 out of 40 in the less intensive intervention. These findings translated to school performance, with 9 children in the intensive therapy group being accepted in the same age class as their peers: only 1 child in the less intensive therapy group achieved this. Four years later, the relative gains made by the children in the intensive therapy had been maintained.

These findings created considerable controversy and have been criticized on methodological grounds (e.g. Gresham and MacMillan 1998). One criticism was that assignment of subjects to treatment and control groups was not random, allowing the possibility that the groups differed on potentially important variables that may have been left uncontrolled. A second criticism was that the pre- and post-treatment measures were not the same for all children. A third criticism was that the study results have not been reliably replicated, nor has a more recently developed non-aversive version of Lovaas's treatment been shown to be effective (Gresham and MacMillan 1998). These criticisms have been strongly refuted by Lovaas (www.feat.org/lovaas). In addition, some studies (e.g. T. Smith et al. 2000) have achieved similar gains to those made in the original Lovaas study. Accordingly, while this approach may not always achieve the therapeutic gains achieved by Lovaas, it does form a potentially effective approach to the treatment of children with autism.

Koegel et al. (2001) further refined the operant approach by targeting a number of what they termed primary factors, which they considered to precede a number of consequent or secondary factors: poor communication skills, for example, typically precede severe behaviour problems. Interventions to improve language and communication skills could, therefore, prevent the need for interventions to deal with disruptive behaviour. Koegel and colleagues argued for targeting a variety of pro-social behaviours that facilitate communication, including improving eye contact, head positioning, reducing stereotypical movements and unusual facial expressions, as well as encouraging children to initiate social interactions.

A second innovation was based on the idea that the goal of any behavioural programme should not just be to modify one particular behaviour, but to increase the individual's motivation to engage in a number of similar behaviours. A key element of their behavioural programmes, therefore, was to provide rewards for behaviours similar to the target one. An example of the difference between this and previous conditioning approaches was reported by Koegel et al. (1988). In this, the traditional operant approach reinforced specified phonetic sounds, as they became increasingly word-like over time. To obtain reinforcement, the child had to produce responses that were at least as good as their previous responses. The newer approach reinforced any attempts to verbalize, however accurate or inaccurate the noise made. In a direct comparison between the two approaches, Koegel et al. (1988) found the newer method to result in more rapid gains in the use of appropriate speech and greater levels of pro-social behaviours than the traditional method.

A final innovation of their approach was to allow the child control over the reward they were given for engaging in the targeted behaviours. Perhaps the most extreme, and ultimately most rewarding, examples of this allowed the child to engage in stereotypical or ritualistic behaviours, which are intrinsically highly rewarding, as a reward for completion of other tasks. This strategy has been shown to reduce the incidence of aggressive tantrums and other 'off-task' behaviours (Charlop-Christy and Haymes 1998).

14.3 Attention-deficit/hyperactivity disorder (ADHD)

DSM-IV-TR identified three categories of attention-deficit/hyperactivity disorder (ADHD): problems of poor attention, hyperactive-impulsive behaviour and a combination of both. Most children with the disorder have both sets of problems. Criteria for each diagnosis are engaging in at least six of the behaviours in Table 14.1 over a period of at least six months.

Table 14.1 Key features of the ADHD diagnostic categories	
Inattention	**Hyperactivity-impulsivity**
· Fails to pay close attention to details or makes careless errors in schoolwork, work or other activities	· Squirms in seat or fidgets
· Has trouble keeping attention on tasks or play	· Inappropriately leaves seat
· Doesn't appear to listen when being told something	· Has trouble playing quietly or engaging in leisure activity
· Neither follows through on instructions nor completes tasks, schoolwork or jobs (not due to oppositional behaviour or failure to understand)	· Runs or climbs inappropriately; in adolescents or adults there may be only a subjective feeling of restlessness
· Has trouble organizing activities and tasks	· Appears driven or 'on the go'
· Dislikes or avoids tasks that involve sustained mental effort (e.g. homework, schoolwork)	· Talks excessively
· Loses materials needed for activities: books, pencils, tools, toys, and so on	· Answers questions before they have been completely asked
· Easily distracted by extraneous stimuli	· Has trouble waiting turn
· Forgetful	· Interrupts or intrudes on others

For a diagnosis to be given, problem behaviours need to have begun before the age of 7 years, be present in school and at home, and significantly impair functioning. Many children with ADHD have difficulty in getting on with their peers and establishing friendships. They fail to recognize when their behaviour is annoying others, and may make significant social mistakes. They can usually understand such issues in hypothetical scenarios, but have trouble translating this understanding into the 'real world'. About 25 per cent of children with ADHD have some form of learning difficulty, and many are placed in special education units as a consequence of their disruptive behaviour. Children with ADHD are more likely to drop out of school than those without the disorder.

An estimated 3–6 per cent of children in the USA could be diagnosed as having ADHD, with significant variation across states and educational systems suggesting differences in the diagnostic criteria being applied (Fulton et al. 2009). However, ADHD is not a uniquely American or Western problem. Kashala et al. (2005), for example, reported a prevalence level of 6 per cent among schoolchildren in the Democratic Republic of Congo. Some, but not all, problems abate as the individual grows older. Of children identified with ADHD, 40 per cent continue to have these problems in late adolescence, and about 10 per cent have some level of symptoms in adulthood (Mannuzza and Klein 2000). Between 1 and 6 per cent of adults meet the criteria for ADHD (Murphy and Barkley 1996). By this time, most people have learned to adapt to their symptoms and can hold down jobs.

Diagnostic versus categorical understandings of ADHD

Many children exhibit some of the characteristics of those diagnosed as having ADHD. This indistinct line between what is 'ordinary' and what is 'pathological' behaviour, and the potential abuse of the diagnosis of ADHD as a justification for medicating disruptive children (see pp. 380–4), have led to strong arguments as to whether ADHD exists as a separate 'condition' or whether the behaviours that comprise ADHD are better thought of as being at the extreme end of the normal distribution of behaviour. That is, the condition may best be considered in dimensional rather than categorical terms (see Chapter 1).

Arguments favouring the dimensional approach are both clinical and empirical. Clinicians note that a child may have significant problems in one particular area, but may not receive help because they do not fulfil the 'diagnostic requirements' for ADHD and therefore may not be considered to have a 'problem'. Similarly, a diagnosis of ADHD may justify drug treatments where other approaches may be more beneficial to the child. Empirical evidence suggests that dimensional scores of behaviours subsumed within ADHD appear to be more predictive of outcome than categorical diagnostic judgements. Fergusson and Horwood (1995), for example, compared the predictive validity of dimensional and categorical ratings/diagnoses of ADHD to predict levels of substance abuse, juvenile offending and school drop-out in a cohort of New Zealand schoolchildren. They found a dose–response relationship between the number and severity of behaviours associated with ADHD and risk of each of these outcomes. Dimensional scores were more predictive of outcome than diagnostic category. These various findings suggest that the behaviours that comprise ADHD are better thought of as towards the end of a distribution of behaviours rather than categorically different from the norm.

Aetiology of ADHD

Genetic factors

Genetic factors appear to contribute to risk of developing ADHD. One early genetic study (Goodman and Stevenson 1989) found a 51 per cent concordance for ADHD between MZ twins and a 31 per cent concordance between DZ twins. More recent studies have found concordance between MZ twins to vary between 58 and 83 per cent compared with between 31 and 47 per cent for DZ twins, with heritability estimates for attention problems varying between 60 and 80 per cent (Wender et al. 2001). Meta-analyses or pooled data analyses have supported association between ADHD and polymorphisms in a number of genes that influence dopamine receptors and transporter processes (Thapar et al. 2005) as well as norepinephrine and serotonin transporter genes (Russell et al. 2005). However, a single gene increasing risk for ADHD has still to be identified, and risk is likely to be associated with a number of genes each contributing a small amount to the disorder (Neale et al. 2010).

Biological mechanisms

The main characteristics of ADHD are thought to reflect problems with behavioural control and management. Impulsivity is not thought to result from an inability to attend, but is the result of problems in executive function: a failure to decide when actions should be taken and how they should be executed. This implicates dysfunction of the frontal lobe as central to the disorder, a hypothesis supported by consistent fMRI findings of hypoactivity within the frontal lobe and its links to other brain areas including the basal ganglia, thalamus, and parietel cortex among people with ADHD (Dickstein et al. 2006). The main neurotransmitter involved in ADHD seems to be dopamine. Data to support this hypothesis mainly stem from animal models and studies that have found drugs that increase dopamine levels to be most effective in reducing or even eliminating the symptoms of ADHD. These include various types of amphetamines, and indirect dopamine agonists. It seems paradoxical that an amphetamine actually reduces levels of physical activity, but it appears to do so by increasing frontal activity and control over executive dysfunctions that underpin the behaviour. In fact, Sagvolden et al. (2005) suggested that dopamine dysregulation in three brain areas may lead to the key symptoms of ADHD:

- *mesocortical system:* responsible for normal cognitive function within the frontal lobe. Dysregulation leads to deficient attention, poor behavioural organization.
- *mesolimbic system:* the reward pathway of the brain, linking (among other brain areas) the limbic and frontal lobes. Dysregulation leads to a shorter 'delay of reinforcement gradient', and deficient extinction. That is, low levels of dopamine increase the salience of short-term rewards and reduce the ability to work towards longer-term rewards, leading to impulsiveness.
- *nigrostriatal system:* dysregulation leads to clumsiness, and poor non-declarative, routine, habit learning.

A second, and still important, neurotransmitter involved in ADHD is norepinephrine. Evidence suggests that there is lower than normal norepinephrine activity within the prefrontal cortex in ADHD, which may amplify responses to attended stimuli, and reduce responses to irrelevant stimuli.

Psychological explanations

As noted above, ADHD can be characterized not by hyperactivity, but by high levels of impulsivity. According to Barkley (1997), children with ADHD do things other children think of doing, but don't actually do. The urge to act is not inhibited. The first response to a situation is the response that is taken. He suggested that the core of ADHD is a failure to inhibit inappropriate responses to environmental events. In addition to this, children with ADHD are more emotionally responsive to events than most children. They are poor at controlling their feelings, and less able to tolerate negative emotions. Their emotions are driven by the moment and the object of their attention at that time. As a consequence, they have difficulties in maintaining goal-oriented behaviour, particularly when this is associated with some type of negative emotion. They have difficulty in sticking to a task in the expectation of future rewards or satisfaction on its completion. Schoolwork or other demanding and sometimes boring or frustrating tasks do not hold their attention and they move rapidly to other more immediately rewarding activities.

Barkley (1997) noted that as children grow older they use an internal dialogue as a means of self-control. This internalized language develops at around the age of 3–4 years, the time that ADHD is often first identified. This is not coincidental: Barkley suggests that children with ADHD have disorganized internal speech, which contributes to their disorganized responses to external events. Barkley noted that children with ADHD often appear 'chatty', but their conversation usually deals with the present rather than the future: thoughts do not lead to planning and future expectations. This disorganization also means that children with ADHD have difficulties in dealing with abstract issues. They find it hard to explain things: they do not get to the point, they talk around it. Of interest is that while Barkley (1997) provided a psychological perspective on ADHD, he considered it to have a biological basis, and to be largely the result of biochemical and neurological factors. He described people with ADHD as 'biochemical outliers', acknowledging a dimensional view of their behaviour rather than a categorical one.

While Barkley's model is probably the most widely acknowledged psychological theory of ADHD, it is not without its critiques. Sagvolden et al. (2005), for example, suggested the biochemical processes that underpin ADHD are more complicated than implied by the relatively simple model of Barkley. They also disagreed on the fundamental processes underpinning the condition. Barkley suggested ADHD involves a failure to inhibit urges to respond to the environment. Sagvolden and colleagues suggested a more complex process involving poor attention and behavioural organization, a failure to learn appropriate behavioural sequences, and a sensitivity to short-term reinforcers and lack of response to longer-term outcomes that rewards rapid, poorly thought through, responses to environmental stimuli. In a more specific examination of the cognitive processes underpinning ADHD, Cornoldi et al. (2001) found that children with ADHD symptoms had working memory problems which led to them having difficulties in suppressing information that initially had to be processed and subsequently excluded from memory, in order to perform a memory task effectively.

A biopsychosocial model

Bettelheim (1973) integrated biochemical models with social and psychological factors in a biopsychosocial model of ADHD. He suggested that ADHD develops when children with a biological predisposition to hyperactivity are raised in an environment with a strong authoritarian ethos or one where there is evident resentfulness at inappropriate behaviour. According to Bettelheim, if a child with a predisposition to hyperactivity is responded to with obvious frustration or impatience by their parents, they may feel unable to respond effectively to their parents' need for controlled behaviour and obedience. As both react to each other in negative ways, this may spiral into a continuous battle between child and parents, that spills over to other settings and eventually results in what may be termed ADHD.

Evidence of a role of family dynamics as a causal factor for ADHD is not strong. Rey et al. (2000) found an adverse family environment was associated with conduct disorder and oppositional defiant disorder, it was not associated with ADHD. A longitudinal social and genetic study by Lifford et al. (2009) found ADHD symptoms, and particularly those of boys, to trigger negative parental responses, but there was no evidence of such responses or family dynamics triggering or impacting on ADHD behaviours. These types of data contributed to the psychosocial model of Sandberg (2005), who suggested that ADHD is an adaptation to defective neurotransmission. The resulting behavioural style is usually maladaptive and not only increases vulnerability to adverse experiences, but also creates a context in which encountering adversity is more likely.

Treatment of ADHD

Pharmacological interventions

Perhaps the best-known pharmacological treatment of ADHD involves methylphenidate hydrachloride, better known as Ritalin. The combined results of studies investigating its efficacy suggest it achieves significant improvements in about 60 per cent of those prescribed it, compared with about 10 per cent of those prescribed placebo (Wender et al. 2001). The key benefit of Ritalin is that it moderates the symptoms of both inattention and hyperactivity, allowing the individual to focus more on educational, social and family issues. Pelham et al. (1993), for example, compared an eight-week school-based behaviour modification programme combined with Ritalin and the same programme combined with placebo in the treatment of a group of 8-year-old boys with ADHD. The behavioural programme involved a points system with both rewards for appropriate behaviour and 'costs' for inappropriate classroom behaviours. Acquisition of a fixed number of points could be exchanged for a variety of items chosen by the child. The effect of the behavioural intervention combined with Ritalin was significantly greater than when it was combined with placebo on measures of both class behaviour and academic performance.

The benefits of Ritalin can be dramatic. Here, a teacher describes the impact of Ritalin on one child and his classmates:

> He just came to us in Year 7, with a real history of paperwork behind him . . . poor behaviour, learning difficulties. He came to the school in September. We thought he had ADHD because he was beyond control, reason. He couldn't stay seated – or wouldn't – he wandered round the class-room, started wandering about the school. He was a powerful lad, and just pushed people out of the way that tried to stop him. By the end of November he had been seen by the doctor. He was given a diagnosis of ADHD and prescribed Ritalin. He stayed at home a couple of days, because he was pretty zonked out on it. Then he came back to school. The change was instantaneous. He was a difficult child, and he still had behavioural problems . . . but you could reason with him.
>
> You could sit him down and talk to him. He decided he liked learning, as for the first time he could understand what he was being taught. He started reading . . . which boosted his self-esteem . . . lots of these kids with ADHD have low self-esteem as they fail in school . . . Ritalin does allow them to access the curriculum. For the first time, they can concentrate on something and make progress. But when the medicine wears off you know about it. We start to give the mid-day dose at about a quarter to twelve. By this time, they [children with ADHD] have got more 'edgy', more loud. Lots of walking, winding people up: 'loud' is the predominant word . . . Sometimes you think the poor kids don't have a chance. It's difficult at home – and they may trash their room. But you think sometimes it's a response to real problems they have with their parents. Some of them are like their child: they go from 'down here' to sky high in seconds. It's got to be bad for the kids.

Of more concern are the findings of King et al. (2009), who found that children with ADHD treated with placebo evidenced the same levels of aggression/hostility to an experimental provocation as typical children: those treated with Ritalin expressed higher levels of aggression/hostility. These results have yet to be replicated in a real life context, but provide a warning of potential problems. Other side-effects have been more widely reported. These include loss of appetite, abdominal pain, weight loss, insomnia and increased heart rate. Retardation of growth may also occur during prolonged therapy in children. Ritalin may also trigger psychotic symptoms. Cherland and Fitzpatrick (1999) reported a 9 per cent prevalence of psychotic symptoms, including hallucinations and paranoia, among their sample of 192 children treated with Ritalin for ADHD, which ceased immediately on withdrawal of the drug. No psychotic symptoms were reported among children with ADHD who did not receive the drug. Other potential problems with Ritalin result from its high level of prescribing. Indeed, many have argued it is over-prescribed, and used to control unruly or unwanted behaviour – not just ADHD. Indeed, some schools in the USA have refused to accept 'difficult' children unless they are treated with Ritalin. Such demands have led pressure groups to lobby the US Congress into considering a bill that prevents school officials from requiring a student take the 'behavioral drugs' in order to attend school (see, for example, www.ritalindeath.com). A final risk associated with Ritalin is its use as a drug of abuse, which is becoming increasingly common in the USA. As an amphetamine, it suppresses appetite, increases wakefulness and produces an emotional high. When abused, tablets are either taken orally or crushed and snorted. Some abusers dissolve the tablets in water and inject the mixture, which can cause complications as insoluble fillers in the tablets can block small blood vessels. Students are also using Ritalin as a so-called 'smart drug' to improve exam performance.

Stop and think...

Treatment with Ritalin has not been without controversy. Searching the web quickly identifies a number of sites of parents and others concerned about its use – one of which is cited in the main text. People worry about its over-prescription, that very young children are being placed on powerful medication, that schooling problems are becoming the remit of medical practitioners. Many people are 'against Ritalin' and similar drugs. But they can work ... So, what are your views, and how would you feel if one of your children was put on this drug?

Other drug treatments are now emerging. The role of norepinephrine in ADHD has resulted in the development and use of a drug designed to increase levels of norepinephrine within the frontal lobe. Atomoxetine is a norepinephrine re-uptake inhibitor which may provide an alternative treatment to methylphenidate and is of similar therapeutic benefit (Gilbert et al. 2007). However, it also has more problematic short-term side-effects including anorexia, nausea and vomiting which are experienced by up to a third of those receiving the drug. Another form of treatment is provided by a drug known as Modafinil. This psychostimulant has been used for treating excessive daytime sleepiness associated with narcolepsy, and is now being used in ADHD. The mechanism of action of Modafinil is unknown, but, unlike other stimulants, the drug is highly selective for the central nervous system and has little effect on dopaminergic activity. Nevertheless, it appears effective in reducing the core symptoms of ADHD (Biederman et al. 2005).

Operant approaches

The behavioural intervention used by Pelham et al. (1993) and described above is typical of operant-conditioning-based interventions. These usually take the form of a token economy, in which the child is rewarded for engaging in specific pre-specified behaviours by receiving a token. Tokens can be collected and, when enough have been accrued, exchanged for a desired item. This approach has a number of variants, including charts on which stars are placed as a reward for appropriate behaviours and, again, exchanged for tangible rewards when enough are displayed. Although this type of intervention can be effective on its own, the results of studies such as that of Pelham and colleagues suggest that operant procedures may be most effective when used in conjunction with treatment by Ritalin.

Training attention

The attention training tasks used to treat head injuries described in Chapter 15 can also be used to help children with ADHD. Semrud-Clikeman et al. (1999), for example, examined the effectiveness of the Attention Process Training Programme (Park et al. 1999: described in more detail in Chapter 15) combined with training in problem-solving in a school setting with children identified as having problems in attention and not completing work. As a result of the training programme, the children improved on the training tasks, completed more tasks in class, and their teachers reported that they seemed more attentive. Using materials specifically developed for young children, Kerns et al. (1999) reported improvements in a group of 7–11-year-old children following a similar attention training programme. By the end of the training period, participants achieved better scores on untrained cognitive tasks, academic performance and on teacher reports of impulsiveness.

Environmental manipulation

As many of the behaviours associated with ADHD are seen as immediate responses to the environment, one way in which they may be influenced is by environmental manipulation. The ERIC (Educational Resources Information Center) Clearinghouse on Disabilities and Gifted Education (www.ericec.org) set out some clear guidelines, including the nature of the learning environment, to help teachers work with children with ADHD. These included:

- sit students with ADHD at the front of the class with their backs to the rest of the class to keep other students out of view
- surround students with ADHD with good role models
- avoid distracting stimuli
- produce a stimuli-reduced study area for teaching (which other children can access) to avoid isolation.

In addition to these environmental factors, they considered a number of other factors, including guidelines for maintaining and enhancing self-esteem, responding to inappropriate behaviour, and the process of teaching, all of which contribute to best practice when teaching children with ADHD.

Working with families

As noted above, the families of children with ADHD experience significant levels of stress and upset. A number of studies have attempted to reduce family problems by working with the whole family. Barkley et al. (2001), for example, compared the effectiveness of problem-solving communication training alone or following training behavioural management skills in an attempt to minimize conflict within families. Problem-solving communication training involved a five-stage process through which the family combined to deal with problems: defining the problem, brainstorming potential solutions, negotiating and deciding within the family which solutions to implement, and then implementing the solution. The behavioural skills management involved learning to change triggers or responses to disruptive behaviour using operant procedures. Both interventions proved equally effective in those that completed them. However, three times as many people dropped out of training when the problem-solving approach was used alone than when the combined intervention was used. More recently, Matos et al. (2009) reported significant improvements on ADHD symptoms, oppositional-defiant behaviours, and family functioning following a similar programe conducted in Puerto Rican pre-school children. Not all studies have shown benefit, however (see Bjornstad and Montgomery 2005), and given the evidence that family dynamics do not directly contribute to the development of ADHD (although they may exacerbate any related problems), this approach may best be used when families are clearly experiencing stress and struggling to cope with a child's behaviour rather than a standard approach given to all.

The MTA Cooperative Group (1999) A 14-month randomized clinical trial of treatment strategies for attention-deficit/hyperactivity disorder: multimodal treatment study of children with ADHD, *Archives of General Psychiatry*, 56: 1073–86.

Molina, B. et al. (2009) The MTA at 8 years: prospective follow-up of children treated for combined-type ADHD in a multisite study, *Journal of the American Academy of Child and Adolescent Psychiatry*, 48: 484–500.

The previous edition of this book reported on the MTA group's 14-month report on their intervention to reduce ADHD. Since then an 8-year follow-up study has been reported. The findings reported in both papers are summarized here.

Method

574 children, aged between 7 and 9.9 years, with a diagnosis of ADHD were randomly assigned to one of four conditions, each lasting 14 months: medication, behavioural treatment, combined medication and behavioural treatment, and community care (essentially, a no treatment control). Each participant met the DSM-IV criteria for ADHD, and had lived with the same caregiver for at least six months. Referral into the study was through 'mental health settings', paediatricians, advertisements and school notices. Exclusion factors were that the family would be unable to fully participate in the study, but did not include other diagnoses such as conduct or oppositional disorder.

Assessments

Six outcome measures were used, with measures before and after the 14-month intervention:

- ADHD symptoms were measured by the parent- and teacher-completed Inattention and Hyperactivity scale of the SNAP

- Oppositional and aggressive behaviour was measured by parent- and teacher-completed Oppositional/defiant Scale of the SNAP
- Social skills were measured with the Social Skills Rating System (SSRS)
- Anxiety and depression were measured by the 'internalizing' scale of the SSRS and the anxiety scale of the Multidimensional Anxiety Scale for Children (MASC).

Interventions

- The behavioural intervention involved parent training following the method of Barkley described in the chapter, comprising a behavioural programme modelling and rewarding appropriate behaviour and not rewarding inappropriate behaviour (as used by Pelham), and a school-based intervention in which teachers were taught classroom management techniques to control impulsive and haphazard behaviour. All the interventions were highly intensive at the beginning of the intervention period, but faded in intensity over time.
- Medication initially involved a double-blind variation of dosages of methylphenidate hydrochloride (Ritalin), given at breakfast, lunch and afternoon. Its impact on behaviour was observed by clinicians, and when they agreed the dosage appeared to be optimal, the blind was broken and this became the standard dose.
- The combined treatment involved both behavioural and medication treatment approaches.
- Community care involved feedback on baseline measures and information on local mental health facilities.

Results

Medication proved superior to psychological therapy on parents' and teachers' ratings of inattention, and teachers' ratings of hyperactivity and impulsivity. There were no differences between the intervention groups on measures of classroom observer ratings of behaviour, parent and teacher ratings of aggression, child mood, social skills and parent–child relationships. Combining the treatments had no additional impact: there were no differences between scores of children in the medication-only group and the combined intervention. Finally, the combined and medical interventions were consistently superior to the community intervention on the measures of inattention and hyperactivity/impulsivity, and at least one measure of mood, oppositional behaviour and reading achievement. However, the psychological treatment was not.

Follow-up

Key results of the follow-up study:

- After the trial, medication was reduced significantly – by 62 per cent: the level of medication had no impact on the study results.

- No study group differed on any measure of social outcome, such as grades at school, arrests, or psychiatric hospitalizations.
- All those in the trial (regardless of treatment group) fared worse than a local normative group of students on 91 per cent of all the measures used in the trial.

Discussion

These data suggest a significant superiority of medication over psychological interventions. However, some caveats may be necessary. The medication was maintained over the entire period of the first study. The psychological intervention was intensive at the beginning of the programme, but by 3–6 months prior to the end of the assessment period had reduced to one-monthly contact. It is not clear how well the two active interventions fared when both were being conducted, or how quickly the benefits of the medication would dissipate once stopped. Pragmatically, though, these data suggest that unless one is concerned about the ethics of medication or its side-effects, this may prove the treatment of choice.

In the longer term, outcomes were disappointing. No group fared differently, and all fared worse than a matched group of 'typical' school children in similar social circumstances. The key predictor of outcome during adolescence was the presence or absence of ADHD.

Working with adults who have ADHD

Self-management strategies

Adults with ADHD can be taught a number of self-management strategies to help them manage their attentional problems (Sohlberg and Mateer 2001). These include *orienting procedures* in which they regularly monitor their activities to ensure they focus on planned activities. An example of this approach may be the use of a watch that beeps every hour, reminding the individual to ask themselves, 'What am I currently doing? What was I doing before doing this? What am I supposed to do next?' An example of another orienting task, used for people who set off to drive somewhere and then forget their destination, is to routinely write down their destination, expected time of arrival, and the time at which it may be useful to ask for help if lost, at the beginning of every trip.

A second approach involves *pacing*. People with attention problems often experience fatigue or problems in maintaining concentration over extended periods of time. To combat this, they may benefit from pacing the demands they place upon themselves, by not setting too high standards of productivity and taking breaks at regular intervals. They can also be taught to monitor fatigue levels and take breaks at appropriate times rather than fighting through the fatigue and being unproductive. People with attention problems also find that they have difficulty in switching from one task to another. The *key ideas log* minimizes the problems associated with this by encouraging people with attention problems to quickly write down or tape-record ideas that spring to mind so they do not disrupt their ongoing task.

Environmental strategies

A final intervention involves thinking through the impact that environmental factors have on attention, and considering ways in which it can be modified to maximize cognitive performance (Sohlberg and Mateer 2001). Central to this approach is avoiding 'busy' or distracting environments and making use of 'quiet' environments when attention is required. This may involve, for example, shopping in quiet local shops rather than attempting to shop in bustling supermarkets. Further strategies may include minimizing the demand on attentional or organizational abilities by setting up standing orders to pay bills or labelling cupboards to ensure maximum organization. The use of 'Do not disturb' signs both at home and at work may also help minimize distraction from ongoing tasks. While these types of approaches would seem logical and likely to be effective, their highly individual nature has meant that their effectiveness has largely been explored through individual case reports rather than controlled trials (Sohlberg and Mateer 2001).

14.4 Chapter summary

1 About 3 per cent of the UK population have learning difficulties.

2 Only about 25 per cent of cases of learning difficulty have an identified cause. These causes include genetic conditions, infectious diseases, environmental hazards and several perinatal factors.

3 Social factors contribute strongly to mild learning difficulties, less so to more severe problems.

4 Down syndrome and Fragile X syndrome are two common conditions resulting from differing genetic factors.

5 The principles of normalization and social role valorization ensure that people with learning difficulties achieve the same respect and rights as the rest of the population.

6 Care of people with learning difficulties includes both social and psychological interventions.

7 Psychological interventions are frequently based on operant conditioning approaches to skills learning or behavioural change, although cognitive behavioural interventions may also prove effective.

8 People with autism have difficulties in three areas: social interaction, communication and obsessive-compulsive or ritualistic acts.

9 When combined with learning difficulties, these may profoundly influence the outcome of affected individuals.

10 The opioid theory of autism suggests that the disorder results from an overdose of opioids as a result of a failure to metabolize gluten and casein from the gut. The MMR vaccine was thought to contribute to this problem – but is no longer seen as a cause of autism.

11 A newly emerging neurological factor appears to be damage to the brain due to high levels of serotonin before birth affecting key brain regions regulating behaviours affected by autism.

12 Bettelheim's psychodynamic model suggests that autism is an escape from an adverse family environment.

▶ 13 The biopsychosocial model of autism proposes that the disorder results from a combination of lack of motivation to engage in social interactions combined with a lack of appropriate responses from the environment.

14 Lovaas's controversial behavioural treatment has proven moderately effective in the treatment of autism. Koegel and colleagues have developed a more strategic approach to such interventions.

15 Pharmacological interventions have also been shown to reduce a number of negative behaviours.

16 An estimated 3–5 per cent of children in the USA have ADHD.

17 ADHD seems to be driven by low levels of dopamine and serotonin and can be treated with drugs that increase these levels.

18 ADHD is driven by high levels of impulsivity, or lack of 'executive control'.

19 Barkley (1997) considered ADHD to reflect failures to control immediate impulses. By contrast, Sagvolden and colleagues considered the problem to reflect behavioural organization, an over-response to immediate reinforcers and a failure to learn routine behavioural sequences.

20 Family factors may also increase risk for ADHD, although relevant data are surprisingly sparse.

21 Treatment by Ritalin and Atomoxetine have been shown to facilitate behavioural interventions and education in children and adults.

22 A variety of self-management programmes may be effective in treating adult ADHD.

14.5 For discussion

1 Do changes in technology and society help or hinder people with learning difficulties to cope with everyday living?

2 What are the implications for a family that has a child with a significant learning disorder?

3 What limits should there be to health professionals' responses to 'challenging behaviour'?

4 What are the implications for a family that has a child with ADHD?

5 Should all families of children with ADHD be encouraged to take part in family therapy to minimize the negative impact of an adverse family environment?

14.6 Key term

Narcolepsy a disorder characterized by sudden and uncontrollable, though often brief, attacks of deep sleep.

14.7 Further reading

Baron-Cohen, S. (2008) *Asperger's Syndrome and Autism.* Oxford: Oxford University Press.

Emerson, E.C., Hatton, J., Felce, D. et al. (2001) *Learning Disabilities: The Fundamental Facts.* London: Mental Health Foundation.

Francis, K. (2005) Autism interventions: a critical update, *Developmental and Medical Child Neurology,* 47: 493–9.

Furman, L.M. (2008) Attention-deficit hyperactivity disorder (ADHD): does new research support old concepts? *Journal of Child Neurology,* 23: 775–84.

Grandin, T. and Scariano, M.M. (1996) *Emergence: Labeled Autistic.* New York: Warner.

Murphy, K. (2005) Psychosocial treatments for ADHD in teens and adults: a practice-friendly review, *Journal of Clinical Psychology,* 61: 607–19.

The following websites also have information about conditions in this chapter, their treatment, and people's experiences of them.

Learning difficulties

www.bild.org.uk/
www.nationalforum.co.uk/view.asp?id=0

Autism

www.autism.org/
www.autism.org.uk/

ADHD

www.adhd.org.uk/
www.pavilion.co.uk/add/english.html
www.ritalindeath.com/

Chapter 15

Neurological disorders

Chapter contents

Neurological disorders are the result of damage or degeneration of the brain following the onset of disease or trauma. This chapter focuses on the consequences of three types of disorder arising from two disease processes, Alzheimer's disease and multiple sclerosis (MS), and from head injury. In the case of Alzheimer's disease and MS, therapy is aimed at maintaining cognitive function and well-being in the face of a progressive deterioration of cognitive processes. Cognitive processes may be markedly impaired following head injury, but recover to some extent over time. Interventions here focus on maximizing the process of recovery and helping the individual cope with any residual cognitive deficits. By the end of the chapter, you should have an understanding of:

- The neurological processes that result in Alzheimer's disease and MS
- The psychological consequences of these diseases
- Interventions aimed at improving or maintaining both cognitive functioning and well-being as the diseases progress

- The immediate and long-term cognitive consequences of head injury
- Interventions used to maximize recovery following head injury.

15.1 Alzheimer's disease

Alzheimer's disease is the most common type of dementia, affecting between 2 and 10 per cent of those aged over 65 years, and at least 20 per cent of those aged over 80 years (e.g. Yamada et al. 2001). Although generally a condition found in elderly people, this is not always the case. Indeed, Alois Alzheimer's first description of the condition in the early years of the twentieth century was of a middle-aged woman. DSM-IV-TR defined Alzheimer's disease as a progressive disease having the following characteristics (often summarized as the 4As):

- *amnesia*: loss of memory
- *aphasia*: language disturbance
- *apraxia*: impaired ability to carry out motor activities despite intact motor function
- *agnosia*: failure to recognize or identify objects despite intact sensory function
- *disturbance in executive functioning* (that is, planning, organizing, sequencing, abstracting).

To achieve a diagnosis of Alzheimer's disease, these deficits should cause significant impairment in social or occupational functioning and represent a significant decline from previous levels of functioning. Memory loss is progressive, with recent memories typically lost before remote ones, which are thought to be preserved as a consequence of rehearsal over life. However, as the disease progresses, even remote and emotionally charged memories are lost. Early forgetfulness becomes a pathologically poor memory for present events, daily routine and even family members. Word-finding difficulties are common. In its final stages, Alzheimer's disease destroys the ability to communicate in any way.

In the early stages of Alzheimer's disease, levels of insight are high and most people are aware of their deficits. However, as the disease progresses, insight is lost, all sense of self seems to vanish, and the individual becomes completely dependent on others for care. Suspiciousness, paranoia and delusions are common. The individual may experience spontaneous changes in mood, including anger and irritability, as well as restlessness and agitation. Confusion is common, and may be worse at night when cues that may orient the individual in time and place are less obvious, and oxygen supply to the brain is at its least. Although most health care services aim to maximize the independence of the individual and maintain them in their own home, there may come a time when they are hospitalized. By this time, they may be confused for much of the time, incontinent, and respond only vaguely to their environment.

The duration of Alzheimer's disease from time of diagnosis to death can be 20 years or more: the typical duration is between 4 and 8 years. Over this time the individual will progress through the following stages:

- *Questionable dementia*: the individual begins to behave 'oddly' and relatives suspect there is a problem.

- *Mild dementia*: there is no question that there is a problem, but the affected individual is able to maintain independence.
- *Moderate dementia*: help is required for routine tasks; 'problem' behaviours such as wandering or aggression may be evident.
- *Severe dementia*: the individual becomes increasingly frail and eventually chair- or bed-bound.

Alzheimer's disease impacts not just on the individual with the disorder. Many elderly people, (the preponderance of them women), care for people with dementia in their own home, often until the disease is far progressed. These people typically experience significant stress (see Box 15.1). Molyneux et al. (2008), for example, reported that 21 per cent of their sample of carers were clinically depressed, and that the higher the functional impairment of the person with Alzheimer's, the greater the risk and level of depression. This stress may spill over into the way they respond to the individual with dementia. Cooper et al. (2009), for example, found that 34 per cent of carers reported abusing the person they were caring for 'at least sometimes' in the three months prior to their survey. Abuse was mainly verbal; only 1 per cent reported physical abuse.

Box 15.1 Focus groups for mild–moderate dementia

Recently, one of my colleagues, Lucie Byrne, ran some focus groups exploring the factors that contributed to the quality of life of people with mild–moderate dementia. Below are some quotes taken from the focus groups, with people telling us what added to or took away from their quality of life. The quotes are actually quite unremarkable, and could be made by virtually anyone of any age. Importantly, what the participants did not say was that their failing memory made their quality of life any worse. Some said that it might in the future. In fact, this became the theme related to this issue: however bad people's cognitive abilities were, they were always said not to be affecting their quality of life at the time, but might in the future. This is not to say that loss of memory is not an issue and concern for people with dementia – and some people may become profoundly depressed as a result of their failing abilities. But many other things contributed to their quality of life – this did not hinge only on their cognitive abilities.

Husband/wife/partner

- Like I said, my husband is still there and so I'm all right.
- All I want is to be with my husband that I've been with practically since I left school.
- I think the majority would say if anything happens to the partner, there's nothing worse could happen, nothing worse could happen.

Children/grandchildren

- You got the love of a family and the grandchildren, like me.
- If I lost one of my children, I would be devastated.

Family

- Lack of friends or relations [would make the quality of life worse].
- I've got a good father and I had a good mother, but I'm afraid I've just lost my mum and dad, you know.

Your friends

- Lack of friends or relations, loneliness, all these things take away the quality of life.
- Friendship, that's very important, isn't it?

Feeling happy

- If you are happy, you are fair enough. Sometimes people are not happy and that must be awful.

Feeling that you are useful

- If you could do a good turn for anybody, do it, that makes the quality of life, don't it?
- If you see a dirty cup there, what's stopping you picking it up and just giving it a swirl, helping that poor lady there? . . . but people walk past . . . and I like [gestures angrily], that's my way.

Feeling content/satisfied

- Well, I could say nothing [could make the quality of life worse], I'm quite contented as I am.
- Whatever I do, I am contented with.

Feeling that you have had a good life

- I'm an extremely lucky person, I think.
- I suppose you don't know me, but over the years I've really enjoyed my life.

Aetiology of Alzheimer's disease

Genetic factors

Up to 50 per cent of first-degree relatives of a person with Alzheimer's disease will develop the disorder (Korten et al. 1993). Genes on chromosomes 14, 21 and in particular the apoE4 gene on chromosome 19 have been implicated in Alzheimer's disease. ApoE4 is one of several forms, or alleles, of the apoE gene, the others being apoE2 and apoE3. People who carry two apoE4 genes are about eight times more likely to develop Alzheimer's disease than those who have two of the E3 allele. The apoE4 gene may bring forward the onset of Alzheimer's disease by as much as 17 years (Warwick Daw et al. 2000). However, it is found in only 40 per cent of people who develop Alzheimer's disease and many people who carry the gene do not develop the condition. In addition, risk of Alzheimer's may be reduced by changing modifiable risk factors even in individuals at genetic risk due to apoE variants (see Table 15.1) (Schipper 2009).

Three other genes have been identified as responsible for the rare early onset familial form of the disease: the amyloid precursor protein (APP) gene, the presenilin 1 (PSEN1) gene, and the presenilin 2 (PSEN2) gene. Mutations in these genes, however, account for less than 5 per cent of the total number of cases of Alzheimer's disease (Rocchi et al. 2003).

Neurological processes

Alzheimer's disease is the result of premature degeneration of brain systems. Degeneration is progressive, and the course of Alzheimer's disease can be mapped against the geography of the brain affected. Problems typically initiate in the entorhinal cortex before proceeding to the hippocampus, and then gradually spread to other regions, particularly the cerebral cortex (Hedden and Gabrieli 2005). As the hippocampal neurons degenerate, short-term memory falters, as does the ability to perform routine tasks. As the disease spreads through the cerebral cortex, it begins to take away language.

The nature of the changes that occur appears to be both structural, including the development of beta amyloid plaques and neurofibrillary tangles, and to involve a number of neurotransmitters. Beta amyloid results from damage to amyloid precursor protein (APT), which lies within the neuron cell membranes. It is a member of a larger family of proteins which enclose cells and act as a barrier to control which substances go in and out of them. Damage to APT results in the formation of beta amyloid fragments, which may clump together to form amyloid plaques and cause neuronal death, perhaps because they form tiny channels in neuron membranes through which uncontrolled amounts of calcium can flow (Sinha et al. 2000). Neuro-fibrillary tangles comprise abnormal collections of twisted threads inside nerve cells. The chief component of these tangles is a protein called tau. In healthy individuals, this binds and stabilizes the microtubules that carry nutrients and molecules from the bodies of the cells to the ends of the axon. In Alzheimer's disease, tau is changed chemically, and this altered tau twists the microfilaments around each other to form tangles. The resultant collapse of the transport system causes errors in communication between nerve cells and neuronal death (Luque and Jaffe 2009).

The most important neurotransmitter implicated in Alzheimer's disease is acetylcholine: levels decline moderately in normal ageing but drop by about 90 per cent in people with Alzheimer's disease (see Luque and Jaffe 2009). Acetylcholine is involved in memory formation and influences neuronal activity in the hippocampus and cerebral cortex. Other neurotransmitters may also be involved. Serotonin and norepinephrine levels are lower than normal in some people with Alzheimer's disease, which may contribute to sensory disturbances and aggressive behaviour (Zarros et al. 2005). They may also be linked to other psychological conditions associated with the early stages of Alzheimer's disease, including depression and anxiety.

Modifiable risk factors

Risk for Alzheimer's disease is determined in part by environmental factors, although their exact roles in its aetiology are little understood. One consistent risk factor appears to be a history of head injury (McDowell 2001). A previous hypothesis that exposure to high levels of aluminium may result in Alzheimer's disease has generally not been supported, although exposure to water massively polluted by aluminium in the UK may have resulted in a measurable decline in cognitive performance in a small number of people (Altmann et al. 1999). Protective factors include high levels of physical activity, moderate levels of red wine, and a diet high in vitamins B6, B12 and folic acid. High levels of consumption of fatty fish may also be of benefit. Huang et al. (2005) found that people who ate fatty fish at least twice a week were 41 per cent less likely to develop Alzheimer's disease than those who ate them less than once a month. A number of medications may also be protective, including non-steroidal anti-inflammatory drugs and oestrogen replacement therapy in post-menopausal women. One particularly important group of drugs which may prevent onset of Alzheimer's disease is known as statins. These drugs are typically used in the treatment of heart disease and reduce levels of cholesterol. Austen et al. (2002) estimated that they may reduce the risk of developing Alzheimer's disease by up to 70 per cent – although the mechanism of this protection is not understood.

Table 15.1 **Relative risk (compared to an individual without each risk factor) of developing Alzheimer's disease attributable to various modifiable factors**

Factors that increase risk	Risk ratio	Factors that decrease risk	Risk ratio
High blood pressure	1.5–2.3	High omega-3 fatty acid/fish in diet	0.3
Diabetes	2.03	Moderate consumption of wine	0.53
Stroke	1.83	High levels of exercise	0.5–0.69
High cholesterol levels	2.1–3.1	Cholesterol-lowering drugs	0.26
Depression	4.2	Anti-inflammatory medication	0.42
Smoking	1.99–2.3	Blood pressure-reducing medication	0.89
Very low vitamin E levels	2.10		
Head injury (serious)	2.32–4.51		

Source: adapted from Schipper (2009)

Treatment of Alzheimer's disease

Pharmacological interventions

If reductions in acetylcholine cause Alzheimer's disease, increasing available acetylcholine levels may reverse its symptoms. Drugs that do so prevent its breakdown in the synaptic cleft by acetyl-cholinesterase and increase uptake in the postsynaptic receptor (see Chapter 4). An important group of drugs, known as acetyl-cholinesterase inhibitors, such as donepezil, generally achieve short-term cognitive improvements in individuals at early and mid-stage Alzheimer's, although they delay rather than prevent cognitive decline, the effects are only modest, and not all people respond to the drugs (see Birks 2006). Unfortunately, many people taking them experience significant side-effects, most notably gastrointestinal tract disturbances, and up to 35 per cent of participants in clinical trials have been withdrawn from medication for this reason (Rogers et al. 1998). A second method of increasing acetylcholine levels is through ingestion of nicotine, which triggers the release of acetylcholine, and has been shown to improve memory in animal experiments (Srivareerat et al. 2009). People with Alzheimer's disease have also shown short-term gains on a number of cognitive tasks and mood following injections of nicotine. However, there are, as yet, insufficient data to decide whether or not nicotine can prove effective in the treatment of Alzheimer's disease.

A different pharmacological approach involves attempts to block the production of beta amyloid within the brain. In evaluating this approach, Sparks et al. (2005) compared the effectiveness of this type of drug (a statin) with that of a placebo intervention in people with mild to moderate Alzheimer's disease. At one-year follow-up, the active intervention proved superior to placebo, with people in this condition showing less disease progression. Whether these initial improvements will be maintained for longer periods is yet to be assessed.

Psychological approaches

Psychological interventions aim to maximize quality of life and functional ability as the disease progresses. Support groups, involving other people with similar problems, may provide support or coping strategies in the early stages of Alzheimer's disease (Yale 1995). Three more formal therapeutic approaches are frequently used in its later stages.

Reality orientation (RO: Holden and Woods 1995) involves providing confused elderly people with relevant information to help them maintain an accurate understanding of the world. There are two types of RO:

- *24-hour RO* involves establishing an environment with multiple cues to orient the individual in time, place and person: large clocks and calendars, reminders of the name of an institution or ward, name badges, and so on. Social interactions with the person are also designed to provide relevant information ('Hello, Mr Jones. It's Tom here . . . It's really cold outside, like it usually is in January . . .'). Sentences are simple and specific, repeating information throughout the day and even within conversations.
- *Classroom RO* involves small groups of people meeting for between 30 and 60 minutes. Despite its name, these are held in comfortable rooms, with easy chairs and a relaxed atmosphere. Attenders are matched according to ability, and sessions involve discussion and information provision, with memory triggered by multiple cues and modes of information: newspapers, pictures, talking, and so on.

In their review of six well-controlled trials of RO, Spector et al. (2000) concluded that RO achieved small but significant gains on measures of verbal orientation in comparison with no treatment or unstructured therapy, but that any gains following the cessation of therapy were soon dissipated. Accordingly, RO may need to be a continous form of intervention. There appears to be limited generalization to other cognitive or behavioural skills, although Reeve and Ivison (1985) did report some improvements on measures of incontinence following a combination of classroom and 24-hour RO. Reality orientation may also combine with other treatments to maximize gains. Onder et al. (2005), for example, found both RO and donepezil contributed independently to cognitive gains made in a group of people with Alzheimer's disease. Perhaps for reasons considered in the Stop and think … box, more recent studies have evaluated a different form of RO, known as cognitive stimulation. A typical programme involves elements of RO combined with less structured approaches to facilitating cognitive processing, including reminiscence (see below). A key difference between the two approaches is that RO encourages rehearsal of knowledge. While this may occur in cognitive stimulation, more emphasis is placed on information *processing*. Thus, an activity known as 'faces' may ask group members 'Who looks the youngest?', 'What do these people have in common?', rather than 'Do you recognize these people?'. In one study of this approach, Spector et al. (2003) found evidence of increases in both quality of life and cognitive performance following one such programme relative to a control group who received no intervention.

Stop and think …

Whatever its outcome, RO can present difficulties for those trying to implement it, particularly when it may be necessary to remind people of distressing information. Many people with Alzheimer's disease, for example, forget about the death of a loved one, and in their confusion may start looking for them or demanding they come and see them. Proper adherence to RO involves a carer telling them that their loved one is dead. This can be devastating news and cause significant distress. Unfortunately, they may forget this information after a period of time and once more start looking for their loved one, requiring the carer to once more break the news of their loved one's death: a cycle that can be distressing for both the individual and carer. Is this fair and a reasonable way to treat people, or, in this case, is ignorance really bliss?

Validation therapy

As a consequence of the potentially problematic aspects of RO, Feil (1990) introduced a very different form of therapy. Validation therapy involves listening to the fears and concerns of the affected individual, taking time to fully understand their problems and to 'validate' them by valuing what they have to say. These conversations can provide opportunities to identify and modify any false beliefs, but this is not a core element of this approach. The focus is on listening and responding to the emotional rather than the factual content of what is said.

In group therapy, small groups of individuals may engage in discussions designed to elicit 'universal' feelings of anger, separation or loss (Bleathman and Morton 1992). Feil suggested that by verbalizing memories and thoughts and having them validated by the group, the person gains a feeling of being accepted. This emphasis on the need to deal with unresolved conflicts has elements of psychodynamic therapy, while the therapeutic use of empathy and acceptance of the individual's personal view of the world provide a strong humanistic element. Evaluation of the effectiveness of this approach is largely anecdotal or based on uncontrolled case histories, although one small randomized controlled trial has been reported (Tondi et al. 2007). In this, older adults with dementia (of various kinds) were randomly allocated to either validation therapy or usual care. Those in the validation therapy experienced reductions in distress, agitation, apathy and irritability. Whether validation therapy is better than other active interventions is not clear.

Reminiscence therapy is based on Erikson's (1980) developmental model in which life-review is considered to occur naturally towards the end of life. This review may be generally positive or negative, with a resultant outcome of ego integrity or despair. In individual therapy, the therapist aids the individual through this already occurring self-analysis in order to make it more conscious and efficient. There are three forms of reminiscence therapy (McMahon and Rhudick 1964). *Story-type reminiscence* involves remembering factual memories for pleasure. *Life-review* involves remembering and discussing memories, both good and bad, which come naturally to consciousness. Finally, *halo reminiscence* involves the repeated recollection of a particular situation involving guilt or despair. Life-review and halo reminiscence are thought to help resolve past conflicts. In group therapy, small groups typically review participants' lives through the use of prompts, including old photographs, television and radio broadcasts, and so on. As with validation therapy, there are few studies of the effectiveness of reminiscence therapy. Participants typically enjoy their involvement in reminiscence groups, and there are reports of small improvements in mood (Wang 2007) and increased self-esteem and life satisfaction (Lai et al. 2004) following group attendance. However, there is little evidence that it is more effective than other group activities, and some studies (e.g. Ito et al. 2007) have reported no benefit.

Helping the carers

Caring for people with Alzheimer's disease at home places enormous strain on the carers, who are usually elderly themselves and often in poor health. Many benefit from some form of support and help. This can be provided by voluntary bodies such as the Alzheimer's Disease Society in the UK, and short periods during which the affected person stays in hospital to provide a break for the carer. They may also benefit from other, more formal interventions. In a meta-analysis of 44 studies designed to provide education and/or support to help carers cope more effectively with their stress, Thompson and Briggs (2000) concluded that group and individual interventions reduced both perceptions of burden and feelings of depression – although the effects across studies were varied and relatively modest. In one interesting study, Gallagher-Thompson and Steffen (1994) contrasted CBT and psychodynamic interventions in the treatment of depressed carers of elderly relatives. By the end of the intervention phase, both interventions proved equally effective: 71 per cent of participants no longer met the criteria for depression. However, those who had been in the caring role for a relatively short time benefited most from dynamic therapy. Those who had cared for their relative for a longer period gained most from the cognitive behavioural intervention. It may be that people relatively new to the caring role benefit from exploration of their new role and its implications, while those who have been involved for longer benefit from learning more practical techniques for coping with their day-to-day stress. A second way of helping carers cope is to provide them with strategies to help them manage the behaviour of their relative more effectively. In one such study Gavrilova et al. (2009) examined the impact of a relatively brief intervention involving two sessions providing basic information about dementia, and two sessions developing personal strategies for coping with problem behaviours. Although measures of distress did not differ between those in the intervention group and a control condition at six month follow-up, those in the intervention group reported signficantly less 'carer burden' (i.e. stress directly related to caring for the individual with dementia).

Case formulation

Mr F was a 74-year-old man, diagnosed with severe dementia, who was now living on a long-stay ward in a hospital in Southampton. He had previously been a Colonel in the army, and had retired to Southampton with his wife, who was physically infirm. His children lived in Yorkshire, and had little contact with him. While living with his wife, he had become increasingly forgetful. Initially, this was attributed to his 'getting on', but it soon became evident that the problem was more severe. Over a period of a year, he began to forget the names of friends, became increasingly lost when away from their home, and lost any sense of time or order in his life. He even forgot the name of his wife, and on occasion did not recognize her, becoming aggressive and challenging the presence of this person in the room with him. His sleep-wake cycle was disrupted, and he was often awake at night, when his confusion became worse. He became verbally aggressive when stopped doing things he wished to do such as leaving the house alone or driving their car and his wife had to hide the house and car keys to avoid such confrontations. At such times he barked orders at her and expected her to do as he wished. She felt intimidated by his behaviour, because she feared physical violence and was herself frail. He was admitted to hospital for a long term as a consequence of his confused and verbally aggressive behaviour. It took some weeks for him to adapt to his new environment, but the transition was eased by the regular visits made by his wife to see him. After a month of being in hospital, however, the ward staff were having increasing difficulties in dealing with his regular outbursts and verbally aggressive behaviour. They reported that these may occur several times a day, and were quite frightening to some of the staff involved.

Assessment and formulation

In response to these episodes of aggressive behaviour, the ward staff asked the ward psychologist to conduct a functional analysis. In this, a psychology assistant observed Mr F's behaviour for a period of two weeks, noting down the antecedents, consequences and nature of his aggressive behaviour at all times. Behaviour was observed at different times in the day – morning, evening and during the night. It became clear that many of the incidents of aggressive behaviour were at times that Mr F went to the toilet – or should have gone. The antecedents to the outbursts were that Mr F would become agitated and start to wander around the ward. Staff would approach him to see why he was walking around the ward, an act that often increased his agitation. If they thought he was going to the toilet, they would take him there, and help him to take his trousers down. This provoked further anger and verbal aggression. If they did not spot that he was walking around the ward and intervene, he was frequently incontinent. His behaviour usually involved him becoming angry and verbally aggressive, demanding that he not be manhandled, and asking to be let out of the ward. The consequences were that Mr F remained agitated for some time after the incident and prone to further outbursts. Once he had been taken from the toilet to the patient seating area, staff generally ignored him.

▶   From these observations, it was hypothesized that Mr F was not responding to early physical cues that he needed to urinate. As a consequence, he did not try to get to the toilet until his bladder was extremely full and he was desperate to go the toilet. His memory was poor, so he was unable to immediately remember the way to the toilet, which was some way from the patient seating area. His desperation led to some of his anger and agitation. In addition, he was unhappy about being helped to go to the toilet, wanting to do this himself, and expressed this anger towards whoever was trying to help him.

Intervention

Following the period of observation, the ward psychologist considered a number of solutions, each of which was relatively simple to initiate (at least in principle). The first involved preventing Mr F reaching the point of desperation before he tried to go the toilet. This could be achieved by instigating a regular series of prompts for him to go the toilet. Mr F could be asked by a designated member of the ward staff whether or not he wanted to go to the toilet on a regular basis throughout the day (every half to one hour). If he said he wanted to go, he would be reminded where the toilets were, but not taken there by a member of staff. If Mr F deviated from going to the toilet on any occasion, the same member of staff would remind him he was going to the toilet and accompany him to it. On a more general level, a coloured line could be painted on the (linoleum) floor between the toilet and the patient seating area. This should be the same colour as the toilets, and Mr F (and other patients with similar memory problems) could be reminded to follow the line to the toilets every time they were directed to them. It was hoped that by ensuring Mr F reached the toilet in plenty of time to sort himself out, help at this time would be less needed. Accordingly, it might not be necessary for staff to help Mr F once at the toilet.

The aims of the intervention were therefore to: (i) increase the time available for Mr F to get to the toilet and obviate the stress and anger that were associated with his being desperate to urinate (and to avoid the risk of incontinence); (ii) provide cues to help Mr F get to the toilet without help; and (iii) minimize his embarrassment at being helped in the toilet by the ward staff.

These intervention strategies were discussed with the ward staff who agreed to implement them. Accordingly, the changes in staff behaviour and the painted line were established, the psychology assistant continued to monitor the behaviour for a further two weeks, and gave feedback to the ward staff and psychologist on any progress or problems they were experiencing. Thankfully, the intervention progressed well. The staff explained to Mr F why they were regularly asking him if he wanted to go to the toilet. He did not always remember this, so they had to explain on a number of occasions. However, after a few days he stopped asking them why they were doing so. He also began to go to the toilet following the prompt. He had to be guided to the toilet on a number of occasions, but was always reminded that the coloured line on the floor led to the toilet – an association helped by the colour of the toilets being the same colour as the line. As a consequence he was not only more likely to get to the toilet and avoid confrontation with staff, the frequency of his incontinence was also markedly reduced.

15.2 Head injury

Closed head injury occurs when an individual is struck on the head with no resultant damage to the skull or specific brain injury. This type of trauma usually results in the whole brain shifting within the skull at the time of the incident, resulting in diffuse damage. About half the cases of closed head injury result from road traffic accidents. The second highest cause is falls, particularly among frail elderly people and young children. Violence accounts for a further 20 per cent of cases, while sports injuries account for about 3 per cent. Alcohol consumption also adds to risk. People aged between 15 and 25 years old are most at risk. In the UK, there are up to 150 cases of closed head injury requiring hospitalization for every 100 000 people each year (Jennett 1996).

One simple index of the severity of injury is that of 'time to follow commands': that is, the time after trauma it takes the head-injured person to be able to respond to simple commands. Mild head injury is indicated by a time to follow commands of less than one hour; for moderate head injury this time is between one hour and 13 days; for severe head injury it is 14 days or more. Between 30 and 50 per cent of people will die as a result of severe head injury. About 10 per cent will still be in a 'vegetative' (non-responsive) state three months after the trauma, decreasing to about 4 per cent at six-month follow-up, and 2–3 per cent one year following injury. For those who survive their injury and recover consciousness, recovery follows a typical pattern. The first phase involves a period of acute confusion and disorientation during which they are unable to form and retain new memories: post-traumatic amnesia. The longer the period of amnesia, the poorer the outcome in the longer term (Willemse-van Son et al. 2007). Following resolution of post-traumatic amnesia, the majority of people with moderate or severe head injuries experience significant physical, cognitive and behavioural impairment, although younger and more intelligent people usually fare better than others due to their 'spare neural capacity' (Green et al. 2008). Most physical problems eventually resolve, although a minority of people continue to experience a wide range of symptoms including persistent muscle spasticity, impaired swallowing and balance disturbances. About 5 per cent of those with moderate to severe closed head injury develop epileptic seizures: this compares with 35–50 per cent of people with penetrating head injuries. Risk for developing epilepsy continues to be higher than the population norm for as long as five years after the original trauma.

Cognitive and neuro-behavioural deficits are the most common residual symptoms of closed head injury. Diffuse brain injury results in a typical pattern of cognitive deficits, including slowed cognitive speed, decreased attention plus impaired memory, complex language skills and impaired 'executive function' (e.g. Malojcic et al. 2008; Schooler et al. 2008). The latter includes problems in working memory, problem-solving, monitoring performance and organizing behaviour. Most recovery occurs in the first six months following injury, although recovery may continue more slowly for a further year. One month following injury, almost all people with moderate to severe injury have detectable cognitive impairments. Six months following injury about 8 per cent of those with moderate injury and 16 per cent of those with severe injury will require hospital care as a result of cognitive disabilities. Ten per cent of people with a severe head injury will still require hospital care one year following the event; only about a quarter will ever return to work (Sherer et al. 2000).

Neuro-behavioural symptoms experienced by people with head injuries include increased irritability, headaches, anxiety, difficulty in concentrating, fatigue, restlessness and depression and poorer quality of life and sleep (e.g. Baumann et al. 2007; Ulvik et al. 2008). These are more common than either physical or cognitive deficits and may have a greater impact on long-term outcome. One important feature of long-term recovery from head injury is a lack of self-awareness (Bach and David 2006). Perhaps for this reason, relatives of people who have sustained a head injury frequently report more psychological changes than the affected individual, as well as high levels of depression (Rivera et al. 2007).

Cognitive rehabilitation following head injury

Rehabilitation following moderate to severe head injury involves a number of treatment approaches provided by a variety of health professionals. Medical treatments include pain control for head-aches, drug treatment of epilepsy and surgical treatment for hydrocephalus. Physiotherapy may maintain muscle flexibility and strength and occupational therapy can teach skills necessary for self-care or return to some form of work. Speech therapists may work with the individual to improve their understanding and articulation of speech. From a psychological perspective, the main intervention is aimed at the cognitive and behavioural consequences of the trauma. The rest of this section will focus on some of the techniques used to improve cognitive function or help the individual cope with enduring cognitive deficits.

Coping with memory problems

A number of general techniques can improve memory, including memory drills, combining imagery with words to improve subsequent recall, and so on. Specific techniques have also been developed for use with people with head trauma. These have frequently involved very specific learning tasks. Wilson (1989), for example, used a preview, question, read, state and test (PQRST) model to improve encoding and recall of lists of words. This involved the participant examining the task, thinking about its requirements, and then reading a list of words over a number of trials both aloud and silently, before testing. The additional cognitive processing required in this approach was thought to enhance learning in comparison with simple repetition of lists of words. Unfortunately, memory gains made in such sessions frequently do not generalize beyond the specific memory task. In addition, as many people with head injuries underestimate their memory loss, attempts to implement such programmes are not always acceptable. These findings led Wilson (2005) to conclude that retraining memory is likely to have little impact on memory *per se*, but teaching people to cope with real-life memory problems, for example, through the use of memory aids, is potentially of benefit. Memory aids may include use of a tape-recorder or hand-written notes, palmtop computers, time reminders such as alarm clocks, phone calls or radio pagers, and the use of personal organizers or orientation boards within the home.

People with significant impairment may need lengthy training in the use of memory aids. Sohlberg et al. (2001), for example, recommended a three-stage process of training to use a memory notebook. The first stage involved systematic training in the contents and purpose of the notebook. This was reinforced by a question-and-answer approach ('What are the five sections of your notebook?'). During the application phase, individuals practised using the book through role play. In one of their studies, it took one participant in their programme as long as 17 days to acquire the skills necessary to use the notebook. External memory aids can also be helpful in reminding the individual to do various tasks they otherwise may have forgotten to do. Wilson et al. (2005), for example, evaluated the use of a paging system that reminded people with head injuries to do various tasks through the day. Most of those given the pager benefited both when they had it and during the seven weeks after returning it. Its use seems to have established behavioural patterns that were self-sustaining, at least in the short term.

Improving 'executive function'

A second problem that people face following head injury is a decrement in problem-solving skills. Interventions designed to compensate for this have focused on breaking down problem-solving into specific stages. One such model, which utilized a simple acronym, *IDEAL*, to trigger each phase, was developed by Bransford and Stein (1984):

I	involved identification of the problem.
D	involved defining the problem (its specific nature and causes).
E	involved exploring alternative approaches to dealing with the problem.
A	involved acting on the plan developed in stage E.
L	involved checking on the effectiveness of any chosen plan.

People with head injuries may also be taught not to try to deal with multiple problems simultaneously, but to identify and deal with specific problems one at a time. Where people lose the attention required for problem-solving and other tasks, attention compensation training may be used. This involves the individual first identifying when they are losing concentration, and then using strategies such as self-instruction (Meichenbaum 1985: 'Come on now, pay attention here . . .') to help remain focused. External cues can also be useful in initiating behaviour (Wilson 2001).

A number of standardized programmes have also been developed to remediate attention problems. The *Attention Process Training programme* (APT) of Park et al. (1999) did so by using a number of differing strategies. Sustained attention was trained by exercises including attention tapes that required listening for target words or word/number sequences and pressing a buzzer when identified, listening to a paragraph and testing comprehension, and mental arithmetic exercises. Shifting attention was trained by exercises including tapes that required identification of one type of target word followed by identification of another. Tasks were presented in order of difficulty and repeated until the individual was able to cope effectively with the task demands. If necessary, they were practised at home with the help of relatives as well as in the clinic. This type of approach has proven moderately effective. Most studies have shown gains on psychometric measures of memory or attention following such interventions. Fewer have looked at 'real-world' improvements, although there is some evidence that improvements can be made on measures as diverse as driving skills, independent living, and return to work (Sohlberg and Mateer 2001). Indeed, relatively few formal randomized trials of any cognitive rehabilitation programme have been conducted, with the majority of studies still involving single cases or small participant groups with no control condition (Cernich et al. 2010). Nevertheless, what evidence there is suggests a small but clinically significant benefit following cognitive rehabilitation.

Coping with negative emotions

Given the high levels of depression and suicide among people who have sustained a significant head injury, there is little doubt that many would benefit from some form of psychological or pharmacological intervention to help moderate their mood. The American National Institutes of Health (NIH Consensus Development Panel 1999), for example, noted that psychotherapy could be an important aid to emotional recovery, reducing depression and improving the low self-esteem associated with cognitive dysfunction. They suggested that such interventions should provide emotional support, explanations of the injury and its likely outcome, help achieve increased self-esteem by maximizing gains towards achievable goals, reduce denial, and increase the individual's ability to relate to family and society. Subsequent research has validated this optimism. Bell et al. (2005), for example, found that a series of telephone calls providing motivational strategies, counselling and education up to nine months following discharge resulted in better outcomes on measures of functional status and well-being than standard care one year following discharge. Bradbury et al. (2008) found that a simplified cognitive behavioural approach delivered either by telephone or live in a group, depending on participant preferences, proved more successful in changing measures of well-being than an educational programme.

Helping the carers

People living with, and caring for, a person who has sustained a head injury may themselves experience significant stress and distress (Harris et al. 2001). While there is some evidence that strain on the family reduces as a consequence of improvements in cognitive deficits and health service input, there is a strong argument for the provision of services to help the family cope with the stress of caring for a person with a head injury more directly. Despite this, just as with studies to help people cope emotionally with the trauma and consequences of head injury, there are few studies of the effectiveness of such programmes, and most of these are uncontrolled and naturalistic studies. As a result, the impact of family or partner support programmes is difficult to judge (Sinnakaruppan and Williams 2001).

15.3 Multiple sclerosis (MS)

Multiple sclerosis is a neurological condition resulting from the destruction of the myelin sheath that surrounds all nerve cells within the brain and central nervous system. Sclerotic plaques develop where this destruction occurs, which block or distort the normal transmission of nerve impulses. As this may occur in any part of the brain or spinal cord, the symptoms they cause differ markedly across individuals, and include loss of limb function, loss of bowel and/or bladder control, blindness due to inflammation of the optic nerve, and cognitive impairment. Muscular spasticity is a common feature, particularly in the upper limbs; 95 per cent of people with MS experience debilitating fatigue. This prevents any sustained physical activity in about 40 per cent of people. Nearly half the people with MS consider this to be their most serious symptom (Rizzo et al. 2004). Between 30 and 50 per cent of people with the condition require walking aids or a wheelchair for mobility.

The course of MS differs across individuals. Onset before the age of 15 years is rare; 20 per cent of those who develop MS have a benign form of the disease in which symptoms show little or no progression after the initial attack. A few people experience malignant MS, resulting in a swift and relentless decline and significant disability or even death shortly after disease onset. Onset of this type of MS is usually after the age of 40 years. The majority of people have an episodic condition, with acute flare-ups followed by periods of remission. Each flare-up is usually followed by a failure to recover to previous levels of function, resulting in a slowly deteriorating condition. Death is usually due to complications of MS, including choking, pneumonia and renal failure.

Suicide rates are significantly higher among people with MS than in the general population (Brønnum-Hansen et al. 2005).

Susan provides a glimpse of what it feels like to have MS. At the time of our talk she was taking antidepressants for her depression and, as you will read, was having problems coming to terms with her disorder:

I developed MS about four years ago. It was odd to start with. I didn't think I had anything serious, although you do worry about symptoms you don't understand. It started when I had some problems with my sight. I couldn't see as well as I used to be able to – it came on suddenly so I didn't think it was age or anything normal. I think at the time I was also a bit more clumsy than I had been – nothing obvious, but I dropped things a bit more than before. Nothing really that you'd notice unless other things were happening as well. I went to my GP about my eyes and he sent me to see a neurologist. He tried to reassure me that there was nothing too badly wrong and that he wanted to check out a few symptoms. But I began to worry then . . . you don't get sent on to see the hospital doctors unless there is anything really wrong with you. He suggested that he thought it might be MS, which was why he was not sending me to an eye specialist.

I got to see the neurologist pretty quickly and she ran a few tests over a few weeks – testing my muscle strength, coordination, scans and so on . . . sticking needles into me at various times. The upshot of this was that I was diagnosed as having MS. My consultant told me and my husband together, and allowed us to ask questions about things. We also got to speak to a specialist nurse who has helped us over the years. She was able to take the time to tell us more than the doctor about what to expect and what support we could have. Although I think it was nice to hear the diagnosis from the doctor.

I must admit that I found it really hard to deal with things at the beginning – you don't know what to expect and perhaps you expect the worst. You hear all sorts of horror stories about people dying with MS and that. And no one can really reassure you that you won't have problems . . . Over the last few years, I've got to know my body and seen things getting worse. But it happens gradually and a lot of the time there are no changes. So that is reassuring that things aren't going to collapse too quickly and I won't be left incontinent and unable to feed myself for a long time – hopefully not ever!

The worse thing is the tiredness and clumsiness. My eyes have actually got better, thank goodness. I use sticks to get around the house. Sometimes I can walk a little out of the house. Often I have to take the wheelchair. I just get exhausted too quickly, there isn't a lot of point trying to walk, because I cannot go far . . .

I hate having MS. I used to take part in sports, go out, be lively. Now I can't do any of that. I'm tired . . . down a lot of the time. I think the two often go together. My memory was never that good, but now it seems to be worse than ever. I can hold conversations, but keeping my concentration up for a long time is difficult. So, people find you difficult to deal with. I know my husband feels that way. He married a lively, sporty, slim woman . . . now I'm lethargic, down, putting on weight because I eat and don't exercise – even though they tell me not to, so I can keep mobile and not develop skin problems. I don't go out very much because it's such a hassle in my wheelchair . . . cities were not designed for people in wheelchairs . . . and people don't like people in wheelchairs. You are ignored . . . and just want to say, 'Hey, I'm here. I have a brain you know . . .' I know this sounds sorry for myself. And sometimes I feel more positive. But I find living with uncertainty difficult. Will I have a bad day today? Will I have a flare-up – have to go to hospital, take mega-steroids, come out worse than when I went in? I guess you have to live for the day . . . but it can be difficult.

Aetiology of MS

Genetic factors

The lifetime risk of developing MS for the general population is 1 in 800. This increases to 1 in 50 for the children of affected individuals and 1 in 20 for their siblings. However, increased concordance among family members may not exclusively indicate a genetic aetiology. Siblings who both develop MS usually do so in the same calendar year rather than the same age, indicating the possibility of common environmental factors impacting on risk for MS (Haines and Pericak-Vance 1999). Other evidence of genetic factors includes the markedly differing rates of the illness across the world (Rosati 2001). Multiple sclerosis is rare among a variety of groups including Uzbeks, Kazakhs, native Siberians, Chinese, Japanese, Africans and New Zealand Maoris. Rates of MS in Sardinia, and among Parsis and Palestinians are particularly high. The specific genes involved are, as is frequently the case, still to be fully understood. However, genes affecting immune processes (including the human leukocyte antigen alleles and interleukin -2 and -7 receptor genes) are clearly implicated in its pathology (Holmøy et al. 2009).

Biological mechanisms

The aetiology of MS is still not fully understood, although the favoured hypotheses are that it is the result of errors in the immune system or viral infection. One chemical within the immune system, called gamma-interferon, is particularly implicated in MS: high levels of gamma-interferon co-occur with high levels of MS activity. How gamma-interferon affects the disease process is not yet fully understood, but it is likely that it stimulates the immune system, through chemical messengers known as interleukins, to produce cytotoxic T cells. These are responsible for attacking and destroying diseased or damaged body cells. These cells can attack cells directly and are usually able to discriminate between 'self' cells (those of the body) and 'non-self' cells (damaged or cancerous cells, or pathogens). In MS, it seems to be that the activated cytotoxic T cells wrongly identify the myelin sheath of nerve cells within the brain and spinal column as 'non-self', and attempt to destroy it. Viral infections may act as a trigger to the production of gamma-interferon: hence, the link between viral infections and MS.

Stress and MS

There is good evidence that stress can influence activity within the immune system. Given the role of the immune system in the aetiology of MS, it is therefore possible that stress may influence the onset and course of the condition. Evidence for the former was provided by Liu et al. (2009) who retrospectively found that the onset of MS was associated with high levels of negative life events, family problems, and a variety of negative emotions – all of which were higher than in a comparable group without MS. Longitudinal studies of the impact of stress on the progression of MS also indicate that stress may have a role in MS. In one such study, Mohr et al. (2000a) took various measures of stress and disease progression every four weeks over periods of up to 100 weeks in a group of people with MS. They found that increases in personal conflict or disruption to routine typically preceded increases in disease activity. Similarly, Ackerman et al. (2002) found that 85 per cent of the exacerbations in symptoms experienced by their cohort of women with MS were preceded by a period of stress. These typically occurred in the two weeks preceding the increase in symptoms. They estimated that participants were 13 times more likely to experience an exacerbation of their condition following an episode of stress than during periods of no stress. Similarly, Brown et al. (2006) found relapse to be predicted by acute, but not chronic, stress. Of course, the exacerbation of symptoms may itself prove stressful. Schwartz et al. (1999) who found a bi-directional relationship between stress and MS: risk of disease progression increased as a consequence of stress, and increases in disease progression contributed to reported levels of stress – a vicious cycle between stress and disease progression.

Psychological sequelae of MS

Cognitive problems

As well as physical problems, people with MS frequently experience a number of cognitive deficits in memory, attention, conceptual reasoning, verbal fluency and abstracting abilities. Nearly half the people with MS complain of some degree of cognitive impairment and memory problems. The latter do not follow a distinct progression, but usually involve problems in retrieval from long-term memory storage: short-term and recognition memory is seldom impaired. Speed of information processing is also slowed in comparison to people without the condition, partly due to slowed psychomotor performance as a result of slowed neuronal activity (Brassington and Marsh 1999). Visual and auditory attention may also be impaired. Perhaps because of the cognitive deterioration they experience, subjective reports of cognitive deficits may differ markedly from more objective measures (Christodoulou et al. 2005). About 20 per cent of people with relatively mild levels of MS experience measurable cognitive deficits (Patti et al. 2009). Increasing cognitive deficits can be charted against progressive brain damage. Feinstein et al. (1993) conducted two-weekly cognitive assessments and magnetic resonance imaging (MRI) scans of brain lesions over a six-month period in a group of people with MS. Performance on the cognitive tasks varied as a function of disease progression as measured by the MRI. The test performance of participants whose MRI scans showed increasing lesions deteriorated over time, despite the practice effects of repeated administration. By contrast, those people whose MS did not progress either maintained or improved their scores. Damage to the corpus callosum, the bundle of fibres connecting both hemispheres of the cortex, appears implicated in a variety of cognitive impairments including visuo-spatial ability and speed of problem-solving. Left parietal lesions are associated with impaired memory and learning (Huber et al. 1992).

Emotional reactions to MS

People with MS experience a variety of emotional responses. The prevalence of depression among people with MS varies between 14 and 57 per cent, higher than among people with other neurological conditions (Schubert and Foliart 1993). About half the people who develop MS will be clinically depressed at some time during the course of the illness (Siegert and Abernethy 2005). Whether this is a direct result of neuronal damage or a psychological reaction to the experience of the disease is not clear. It may, of course, be both.

Perhaps the strongest indicator that depression can be the result of neurological changes is that depression can be the first sign of MS, preceding obvious neurocognitive symptoms by months or years (Berrios and Quemada 1990). Proponents of the neurological model have suggested that this is the result of sclerotic plaques in brain areas, such as the limbic system, that mediate mood, prior to any obvious disorder to which the individual will react. An alternative explanation could be that depression provides a trigger to the onset of MS (as may stress) rather than being an early indicator of its presence.

Evidence of a psychological aetiology is suggested by the findings of Patti et al. (2009) who found no relationship between depression and level of neurological involvement, suggesting a degree of independence between the two. By contrast, Kindrat (2007) found a positive association between disturbed body image and depression in women with relapsing remitting MS, again suggesting a psychological causation.

In sharp contrast to the previous discussion, some people with MS experience periods of euphoria. This is found in people with advanced disease and is thought to be a consequence of scarring in the limbic system isolating it from frontal control, although this has not been confirmed by MRI studies (Minden and Schiffer 1990). Steroids used to treat MS during acute flare-ups may also trigger such episodes. Finally, people with MS may experience significant levels of anger, possibly as a consequence of neuronal damage (Nocentini et al. 2009).

Christodoulou, C., Melville, P., Scherl, W.F. et al. (2009) Negative affect predicts subsequent cognitive change in multiple sclerosis, *Journal of the International Neuropsychological Society*, 15: 53–61.

The authors note that although cognitive impairment associated with MS may take many forms, the most common involve episodic memory and memory for newly learned verbal and visuospatial information. This study examined changes of memory function over time, and also the relationship between depression and memory. Depression has been shown to predict cognitive decline in conditions other than MS. However, no studies have examined whether this is the case in patients with MS. The present study aimed to fill this research gap.

Method

Participants

Participants were patients with MS living in New York. They had all been 'neurologically stable' for at least 30 days before entry into the study. People meeting the DSM-IV criteria for a diagnosis of depression were excluded.

Procedure

Participants were tested at baseline and one year later. Cognitive tests they completed included:

- Parts of the Brief Repeatable Battery:
  - two measures of episodic learning and recall,
  - the Selective Reminding Test (SRT) which measures verbal memory
  - the 10/36 Spatial Recall Test (SRT) which measures visuospatial memory
- Parts of the Minimal Assessment of Cognitive Function in MS:
  - Delpis-Kaplan Executive Function Test
  - Symbol-digit modalities test measuring sustained concentration and speed of visual information

Measures of mood included:

- The Center for Epidemiological Studies Depression Scale (CESD)
- The Chicago Multiscale Depression Inventory (CMDI)
- State version of the State-Trait Anxiety Inventory (STAI)
- Positive and Negative Affect Scale (PANAS)

Results

Sample characteristics

The 38 participants were predominantly female (58 per cent) and Caucasian (97 per cent), with a mean age of 45.5 years, as were the 38 people in the healthy control group. The MS participants were diagnosed with relapsing-remitting MS ($n = 28$) or progressive MS ($n = 10$).

Baseline cognitive and affective scores

The sample had 'mild difficulties' in comparison to the control group on key cognitive measures, scoring an average of 1.5 standard deviations below the mean scores of the healthy sample. By contrast, they showed significantly higher levels of psychopathology. Table 15.1 shows the mean scores of the MS group and z scores showing their performance relative to that of the comparison group (for whom data was not reported).

Table 15.1 **Mean and z scores for each key cognitive measure at baseline and one year follow-up**

	Baseline		One year	
	Mean	z score	Mean	z score
Cognitive function tests				
SRT total	49.92	−.80	50.71	−.72
10/36 SRT total	19.84	−.88	20.05	−.84
DKEFS	8.92	−.41	9.66	−.10
Symbol-digit	49.39	−1.14	51.55	−.95
Measures of mood				
CESD	11.89	.92	10.70	.72
CMDI	13.74	.47	12.81	.21
STAI	27.79	.048	24.47	.021

Associations between mood and cognitive function

No significant associations were found between baseline measures of mood and any measure of cognitive performance. However, significant correlations were found between baseline measures of mood and changes in cognitive function between time 1 and time 2 (see Table 15.2). To summarize the overall impact of mood on cognition, the authors formed a composite mood score based on a combination of scores of the CMDI mood, STAI and PANAS negative affect scale. This was significantly associated with changes on the 10/36 SRT scores ($r = -.567$), DKES ($r = -.357$), symbol-digit ($r = -.327$), but not SRT total ($r = -.221$).

Table 15.2 Correlations between various measures of mood measured at baseline and cognition change scored between time 1 and time 2

	CDMI Mood	CESD	PANAS (-ve)	STAI
Cognitive function tests				
SRT total	−.217	−.025	−.221	−.164
10/36 SRT total	−.343*	−.270	−.567**	−.474**
DKEFS	−.272	−.262	−.357"	−.280
Symbol-digit	−.208	−.229	−.327*	−.358

Discussion

Although it had relatively small sample, this was the first study to show that baseline measures of negative affect consistently predicted cognitive decline in the year following assessment, despite there being no association between measures of mood and cognitive performance at baseline. High baseline negative affect, as measured by the PANAS, was particularly associated with decline in performance in tasks involving episodic memory of newly learned verbal and visuospatial information. While this is an important finding, the authors do not propose any mechanisms through which these associations may have occurred, although the lack of association between baseline performance and mood suggests it is not simply that low mood leads to poor performance due to lack of concentration or focus on the tasks, and implies some form of organic mechanism. The exclusion of individuals with clinical levels of depression suggests that even relatively low levels of anxiety or depression may impact significantly on cognitive processes. However, a larger study involving a wider range of depression or anxiety scores needs to confirm these preliminary findings.

Treatment of psychological problems associated with MS

Psychological interventions in MS have two primary foci: first, to help people manage the cognitive and other symptoms of MS, and, second, to help people cope emotionally with the impact of the disease.

Coping with cognitive changes

A number of studies have examined the impact of neurological rehabilitation techniques on cognitive abilities in MS, although the number of high quality studies is limited (O'Brien et al. 2008). These high quality studies have focused on interventions designed to improve attention, memory and learning, and 'non-specific' factors. Evidence of benefit is fairly limited. In her review, O'Brien reviewed reported that one study Solari et al. (2004) found little gain on measures of attention, while of the two studies focusing on improving memory, Solari et al. (2004) found no gain while Chiaravalloti et al. (2005) found evidence of short-term benefits which had attenuated by five week follow-up.

Coping with emotional problems

A number of interventions can be used to help people cope with the symptoms of MS. One relatively simple method involves providing information about the likely course of the disease, as uncertainty is associated with lower mood. There is consistent evidence that more sophisticated interventions can also alleviate depressive symptoms experienced by people with MS. In a meta-analysis of the evidence, Thomas et al. (2006) found a number of, primarily cognitive behavioural, psychological interventions to be effective in treating depression – just as in patients without MS, and supporting the argument for a psychological aetiology. Responding to the specific needs of this population, who may find it difficult to attend outpatient therapy appointments due to fatigue and poor mobility, Mohr et al. (2000b) examined the effectiveness of a cognitive behavioural programme for the treatment of depression delivered by telephone. The intervention lasted eight weeks and involved a workbook with standardized assignments combined with telephone contacts. Assignments focused on identifying and modifying dysfunctional thoughts, increasing pleasant events, and developing strategies to manage fatigue. The latter included scheduling achievable amounts of exercise, scheduling breaks, and learning to identify physical cues to determine when to take breaks. The usual care control involved routine outpatient appointments. By the end of the intervention, participants in the cognitive behavioural programme reported lower levels of depression and were more likely to adhere to their interferon therapy than those in the normal care condition. A more direct approach reported by Sauter et al. (2008) involved training people with MS specific strategies to minimize fatigue. As well as improvements in fatigue, the intervention also improved mood.

Pharmacological interventions

Medical interventions have been used to combat deteriorations in memory and depression in people with MS. Treatment of memory problems has mirrored treatment of Alzheimer's disease, by using donepezil. Krupp et al. (2004) found that twice as many participants reported improvements in memory following treatment with donepezil than when treated with placebo. Unfortunately, these improvements were not accompanied by improvements on objective tests of memory. A potentially useful intervention involves using cannabinoids to control the pain that is sometimes associated with MS, which have been found to be effective without inducing any psychopathy (Aragona et al. 2009).

In terms of depression, Minden and Schiffer (1990) found desipramine (a tricyclic) to be superior to placebo. However, nearly half those in the trial experienced significant side-effects, even at less than optimum treatment levels of the drug. This sensitivity to medication has also been found in the treatment of depression following head injury, and may make psychological interventions the therapy of choice in such cases. SSRIs may also be of benefit in some, but by no means all, patients (Ehde et al. 2008) and there is limited animal evidence that they may also improve cognitive function (Mostert et al. 2008). Whatever the scientific evidence, pharmaceutical treatments are frequently prescribed for MS. Tremlett et al. (2001) found that, relative to a non-MS comparison group, people with MS were more likely to be prescribed a variety of medications including hypnotics, anxiolytics and antidepressants.

15.4 Chapter summary

1 Alzheimer's disease affects a significant proportion of elderly people.

2 It is characterized by a progressive process of cognitive and behavioural degeneration following a regular pattern as differing brain systems become involved.

3 The neurological processes underpinning the disorder appear to be neurofibrillary tangles and beta amyloid plaques. Reductions in levels of the neurotransmitter acetylcholine also appear to be implicated.

4 There is, as yet, no cure for Alzheimer's disease. In its early stages, interventions are aimed at maximizing cognitive abilities. As the illness progresses, interventions focus on minimizing cognitive load and maintaining independence.

5 Closed head injuries can result in profound and long-lasting cognitive deficits.

6 Psychological interventions in this population focus on cognitive retraining, although any gains often fail to generalize beyond the training context. Accordingly, many interventions incorporate the use of external aids to trigger routine behaviours as well as cognitive strategies for maintaining concentration.

7 Multiple sclerosis is a degenerative disease of varying course.

8 It impacts on both the cognitive and emotional life of people with the disease.

9 Stress may exacerbate or trigger the symptoms of MS.

10 Interventions are therefore aimed at developing strategies for coping with both cognitive impairments and depression. Both appear to be effective.

15.5 For discussion

1 Many frail and elderly people act as carers for people with Alzheimer's disease. How can their stress be minimized?

2 Does cognitive retraining really provide meaningful benefit to people who have had a head injury, or are its effects too limited?

3 How may people with MS be helped to cope effectively with their disease?

15.6 Key terms

Alzheimer's disease the most common cause of dementia in old age.

Hydrocephalus retention of cerebrospinal fluid within the ventricles of the brain. The fluid is often under increased pressure and can compress and damage the brain.

15.7 Further reading

Brown, R.F., Tennant, C.C., Dunn, S.M. et al. (2005) A review of stress-relapse interactions in multiple sclerosis: important features and stress-mediating and -moderating variables, *Multiple Sclerosis*, 11: 477–84.

Cicerone, K.D., Dahlberg, C., Malec, J.F. et al. (2005) Evidence-based cognitive rehabilitation: updated review of the literature from 1998 through 2002, *Archives of Physical Medical Rehabilitation*, 86: 1681–92.

Dennison, L., Moss-Morris, R. and Chalder, T. (2009) A review of psychological correlates of adjustment in patients with multiple sclerosis, *Clinical Psychology Review*, 29: 141–53.

Mateer, C.A., Sira, C.S. and O'Connell, M.E. (2005) Putting Humpty Dumpty together again: the importance of integrating cognitive and emotional interventions, *Journal of Head Trauma Rehabilitation*, 20: 62–75.

Ouldred, E. and Bryant, C. (2008) Dementia care. Part 2: understanding and managing behavioural challenges, *British Journal of Nursing*, 17: 242–7.

Wilcock, G.K., Bucks, R.S. and Rockwood, K. (eds) (1999) *Diagnosis and Management of Dementia: A Manual for Memory Disorders Teams*. Oxford: Oxford University Press.

The following websites also have information about conditions in this chapter, their treatment, and people's experiences them.

Multiple sclerosis

lib.bioinfo.pl/meid:171355
www.msrc.co.uk/index.cfm?fuseaction=show&pageid=2304&CFID=4436191&CFTOKEN=85855848

Alzheimer's disease

alzheimers.org.uk/
alzheimersdad.blogspot.com/

Head injury

www.headway.org.uk/home.aspx
www.brainandspine.org.uk/information/publications/brain_and_spine_booklets/head_injury_and_concussion/index.html

16

Addictions

Chapter contents

Ask someone to describe an addict, and they will usually give a stereotypical description of someone addicted to 'hard' drugs such as heroin or cocaine. However, most chemical addictions are to legal drugs such as coffee, cigarettes and alcohol. People may also be addicted to a variety of behaviours, including exercise or gambling. For these people, the neurochemical reaction to their behaviour is similar to that induced by drugs. After a brief introduction to drugs and drug dependence, this chapter considers the aetiology, implications and treatment of three types of addiction: to alcohol, heroin and gambling. By the end of the chapter, you should have an understanding of:

- Why people take drugs, and the nature of dependence
- Factors leading to alcohol and opiate abuse, and gambling disorders
- The types of interventions used to treat each disorder, and their relative effectiveness.

16.1 Drugs and drug dependence

Many people take drugs, and start taking them at a relatively young age. In the UK, 41 per cent of 16-year-olds report having used cannabis, in comparison with 34 per cent of US, 10 per cent of Italian and 2 per cent of Greek teenagers (Hibell et al. 1997). Similar cross-cultural differences emerge when considering the use of cocaine in various European countries. Haasen et al. (2004), for example, found the percentage of individuals within a general population sample of people aged between 15 and 64 years having used cocaine on at least one occasion varied across countries: UK 5.2 per cent; Spain 4.9 per cent; Germany 2.3 per cent; Italy 1.1 per cent. Use of cocaine was highest among young people and socially marginalized groups such as the homeless and prostitutes. A smaller percentage of older people also use drugs such as alcohol (60 per cent), cannabis (2.6 per cent) and cocaine (0.41 per cent) in the USA (Blazer and Wu 2009). Specific subcultures may also be associated with specific drug use. Participants in the rave culture typically report having used over ten drugs, including alcohol, cannabis, ecstasy, tobacco, LSD, amphetamine and cocaine (Grov et al. 2009). Only 3 per cent of the drug-using population injects.

Drugs impact through changes in neurotransmitters within brain systems (see Table 16.1). With few exceptions, the quicker a drug's action, the more addictive it is. Cocaine, for example, was originally ingested by chewing coca leaves. This produced an increase in vigour and resistance to fatigue but little pleasure. More recently, it has been made into cocaine hydrochloride powder which, when taken nasally, impacts on the brain within 4–10 minutes of ingestion. Crack cocaine is a further refinement that allows it to be smoked and to impact on the brain in seconds. Each form of cocaine is thought to be increasingly addictive.

Table 16.1 **The neurotransmitters involved and 'addictiveness' of various drugs**

Drug class	Neurotransmitter involved	Physical withdrawal problems	Psychological withdrawal problems
Mimic natural transmitters			
Opiates	Endorphins	+++	+++
Cannabis	Anandamide	+	+
Alcohol	GABA	+++	++
Nicotine	Acetylcholine	+	+++
Release transmitters			
Cocaine	Dopamine	++	+++
Amphetamines	Dopamine	+	++
Nicotine	Dopamine	+	+++
Ecstasy	Dopamine; serotonin	+	0
Block transmitters			
Barbiturates	Glutamate	+++	++
Psychedelics (incl.LSD)	Serotonin	+	0

Source: adapted from Nutt and Law (2000).

Problems arising from drug use defy simple categorization. They may be social, physical, legal, interpersonal or psychological. DSM-IV-TR (APA 2000) acknowledged these factors in its definition of 'abuse or harmful use of substances' as a maladaptive pattern of substance use leading to clinically significant impairment or distress and one or more of the following:

- failure to fulfil major role obligations at work, school or home
- use in situations in which it is physically hazardous
- legal problems
- social or interpersonal problems.

DSM-IV-TR also identified a more problematic level of dependence, in which the individual becomes psychologically or physically dependent on a particular drug. The key factor here is the development of a tolerance to the drug, involving a need for more of it to achieve the desired experience, and withdrawal symptoms if use of the drug is ceased. Other criteria include social impairment, devoting substantial time and effort to obtaining the drug, and a history of repeated, unsuccessful attempts to stop using.

16.2 Excess alcohol consumption

Alcohol is a socially sanctioned drug. Drunk at moderate levels, certain types of alcohol, such as red wine, may benefit health. Excess consumption may be harmful. Defining what is meant by excess alcohol consumption has proven far from simple. This confusion is illustrated by changes to health advice made by the UK government in 1995. Between 1986 and 1995 the recommended limits for weekly consumption were 21 units of alcohol or less for men, and 14 units or less for women. In 1995, a government committee established to review these guidelines recommended they be increased to 28 and 21 units per week respectively. These changes caused a furore and much criticism among alcohol experts, particularly as they were not based on any new evidence (see, for example, *British Medical Journal*, volume 293). Consequently, a number of health promotion and alcohol agencies have been reluctant to adopt these guidelines and there is a lack of clear advice concerning the recommended limits to consumption.

Acute intoxication can result in risk-taking or other behaviours that may damage the individual or others. Twenty-two per cent of deaths in road accidents in Sweden, for example, are associated with high levels of driver alcohol consumption (Jones et al. 2009), while more generally alcohol consumption has also been associated with an increased risk for violent crime, accidents at work, admissions for mental health problems, drownings, burns and suicide (Allan et al. 2001).

Long-term dangers include physical health problems such as liver cirrhosis, hypertension and various cancers. Long-term excess consumption may also result in significant neurological problems. Wernicke's encephalopathy is caused by thiamine deficiencies common in heavy drinkers as a consequence of poor diet, and results from degenerative changes and small bleeds in the brain. Its symptoms include memory deficits, ataxia and confusion. If not treated, it may progress to a more problematic disorder known as Korsakoff's syndrome. This irreversible condition affects about 5 per cent of heavy drinkers and involves significant retrograde amnesia and anterograde amnesia. Anterograde memory deficits are usually the most marked problems, and individuals with the condition live a very 'minute-by-minute' existence, frequently confabulating in an effort to replace the memories they fail to sustain.

Problem drinking is usually the end-point of a progression from social drinking to drinking at times of stress or difficulty, through to an increasing 'need' to drink to cope with social or psychological problems or prevent the onset of withdrawal symptoms. In the early stages of dependence, individuals may need a drink at lunchtime to alleviate discomfort. As they become more dependent, they may need an early morning drink or one during the night to avoid withdrawal. Periods of abstinence of three to four hours may be difficult. Withdrawal results in a variety of symptoms, including tremor, nausea, sweating and mood disturbance. Delirium tremens ('the DTs') is the most extreme element of withdrawal. It usually begins within three to four days of abstinence and lasts between two and three days. It involves reductions in consciousness, impairment of memory, insomnia and frightening auditory and/or visual hallucinations. Interestingly, drinking early in life is not necessarily predictive of subsequent dependence. A German study, reported by Behrendt et al. (2008), for example, found that the speed of transition from an alcohol user to early signs of alcohol dependence was quicker among young people who were older when they started to drink than those who were younger.

The story of Anne is typical of many people who drink to excess:

First started drinking when I was 18. I was at college at the time – a part of the norm – drinking cider or lager at weekends. I met my first partner out drinking when I was about 22. We got into a crowd who were wine drinkers and so we started drinking more wine. He'd always been a heavy drinker – more than I ever did. And often as a result of his drinking he'd become quite violent towards me and arguments would follow after drinking. As a result of this, I began to drink more – to join him, to keep up. My violent marriage made me think about my childhood – which had been very unstable and unhappy for various reasons – and the more I brooded on that, the more I drank. I was drinking about two bottles of wine a night at this time. Drinking helped me cope with my marriage and memories of my childhood. It also made things in the relationship worse, of course.

By the time I was 28–29, the relationship had broken down, and my drinking fell a little – but not that much. Then one night, I was followed home by a man from a nightclub and sexually assaulted by him. My drinking escalated again. I felt I couldn't go out of the house. I was scared and felt trapped. I lost my job as a care worker with children and then I had nothing to keep me going, so I just drank through the day. I was drinking a couple of bottles of wine and perhaps a flagon of cider a day at this time. I did this for about six months or so, when I met my next partner, and I began to drink less. I managed to get another job. But the drinking was always there. I managed to get another job – as a health care assistant in an old people's home. I had a child – but things were never good in the relationship I suppose. For the last 20 years, things have pretty much been the same. I drink all the time – sometimes more, sometimes less. Drinking helps me forget my problems and go into oblivion – it blocks things out. And there's a lot to block out. I thought I had been an OK mother – perhaps not the best, but OK. But my son doesn't want to know me any more. My partner has long gone. I've had jobs on and off over this time – that last one, about eight years ago.

I feel guilty about my drinking. I've never really been there for my family – I've always been the drunk that doesn't fit in. I suppose if you are always drunk – quietly not loudly – you still can't do your best. Now, I stay in – I don't go out much. I'm ashamed when I go to the shops – people looking at me, talking about me. I feel they are looking at me – judging me. I don't feel good when I'm drunk, but I do feel in oblivion. I just sit there – or lie in bed all day. I'm drinking from the moment I get up – I have to control the tremors.

I want to stop drinking. I feel despair at the circle I'm caught up in – there's no way out. I try – I do all the right things from pouring the drink down the sink, going to the GP for help and so on. But when I stop drinking I get violent stomach cramps. I shake. I get headaches. I feel paranoid, that people are talking about me. I can't cope with these withdrawals, so I end up drinking again.

Since telling her story, Anne has been through in-patient detoxification and a six-month programme in a residential setting involving both exploratory psychotherapy and a cognitive behavioural relapse prevention programme. At the time of writing all is going well.

Aetiology of excess alcohol consumption

Many people drink excessively for years without becoming dependent on alcohol. Most reduce their consumption as they grow older. Young people who drink excessively while single, for example, may moderate their consumption as they develop long-term relationships, start families, and so on. Any explanation of alcohol-related problems needs therefore to explain factors that contribute to the early stages of alcohol use as well as why some people continue to use and then abuse alcohol. The biopsychosocial model appears to be the most appropriate model, as it may explain why some people are more prone to alcohol dependence than others, as well as the social and psychological factors that may independently and together lead to this state.

Genetic factors

There is some evidence of a genetic predisposition to alcohol problems. Prescott and Kendler (1999), for example, reported concordance for 'high lifetime alcohol consumption' of 47 per cent in MZ and 32 per cent in DZ twins. Adoption studies have also shown the adopted children of parents with alcohol problems to have higher rates of alcohol problems than those of parents without this history (e.g. Cadoret et al. 1995).

This evidence does not necessarily point to a gene for alcoholism: alcohol problems may be secondary to other genetically mediated traits, including poor impulse control or emotional problems. However, there is evidence implicating a specific gene or genes related to alcohol dependence. One important genetic process involves the dopamine D2 receptor gene. This gene can take a number of forms: it is polymorphic. One variant of the D2 dopamine receptor gene, the DRD2 A1 allele, has been found to be more prevalent in individuals with a dependence on alcohol than those without such a dependence (Lawford et al. 1997). The gene may also influence the initiation and effect of a variety of drugs. Conner et al. (2005), for example, found that male adolescents with this allele tried alcohol and became intoxicated more often than those without it. In addition, they were more likely to develop a smoking habit and experience a marijuana 'high'. This link between sensitivity to cannabis and alcohol may work both ways. Hutchison et al. (2008) reported that a variant of the CNR1 gene (cannabinoid receptor 1) was equally associated with higher levels of alcohol consumption.

Biological factors

The DRD2 A1 allele and variants of the CNR1 gene impact through their effect on the dopamine receptors (Bowirrat and Oscar-Berman 2005). Consumption of alcohol triggers a cascade of chemical events resulting in the release of dopamine within the reward or 'pleasure centre' of the brain: a complex of structures that includes the basal ganglia, thalamus, amygdala, hypothalamus and nucleus accumbens. People with these genes may be more sensitive to the effects of alcohol than those without it (a potential explanation of the findings of Finn et al. 1992). Thus, they may be encouraged to initiate alcohol and other drug use because they find it easy to gain a 'high' from their alcohol consumption. This mechanism suggests that such individuals may need relatively little alcohol to provide an emotional reward, and therefore maintain their consumption. However, continued use of alcohol is thought to reduce the response of this reward system to other potential reinforcers, leading to a dependence on alcohol to maintain a desired mood state. In addition, other neurotransitters may be involved in maintaining alcohol consumption. Alcohol also enhances the action of GABA within the hypothalamus and sympathetic nervous system (see Chapter 3), helping calm mood and behaviour. Over time, this results in a reduction in the natural production of GABA, leading to a dependence on alcohol to maintain desired emotional states. Abstinence results in sub-optimal levels of GABA, increases in anxiety and agitation, and the onset of physical withdrawal symptoms. These are relieved by continued drinking or, in time, the body's resumption of normal levels of GABA.

Socio-cultural factors

Alcohol is a socially sanctioned drug, and consumption is markedly influenced by social and environmental factors. Beginning to drink alcohol is seen as one of the transitions from childhood to adulthood, although this may happen relatively early in life: about one-third of British 13–14-year-olds report having been drunk on more than one occasion (Sutherland and Willner 1998). The early consumption of alcohol by young people is associated with positive attitudes to alcohol use, some of which are linked to family and peer attitudes and behaviours, and may result from the positive images of consumption seen on television, in films, and so on (Engels et al. 2009). Social factors influence consumption once initiated. Round buying, for example, may increase consumption among young social drinkers, for whom alcohol is frequently linked to social and group activities. Life transitions, both good and bad, may also influence consumption: developing relationships and families, or getting and maintaining a job, may inhibit consumption. Adverse life-events may increase consumption, particularly among people who use alcohol as a means of coping with stress (Perreira and Sloan 2001).

Within countries, rates of drinking vary across cultural and social groups. Men are more likely to drink heavily than women. Blue-collar workers are more likely than white-collar workers to report problem drinking, as are workers with access to alcohol as part of their job. Among men, binge drinking is most frequent among the young, lower-income and lower-educated groups (Bloomfield et al. 2006). There is less evidence of such a social gradient among females. Levels of alcohol consumption may be particularly high in marginalized groups or groups under social pressure, such as the Native Americans in the USA (e.g. Bursac and Campbell 2003). Similarly, Latinas had a higher risk for alcohol use than their African and Asian-American peers in a survey of alcohol consumption in the southern USA (Guiao and Thompson 2004). Not surprisingly, levels of alcohol consumption vary across countries also. The Japanese, for example, drink more alcohol than US or British people (Ueshima 2005).

Psychological factors

Behavioural explanations of alcohol consumption consider it to be the consequence of both operant and classical conditioning. Consumption is rewarded by both the pleasure associated with drinking, which may be physiological or social. Once an individual has developed a dependence on alcohol, a further motivator to drink is the avoidance of withdrawal symptoms. Classical conditioning may occur as drinking becomes associated with particular cues or events, subsequent exposure to which may trigger episodes of drinking. As noted above, some individuals may be genetically more susceptible to these effects than others. In addition to this learning approach, cognitive theorists suggest that beliefs about alcohol, known as *addictive beliefs* (Beck et al. 1993), are important determinants of consumption at all stages in a drinking career. Expectancy theory (Goldman 1999a) suggests that our expectations of the outcome of drinking ('If I drink this beer, then I will be more outgoing') play a significant role in the development of drinking histories and alcohol dependence. At the beginning of a history of alcohol use, positive beliefs such as 'It will be fun to get drunk' predominate. As the individual begins to rely on alcohol to counteract feelings of distress, relief-oriented thoughts ('I need a drink to get through the day') may predominate. Addictive beliefs are frequently accompanied by a wider set of negative core beliefs, including a negative view of oneself, one's circumstances and environment, which may contribute to depression or anxiety. Both addictive and negative beliefs may be triggered by external cues, including walking past a bar, or internal ones, such as adverse mood states. Toneatto (1999) identified a number of types of thoughts that trigger consumption and the expected impact that such consumption would have on long-term drug and alcohol users (see Table 16.2). Goldman (1999b) theorized that previous memories of consumption act as triggers that directly drive subsequent drinking behaviour. These may involve images of previous drinking, memories of affective experiences associated with consumption, or verbal representations of these concepts, acquired from sources such as family members, the media or peer groups. Activation of particular memories ('. . . drinking really makes me feel good') occur when the individual encounters stimuli previously associated with drinking, and influence the onset and pattern of drinking.

Many people consider drinking alcohol to be a means of stress reduction. In a more scientific description of this hypothesis, Levenson's stress-response dampening (SRD) model suggests that alcohol reduces stress-related emotions and the sympathetic arousal associated with stress. However, evidence for this model has proven surprisingly mixed. Alcohol has been shown to reduce stress, increase stress, or have no impact on stress at all (Sayette 1999). In an attempt to explain these findings, Sayette's (1993) appraisal-disruption model suggested that alcohol impairs the cognitive processes involved in the appraisal of new information. In the context of stress reduction, drinking may interfere with the initial perception of stressful information by preventing the activation of associated stressful memories and concepts. Sayette (1999) noted that this process of appraisal can lead to specific testable hypotheses in relation to the effects of alcohol on mood and behaviour. He noted, for example, that the time of alcohol consumption of someone invited to a party who feels nervous about dancing with unknown partners may impact on their anxiety levels and behaviour. If they consume alcohol *before* attending, they will experience lower levels of anxiety-related appraisals while dancing as they are likely to be relatively insensitive to their dance partners' behaviour that could be appraised in a negative way. If, however, they only start to drink *after* they are at the party and have started to dance, then they will not experience lower anxiety after drinking as they will have already processed this negative information. A series of studies using tasks analogous to this situation have found such an outcome (see Sayette 1999). This, Sayette suggested, goes some way to explain the mixed findings of the relationship between alcohol and stress.

Table 16.2 **Type of thoughts leading to alcohol consumption and their impact**

Cognitive state	Likelihood of consumption (%)	Expected consequence
Depression	74	Detachment
Stress	71	Reduction
Anxiety	67	Reduction
Grief	62	Detachment
Unpleasant thoughts	62	Detachment
Anger	51	Reduction
Unpleasant memories	50	Reduction
Boredom	49	Reduction
Pain	48	Intensification
Guilt	47	Detachment

Interventions in excess alcohol consumption

Prevention: the socio-cultural approach

Approaches to preventing excess alcohol consumption have generally assumed that controls over drinking that affect the whole population will also impact on heavy or problem drinkers. As a result, preventive approaches have typically focused on all drinkers rather than just those who drink to excess (see also Chapter 4). These have generally attempted to change the context or rules surrounding consumption. Many have met with success. Increasing pricing, reducing availability and advertising, and implementing strong drink–drive laws have, for example, been shown to reduce consumption or the negative outcomes of drinking such the number of alcohol-related accidents cross a number of countries (see Anderson et al. 2009). Conversely, reductions in pricing in alcohol, which happened in Sweden due to taxation changes may result in an increase in consumption (Norström and Skog 2005).

Stop and think...

At the time of writing, UK pubs and clubs can be open for much of the day (potentially up to 24 hours), leading to fears that binge drinking and public disorder may rise to unprecedented levels. But is this necessarily the case? Between 1980 and 2000, Australia increased the availability of alcohol, liberalized trading hours, and did not increase overall taxation on alcohol – changes associated with a *fall* in per-capita alcohol consumption of 24 per cent (Stockwell 2004). Television programmes focusing on binge drinking and violence give the impression that the UK experience has been less positive. But is this simply press sensationalism? El-Maaytah et al. (2008) reported a *reduction* in the number of alcohol-related assaults attending one London hospital following the change in licensing laws. By contrast, another London hospital reported a significant increase of alcohol-related injuries (Newton et al. 2007).

So, availability of alcohol can increase, while its harmful effects on individuals and society can decrease. But are these effects specific to Australian culture? Or can drinking policies that enable wide access to alcohol accompany policies that reduce potential harm elsewhere?

Alcoholism versus problem drinking

A sharp divide can be found between the beliefs that different practitioners hold about the nature and treatment of alcohol-associated problems, and the terminology they use. Some consider what they term 'alcoholism' to be a biological disease. Interventions based on this approach usually involve medical treatments or programmes of complete abstinence, such as that followed by Alcoholics Anonymous (AA). Others consider what they term 'problem drinking' to be the result of psychological and social factors, and argue that most people can learn to drink alcohol in moderation and appropriately. Interestingly, there is a substantial transatlantic split on this issue. A majority of US practitioners subscribe to the medical, abstinence model; most Europeans subscribe to the psychosocial, controlled drinking model (Peele 1992). Advocates of the latter (e.g. Heather 1995) contend that many problem drinkers can moderate their consumption whereas others may refuse to consider abstinence. Attempts at abstinence by these people may result in more problems, not fewer. Trials that have offered dependent drinkers a choice between controlled drinking and abstinence (e.g. Booth et al. 1992) have resulted in similar gains in both conditions. The best treatment goal may therefore be the choice of the client, not the therapist.

Withdrawal

The initial treatment of people with alcohol problems may involve a period of withdrawal. This may take three to four days, and is usually aided by the use of sedatives such as diazepam (Valium) which moderate the severity of any withdrawal symptoms (Favre et al. 2005). Once they have withdrawn from alcohol, many people will receive one or more of the interventions described below.

Drug therapy

Antidipstrotrophics deter consumption by causing the drinker to feel ill if they consume alcohol while taking them. The most commonly used drug of this type is disulfiram (Antabuse).

It prevents alcohol being broken down further than its intermediate metabolite acetaldehyde. This accumulates in the body and causes a number of symptoms, including flushing, headache, pounding in the head or chest, nausea and occasional vomiting, about 15–20 minutes after consumption of alcohol. Patients may be given a test reaction to alcohol to alert them to the consequences of consumption. The benefits of disulfiram depend on its regular consumption. Where this is enforced, it appears an effective barrier to consumption. It is less effective when taken voluntarily (Hughes and Cook 1997). Its use clearly follows a biological, abstinence model. However, some studies have evaluated the effectiveness of similar drugs in programmes that accept that participants may choose to drink on occasion. In these, it may be used as an occasional control to consumption, particularly when users feel they are losing control over their drinking (Sinclair 2001).

A second type of drug treatment for alcohol abuse involves the use of opioid agonists, such as naltrexone, which are thought to reduce cravings. Such programmes, of course, encounter the same problems as antabuse programmes: if people want to drink, they simply stop taking the medication, although the advent of an extended release version of the drug which is therapeutically effective for one month promises to be potentially more effective. In one study of its effectiveness, Garbutt et al. (2005) found that compared with placebo, long-acting naltrexone resulted in a 25 per cent decrease in heavy drinking days over a six-month period, while Pettinati et al. (2009) found a high dose of the drug to result in higher levels of quality of life as well as reduced drinking when compared to placebo. A final drug type used to treat alcohol dependence, including acamprosate and baclofen reduces cravings through its action on GABA receptors. Boothby and Doering (2005) reviewed the evidence of the effectiveness of acamprosate, and found it to be of significant benefit. The percentage of patients who were completely abstinent when prescribed acamprosate throughout the different durations of the studies varied from 18 per cent to 61 per cent, compared with 4 per cent to 45 per cent with placebo. High quality studies of the effectiveness of baclofen are still lacking.

The 12-step approach

The 12-step approach is the treatment programme of AA. It is based on a belief that alcoholism is a physical, psychological and spiritual illness that cannot be cured, but can be controlled by total abstinence from alcohol. The organization provides a strong social support network that encourages emotional expression and the admission of failure. Attenders at group meetings are encouraged to accept that they are powerless to control their drinking, to cease their struggle and to allow a 'higher power' to take control (Gorski 1989).

The millions of attenders of AA meetings across the world attest to the potential benefits of this approach. More empirical data provide mixed support. In a meta-analysis of research, Ferri et al. (2006) concluded that attendance at AA had not been shown to unequivocally demonstrated the effectiveness of the AA (or twelve-step) programmes. However, the mixed outcomes of the studies they reviewed may have resulted, at least in part, from the inclusion of many programmes in which attendance at AA was compulsory – a factor that is likely to reduce the impact of any programme. More positive results were reported by Timko et al. (2000), who compared outcomes on people who self-selected either into AA or a variety of formal treatment programmes including residential, psychological or psychiatric treatments. At one-year follow-up, 56 per cent of the participants in AA had a 'benign' drinking pattern in comparison with 33 per cent of those who received other formal interventions. At three-year follow-up, the figures were 64 and 43 per cent respectively. Note that while AA follows a model of abstinence, many of the people who engaged in this approach seemingly learned to drink within reasonable limits.

Cognitive behavioural approaches

A number of aversive approaches have been used in the treatment of alcohol-related problems, including presenting alcohol-related stimuli at the same time as mild electrical shocks or inducing feelings of suffocation by injection of succinylcholine. These have proven, at best, moderately effective in the short but not the long term, and are now considered ethically questionable. More recent cognitive behavioural programmes have involved training in social skills and strategies for preventing relapse (see Longabough and Morgenstern 2000). Social skills training involves teaching interpersonal and assertive skills to help participants cope more effectively with stressful situations, refuse drinks, and so on. In relapse prevention programmes, high-risk situations are identified, and the individual develops and rehearses strategies to help them cope with them should they arise. These may include specific strategies to challenge addictive beliefs and to cope with cravings to drink. These may be combined with drug therapies. Feeney et al. (2002), for example, reported abstinence rates of 14 per cent following a CBT relapse prevention programme, compared with one of 38 per cent in a CBT plus acamprosate in a group of patients considered to be at high risk of relapse. By contrast, the combined intervention was no more effective in improving psychological well-being and health status than cognitive behaviour therapy alone (Feeney et al. 2006).

Relapse is frequently associated with marital problems and prevented by strong marital cohesion. For this reason, some programmes involve the problem drinker's partner where this is possible. O'Farrell and Fals-Stewart (2000), for example, described an intervention intended to increase the communication and problem-solving skills of couples rather than just the individual. Both the problem drinker and their partner learned strategies to reduce consumption, including the partner changing behaviours that may trigger alcohol use, finding new ways to discuss drinking and situations involved with it, and new responses to their partner's drinking. A further strand of therapy focused on the type and quality of communication between the partners. In their review of the effectiveness of this approach, O'Farrell and Fals-Stewart (2000) concluded that it was consistently more effective than individual therapy on measures of alcohol consumption, abstinence, alcohol-related problems and the quality of marital relationships.

Brief therapies

A number of early studies (e.g. Chick 1991) showed that interventions as brief as one session could be effective in reducing some individuals' levels of alcohol consumption. One approach has proven very popular, and is now widely used. Motivational interviewing (Miller and Rollnick 2002) is a non-confrontational approach in which the therapist allows the drinker to explore their reasons for drinking and the advantages (and disadvantages) associated with reducing their consumption. The aim is to trigger a state of dissonance in which the individual actively considers two sets of opposing beliefs and attitudes towards a particular issue (in this case, the 'good' and 'not so good' things about drinking). According to cognitive dissonance theory, this is an aversive state and motivates cognitive work to reduce the discomfort. It may result in a rejection of the newly considered arguments, or the adoption of new beliefs or behaviours – in this case, a reduction in alcohol consumption. The second phase of this approach can involve problem-solving how to achieve change should the individual choose to do so. It has proven an effective intervention. Monti et al. (1999), for example, evaluated the effect of this among adolescents treated in a casualty department following an alcohol-related incident. Those who received the intervention had a significantly lower incidence of drinking and driving, traffic violations, alcohol-related injuries and alcohol-related problems over the following year than those who received no intervention. A similar intervention provided by peers instead of health professionals has also proven of benefit (Bazargan-Hejazi et al. 2005). In a more chronic population in which alcohol consumption was high and problematic, Sellman et al. (2001) compared the effects of motivational therapy, non-directive reflective listening and a no-treatment control among problem drinkers. The goal of therapy was controlled drinking, and the key outcome was the frequency of binge drinking. In the six months following the interventions, 43 per cent of people who received the motivational intervention had engaged in binge drinking, in comparison with over 63 per cent of those in the other conditions. One of the questions frequently asked of the founders of motivational interviewing and its practitioners is, how does it work? It has no strong theoretical base, and evolving from practice rather than a particular theoretical perspective. A number of studies have begun to address this issue, one of which was in heavy drinking college students. Walters et al. (2009) argued that motivational interviewing often contains two elements. First, an educational element comparing the client's drinking with relevant others. Second, an attempt to motivate change based at least partly on this feedback. They considered the relevance of each element by comparing the effects of feedback on heavy drinking college students provided through a web, a single motivational interview with no feedback, and a single motivational interview plus feedback. At 6-month follow-up the combined intervention proved more effective than either of the single approaches, which did not differ in their effectiveness.

Project MATCH

Despite the differences in philosophy and strategies of the various treatment approaches, their effectiveness appears to be very similar. In order to tease out exactly which is the best, Project MATCH, the largest ever alcohol-treatment trial, involving over 1500 participants (Project MATCH Research Group 1998), compared the effectiveness of a number of interventions, including motivational enhancement therapy (an enhanced longer-term version of motivational interviewing), cognitive behavioural and 12-step approaches. By one-year follow-up, 35 per cent of all participants reported complete abstinence over the previous year; a further 25 per cent reported having not having drunk heavily on more than two consecutive days in this time, a measure considered to reflect some degree of control over their alcohol consumption. At one-year and three-year follow-ups, there were, again, no differences between the three intervention groups. The principal purpose of the study, however, was to determine which clients responded best to which treatments. Four such effects were found. People who entered treatment with a high level of state/trait anger fared best in motivational enhancement therapy through the three years of follow-up (Waldron et al. 2001). Those whose social support systems favoured continued drinking rather than abstinence, who had higher levels of dependence, and who had higher levels of mental health problems benefited most from the 12-step approach. People with lower levels of dependence fared better if they received cognitive behavioural therapy (Babor et al. 1999). So, it seems that the approach of choice is probably that which is chosen by the client.

Case formulation

Mr C is a 33-year-old married man with significant alcohol problems. At the time he was seen by a psychologist he was unemployed as a result of drunken behaviour and lack of discipline in a variety of jobs, with financial problems due to his loss of employment and continued spending of money on alcohol, and was experiencing significant marital problems. He was seeking treatment because his partner of eight years had threatened to leave the relationship if he continued to drink.

Long-term antecedents

Mr C first experienced alcohol consumption at the age of 14 years. His father and partner regularly drank around the house, and he was soon regularly accessing his father's alcohol at home, or was either able to buy alcohol from local off licences or friends bought it for him. By the age of 15, he was a regular drinker. He got high on alcohol, but was able to tolerate its effects rather more than the friends with whom he drank. He became a member of a group of young heavy drinkers on his local estate, with whom he regularly drank cheap alcohol, such as beer or strong cider. By the age of 18, he was drinking every day and night, drinking several pints of beer/cider per night combined with significant intake of short drinks (Jack Daniels, etc.). He had left school at 16, and had held a series of short-term manual jobs, losing each due to poor time keeping and lack of commitment. He had a series of girlfriends, but no committed relationship and was prioritizing spending his money on alcohol to the exclusion of other things. He was also taking various other drugs and regularly smoking cannabis.

At the age of 25 his behaviour continued much as before. However, he then met a woman (in a bar) with whom he began a long-term relationship, moving in with her after three months. She had a job in a local hairdresser and was earning a modest but regular income. He was still drifting from job to job. In the first months of the relationship he reduced his alcohol consumption, made a significant attempt to get and hold down a longer-term job and attempted to establish a good relationship with his new partner. He succeeded in doing so for a number of months, but gradually began to drink more, began to re-establish old relationships with his drinking friends, and eventually lost his job due to drinking alcohol while at work and previous irregular time-keeping. He then began to drink more in the day as well as during the evenings and nights. He tried to hide his consumption from his partner by drinking spirits in the day and hiding bottles around the house. However, he increasingly needed to drink during the day, starting when he woke up. His mood was becoming erratic and contributing to frequent highly verbally aggressive rows with his partner who was becoming increasingly frustrated by his drinking, lying about his drinking, the money (her money!) spent on his drinking and their poor relationship.

Short-term antecedents

The trigger to his seeking help for his alcohol problems was a row with his partner, who moved back to her mother's flat saying she could no longer tolerate his drinking. He had told her that he would seek help for his drinking many times and had not done so. But in an attempt at one last reconciliation he agreed to seek help. He did so somewhat reluctantly, and felt rather anxious and unsure of how much benefit this may prove. Nevertheless, he and his partner went to his local doctor and asked to be referred to the local alcohol treatment programme. Referral was delayed due to the waiting list of the services and he was eventually seen some three months later. In this time, he tried to reduce his alcohol consumption, but had struggled to do so, and his partner (and now more accurately his ex-partner) was still living with her mother – although she had agreed to reconsider her decision if he were to change his drinking behaviour.

Formulation

Mr C was a fairly typical man with drinking problems, in that there was no one trigger to his problems, but he had rather drifted over a period of years into high levels of drinking. He found the process of drinking rewarding, as it made him feel good, and when he drank with his friends there was an added social bonding. Eventually, he also found that drinking relieved the discomfort of withdrawal symptoms and the low moods he experienced when not drinking. These immediate rewards became more powerful determinants of his behaviour than the longer-term and more incremental problems drinking was causing in the rest of his life.

Intervention

Mr C was drinking high levels of alcohol when he first came to the service, so he underwent a home detoxification programme, overseen by a community psychiatric nurse. This involved him stopping drinking, while taking fairly high dosages of drugs designed to minimize any withdrawal effects, and which also made him very sleepy. As a result, he was visited a number of times a day by the nurse, and over a period of three days the level of drug dosage was gradually reduced as did his withdrawal symptoms. Once he was detoxed, Mr C was seen by a drug and alcohol counsellor for a period of psychological treatment.

The first phase of treatment involved a motivational interview, designed to identify and hopefully increase his motivation to change his drinking behaviour. This identified key motivators of his desire to change as his relationship with his partner, lack of success in having children and providing a stable background for them, and the lack of money to spend on other parts of his life. He wanted to succeed and to be seen to be succeeding very quickly so that he could reinstate his relationship with his estranged partner, so he initially opted to aim for total alcohol abstinence, using Antabuse as a means of ensuring abstinence. He also wanted to involve his partner in any treatment programme so she would have confidence that he was improving. Accordingly he was seen with his partner on four occasions, and on his own for a similar number. In the joint sessions, the counsellor addressed a number of issues particular pertinent to the relationship, including issues related to intimacy and sexual matters as well as developing strategies to reduce the intensity and number of arguments they had been having – all of which were triggers to his drinking. They also negotiated a plan for coming to live back together. Mr C also developed strategies for coping with urges to drink and to prevent his relapse. These involved both strategies he could use on his own, including going to see his father or getting a buzz from involvement in other activities such as jogging (which he had started to do following his withdrawal), and activities involving his partner, that could be as simple as watching TV together or talking. He initially avoided people he associated with drinking, although this was not easy as most of his friends were heavy drinkers. Over time, when he was confident he could resist a drink, he began to see some of them, but not in drinking contexts. Over time, he also developed strategies to engage in if he did have a drink, which included talking about this with his partner, ensuring regular use of Antabuse, re-invoking strategies of abstinence if he had begun to relax and not use them, and seeing his counsellor if necessary. He also was helped by a social worker to find a job, allowing some stability in his life.

16.3 Using heroin

Opiates are a group of drugs derived from the opium poppy. The key derivatives, in order of strength and addictiveness, are opium, morphine and heroin. The most widely used form of the drug is heroin. Initially widely used as a sedative, the non-medical use of all opiates is now illegal across the world. Taking heroin results in profound feelings of warmth, relaxation and euphoria. Worries, fears and concerns are forgotten, and self-confidence increases. These effects last for between 4 and 6 hours, before the individual 'comes down' from the drug. Once dependent on the drug, withdrawal usually begins about 8 hours after an injection, and results in muscle pain, sweats, sneezes and uncontrollable yawning. Within 36 hours, the symptoms become increasingly severe, and include uncontrollable muscle twitching, cramps, chills, sweats and a rise in heart rate. The person is unable to sleep, vomits and has diarrhoea. These symptoms typically last for about 72 hours, and then gradually reduce over a period of between 5 and 10 days.

For obvious reasons, it is difficult to estimate the use of heroin within the general population. However, a number of estimates have been made drawing on evidence from sources such as the number of people in treatment, police records, mortality data and/or AIDS/HIV data. These types of data led Kraus et al. (2003) to estimate the prevalence of drug injectors (usually opiates, but including amphetamine) within the populations of differing countries across Europe to lie somewhere between the extremes of 0.26 per cent of the population of Germany and 0.48 per cent of those in Luxembourg. Still in Europe, Bargagli et al. (2006) estimated mortality rates from drug overdoses and AIDS as a result of opiate use to be highest in Barcelona, with a rate of 10 deaths per 1000 person-years. Countries, such as Italy, the UK and Austria had a rate of about 7 deaths per 1000 person-years.

In the 1960s to the early 1990s, heroin was taken predominantly through intravenous injection. Now it is more frequently smoked, a practice known as 'chasing the dragon'. In Dublin, for example, Smyth et al. (2000) reported a 330 per cent increase in the number of new attenders of drug clinics between 1991 and 1996. Over this time, the age of initiating heroin use fell, and users were more likely to smoke than inject it. Changing from being an injector to a smoker of heroin is associated with an increased drug effect and perceived cost-effectiveness (Swift et al. 1999). Chasers were more likely to be employed, younger, use fewer other drugs, and to be more educated and have a shorter history of use than people who injected. Cultural differences may also influence mode of consumption. Golub and Johnson (2005), for example, found that in New York, black and Hispanic men were more likely to smoke heroin, while white men continued to inject heroin over this period.

Most heroin users use other drugs. Beswick et al. (2001) reported that 60 per cent of their sample of attenders at a London clinic used crack cocaine, 58 per cent used alcohol, 11 per cent diazepam, 9 per cent methadone and 8 per cent used cocaine powder at the same time as taking heroin. Of note are the findings of Degenhardt et al. (2005) who found that users may switch between quite different drugs such as heroin, metamphetamine and cocaine, depending on their relative availability and price.

Aetiology of heroin use

Genetic factors

Although environmental factors predominate in the development of drug addiction, there is evidence of a genetic vulnerability to drug abuse involving two pathways (Cadoret et al. 1995). The first involves a direct pathway of drug dependence. Cadoret and colleagues found that the adopted children of parents who evidenced alcohol abuse or dependence were three times more likely to develop drug dependence than those from non-alcohol-dependent parents, suggesting the potential of a gene for an 'addictive personality' rather than one for opiate addiction in particular. The second, indirect route identified by Cadoret involved genetic linkages of antisocial behaviour (see Chapter 12) that led to aggression, conduct disorder, antisocial personality and eventually drug or alcohol abuse. As with addiction to alcohol, the DRD2 dopamine gene may be involved in determining risk for opiate dependence, although the gene may work in different ways in different phenotypes: Xu et al. (2004) found that variants of the gene typically increased susceptibility to dependence in people of Chinese origin, but were associated with a low risk of dependence in Germans. Other genes may also be involved with opiate dependence, including genes involved with serotonin (Saiz et al. 2009) and endorphin activity (Shi et al. 2002).

Biological factors

Just as with alcohol, the action of opiates results from their impact on dopamine systems within the 'pleasure centre'. A second mechanism through which they influence mood and well-being is through their chemical similarity to chemicals known as endorphins and enkephalins. These moderate pain and produce feelings of well-being, contributing, for example, to the 'runner's high' that can accompany intense prolonged physical exercise. Opiates bind to the same receptor sites as endorphins and enkephalins, resulting in a state of well-being, as well as having a sedating effect. Both chemicals are found throughout the brain, although there are high concentrations in the midbrain, hypothalamus and thalamus, as well as the spinal cord. Positron emission tomography (PET) scans of opiate receptors in the human brain show the highest concentrations in the thalamus which is involved in pain, intermediate concentrations in the basal ganglia, which play an important role in movement and emotions, and low levels in the visual cortex (Lingford-Hughes 2005). Of note also, is that fMRI scans appear to reveal that regular heroin users evidence generalized dysfunctional connectivity throughout the brain, including the pre-frontal cortex, amygdala, hippocampus and corpus callosum. These may contribute to decreased self-control, impaired inhibitory function as well as deficits in stress regulation in chronic heroin users (Liu et al. 2009).

Socio-cultural factors

Only about 20 per cent of those who initiate drug use do so with the primary goal of pleasure seeking (Nutt and Law 2000). Other reasons include self-medication, social pressure and the search for 'meaning' or mystical experiences. Evidence of the use of heroin as a means of self-medication or as a means of reducing stress can be found in studies that show higher rates of heroin use in populations who live in stressful environments. Perhaps the most dramatic evidence of this is the estimated 40 per cent of American soldiers who used heroin during the Vietnam War, and the approximately 1 per cent who continued to use it when back in the USA (Grinspoon and Bakalar 1986). Further support for this hypothesis can be found in the high use of heroin and other drugs among people with conditions as varied as post-traumatic stress, eating disorders and schizophrenia (e.g. Johnson et al. 2006).

A second route to the use of heroin is as a progression from the use of other drugs, as users seek a greater 'high' than or different experience from those already achieved. Use can escalate to abuse, and then to dependence, involving increased tolerance of the drug, compulsive drug taking and withdrawal symptoms if the drug is not taken regularly. Sharing needles is relatively common and may contain a social or ritual element. For many addicts, maintaining a drug habit can be expensive, and beyond their financial resources, particularly where they find it difficult or choose not to hold down a job. As a result, use is often maintained by stealing: more than 95 per cent of American opiate-dependent individuals reported committing crimes to maintain their drug use (NIH Consensus Development Panel on Effective Treatment of Opiate Addiction 1998). Many users cannot maintain jobs, as much of their day is spent seeking and then taking drugs. The 'addiction career' often involves cycles of cessation and relapse, often over many years. Between one-quarter and one-third of users will die of a drug-related cause, generally an over-dose. An example of this history is afforded by Dai, a 29-year-old brought up in an economically marginalized council estate in South Wales. Here is the story of his drug taking, its associated problems, and how it was at least partly maintained by the social world he inhabited:

> Started smoking ciggies when I was 9 . . . bunk off school – hang around with me mates – some of the older kids – just hang around all day – no worries – just wander the streets all day. Soon got into sniffing glue – did it for about a year, year and a half. Didn't start as a regular thing – every now and then – but did it most days after a while. Used to be one of us would have a bag and some glue. Gave us a buzz. Yeah! Move on to dope at about 12. Did it with my mates. Spend a day in someone's house shitless on dope. F. . .cking good! Still smoke. Mellows me out. But then went on to speed. Took it about when I was 12 and something. Only took it at weekends, washed down with lager. Billy whiz . . . keeps you going, going, going. Good for dancing . . . After a while, taking the stuff everyday – starts getting expensive, so start lifting things, nicking, TWOCing [taking without consent: stealing cars]. Problems with the police – in front of the bench a few times. Got a fine, so have to nick again! Parents found out once got to police. Went ballistic when they found

out. First time they knew I was taking drugs. Beaten shitless by my father. Grounded – not that that did much good. Old man's a hypocrite anyway – drinks loads, but dead against drugs. Anyway, tried loads of other shit after that – LSD, tabs [benzodiazepines], Temazies, E's, uppers, downers. Sixteen. Stoned out of my mind on dope, one of my mates asked if I wanted some smack. So I said, 'Yeah!' Anything for a buzz. He injected me. That did it. What a rush! I felt I was superman! I could do anything. That was it. Hooked. Stopped taking speed – smack was it.

Left school at 16. Parents knew I was taking smack. Took me to loads of docs, but didn't do anything. So, they washed their hands of me – didn't want to know – chucked me out. Crashed on my mates' floors for a while. Got a council house pretty quickly. Got chucked out pretty quickly too – didn't pay the rent! Not good at paying rent! Smack had me hooked. The more I used, the more money I needed. So, I got into breaking and entering – always getting caught. Fines, probation, then time in prison. But that didn't stop me taking the stuff. You can get anything you want inside if you know the right people. Went to prison for the first time just before my 18th birthday – four months for burglary.

Cut a long story short – been in and out of prison for the last 12 years. Had girlfriends. Lived with one woman for about three years. Got a daughter with her – see her sometimes, but not a lot. They don't come and see me when I'm inside . . . Smack has a hold on me and I can't let go. My mates all take the stuff. I don't know anyone that doesn't use. So, I've nothing else. Did give up once. Went on a programme in prison. Came out clean – stayed clean for about three months. They put me up in a hostel when I came out – so I could stay away from my mates . . . Stop using in the 'real world' . . . But then I had to leave as they didn't have money to keep me there. So, I went back to my old haunts. Soon back to jacking up . . .

Don't enjoy the dope now. I'm pissed with the routine – take drugs, steal, go to prison, take drugs . . . Don't get the buzz from using. I've got to take it so it doesn't do my head in. I'm trying to get out of it – stop using. I'm on methadone [see p. 433], so I can stop taking the stuff. But they don't give enough . . . still get withdrawals – heart pounding, sweats, cramps. So I'm still using – but less than I was – was using about three bags a day, now it's a bag, bag and a half. I'll try to get more methadone – try to keep off the smack altogether, but they don't like to give you too much.

Psychological factors

The psychological factors associated with opiate use are similar to those involved in alcohol use. That is, in the case of the conditioning model, the pleasure of taking the drug establishes an operant conditioning process in which the individual is rewarded for taking the drug by the pleasant effects and reductions in tension associated with its use, and then the avoidance of withdrawal symptoms. Classical conditioning triggers cravings for heroin when a user encounters conditions similar to its previous use. These conditioned responses may be both powerful and sustained over time. Meyer (1995), for example, reported that the sight of a needle may decrease the severity of withdrawal symptoms while coming off heroin. Conversely, cues conditioned to withdrawal may trigger its symptoms, even years after heroin use has been stopped. Cognitive factors are also involved in expectancies of both pleasure and ultimately, fear of withdrawal. Expectancy theory (Goldman 1999a) is also relevant in this context.

A biopsychosocial model

Combining pharmacological and psychological processes within one model, the incentive sensitization theory of Robinson and Berridge (2008) contended that the most important psychological changes associated with drug use is a 'sensitization' or hypersensitivity, at a neurological level, to what they termed the incentive motivational effects of drugs and drug-associated stimuli. Incentive sensitization involves a bias of attentional processing towards drug-associated stimuli and a pathological motivation for drugs (compulsive 'wanting'). When combined with impaired executive control over behaviour, incentive sensitization culminates in the core symptoms of addiction. As this is a partly (Pavlovian) conditioned process, this may be particularly triggered by contexts associated with previous drug use. Behavioural evidence of this sensitization can be found in drug addicts whose attention is biased to visual drug-associated cues at an overt and implicit level (Wiers and Stacy 2006). Neural evidence of sensitization can be found in studies that have shown repeated intermittent administration of amphetamine causes increased dopamine release in humans, even when a drug is given a year after the initial administration, while drug cues can also elicit a significant conditioned dopamine response even in the absence of the drug (Boileau et al. 2006, 2007).

Treatment of heroin use

Harm minimization approaches: the socio-cultural approach

Harm minimization strategies do not attempt to 'treat' addiction. Instead, they reduce the harm associated with the continued use of drugs either by substituting the use of heroin with a safer oral medication, known as methadone, or reducing risk of infection by ensuring those who continue to inject do so using clean needles.

Methadone maintenance   Methadone is an opiate agonist. Methadone replacement programmes provide opiate users with an orally taken drug that does not give them the high associated with opiate use, but does prevent withdrawal symptoms when opiates are not taken. Its use is intended to prevent the risks of needle sharing and overdose, and to prevent withdrawal when individuals initially seek help: a time that may be particularly chaotic in their lives. Methadone can be prescribed for periods of a year or more, during which time the recipient is expected to 'stabilize' their life and prepare for subsequent withdrawal from it. Users typically have to report to a drug centre on a daily basis – where they are given sufficient methadone to get them through to the next day, to try to maintain contact with support services and to stop them selling it on the black market – or, in the UK, a pharmacist or family doctor. About half of UK family doctors are providing methadone to opiate users at any one time (Strang et al. 2005).

This approach appears to be successful. Indeed, Mattick et al. (2009), in their Cochrane review of the intervention concluded that methadone was superior to non-pharmacological approaches and placebo in retaining patients in treatment and in the suppression of heroin use measured by both self-report use and urine/hair analysis. In the largest study of its use, the Drug Abuse Treatment Outcome Study (Hubbard et al. 1997) followed nearly 3000 people receiving outpatient methadone treatment. In the year following its prescription, the percentage of people to use heroin weekly or daily fell from 90 to 30 per cent. Only 17 per cent of those who remained in the programme for a year were still using heroin at follow-up. Reasons given for continued use of heroin included being maintained on too low a dose of methadone, the desire for the 'high' achieved with opiates, the strength of self-identity as an 'addict', and living with a partner or continued social relationships with people who took intravenous drugs (Avants et al. 1999).

Needle-exchange schemes   Needle-exchange schemes exchange old for new needles and prevent the need for sharing, reducing risk of cross-infection of various blood-borne viruses including HIV and hepatitis. Some right-wing and church groups in the USA have condemned this approach, claiming that it maintains, or even encourages, the use of drugs. As a result, needle-exchange schemes are legal in some US states and illegal in others. A report by the North American Syringe Exchange Network (in Yoast et al. 2001), for example, found that of a sample of 100 US programmes, 52 were legal, 16 were illegal but 'tolerated', while 32 were 'underground'. Longitudinal studies suggest that where syringes cannot legally be obtained elsewhere, needle-exchange programmes are effective in reducing use of shared needles (Kerr et al. 2005), although use is not always high. Gindi et al. (2009), for example, reported the median number of return visits in one year among people who had used the Baltimore needle exchange programme was one. More worryingly, Taylor et al. (2001) reported the prevalence of shared needle use between 1990 and 1999 in Scotland, which showed a reduction in the use of shared needles between 1990 and 1992 following the introduction of needle-exchange schemes, but then a gradual increase in sharing whether from a partner or 'casual acquaintance' in the following years despite their continued provision. These data mirror some of the changes in risk behaviours in other populations at risk for HIV, where initial changes towards safer behaviours have dwindled and more risky behaviours have returned over time. The reasons for this are unclear, but may relate to the relatively low profile given to HIV/AIDS awareness in the UK and increasing beliefs that AIDS can be 'cured'.

Withdrawal

Most of the interventions described below follow a period of withdrawal. This often involves levels of methadone being gradually reduced over a period of weeks, to minimize withdrawal symptoms. A shorter-term withdrawal involves rapid detoxification, with withdrawal symptoms controlled by other opiate agonists such as clonidine hydrochloride (Marsch et al. 2005). This reduces, but does not totally prevent, many of the symptoms of withdrawal. These strategies can be used in both in-patient and outpatient settings, and can achieve total withdrawal within three days.

Drug therapy

Longer-term use of drug therapy may involve the use of drugs that negate the effects of heroin. Naltrexone is an opiate antagonist that binds with opioid receptors in the brain and blocks the effect of opiate drugs. It is taken on a regular basis and prevents the 'high' associated with opiates if taken. As few as 3 per cent of people offered this form of intervention chose to take it up, and many fail to take the drug regularly. This may be the consequence of an inability to withdraw from opiates, fear of a new drug and residual dependence, or a lack of genuine motivation to remain drug-free (Tucker and Ritter 2000). Among highly motivated individuals who actually use naltrexone, outcomes are relatively good. It results in lower cravings for opiates, longer periods of abstinence, and greater improvements in psychosocial functioning than placebo. Despite these successes, many people will restart or continue using opiates following treatment. Abstinence rates as high as 64 per cent have been found in well-supported and 'high coping' individuals at 18-month follow-up, although rates between 31 and 53 per cent are more typical (Tucker and Ritter 2000). The effects of naltrexone may be added to by combining it with a benzodiazepine to reduce insomnia and 'excitability' that may accompany its use (Stella et al. 2005).

Psychological approaches

Operant programmes   Many people who take methadone also continue to use opiates (see the case of Dai, pp. 431–2). In an attempt to minimize this, Gruber et al. (2000) investigated whether providing extrinsic rewards to people attending methadone clinics could increase attendance and drug abstinence. Their incentives to attend counselling sessions included bus tokens and vouchers to be spent on activities or items agreed by their counsellor. As incentives for abstinence, participants received free weekend recreational activities, lunches, a modest financial sum per week in vouchers and rent payment. This approach was compared with a standard treatment approach in which clients were encouraged to attend routine methadone clinics but were not rewarded for doing so. One month after entry, 61 per cent of participants in this condition, compared with 17 per cent of those in the standard treatment, were enrolled in treatment; 50 per cent of participants compared with 21 per cent of controls had achieved 30 days of abstinence from heroin.

Cognitive behavioural therapy   Despite their effectiveness in the treatment of alcohol problems, there are relatively few studies of the effectiveness of cognitive behavioural programmes in injecting drug users – although several studies in other drug-dependent populations such as cocaine or amphetamine users suggest they would be of benefit (e.g. Baker et al. 2005), and psychosocial interventions in general appear to add to the benefits of medication alone (Amatom et al. 2008). In one study, Scherbaum et al. (2005) compared group cognitive therapy with standard treatment and, although they found no immediate benefits, people who participated in the therapy were using fewer opiates than the standard treatment group six months following the intervention. However, data from Gruber et al. (2000) who found that a brief one-session counselling intervention was as effective as a longer-term counselling programme suggests that complex cognitive behavioural programmes may not be the treatment of choice for many programmes.

Couples therapy   Just as for alcohol problems, couples therapy may be more effective in the treatment of drug dependence than individual therapy. In their review of interventions, O'Farrell and Fals-Stewart (2000) reported that those people who received couples therapy had improved relationships and used fewer drugs, in both the short and the long term, than comparative groups in either no-treatment or individual therapy conditions. In addition, drop-out rates were significantly lower than for any other treatment approaches. This has important implications, as it means that more people received a beneficial 'level' of intervention, some of whom may have been 'less motivated' individuals who would have dropped out of other forms of intervention. That couples therapy still appears more effective than the other treatment approaches, while including a 'harder to treat' group of clients, reinforces its high success levels.

16.4 Pathological gambling

Most of us gamble at some time. However, for some, gambling becomes addictive and is as difficult to stop as the use of drugs. Although it is identified as an impulse disorder in DSM-IV-TR (APA 2000), pathological gambling is considered in the same behavioural terms as an addiction. Its diagnosis requires five or more of the following:

- a preoccupation with gambling
- a need to gamble with increasing amounts of money in order to achieve the desired excitement
- repeated, unsuccessful efforts to control, cut back or stop gambling
- its use as a way of escaping from problems or relieving dysphoric mood states
- a return to gambling following losses in the hope of 'getting even' ('chasing')
- lying to family members or others to conceal the extent of gambling
- committing illegal acts such as forgery or fraud to continue gambling
- jeopardizing or losing significant relationships as a result of gambling.

Pathological gambling is usually the end-point of a gradual shift through social, frequent, problem and finally pathological gambling. Each 'stage' involves a greater psychological and financial commitment to gambling, and an increase in associated problems. A survey commissioned by the British gambling charity GamCare (National Centre for Social Research 1999), reported that 0.8 per cent of British gamblers could be classified as 'problem gamblers': lower than the USA (1.1 per cent), Australia (2.3 per cent) and Spain (1.4 per cent).

Pathological gambling can result in the individual jeopardizing or losing a significant relationship or job. When they can no longer raise the money needed, they may turn to criminal activity to obtain money: an estimated 60–5 per cent of pathological gamblers have committed criminal offences in order to continue gambling (Turner et al. 2009). It has been linked to antisocial, narcissistic and borderline personality disorders. In addition, up to 30 per cent of pathological gamblers may have alcohol-related problems. The relationship with alcohol is important, as some have taken it to suggest that both alcohol and gambling problems are indicative of a more general 'addictive' personality.

Aetiology of pathological gambling

Genetic factors

Family studies (e.g. Slutske et al. 2009) involving large numbers of twin pairs have found genetic factors to account for between around 45 per cent of the vulnerability to various types of pathological gambling. Summarizing the evidence, Comings et al. (2001) reported that the DRD2, DRD4, DAT1, TPH, ADRA2C, NMDA1, and PS1 genes (moderating dopamine, serotonin and norepinephrine metabolism) were involved in moderating risk of pathological gambling – although the variance in behaviour explained by each gene was very low (less than 1 per cent).

Biological factors

One of the factors thought to be associated with gambling is the 'buzz' of winning or coming close to winning, which has been equated with the 'high' achieved through taking drugs. A number of neurotransmitters seem to mediate this response. Dopamine levels have been found to rise after a winning streak, with activation of the reward system common to other addictions (Zack and Poulos 2009). Raised levels of norepinephrine have also been found following episodes of gambling. These may impact on activity within both the brain and the sympathetic nervous system (see Chapter 4 and Research box 16). In social gamblers, these neurochemical processes typically occur while gambling. Among pathological gamblers, they occur while anticipating gambling or as a classically conditioned response to gambling-related stimuli (Sharpe et al. 1995). These effects are not trivial, and withdrawal from gambling may result in symptoms similar, or even more severe, to those experienced while coming off drugs. Rosenthal and Lesieur (1992), for example, found that two-thirds of pathological gamblers reported at least one physical side-effect during withdrawal. These included insomnia, headaches, loss of appetite, physical weakness, heart racing, muscle aches, breathing difficulty and chills, and were often more severe than those experienced by a comparison group reporting their experiences of withdrawal from drugs.

Meyer, G., Schwertfeger, J., Exton, M.S. et al. (2004) Neuroendocrine response to casino gambling in problem gamblers, *Psychoneuroendocrinology*, 29: 1272–80.

According to the authors, self-reports and observations of gamblers attending casinos indicate that gambling can directly affect physiological, emotional and mental states. The monetary stakes, recognition of risk, and the hope of winnings produce stimulation, arousal, well-being and euphoria. To date, however, only a few studies have investigated the effect of gambling on physiological emotional states. Their study examined the effect of gambling on cardiovascular (heart rate) and neuroendocrine activity (cortisol – a stress hormone) in a real gambling situation.

Method

Participants

Fourteen regular blackjack players were approached in a casino and agreed to participate in the study. Two were subsequently excluded from analyses due to alcohol consumption, one had a viral infection, and one was taking blood pressure medication. As a consequence, a final group of 10 male gamblers (mean age 44.5 years) participated in the study.

Measures

Heart rate was continuously measured using a portable heart rate monitor. The ECG was transmitted from a chest patch to a receiver that was worn around the wrist in the mode of a watch. Saliva samples were collected for the detection of cortisol using a cotton wool swab placed in participants' mouths for 2 minutes. The swab was subsequently placed into a prepared tube and stored on ice until assessment of cortisol levels. The severity of pathological gambling was assessed using a 20-item questionnaire which assessed items including preoccupation with gambling, loss of control, escapism, financial indebtedness, 'chasing one's losses', illegal acts and feelings of guilt.

Procedure

Each person participated in a gambling and a control session, with both sessions occurring in the same casino environment. In each condition they sat at a blackjack table and either participated in the game using their own money or played a game of cards without any monetary stakes for a period of two hours. In both conditions, salivary measures of cortisol were taken at baseline, after 30 and 60 minutes, and following the end of play. Heart rate was measured continuously, with data reported at the same times as the cortisol was measured.

Results

Figure 16.1 shows the heart rate during gambling and the control condition. Salivary cortisol was also elevated in the period of gambling compared with control conditions. Peak cortisol increase at 60 minutes was significantly higher than control levels. Although salivary cortisol levels dropped following completion of the gambling session, cortisol remained significantly elevated compared with levels at the end of play. Severity of pathological gambling was unrelated to the reactivity of heart rate during gambling.

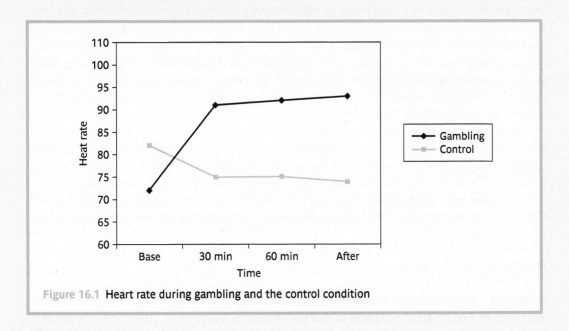

Figure 16.1 Heart rate during gambling and the control condition

Discussion

The degree of increased heart rate during gambling was lower than that associated with the acute stress of parachute jumping, but was comparable to that evoked by the stress of public speaking and mental arithmetic – but lasted much longer. In addition, and unlike these previous stressors, heart rate elevations continued following termination of gambling. Severity of pathological gambling was unrelated to the reactivity of heart rate during gambling.

The study provided the first demonstration that the arousal of gambling induces a secretion of salivary cortisol. This was lower than salivary cortisol responses to very brief, intense stressors. Instead, the cortisol profile was similar to that observed in acute stress situations that last between 1 and 2 hours.

The sympathetic (and unmeasured dopaminergic and endorphin activity) consequences of gambling may reinforce and encourage future gambling. However, the relevance of increased cortisol for the maintenance of gambling behaviour is unclear. Physiological responses to gambling enhance mood, and winning can produce a 'euphoric' state. Cortisol may contribute to such mood alterations because acute cortisol administration has been shown to enhance positive feelings – although longer-term secretion may be associated with lowering of mood.

Socio-cultural factors

In general, greater access to gambling opportunities seems to increase both social and problem gambling. Ladouceur et al. (1999), for example, found that as availability of gambling increased over time in a number of countries, so too did rates of pathological gambling. In Australia, the Productivity Commission (1999), however, found little difference in levels of gambling-related expenditure and problem gambling as a consequence of significant differences in access to gambling across various Australian states. The one exception to this was access to gaming machines. In this case, greater availability was associated with higher rates of problem gambling. By contrast, removal of gambling machines in Norway resulted in a reduction in gambling and no substitution to other types of gambling (Lund 2009).

Once in a gambling context, a number of factors, and in particular alcohol consumption, may influence the extent of gambling. Ellery et al. (2005), for example, found that alcohol increased the time videopoker players spent gambling and the frequency with which they placed 'power bets', as well as increasing the time played while losing money. It is perhaps noteworthy that many regular casino gamblers drink less while gambling than they usually do: a finding that led Dickerson and Baron (2000) to challenge the notion that gambling and alcohol consumption share a common genetic risk.

Psychological factors

Impulsivity High levels of impulsivity in childhood may be a risk factor for pathological gambling. In one longitudinal study of this phenomenon, Vitaro et al. (1999) investigated the predictive strength of four measures of impulsivity in 13–14-year-olds: teacher ratings, self-report and performance on a card-playing task and a 'delay in gratification task'. Gambling was subsequently measured at the age of 17 years. Among the factors that predicted gambling were perseveration on the card-playing task and an inability to delay gratification. These findings were considered indicative of a tendency to respond excessively to positive outcomes, to require immediate reinforcement, and insensitivity to negative consequences: characteristics of the pathological gambler.

Learning history   As with other addictions, operant and classical conditioning serve to maintain gambling behaviour. Early models of gambling assumed that gambling was essentially maintained by the intermittent reinforcement – both biological and economic – inherent in gambling. Losses would be sustained in the hope of later gains. Variable and intermittent reinforcement schedules lead to the rapid acquisition of behaviour and render it resistant to extinction. Sharpe (2002) suggested that while these undoubtedly contribute to high levels of social gambling, they do not fully explain pathological gambling, where consistent and significant losses do not result in a cessation of gambling. Sharpe suggested that large pay-outs, and in particular a 'big win' early in a gambling career, establish and sustain pathological gambling. These presumably distort expectations of the outcomes of gambling, and support losses in the expectation of future 'big wins'.

Cognitive processes   Differing cognitive processes instigate and maintain gambling. Pro-gambling attitudes increase the likelihood of gambling, and may be a consequence of early exposure to family influences. Oei and Raylu (2004), for example, found that parents', and especially fathers', attitudes towards gambling were predictive of their children's beliefs and attitudes. Although pro-gambling attitudes appear to lead to participation in gambling activities, they do not sustain gambling once initiated (Sharpe 2002). Other forms of cognitive self-talk may be important at this time. Delfabbro and Winefield (1999), for example, found that 75 per cent of all game-related cognitions during gambling were irrational in nature and supportive of continued gambling. Such thoughts may stimulate impulsivity, discount losses and even lead the individual to feel that they have some degree of control over their fate. This type of self-talk may also sustain arousal while gambling: several studies (e.g. Sharpe et al. 1995) have found a relationship between the frequency of irrational verbalizations and arousal levels.

Negative emotions   Low mood or anxiety appear to be triggers to gambling among many pathological, but not casual, gamblers (Skokauskas and Satkeviciute 2007). Dysphoric mood before gambling may also result in more persistent gambling following losses. As a partial explanation for this phenomenon, Dickerson and Baron (2000) suggested that low mood may reduce perceptions of control over gambling, and hence reduce attempts to curtail the activity even when losing.

A biopsychosocial model of gambling

These various findings each contributed to Sharpe's (2002) biopsychosocial model of gambling. She suggested that this may involve three early risk factors:

- a biological vulnerability involving the dopaminergic and serotonergic systems
- family attitudes that support gambling
- high levels of impulsivity.

These factors may lead to a number of gambling experiences as a relatively young individual. In these, the individual becomes socialized into a gambling culture. A pattern of early wins may also reinforce gambling and distort beliefs about, and attitudes towards, it. More attention may be paid, for example, to success than failures. At the same time, the individual may become pleasantly physiologically aroused while gambling. All of these factors serve to maintain an interest. As a gambling career progresses, episodes may be triggered by hopes of avoiding stress, boredom or improving mood. Gambling is used to increase arousal and as a means of escape from reality. Once in the gambling situation, cognitive biases and the arousal experienced serve to maintain the behaviour, whether winning or losing.

Stop and think...

Gambling has never been easier. Internet gambling, in particular, allows the possibility of winning, or losing, significant amounts of money in the comfort of your own home. Mark Griffiths, a well-known UK gambling researcher, identified a number of factors associated with internet gambling that makes this potentially tempting and risky for people with gambling problems: accessibility, affordability, anonymity, convenience, escape immersion/dissociation, disinhibition, event frequency, asociability and interactivity (Griffiths 2003).

Given these risks, should there be controls over who can gamble on the internet? If so, how should such controls be determined? Or should such gambling be open to all . . . and at their own risk?

Treatment of pathological gambling

Empirical evaluations of treatments for pathological gambling are still relatively rare, although what evidence there is, is encouraging (Pallesen et al. 2005). Self-help programmes such as the Gamblers Anonymous 12-step programme have achieved abstinence rates of about 8 per cent over a one-year period and 7 per cent over two years (Stewart and Brown 1988). More formal interventions have reported one-year abstinence rates as high as 55 per cent.

Behavioural approaches

One of the earliest treatment studies, reported by McConaghy et al. (1983), compared the effectiveness of aversion therapy and imaginal desensitization. Aversion therapy involved participants reading aloud words on a series of cards, some of which were related to gambling activities and some of which described alternative actions such as 'went straight home'. Each time they read out a gambling-related phrase they received a mild electric shock described as 'unpleasant but not emotionally upsetting' (McConaghy et al. 1983: 367) for two seconds. Imaginal desensitization involved participants imagining a variety of gambling-related scenarios at the same time as using relaxation procedures to reduce arousal. The latter approach proved the most effective on measures of gambling urge and behaviour over the year following treatment. Long-term follow-up, conducted between two and nine years after the end of therapy, found that 79 per cent of those who took part in the desensitization programme reported control over or having stopped gambling. Just over 50 per cent of the aversion therapy group reported the same outcomes (McConaghy et al. 1991).

Cognitive behavioural approaches

A number of studies have reported positive results following cognitive behavioural procedures. Gooding and Tarrier (2009) summarized data from 25 studies involving the use of cognitive therapies, including cognitive therapy, motivational interviewing and imaginal desensitization (see above) and found that they all showed evidence of effect up to two years following the intervention. Although the data were not conclusive, they also seemed to indicate that cognitive therapy was the most effective of the three. In one such study, Ladouceur et al. (2001) randomly allocated pathological gamblers into either cognitive therapy or waiting list control group. The cognitive intervention had two elements. The first involved cognitive correction, in which participants' misconceptions on randomness were challenged. This involved both an educational component on the nature of randomness and the identification and challenge of erroneous cognitions made while gambling. This was achieved by tape-recording verbalizations ('. . . if I lose four times in a row, I will definitely win the next time . . .') made during a session of imaginal gambling followed by the therapist 'correcting' them within the therapy session. The second element involved training in relapse prevention. In this, participants identified high-risk situations and planned how to cope with them should they arise. The intervention was successful: 54 per cent of participants in the cognitive intervention improved by at least 50 per cent on a composite measure of recovery which included frequency of gambling and perceived control over gambling behaviour, compared with only 7 per cent of those in the control group. Furthermore, 85 per cent of participants in the treatment programme compared with only 14 per cent of those in the control group achieved 50 per cent improvements on at least three of the four measures. These gains were generally maintained at six-month, twelve-month and two-year follow-up (Ladouceur et al. 2003). Petry et al. (2008) reported greater benefits than brief advice following both one-session motivational intervention and one combining motivation plus three sessions of cognitive behavioural therapy. Interestingly, the single session proved the most effective in the short term, although the combined intervention proved equally successful over a longer follow-up period.

Pharmacological therapies

Given the multiple biochemical pathways that drive pathological gambling, a number of medications may be of benefit. Despite this, few controlled studies of their effects have been conducted. Early studies focused on the use of SSRIs, and found them to be relatively successful. In a total population of 10 participants, Hollander et al. (2000) found modest gains following treatment with fluvoxamine. More recently, Dannon et al. (2007) compared the effects of two drug types: an SSRI (fluvoxamine) and the opiate antagonist (naltrexone). In a small, uncontrolled, study, they measured outcomes in a group of gamblers who had been previously successfully treated using the same medication they were given during the trial both during further treatment and in a 6-month no treatment follow-up period. During this time, just under half the participants relapsed (i.e. gambled on at least one occasion): 3 out of 6 in the fluvoxamine group, and 4 out of 10 in the naltroxelone. However, those that did gamble reported a reduction in their gambling losses.

16.5 Chapter summary

1 Drug use is relatively common throughout most social groups, although some groups use more than others do.

2 Excess alcohol consumption results in a number of negative short-term social consequences, including risky or dangerous behaviours, and long-term health consequences, such as cirrhosis and Korsakoff's syndrome.

3 Genetic factors may influence risk for high levels of alcohol.

4 Alcohol influences mood through its impact on levels of GABA and dopamine.

5 Social factors, including ease of access, peer influence, cost and advertising, influence levels of consumption.

6 Psychological explanations of drinking include operant and classical conditioning experiences and cognitions that support consumption.

7 Legal and social interventions impact on drinking levels throughout the population.

8 Treatment of alcohol-dependent individuals usually begins with a period of withdrawal.

9 Antidipstrotrophics can help maintain abstinence in highly motivated groups or where its use is compulsory.

10 Both the 12-step model which advocates abstinence and cognitive behavioural interventions that can support abstinence or controlled drinking appear equally effective in maintaining abstinence or appropriate drinking levels.

11 Couples therapy is particularly effective for people with drinking problems.

12 Opiates exert their action through dopamine levels, endorphins and enkephalins.

13 Harm reduction strategies, including methadone maintenance and needle-exchange schemes, can be successful in reducing opiate use-related harm.

14 As with alcohol, behavioural therapy and social approaches can be effective in the treatment of opiate dependence: couples therapy may be the most effective intervention where appropriate.

15 Gambling results in similar neurochemical changes to those associated with drug use.

16 The biopsychosocial model implicates biological, family, psychological and learning history factors in the aetiology of problem gambling.

17 Cognitive behavioural therapy, antidepressants and opiate antagonists may prove effective in reducing gambling-related problems.

16.6 For discussion

1 Why might the various approaches to the treatment of alcohol-related problems differ little in their effectiveness?

2 Switzerland legalized opiate use in 2004. What are the costs and benefits of this approach for the individual and society?

3 Many people receiving treatment for addictions continue to engage in their addiction. Is this an acceptable behaviour within therapy?

4 Should access to gaming machines be controlled?

16.7 Key terms

Anterograde amnesia lack of memory for events that occur after an event that causes amnesia.

Ataxia an incoordination and unsteadiness due to brain's failure to regulate posture and strength and direction of limb movement.

Confabulate to make up 'facts', usually to hide confusion or poor memory.

Dysphoric unhappy, but not sufficiently so to warrant a diagnosis of depression.

Retrograde amnesia lack of memory for events that occurred before an event that causes amnesia.

16.8 Further reading

Anderson, P., Chisholm, D. and Fuhr D.C. (2009) Effectiveness and cost-effectiveness of policies and programmes to reduce the harm caused by alcohol, *Lancet*, 373: 2234–46.

Nutt, D. and Lingford-Hughes, A. (2008) Addiction: the clinical interface, *British Journal of Pharmacology*, 154: 397–405.

Petersen, T. and McBride, A. (2002) *Working with Substance Misusers: A Guide to Theory and Practice*. London: Routledge.

Petry, N.M., Weinstock, J., Ledgerwood, D.M. et al. (2008) A randomized trial of brief interventions for problem and pathological gamblers, *Journal of Consulting and Clinical Psychology*, 76: 318–28.

Robinson, T.E. and Berridge, K.C. (2008) Review. The incentive sensitization theory of addiction: some current issues, *Philosophical Transactions of the Royal Society of London: Series B, Biological Sciences*, 363: 3137–46.

Sharpe, L. (2002) A reformulated cognitive-behavioural model of problem gambling: a biopsychosocial perspective, *Clinical Psychology Review*, 22: 1–25.

Wesst, R. (2006) *A Theory of Addiction*. Chichester: John Wiley.

The following websites also have information about conditions in this chapter, their treatment, and people's experiences of them.

Alcohol

www.aa.org/?Media=PlayFlash
www.drinkaware.co.uk/facts/factsheets/alcohol-dependence
hpretreats.com/?gclid=CMXQw6DF-aICFQiX2AodWnQgjA

Heroin

www.drugrehab.co.uk/FAQ-heroin.htm
www.youtube.com/watch?v=OIUASXb0Jrk

Gambling

www.21stepstostopgambling.com/
www.gamcare.org.uk/

A

Aetiology explanations of the causes of disease.

Agonist drug that increases the action of a neurotransmitter.

Agranulocytosis condition in which the bone marrow fails to produce enough white blood cells called neutrophils. Leaves the individual prone to infection.

Alexithymia a paucity of emotional experience and awareness, with an associated poverty of imagination and a tendency to focus upon the tangible and mundane.

Alogia poverty of speech; literally, 'no words'.

Alzheimer's disease the most common cause of dementia in old age.

Antagonist drug that inhibits the action of a neurotransmitter.

Anterograde amnesia lack of memory for events that occur after an event that causes amnesia.

Aphonia inability to speak.

Ataxia an incoordination and unsteadiness due to brain's failure to regulate posture and strength and direction of limb movement.

Avolition lack of volition, or voluntary motivation.

B

Behaviour therapy form of therapy that targets behavioural change by changing the triggers or consequences of behaviour using operant or classical conditioning-based interventions.

C

Catatonic behaviour behaviour found in one form of schizophrenia; includes posturing, or 'waxy flexibility', mutism and stupor.

Catharsis reliving past repressed emotions in order to come to terms with past conflicts.

Chromosome structures within a cell that contain genes.

Classical conditioning the learned association between two co-occurring stimuli, such that a similar response is evoked by either.

Client a term often used to denote an individual in therapy. In contrast to words such as patient or subject, it is used to indicate the helping, non-hierarchical nature of the therapeutic relationship between therapist and individual.

Clinical supervision discussion and feedback on therapy by peers or experts intended to improve therapeutic formulation and treatment.

Cognitive challenge the identification and disputation of maladaptive cognitions.

Cognitive schema a consistent set of beliefs that influence mood and behaviour.

Community Mental Health Team a multidisciplinary team providing mental health care within the community. Usually includes psychiatrists, community psychiatric nurses, psychologists and other therapists.

Confabulate to make up 'facts', usually to hide confusion or poor memory.

D

Defence mechanism an unconscious mental act that prevents the individual from psychological harm.

Delusion a strongly held inappropriate belief; usually a belief that is normally considered impossible.

Depot injection injection of a slow-release drug that will provide a therapeutic dose for days or weeks.

Disorganized symptoms (of schizophrenia) include confused thinking and speech and behaviour that do not make sense.

DSM-IV-TR the *Diagnostic and Statistical Manual* (fourth edition with text revision: APA 2000) – US system of classification of mental health disorders.

Dysphoric unhappy, but not sufficiently so to warrant a diagnosis of depression.

Dyzygotic (DZ) twins non-identical twins.

E

Effect size provides a measure of the effect of an intervention; 0.2 is considered small, above 0.6 is a large effect, and between is moderate.

Ego according to Freud, the part of the personality that operates under the reality principle and works to maximize gratification within the constraints of the 'real world'.

Electroconvulsive therapy (ECT) treatment involving passing a brief electric current through the temporal lobe(s) as a treatment for depression and schizophrenia.

Executive function neurological coordination of a number of complex processes, including speech, motor coordination and behavioural planning.

Extrapyramidal symptoms symptoms that result from low levels of dopamine in the extrapyramidal regions of the brain, often as a result of long-term phenothiazine use. Include Parkinsonism and tardive dyskinesia.

F

Flattened mood lack of emotional response, either positive or negative, to events.

G

Glucocorticoid a corticosteroid. Has anti-inflammatory and immunosuppressive effect.

H

Half-life the time required for half the quantity of a drug to be metabolized or eliminated by normal biological processes.

Hallucination the experience of touch, visions or sounds in the absence of external stimuli.

Heritability coefficient the degree to which individual differences are due to genetic factors.

Hydrocephalus retention of cerebrospinal fluid within the ventricles of the brain. The fluid is often under increased pressure and can compress and damage the brain.

Hyperalgesia abnormally increased pain sensation – a lowered pain threshold.

Hyperventilation short rapid breaths that lead to low levels of carbon dioxide in the blood and physical sensations including tingling in the arms,

dizziness and feelings of an inability to breathe.

Hysterical disorder physical symptoms in the absence of physical pathology.

I

Id according to Freud, the personality component driven by the basic instincts of sex and aggression.

Ideas of reference the, inappropriate, belief that objects, events or people are of personal significance. For example, a person may think that a television programme he is watching is all about him. May reach sufficient intensity to constitute delusions.

Incidence the frequency with which new cases of a condition arise within the population.

Interpersonal psychotherapy a form of therapy focusing exclusively on changing interpersonal problems that contribute to mental health problems.

L

Learned helplessness a belief that one has no control over events; results in a cessation of attempts at control.

Lobotomy an early form of psychosurgery.

M

Major tranquillizers see phenothiazines.

MAOI (monoamine oxidase inhibitor) a form of antidepressant, whose action is on the norepinephrine system.

Meta-analysis a statistical method of combining the data from several studies using similar measures that allows a more powerful analysis of the effect of the intervention than that provided by single, relatively small studies.

Monozygotic (MZ) twins identical twins, with identical genetic structure.

N

Narcolepsy a disorder characterized by sudden and uncontrollable, though often brief, attacks of deep sleep.

Negative symptoms (of schizophrenia) include absence of activation, and include apathy, lack of motivation or poverty of speech.

Neologism making up new words.

Neuroleptics a broad class of drugs used to treat psychotic condition such as schizophrenia; otherwise known as major tranquillizers or phenothiazines.

Neurotransmitter chemical involved in maintaining neuronal activity; transmits information across the synaptic cleft.

O

Operant (Skinnerian) conditioning manipulation of behaviour through the use of reinforcement and punishment schedules.

P

Perseveration inability to shift from a cognitive set, resulting in inappropriate repetitive behaviour, including speech.

Pharmacotherapy treatment with drugs.

Phenothiazines major tranquillizers used to treat schizophrenia, of which the best known is chlorpromazine; their action is usually on the dopaminergic system.

Placebo inactive treatments (either pharmacological or psychological) against which active treatment trials are often evaluated. These allow the assessment of the general effects of receiving some form of attention or 'treatment'. Differences in outcomes between placebo conditions and active interventions are considered to show the specific effects of the therapy against which it is compared.

Polygenic caused by multiple genes.

Positive symptoms (of schizophrenia) include hallucinations, delusions, disorganized speech or positive thought disorder.

Prevalence the frequency with which a particular condition is found within the population at any one time.

Primary care basic or general health care focused on the point at which a patient ideally first seeks assistance from the medical care system.

Psychoanalysis there are a number of different psychoanalytic therapies. Most share a number of therapeutic goals, including gaining insight into the nature of the original trauma and bringing troubling material to consciousness so the individual can cope with it without the use of ego defence mechanisms.

Psycho-educational programme a treatment usually combining elements of education about a problem or means of coping with it with cognitive behavioural strategies of change.

Psychomotor movements involving both mental and motor processes.

Psychosis includes a number of mental health conditions, such as schizophrenia, each of which has the common symptom of a loss of contact with reality.

Psychotherapist a generic term for someone who provides some form of therapy. In this book, it does not denote any particular therapeutic orientation, and may include therapists as diverse as cognitive and psychoanalytic in practice.

Psychotic the presence of a mental health condition, such as schizophrenia, of which the main symptom is a loss of contact with reality.

Psychotropic medication drugs used to treat mental health problems by their action on neurotransmitter levels.

R

Retrograde amnesia lack of memory for events that occurred before an event that causes amnesia.

S

Self-actualization described by the humanists as the experience of fulfilling one's potential for growth.

Self-instruction training developed by Meichenbaum, involves the use of coping self-statements at times of stress.

SNRIs (serotonin/norepinephrine re-uptake inhibitors) antidepressants thought to inhibit neuronal uptake of serotonin, norepinephrine and dopamine in the central nervous system.

Spillover here, a failure to separate work and home life, such that each intrudes on the other.

SSRIs (selective serotonin re-uptake inhibitors) a form of antidepressant, whose action is on the serotinergic system.

Stereotypic behaviours repetitive, non-spontaneous, apparently non-functional behaviours.

Stress management a specialist cognitive behavioural intervention focusing on teaching people to cope with stress; includes the usual elements of this approach, including relaxation, self-instruction and cognitive challenge.

Superego according to Freud, contains the individual's morals and societal values; the psychoanalytical equivalent of the conscience.

T

Transference the unconscious transfer of experience from one interpersonal context to another, i.e. the reliving of past interpersonal relationships in current situations, including therapies.

Tricyclic a form of antidepressant whose action is on the serotonin and norepinephrine systems.

V

Ventricle one of a system of four communicating cavities within the brain that are continuous with the central canal of the spinal cord.

Vicarious learning learning the outcomes of behaviour or situations from observation of others.

W

Waiting list control used in randomized controlled trial; provides a group whose treatment is delayed, so comparisons can be made between treatment and no-treatment conditions without withholding treatment to some people.

Waxy flexibility a condition found in schizophrenia in which individuals maintain the posture in which they are placed for prolonged periods of time.

Bibliography

Abela, J.R.Z. and D'Allesandro, D.U. (2002) Beck's cognitive theory of depression: the diathesis-stress and causal mediation components, *British Journal of Clinical Psychology*, 41: 111–28.

Abela, J.R.Z. and Seligman, M.E.P. (2000) The hopelessness theory of depression: a test of the diathesis-stress component in the interpersonal and achievement domains, *Cognitive Therapy and Research*, 23: 361–78.

Abiodun, O.A. (1995) Pathways to mental health care in Nigeria, *Psychiatric Services*, 46: 823–6.

Abraham, H.C. (1956) Therapeutic and psychological approach to cases of unconsummated marriage, *British Medical Journal*, 1: 837–9.

Abramson, L.Y., Alloy, L.B., Hankin, B.L. et al. (2002) Cognitive vulnerability–stress models of depression in a self-regulatory and psychobiological context, in I.H. Gotlib and C.L. Hammen (eds) *Handbook of Depression*. New York: Guilford.

Abramson, L.Y., Seligman, M.E. and Teasdale, J.D. (1978) Learned helplessness in humans: critique and reformulation, *Journal of Abnormal Psychology*, 87: 49–74.

Ackerman, K.D., Heyman, R., Rabin, B.S. et al. (2002) Stressful life events precede exacerbations of multiple sclerosis, *Psychosomatic Medicine*, 64: 916–20.

Adebowale, T.O. and Ogunlesi, A.O. (1999) Beliefs and knowledge about aetiology of mental illness among Nigerian psychiatric patients and their relatives, *African Journal of Medicine and Medical Science*, 28: 35–41.

Agras, W.S., Rossiter, E.M. and Arnow, B. (1994) One-year follow-up of psychosocial and pharmacologic treatments for bulimia nervosa, *Journal of Clinical Psychiatry*, 55: 179–83.

Agras, W.S., Walsh, T., Fairburn, C.G. et al. (2000) A multicenter comparison of cognitive behavioral therapy and interpersonal psychotherapy for bulimia nervosa, *Archives of General Psychiatry*, 57: 459–66.

Ahern, J., Galea, S., Resnick, H. et al. (2002) Television images and psychological symptoms after the September 11 terrorist attacks, *Psychiatry*, 65: 289–300.

Ahmad, F., Quinn, T.J., Dawson, J. et al. (2008) A link between lunar phase and medically unexplained stroke symptoms: an unearthly influence? *Journal of Psychosomatic Research*, 65: 131–3.

Ahmed, S.M. (2001) Differing health and health-seeking behaviour: ethnic minorities of the Chittagong Hill Tracts, Bangladesh, *Asian Pacific Journal of Public Health*, 13: 100–8.

Ahn, W., Novick, L. and Kim, N. (2003) Understanding behavior makes it more normal, *Psychonomic Bulletin and Review*, 10: 746–52.

Allan, A., Roberts, M.C., Allan, M.M. et al. (2001) Intoxication, criminal offences and suicide attempts in a group of South African problem drinkers, *South African Medical Journal*, 91: 145–50.

Allen, A., Hadley, S.J., Kaplan, A. et al. (2008) An open-label trial of venlafaxine in body dysmorphic disorder, *CNS Spectrum*, 13: 138–44.

Allen, L.A., Woolfolk, R.L., Escobar, J.I. et al. (2006) Cognitive-behavioral therapy for somatization disorder: a randomized controlled trial, *Archives of Internal Medicine*, 166: 1512–18.

Allen, M.G. (1976) Twin studies of affective illness, *Archives of General Psychiatry*, 33: 1476–8.

Alloy, L.B. and Abramson, L.Y. (1979) Judgement of contingency in depressed and nondepressed students: sadder but wiser?, *Journal of Experimental Psychology: General*, 108: 441–85.

Altmann, P., Cunningham, J., Dhanesha, U. et al. (1999) Disturbance of cerebral function in people exposed to drinking water contaminated with aluminium sulphate: retrospective study of the Camelford water incident, *British Medical Journal*, 319: 807–11.

Amatom, L., Minozzi, S., Davoli, M. et al. (2008) Psychosocial and pharmacological treatments versus pharmacological treatments for opioid detoxification, *Cochrane Database of Systematic Reviews*, 4: CD005031.

American Psychiatric Association (APA) (1968) *Diagnostic and Statistical Manual of Mental Disorders*, 2nd edn. Washington, DC: APA.

American Psychiatric Association (APA) (1987) *Diagnostic and Statistical Manual of Mental Disorders*, 3rd edn, text revision. Washington, DC: APA.

American Psychiatric Association (APA) (1994) *Diagnostic and Statistical Manual of Mental Disorders*, 4th edn. Washington, DC: APA.

American Psychiatric Association (APA) (2000) *Diagnostic and Statistical Manual of Mental Disorders*, 4th edn, text revision (DSM-IV-TR). Washington, DC: APA.

Andersen, I., Thielen, K., Nygaard, E. et al. (2009) Social inequality in the prevalence of depressive disorders, *Journal of Epidemiology and Community Health*, 63: 575–81.

Anderson, D.A. and Maloney, K.C. (2001) The efficacy of cognitive-behavioral therapy on the core symptoms of bulimia nervosa, *Clinical Psychology Review*, 21: 971.

Anderson, I.M. (1998) SSRIS versus tricyclic antidepressants in depressed inpatients: a meta-analysis of efficacy and tolerability, *Depression and Anxiety*, 7 (Suppl. 1): 11–17.

Anderson, P., Chisholm, D. and Fuhr, D.C. (2009) Effectiveness and cost-effectiveness of policies and programmes to reduce the harm caused by alcohol, *Lancet*, 373: 2234–46.

Anderson, R.N. and Smith, B.L. (2003) Deaths: leading causes for 2001, *National Vital Statistics Report*, 52: 1–86.

Andreasson, S., Allebeck, P. and Engstrom, A. (1987) Cannabis and schizophrenia: a longitudinal study of Swedish conscripts, *Lancet*, 2: 1483–6.

Andrews, B., Brewin, C.R. and Rose, S. (2003) Gender, social support, and PTSD in victims of violent crime, *Journal of Traumatic Stress*, 16: 421–7.

Andrews, B., Brewin, C.R., Rose, S. and Kirk, M.P. (2000) Predicting PTSD symptoms in victims of violent crime: the role of shame, anger, and childhood abuse, *Journal of Abnormal Psychology*, 109: 69–73.

Andrews, G., Stewart, G., Allen, R. et al. (1990) The genetics of six neurotic disorders: a twin study, *Journal of Affective Disorders*, 19: 23–9.

Angst, J. (1999) The epidemiology of depressive disorders, *European Neuropharmacology* (Suppl.): 95–8.

Aouizerate, B., Pujol, H., Grabot, D. et al. (2003) Body dysmorphic disorder in a sample of cosmetic surgery applicants, *European Psychiatry*, 18: 365–8.

Appiah-Poku, J., Laugharne, R., Mensah, E. et al. (2004) Previous help sought by patients presenting to mental health services in Kumasi, Ghana, *Social Psychiatry and Psychiatric Epidemiology*, 39: 208–11.

Aragona, M., Onesti, E., Tomassini, V. et al. (2009) Psychopathological and cognitive effects of therapeutic cannabinoids in multiple sclerosis: a double-blind, placebo controlled, crossover study, *Clinical Neuropharmacology*, 32: 41–7.

Arntz, A., Klokman, J. and Sieswerda, S. (2005) An experimental test of the schema mode model of borderline personality disorder, *Journal of Behavior Therapy and Experimental Psychiatry*, 36: 226–39.

Asen, E. (2002) Outcome research in family therapy, *Advances in Psychiatric Treatment*, 8: 230–8.

Ataoglu, A., Ozcetin, A., Icmeli, C. et al. (2003) Paradoxical therapy in conversion reaction, *Journal of Korean Medical Science*, 18: 581–4.

Attia, E. and Schroeder, L. (2005) Pharmacologic treatment of anorexia nervosa: where do we go from here?, *International Journal of Eating Disorders*, 37 (Suppl.): S60–3.

Austen, B., Christodoulou, G. and Terry, J.E. (2002) Relation between cholesterol levels, statins and Alzheimer's disease in the human population, *Journal of Nutrition, Health and Aging*, 6: 377–82.

Avants, S.K., Margolin, A. and McKee, S. (1999) A path analysis of cognitive, affective, and behavioral predictors of treatment response in a methadone maintenance program, *Journal of Substance Abuse*, 11: 215–30.

Awad, A.D. and Vorungati, L.N. (1999) Quality of life and new antipsychotics in schizophrenia: are patients better off?, *International Journal of Social Psychiatry*, 45: 268–75.

Babor, T.F., Miller, W.R., DiClemente, C.C. and Longabaugh, R. (1999) A study to remember: Response of the Project MATCH Research Group, *Addiction*, 94: 66–9.

Bacaltchuk, J. and Hay, P. (2003) Antidepressants versus placebo for people with bulimia nervosa. *Cochrane Database of Systematic Reviews*, 4: CD003391.

Bacaltchuk, J., Hay, P. and Trefiglio, R. (2002) Antidepressants versus psychological treatments and their combination for bulimia nervosa, *Cochrane Database of Systematic Reviews*, 1.

Bacaltchuk, J., Trefiglio, R., Lima, M.S. et al. (1999) Antidepressants versus psychotherapy for bulimia nervosa: a systematic review, *Journal of Clinical Pharmacy and Therapeutics*, 24: 23–31.

Bach, L.J. and David, A.S. (2006) Self-awareness after acquired and traumatic brain injury, *Neuropsychological Rehabilitation*, 16(4): 397–414.

Bachner-Melman, R., Lerer, E., Zohar, A.H. et al. (2007) Anorexia nervosa, perfectionism, and dopamine D4 receptor (DRD4), *American Journal of Medical Genetics B Neuropsychiatric Genetics*, 144B: 748–56.

Bailey, A., Le Couteur, A., Gottesman, I. et al. (1995) Autism as a strongly genetic disorder: evidence from a British twin study, *Psychological Medicine*, 25: 63–77.

Baker, A., Lee, N.K. and Claire, M. (2005) Brief cognitive behavioural interventions for regular amphetamine users: a step in the right direction, *Addiction*, 100: 367–78.

Bakker, A., Van Dyck, R., Spinhoven, P. et al. (1999) Paroxetine, clomipramine, and cognitive therapy in the treatment of panic disorder, *Journal of Clinical Psychiatry*, 60: 831–8.

Ballenger, J.C. (2000) Panic disorder and agoraphobia, in M.G. Gelder, J.J. Lopez-Ibor Jr and N.C. Andreasen (eds) *New Oxford Textbook of Psychiatry*. Oxford: Oxford University Press.

Ballenger, J.C. (2004) Remission rates in patients with anxiety disorders treated with paroxetine, *Journal of Clinical Psychiatry*, 65: 1696–707.

Bancroft, J. (1999) Central inhibition of sexual response in the male: a theoretical perspective, *Neuroscience Biobehavioral Review*, 23: 763–84.

Bandelow, B. (2008) The medical treatment of obsessive-compulsive disorder and anxiety, *CNS Spectrum*, 13: 37–46.

Bandelow, B., Krause, J., Wedekind, D. et al. (2005) Early traumatic life events, parental attitudes, family history, and birth risk factors in patients with borderline personality disorder and healthy controls, *Psychiatry Research*, 134: 169–79.

Bandura, A. (1977) Self-efficacy: toward a unifying theory of behavioural change, *Psychological Review*, 84: 191–215.

Bandura, A. (1982) Self-efficacy mechanism in human agency, *American Psychologist*, 37: 122–47.

Banerjee, T. and Banerjee, G. (1995) Determinants of help-seeking behaviour in cases of epilepsy attending a teaching hospital in India: an indigenous explanatory model, *International Journal of Social Psychiatry*, 41: 217–30.

Barbaree, H.E. (1990) Stimulus control of sexual arousal, in W.L. Marshall, D.R. Laws and H.E. Barbaree (eds) *Handbook of Sexual Assault: Issues, Theories, and Treatment of the Offender*. New York: Plenum.

Barbaree, H.E. (1991) Denial and minimization among sex offenders: assessment and treatment outcome, *Forum on Corrections Research*, 3: 30–3.

Barbaree, H.E. and Marshall, W.L. (1989) Erectile responses among heterosexual child molesters, father–daughter incest offenders and matched nonoffenders: five distinct age preference profiles, *Canadian Journal of Behavioural Science*, 21: 70–82.

Barbaree, H.E. and Seto, M.C. (1997) Pedophila: assessment and treatment, in D.R. Laws and W. O'Donohue (eds) *Sexual Deviance: Theory, Assessment, and Treatment*. New York: Guilford.

Barber, J.P. and Luborsky, L. (1991) A psychodynamic view of simple phobias and prescriptive matching: a commentary, *Psychotherapy*, 28: 469–72.

Bargagli, A.M., Hickman, M., Davoli, M. et al. (2006) Drug-related mortality and its impact on adult mortality in eight European countries, *European Journal of Public Health*, 16: 198–202.

Barker, C., Pistrang, N., Shapiro, D.A. et al. (1993) You in Mind: a preventive mental health television series, *British Journal of Clinical Psychology*, 32: 281–93.

Barkley, A. (1997) Behavioral inhibition, sustained attention and executive functions: constructing a unifying theory of ADHD, *Psychological Bulletin*, 121: 65–94.

Barkley, R.A., Edwards, G., Laneri, M. et al. (2001) The efficacy of problem solving communication training alone, behavior management training alone, and their combination for parent–adolescent conflict in teenagers with ADHD and ODD, *Journal of Consulting and Clinical Psychology*, 69: 926–41.

Barlow, D.H., Gorman, J.M., Shear, M.K. et al. (2000) Cognitive-behavioral therapy, imipramine, or their combination for panic disorder: a randomized controlled trial, *Journal of the American Medical Association*, 283: 2573–4.

Barnes, A. (2007) Race and hospital diagnoses of schizophrenia and mood disorders, *Social Work*, 53: 77–83.

Barr, L.C., Goodman, W.K. and Price, L.H. (1992) Acute exacerbation of body dysmorphic disorder during tryptophan depletion, *American Journal of Psychiatry*, 149: 1406–7.

Barsky, A.J. and Ahern, D.K. (2004) Cognitive behavior therapy for hypochondriasis: a randomized controlled trial, *Journal of the American Medical Association*, 291: 1464–70.

Barsky, A.J., Ahern, D.K., Bailey, E.D. et al. (2001) Hypochondriacal patients' appraisal of health and physical risks, *American Journal of Psychiatry*, 158: 783–7.

Barsky, A.J., Brener, J., Coeytaux, R.R. et al. (1995) Accurate awareness of heartbeat in hypochondriacal and non-hypochondriacal patients, *Psychosomatic Medicine*, 39: 489–97.

Bass, C. and Murphy, M. (1995) Somatoform and personality disorders: syndromal comorbidity and overlapping developmental pathways, *Journal of Psychosomatic Research*, 39: 405–27.

Bass, E. and Davis, L. (1988) *The Courage to Heal: A Guide for Women Survivors of Sexual Abuse*. New York: Harper and Row.

Basso, M.R., Nasrallah, H.A., Olson, S.C. et al. (1998) Neuropsychological correlates of negative, disorganized and psychotic symptoms in schizophrenia, *Schizophrenia Research*, 25: 99–111.

Batelaan, N.M., De Graaf, R. and Van Balkom, A.J. (2006) Epidemiology of panic, *Tijdschrift voor Psychiatrie*, 48: 195–205.

Bateson, G., Jackson, D., Haley, J. et al. (1956) Toward a theory of schizophrenia, *Behavioural Science*, 1: 251–64.

Battaglia, M., Pesenti-Gritti, P., Medland, S.E. et al. (2009) A genetically informed study of the association between childhood separation anxiety, sensitivity to CO(2), panic disorder, and the effect of childhood parental loss, *Archives of General Psychiatry*, 66: 64–71.

Bauer, P.J. (2006) *Remembering the Time of Our Lives: Memory in Infancy and Beyond*. Mahwah, NJ: Erlbaum.

Baumann, C.R., Werth, E., Stocker, R. et al. (2007) Sleep-wake disturbances 6 months after traumatic brain injury: a prospective study, *Brain*, 130: 1873–83.

Bazargan-Hejazi, S., Bing, E., Bazargan, M. et al. (2005) Evaluation of a brief intervention in an inner-city emergency department, *Annals of Emergency Medicine*, 46: 67–76.

Bebbington, P. and Ramana, R. (1995) The epidemiology of bipolar affective disorder, *Social Psychiatry and Psychiatric Epidemiology*, 30: 279–92.

Beck, A.T. (1977) *Cognitive Therapy of Depression*. New York: Guilford.

Beck, A.T. (1997) Cognitive therapy: reflections, in J.K. Zeig (ed.) *The Evolution of Psychotherapy: The Third Conference*. New York: Brunner/Mazel.

Beck, A.T., Freeman, A. and associates (1990) *Cognitive Therapy of Personality Disorders*. New York: Guilford.

Beck, A.T., Mendelson, M., Mock, J. et al. (1961) Inventory for measuring depression, *Archives of General Psychiatry*, 4: 561–71.

Beck, A.T., Rush, A.J., Shaw, B.F. and Emery, G. (1979) *Cognitive Therapy for Depression*. New York: Guilford.

Beck, A.T., Steer, R.A., Ball, R. and Ranieri, W. (1996) Comparison of Beck Depression Inventories -IA and -II in psychiatric outpatients, *Journal of Personality Assessment*, 67: 588–97.

Beck, A.T., Wright, F.D., Newman, C.F. et al. (1993) *Cognitive Therapy of Substance Abuse*. New York: Guilford.

Behrendt, S., Wittchen, H-U., Hofler, M. et al. (2008) Risk and speed of transitions to first alcohol dependence symptoms in adolescents: a 10-year longitudinal community study in Germany, *Addiction*, 103: 1638–47.

Beidel, D.C. and Turner, S.M. (1986) A critique of the theoretical bases of cognitive-behavioral theories and therapy, *Clinical Psychology Review*, 6: 177–97.

Bell, K.R., Temkin, N.R. and Esselman, P.C. (2005) The effect of a scheduled telephone intervention on outcome after moderate to severe traumatic brain injury: a randomized trial, *Archives of Physical Medicine and Rehabilitation*, 86: 851–6.

Benbadis, S.R. and Allen Hauser, W. (2000) An estimate of the prevalence of psychogenic nonepileptic seizures, *Seizure*, 9: 280–1.

Bennett, P., Conway, M. and Clatworthy, J. (2001) Predicting post-traumatic symptoms in cardiac patients, *Heart and Lung*, 30: 458–65.

Bennett, P., Lowe, R. and Honey, K. (2002) Appraisals and emotions: a test of the consistency of reporting and their associations, *Cognition and Emotion*, 17: 511–20.

Bennett, P., Parsons, E., Brain, K. et al. (2010) Long-term cohort study of women at intermediate risk of familial breast cancer: experiences of living at risk, *Psycho-Oncology*, 19: 390–8.

Bennett, P., Smith, C., Nugent, Z. et al. (1991) 'Pssst . . . the really useful guide to alcohol': evaluation of an alcohol education television series, *Health Education Research, Theory and Practice*, 6: 57–64.

Bennett, P., Williams, Y., Page, N. et al. (2001) Associations between organizational and incident factors and emotional distress in emergency ambulance personnel, *British Journal of Clinical Psychology*, 12: 215–26.

Bennett, P., Williams, Y., Page, N. et al. (2004) Levels of mental health problems among UK emergency ambulance workers, *Emergency Medicine Journal*, 21: 235–6.

Ben-Shachar, D., Gazawi, H., Riboyad-Levin, J. et al. (1999) Chronic repetitive transcranial magnetic stimulation alters beta-adrenergic and 5-HT2 receptor characteristics in rat brain, *Brain Research*, 816: 78–83.

Bentall, R.P. (1993) Deconstructing the concept of 'schizophrenia', *Journal of Mental Health*, 2: 223–38.

Bentall, R.P., Corcoran, R., Howard, R. et al. (2001) Persecutory delusions: a review and theoretical integration, *Clinical Psychology Review*, 21: 1143–92.

Bentall, R.P. and Fernyhough, C. (2008) Social predictors of psychotic experiences: specificity and psychological mechanisms, *Schizophrenia Bulletin*, 34: 1012–20.

Bentall, R.P. and Slade, P.D. (1985) Reality testing and auditory hallucinations, *British Journal of Clinical Psychology*, 24: 159–69.

Berlin, F.S. and Meinecke, C.F. (1981) Treatment of sex offenders with antiandrogenic medication: conceptualization, review of treatment modalities and preliminary findings, *American Journal of Psychiatry*, 138: 601–8.

Bernard-Bonnin, A.C., Hébert, M., Daignault, I.V. et al. (2008) Disclosure of sexual abuse, and personal and familial factors as predictors of post-traumatic stress disorder symptoms in school-aged girls, *Paediatric Child Health*, 13: 479–86.

Berretini, W.H. (2000) Susceptibility loci for bipolar disorder: overlap with inherited vulnerability to schizophrenia, *Biological Psychiatry*, 47: 245–51.

Berrios, G.E. and Quemada, J.I. (1990) Depressive illness in multiple sclerosis: clinical and theoretical aspects of the association, *British Journal of Psychiatry*, 156: 10–16.

Berrios, R.P. (1991) Delusions as 'wrong beliefs': a conceptual history, *British Journal of Psychiatry*, 159: 6–13.

Beswick, T., Best, D., Rees, S. et al. (2001) Multiple drug use: patterns and practices of heroin and crack use in a population of opiate addicts in treatment, *Drug and Alcohol Review*, 20: 201–4.

Bettelheim, B. (1967) *The Empty Fortress*. New York: Free Press.

Bettelheim, B. (1973) Bringing up children, *Ladies Home Journal*, 90: 28.

Beutler, L. and Consoli, A. (1993) Matching the therapist's interpersonal stance to clients' characteristics: contributions from systemic eclectic psychotherapy, *Psychotherapy: Theory, Research and Practice*, 30: 417–22.

Beynon, S., Soares-Weiser, K., Woolacott, N. et al. (2008) Psychosocial interventions for the prevention of relapse in bipolar disorder: systematic review of controlled trials, *British Journal of Psychiatry*, 192: 5–11.

Bezchlibuyle-Butler, K.Z. and Jeffries, J.J. (2003) *Clinical Handbook of Psychotropic Drugs*, 13th edn, Cambridge, MA: Hogrefe and Huber.

Bhatt, A., Tomenson and Benjamin, S. (1989) Transcultural patterns of somatization in primary care: a preliminary report, *Journal of Psychosomatic Research*, 33: 671–80.

Biederman, J., Petty, C., Faraone, S.V. et al. (2005) Childhood antecedents to panic disorder in referred and nonreferred adults, *Journal of Child and Adolescent Psychopharmacology*, 15: 549–61.

Biederman, J., Swanson, J.M., Wigal, S.B. et al. (2005) Efficacy and safety of modafinil filmcoated tablets in children and adolescents with attention-deficit/hyperactivity disorder: results of a randomized, double-blind, placebo-controlled, flexible-dose study, *Pediatrics*, 116: 777–84.

Biondi, M. and Picardi, A. (2003) Increased probability of remaining in remission from panic disorder with agoraphobia after drug treatment in patients who received concurrent cognitive-behavioural therapy: a follow-up study, *Psychotherapy and Psychosomatics*, 72: 34–42.

Birbaumer, N., Veit, R., Lotze, M. et al. (2005) Deficient fear conditioning in psychopathy: a functional magnetic resonance imaging study, *Archives of General Psychiatry*, 62: 799–805.

Birch, H., Richardson, S.A., Baird, D. et al. (1970) *Mental Subnormality in the Community: A Clinical and Epidemiological Study*. Baltimore, MD: Williams and Wilkins.

Birchwood, M., Fowler, D. and Jackson, C. (eds) (2000) *Early Intervention in Psychosis*. London: Wiley.

Bird, C.E. and Rieker, P.P. (1999) Gender matters: an integrated model for understanding men's and women's health, *Social Science and Medicine*, 48: 745–55.

Birks, J. (2006) Cholinesterase inhibitors for Alzheimer's disease, *Cochrane Database of Systematic Reviews*, 1: CD005593.

Birmingham, C.L., Su, J., Hlynsky, J.A. et al. (2005) The mortality rate from anorexia nervosa, *International Journal of Eating Disorders*, 38: 143–6.

Bishop, S.R., Lau, M., Shapiro, S. et al. (2004) Mindfulness: a proposed operational definition, *Clinical Psychology Science and Practice*, 11: 230–41.

Bissada, H., Tasca, G.A., Barber, A.M. et al. (2008) Olanzapine in the treatment of low body weight and obsessive thinking in women with anorexia nervosa: a randomized, double-blind, placebo controlled trial, *American Journal of Psychiatry*, 165: 1281–8.

Bisson, J. and Andrew, M. (2007) Psychological treatment of post-traumatic stress disorder (PTSD), *Cochrane Database of Systematic Reviews*, 3: CD003388.

Bisson, J.I., Ehlers, A., Matthews, R. et al. (2007) Psychological treatments for chronic post-traumatic stress disorder: systematic review and meta-analysis, *British Journal of Psychiatry*, 190: 97–104.

Bjornstad, G. and Montgomery, P. (2005) Family therapy for attention-deficit disorder or attention-deficit/hyperactivity disorder in children and adolescents, *Cochrane Database of Systematic Reviews*, 2.

Black, D.W., Noyes, R. Jr, Goldstein, R.B. et al. (1992) A family study of obsessive-compulsive disorder, *Archives of General Psychiatry*, 49: 362–8.

Blaszczynski, A. (1995) Criminal offences in pathological gamblers, *Psychiatry, Psychology and Law*, 1: 129–38.

Blazer, D.G. and Wu, L.T. (2009) The epidemiology of substance use and disorders among middle aged and elderly community adults: national survey on drug use and health, *American Journal of Geriatric Psychiatry*, 17: 237–45.

Bleathman, C. and Morton, I. (1992) Validation therapy: extracts from 20 groups with dementia sufferers, *Journal of Advanced Nursing*, 17: 658–66.

Bleich-Cohen, M., Strous, R.D., Even, R. et al. (2009) Diminished neural sensitivity to irregular facial expression in first-episode schizophrenia, *Human Brain Mapping*, 30: 2606–16.

Bleuler, E. (1908) Die Prognose der Dementia praecox – Schizophreniegruppe, *Präger Medizinische Wochenschrift*, 16: 321–5.

Bliss, E.L. (1986) *Multiple Personality, Allied Disorders and Hypnosis*. New York: Oxford University Press.

Bloch, M.H., Landeros-Weisenberger, A., Rosario M.C. et al. (2008) Meta-analysis of the symptom structure of obsessive-compulsive disorder, *American Journal of Psychiatry*, 165: 1532–42.

Block, R., Slomp, M., Patten, S. et al. (2009) Disability payments for persons with severe mental illness in Alberta, Canada, *Psychiatric Services*, 60: 686–8.

Bloomfield, K., Grittner, U., Kramer, S. et al. (2006) Social inequalities in alcohol consumption and alcohol-related problems in the study countries of the EU concerted action 'Gender, Culture and Alcohol Problems: a Multi-national Study', *Alcohol and Alcoholism*, 41: i26–36.

Blum, N., St John, D., Pfohl, S. et al. (2008) Systems training for emotional predictability and problem solving (STEPPS) for outpatients with borderline personality disorder: a randomized controlled trial and 1-year follow-up, *American Journal of Psychiatry*, 165: 468–78.

Bohne, A., Keuthen, N.J., Wilhelm, S. et al. (2002) Prevalence of symptoms of body dysmorphic disorder and its correlates: a cross-cultural comparison, *Psychosomatics*, 43: 486–90.

Boileau, I., Dagher, A., Leyton, M. et al. (2006) Modeling sensitization to stimulants in humans: an [11C]raclopride/positron emission tomography study in healthy men, *Archives of General Psychiatry*, 63: 1386–95.

Bonne, O., Vythilingam, M., Inagaki, M. et al. (2008) Reduced posterior hippocampal volume in posttraumatic stress disorder, *Journal of Clinical Psychiatry*, 69: 1087–91.

Boon, S. and Draijer, N. (1993) Multiple personality disorder in The Netherlands: a clinical investigation of 71 patients, *American Journal of Psychiatry*, 150: 489–94.

Boone, M.L., McNeil, D.W., Masia, C.L. et al. (1999) Multimodal comparisons of social phobia subtypes and avoidant personality disorder, *Journal of Anxiety Disorders*, 13: 271–92.

Borduin, C.M. (1999) Multisystemic treatment of criminality and violence in adolescents, *Journal of Consulting and Clinical Psychology*, 63: 569–78.

Borduin, C.M., Mann, B.J., Cone, L.T. et al. (1995) Multisystemic treatment of serious juvenile offenders: long-term prevention of criminality and violence, *Journal of Consulting and Clinical Psychology*, 63: 569–78.

Boury, M., Treadwell, T. and Kumar, V.K. (2001) Integrating psychodrama cognitive therapy: an exploratory study, *International Journal of Action Methods*, 54: 13–28.

Bower, G.H. (1981) Mood and memory, *American Psychologist*, 36: 129–48.

Bowirrat, A. and Oscar-Berman, M. (2005) Relationship between dopaminergic neurotransmission, alcoholism, and Reward Deficiency syndrome, *American Journal of Medical Genetics. B: Neuropsychiatric Genetics*, 132: 29–37.

Bradbury, C.L., Christensen, B.K., Lau, M.A. et al. (2008) The efficacy of cognitive behavior therapy in the treatment of emotional distress after acquired brain injury, *Archives of Physical Medicine and Rehabilitation*, 89: S61–8.

Brain, K., Norman, P., Gray, J. et al. (2002) A randomized trial of specialist genetic assessment: psychological impact on women at different levels of familial breast cancer risk, *British Journal of Cancer*, 86: 233–8.

Brambilla, F., Bellodi, L., Arancio, C. et al. (2001) Central dopaminergic function in anorexia and bulimia nervosa: a psychoneuroendocrine approach, *Psychoneuroendocrinology*, 26: 293–409.

Bransford, J.D. and Stein, B.S. (1984) *The Ideal Problem Solver: A Guide for Improving Thinking, Learning, and Creativity.* New York: W.H. Freeman.

Brassington, J.C. and Marsh, N.V. (1999) Neuropsychological aspects of multiple sclerosis, *Neuropsychology Review*, 8: 43–77.

Brenneis, C.B. (2000) Evaluating the evidence: can we find authenticated recovered memory? *Journal of the American Psychoanalytical Association*, 17: 61–77.

Brewin, C.R. (2001) A cognitive neuroscience account of posttraumatic stress disorder and its treatment, *Behaviour Research and Therapy*, 39: 373–93.

Brewin, C.R. and Andrews, B. (1998) Recovered memories of trauma: phenomenology and cognitive mechanisms, *Clinical Psychology Review*, 18: 949–70.

Briken, P., Hill, A. and Berner, W. (2003) Pharmacotherapy of paraphilias with long-acting agonists of luteinizing hormone-releasing hormone: a systematic review, *Journal of Clinical Psychiatry*, 64: 890–7.

Broadbent, D.E. (1971) *Decision and Stress.* London: Academic Press.

Bronisch, T. (1996) The relationship between suicidality and depression, *Archives of Suicide Research*, 2: 235–54.

Bronisch, T. and Wittchen, H.U. (1994) Suicidal ideation and suicide attempts: comorbidity with depression, anxiety disorders, and substance abuse disorder, *European Archives of Psychiatry and Clinical Neuroscience*, 244: 93–8.

Brønnum-Hansen, H., Stenager, E. et al. (2005) Suicide among Danes with multiple sclerosis, *Journal of Neurology, Neurosurgery, and Psychiatry*, 76: 1457–9.

Brown, G.K., Newman, C.F., Charlesworth, S.E. et al. (2004) An open clinical trial of cognitive therapy for borderline personality disorder, *Journal of Personality Disorders*, 18: 257–71.

Brown, G.K., Ten Have, T., Henriques, G.R. et al. (2005) Cognitive therapy for the prevention of suicide attempts: a randomized controlled trial, *Journal of the American Medical Association*, 294: 563–70.

Brown, G.R. and Anderson, B. (1991) Psychiatric morbidity in adult clients with childhood histories of sexual and physical abuse, *American Journal of Psychiatry*, 148: 55–61.

Brown, G.W., Birley, J.L.T. and Wing, J.K. (1972) The influence of family life on the course of schizophrenic disorders: a relocation, *British Journal of Psychiatry*, 121: 241–58.

Brown, G.W. and Harris, T.O. (1978) *Social Origins of Depression: A Study of Psychiatric Disorder in Women.* London: Tavistock.

Brown, J.S.L., Cochrane, R. and Hancox, T. (2000) Large-scale health promotion stress workshops for the general public: a controlled evaluation, *Behavioural and Cognitive Psychotherapy*, 28: 139–51.

Brown, M. and Barraclough, B. (1997) Epidemiology of suicide pacts in England and Wales, 1988–92, *British Medical Journal*, 315: 286–7.

Brown, R.F., Tennant, C.C., Sharrock, M. et al. (2006) Relationship between stress and relapse in multiple sclerosis: Part II. Direct and indirect relationships, *Multiple Sclerosis*, 12: 465–75.

Bruch, H. (1982) Anorexia nervosa: therapy and theory, *American Journal of Psychiatry*, 139: 1531–8.

Brüne, M. (2005) 'Theory of mind' in schizophrenia: a review of the literature, *Schizophrenia Bulletin*, 31: 21–42.

Bryant, M.J., Simons, A.D. and Thase, M.E. (1999) Therapist skill and patient variables in homework compliance: controlling an uncontrolled variable in cognitive therapy outcome research, *Cognitive Therapy and Research*, 23: 381–99.

Bucci, W. (1997) Symptoms and symbols: a multiple code theory of somatization, *Psychoanalytic Enquiry*, 2: 151–72.

Buckley, S., Bird, G., Sacks, B. et al. (2007) Mainstream or special education for teenagers with Down syndrome, in J-A. Rondal and A. Rasore-Quartino (eds) *Therapies and Rehabilitation in Down Syndrome.* Chichester: Wiley.

Buhlmann, U., Cook, L.M., Fama, J.M. et al. (2007) Perceived teasing experiences in body dysmorphic disorder, *Body Image*, 4: 381–5.

Buhlmann, U., Etcoff, N.L. and Wilhelm, S. (2006) Emotion recognition bias for contempt and anger in body dysmorphic disorder, *Journal of Psychiatric Research*, 40: 105–11.

Bulik, C.M., Prescott, C.A. and Kendler, K.S. (2001) Features of childhood sexual abuse and the development of psychiatric and substance use disorders, *British Journal of Psychiatry*, 179: 444–9.

Bulloch, A.G., and Patten, S.B. (2010) Non-adherence with psychotropic medications in the general population, *Social Psychiatry and Psychiatric Epidemiology*, 45: 47–56.

Bullough, V. and Weinberg, T. (1988) Women married to transvestites: problems and adjustments, *Journal of Psychology and Human Sexuality*, 1: 83–6.

Burke, B.L., Arkowitz, H., Menchola, M. (2003) The efficacy of motivational interviewing: a meta-analysis of controlled clinical trials, *Journal of Consulting and Clinical Psychology*, 71: 843–61.

Burneo, J.G., Martin, R., Powell, T. et al. (2003) Teddy bears: an observational finding in patients with nonepileptic events, *Neurology*, 61: 714–15.

Bursac, Z. and Campbell, J.E. (2003) From risky behaviors to chronic outcomes: current status and Healthy People 2010 goals for American Indians in Oklahoma, *Journal of the Oklahoma State Medical Association*, 96: 569–73.

Butler, A.C., Chapman, J.E., Forman, E.M. et al. (2006) The empirical status of cognitive behavioral therapy: a review of meta-analyses, *Clinical Psychology Review*, 26: 17–31.

Butler, G., Fennell, M., Robson, P. et al. (1991) A comparison of behavior therapy and cognitive behavior therapy in the treatment of generalized anxiety disorder, *Journal of Consulting and Clinical Psychology*, 59: 167–75.

Byerly, M.J., Fisher, R., Carmody, T. and Rush, A.J. (2005) A trial of compliance therapy in outpatients with schizophrenia or schizoaffective disorder, *Journal of Clinical Psychiatry*, 66: 997–1001.

Cadoret, R.J. (1982) Genotype–environment interaction in antisocial behavior, *Psychological Medicine*, 12: 235–9.

Cadoret, R.J., Yates, G.A., Geyer, M.A. et al. (1995) Adoption study demonstrating two genetic pathways to drug abuse, *Archives of General Psychiatry*, 52: 45–52.

Calhoun, L.G. and Tedeschi, R.G. (1999) *Facilitating Posttraumatic Growth: A Clinician's Guide*. Mahwah, NJ: Lawrence Erlbaum Associates.

Campbell, M., Adams, P., Perry, R. et al. (1988) Tardive and withdrawal dyskinesias in autistic children: a prospective study, *Psychopharmacology Bulletin*, 24: 251–5.

Campbell, M., Anderson, L.T., Small, A.M. et al. (1993) Naltrexone in autistic children: behavioral symptoms and attentional learning, *Journal of the American Academy of Child and Adolescent Psychiatry*, 32: 1283–91.

Campion, J. and Bhugra, D. (1997) Experiences of religious healing in psychiatric patients in south India, *Social Psychiatry and Psychiatric Epidemiology*, 32: 215–21.

Cannon, M., Moffitt, T.E., Caspi, A. et al. (2006) Neuropsychological performance at the age of 13 years and adult schizophreniform disorder: prospective birth cohort study, *British Journal of Psychiatry*, 189: 463–4.

Carey, G. and Gottesman, I.I. (1981) Twin and family studies of anxiety, phobic and obsessive disorders, in D.F. Klein and J. Rabkin (eds) *Anxiety: New Research and Changing Concepts*. New York: Raven.

Carlton, P.L. and Manowicz, P. (1994) Factors determining the severity of pathological gambling in males, *Journal of Gambling Studies*, 10: 147–57.

Carney, T., Tait, D., Richardson, A. et al. (2008) Why (and when) clinicians compel treatment of anorexia nervosa patients, *European Eating Disorders Review*, 16: 199–206.

Carr, A. (2008) Depression in young people: description, assessment and evidence-based treatment, *Developmental Neurorehabilitation*, 11: 3–15.

Carr, A.T. (1974) Compulsive neurosis: a review of the literature, *Psychological Bulletin*, 81: 311–18.

Carter, J.C., McFarlane, T.L., Bewell, C. et al. (2009) Maintenance treatment for anorexia nervosa: a comparison of cognitive behavior therapy and treatment as usual, *International Journal of Eating Disorders*, 42: 202–7.

Cartwright-Hatton, S. and Wells, A. (1997) Beliefs about worry and intrusions: the meta-cognitions questionnaire and its correlates, *Journal of Anxiety Disorders*, 11: 279–96.

Caspi, A., Mofftt, T.E., Cannon, M. et al. (2005) Moderation of the effect of adolescent-onset cannabis use on adult psychosis by a functional polymorphism in the catechol-Omethyltransferase gene: longitudinal evidence of a gene X environment interaction, *Biological Psychiatry*, 57: 1117–27.

Cassady, J.D., Kirschke, D.L., Jones, T.F. et al. (2005) Case series: outbreak of conversion disorder among Amish adolescent girls, *Journal of the American Academy of Child and Adolescent Psychiatry*, 44: 291–7.

Cassin, S.E. and von Ranson, K.M. (2005) Personality and eating disorders: a decade in review, *Eating and Weight Disorders*, 10: 98–106.

Castellanos, F.X., Giedd, J.N., Marsh, W.L. et al. (1996) Quantitative brain magnetic resonance imaging in attention-deficit hyperactivity disorder, *Archives of General Psychiatry*, 53: 607–16.

Castellanos, F.X., Xavier, L., Sharp, P.P. et al. (2002) Developmental trajectories of brain volume abnormalities in children and adolescents with attention-deficit/hyperactivity disorder, *Journal of the American Medical Association*, 288: 1740–8.

Cernich, A.N., Kurtz, S.M. and Mordecai, K.L. (2010) Cognitive rehabilitation in traumatic brain injury, *Current Treatment Options in Neurology*, 12: 412–23.

Chaix, B., Rosvall, M. and Merlo, J. (2007) Neighborhood socioeconomic deprivation and residential instability: effects on incidence of ischemic heart disease and survival after myocardial infarction, *Epidemiology*, 18: 104–11.

Charlop-Christy, M.H. and Haymes, L.K. (1998) Using obsessions as reinforcers with and without mild reductive procedures to decrease inappropriate behaviors of children with autism, *Journal of Autism and Developmental Disorders*, 26: 527–46.

Chemtob, C., Roitblatt, H., Hamada, J. et al. (1988) A cognitive action theory of posttraumatic stress disorder, *Journal of Anxiety Disorders*, 2: 253–75.

Chen, Y.R., Swann, A.C. and Burt, D.B. (1996) Stability of diagnosis in schizophrenia, *American Journal of Psychiatry*, 153: 682–6.

Cherland, E. and Fitzpatrick, R. (1999) Psychotic side effects of psychostimulants: a 5-year review, *Canadian Journal of Psychiatry*, 44: 811–13.

Chiang, Y.L., Yeh, S.S., Hsiao, C.C. et al. (1999) Treatment of a transvestic fetishist with cognitive-behavioral therapy and supportive psychotherapy: case report, *Changgeng Yi Xue Za Zhi*, 22: 299–312.

Chiaravalloti, N., DeLuca, J., Moore, N.B. et al. (2005) Treating learning impairments improves memory performance in multiple sclerosis: a randomized controlled trial, *Multiple Sclerosis*, 11: 58–68.

Chick, J. (1991) Early intervention for hazardous drinking in the general hospital, *Alcohol and Alcoholism*, 1: 477–9.

Chorpita, B.F. and Barlow, D.H. (1998) The development of anxiety: the role of control in the early environment, *Psychological Bulletin*, 124: 3–21.

Chosak, A., Marques, L., Greenberg, J.L. et al. (2008) Body dysmorphic disorder and obsessive-compulsive disorder: similarities, differences and the classification debate, *Expert Review of Neurotherapeutics*, 8: 1209–18.

Chretien, R.D. and Persinger, M.A. (2000) 'Prefrontal deficits' discriminate young offenders from age-matched cohorts: juvenile delinquency as an expected feature of the normal distribution of prefrontal cerebral development, *Psychological Reports*, 87: 1196–202.

Christian, C.J., Lencz, T., Robinson, D.G. et al. (2008) Gray matter structural alterations in obsessive-compulsive disorder: relationship to neuropsychological functions, *Psychiatry Research*, 164: 123–31.

Christodoulou, C., Melville, P., Scherl, W.F. et al. (2005) Perceived cognitive dysfunction and observed neuropsychological performance: longitudinal relation in persons with multiple sclerosis, *Journal of the International Neuropsychological Society*, 11: 614–19.

Chugani, D.C. (2004) Serotonin in autism and pediatric epilepsies, *Mental Retardation and Developmental Disabilities Research Reviews*, 10: 112–16.

Ciudad, A., Alvarez, E., Bobes, J. et al. (2009) Remission in schizophrenia: results from a 1-year follow-up observational study, *Schizophrenia Research*, 108: 214–22.

Clark, D.M. (1986) A cognitive approach to panic disorder, *Behaviour Research and Therapy*, 24: 461–70.

Clark, D.M., Salkovskis, P.M., Gelder, M. et al. (1988) Tests of a cognitive model of panic, in I. Hand and U. Wittchen (eds) *Panic and Phobias*, Vol. 2. Berlin: Springer Verlag.

Clark, D.M., Salkovskis, P.M., Hackmann, A. et al. (1994) A comparison of cognitive therapy, applied relaxation and imipramine in the treatment of panic disorder, *British Journal of Psychiatry*, 164: 759–69.

Clark, D.M., Salkovskis, P.M., Hackmann, A. et al. (1998) Two psychological treatments for hypochondriasis: a randomised controlled trial, *British Journal of Psychiatry*, 173: 218–25.

Clark, L.A., Watson, D. and Reynolds, S. (1995) Diagnosis and classification of psychopathology: challenges to the current system and future directions, *Annual Review of Psychology*, 46: 121–53.

Clarke, R. (2000) Perceptions of interethnic group racism predict increased vascular reactivity to a laboratory challenge in college women, *Annals of Behavioral Medicine*, 22: 214–22.

Clarkin, J.F., Levy, K.N., Lenzenweger, M.F. et al. (2007) Evaluating three treatments for borderline personality disorder: a multiwave study, *American Journal of Psychiatry*, 164: 922–8.

Clomipramine Collaborative Study Group (1991) Clomipramine in the treatment of patients with OCD, *Archives of General Psychiatry*, 48: 730–8.

Cloutier, S., Martin, S.L. and Poole, C. (2002) Sexual assault among North Carolina women: prevalence and health risk factors, *Journal of Epidemiology and Community Health*, 56: 265–71.

Coelho, H.F., Canter, P.H. and Ernst, E. (2007) Mindfulness-based cognitive therapy: evaluating current evidence and informing future research, *Journal of Consulting and Clinical Psychology*, 75: 1000–5.

Coffey, M. (1999) Psychosis and medication: strategies for improving adherence, *British Journal of Nursing*, 8: 225–30.

Cohen, H. (1981) The evolution of the concept of disease, in A. Caplan, H. Engelhardt, and J. McCarthy (eds) *Concepts of Health and Disease: Interdisciplinary Perspectives*. Reading, MA: Addison-Wesley.

Cohen, L.J., McGeoch, P.G., Gans, S.W. et al. (2002a) Childhood sexual history of 20 male pedophiles vs. 24 male healthy control subjects, *Journal of Nervous and Mental Diseases*, 190: 757–66.

Cohen, L.J., Nikiforov, K., Gans, S. et al. (2002b) Heterosexual male perpetrators of childhood sexual abuse: a preliminary neuropsychiatric model, *Psychiatric Quarterly*, 73: 313–36.

Cohen-Kettenis, P.T., Van Goozen, S.H., Doorn, C.D. et al. (1998) Cognitive ability and cerebral lateralisation in transsexuals, *Psychoneuroendocrinology*, 23: 631–41.

Cole, S.W., Kemeny, M.E., Taylor, S.E. and Visscher, B.R. (1996) Elevated physical health risk among gay men who conceal their homosexual identity, *Health Psychology*, 15: 243–51.

Collins, A.M. and Loftus, E.F. (1975) A spreading activation theory of semantic memory, *Psychological Review*, 82: 407–28.

Comings, D.E., Blake, H., Dietz G. et al. (1999) The proenkephalin gene (PENK) and opioid dependence, *Neuroreport*, 10: 1133–5.

Comings, D.E., Gade-Andavolu, R., Gonzalez, N. et al. (2001) The additive effect of neurotransmitter genes in pathological gambling, *Clinical Genetics*, 60: 107–16.

Comings, D.E., Rosenthal, R.J., Lesieur, H.R. et al. (1996) A study of the dopamine D2 receptor gene in pathological gambling, *Pharmacogenetics*, 6: 223–34.

Commander, M.J., Odell, S.M., Surtees, P.G. et al. (2004) Care pathways for south Asian and white people with depressive and anxiety disorders in the community, *Social Psychiatry and Psychiatric Epidemiology*, 39: 259–64.

Compton, W.M., Conway, K.P., Stinson, F.S. et al. (2005) Prevalence, correlates, and comorbidity of DSM-IV antisocial personality syndromes and alcohol and specific drug use disorders in the United States: results from the national epidemiologic survey on alcohol and related conditions, *Journal of Clinical Psychiatry*, 66: 677–85.

Conner, B.T., Noble, E.P., Berman, S.M. et al. (2005) DRD2 genotypes and substance use in adolescent children of alcoholics, *Drug and Alcohol Dependency*, 79: 379–87.

Conway, K., Compton, W., Stinson, F. et al. (2006) Lifetime comorbidity of DSM-IV mood and anxiety disorders and specific drug use disorder: results from the national epidemiologic survey of alcohol and related conditions, *Journal of Clinical Psychiatry*, 67: 247–57.

Coolidge, F.L., Thede, L.L. and Young, S.E. (2002) The heritability of gender identity disorder in a child and adolescent twin sample, *Behavioral Genetics*, 32: 251–7.

Cooper, C., Selwood, A., Blanchard, M. et al. (2009) Abuse of people with dementia by family carers: representative cross sectional survey, *British Medical Journal*, 338: b115.

Cornoldi, C., Marzocchi, G.M., Belotti, M. et al. (2001) Working memory interference control deficit in children referred by teachers for ADHD symptoms, *Neuropsychology, Development, and Cognition. Section C: Child Neuropsychology*, 7: 230–40.

Cororve, M.B. and Gleaves, D.H. (2001) Body dysmorphic disorder: a review of conceptualizations, assessment, and treatment strategies, *Clinical Psychology Review*, 6: 949–70.

Corrigan, P.W. (1991) Social skills training in adult psychiatric populations: a meta-analysis, *Journal of Behavior Therapy and Experimental Psychiatry*, 22: 203–10.

Corrigan, P.W., Larson, J., Sells, M. et al. (2007) Will filmed presentations of education and contact diminish mental illness stigma? *Community Mental Health Journal*, 43: 171–81.

Cory, F., Newman, L., Beck, R.L. et al. (2001) *Bipolar Disorder: A Cognitive Therapy Approach*. Washington, DC: American Psychological Association.

Costa, P.T. and McCrae, R.R. (1992) The five-factor model of personality and its relevance to personality disorders, *Journal of Personality Disorders*, 6: 343–59.

Costa, P.T. and McCrae, R.R. (1995) Domains and facets: hierarchical personality assessment using the Revised NEO Personality Inventory, *Journal of Personal Assessment*, 64: 21–50.

Costello, C. (1982) Fears and phobias in women: a community study, *Journal of Abnormal Psychology*, 91: 280–6.

Costello, E.J., Edelbrock, C.S. and Costello, A.J. (1985) Validity of the NIMH Diagnostic Interview Schedule for Children: a comparison between psychiatric and pediatric referrals, *Journal of Abnormal Child Psychology*, 13: 579–95.

Cottraux, J., Note, I., Yao, S.N. et al. (2001) A randomized controlled trial of cognitive therapy versus intensive behavior therapy in obsessive-compulsive disorder, *Psychotherapy and Psychosomatics*, 70: 288–97.

Cox, A., Rutter, M., Newman, S. et al. (1975) A comparative study of infantile autism and specific developmental language disorders. 2: Parental characteristics, *British Journal of Psychiatry*, 126: 146–59.

Cox, B.J., Kuch, K., Parker, J.D.A. et al. (1994) Alexithymia in somatoform disorder patients with chronic pain, *Journal of Psychosomatic Research*, 35: 523–7.

Craddock, N. and Jones, I. (1999) Genetics of bipolar disorder, *Journal of Medical Ethics*, 36: 585–94.

Craddock, N. and Sklar, P. (2009) Genetics of bipolar disorder: successful start to a long journey, *Trends in Genetics*, 25: 99–105.

Craig, J.S., Hatton, C., Craig, F.B. et al. (2004a) Persecutory beliefs, attributions and theory of mind: comparison of patients with paranoid delusions, Asperger's syndrome and healthy controls, *Schizophrenia Research*, 69: 29–33.

Craig, T.K., Bialas, I., Hodson, S. et al. (2004b) Intergenerational transmission of somatization behaviour. 2: Observations of joint attention and bids for attention, *Psychological Medicine*, 34: 199–209.

Craig, T.K., Boardman, A.P., Mills, K. et al. (1993) The South London Somatization Study. I: Longitudinal course and the influence of early life experiences, *British Journal of Psychiatry*, 163: 579–88.

Craig, T.K., Cox, A.D. and Klein, K. (2002) Intergenerational transmission of somatization behaviour: a study of chronic somatizers and their children, *Psychological Medicine*, 32: 805–16.

Cranston-Cuebas, M.A. and Barlow, D.H. (1990) Cognitive and affective contributions to sexual functioning, *Annual Review of Sexual Research*, 1: 119–61.

Craske, M.G., Golinelli, D., Stein, M.B. et al. (2005) Does the addition of cognitive behavioral therapy improve panic disorder treatment outcome relative to medication alone in the primary-care setting? *Psychological Medicine*, 35: 1645–54.

Craven, J.L. and Rodin, G.M. (1987) Cyproheptadine dependence associated with an atypical somatoform disorder, *Canadian Journal of Psychiatry*, 32: 143–5.

Crawford, L.L., Holloway, K.S. and Domjan, M. (1993) The nature of sexual reinforcement, *Journal of Experimental Analysis of Behaviour*, 60: 55–66.

Creed, F. and Barsky, A. (2004) Systematic review of the epidemiology of somatisation disorder and hypochondriasis, *Journal of Psychosomatic Research*, 56: 391–408.

Crimlisk, H.L., Bhatia, K., Cope, H. et al. (1998) Slater revisited: 6 year follow up study of patients with medically unexplained motor symptoms, *British Medical Journal*, 316: 582–6.

Crimlisk, H.L. and Ron, M.A. (1999) Conversion hysteria: history, diagnostic issues and clinical practice, in P. Halligan (ed.) *Conversion Hysteria: Towards a Cognitive Neuropsychological Account*. Hove: Psychology Press.

Crits-Cristoph, P., Cooper, A. and Luborsky, L. (1988) The accuracy of therapists' interpretations and the outcome of dynamic psychotherapy, *Journal of Consulting and Clinical Psychology*, 56: 490–5.

Cromarty, P. and Marks, I. (1995) Does rational role-play enhance the outcome of exposure therapy in dysmorphophobia? A case study, *British Journal of Psychiatry*, 167: 399–402.

Crowe, R. (1974) An adoption study of antisocial personality disorder, *Archives of General Psychiatry*, 31: 785–91.

Cummins, L.F., Nadorff, M.R. and Kelly, A.E. (2009) Winning and positive affect can lead to reckless gambling. *Psychology of Addictive Behaviors*, 23: 287–94.

Cunningham-Williams, R.M., Gattis, M.N., Dore, P.M. et al. (2009) Towards DSM-V: considering other withdrawal-like symptoms of pathological gambling disorder. *International Journal of Methods in Psychiatric Research*, 18: 13–22.

Curran, H.V. (1991) Benzodiazepines, memory and mood: a review, *Psychopharmacology*, 105: 1–8.

Dalgleish, T., Rosen, K. and Marks, M. (1996) Rhythm and blues: the theory and treatment of seasonal affective disorder, *British Journal of Clinical Psychology*, 35: 163–82.

Dannon, P.N., Lowengrub, K., Musin, E. et al. (2005) Sustained-release bupropion versus naltrexone in the treatment of pathological gambling: a preliminary blind-rater study, *Journal of Clinical Psychopharmacology*, 25: 593–6.

Dannon, P.N., Lowengrub, K., Musin, E. et al. (2007) 12-month follow-up study of drug treatment in pathological gamblers: a primary outcome study, *Journal of Clinical Psychopharmacology*, 27: 620–4.

Dare, C., Eisler, I., Russell, G. et al. (2001) Psychological therapies for adults with anorexia nervosa, *British Journal of Psychiatry*, 178: 216–21.

Davey, G.C.L. (1989) Dental phobias and anxieties: evidence for conditioning processes in the acquisition and modulation of a learned fear, *Behaviour Research Therapy*, 27: 51–8.

Davey, G.C.L. (1997) A conditioning model of phobias, in G.C.L. Davey (ed.) *Phobias: A Handbook of Theory, Research and Treatment*. Chichester: Wiley.

Davey Smith, G., Dorling, D., Gordon, D. et al. (1999) The widening health gap: what are the solutions?, *Critical Public Health*, 9: 151–70.

Davidson, J.R.T. (2001) Pharmacotherapy of Generalised Anxiety Disorder, *Journal of Clinical Psychiatry*, 62 (Suppl. 11): 46–50.

Davidson, K. (2000) *Cognitive Therapy for Personality Disorders*. Oxford: Butterworth-Heinemann.

Davidson, K.M., Tyrer, P., Tata, P. et al. (2008) Cognitive behaviour therapy for violent men with antisocial personality disorder in the community: an exploratory randomized controlled trial, *Psychological Medicine*, Jul (30): 1–9.

Davidson, P.R. and Parker, K.C.H. (2001) Eye movement desensitization and reprocessing (EMDR): a meta-analysis, *Journal of Consulting and Clinical Psychology*, 69: 305–16.

Day, J.C., Bentall, R.P., Roberts, C. et al. (2005) Attitudes toward antipsychotic medication: the impact of clinical variables and relationships with health professionals, *Archives of General Psychiatry*, 62: 717–24.

Degenhardt, L., Day, C., Dietze, P. et al. (2005) Effects of a sustained heroin shortage in three Australian States, *Addiction*, 100: 908–20.

De la Fuente, J.M. Goldman, S. Stanus, E. et al. (1997) Brain glucose metabolism in borderline personality disorder, *Journal of Psychiatric Research*, 31: 531–41.

Delfabbro, P.H. and Winefield, A.H. (1999) Poker machine gambling: an analysis of within session characteristics, *British Journal of Psychology*, 90: 425–32.

Deltito, J.A. and Stam, M. (1989) Psychopharmacological treatment of avoidant personality disorder, *Comprehensive Psychiatry*, 30: 498–504.

DeMarco, R.R. (2000) The epidemiology of major depression: implications of occurrence, recurrence, and stress in a Canadian community sample, *Canadian Journal of Psychiatry*, 45: 67–74.

Demicheli, V., Jefferson, T., Rivetti, A. et al. (2005) Vaccines for measles, mumps and rubella in children, *Cochrane Database of Systematic Reviews*, 5.

Demyttenaere, K., Van Ganse, E., Gregoirre, J. et al. (1998) Compliance in depressed patients treated with fluoxetine or amitriptyline. Belgian Compliance Study Group, *International Clinical Psychopharmacology*, 13: 11–17.

DeRubeis, R.J., Gelfand, L.A., Tang, T.Z. et al. (1999) Medications versus cognitive behavior therapy for severely depressed outpatients: mega-analysis of four randomized comparisons, *American Journal of Psychiatry*, 156: 1007–13.

Dettmer, K., Hanna, D., Whetstone, P. et al. (2007) Autism and urinary exogenous neuropeptides: development of an on-line SPE-HPLC-tandem mass spectrometry method to test the opioid excess theory, *Analytical and Bioanalytical Chemistry*, 388: 1643–51.

Devanand, D.P., Dwork, A.J., Hutchinson, E.R. et al. (1994) Does ECT alter brain structure?, *American Journal of Psychiatry*, 151: 957–70.

Deveney, C.M. and Deldin, P.J. (2006) A preliminary investigation of cognitive flexibility for emotional information in major depressive disorder and non-psychiatric controls, *Emotion*, 6: 429–37.

Devilly, G.J. and Spence, S.H. (1999) The relative efficacy and treatment distress of EMDR and a cognitive-behavior trauma treatment protocol in the amelioration of posttraumatic stress disorder, *Journal of Anxiety Disorders*, 13: 131–57.

Dhawan, S. and Marshall, W.L. (1996) Sexual abuse histories of sexual offenders, *Sexual Abuse: A Journal of Research and Treatment*, 8: 7–15.

Dickerson, M. and Baron, E. (2000) Contemporary issues and future directions for research into pathological gambling, *Addiction*, 95: 1145–59.

Dickerson, M.G., Baron, E., Hong, S-M. et al. (1996) Estimating the extent and degree of gambling related problems in the Australian population: a national survey, *Journal of Gambling Studies*, 12: 161–78.

Dickstein, S.G., Bannon, K., Castellanos, F.X. et al. (2006) The neural correlates of attention deficit hyperactivity disorder: an ALE meta-analysis, *Journal of Child Psychology and Psychiatry*, 47: 1051–62.

Didie, E.R., Menard, W., Stern, A.P. et al. (2008) Occupational functioning and impairment in adults with body dysmorphic disorder, *Comprehensive Psychiatry*, 49: 561–9.

Distel, M.A., Hottenga, J.J., Trull, T.J. et al. (2008b) Chromosome 9: linkage for borderline personality disorder features, *Psychiatric Genetics*, 18: 302–7.

Distel, M.A., Trull, T.J., Derom, C.A. et al. (2008a) Heritability of borderline personality disorder features is similar across three countries, *Psychological Medicine*, 38: 1219–29.

Docter, R.F. and Prince, V. (1997) Transvestism: a survey of 1032 crossdressers, *Archives of Sexual Behavior*, 26: 589–605.

Dolan, M., Deakin, W.J., Roberts, N. et al. (2002) Serotonergic and cognitive impairment in impulsive aggressive personality disordered offenders: are there implications for treatment? *Psychological Medicine*, 32: 105–17.

Dollard, J. and Miller, N.E. (1950) *Personality and Psychotherapy*. New York: McGraw-Hill.

Dong, X., Beck, T. and Simon, M.A. (2010) The associations of gender, depression and elder mistreatment in a community-dwelling Chinese population: the modifying effect of social support, *Archives of Gerontology and Geriatrics*, 50: 202–8.

Donohoe, G., Owens, N., O'Donnell, C. et al. (2001) Predictors of compliance with neuroleptic medication among inpatients with schizophrenia: a discriminant function analysis, *European Psychiatry*, 16: 293–8.

Driessen, M., Herrmann, J., Stahl, K. et al. (2000) Magnetic resonance imaging volumes of the hippocampus and the amygdala in women with borderline personality disorder and early traumatization, *Archives of General Psychiatry*, 57: 1115–22.

Drury, V., Birchwood, M. and Cochrane, R. (2000) Cognitive therapy and recovery from acute psychosis: a controlled trial. 3: Five-year follow-up, *British Journal of Psychiatry*, 177: 8–14.

Dugas, M.J., Marchand, A., Ladouceur, R. et al. (2005) Further validation of a cognitive behavioral model of generalized anxiety disorder: diagnostic and symptom specificity, *Journal of Anxiety Disorders*, 19: 329–43.

Dumais, A., Lesage, A.D., Alda, M. et al. (2005) Risk factors for suicide completion in major depression: a case-control study of impulsive and aggressive behaviors in men, *American Journal of Psychiatry*, 162: 2116–24.

Duncan, G.E., Sheitman, B.B. and Lieberman, J.A. (1999) An integrated view of pathophysiological models of schizophrenia, *Brain Research Reviews*, 29: 250–64.

Duncan, R. and Oto, M. (2008) Predictors of antecedent factors in psychogenic nonepileptic attacks: multivariate analysis, *Neurology*, 71: 1000–5.

Durham, R.C., Murphy, T., Allan, T. et al. (1994) Cognitive therapy, analytic psychotherapy and anxiety management training for generalised anxiety disorder, *British Journal of Psychiatry*, 16: 315–23.

Durkheim, E. ([1897] 1951) *Suicide*. New York: Free Press.

Dyck, M., Habel, U., Slodczyk, J. et al. (2009) Negative bias in fast emotion discrimination in borderline personality disorder, *Psychological Medicine*, 39: 855–64.

Dyer, C. (1997) High court detains girl with anorexia, *British Medical Journal*, 314: 845.

Eagles, J.M., Wileman, S.M., Cameron, I.M. et al. (1999) Seasonal affective disorder among primary care attenders and a community sample in Aberdeen, *British Journal of Psychiatry*, 175: 472–5.

Eamon, M.K. and Mulder, C. (2005) Predicting antisocial behavior among Latino young adolescents: an ecological systems analysis, *American Journal of Orthopsychiatry*, 75: 117–27.

Eaton, W.W., Kramer, M., Anthony, J.C. et al. (1989) The incidence of specific DIS/DSM-III mental disorders: data from the NIMH Epidemiologic Catchment Area Program, *Acta Psychiatrica Scandinavica*, 79: 163–78.

Ebert, A. and Dyck, M.J. (2004) The experience of mental death: the core feature of complex posttraumatic stress disorder, *Clinical Psychology Review*, 24: 617–35.

Eddy, J.M. and Chamberlain, P. (2000) Family management and deviant peer associations as mediators of the impact of treatment condition on youth antisocial behavior, *Journal of Consulting and Clinical Psychology*, 68: 857–63.

Eddy, K.T., Dorer, D.J., Franko, D.L. et al. (2008) Diagnostic crossover in anorexia nervosa and bulimia nervosa: implications for DSM-V, *American Journal of Psychiatry*, 165: 245–50.

Edwards, G., Anderson, P., Babor, T.F. et al. (1994) *Alcohol Policy and the Public Good*. Oxford: Oxford University Press.

Ehde, D.M., Kraft, G.H., Chwastiak, L. et al. (2008) Efficacy of paroxetine in treating major depressive disorder in persons with multiple sclerosis, *General Hospital Psychiatry*, 30: 40–8.

Ehlers, A., Mayou, R.A. and Bryant, B. (1998) Psychological predictors of chronic posttraumatic stress disorder after motor vehicle accidents, *Journal of Abnormal Psychology*, 107: 508–19.

Ehrhardt, A. and Money, J. (1967) Progestin-induced hermaphroditism: IQ and psychosexual identity in a study of ten girls, *Journal of Sex Research*, 3: 83–100.

Eisler, I., Simic, M., Russell, G.F.M. et al. (2007) A randomized controlled trial of two forms of family therapy in adolescent anorexia nervosa: a five-year follow-up, *Journal of Child Psychology and Psychiatry*, 48: 552–60.

El-Maaytah, M., Smith, S.F., Jerjes, W. et al. (2008) The effect of the new '24 hour alcohol licensing law' on the incidence of facial trauma in London, *British Journal of Oral Maxillofacial Surgery*, 46: 460–3.

Elkin, I., Shea, T., Watkins, J.T. et al. (1989) National Institute of Mental Health Treatment of Depression Collaborative Research Program: general effectiveness of treatments, *Archives of General Psychiatry*, 46: 971–82.

Elkins, G., Rajab, M.H. and Marcus, J. (2005) Complementary and alternative medicine use by psychiatric inpatients, *Psychological Reports*, 96: 163–6.

Ellery, M., Stewart, S.H. and Loba, P. (2005) Alcohol's effects on video lottery terminal (VLT) play among probable pathological and non-pathological gamblers, *Journal of Gambling Studies*, 21: 299–324.

Elliott, M. (2000) Gender differences in the causes of depression, *Women and Health*, 33: 163–77.

Ellis, A. (1977) The basic clinical theory of rational-emotive therapy, in A. Ellis and R. Grieger (eds) *Handbook of Rational-Emotive Therapy*. New York: Springer.

Elzinga, B.M., Phaf, R.H., Ardon, A.M. et al. (2003) Directed forgetting between, but not within, dissociative personality states, *Journal of Abnormal Psychology*, 112: 237–43.

Emerson, E. (1998) Working with people with challenging behaviour, in E. Emerson, C. Hatton, J. Bromley et al. (eds) *Clinical Psychology and People with Intellectual Disabilities*. Chichester: Wiley.

Emerson, E., Hatton, C., Felce, D. et al. (2001) *Learning Disabilities: The Fundamental Facts*. London: Mental Health Foundation.

Emmelkamp, P.M., Benner, A., Kuipers, A. et al. (2006) Comparison of brief dynamic and cognitive-behavioural therapies in avoidant personality disorder, *British Journal of Psychiatry*, 189: 60–4.

Endicott, J. and Spitzer, R.L. (1978) A diagnostic interview: the schedule for affective disorders and schizophrenia, *Archives of General Psychiatry*, 35: 873–4.

Engel, S.M., Berkowitz, G.S., Wol., M.S. et al. (2005) Psychological trauma associated with the World Trade Center attacks and its effect on pregnancy outcome, *Paediatric and Perinatal Epidemiology*, 19: 334–41.

Engels, R.C., Hermans, R., van Baaren, R.B. et al. (2009) Alcohol portrayal on television affects actual drinking behaviour, *Alcohol and Alcoholism*, 44: 244–9.

Epstein, J., Wiseman, C.V., Sunday, S.R. et al. (2001) Neurocognitive evidence favors 'top down' over 'bottom up' mechanisms in the pathogenesis of body size distortions in anorexia nervosa, *Eating and Weight Disorders*, 6: 140–7.

Erikson, E. (1980) *Growth and Crisis of the Healthy Personality: Identity and the Life Cycle*. New York: W.W. Norton.

Essali, A., Al-Haj Haasan, N., Li, C. et al. (2009) Clozapine versus typical neuroleptic medication for schizophrenia, *Cochrane Database of Systematic Reviews*, 1: CD000059.

Evans, E., Kupfer, D.J., Perel, J.M. et al. (1992) Three-year outcomes for maintenance therapies in recurrent depression, *Archives of General Psychiatry*, 47: 1093–9.

Evans, K.C., Simon, N.M., Dougherty, D.D. et al. (2009) A PET study of tiagabine treatment implicates ventral medial prefrontal cortex in generalized social anxiety disorder, *Neuropsychopharmacology*, 34: 390–8.

Evans, S., Ferrando, S., Findler, M. et al. (2008) Mindfulness-based cognitive therapy for generalized anxiety disorder, *Journal of Anxiety Disorders*, 22: 716–21.

Fagan, P.J., Wise, T.N., Schmidt, C.W. Jr., et al. (2002) Pedophilia, *Journal of the American Medical Association*, 288: 2458–65.

Fahlen, T. (1995) Personality traits in social phobia. II: changes during drug treatment, *Journal of Clinical Psychiatry*, 56: 569–73.

Fairburn, C.G. (1997) Eating disorders, in D.M. Clark and C.G. Fairburn (eds) *Science and Practice of Cognitive Behaviour Therapy*. Oxford: Oxford University Press.

Fairburn, C.G. (1998) *Cognitive Behaviour Therapy and Eating Disorders.* New York: Guilford Press.

Fairburn, C.G., Jones, R., Peveler, R.C. et al. (1993) Psychotherapy and bulimia nervosa: the longer-term effects of interpersonal psychotherapy, behaviour therapy and cognitive behaviour therapy, *Archives of General Psychiatry*, 50: 419–28.

Fairburn, C.G., Norman, P.A. and Welch, S.L. (1995) A prospective study of outcome in bulimia nervosa and the long-term effects of three psychological treatments, *Archives of General Psychiatry*, 52: 304–12.

Fallon, B.A., Petkova, E., Skritskaya, N. et al. (2008) A double-masked, placebo-controlled study of fluoxetine for hypochondriasis, *Journal of Clinical Psychopharmacology*, 28: 638–45.

Fallon, B.A., Qureshi, A.I., Schneier, F.R. et al. (2003) An open trial of fluvoxamine for hypochondriasis, *Psychosomatics*, 44: 298–303.

Falloon, I.R., Boyd, J.L., McGill, C.W. et al. (1982) Family management in the prevention of exacerbations of schizophrenia: a controlled study, *New England Journal of Medicine*, 306: 1437–40.

Faraone, S.V., Biederman, J., Spencer, T. et al. (2005) Efficacy of atomoxetine in adult attention-deficit/hyperactivity disorder: a drug-placebo response curve analysis, *Behavioral and Brain Functions*, 1: 16–20.

Farber, S. (1990) Institutional mental health and social control: the ravages of epistemological hubris, *Journal of Mind and Behavior*, 11: 285–300.

Farrington, D.P. (2000) Psychosocial predictors of adult antisocial personality and adult convictions, *Behavioral Sciences and the Law*, 18: 605–22.

Farris, B. and Stancliffe, R.J. (2001) The co-worker training model: outcomes of an open employment pilot project, *Journal of Intellectual and Developmental Disability*, 26: 143–59.

Favarelli, C., Salvatori, S., Galassi, F. et al. (1997) Epidemiology of somatoform disorders: a community survey in Florence, *Social Psychiatry and Psychiatric Epidemiology*, 32: 24–9.

Favre, J.D., Allain, H., Aubin, H.J. et al. (2005) Double-blind study of cyamemazine and diazepam in the alcohol withdrawal syndrome, *Human Psychopharmacology*, 20: 511–19.

Feeney, G.F., Connor, J.P., Young, R. et al. (2006) Is acamprosate use in alcohol dependence treatment reflected in improved subjective health status outcomes beyond cognitive behavioural therapy alone? *Journal of Addictive Diseases*, 25: 49–58.

Feeney, G.F., Young, R.M., Connor, J.P. et al. (2002) Cognitive behavioural therapy combined with the relapse-prevention medication acamprosate: are short-term treatment outcomes for alcohol dependence improved?, *Australian and New Zealand Journal of Psychiatry*, 36: 622–8.

Feil, N. (1990) Validation therapy helps staff reach confused patients, *Nursing*, 16: 33–4.

Feingold, B.F. (1979) *The Feingold Cookbook for Hyperactive Children.* New York: Random House.

Feinstein, A., Ron, M. and Thompson, A. (1993) A serial study of psychometric and magnetic resonance imaging changes in multiple sclerosis, *Brain*, 116: 569–602.

Feiring, C., Taska, L. and Lewis, M. (2002) Adjustment following sexual abuse discovery: the role of shame and attributional style, *Developmental Psychology*, 38: 79–92.

Feldman-Summers, S. and Pope, K.S. (1994) The experience of 'forgetting' childhood abuse: a national survey of psychologists, *Journal of Consulting and Clinical Psychology*, 62: 636–9.

Feliu, M., Edwards, C.L., Sudhakar, S. et al. (2008) Neuropsychological effects and attitudes in patients following electroconvulsive therapy, *Neuropsychiatric Diseases and Treatment*, 4: 613–17.

Felner, R.D., Brand, S., Adan, A.M. et al. (1993) Restructuring the ecology of the school as an approach to prevention during school transitions: longitudinal follow-ups and extensions of the School Transitional Environment Project (STEP), *Prevention in Human Services*, 10: 103–9.

Ferguson, C.P., La Via, M.C., Crossan, P.J. et al. (1999) Are serotonin selective reuptake inhibitors effective in underweight anorexia nervosa?, *International Journal of Eating Disorders*, 25: 7–11.

Fergusson, D., Doucette, S., Glass, K.C. et al. (2005) Association between suicide attempts and selective serotonin reuptake inhibitors: systematic review of randomised controlled trials, *British Medical Journal*, 330: 396–9.

Fergusson, D.M. and Horwood, L.J. (1995) Predictive validity of categorically and dimensionally scored measures of disruptive childhood behaviors, *Journal of the American Academy of Child and Adolescent Psychiatry*, 34: 477–85.

Ferri, M., Amato, L. and Davoli, M. (2006) Alcoholics Anonymous and other 12-step programmes for alcohol dependence, *Cochrane Database of Systematic Reviews*, 3: CD005032.

Ferrie, J.E., Martikainen, P., Shipley, M.J. et al. (2001) Employment status and health after privatisation in white collar civil servants: prospective cohort study, *British Medical Journal*, 322: 647–51.

Fineberg, N.A., Saxena, S. and Zohar, J. (2007) Obsessive-compulsive disorder: boundary issues, *CNS Spectrum*, 12: 359–64, 367–75.

Fink, D. and Golinkoff, M. (1990) Multiple personality disorder, borderline personality disorder, and schizophrenia: a comparative study of clinical features, *Dissociation*, 3: 127–34.

Fink, P., Hansen, M.S. and Oxhoj, M-L. (2004) The prevalence of somatoform disorders among internal medical inpatients, *Journal of Psychosomatic Research*, 56: 413–18.

Fink, P., Ornbol, E., Toft, T. et al. (2004) A new, empirically established hypochondriasis diagnosis, *American Journal of Psychiatry*, 161: 1680–91.

Finkelhor, D. (1984) *Child Sexual Abuse: New Theory and Research*. New York: Free Press.

Finn, P.R., Earleywine, M. and Pihl, R.O. (1992) Sensation seeking, stress reactivity, and alcohol dampening discriminate the density of a family history of alcoholism, *Alcoholism: Clinical and Experimental Research*, 16: 585–90.

First, M.B., Spitzer, R.L., Gibbon, M. et al. (1996) *Structured Clinical Interview for DSM-IV Axis I Disorders. Clinical Version (SCID-CV)*. Washington, DC: American Psychiatric Press.

Fishbain, D.A. and Aldrich, T.E. (1985) Suicide pacts: international comparisons, *Journal of Clinical Psychiatry*, 46: 11–15.

Foa, E.B. and Kozak, M.J. (1986) Emotional processing of fear: exposure to corrective information, *Psychological Bulletin*, 99: 20–35.

Foa, E.B., Liebowitz, M.R., Kozak, M.J. et al. (2005) Randomized, placebo-controlled trial of exposure and ritual prevention, clomipramine, and their combination in the treatment of obsessive-compulsive disorder, *American Journal of Psychiatry*, 162: 151–61.

Foa, E.B., Rothbaum, B.O., Riggs, D.S. et al. (1991) Treatment of posttraumatic stress disorder in rape victims: a comparison between cognitive and behavioral procedures and counselling, *Journal of Consulting and Clinical Psychology*, 59: 715–23.

Foa, E.B., Steketee, G. and Rothbaum, B.O. (1989) Behavioral/cognitive conceptualizations of post-traumatic stress disorder, *Behavior Therapy*, 20: 155–76.

Foote, B., Smolin, Y., Kaplan, M. et al. (2006) Prevalence of dissociative disorders in psychiatric outpatients, *American Journal of Psychiatry*, 163: 623–9.

Fox, J.C., Blank, M., Berman, J. et al. (1999) Mental disorders and help seeking in a rural impoverished population, *International Journal of Psychiatry in Medicine*, 29: 181–95.

Fox, J.W. (1990) Social class, mental illness, and social mobility: the social selection-drift hypothesis for serious mental illness, *Journal of Health and Social Behavior*, 31: 344–53.

Frank, J.D. (1961) *Persuasion and Healing: A Comparative Study of Psychotherapy*. Baltimore, MD: Johns Hopkins University Press.

Fraser, G.A. (1992) Multiple personality disorder, *British Journal of Psychiatry*, 161: 416–17.

Freedy, J.R., Resnick, H.S. and Kilpatrick, D.G. (1992) Conceptual framework for evaluating disaster impact: implications for clinical intervention, in L.S. Austin (ed.) *Responding to Disaster: A Guide for Mental Health Professionals*. Washington, DC: American Psychiatric Press.

Freeman, C. (1995) *The ECT Handbook*. London: Royal College of Psychiatrists.

Freud, S. (1900) *The Interpretation of Dreams*. New York: Wiley.

Freud, S. (1906) Analysis of a phobia in a five-year-old boy, in J. Strachey (ed. and trans.) *Standard Edition of Complete Psychological Works*, Vol. 10. London: Hogarth Press, pp. 5–149.

Freud, S. (1914) On narcissism: an introduction, *The Standard Edition of Complete Psychological Works*, 14: 67–102.

Freud, S. (1922) *Introductory Lectures on Psychoanalysis*. London: George Allen and Unwin.

Freud, S. ([1917] 1957) Mourning and melancholia, in J. Strachey (ed. and trans.) *The Standard Edition of Complete Psychological Works*, Vol. 14. London: Hogarth Press.

Freud, S. ([1920] 1990) *Beyond the Pleasure Principle*. New York: W.W. Norton.

Freud, S. and Breur, J. (2004) *Studies in Hysteria*. New York: Penguin.

Freyd, J.J. (1996) *Betrayal Trauma: The Logic of Forgetting Childhood Abuse*. Cambridge, MA: Harvard University Press.

Friedberg, J. (1977) Shock treatment, brain damage, and memory loss: a neurological perspective, *American Journal of Psychiatry*, 13: 1010–14.

Frith, C.D. and Corcoran, R. (1996) Exploring 'theory of mind' in people with schizophrenia, *Psychological Medicine*, 26: 521–30.

Fromm-Reichman, F. (1948) Notes on the development of treatment of schizophrenia by psycho-analytic psychotherapy, *Psychiatry*, 11: 263–73.

Frost, A. (2004) Therapeutic engagement styles of child sexual offenders in a group treatment program: a grounded theory study, *Sexual Abuse*, 16: 191–208.

Fryers, T., Melzer, D., Jenkins, R. et al. (2005) The distribution of the common mental disorders: social inequalities in Europe, *Clinical Practice and Epidemiology in Mental Health*, 1: 14.

Fukunishi, I. (1997) Alexithymic characteristics of bulimia nervosa in diabetes mellitus with end-stage renal disease, *Psychological Reports*, 81: 627–33.

Fukunishi, I., Sasaki, K., Chisima, Y. et al. (1996) Emotional disturbances in trauma patients during the rehabilitation phase: studies of post-traumatic stress disorder and alexithymia, *General Hospital Psychiatry*, 18: 121–7.

Fulton, B.D., Scheffler, R.M., Hinshaw, S.P. et al. (2009) National variation of ADHD diagnostic prevalence and medication use: health care providers and education policies, *Psychiatric Services*, 60: 1075–83.

Gada, M.T. (1982) A cross-cultural study of symptomatology of depression: eastern versus western patients, *International Journal of Social Psychology*, 28: 195–202.

Gaebel, W., Janner, M., Frommann, N. et al. (2002) First vs multiple episode schizophrenia: two-year outcome of intermittent and maintenance medication strategies, *Schizophrenia Research*, 53: 145–59.

Gaebel, W. and Riesbeck, M. (2007) Revisiting the relapse predictive validity of prodromal symptoms in schizophrenia, *Schizophrenia Research*, 95: 19–29.

Gagné, G.G., Furman, M.J., Carpenter, L.L. et al. (2000) Efficacy of continuation ECT and antidepressant drugs compared to long-term antidepressants alone in depressed patients, *American Journal of Psychiatry*, 157: 1960–9.

Galea, S., Vlahov, D., Resnick, H. et al. (2003) Trends of probable post-traumatic stress disorder in New York City after the September 11 terrorist attacks, *American Journal of Epidemiology*, 158: 514–24.

Gallagher-Thompson, D. and Steffen, A.M. (1994) Comparative effects of cognitive behavioral and brief psychodynamic psychotherapies for depressed family caregivers, *Journal of Consulting and Clinical Psychology*, 62: 543–9.

Gannon, T.A., Ward, T. and Polaschek, D.L.L. (2004) Child sexual offenders, in M. Connolly (ed.) *Violence in Society: New Zealand Perspectives*. Christchurch: Te Awatea Press.

Garbutt, J.C., Kranzler, H.R., O'Malley, S.S. et al. (2005) Efficacy and tolerability of longacting injectable naltrexone for alcohol dependence: a randomized controlled trial, *Journal of the American Medical Association*, 293: 1617–25.

Garcia-Palacios, A., Botella, C., Hoffman, H. et al. (2007) Comparing acceptance and refusal rates of virtual reality exposure vs. in vivo exposure by patients with specific phobias, *Cyberpsychology and Behavior*, 10: 722–4.

Garner, D.M. and Bemis, K.M. (1985) Cognitive therapy for anorexia nervosa, in D.M. Garner and P.E. Garfinkel (eds) *Handbook of Psychotherapy for Anorexia Nervosa and Bulimia*. New York: Guilford.

Gava, I., Barbui, C., Aguglia, E. et al. (2007) Psychological treatments versus treatment as usual for obsessive compulsive disorder (OCD), *Cochrane Database of Systematic Reviews*, 2: CD00533.

Gavrilova, S.I., Ferri, C.P., Mikhaylova, N. et al. (2009) Helping carers to care – the 10/66 dementia research group's randomized control trial of a caregiver intervention in Russia, *International Journal of Geriatric Psychiatry*, 24(4): 347–54.

Geddes, J.R., Verdoux, H., Takei, N. et al. (1999) Schizophrenia and complications of pregnancy and labor: an individual patient data meta-analysis, *Schizophrenia Bulletin*, 25: 413–23.

Gena, A., Couloura, S. and Kymissis, E. (2005) Modifying the affective behavior of preschoolers with autism using in-vivo or video modeling and reinforcement contingencies, *Journal of Autism and Developmental Disorders*, 35: 1–12.

Gentile, M.G., Manna, G.M., Ciceri, R. et al. (2008) Efficacy of inpatient treatment in severely malnourished anorexia nervosa patients, *Eating and Weight Disorders*, 13: 191–7.

Geoffrey, C. (1991) A Prozac backlash, *Newsweek*, 1 April, p. 64.

Geraerts, E., Lindsay, D.S., Merckelbach, H. et al. (2009) Cognitive mechanisms underlying recovered-memory experiences of childhood sexual abuse, *Psychological Science*, 20: 92–7.

Gerra, G., Garofano, L., Santoro, G. et al. (2004) Association between low-activity serotonin transporter genotype and heroin dependence: behavioral and personality correlates, *American Journal of Medical Genetics. B: Neuropsychiatric Genetics*, 126: 37–42.

Gibson, D.R., Flynn, N.M. and Perales, D. (2001) Effectiveness of syringe exchange programs in reducing HIV risk behavior and HIV seroconversion among injecting drug users, *AIDS*, 15: 1329–41.

Giesen-Bloo, J., van Dyck, R., Spinhoven, P. et al. (2006) Outpatient psychotherapy for borderline personality disorder: randomized trial of schema-focused therapy vs transference-focused psychotherapy, *Archives of General Psychiatry*, 63: 649–58.

Gilbert, D.L., Zhang, J., Lipps, T.D. et al. (2007) Atomoxetine treatment of ADHD in Tourette syndrome: reduction in motor cortex inhibition correlates with clinical improvement, *Clinical Neurophysiology*, 118: 1835–41.

Gillespie, K., Duffy, M., Hackmann, A. et al. (2002) Community based cognitive therapy in the treatment of post-traumatic stress disorder following the Omagh bomb, *Behaviour Research and Therapy*, 40: 345–57.

Gillespie, N.A., Zhu, G., Heath, A.C. et al. (2000) The genetic aetiology of somatic distress, *Psychological Medicine*, 30: 1051–61.

Gillman, P.K. (2007) Tricyclic antidepressant pharmacology and therapeutic drug interactions updated, *British Journal of Pharmacology*, 151: 737–48.

Gindi, R.M., Rucker, M.G., Serio-Chapman, C.E. et al. (2009) Utilization patterns and correlates of retention among clients of the needle exchange program in Baltimore, Maryland, *Drug and Alcohol Dependence*, 103: 93–8.

Gladue, B.A. (1985) Neuroendocrine response to estrogen and sexual orientation, *Science*, 230: 961.

Gleaves, D.H. (1996) The sociocognitive model of dissociative identity disorder: a reexamination of the evidence, *Psychological Bulletin*, 120: 42–59.

Gleaves, D.H., May, M.C. and Cardena, E. (2001) An examination of the diagnostic validity of dissociative identity disorder, *Clinical Psychology Review*, 21: 577–608.

Goddard, A.W., Mason, G.F., Almai, A. et al. (2001) Reductions in occipital cortex GABA levels in panic disorder detected with 1H-magnetic resonance spectroscopy, *Archives of General Psychiatry*, 58: 556–61.

Goldbloom, D.S., Hicks, L.K. and Garfinkel, P.E. (1990) Platelet serotonin uptake in bulimia nervosa, *Biological Psychiatry*, 28: 644–7.

Golding, L., Emerson, E. and Thornton, A. (2005) An evaluation of specialized community-based residential supports for people with challenging behaviour, *Journal of Intellectual Disability*, 9: 145–54.

Goldman, A. and Carroll, J.L. (1990) Educational intervention as an adjunct to treatment of erectile dysfunction in older couples, *Journal of Sexual and Marital Therapy*, 16: 127–41.

Goldman, M.S. (1999a) Expectancy operation: cognitive and neural models and architectures, in I. Kirsch (ed.) *Expectancy, Experience, and Behavior.* Washington, DC: APA Books.

Goldman, M.S. (1999b) Risk for substance abuse: memory as a common etiological pathway, *Psychological Science*, 10: 196–8.

Goldstein, I., Lue, T.F., Padma-Nathan, H. et al. (1998) Oral sildenafil in the treatment of erectile dysfunction: Sildenafil Study Group, *New England Journal of Medicine*, 338: 1397–404.

Golub, A. and Johnson, B.D. (2005) The new heroin users among Manhattan arrestees: variations by race/ethnicity and mode of consumption, *Journal of Psychoactive Drugs*, 37: 51–61.

Gomez-Perez, J.C., Marks, I.M. and Gutierrez-Fisac, J.L. (1994) Dysmorphophobia: clinical features and outcome with behavior therapy, *European Psychiatry*, 9: 229–35.

Gooding, P. and Tarrier, N. (2009) A systematic review and meta-analysis of cognitive-behavioural interventions to reduce problem gambling: hedging our bets? *Behaviour Research and Therapy*, 47: 592–607.

Goodman, G.S., Ghetti, S., Quas, J.A. et al. (2003) A prospective study of memory for abuse: new findings relevant to the repressed memory debate, *Psychological Science*, 14: 113–18.

Goodman, R. and Stevenson, J. (1989) A twin study of hyperactivity – II: the etiological role of genes, family relationships, and perinatal adversity, *Journal of Child Psychology and Psychiatry*, 30: 691–709.

Goodwin, R.D. (2003) The prevalence of panic attacks in the United States: 1980 to 1995, *Journal of Clinical Epidemiology*, 56: 914–16.

Goodyear-Smith, F.A., Laidlaw, T.M. and Large, R.G. (1997) Memory recovery and repression: what is the evidence?, *Health Care Analysis*, 5: 99–111.

Gordon, C.T., State, R.C., Nelson, J.E. et al. (1993) A double-blind comparison of clomipramine, desipramine, and placebo in the treatment of autistic disorder, *Archives of General Psychiatry*, 50: 441–7.

Gorski, T.T. (1989) *Understanding the Twelve Steps.* New York: Prentice Hall/Parkside.

Goudriaan, A.E., Oosterlaan, J., de Beurs, E. et al. (2004) Pathological gambling: a comprehensive review of biobehavioral findings, *Neuroscience and Biobehavioral Review*, 28: 123–41.

Gould, R.A., Otto, M.W. and Pollack, M.H. (1995) A meta-analysis of treatment outcome for panic disorder, *Clinical Psychology Review*, 15: 819–44.

Gowers, S.G., Clark, A., Roberts, C. et al. (2007) Clinical effectiveness of treatments for anorexia nervosa in adolescents, *British Journal of Psychiatry*, 191: 427–35.

Goyer, P., Andreason, P.J., Semple, W.E. et al. (1994) Positron-emission tomography and personality disorders, *Neuropsychopharmacology*, 10: 21–8.

Grant, B.F., Hasin, D.S., Stinson, F.S. et al. (2005) Prevalence, correlates, co-morbidity, and comparative disability of DSM-IV generalized anxiety disorder in the USA: results from the National Epidemiologic Survey on Alcohol and Related Conditions, *Psychological Medicine*, 35: 1747–59.

Grant, B.F., Stinson, F.S., Hasin, D.S. et al. (2005) Prevalence, correlates, and comorbidity of bipolar I disorder and axis I and II disorders: results from the National Epidemiologic Survey on Alcohol and Related Conditions, *Journal of Clinical Psychiatry*, 66: 1205–15.

Grant, J.E., Kim, S.W. and Potenza, M.N. (2003) Paroxetine treatment of pathological gambling: a multi-centre randomized controlled trial, *International Clinical Psychopharmacology*, 18: 243–9.

Gray, J.A. (1983) A theory of anxiety: the role of the limbic system, *Encephale*, 9 (Suppl. 2): 161B–6B.

Gray, N.S., Brown, A.S., MacCulloch, M.J. et al. (2005) Implicit test of the associations between children and sex in pedophiles, *Journal Abnormal Psychology*, 114: 104–8.

Green, R. (1987) *The 'Sissy Boy Syndrome' and the Development of Homosexuality.* New Haven, CT: Yale University Press.

Green, R. and Blanchard, R. (1995) Gender identity disorders, in H.I. Kaplan and B.J. Sadock (eds) *Comprehensive Textbook of Psychiatry.* Baltimore, MD: Williams and Wilkins.

Green R.E., Colella B., Christensen, B. et al. (2008) Examining moderators of cognitive recovery trajectories after moderate to severe traumatic brain injury, *Archives of Physical Medicine and Rehabilitation*, 89 (12 Suppl.): S16–24.

Greenberg, D.M., Bradford, J. and Curry, S. (1993) A comparison of sexual victimizations in the childhoods of pedophiles and hebephiles, *Journal of Forensic Sciences*, 38: 432–6.

Greenberg, P. and Kusche, C. (1998) Preventive intervention for school-age deaf children: the PATHS curriculum, *Journal of Deaf Studies and Deaf Education*, 3: 49–63.

Greenhalgh, J., Knight, C., Hind, D. et al. (2005) Clinical and cost-effectiveness of electroconvulsive therapy for depressive illness, schizophrenia, catatonia and mania: systematic reviews and economic modelling studies, *Health Technology Assessment*, 9: 1–156.

Greeven, A., van Balkom, A.J., Visser, S. et al. (2007) Cognitive behavior therapy and paroxetine in the treatment of hypochondriasis: a randomized controlled trial, *American Journal of Psychiatry*, 164: 91–9.

Gresham, F.M. and MacMillan, D.L. (1998) Early intervention project: can its claims be substantiated and its effects replicated?, *Journal of Autism and Developmental Disorders*, 28: 5–13.

Griffiths, M. (2003) Internet gambling: issues, concerns, and recommendations, *Cyber Psychology and Behavior*, 6: 557–68.

Grilo, C.M., Pagano, M.E., Skodol, A.E. et al. (2007) Natural course of bulimia nervosa and of eating disorder not otherwise specified: 5-year prospective study of remissions, relapses, and the effects of personality disorder psychopathology, *Journal of Clinical Psychiatry*, 68: 738–46.

Grimland, M., Apter, A. and Kerkhof, A. (2006) The phenomenon of suicide bombing: a review of psychological and nonpsychological factors, *Crisis*, 27: 107–18.

Grinspoon, L. and Bakalar, J.B. (1986) Can drugs be used to enhance the psychotherapeutic process? *American Journal of Psychotherapy*, 40: 393–404.

Grov, C., Kelly, B.C., Parsons, J.T. (2009) Polydrug use among club-going young adults recruited through time-space sampling, *Substance Use and Misuse*, 44: 848–64.

Gruber, K., Chutuape, M.A. and Stitzer, M.L. (2000) Reinforcement-based intensive outpatient treatment for inner city opiate abusers: a short-term evaluation, *Drug and Alcohol Dependence*, 57: 211–23.

Gruber, S.A., Tzilos, G.K., Silveri, M.M. et al. (2006) Methadone maintenance improves cognitive performance after two months of treatment, *Experimental and Clinical Psychopharmacology*, 14: 157–64.

Grzywacz, J.G., Almeida, D.M., Neupert, S.D. et al. (2004) Socioeconomic status and health: a micro-level analysis of exposure and vulnerability to daily stressors, *Journal of Health and Social Behavior*, 45: 1–16.

Guastella, A.J., Carson, D.S., Dadds, M.R. et al. (2009) Does oxytocin influence the early detection of angry and happy faces? *Psychoneuroendocrinology*, 34: 220–5.

Gude, T. and Vaglum, P. (2001) One-year follow-up of patients with cluster C personality disorders: a prospective study comparing patients with 'pure' and comorbid conditions within cluster C, and 'pure' C with 'pure' cluster A or B conditions, *Journal of Personality Disorders*, 15: 216–28.

Guiao, I.Z. and Thompson, E.A. (2004) Ethnicity and problem behaviors among adolescent females in the United States, *Health Care for Women International*, 25: 296–310.

Guo, X., Hamilton, P.J., Reish, N.J. et al. (2009) Reduced expression of the NMDA receptor-Interacting protein SynGAP causes behavioral abnormalities that model symptoms of schizophrenia, *Neuropsychopharmacology*, 34: 1659–72.

Gunnell, D., Magnusson, P.K. and Rasmussen, F. (2005) Low intelligence test scores in 18 year old men and risk of suicide: cohort study, *British Medical Journal*, 30: 67.

Gunnell, D., Saperia, J. and Ashby, D. (2005) Selective serotonin reuptake inhibitors (SSRIs) and suicide in adults: meta-analysis of drug company data from placebo controlled, randomized controlled trials submitted to the MHRA's safety review, *British Medical Journal*, 330: 385–90.

Gupta, M.A. and Johnson, A.M. (2000) Nonweight-related body image concerns among female eating-disordered patients and nonclinical controls: some preliminary observations, *International Journal of Eating Disorders*, 27: 304–9.

Gureje, O., Acha, R.A. and Odejide, O.A. (1995) Pathways to psychiatric care in Ibadan, Nigeria, *Tropical and Geographical Medicine*, 47: 125–9.

Gurvits, I.G., Koenigsberg, H.W. and Siever, L.J. (2000) Neurotransmitter dysfunction in patients with borderline personality disorder, *Psychiatric Clinics of North America*, 23: 27–40.

Guscott, R. and Taylor, L. (1994) Lithium prophylaxis in recurrent affective illness: efficacy, effectiveness and efficiency, *British Journal of Psychiatry*, 164: 741–6.

Guthrie, E. (1996) Psychotherapy for somatisation disorders, *Current Opinion in Psychiatry*, 9: 182–7.

Haaga, D.A. and Beck, A.T. (1995) Perspectives on depressive realism: implications for cognitive theory of depression, *Behaviour Research and Therapy*, 33: 41–8.

Haasen, C., Prinzleve, M., Zurhold, H., et al. (2004) Cocaine use in Europe – a multi-centre study: methodology and prevalence estimates, *European Addiction Research*, 10: 139–46.

Haenen, M-A., Schmidt, A.J., Schoenmakers, M. et al. (1997) Tactual sensitivity in hypochondriasis, *Psychotherapy and Psychosomatics*, 66: 128–32.

Haines, J.L. and Pericak-Vance, M.A. (1999) Genetics of multiple sclerosis, *Current Directions in Autoimmunology*, 1: 273–88.

Hall, G.C.N. (1995) Sexual offender recidivism revisited: a meta-analysis of recent treatment studies, *Journal of Consulting and Clinical Psychology*, 63: 802–9.

Halliburton, M. (2005) 'Just some spirits': the erosion of spirit possession and the rise of 'tension' in South India, *Medical Anthropology*, 24: 111–44.

Halligan, P.W., Athwal, B.S., Oakley, D.A. et al. (2000) Imaging hypnotic paralysis: implications for conversion hysteria, *Lancet*, 355: 986–7.

Halmi, K.A., Sunday, S.R., Strober, M. et al. (2000) Perfectionism in anorexia nervosa: variation by clinical subtype, obsessionality, and pathological eating behavior, *American Journal of Psychiatry*, 157: 1799–805.

Hansen, B., Vogel, P.A., Stiles, T.C. et al. (2007) Influence of co-morbid generalized anxiety disorder, panic disorder and personality disorders on the outcome of cognitive behavioural treatment of obsessive-compulsive disorder, *Cognitive Behaviour Therapy*, 36: 145–55.

Hanson, R.K. and Slater, S. (1988) Sexual victimization in the history of child sexual abusers: a review, *Annals of Sex Research*, 1: 485–99.

Haraldsen, I.R., Egeland, T., Haug, E. et al. (2005) Cross-sex hormone treatment does not change sex-sensitive cognitive performance in gender identity disorder patients, *Psychiatry Research*, 137: 161–74.

Haraldsen, I.R., Opjordsmoen, S., Egeland, T. et al. (2003) Sex-sensitive cognitive performance in untreated patients with early onset gender identity disorder, *Psychoneuroendocrinology*, 28: 906–15.

Hardy, G., Aldridge, J., Davidson, C. et al. (1999) Therapist responsiveness to client attachment styles and issues observed in client-identified significant events in psychodynamic interpersonal psychotherapy, *Psychotherapy Research*, 9: 36–53.

Hare, R.D. (1991) *The Hare Psychopathy Checklist-Revised (PCL-R)*. Toronto: Multi-Health Systems.

Hare, R.D., Clark, D., Grann, M. et al. (2000) Psychopathy and the predictive utility of the PCL-R: an international perspective, *Behavioural Sciences and the Law*, 18: 623–45.

Harford, T.C., Yi, H.Y., Faden, V.B. and Chen, C.M. (2009) The dimensionality of DSM-IV alcohol use disorders among adolescent and adult drinkers and symptom patterns by age, gender, and race/ethnicity, *Alcoholism: Clinical and Experimental Research*, 33: 868–78.

Harris, J.K., Godfrey, H.P., Partridge, F.M. et al. (2001) Caregiver depression following traumatic brain injury (TBI): a consequence of adverse effects on family members?, *Brain Injury*, 15: 223–38.

Harris, M.B., Deary, I.J. and Wilson, J.A. (1996) Life events and difficulties in relation to the onset of globus pharynges, *Journal of Psychosomatic Research*, 40: 603–15.

Harrow, M., Grossman, L.S., Jobe, T.H. and Herbener, E.S. (2005) Do patients with schizophrenia ever show periods of recovery? A 15-year multi-follow-up study, *Schizophrenia Bulletin*, 31: 723–34.

Harvey, A., Watkins, E., Mansell, W. and Shafran, R. (2004) *Cognitive Behavioural Processes Across Psychological Disorders: A Transtheoretical Approach to Research and Treatment.* Oxford: Oxford University Press.

Hassiotis, A.A. and Hall, I. (2008) Behavioural and cognitive-behavioural interventions for outwardly-directed aggressive behaviour in people with learning disabilities. *Cochrane Database of Systematic Reviews*, 3: CD003406.

Haworth-Hoeppner, S. (2000) The critical shapes of body image: the role of culture and family in the production of eating disorders, *Journal of Marriage and the Family*, 62: 212–27.

Hawton, K. (1997) Attempted suicide, in D.M. Clark and C.G. Fairburn (eds) *Science and Practice of Cognitive Behaviour Therapy*. Oxford: Oxford University Press.

Hawton, K., Catalan, J. and Fagg, J. (1992) Sex therapy for erectile dysfunction: characteristics of couples, treatment outcome and prognostic factors, *Archives of Sexual Behavior*, 21: 161–75.

Hawton, K., Catalan, J., Martin, P. et al. (1986) Long-term outcome of sex therapy, *Behaviour Research and Therapy*, 24: 665–75.

Hayes, S.C., Luoma, J.B., Bond, F.W. et al. (2006) Acceptance and commitment therapy: model, processes and outcomes, *Behaviour Research and Therapy*, 44: 1–25.

Hayes, S.C., Strosahl, K.D., Bunting, K., Twohig, M. and Wilson, K.G. (2004) What is acceptance and commitment therapy?, in S.C. Hayes and K.D. Strosahl (eds) *A Practical Guide to Acceptance and Commitment Therapy*. New York: Springer.

Hayward, P. and Wardle, J. (1999) The use of medication in the treatment of phobias, in G.C.L. Davey (ed.) *Phobias: A Handbook of Theory, Research, and Treatment*. Chichester: Wiley.

Hayward, P., Wardle, J. and Gray, J. (1996) The use of medication in the treatment of phobias, in G.C.L. Davey (ed.) *Phobias: A Handbook of Description, Theory and Treatment*. New York: Wiley.

Heather, N. (1995) The great controlled drinking consensus: is it premature?, *Addiction*, 90: 1160–3.

Hedden, T. and Gabrieli, J.D. (2005) Healthy and pathological processes in adult development: new evidence from neuroimaging of the aging brain, *Current Opinion in Neurology*, 18: 740–7.

Heiman, J.R. and LoPiccolo, J. (1988) *Becoming Orgasmic*. London: Piatkus.

Hellawell, S.J. and Brewin, C.R. (2002) A comparison of flashbacks and ordinary autobiographical memories of trauma: cognitive resources and behavioural observations, *Behaviour Research and Therapy*, 40: 1143–56.

Hellawell, S.J. and Brewin, C.R. (2004) A comparison of flashbacks and ordinary autobiographical memories of trauma: content and language, *Behaviour Research and Therapy*, 42: 1–12.

Hellstrom, K., Fellenius, J. and Öst, L-G. (1996) One versus five sessions of applied tension in the treatment of blood phobia, *Behaviour Research and Therapy*, 34: 101–12.

Hemsley, D.R. (1996) Schizophrenia: a cognitive model and its implications for psychological intervention, *Behavior Modification*, 20: 139–69.

Hemsley, D.R. (1998) The disruption of the 'sense of self' in schizophrenia: potential links with disturbances of information processing, *British Journal of Medical Psychology*, 71: 115–24.

Hemsley, D.R. (2005) The development of a cognitive model of schizophrenia: placing it in context, *Neuroscience and Biobehavioral Reviews*, 29: 977–88.

Hemsley, D.R. and Murray, R.M. (2000) Commentary: psychological and social treatments for schizophrenia: not just old remedies in new bottles, *Schizophrenia Bulletin*, 26: 145–51.

Hendin, H. (1992) The psychodynamics of suicide, *International Review of Psychiatry*, 4: 157–67.

Henggeler, S.W., Melton, G.B. and Smith, L.A. (1992) Family preservation using multisystemic therapy: an effective alternative to incarcerating serious juvenile offenders, *Journal of Consulting and Clinical Psychology*, 60: 953–61.

Henken, H.T., Huibers, M.J., Churchill, R. et al. (2007) Family therapy for depression, *Cochrane Database of Systematic Reviews*, 2: CD006728.

Henningsen, P., Zimmerman, T. and Sattel, H. (2003) Medically unexplained physical symptoms, anxiety, and depression: a meta-analysis, *Psychosomatic Medicine*, 65: 528–33.

Henquet, C., Murray, R., Linszen, D. et al. (2005) The environment and schizophrenia: the role of cannabis use, *Schizophrenia Bulletin*, 31: 608–12.

Henry, D.B., Tolan, P.H. and Gorman-Smith, D. (2001) Longitudinal family and peer group effects on violence and nonviolent delinquency, *Journal of Clinical Child Psychology*, 30: 172–86.

Hepp, U., Kraemer, B., Schnyder, U. et al. (2005) Psychiatric comorbidity in gender identity disorder, *Journal of Psychosomatic Research*, 58: 259–61.

Hermann, B.P. and Chabria, S. (1980) Interictal psycho-pathology in patients with ictal fear, *Archives of Neurology*, 37: 667–8.

Herrera-Guzmán, I., Gudayol-Ferré, E., Herrera-Guzmán D. et al. (2009) Effects of selective serotonin reuptake and dual serotonergic-noradrenergic reuptake treatments on memory and mental processing speed in patients with major depressive disorder, *Journal of Psychiatric Research*, 43: 855–63.

Hettema, J.M., Neale, M.C. and Kendler, K.S. (2001a) A review and meta-analysis of the genetic epidemiology of anxiety disorders, *American Journal of Psychiatry*, 158: 1568–78.

Hettema, J.M., Prescott, C.A. and Kendler, K.S. (2001b) A population-based twin study of generalized anxiety disorder in men and women, *Journal of Nervous and Mental Disorders*, 189: 413–20.

Hibell, B., Andersson, B., Bjarnasson, T. et al. (1997) *The 1995 ESPAD Report: Alcohol and Other Drug Use Among Students in 26 European Countries*. Stockholm: Council of Europe Pompidou Group.

Hill, C.E., Nutt-Williams, E., Heaton, K.J. et al. (1996) Therapist retrospective recall of impasses in long-term psychotherapy: a qualitative analysis, *Journal of Counseling Psychology*, 43: 207–17.

Hill, P. (1998) Attention deficit hyperactivity disorder, *Archives of Diseases of Childhood*, 79: 381–5.

Hiller, W., Leibbrand, R., Rief, W. et al. (2002) Predictors of course and outcome in hypochondriasis after cognitive-behavioral treatment, *Psychotherapy and Psychosomatics*, 71: 318–25.

Hiller, W., Rief, W. and Brähler, E. (2006) Somatization in the population: from mild bodily misperceptions to disabling symptoms, *Social Psychiatry and Psychiatric Epidemiology*, 41: 704–12.

Hirschfield, R.M.A. (1999) Efficacy of SSRIs and newer antidepressants in severe depression: comparison with TCAs, *Journal of Clinical Psychiatry*, 60: 326–35.

Ho, B.C., Alicata, D., Mola, C. and Andreasen, N.C. (2005) Hippocampus volume and treatment delays in first-episode schizophrenia, *American Journal of Psychiatry*, 162: 1527–9.

Hobfoll, S.E. (1989) Conservation of resources: a new attempt at conceptualizing stress, *American Psychologist*, 44: 513–24.

Hoffman, R.E., Rapaport, J., Mazure, C.M. et al. (1999) Selective speech perception alterations in schizophrenic patients reporting hallucinated 'voices', *American Journal of Psychiatry*, 156: 393–9.

Hofmann, S.G. and Asmundson, G.J. (2008) Acceptance and mindfulness-based therapy: new wave or old hat? *Clinical Psychology Review*, 28: 1–16.

Hoge, E.A., Tamrakar, S.M., Christian, K.M. et al. (2006) Cross-cultural differences in somatic presentation in patients with generalized anxiety disorder, *Journal of Nervous and Mental Disease*, 194: 962–6.

Holden, U.P. and Woods, R.T. (1995) *Positive Approaches to Dementia Care*. Oxford: Churchill Livingstone.

Holen-Hoeksema, S. (1990) *Sex Difference in Depression*. Stanford, CA: Stanford University Press.

Hollander, E., Allen, A., Kwon, J. et al. (1999) Clomipramine vs desipramine crossover trial in body dysmorphic disorder: selective efficacy of a serotonin reuptake inhibitor in imagined ugliness, *Archives of General Psychiatry*, 56: 1033–42.

Hollander, E., DeCaria, C.M., Finkell, J.N. et al. (2000) A randomized double blind fluvoxamine/placebo crossover trial in pathologic gambling, *Biological Psychiatry*, 47: 813–17.

Hollander, E., Tracy, K.A., Swann, A.C. et al. (2003) Divalproex in the treatment of impulsive aggression: efficacy in cluster B personality disorders, *Neuropsychopharmacology*, 28: 1186–97.

Hollon, S.D., DeRubeis, R.J., Shelton, R.C. et al. (2005) Prevention of relapse following cognitive therapy vs medications in moderate to severe depression, *Archives of General Psychiatry*, 62: 417–22.

Holmes, S. (2000) Treatment of male sexual dysfunction, *British Medical Bulletin*, 56: 798–808.

Holmøy, T., Harbo, H., Vartdal, F. et al. (2009) Genetic and molecular approaches to the immunopathogenesis of multiple sclerosis: an update, *Current Molecular Medicine*, 9: 591–611.

Holtzman, D., Barry, V., Ouellet, L.J. et al. (2009) The influence of needle exchange programs on injection risk behaviors and infection with hepatitis C virus among young injection drug users in select cities in the United States, 1994–2004, *Preventive Medicine*, 49: 68–73.

Honda, H., Shimizu, Y., Rutter, M. (2005) No effect of MMR withdrawal on the incidence of autism: a total population study, *Journal of Child Psychology and Psychiatry*, 46: 72–9.

Horn, W.F., Ialongo, N.S., Pascoe, J.M. et al. (1991) Additive effects of psychostimulants, parent training, and self-control therapy with ADHD children, *Journal of the American Academy of Child and Adolescent Psychiatry*, 30: 233–40.

Horowitz, M.J. (1986) Stress-response syndromes: a review of posttraumatic and adjustment disorders, *Hospital and Community Psychiatry*, 37: 241–9.

Hoven, C.W., Duarte, C.S., Lucas, C.P. et al. (2005) Psychopathology among New York City public school children 6 months after September 11, *Archives of General Psychiatry*, 62: 545–52.

Hrabosky, J.I., Cash, T.F., Veale, D. et al. (2009) Multidimensional body image comparisons among patients with eating disorders, body dysmorphic disorder, and clinical controls: a multisite study, *Body Image*, 6: 155–63.

Huang, T.L., Zandi, P.P., Tucker, K.L. et al. (2005) Benefits of fatty fish on dementia risk are stronger for those without APOE epsilon4, *Neurology*, 65: 1409–14.

Huang, X., Lei, Z., Li, X.P. et al. (2009) Response of sodium pump to ouabain challenge in human glioblastoma cells in culture, *World Journal of Biological Psychiatry*, 10: 884–92.

Hubbard, R.L., Craddock, S.G., Flynn, P.M. et al. (1997) Overview of 1-year follow-up outcomes in the Drug Abuse Treatment Outcome Study (DATOS), *Psychological Addiction and Behavior*, 4: 1303–10.

Huber, S.J., Bornstein, R.A., Rammohan, K.W. et al. (1992) Magnetic resonance imaging and correlates of neuropsychological impairment in multiple sclerosis, *Journal of Neuropsychiatry and Clinical Neurosciences*, 4: 152–8.

Hudson, C.G. (2005) Socioeconomic status and mental illness: tests of the social causation and selection hypotheses, *American Journal of Orthopsychiatry*, 75: 3–18.

Hughes, J.C. and Cook, C. (1997) The efficacy of disulfram – a review of outcome studies, *Addictions*, 92: 381–96.

Hunot, V., Churchill, R., Silva de Lima, M. et al. (2007) Psychological therapies for generalised anxiety disorder, *Cochrane Database Systematic Reviews*, 1: CD001848.

Hunter, E. (1997) Memory loss for childhood sexual abuse: distinguishing between encoding and retrieval factors, in D. Read and D.S. Lindsay (eds) *Recollections of Trauma: Scientific Research and Clinical Practice*. New York: Plenum.

Hunter, L.C., O'Hare, A., Herron, W.J. et al. (2003) Opioid peptides and dipeptidyl peptidase in autism, *Developmental Medicine and Child Neurology*, 45: 121–8.

Huntjens, R.J., Peters, M.L., Woertman, L. et al. (2006) Inter-identity amnesia in dissociative identity disorder: a simulated memory impairment? *Psychological Medicine*, 36: 857–63.

Huprich, S.K. (2009) What should become of depressive personality disorder in DSM-V? *Harvard Review of Psychiatry*, 17: 41–59.

Hutchison, K.E., Haughey, H., Niculescu, M. et al. (2008) The incentive salience of alcohol: translating the effects of genetic variant in CNR1, *Archives of General Psychiatry*, 65: 841–50.

Hyman, I.E., Husband, T.H. and Billings, F.J. (1995) False memories of childhood experiences, *Applied Cognitive Psychology*, 9: 181–97.

International Molecular Genetic Study of Autism Consortium (1998) A full genome screen for autism with evidence for linkage to a region on chromosome 7q, *Human Molecular Genetics*, 7: 571–8.

Intrator, J., Hare, R., Strizke, P. et al. (1997) A brain imaging (single photon emission computerized tomography) study of semantic and affective processing in psychopaths, *Biological Psychiatry*, 42: 96–103.

Ipser, J.C., Sander, C. and Stein, D.J. (2009) Pharmacotherapy and psychotherapy for body dysmorphic disorder, *Cochrane Database of Systematic Reviews*, 1: CD005332.

Ipser, J., Seedat, S. and Stein D.J. (2006) Pharmacotherapy for post-traumatic stress disorder – a systematic review and meta-analysis, *South Africa Medical Journal*, 96: 1088–96.

Ishihara, K. and Sasa, M. (1999) Mechanism underlying the therapeutic effects of electroconvulsive therapy (ECT) on depression, *Japanese Journal of Pharmacology*, 80: 185–9.

Ito, T., Meguro, K., Akanuma, K. et al. (2007) A randomized controlled trial of the group reminiscence approach in patients with vascular dementia, *Dementia and Geriatric Cognitive Disorders*, 24: 48–54.

Jacobson, N.S. and Hollon, S.D. (1996) Cognitive-behavior therapy versus pharmacotherapy: now that the jury's returned its verdict, it's time to present the rest of the evidence, *Journal of Consulting and Clinical Psychology*, 64: 74–80.

Jaffe, S.R., Moffitt, T.E., Caspi, A. et al. (2002) Differences in early childhood risk factors for juvenile-onset and adult-onset depression, *Archives of General Psychiatry*, 59: 215–22.

Jansen, A., Van den Hout, M.A. and Griez, E. (1989) Does bingeing restore bulimic's alleged 5-HT deficiency?, *Behaviour Research and Therapy*, 27: 555–60.

Janssen, P.L. (1985) Psychodynamic study of male potency disorders: an overview, *Psychotherapy and Psychosomatics*, 44: 6–17.

Jenike, M.A. (1998) Neurosurgical treatment of obsessive-compulsive disorder, *British Medical Journal*, 163 (Suppl. 35): 75–90.

Jenike, M.A., Ballantine, H.T., Martuza, R.L. et al. (1991) Cingulotomy for refractory obsessive-compulsive disorder: a long-term follow-up of 33 patients, *Archives of General Psychiatry*, 48: 548–55.

Jenkins, R., Bebbington, P., Brugha, T.S. et al. (1998) British psychiatric morbidity survey, *British Journal of Psychiatry*, 173: 4–7.

Jenkins, R.L., Lewis, G., Bebbington, P. et al. (1997) The National Psychiatric Morbidity Surveys of Great Britain: initial findings from the household survey, *Psychology and Medicine*, 27: 775–89.

Jennett, B. (1996) Epidemiology of head injury, *International Journal of Neurology, Neurosurgery and Psychiatry*, 60: 362–9.

Jensen, P.S., Arnold, L.E., Richters, J.E. et al. (1999) A 14-month randomized clinical trial of treatment strategies for attention-deficit/hyperactivity disorder, *Archives of General Psychiatry*, 56: 1073–86.

Jick, S.S., Dean, A.D. and Jick, H. (1995) Antidepressants and suicide, *British Medical Journal*, 310: 215–18.

Jimerson, D.C., Lesem, M.D., Kaye, W.H. et al. (1992) Low serotonin and dopamine metabolite concentrations in cerebrospinal fluid from bulimic patients with frequent bulimic episodes, *Archives of General Psychiatry*, 49: 132–8.

Johnson, S.D., Striley, C. and Cottler, L.B. (2006) The association of substance use disorders with trauma exposure and PTSD among African American drug users, *Addictive Behaviors*, 31: 2063–73.

Johnstone, L. (2000) *Users and Abusers of Psychiatry: A Critical Look at Psychiatric Practice*. London: Routledge.

Jones, C., Cormac, I., Mota, J. et al. (2000) Cognitive behaviour therapy for schizophrenia, *The Cochrane Library*, Issue 3. Oxford: Update Software.

Jones, P. and Cannon, M. (1998) The new epidemiology of schizophrenia, *Psychiatric Clinics of North America*, 21: 1–25.

Jónsdóttir, H., Friis S., Horne, R. et al. (2008) Beliefs about medications: measurement and relationship to adherence in patients with severe mental disorders, *Acta Psychiatrica Scandinavica*, 118: 78–84.

Jorge, R.E., Robinson, R.G., Moser, D. et al. (2004) Major depression following traumatic brain injury, *Archives of General Psychiatry*, 61: 42–50.

Joseph, S., Dalgleish, T., Thrasher, S. et al. (1996) Crisis support following the Herald of Free Enterprise disaster: a longitudinal perspective, *Journal of Traumatic Stress*, 9: 833–45.

Joseph, S., Williams, R. and Yule, W. (1995) Psychosocial perspectives on posttraumatic stress, *Clinical Psychology Review*, 15: 515–44.

Jung, C.G. ([1912] 1956) *Symbols of Transformation*. New York: Bollingen, no. 5. (Original edition published in 1912 as *The Psychology of the Unconscious*.)

Kabat-Zinn, J. (1990) *The Full Catastrophe Living: Using the Wisdom of Your Body and Mind to Face Stress, Pain, and Illness*. New York: Delacorte.

Kabat-Zinn, J., Massion, A.O., Kristeller, J. et al. (1992) Effectiveness of a meditation-based stress reduction program in the treatment of anxiety disorders, *American Journal of Psychiatry*, 149: 936–43.

Kalyna, Z., Bezchlibnyk-Butler, J. and Jeffries, J. (eds) (2003) *Clinical Handbook of Psychotropic Drugs*. Cambridge, MA: Hogrefe and Huber.

Kamann, M.P. and Wong, B.Y. (1993) Inducing adaptive coping self-statements in children with learning disabilities through self-instruction training, *Journal of Learning Disabilities*, 26: 630–8.

Kamphuis, J.H., Emmelkamp, P.M. and Bartak, A. (2003) Individual differences in posttraumatic stress following post-intimate stalking: stalking severity and psychosocial variables, *British Journal of Clinical Psychology*, 42: 145–56.

Kanno, M., Matsumoto, M., Togashi, H. et al. (2003) Effects of repetitive transcranial magnetic stimulation on behavioral and neurochemical changes in rats during an elevated plus-maze test, *Journal of Neurological Sciences*, 211: 5–14.

Karasz, A. (2005) Cultural differences in conceptual models of depression, *Social Science and Medicine*, 60: 1625–35.

Karno, M., Golding, J.M., Sorensen, S.B. et al. (1988) The epidemiology of OCD in five US communities, *Archives of General Psychiatry*, 45: 1094–9.

Kashala, E., Tylleskar, T., Elgen, I. et al. (2005) Attention deficit and hyperactivity disorder among school children in Kinshasa, Democratic Republic of Congo, *African Health Sciences*, 5: 172–81.

Kasper, S. and Resinger, E. (2001) Panic disorder: the place of benzodiazepines and selective serotonin reuptake inhibitors, *European Neuropsychopharmacology*, 11: 307–21.

Katan, M. (1953) Mania and the pleasure principle, in P. Greenacre (ed.) *Affective Disorders*. New York: International University Press.

Kaye, W.H. (1997) Anorexia nervosa, obsessional behaviour, and serotonin, *Psychopharmacology Bulletin*, 33: 335–44.

Kaye, W.H. (2008) Neurobiology of anorexia and bulimia nervosa, *Physiology and Behavior*, 94: 121–35.

Kaye, W.H., Frank, G.K., Bailer, U.F. et al. (2005) Serotonin alterations in anorexia and bulimia nervosa: insights from imaging studies, *Physiology and Behavior*, 85: 73–81.

Kaye, W.H., Gwirtsman, H.E., Brewerton, T.D. et al. (1988) Bingeing behaviour and plasma amino acids: a possible involvement of brain serotonin in bulimia nervosa, *Psychiatry Research*, 23: 31–43.

Kaye, W.H., Gwirtsman, H.E., Brewerton, T.D. et al. (1991) Altered serotonin activity in anorexia nervosa after long-term weight restoration. Does elevated cerebrospinal fluid 5-hydroxyindoleacetic acid level correlate with rigid and obsessive behaviour?, *Archives of General Psychiatry*, 48: 556–62.

Kaye, W.H., Klump, K.L., Frank, G.K. et al. (2001a) Anorexia and bulimia nervosa, *Annual Review of Medicine*, 51: 299–313.

Kaye, W.H., Nagata, T., Weltzin, T.E. et al. (2001b) Double-blind placebo-controlled administration of fluoxetine in restricting- and restricting-purging-type anorexia nervosa, *Biological Psychiatry*, 49: 644–52.

Kaye, W.H. and Weltzin, T.E. (1991) Serotonin activity in anorexia and bulimia nervosa: relationship to the modulation of feeding and mood, *Journal of Clinical Psychiatry*, 52 (Suppl.): 41–8.

Keck, P.E. Jr, McIntyre, R.S. and Shelton, R.C. (2007) Bipolar depression: best practices for the outpatient, *CNS Spectrum*, 12(12 Suppl 20): 1–14.

Keel, P.K. and Haedt, A. (2008) Evidence-based psychosocial treatments for eating problems and eating disorders, *Journal of Clinical Child and Adolescent Psychology*, 37: 39–61.

Keel, P.K., Klump, K.L., Miller, K.B. et al. (2005) Shared transmission of eating disorders and anxiety disorders, *International Journal of Eating Disorders*, 38: 99–105.

Keesey, R.E. and Corbett, S.W. (1984) Metabolic defense of the body weight set-point, *Research Publications: Association of Research in Nervous and Mental Disease*, 62: 87–96.

Keijsers, G.P.J., Schaap, C.P.D.R. and Hoogduin, C.A.L. (2000) The impact of interpersonal patient and therapist behavior on outcome in cognitive-behavioral therapy: a review of empirical studies, *Behavior Modification*, 24: 264–97.

Keller, M.B., Klerman, G.L., Lavori, P.W. et al. (1984) Long-term outcome of episodes of major depression: clinical and public health significance, *Journal of the American Medical Association*, 252: 788–92.

Kellett, S. (2005) The treatment of dissociative identity disorder with cognitive analytic therapy: experimental evidence of sudden gains, *Journal of Trauma and Dissociation*, 6: 55–81.

Kelly, K.A. (1993) Multiple personality disorders: treatment coordination in a partial hospital setting, *Bulletin of the Menninger Clinic*, 57: 390–8.

Kemp, R., Kirov, G., Everitt, B. et al. (1998) Randomised controlled trial of compliance therapy: 18-month follow-up, *British Journal of Psychiatry*, 172: 413–19.

Kendler, K.S., Jacobson, K.C., Myers, J. et al. (2002) Sex differences in genetic and environmental risk factors for irrational fears and phobias, *Psychological Medicine*, 32: 209–17.

Kendler, K.S., MacLean, C., Neale, M. et al. (1991) The genetic epidemiology of bulimia nervosa, *American Journal of Psychiatry*, 148: 1627–37.

Kendler, K.S., Neale, M.C., Kessler, R.C. et al. (1993) Panic disorder in women: a population-based twin study, *Psychological Medicine*, 40: 397–406.

Kenworthy, T., Adams, C.E., Bilby, C. et al. (2004) Psychological interventions for those who have sexually offended or are at risk of offending, *The Cochrane Library*, 3.

Kéri, S. and Kelemen, O. (2009) The role of attention and immediate memory in vulnerability to interpersonal criticism during family transactions in schizophrenia, *British Journal of Clinical Psychology*, 48: 21–9.

Kernberg, O.F. (1985) *Borderline Conditions and Pathological Narcissism*. Northvale, NJ: Jason Aronson.

Kerns, A., Eso, K., Thomson, J. et al. (1999) Investigation of a direct intervention for improving attention in young children with ADHD, *Developmental Neuropsychology*, 16: 273–95.

Kerr, T., Tyndall, M., Li, K. et al. (2005) Sager injection facility use and syringe sharing in injection drug users. *Lancet*, 366: 316–18.

Kessler, R.C., McGonagle, K.A., Zhao, S. et al. (1994) Lifetime and 12-month prevalence of DSM-III-R psychiatric disorders in the United States. Results from the National Comorbidity Survey, *Archives of General Psychiatry*, 5: 8–19.

Kessler, R.C., Sonnega, A., Bromet, E. et al. (1995) Posttraumatic stress disorder in the national comorbidity survey, *Archives of General Psychiatry*, 52: 1048–60.

Kety, S.S., Rosenthal, D., Wender, P.H. et al. (1975) Mental illness in the biological and adoptive families of adopted individuals who become schizophrenic: a preliminary report based on psychiatric interviews, in R.R. Fieve, D. Rosenthal and H. Brill (eds) *Genetic Research in Psychiatry*. Baltimore, MD: Johns Hopkins University Press.

Kiehl, K.A., Smith, A.M., Hare, R.D. et al. (2001) Limbic abnormalities in affective processing by criminal psychopaths as revealed by functional magnetic resonance imaging, *Biological Psychiatry*, 50: 677–84.

Kihlstrom, J.F. (2005) Dissociative disorders, *Annual Review of Clinical Psychology*, 1: 227–53.

Kilic, C., Rezaki, M., Ustun, T.B. et al. (1994) Pathways to psychiatric care in Ankara, *Social Psychiatry and Psychiatric Epidemiology*, 29: 131–6.

Kim, Y.K., Lee, H.J., Yang, J.C. et al. (2009) A tryptophan hydroxylase 2 gene polymorphism is associated with panic disorder, *Behavioral Genetics*, 39: 170–5.

Kinderman, P., Prince, S., Waller, G. et al. (2003) Self-discrepancies, attentional bias and persecutory delusions, *British Journal of Clinical Psychology*, 42: 1–12.

Kindrat, S. (2007) The relationship between body image and depression in women diagnosed with relapsing remitting multiple sclerosis, *Canadian Journal of Neuroscience Nursing*, 29: 8–13.

King, M., Semlyen, J., Tai, S.S. et al. (2008) A systematic review of mental disorder, suicide, and deliberate self harm in lesbian, gay and bisexual people, *BMC Psychiatry*, 8: 70.

King, S., Waschbusch, D.A., Pelham, W.E. et al. (2009) Subtypes of aggression in children with attention deficit hyperactivity disorder: medication effects and comparison with typical children, *Journal of Clinical Child and Adolescent Psychology*, 38: 619–29.

Kinnunen, U., Feldt, T., Geurts, S. et al. (2006) Types of work-family interface: well-being correlates of negative and positive spillover between work and family, *Scandinavian Journal of Psychology*, 47: 149–62.

Kirkpatrick, D.R. (1984) Age, gender, and patterns of common intense fears among adults, *Behaviour Research and Therapy*, 22: 141–50.

Kirmayer, L.F. (1991) The place of culture in psychiatric nosology: taijin kyofusho and DSM-III-R, *The Journal of Nervous and Mental Disease*, 179: 19–28.

Kirmayer, L.J., Groleau, D., Looper, K.J. et al. (2004) Explaining medically unexplained symptoms, *Canadian Journal of Psychiatry*, 49: 663–72.

Kirmayer, L.J., Robbins, J.M. and Paris, J. (1994) Somatoform disorders: personality and social matrix of somatic disorder, *Journal of Abnormal Psychology*, 103: 125–36.

Klein, M. (1927) The psychological principles of infant analysis, *International Journal of Psychoanalysis*, 8: 25–37.

Kleindienst, N., Engel, R.R. and Greil, W. (2005) Psychosocial and demographic factors associated with response to prophylactic lithium: a systematic review for bipolar disorders, *Psychological Medicine*, 35: 1685–94.

Kleinman, A.M. (1977) Depression, somatization and the 'new cross-cultural psychiatry', *Social Science and Medicine*, 11: 3–10.

Kleinman, A. (1988) *Rethinking Psychiatry*. New York: Macmillan.

Kluft, R.P. (1994) Multiple personality disorder: observations on the etiology, natural history, recognition, and resolution of a long-neglected condition, in R. Klein and B.K. Doane (eds) *Psychological Concepts and Dissociative Disorders*. Hillsdale, NJ: Erlbaum.

Kluft, R.P. (1996) Multiple personality disorder: a legacy of trauma, in C.R. Pfeffer (ed.) *Severe Stress and Mental Disorder in Children*, Washington, DC: American Psychiatric Press.

Kluft, R.P. (1999) An overview of the psychotherapy of dissociative identity disorder, *American Journal of Psychotherapy*, 53: 289–319.

Klump, K.L., Miller, K.B., Keel, P.K. et al. (2001) Genetic and environmental influences on anorexia nervosa syndromes in a population-based twin sample, *Psychological Medicine*, 31: 737–40.

Knivsberg, A.M., Reichelt, K.L., Høien, T. et al. (1998) Parents' observations after one year of dietary intervention for children with autistic syndromes, *Psychobiology of Autism: Current Research and Practice*, 13–24.

Koegel, R.L., Koegel, L.K. and McNerney, E.K. (2001) Pivotal areas in intervention for autism, *Journal of Clinical Child Psychology*, 30: 19–32.

Koegel, R.L., O'Dell, M.C. and Dunlap, G. (1988) Producing speech use in nonverbal autistic children by reinforcing attempts, *Journal of Autism and Developmental Disorders*, 18: 525–38.

Koenen, K.C., Amstadter, A.B., Ruggiero, K.J. et al. (2009) RGS2 and generalized anxiety disorder in an epidemiologic sample of hurricane-exposed adults, *Depression and Anxiety*, 26: 309–15.

Kolevzon, A., Mathewson, K.A. and Hollander, E. (2006) Selective serotonin reuptake inhibitors in autism: a review of efficacy and tolerability, *Journal of Clinical Psychiatry*, 67: 407–14.

Koran, L.M., Abujaoude, E., Large, M.D. (2008) The prevalence of body dysmorphic disorder in the United States adult population, *CNS Spectrum*, 13: 316–22.

Korten, A.E., Jorm, A.F., Henderson, A.S. et al. (1993) Assessing the risk of Alzheimer's disease in first-degree relatives of Alzheimer's disease cases, *Psychological Medicine*, 23: 915–23.

Kovach, C. (1990) Promise and problems in reminiscence research, *Journal of Gerontological Nursing*, 16: 10–14.

Kownacki, R.J. and Shadish, W.R. (1999) Does Alcoholics Anonymous work? The results from a meta-analysis of controlled experiments, *Substance Use and Misuse*, 34: 1897–916.

Kraepelin, E. ([1883] 1981) *Clinical Psychiatry* (trans. A.R. Diefendorf). Delmar, NY: Scholar's Facsimiles and Reprints.

Kraus, L., Augustan, R., Frischer, M. et al. (2003) Estimating prevalence of problem drug use at national level in countries of the European Union and Norway, *Addiction*, 98: 471–85.

Kringlen, E. (1993) Genes and environment in mental illness: perspectives and ideas for future research, *Acta Psychiatrica Scandinavica*, 370: 79–84.

Kripke, D.F., Nievergelt, C.M., Joo, E. et al. (2009) Circadian polymorphisms associated with affective disorders, *Journal of Circadian Rhythms*, 23: 2.

Krueger, T.H., Schedlowski, M. and Meyer, G. (2005) Cortisol and heart rate measures during casino gambling in relation to impulsivity, *Neuropsychobiology*, 52: 206–11.

Kruijver, F.P., Zhou, J.N., Pool, C.W. et al. (2000) Male-to-female transsexuals have female neuron numbers in a limbic nucleus, *Journal of Clinical Endocrinology and Metabolism*, 85: 2034–41.

Krupp, L.B., Christodoulou, C., Melville, P. et al. (2004) Donepezil improved memory in multiple sclerosis in a randomized clinical trial, *Neurology*, 63: 1579–85.

Kuhn, A., Bodmer, C., Stadlmayr, W. et al. (2008) Quality of life 15 years after sex reassignment surgery for transsexualism, *Fertility and Sterility*, 92: 1685–9.

Kulka, R.A., Schlenger, W.E., Fairbank, J.A. et al. (1990) *Trauma and the Vietnam War Generation: Report of Findings from the National Vietnam Veterans Readjustment Study*. New York: Brunner/Mazel.

Kwon, P. and Laurenceau, J-P. (2002) A longitudinal study of the hopelessness theory of depression: testing the diathesis-stress model within a differential reactivity and exposure framework, *Journal of Clinical Psychology*, 58: 1305–21.

Laakso, M.P., Vaurio, O., Koivisto, E. et al. (2001) Psychopathy and the posterior hippocampus, *Behavioural Brain Research*, 118: 187–93.

Lackner, J.M., Gudleski, G.D. and Blanchard, E.B. (2004) Beyond abuse: the association among parenting style, abdominal pain, and somatization in IBS patients, *Behaviour Research and Therapy*, 42: 41–56.

Ladouceur, R., Jacques, C., Ferland, F. et al. (1999) Prevalence of problem gambling: a replication study 7 years later, *Canadian Journal of Psychiatry*, 44: 802–4.

Ladouceur, R., Sylvain, C., Boutin, C. et al. (2001) Cognitive treatment of pathological gambling, *Journal of Nervous and Mental Disease*, 189: 774–80.

Ladouceur, R., Sylvain, C., Boutin, C. et al. (2003) Group therapy for pathological gamblers: a cognitive approach, *Behavioural Research and Therapy*, 41: 87–96.

Lai, C.K., Chi, I. and Kayser-Jones, J. (2004) A randomized controlled trial of a specific reminiscence approach to promote the well-being of nursing home residents with dementia, *International Psychogeriatrics*, 16: 33–49.

Lai, D.W. (2004) Impact of culture on depressive symptoms of elderly Chinese immigrants, *Canadian Journal of Psychiatry*, 49: 820–7.

Lam, D.H., Hayward, P., Watkins, E.R. et al. (2005) Relapse prevention in patients with bipolar disorder: cognitive therapy outcome after 2 years, *American Journal of Psychiatry*, 162: 324–9.

Lam, D.H., Watkins, E.R., Hayward, P. et al. (2003) A randomized controlled study of cognitive therapy for relapse prevention for bipolar affective disorder, *Archives of General Psychiatry*, 60: 145–52.

Laney, C. and Loftus, E.F. (2005) Traumatic memories are not necessarily accurate memories, *Canadian Journal of Psychiatry*, 50: 823–8.

Langstrom, N. and Zucker, K.J. (2005) Transvestic fetishism in the general population: prevalence and correlates, *Journal of Sexual and Marital Therapy*, 31: 87–95.

Lanning, K.V. (2001) *Child Molesters: A Behavioral Analysis*, 4th ed. Alexandria, VA: National Center for Missing & Exploited Children.

Larsson, H., Tuvblad, C., Rijsdijk, F.V. et al. (2007) A common genetic factor explains the association between psychopathic personality and antisocial behavior, *Psychological Medicine*, 37: 15–26.

Laumann, E.O., Paik, A. and Rosen, R. (1999) Sexual dysfunction in the United States: prevalence and predictors, *Journal of the American Medical Association*, 21: 537–44.

Lawford, B.R., Young, R., Rowell, J.A. et al. (1997) D2 dopamine receptor A1 allele with alcoholism: medical severity of alcoholism and type of controls, *Biological Psychiatry*, 41: 386–93.

Laws, D.R. and Marshall, W.L. (1991) Masturbatory reconditioning with sexual deviates: an evaluative review, *Advances in Behavior Research and Therapy*, 13: 13–25.

Lazarus, R.S. (1991) *Emotion and Adaptation*. New York: Oxford University Press.

Lechtenberg, R. (1988) *Multiple Sclerosis Fact Book*. Philadelphia, PA: F.A. Davis.

Lee, J., Sartorius, N., Jablensky, A. et al. (1992) The International Pilot Study of Schizophrenia: five-year follow-up findings, *Psychological Medicine*, 22: 131–45.

Lee, R., Kavoussi, R.J. and Coccaro, E.F. (2008) Placebo-controlled, randomized trial of fluoxetine in the treatment of aggression in male intimate partner abusers, *International Clinical Psychopharmacology*, 23: 337–41.

Lee, S., Tsang, A., Zhang, M.Y. et al. (2007) Lifetime prevalence and inter-cohort variation in DSM-IV disorders in metropolitan China, *Psychological Medicine*, 37: 61–71.

Leff, J. and Vaughn, C. (1985) *Expressed Emotions in Families: Its Significance for Mental Illness*. New York: Guilford.

Legrand, L.N., Keyes, M., McGue, M. et al. (2008) Rural environments reduce the genetic influence on adolescent substance use and rule-breaking behavior, *Psychological Medicine*, 38: 1341–50.

Le Grange, D., Crosby, R.D., Rathouz, P.J. et al. (2007) A randomized controlled comparison of family-based treatment and supportive psychotherapy for adolescent bulimia nervosa, *Archives of General Psychiatry*, 64: 1049–56.

Lengua, L.J., Long, A.C., Smith, K.I. et al. (2005) Pre-attack symptomatology and temperament as predictors of children's responses to the September 11 terrorist attacks, *Journal of Child Psychology and Psychiatry*, 46: 631–45.

Lenox, R.H., McNamara, R.F., Papke, R.L. et al. (1998) Neurobiology of lithium: an update, *Journal of Clinical Psychiatry*, 59 (Suppl. 6): 37–47.

Leskin, G.A., Kaloupek, D.G. and Keane, T.M. (1998) Treatment for traumatic memories: review and recommendations, *Clinical Psychology Review*, 18: 983–1002.

Letonoff, E.J., Williams, T.R., Sidhu, K.S. (2002) Hysterical paralysis: a report of three cases and a review of the literature, *Spine*, 27: E441–5.

Levenson, R.W., Sher, K.J., Grossman, L.M. et al. (1980) Alcohol and stress response dampening: pharmacological effects, expectancy, and tension reduction, *Journal of Abnormal Psychology*, 89: 528–38.

Levin, H.S. (1993) Neurobehavioral sequelae of closed head injury, in P.R. Cooper (ed.) *Head Injury*. Baltimore, MD: Williams and Wilkins.

Lewinsohn, P.M., Youngren, M.A. and Grosscup, S.J. (1979) Reinforcement and depression, in A. Depue (ed.) *The Psychobiology of the Depressive Disorders*. New York: Academic Press.

Lewy, A.J., Bauer, V.K. and Cutler, N.L. (1998) Morning vs evening light treatment of patients with winter depression, *Archives of General Psychiatry*, 55: 890–6.

Ley, P. (1997) Compliance among patients, in A. Baum, S. Newman, J. Weinman et al. (eds) *Cambridge Handbook of Psychology, Health and Medicine*. Cambridge: Cambridge University Press.

Liau, A.K., Barriga, A.Q. and Gibbs, J.C. (1998) Relations between self-serving cognitive distortions and overt vs. covert antisocial behavior in adolescents, *Aggressive Behavior*, 24: 335–46.

Lidbeck, J. (2003) Group therapy for somatization disorders in primary care: maintenance of treatment goals of short cognitive-behavioural treatment one-and-a-half-year follow-up, *Acta Psychiatrica Scandinavica*, 107: 449–56.

Liddle, P., Carpenter, W.T. and Crow, T. (1994) Syndromes of schizophrenia: classic literature, *British Journal of Psychiatry*, 165: 721–7.

Lieberman, J.A., Kinon, B.J. and Loebel, A.D. (1990) Dopaminergic mechanisms in idiopathic and drug-induced psychoses, *Schizophrenia Bulletin*, 16: 97–109.

Lifford, K.J., Harold, G.T. and Thapar, A. (2009) Parent-child hostility and child ADHD symptoms: a genetically sensitive and longitudinal analysis, *Journal of Child Psychology and Psychiatry*, 50: 1468–76.

Lilienfeld, S.O., Lynn, S.J., Kirsch, I. et al. (1999) Dissociative identity disorder and the sociocognitive model: recalling the lessons of the past, *Psychological Bulletin*, 125: 507–23.

Lilienfeld, S.O. and Marino, L. (1995) Mental disorder as a Roschian concept: a critique of Wakefield's 'harmful dysfunction' analysis, *Journal of Abnormal Psychology*, 104: 411–20.

Lim, L., Ng, T.P., Chua, H.C. et al. (2005) Generalised anxiety disorder in Singapore: prevalence, co-morbidity and risk factors in a multi-ethnic population, *Social Psychiatry and Psychiatric Epidemiology*, 40: 972–9.

Lin, K.M., Inui, T.S., Kleinman, A.M. et al. (1982) Sociocultural determinants of the helpseeking behavior of patients with mental illness, *Journal of Nervous and Mental Disorders*, 170: 78–85.

Linde, K. and Mulrow, C.D. (2002) St John's wort for depression, *Cochrane Database of Systematic Reviews*, Issue 1.

Lindsay, S. and Jackson, C. (1993) Fear of routine dental treatment in adults: its nature and management, *Psychology and Health*, 8: 135–53.

Linehan, M.M. (1993) *Cognitive Behavioral Treatment of Borderline Personality Disorder*. New York: Guilford Press.

Linehan, M.M., Comtois, K.A., Murray, A.M. et al. (2006) Two-year randomized controlled trial and follow-up of dialectical behavior therapy vs therapy by experts for suicidal behaviors and borderline personality disorder, *Archives of General Psychiatry*, 63: 757–66.

Linehan, M.M., Heard, H.L. and Armstrong, H.E. (1993) Naturalistic follow-up of a behavioral treatment for chronically parasuicidal borderline patients, *Archives of General Psychiatry*, 50: 971–4.

Linehan, M.M., McDavid, J.D., Brown, M.Z. et al. (2008) Olanzapine plus dialectical behavior therapy for women with high irritability who meet criteria for borderline personality disorder: a double-blind, placebo-controlled pilot study, *Journal of Clinical Psychiatry*, 69: 999–1005.

Lingford-Hughes, A. (2005) Human brain imaging and substance abuse, *Current Opinion in Pharmacology*, 5: 42–6.

Lingjaerde, O., Ahlfors, U.G., Bech, P. et al. (1987) The UKU side effect rating scale: a new comprehensive rating scale for psychotropic drugs and a cross-sectional study of side effects in neuroleptic-treated patients, *Acta Psychiatrica Scandinavica*, 334: 1–100.

Lipinski, J.F., Mallya, G., Zimmerman, P. et al. (1989) Fluoxetine-induced akathisia: clinical and theoretical implications, *Journal of Clinical Psychiatry*, 59: 339–42.

Lisanby, S.H., Maddox, J.H., Prudic, J. et al. (2000) The effects of electroconvulsive therapy on memory of autobiographical and public events, *Archives of General Psychiatry*, 57: 581–90.

Liu, S.K., Fitzgerald, P.B., Daigle, M. et al. (2009) The relationship between cortical inhibition, antipsychotic treatment, and the symptoms of schizophrenia, *Biological Psychiatry*, 65: 503–9.

Liu, X.J., Ye, H.X., Li, W.P. et al. (2009) Relationship between psychosocial factors and onset of multiple sclerosis, *European Neurology*, 62: 130–6.

Lloyd, G.G. and Lishman, W.A. (1975) Effect of depression on the speed of recall of pleasant and unpleasant experiences, *Psychological Medicine*, 5: 173–80.

Lobo, D.S. and Kennedy, J.L. (2009) Genetic aspects of pathological gambling: a complex disorder with shared genetic vulnerabilities, *Addiction*, 104: 1454–65.

Loebel, J.P., Loebel, J.S., Dager, S.R. et al. (1991) Anticipation of nursing home placement may be a precipitant of suicide among the elderly, *Journal of the American Geriatric Society*, 39: 407–8.

Loewe, B., Zipfel, S., Buchholz, C. et al. (2001) Long-term outcome of anorexia nervosa in a prospective 21-year follow-up study, *Psychological Medicine*, 31: 881–90.

Loftus, E.F. and Coan, D. (1998) The construction of childhood memories, in D. Peters (ed.) *The Child Witness in Context: Cognitive, Social, and Legal Perspectives*. New York: Kluwer.

Loftus, E. and Davis, D. (2006) Recovered memories, *Annual Review of Clinical Psychology*, 2: 469–98.

Loftus, E.F. and Ketcham, K. (1994) *The Myth of Repressed Memory*. New York: St Martin's Press.

Longabaugh, R. and Morgenstern, J. (2000) Cognitive-behavioral coping skills therapy for alcohol dependence: current status and future directions, *Alcohol Research and Health*, 23: 78–87.

Lopez, V.A. and Emmer, E.T. (2002) Influences of beliefs and values on male adolescents' decision to commit violent offenses, *Psychology of Men and Masculinity*, 3: 28–40.

Lösel, F. and Schmucker, M. (2005) The effectiveness of treatment for sexual offenders: a comprehensive meta-analysis, *Journal of Experimental Criminology*, 1: 117-46.

Lovaas, O.I. (1987) Behavioral treatment and normal educational and intellectual functioning in young autistic children, *Journal of Consulting and Clinical Psychology*, 55: 3–9.

Lowe, K., Allen, D., Jones, E. et al. (2007) Challenging behaviours: prevalence and topographies, *Journal of Intellectual Disability Research*, 51: 625–36.

Lu, C.L., Wang, Y.C., Chen, J.Y., Lai, I.C. and Liou, Y.J. (2010) Support for the involvement of the ERBB4 gene in schizophrenia: a genetic association analysis, *Neuroscience Letters*, 26 June.

Lund, I. (2009) Gambling behaviour and the prevalence of gambling problems in adult EGM gamblers when EGMs are banned: a natural experiment, *Journal of Gambling Studies*, 25: 215–25.

Luque, F.A. and Jaffe, S.L. (2009) The molecular and cellular pathogenesis of dementia of the Alzheimer's type an overview, *International Review of Neurobiology*, 84: 151–65.

Lynam, D.R., Caspi, A., Moffitt, T.E. et al. (2005) Adolescent psychopathy and the big five: results from two samples, *Journal of Abnormal Child Psychology*, 33: 431–43.

Lyon, H.M., Startup, M. and Bentall, R.P. (1999) Social cognition and the manic defense: attributions, selective attention, and self-schema in bipolar affective disorder, *Journal of Abnormal Psychology*, 108: 273–82.

Lyon-Caen, O., Jouvent, R., Hauser, S. et al. (1986) Cognitive function in recent onset demyelinating diseases, *Archives of Neurology*, 43: 1138–41.

Lyons-Ruth, K., Holmes, B.M., Sasvari-Szekely, M. et al. (2007) Serotonin transporter polymorphism and borderline or antisocial traits among low-income young adults, *Psychiatric Genetics*, 17: 339–43.

Madden, P.A.F., Heath, A.C., Rosenthal, N.E. et al. (1996) Seasonal changes in mood and behavior: the role of genetic factors, *Archives of General Psychiatry*, 53: 47–55.

Maes, S., Verhoeven, C., Kittel, F. et al. (1998) Effects of the Brabantia-project, a Dutch wellness-health programme at the worksite, *American Journal of Public Health*, 88: 1037–41.

Magnusson, A. and Partonen, T. (2005) The diagnosis, symptomatology, and epidemiology of seasonal affective disorder, *CNS Spectrum*, 10: 625–34.

Mahmood, T. and Silverstone, T. (2001) Serotonin and bipolar disorder, *Journal of Affective Disorders*, 66: 1–11.

Malaspina, C., Corcoran, K.R., Kleinhaus, M.C. et al. (2008) Acute maternal stress in pregnancy and schizophrenia in offspring: a cohort prospective study, *BMC Psychiatry*, 8: 71.

Malizia, A.L. (2000) Neurosurgery for psychiatric disorders, in M.G. Gelder, J.J. Lopez-Ibor Jr and N.C. Andreasen (eds) *New Oxford Textbook of Psychiatry*. Oxford: Oxford University Press.

Malizia, A.L. and Bridges, P.K. (1991) The management of treatment resistant affective disorders: clinical perspectives, *Journal of Psychopharmacology*, 6: 145–55, 172–5.

Malojcic, B., Mubrin, Z., Coric, B. et al. (2008) Consequences of mild traumatic brain injury on information processing assessed with attention and short-term memory tasks, *Journal of Neurotrauma*, 25: 30–7.

Mannuzza, S., Fyer, A.J., Klein, D.F. et al. (1986) Schedule for Affective Disorders and Schizophrenia – Lifetime Version modified for the study of anxiety disorders (SADS-A): rationale and conceptual development, *Journal of Psychiatric Research*, 20: 317–25.

Mannuzza, S. and Klein, R.G. (2000) Long-term prognosis in attention-deficit/hyperactivity disorder, *Child and Adolescent Psychiatric Clinics of North America*, 9: 711–26.

Marcus, D.K., Gurley, J.R., Marchi, M.M. and Bauer, C. (2006) Cognitive and perceptual variables in hypochondriasis and health anxiety: a systematic review, *Clinical Psychology Review*, 27: 127–39.

Marjoram, D., Tansley, H., Miller, P. et al. (2005) A Theory of Mind investigation into the appreciation of visual jokes in schizophrenia, *BMC Psychiatry*, 5: 12–20.

Marks, I. (1977) Phobias and obsessions: clinical phenomena in search of laboratory models, in J.D. Maser and M.E.P. Seligman (eds) *Psychopathology: Experimental Models*. San Francisco, CA: Freeman.

Marks, I., Gelder, M. and Bancroft, J. (1970) Sexual deviants two years after electric shock aversion, *British Journal of Psychiatry*, 117: 173–85.

Marks, I., Green, R. and Mataix-Cols, D. (2000) Adult gender identity disorder can remit, *Comprehensive Psychiatry*, 41: 273–5.

Marks, I., Lovell, K., Noshirvani, H. et al. (1996) Treatment of post-traumatic stress disorder by exposure and/or cognition restructuring, *Archives of General Psychiatry*, 55: 317–25.

Marmar, C.R. (1991) Brief dynamic psychotherapy for post-traumatic stress disorder, *Psychiatric Annals*, 21: 405–14.

Maron, E. and Shlik, J. (2005) Serotonin function in panic disorder: important, but why? *Neuropsychopharmacology*, 31 Aug.

Marques, J.K., Nelson, C., Alaarcon, J-M. and Day, D.M. (2000) Preventing relapse in sex offenders: what we learned from SOTEP's experimental treatment program, in D.R. Laws, S.M. Hudson and T. Ward (eds) *Remaking Relapse Prevention with Sex Offenders: A Sourcebook*. Thousand Oaks, CA: Sage.

Marques, J.K., Wiederanders, M., Day, D.M. et al. (2005) A Effects of a relapse prevention program on sexual recidivism: final results from California's sex offender treatment and evaluation project (SOTEP), *Sexual Abuse*, 17: 79–107.

Marsch, L.A., Bickel, W.K., Badger, G.J. et al. (2005) Comparison of pharmacological treatments for opioid-dependent adolescents: a randomized controlled trial, *Archives of General Psychiatry*, 62: 1157–64.

Marshall, J.C., Halligan, P.W., Fink, G.R. et al. (1997) The functional anatomy of a hysterical paralysis, *Cognition*, 64: B1–8.

Marshall, W.L. (1994) Treatment effects on denial and minimization in incarcerated sex offenders, *Behaviour Research and Therapy*, 32: 559–64.

Martin, A., Rauh, E., Fichter, M. and Rief, W. (2007) A one-session treatment for patients suffering from medically unexplained symptoms in primary care: a randomized clinical trial, *Psychosomatics*, 48: 294–303.

Maslow, A.H. (1970) *Motivation and Personality*. New York: Harper and Row.

Masters, W.H. and Johnson, V.E. (1970) *Human Sexual Inadequacy*. Boston, MA: Little, Brown.

Matthews, K.A., Räikkönen, K., Gallo, L. et al. (2008) Association between socioeconomic status and metabolic syndrome in women: testing the reserve capacity model, *Health Psychology*, 27: 576–83.

Mattick, R.P., Breen, C., Kimber, J. et al. (2009) Methadone maintenance therapy versus no opioid replacement therapy for opioid dependence, *Cochrane Database of Systematic Reviews*, 3: CD002209.

Mayou, R., Bryant, B. and Ehlers, A. (2001) Prediction of psychological outcomes one year after a motor vehicle accident, *American Journal of Psychiatry*, 158: 1231–8.

McBride, P.A., Anderson, G.M. and Shapiro, T. (1996) Autism research: bringing together approaches to pull apart the disorder, *Archives of General Psychiatry*, 53: 980–3.

McCabe, R., Leudar, I. and Antaki, C. (2004) Do people with schizophrenia display theory of mind deficits in clinical interactions?, *Psychological Medicine*, 34: 401–12.

McCall, W.V. (2001) Electroconvulsive therapy in the era of modern psychopharmacology, *International Journal of Neuropsychopharmacology*, 4: 315–24.

McClure, G.M. (2000) Changes in suicide in England and Wales, 1960–1997, *British Journal of Psychiatry*, 176: 64–7.

McConaghy, N., Armstrong, M.S., Blaszczynski, A. et al. (1983) Controlled comparison of aversive therapy and imaginal desensitization in compulsive gambling, *British Journal of Psychiatry*, 142: 366–72.

McConaghy, N., Blaszczynski, A. and Frankova, A. (1991) Comparison of imaginal desensitization with other behavioural treatments of pathological gambling: a two to nine year follow-up, *British Journal of Psychiatry*, 159: 390–3.

McDaid, C., Trowman, R., Golder, S. et al. (2008) Interventions for people bereaved through suicide: systematic review, *British Journal of Psychiatry*, 193: 438–43.

McDougle, C.J., Naylor, S.T., Volkmar, F.R. et al. (1994) A double-blind, placebo-controlled investigation of fluvoxamine in adults with autism, *Society for Neuroscience Abstracts*, 20: 396.

McDowell, I. (2001) Alzheimer's disease: insights from epidemiology, *Aging*, 13: 143–62.

McGhie, A. and Chapman, J. (1961) Disorders of attention and perception in early schizophrenia, *British Journal of Medical Psychology*, 34: 103–16.

McGorry, P.D., Yung, A.R., Phillips, L.J. et al. (2002) Randomized controlled trial of interventions designed to reduce the risk of progression to first-episode psychosis in a clinical sample with subthreshold symptoms, *Archives of General Psychiatry*, 59: 921–8.

McGuffin, P., Katz, R., Watkins, S. et al. (1996) A hospital-based twin register of the heritability of DSM-IV unipolar depression, *Archives of General Psychiatry*, 53: 129–36.

McGuire, P.K., Silbersweig, D.A., Wright, I. et al. (1996) The neural correlates of inner speech and auditory verbal imagery in schizophrenia: relationship to auditory verbal hallucinations, *British Journal of Psychiatry*, 169: 148–59.

McGunn, P., Katz, R., Watkins, S. et al. (1996) A hospital-based twin register of the heritability of DSM-IV unipolar depression, *Archives of General Psychiatry*, 53: 129–36.

McIntosh, V.W., Jordan, J., Carter, F.A. et al. (2005) Three psychotherapies for anorexia nervosa: a randomized, controlled trial, *American Journal of Psychiatry*, 162: 741–7.

McKay, D., Todaro, J., Neziroglu, F. et al. (1997) Body dysmorphic disorder: a preliminary evaluation of treatment and maintenance using exposure with response prevention, *Behaviour Research and Therapy*, 35: 67–70.

McKay, R., Langdon, R. and Coltheart, M. (2005) Paranoia, persecutory delusions and attributional biases, *Psychiatry Research*, 136: 233–45.

McLean, A. and Broomfield, N.M. (2007) How does thought suppression impact upon beliefs about uncontrollability of worry? *Behaviour Research and Therapy*, 45: 2938–49.

McLean, P.D., Whittal, M.L., Thordarson, D.S. et al. (2001) Cognitive versus behavior therapy in the group treatment of obsessive-compulsive disorder, *Journal of Consulting and Clinical Psychology*, 69: 205–14.

McMahon, A. and Rhudick, P. (1964) Reminiscing, *Archives of General Psychiatry*, 10: 292–8.

McNally, R.J., Lasko, N.B., Clancy, S.A. et al. (2004) Psychophysiological responding during script-driven imagery in people reporting abduction by space aliens, *Psychological Science*, 15: 493–7.

Meehl, P.E. (1990) Towards an integrated theory of schizotaxia, schizotypy, and schizophrenia, *Journal of Personality Disorders*, 4: 1–99.

Meichenbaum, D. (1985) *Stress Inoculation Training*. New York: Pergamon.

Melchior, M., Caspi, A., Milne, B.J. et al. (2007) Work stress precipitates depression and anxiety in young, working women and men, *Psychological Medicine*, 37: 1119–29.

Meltzer, H.Y. (1998) Suicide in schizophrenia: risk factors and clozapine treatment, *Archives of General Psychiatry*, 52: 200–2.

Menzies, R.G. and Clarke, J.C. (1995) The etiology of phobias: a non-associative account, *Clinical Psychology Review*, 15: 23–48.

Merckelbach, H. and de Jong, P.J. (1999) Evolutionary models of phobias, in G.C.L. Davey (ed.) *Phobias: A Handbook of Theory, Research, and Treatment*. Chichester: Wiley.

Merckelbach, H., Devilly, G.J. and Rassin, E. (2002) Alters in dissociative identity disorder: metaphors or genuine entities?, *Clinical Psychology Review*, 22: 481–97.

Merskey, H. (1992) The manufacture of personalities: the production of multiple personality disorder, *British Journal of Psychiatry*, 160: 327–40.

Merskey, H. (1995) *The Analysis of Hysteria: Understanding Conversion and Dissociation*, 2nd edn. London: Gaskell.

Meyer, R.E. (1995) Biology of psychoactive substance dependence disorders: opiates, cocaine, ethanol, in A.F. Schatzberg and C.B. Nemeroff (eds) *The American Psychiatric Press Handbook of Psychopharmacology*. Washington, DC: American Psychiatric Press.

Meyer, U. and Feldon, J. (2009) Neural basis of psychosis-related behaviour in the infection model of schizophrenia, *Behavioural Brain Research*, 204: 322–34.

Meyer-Bahlburg, H. (1979) Sex hormones and female homosexuality: a critical examination, *Archives of Sexual Behavior*, 8: 101–19.

Meyer-Bahlburg, H.F.L. (2002) Gender identity disorder in young boys: a parent- and peer-based treatment protocol, *Clinical Child Psychology and Psychiatry*, 7: 1359–45.

Mihailides, S., Devilly, G.J. and Ward, T. (2004) Implicit cognitive distortions and sexual offending, *Sexual Abuse: A Journal of Research and Treatment*, 16: 333–50.

Miklowitz, D.J. (2004) The role of family systems in severe and recurrent psychiatric disorders: a developmental psychopathology view, *Developmental Psychopathology*, 16: 667–88.

Miklowitz, D.J., Simponeau, T.L., George, E.L. et al. (2003) Family-focused treatment of bipolar disorder: 1-year effects of a psychoeducational program in conjunction with pharmacotherapy, *Biological Psychiatry*, 48: 582–92.

Miles, C., Green, R., Sanders, G. et al. (1998) Estrogen and memory in a transsexual population, *Hormones and Behavior*, 34: 199–208.

Miller, E. (1999) Conversion hysteria: is it a viable concept?, in P. Halligan (ed.) *Conversion Hysteria: Towards a Neuropsychological Account*. Hove: Psychology Press.

Miller, W.R. and Rollnick, S. (2002) *Motivational Interviewing: Preparing People for Change*. New York: Guilford Press.

Millward, C., Ferriter, M., Calver, S. et al. (2004) Gluten- and casein-free diets for autistic spectrum disorder, *Cochrane Database of Systematic Reviews*, 2.

Minden, S.L. and Schiffer, R.B. (1990) Affective disorders in multiple sclerosis: review and recommendations for clinical research, *Archives of Neurology*, 47: 98–104.

Minuchin, S. (1974) *Families and Family Therapy*. London: Tavistock.

Minuchin, S., Rosman, B. and Baker, L. (1978) *Psychosomatic Families: Anorexia Nervosa in Context*. Cambridge, MA: Harvard University Press.

Miranda, J. and Gross, J.J. (1997) Cognitive vulnerability depression, and the mood-state dependent hypothesis: is it out of sight out of mind?, *Cognition and Emotion*, 11: 585–605.

Mitte, K., Noack, P., Steil, R. and Hautzinger, M. (2005) A meta-analytic review of the efficacy of drug treatment in generalized anxiety disorder, *Journal of Clinical Psychopharmacology*, 25: 141–50.

Modestin, J. (1992) Multiple personality disorder in Switzerland, *American Journal of Psychiatry*, 149: 88–92.

Modestin, J., Furrer, R. and Malti, T. (2005) different traumatic experiences are associated with different pathologies, *Psychiatry Quarterly*, 76: 19–32.

Moene, F.C., Spinhoven, P., Hoogduin, K.A. and Van Dyck, R. (2003) A randomized controlled clinical trial of a hypnosis-based treatment for patients with conversion disorder, motor type, *International Journal of Clinical and Experimental Hypnosis*, 51: 29–50.

Mogg, K., Baldwin, D.S., Brodrick, P. et al. (2004) Effect of short-term SSRI treatment on cognitive bias in generalised anxiety disorder, *Psychopharmacology*, 176: 466–70.

Mohr, D.C., Goodkin, D.E., Bacchetti, P. et al. (2000a) Psychological stress and the subsequent appearance of new brain MRI lesions in MS, *Neurology*, 55: 55–61.

Mohr, D.C., Likosky, W., Bertagnolli, A. et al. (2000b) Telephone-administered cognitive-behavioral therapy for the treatment of depressive symptoms in multiple sclerosis, *Journal of Consulting and Clinical Psychology*, 68: 356–61.

Molyneux, G.J., McCarthy, G.M., McEniff, S. et al. (2008) Prevalence and predictors of carer burden and depression in carers of patients referred to an old age psychiatric service, *International Psychogeriatrics*, 20: 1193–202.

Mondraty, N., Birmingham, C.L., Touyz, S. et al. (2005) Randomized controlled trial of olanzapine in the treatment of cognitions in anorexia nervosa, *Australasian Psychiatry: Bulletin of Royal Australian and New Zealand College of Psychiatrists*, 13: 72–5.

Monroe, S.M., Slavich, G.M., Torres, L.D. et al. (2007) Severe life events predict specific patterns of change in cognitive biases in major depression, *Psychological Medicine*, 37: 863–71.

Monteleone, P. and Maj, M. (2008) Genetic susceptibility to eating disorders: associated polymorphisms and pharmacogenetic suggestions, *Pharmacogenomics*, 9: 1487–520.

Montgomery, S.A., Dufour, H., Brion, S. et al. (1993) Guidelines for treatment of depressive illness with antidepressants, *Journal of Psychopharmacology*, 7: 19–23.

Monti, P.M., Colby, S.M., Barnett, N.P. et al. (1999) Brief intervention for harm reduction with alcohol-positive older adolescents in a hospital emergency department, *Journal of Consulting and Clinical Psychology*, 67: 989–94.

Moore, M.L., Eichner, S.F., Jones, J.R. (2004) Treating functional impairment of autism with selective serotonin-reuptake inhibitors, *Annals of Pharmacotherapy*, 38: 1515–19.

Moores, B. and Grant, G.W.B. (1976) Nurses' expectations for accomplishment of mentally retarded patients, *American Journal of Mental Deficiency*, 80: 644–9.

Morey, L.C. (1988) Personality disorders in DSM-III and DSM-IIIR: convergence, coverage, and internal consistency, *American Journal of Psychiatry*, 145: 573–7.

Morimoto, T., Hashimoto, K., Yasumatsu, H. et al. (2002) Neuropharmacological profile of a novel potential atypical antipsychotic drug Y-931 (8-fluoro-12-(4-methylpiperazin-1-yl)-6H-[1]benzothieno[2,3-b][1,5] benzodiazepine maleate), *Neuropsychopharmacology*, 26: 456–67.

Morrison, A.P., French, P., Parker, S. et al. (2006) Three-year follow-up of a randomized controlled trial of cognitive therapy for the prevention of psychosis in people at ultrahigh risk, *Schizophrenia Bulletin*, 33: 682–7.

Morton, J., Andrews, B., Bekerian, D. et al. (1995) *Recovered Memories*. Leicester: British Psychological Society.

Mostert, J.P., Koch, M.W., Heerings, M. et al. (2008) Therapeutic potential of fluoxetine in neurological disorders, *CNS Neuroscience and Therapeutics*, 14: 153–64.

Mowrer, O.H. (1947) On the dual nature of learning: a reinterpretation of 'conditioning' and 'problem-solving', *Harvard Education Review*, 17: 102–48.

Muhle, R., Trentacoste, S.V. and Rapin, I. (2004) The genetics of autism, *Pediatrics*, 113: 472–86.

Murad, M.H., Elamin, M.B., Garcia, M.Z. et al. (2009) Hormonal therapy and sex reassignment: a systematic review and meta-analysis of quality of life and psychosocial outcomes, *Clinical Endocrinology*, 16 May.

Muris, P., de Jongh, A., Merckelbach, H., Postema, S. and Vet, M. (1998) Thought suppression in phobic and nonphobic dental patients, *Anxiety, Stress and Coping*, 11: 275–87.

Murphy, J.M. (1976) Psychiatric labelling in cross-cultural perspective, *Science*, 191: 1019–28.

Murphy, K. and Barkley, R.A. (1996) Attention deficit hyperactivity disorder adults: comorbidities and adaptive impairments, *Comprehensive Psychiatry*, 37: 393–401.

Murphy, P.M., Cramer, D. and Lillie, F.J. (1984) The relationship between curative factors perceived by patients in their psychotherapy and treatment outcome: an exploratory study, *British Journal of Medical Psychology*, 57: 187–92.

Murray, E.J. and Foote, F. (1979) The origins of fear of snakes, *Behaviour Research and Therapy*, 17: 489–93.

Murray, J.B. (2000) Psychological profiles of pedophiles and child molesters, *Journal of Psychology*, 134: 211–24.

Mustapić, M., Pivac, N., Kozarić-Kovacić, D. et al. (2007) Dopamine beta-hydroxylase (DBH) activity and -1021C/T polymorphism of DBH gene in combat-related post-traumatic stress disorder, *American Journal of Medical Genetics B Neuropsychiatric Genetics*, 144B: 1087–9.

Myers, E.D. and Branthwaite, A. (1992) Out-patient compliance with antidepressant medication, *British Journal of Psychiatry*, 160: 83–6.

Nagel, B. and Leiper, R. (1999) A national survey of psychotherapy with people with learning disabilities, *Clinical Psychology Forum*, 129: 14–18.

Najavitis, L.M., Gastfriend, D.R., Barber, J.P. et al. (1998) Cocaine dependence with and without PTSD among subjects in the National Institute on Drug Abuse collaboration cocaine treatment study, *American Journal of Psychiatry*, 155: 214–19.

Naranjo, C.A. and Bremner, K.E. (1993) Behavioural correlates of alcohol intoxication, *Addiction*, 88: 25–35.

Nash, J.R., Sargent, P.A., Rabiner, E.A. et al. (2008) Serotonin 5-HT1A receptor binding in people with panic disorder: positron emission tomography study, *British Journal of Psychiatry*, 193: 229–34.

Nathan, P.E. and Langenbucher, J. (2003) Diagnosis and classification, in I.B. Weiner, D.K. Freedheim, J.A. Schinka and W.F. Velicer (eds) *Handbook of Psychology*. New York: John Wiley.

National Centre for Social Research (1999) *British Gambling Prevalence Survey*. London: National Centre for Social Research.

National Institute for Clinical Excellence (2009) *Core Interventions in the Treatment and Management of Schizophrenia in Primary and Secondary Care* (update). London: NICE.

National Institutes of Health (NIH) (1985) Electroconvulsive therapy, *NIH Consensus Statement Online*, 5: 1–23.

Neale, B.M., Medland, S., Ripke, P. et al. (2010) Case-control genome-wide association study of attention-deficit/hyperactivity disorder, *Journal of the American Academy of Child and Adolescent Psychiatry*, 49: 906–20.

Neisser, U. and Harsch, N. (1992) Phantom flashbulbs: false recollections of hearing the news about Challenger, in E. Winograd and U. Neisser (eds) *Affect and Accuracy in Recall: Studies in Flashbulb Memories*. Cambridge: Cambridge University Press.

Nelson, E. and Rice, J. (1997) Stability of diagnosis of obsessive-compulsive disorder in the Epidemiologic Catchment Area study, *American Journal of Psychiatry*, 154: 826–31.

Neto, D., Lambaz, R., Aguiar, P. et al. (2008) Effectiveness of sequential combined treatment in comparison with treatment as usual in preventing relapse in alcohol dependence, *Alcohol and Alcoholism*, 43: 661–8.

Neumeister, A., Praschak-Rieder, N., Hesselmann, B. et al. (1997) Rapid tryptophan depletion in drug-free depressed patients with seasonal affective disorder, *American Journal of Psychiatry*, 154: 1153–5.

Nevonen, L. and Broberg, A.G. (2005) A comparison of sequenced individual and group psychotherapy for patients with bulimia nervosa, *International Journal of Eating Disorders*, 17 October.

New, A.S., Buchsbaum, M.S., Hazlett, E.A. et al. (2004) Fluoxetine increases relative metabolic rate in prefrontal cortex in impulsive aggression, *Psychopharmacology (Berl)*, 176: 451–8.

New, A.S., Hazlett, E.A., Buchsbaum, M.S. et al. (2003) m-CPP PET and impulsive aggression in borderline personality disorder, *Biological Psychiatry*, 53: S104.

Newcomb, M.D. (1985) The role of perceived relative parent personality in the development of heterosexuals, homosexuals, and transvestites, *Archives of Sexual Behavior*, 14: 147–64.

Newman, C.F., Leahy, R.L., Beck, A.T. et al. (2002) *Bipolar Disorder: A Cognitive Therapy Approach*. Washington, DC: American Psychological Association.

Newton, A., Sarker, S.J., Pahal, G.S. et al. (2007) Impact of the new UK licensing law on emergency hospital attendances: a cohort study, *Emergency Medical Journal*, 24: 532–4.

Neziroglu, F., McKay, D., Todaro, J. et al. (1996) Effect of cognitive behavior therapy on persons with body dysmorphic disorder and comorbid axis II diagnoses, *Behavior Therapy*, 27: 67–77.

NICE (National Institute for Clinical Excellence) (2000) *Guidance on the Use of Electroconvulsive Therapy*. London: NICE.

Nickell, A.D., Waudby, C.J. and Trull, T.J. (2002) Attachment, parental bonding and borderline personality disorder features in young adults, *Journal of Personality Disorders*, 16: 148–59.

Nigg, J.T. and Goldsmith, H.H. (1994) Genetics of personality disorders: perspectives from personality and psychopathology research, *Psychological Bulletin*, 115: 346–80.

NIH Consensus Development Panel on Effective Treatment of Opiate Addiction (1998) Effective medical treatment of opiate addiction, *Journal of the American Medical Association*, 280: 1936–43.

NIH Consensus Development Panel on Rehabilitation of Persons with Traumatic Brain Injury (1999) Rehabilitation of persons with traumatic brain injury, *Journal of the American Medical Association*, 282: 974–83.

Noblitt, J.R. and Perskin, P.S. (2000) *Cult and Ritual Abuse: Its History, Anthropology, and Recent Discovery in Contemporary America*. Westport, CT: Praeger.

Nocentini, U., Tedeschi, G., Migliaccio, R. et al. (2009) An exploration of anger phenomenology in multiple sclerosis, *European Journal of Neurology*, 29 June.

Nock, M.K. and Kazdin, A.E. (2005) Randomized controlled trial of a brief intervention for increasing participation in parent management training, *Journal of Consulting and Clinical Psychology*, 73: 872–9.

Noh, S., Kaspar, V., Wickrama, K.A. (2007) Overt and subtle racial discrimination and mental health: preliminary findings for Korean immigrants, *American Journal of Public Health*, 97: 1269–74.

Nordahl, H.M. and Nysaeter, T.E. (2005) Schema therapy for patients with borderline personality disorder: a single case series, *Journal of Behavior Therapy and Experimental Psychiatry*, 36: 254–64.

Nordahl, H.M. and Stiles, T.C. (1997) Perceptions of parental bonding in patients with various personality disorders, lifetime depressive disorders, and healthy controls, *Journal of Personality Disorders*, 11: 391–402.

Norström, T. and Skog, O.J. (2005) Saturday opening of alcohol retail shops in Sweden: an experiment in two phases, *Addiction*, 100: 767–76.

Noyes, R., Happel, R., Muller, B. et al. (1998) Fluvoxamine for somatoform disorders: an open trial, *General Hospital Psychiatry*, 20: 339–44.

Noyes, R., Stuart, S.P., Langbehn, D.R. et al. (2003) Test of an interpersonal model of hypochondriasis, *Psychosomatic Medicine*, 65: 292–300.

Nugent, A.C., Milham, M.P., Bain, E.E. et al. (2006) Cortical abnormalities in bipolar disorder investigated with MRI and voxel-based morphometry, *Neuroimage*, 30: 485–97.

Nutt, D.J. (2005) Overview of diagnosis and drug treatments of anxiety disorders, *CNS Spectrum*, 10: 49–56.

Nutt, D.J. and Law, F.D. (2000) Pharmacological and psychological aspects of drugs of abuse, in M.G. Gelder, J.J. Lopez-Ibor Jr and N.C. Andreasen (eds) *New Oxford Textbook of Psychiatry*. Oxford: Oxford University Press.

Oades, R.D., Lasky-Su, J., Christiansen, H., et al. (2008) The influence of serotonin- and other genes on impulsive behavioral aggression and cognitive impulsivity in children with attention-deficit/hyperactivity disorder (ADHD): findings from a family-based association test (FBAT) analysis, *Behavioral and Brain Functions*, 4: 48.

Oakley, D.A. (1999) Hypnosis and conversion hysteria: a unifying model, in P. Halligan and A.S. David (eds) *Conversion Hysteria: Towards a Neuropsychological Account*. Hove: Psychology Press.

O'Brien, A.R., Chiaravalloti, N., Goveover, Y. et al. (2008) Evidenced-based cognitive rehabilitation for persons with multiple sclerosis: a review of the literature, *Archives of Physical Medicine and Rehabilitation*, 89: 761–9.

O'Connor, T.G., Deater-Deckard, K., Fulker, D. et al. (1998) Genotype–environment correlations in late childhood and early adolescence: antisocial behavioral problems and coercive parenting, *Developmental Psychology*, 34: 970–81.

Oei, T.P. and Raylu, N. (2004) Familial influence on offspring gambling: a cognitive mechanism for transmission of gambling behavior in families, *Psychological Medicine*, 34: 1279–88.

O'Farrell, T.J. and Fals-Stewart, W. (2000) Behavioral couples therapy for alcoholism and drug abuse, *Journal of Drug Abuse Treatment*, 18: 51–4.

Öhman, A. (1986) Face the beast and fear the face: animal and social fears as the prototypes for evolutionary analyses of emotion, *Psychophysiology*, 23: 123–45.

Oke, S. and Kanigsberg, E. (1991) Occupational therapy in the treatment of individuals with multiple personality disorder, *Canadian Journal of Occupational Therapy*, 58: 234–40.

Oldenburg, B. and Harris, D. (1996) The workplace as a setting for promoting health and preventing disease, *Homeostasis in Health and Disease*, 37: 226–32.

Onder, G., Zanetti, O., Giacobini, E. et al. (2005) Reality orientation therapy combined with cholinesterase inhibitors in Alzheimer's disease: randomised controlled trial, *British Journal of Psychiatry*, 187: 450–5.

Ono, Y., Yoshimura, K., Sueoka, R. et al. (1996) Avoidant personality and taijin kyoufu: sociocultural implications of the WHO/ADAMHA International Study of Personality Disorders in Japan, *Acta Psychiatrica Scandinavica*, 93: 172–6.

Oosthuizen, P.P. and Castle, D. (1998) Body dysmorphic disorder – a distinct entity? *South African Medical Journal*, 88: 766–9.

Oosthuizen, P., Lambert, T. and Castle, D.J. (1998) Dysmorphic concern: prevalence and associations with clinical variables, *Australian and New Zealand Journal of Psychiatry*, 32: 129–32.

Oppenheimer, R., Howells, K., Palmer, R.L. et al. (1985) Adverse sexual experience in childhood and clinical eating disorders: a preliminary description, *Journal of Psychiatric Research*, 19: 357–61.

Osman, S., Cooper, M., Hackmann, A. and Veale, D. (2004) Spontaneously occurring images and early memories in people with body dysmorphic disorder, *Memory*, 12: 428–36.

Ost, J., Costall, A. and Bull, R. (2005) A perfect symmetry? A study of retractors' experiences of making and then repudiating claims of early sexual abuse, *Psychology, Crime and Law*, 8: 155–81.

Öst, L-G. (1987) Age of onset of different phobias, *Journal of Abnormal Psychology*, 96: 223–9.

Öst, L-G. (1996) One-session group treatment of spider phobia, *Behaviour Research and Therapy*, 34: 707–15.

Öst, L.G. and Hellström, K. (1997) Blood-injury-injection phobia, in G.C.L. Davey (ed.) *Phobias: A Handbook of Theory, Research & Treatment*. New York: Wiley.

Öst, L-G., Salkovskis, P.M. and Hellström, K. (1991) One-session therapist-directed exposure vs. self-exposure in the treatment of spider phobia, *Behavior Therapy*, 22: 407–22.

Ovesey, L. and Person, E. (1973) Gender identity and sexual pathology in men: a psychodynamic analysis of heterosexuality, transsexualism, and transvestism, *Journal of the American Academy of Psychoanalysis*, 1: 53–72.

Ovuga, E., Oyok, T.O. and Moro, E.B. (2008) Post traumatic stress disorder among former child soldiers attending a rehabilitative service and primary school education in northern Uganda, *African Health Sciences*, 8: 136–41.

Owen, M., Liddell, M. and McGuffin, P. (1994) Alzheimer's disease, *British Medical Journal*, 308: 672–3.

Pallesen, S., Mitsem, M., Kvale, G. et al. (2005) Outcome of psychological treatments of pathological gambling: a review and meta-analysis, *Addiction*, 100: 1412–22.

Papageorgiou, C. and Wells, A. (1998) Effects of attention training on hypochondriasis: a brief case series, *Psychological Medicine*, 28: 193–200.

Papakostas, G.I., Thase, M.E., Fava, M. et al. (2007) Are antidepressant drugs that combine serotonergic and noradrenergic mechanisms of action more effective than the selective serotonin reuptake inhibitors in treating major depressive disorder? A meta-analysis of studies of newer agents, *Biological Psychiatry*, 62: 1217–27.

Parikh, M.S., Kolevzon, A. and Hollander, E. (2008) Psychopharmacology of aggression in children and adolescents with autism: a critical review of efficacy and tolerability, *Journal of Child and Adolescent Psychopharmacology*, 18: 157–78.

Paris, J. (1991) Personality disorders, parasuicide, and culture, *Transcultural Psychiatric Research*, 28: 25–39.

Paris, J. (1996) Antisocial personality disorder: a biopsychosocial model, *Canadian Journal of Psychiatry*, 41: 75–80.

Paris, J. (2008) Clinical trials of treatment for personality disorders, *Psychiatric Clinics of North America*, 31: 517–26.

Paris, J. and Zweig-Frank, H. (2001) A 27-year follow-up of patients with borderline personality disorder, *Comprehensive Psychiatry*, 42: 482–7.

Park, N.W., Proulx, G.B. and Towers, W.M. (1999) Evaluation of the Attention Process Training programme, *Neuropsychological Rehabilitation*, 9: 135–54.

Parker, G. and Lipscombe, P. (1980) The relevance of early parental experiences to adult dependency, hypochondriasis and utilization of primary physicians, *British Journal of Medical Psychology*, 53: 355–63.

Parker, G., Roy, K., Wilhelm, K. et al. (1999) An exploration of links between early parenting experiences and personality disorder type and disordered personality functioning, *Journal of Personality Disorders*, 13: 361–74.

Parnas, J., Cannon, T., Schulsinger, F. and Mednick, S.A. (1995) Early predictors of onset and course of schizophrenia: results from the Copenhagen High-Risk Study, in H. Häfner and W.F. Gattaz (eds) *Search for the Causes of Schizophrenia*, Vol. 3. Berlin: Springer Verlag.

Parnas, J., Licht, D. and Bovet, P. (2005) Cluster A personality disorders: a review, in M. Maj, H.S. Akiskal, J.E. Mezzich and A. Okasha (eds) *Personality Disorders*. Chichester: Wiley.

Partonen, T. and Lonnqvist, J. (1998) Seasonal affective disorder, *Lancet*, 352: 1369–74.

Partonen, T., Treutlein, J., Alpman, A. et al. (2007) Three circadian clock genes Per2, Arntl, and Npas2 contribute to winter depression, *Annals of Medicine*, 39: 229–38.

Patel, V., Musara, T., Butau, T. et al. (1995) Concepts of mental illness and medical pluralism in Harare, *Psychological Medicine*, 25: 485–93.

Pato, M.T., Zohar-Kadouch, R., Zohar, J. et al. (1988) Return of symptoms after discontinuation of clomipramine in patients with obsessive-compulsive disorder, *American Journal of Psychiatry*, 145: 1521–5.

Patterson, T.L. and Leeuwenkamp, O.R. (2008) Adjunctive psychosocial therapies for the treatment of schizophrenia, *Schizophrenia Research*, 100: 108–19.

Patti, F., Amato, M., Trojano, M. et al. (2009) Cognitive impairment and its relation with disease measures in mildly disabled patients with relapsing-remitting multiple sclerosis: baseline results from the Cognitive Impairment in Multiple Sclerosis (COGIMUS) study, *Multiple Sclerosis*, 15: 779–88.

Pavlov, I.P. ([1927] 1960) *Conditioned Reflexes* (ed. and trans. G.V. Anrep). New York: Dover.

Paykel, E.S. (1994) Life events, social support and depression, *Acta Psychiatrica Scandinavica*, 377: 50–8.

Paykel, E.S., Brugha, T. and Fryers, T. (2005) Size and burden of depressive disorders in Europe, *European Neuropsychopharmacology*, 15: 411–23.

Peele, S. (1992) Alcoholism, politics, and bureaucracy: the consensus against controlled drinking therapy in America, *Addictive Behaviors*, 17: 49–62.

Pehek, E.A., Nocjar, C., Roth, B.L. et al. (2006) Evidence for the preferential involvement of 5-HT2A serotonin receptors in stress- and drug-induced dopamine release in the rat medial prefrontal cortex, *Neuropsychopharmacology*, 31: 265–77.

Pelham, W.E., Carlson, C., Sams, S.E. et al. (1993) Separate and combined effects of methylphenidate and behavior modification on boys with attention deficit/hyperactivity in the classroom, *Journal of Consulting and Clinical Psychology*, 61: 506–15.

Peralta, V. and Cuesta, M.J. (1992) Influence of cannabis abuse on schizophrenic psychopathology, *Acta Psychiatrica Scandinavica*, 85: 127–30.

Perkin, G.D. (1989) An analysis of 7936 successive new outpatient referrals, *Journal of Neurology, Neurosurgery and Psychiatry*, 52: 44–78.

Perkins, S., Schmidt, U., Eisler, I. et al. (2005) Why do adolescents with bulimia nervosa choose not to involve their parents in treatment?, *European Child and Adolescent Psychiatry*, 14: 376–85.

Perkonigg, A., Kessler, R.C. and Wittchen, H-U. (2000) Traumatic events and post-traumatic stress disorder in the community: prevalence, risk factors and comorbidity, *Acta Psychiatrica Scandinavica*, 101: 46–59.

Perreira, K.M. and Sloan, F. (2001) Life events and alcohol consumption among mature adults: a longitudinal analysis, *Journal of Studies on Alcohol*, 62: 501–8.

Perry, A., Tarrier, N., Morris, R. et al. (1999) Randomised controlled trial of efficacy of teaching patients with bipolar disorder to identify early symptoms of relapse and obtain treatment, *British Medical Journal*, 318: 149–53.

Peterson, C., Semmel, A., von Baeyer, C. et al. (1982) The Attributional Style Questionnaire, *Cognitive Therapy and Research*, 6: 287–300.

Petras, H., Kellam, S.G., Brown, C.H. et al. (2008) Developmental epidemiological courses leading to antisocial personality disorder and violent and criminal behavior: effects by young adulthood of a universal preventive intervention in first- and second-grade classrooms, *Drug and Alcohol Dependence*, 95 Suppl. 1: S45–59.

Petry, N.M., Weinstock, J., Ledgerwood, D.M. et al. (2008) A randomized trial of brief interventions for problem and pathological gamblers, *Journal of Consulting and Clinical Psychology*, 76: 318–28.

Pettinati, H.M., Gastfriend, D.R., Dong, Q. et al. (2009) Effect of extended-release naltrexone (XR-NTX) on quality of life in alcohol-dependent patients, *Alcoholism: Clinical and Experimental Research*, 33: 350–6.

Pharoah, F.M., Mari, J.J. and Streiner, D. (2000) Family intervention for schizophrenia, *The Cochrane Library*, Issue 4. Oxford: Update Software.

Phillips, K.A. (1991) Body dysmorphic disorder: the distress of imagined ugliness, *American Journal of Psychiatry*, 148: 1138–49.

Phillips, K.A. (1996a) *The Broken Mirror*. New York: Oxford University Press.

Phillips, K.A. (1996b) Pharmacologic treatment of body dysmorphic disorder, *Psychopharmacology Bulletin*, 32: 597–605.

Phillips, K.A. (2004) Psychosis in body dysmorphic disorder, *Journal of Psychiatric Research*, 38: 63–72.

Phillips, K.A., Albertini, R.S. and Rasmussen, S.A. (2002) A randomized placebo-controlled trial of fluoxetine in body dysmorphic disorder, *Archives of General Psychiatry*, 59: 381–8.

Phillips, K.A., Albertini, R.S., Siniscalchi, J.M. et al. (2001) Effectiveness of pharmacotherapy for body dysmorphic disorder: a chart-review study, *Journal of Clinical Psychology*, 62: 721–7.

Phillips, K.A., Menard, W., Fay, C. et al. (2006a) Gender similarities and differences in 200 individuals with body dysmorphic disorder, *Comprehensive Psychiatry*, 47: 77–87.

Phillips, K.A., Menard, W., Pagano, M.E. et al. (2006b) Delusional versus nondelusional body dysmorphic disorder: clinical features and course of illness, *Journal of Psychiatric Research*, 40: 95–104.

Phillips, K.A., Pinto, A., Menard, W. et al. (2007) Obsessive-compulsive disorder versus body dysmorphic disorder: a comparison study of two possibly related disorders, *Depression and Anxiety*, 24: 399–409.

Phillips, K.A., Quinn, G. and Stout, R.L. (2008) Functional impairment in body dysmorphic disorder: a prospective, follow-up study, *Journal of Psychiatric Research*, 42: 701–7.

Phillips, K.A. and Rasmussen, S.A. (2004) Change in psychosocial functioning and quality of life of patients with body dysmorphic disorder treated with fluoxetine: a placebo-controlled study, *Psychosomatics*, 45: 438–44.

Phillips, L.J., Francey, S.M., Edwards, J. et al. (2007) Stress and psychosis: towards the development of new models of investigation, *Clinical Psychology Review*, 27: 307–17.

Phongsavan, P., Chey, T., Bauman, A. et al. (2006) Social capital, socio-economic status and psychological distress among Australian adults, *Social Science and Medicine*, 63: 2546–61.

Piaget, J. (1954) *The Child's Construction of Reality*. London: Routledge and Kegan Paul.

Pigot, M., Loo, C. and Sachdev, P. (2008) Repetitive transcranial magnetic stimulation as treatment for anxiety disorders, *Expert Review of Neurotherapeutics*, 8: 1449–55.

Pike, K.M. (1998) Long-term course of anorexia nervosa: response, relapse, remission, and recovery, *Clinical Psychology Review*, 18: 447–75.

Pike, K.M., Hilbert, A., Wilfley, D.E. et al. (2008) Toward an understanding of risk factors for anorexia nervosa: a case-control study, *Psychological Medicine*, 38: 1443–53.

Pike, K.M., Walsh, B.T., Vitousek, K. et al. (2003) Cognitive behaviour therapy in the post hospitalisation treatment of anorexia nervosa, *American Journal of Psychiatry*, 160: 2046–9.

Piotrkowski, C.S. and Brannen, S.J. (2002) Exposure, threat appraisal, and lost confidence as predictors of PTSD symptoms following September 11, 2001, *American Journal of Orthopsychiatry*, 72: 476–85.

Piper, A. and Merskey, H. (2004) The persistence of folly: a critical examination of dissociative identity disorder. Part I. The excesses of an improbable concept, *Canadian Journal of Psychiatry*, 49: 592–600.

Piper, W.E., Joyce, A.S., McCallum, M. et al. (1993) Concentration and correspondence of transference interpretations in short-term psychotherapy, *Journal of Consulting and Clinical Psychology*, 61: 586–95.

Piper, W.E., Ogrodniczuk, J.S., Joyce, A.S. et al. (1999b) Prediction of dropping out in timelimited, interpretive individual psychotherapy, *Psychotherapy*, 36: 114–22.

Pithers, W.D. (1990) Relapse prevention with sexual aggressors: a method for maintaining therapeutic gain and enhancing external supervision, in W.L. Marshall, D.R. Laws and H.E. Barbaree (eds) *Handbook of Sexual Assault: Issues, Theories, and Treatment of the Offender*. New York: Plenum.

Pjrek, E., Konstantinidis, A., Assem-Hilger, E. et al. (2009) Therapeutic effects of escitalopram and reboxetine in seasonal affective disorder: a pooled analysis, *Journal of Psychiatric Research*, 43: 792–7.

Pjerk, E., Winkler, D. and Kasper, S. (2005) Pharmacotherapy of seasonal affective disorder, *CNS Spectrums*, 10: 664–9.

Pjerk, E., Winkler, D., Statsny, J. et al. (2004) Bright light therapy in seasonal affective disorder – does it suffice?, *European Neuropsychopharmacology*, 14: 347–51.

Pols, R. and Hawks, D. (1991) *Is There a Safe Level of Daily Consumption of Alcohol for Men and Women?* Canberra: Australian Government Publishing Service.

Pope, K.S. and Feldman-Summers, S. (1992) National survey of psychologists' sexual and physical abuse history and their evaluation of training and competence in these areas, *Professional Psychology: Research and Practice*, 23: 353–61.

Potenza, M.N. (2001) The neurobiology of pathological gambling, *Seminars in Clinical Neuropsychiatry*, 6: 217–26.

Poulton, R., Caspi, A., Moffitt, T.E. et al. (2000) Children's self-reported psychotic symptoms and adult schizophreniform disorder: a 15-year longitudinal study, *Archives of General Psychiatry*, 57: 1053–8.

Poulton, R. and Menzies, R.G. (2002) Fears born and bred: toward a more inclusive theory of fear acquisition, *Behaviour Research and Therapy*, 40: 197–208.

Powell, G.E. and Lindsay, S.J.E. (1994) *The Handbook of Clinical Adult Psychology*. London: Routledge.

Power, K.G., Simpson, R.J., Swanson, V. et al. (1990) A controlled study of cognitive behavior therapy, diazepam, and placebo in the management of generalized anxiety, *Behavioural Psychotherapy*, 17: 10–14.

Prescott, C.A. and Kendler, K.S. (1999) Genetic and environmental contributions to alcohol abuse and dependence in a population-based sample of male twins, *American Journal of Psychiatry*, 156: 34–40.

Preti, A., Girolamo, G.D., Vilagut, G. et al. (2009) The epidemiology of eating disorders in six European countries: results of the ESEMeD-WMH project, *Journal of Psychiatric Research*, 7 May.

Price, V.A. (1982) *Type A Behavior Pattern: A Model for Research and Practice*. New York: Academic Press.

Productivity Commission (1999) *Australia's Gambling Industries: Inquiry Report*. Melbourne: Productivity Commission.

Project MATCH Research Group (1998) Matching alcoholism treatments to client heterogeneity: project MATCH three-year drinking outcomes, *Alcoholism: Clinical and Experimental Research*, 22: 1300–11.

Putnam, F.W. (1997) *Dissociation in Children and Adolescents*. New York: Guilford.

Quinsey, V.I., Harris, G.T. and Rice, M.E. (1995) Actuarial prediction of sexual recidivism, *Journal of Interpersonal Violence*, 10: 85–105.

Rachman, S. (2003) *The Treatment of Obsessions*. Oxford: Oxford University Press.

Rachman, S.J. and de Silva, P. (1978) Abnormal and normal obsessions, *Behaviour Research and Therapy*, 16: 233–8.

Raine, A., Lencz, T., Bihrle, S. et al. (2000) Reduced prefrontal gray matter volume and reduced autonomic activity in antisocial personality disorder, *Archives of General Psychiatry*, 57: 119–27.

Raine, A., Reynolds, C. and Venables, P.H. (1998) Fearlessness, stimulation seeking, and large body size at 3 years as early predispositions to childhood aggression at age 11 years, *Archives of General Psychiatry*, 55: 745–51.

Rajagopal, S. (2004) Suicide pacts and the internet, *British Medical Journal*, 329: 1298–9.

Ralevski, E., Sanislow, C.A. and Grilo, C.M. (2005) Avoidant personality disorder and social phobia: distinct enough to be separate disorders?, *Acta Psychiatrica Scandinavica*, 112: 208–14.

Ralph, D. and McNicholas, T. (2000) UK management guidelines for erectile dysfunction, *British Medical Journal*, 321: 499–503.

Rampello, L., Nicoletti, F. and Nicoletti, F. (2000) Dopamine and depression: therapeutic implications, *CNS Drugs*, 13: 35–45.

Ramsay, M. (2001) Genetic susceptibility for panic and phobic disorders, *Trends in Molecular Medicine*, 7: 539.

Rao, D., Young, M. and Raguram, R. (2007) Culture, somatization, and psychological distress: symptom presentation in South Indian patients from a public psychiatric hospital, *Psychopathology*, 40: 349–55.

Rapee, R., Mattick, R. and Murrell, E. (1986) Cognitive mediation of anxiety and panic: a cognitive account, *Journal of Behavior Therapy and Experimental Psychiatry*, 17: 245–53.

Raskin, M., Peeke, H.Y., Dickman, W. et al. (1982) Panic and generalized anxiety disorders. Developmental antecedents and precipitants, *Archives of General Psychiatry*, 39: 687–9.

Rassin, E., Muris, P., Franken, I. et al. (2008) The feature-positive effect and hypochondriacal concerns, *Behaviour Research and Therapy*, 46: 263–9.

Rauch, S.L., Shin, L.M., Dougherty, D.D. et al. (2002) Predictors of fluvoxamine response in contamination-related obsessive compulsive disorder: a PET symptom provocation study, *Neuropsychopharmacology*, 27: 782–91.

Ray, L.A. and Oslin, D.W. (2009) Naltrexone for the treatment of alcohol dependence among African Americans: results from the COMBINE Study, *Drug and Alcohol Dependence*, 28 August.

Rayworth, B.B., Wise, L.A. and Harlow, B.L. (2004) Childhood abuse and risk of eating disorders in women, *Epidemiology*, 15: 271–8.

Razali, M.S. (1995) Psychiatrists and folk healers in Malaysia, *World Health Forum*, 16: 56–8.

Razali, S.M., Khan, U.A. and Hasanah, C.I. (1996) Belief in supernatural causes of mental illness among Malay patients: impact on treatment, *Acta Psychiatrica Scandinavica*, 94: 229–33.

Razali, S.M. and Najib, M.A. (2000) Help-seeking pathways among Malay psychiatric patients, *International Journal of Social Psychiatry*, 46: 281–9.

Rea, M., Tompson, M., Miklowitz, D. et al. (2003) Family-focused treatment versus individual treatment for bipolar disorder: results of a randomized clinical trial, *Journal of Consulting and Clinical Psychology*, 71: 482–92.

Reeve, W. and Ivison, D. (1985) Use of environmental manipulation and classroom and modified informal reality orientation with institutionalized, confused elderly patients, *Age and Ageing*, 14: 119–21.

Regier, D.A., Rae, D.S., Narrow, W.E. et al. (1998) Prevalence of anxiety disorders and their comorbidity with mood and addictive disorders, *British Journal of Psychiatry*, 173 (Suppl. 34): 24–6.

Reichborn-Kjennerud, T., Czajkowski, N., Neale, M.C. et al. (2007) Genetic and environmental influences on dimensional representations of DSM-IV cluster C personality disorders: a population-based multivariate twin study, *Psychological Medicine*, 37: 645–53.

Reichelt, K.L., Knivsberg, A.M., Lind, G. et al. (1991) Probable etiology and possible treatment of childhood autism, *Brain Dysfunction*, 4: 308–19.

Reid, W.H. and Gacono, C. (2000) Treatment of antisocial personality, psychopathy, and other characterologic antisocial syndromes, *Behavioral Science and Law*, 18: 647–62.

Reimherr, F.W., Wender, P.H., Wood, D.R. et al. (1987) An open trial of L-tyrosine in the treatment of attention deficit disorder, residual type, *American Journal of Psychiatry*, 144: 1071–3.

Remafedi, G., French, S., Story, M. et al. (1998) The relationship between suicide risk and sexual orientation: results of a population-based study, *American Journal of Public Health*, 88: 57–60.

Research Units on Pediatric Psychopharmacology Autism Network (2005) Risperidone treatment of autistic disorder: longer-term benefits and blinded discontinuation after 6 months, *American Journal of Psychiatry*, 162: 1361–9.

Revill, S. and Blunden, R. (1977) *Home Training of Pre-school Children with Developmental Delay: Report of the Development and Evaluation of the Portage Service in South Glamorgan*. Cardiff: Mental Handicap in Wales Applied Research Unit.

Rey, J.M., Walter, G., Plapp, J.M. et al. (2000) Family environment in attention deficit hyperactivity, oppositional defiant and conduct disorders, *Australia and New Zealand Journal of Psychiatry*, 34: 453–7.

Rice, M.E., Harris, G.T. and Cormier, C.A. (1992) An evaluation of a maximum security therapeutic community for psychopaths and other mentally disordered offenders, *Law and Human Behavior*, 16: 399–412.

Rice, M.E., Quinsey, V.L. and Harris, G.T. (1991) Sexual recidivism among child molesters released from a maximum security psychiatric institution, *Journal of Consulting and Clinical Psychology*, 59: 381–6.

Rief, W. and Barsky, A.J. (2005) Psychobiological perspectives on somatoform disorders, *Psychoneuroendocrinology*, 30: 996–1002.

Rief, W. and Broadbent, E. (2007) Explaining medically unexplained symptoms-models and mechanisms, *Clinical Psychology Review*, 27: 821–41.

Rief, W., Pilger, F., Ihle, D. et al. (2004) Psychobiological aspects of somatoform disorders: contributions of monoaminergic transmitter systems, *Neuropsychobiology*, 49: 24–9.

Rieker, P.P. and Bird, C.E. (2000) Sociological explanations of gender differences in mental and physical health, in C.E. Bird, P. Conrad and A.M. Fremont (eds) *Handbook of Medical Sociology*. Upper Saddle River, NJ: Prentice Hall.

Riley, D.E. (2002) Reversible transvestic fetishism in a man with Parkinson's disease treated with selegiline, *Clinical Neuropharmacology*, 25: 234–7.

Rinne, T., Van den Brink, W., Wouters, L. et al. (2002) SSRI treatment of borderline personality disorder: a randomized, placebo-controlled clinical trial for female patients with borderline personality disorder, *American Journal of Psychiatry*, 159: 2048–54.

Ritsher, J.E.B., Warner, V., Johnson, J.G. et al. (2001) Inter-generation longitudinal study of social class and depression: a test of social causation and social selection models, *British Journal of Psychiatry*, 178 (Suppl. 40): S84–S90.

Rivera, P., Elliott, T.R., Berry, J.W. et al. (2007) Predictors of caregiver depression among community-residing families living with traumatic brain injury, *NeuroRehabilitation*, 22: 3–8.

Rizzo, M.A., Hadjimichael, O.C., Preiningerova, J. et al. (2004) Prevalence and treatment of spasticity reported by multiple sclerosis patients, *Multiple Sclerosis*, 10: 589–95.

Roberts, J.S. (2000) Schizophrenia epigenesis?, *Theoretical Medicine and Bioethics*, 21: 191–215.

Robins, A.L., Siegel, P.T. and Moye, A. (1995) Family therapy versus individual therapy for anorexia: impact on family conflict, *International Journal of Eating Disorders*, 17: 313–22.

Robins, L.N., Helzer, J.E., Croughan, J. et al. (1981) National Institute of Mental Health Diagnostic Interview Schedule: its history, characteristics, and validity, *Archives of General Psychiatry*, 38: 381–9.

Robinson, D.G., Woerner, M.G., McMeniman, M. et al. (2004) Symptomatic and functional recovery from a first episode of schizophrenia or schizoaffective disorder, *American Journal of Psychiatry*, 161: 473–9.

Robinson, T.E. and Berridge, K.C. (2008) The incentive sensitization theory of addiction: some current issues, *Philosophical Transactions of the Royal Society*, 363: 3137–46.

Rocca, P., Fonzo, V., Scotta, M. et al. (1997) Paroxetine efficacy in the treatment of generalized anxiety disorder, *Acta Psychiatrica Scandinavica*, 95: 444–50.

Rocca, P., Marchiaro, L., Cocuzza, E. et al. (2002) Treatment of borderline personality disorder with risperidone, *Journal of Clinical Psychiatry*, 63: 241–4.

Rocchi, A., Pellegrini, S. and Siciliano, G. (2003) Causative and susceptibility genes for Alzheimer's disease: a review, *Brain Research Bulletin*, 61: 1–24.

Roeleveld, N., Zielhuis, G.A. and Gabreels, F. (1997) The prevalence of mental retardation: a critical review of recent literature, *Developmental Medicine and Child Neurology*, 39: 125–32.

Roelofs, K., Spinhoven, P., Sandijck, P. et al. (2005) The impact of early trauma and recent life events on symptom severity in patients with conversion disorder, *Journal of Nervous and Mental Disease*, 193: 508–14.

Roemer, L., Orsillo, S.M. and Salters-Pedneault, K. (2008) Efficacy of an acceptance-based behavior therapy for generalized anxiety disorder: evaluation in a randomized controlled trial, *Journal of Consulting and Clinical Psychology*, 76: 1083–9.

Roener, E., Salters-Pedneault, K. and Orsillo, S.M. (2006) Incorporating mindfulness- and acceptance-based strategies in the treatment of generalized anxiety disorder, in R.A. Baer (ed.) *Mindfulness Based Treatment Approaches: Clinician's Guide to Evidence Base and Applications*. London: Academic Press.

Roepke, S., Merkl, A., Dams, A. et al. (2008) Preliminary evidence of improvement of depressive symptoms but not impulsivity in cluster B personality disorder patients treated with quetiapine: an open label trial, *Pharmacopsychiatry*, 41: 176–81.

Rogers, C.R. (1961) *On Becoming a Person*. Boston, MA: Houghton Mifflin.

Rogers, S.L., Farlow, M.R., Doody, R.S. et al. (1998) A 24-week, double-blind, placebo-controlled trial of donepezil in patients with Alzheimer's disease, *Neurology*, 50: 136–45.

Roggla, H. and Uhl, A. (1995) Depression and relapses in treated alcoholics, *International Journal of Addictions*, 30: 337–49.

Romme, M. and Escher, S. (2000) *Making Sense of Voices*. London: Mind Publications.

Rosati, G. (2001) The prevalence of multiple sclerosis in the world: an update, *Neurological Sciences*, 22: 117–39.

Rose, S., Bisson, J. and Wessely, W. (2002) Psychological debriefing for preventing post traumatic stress disorder (PTSD), *Cochrane Database of Systematic Reviews*, 1.

Rose, S., Lewontin, R.C. and Kamin, L.J. (1984) *Not in Our Genes: Biology, Ideology, and Human Nature*. New York: Penguin.

Rosen, J.C. (1996) Body dysmorphic disorder: assessment and treatment, in J.K. Thompson (ed.) *Body Image, Eating Disorders, and Obesity*. Washington, DC: American Psychological Association.

Rosen, J.C. and Ramirez, E. (1998) A comparison of eating disorders and body dysmorphic disorder on body image and psychological adjustment, *Journal of Psychosomatic Research*, 44: 441–9.

Rosen, J.C., Reiter, J. and Orosan, P. (1995) Cognitive-behavioral body image therapy for body dysmorphic disorder, *Journal of Consulting and Clinical Psychology*, 63: 263–9.

Rosen, R. and Garety, P. (2005) Predicting recovery from schizophrenia: a retrospective comparison of characteristics at onset of people with single and multiple episodes, *Schizophrenia Bulletin*, 31: 735–50.

Rosen, R.C. (2001) Psychogenic erectile dysfunction: classification and management, *Urologic Clinics of North America*, 28: 269–78.

Rosenhan, D.L. (1973) On being sane in insane places, *Science*, 179: 250–8.

Rosenthal, N.E., Sack, D.A., Gillin, J.C. et al. (1984) Seasonal affective disorder: a description of the syndrome and preliminary findings with light therapy, *Archives of General Psychiatry*, 41: 72–80.

Rosenthal, R. and Lesieur, H. (1992) Self-reported withdrawal symptoms and pathological gambling, *American Journal of Addiction*, 1: 150–4.

Ross, C.A., Miller, S.D., Reagor, P. et al. (1991) Structured interview data on 102 cases of multiple personality disorder from four centres, *American Journal of Psychiatry*, 147: 596–600.

Ross, C.A., Norton, R. and Wozney, K. (1989) Multiple personality disorder: an analysis of 236 cases, *Canadian Journal of Psychiatry*, 34: 97–101.

Rossel, R. (1998) Multiplicity: the challenges of finding place in experience, *Journal of Constructivist Psychology*, 11: 221–40.

Rossell, S.L. and Boundy, C.L. (2005) Are auditory-verbal hallucinations associated with auditory affective processing deficits?, *Schizophrenia Research*, 78: 95–106.

Roth, A. and Fonagy, P. (1998) *What Works for Whom? A Critical Review of Psychotherapy Research*. New York: Guilford.

Rothschild, A.J. and Locke, C.A. (1991) Reexposure to fluoxetine after serious suicide attempts by three patients: the role of akathisia, *Journal of Clinical Psychiatry*, 12: 491–3.

Routsalainen, J., Serra, C., Marine, A. et al. (2008) Systematic review of interventions for reducing occupational stress in health care workers, *Scandinavian Journal of Work, Environment, and Health*, 34: 169–78.

Royal College of Psychiatrists (RCP) (1986) *Alcohol: Our Favourite Drug*. London: RCP.

Roy-Byrne, P.P., Craske, M.G., Stein, M.B. et al. (2005) Randomized effectiveness trial of cognitive-behavioral therapy and medication for primary care panic disorder, *Archives of General Psychiatry*, 62: 290–8.

Rubinstein, S. and Caballero, B. (2000) Is Miss America an undernourished role model?, *Journal of the American Medical Association*, 283: 1569.

Rudd, M.D. (2000) The suicidal mode: a cognitive-behavioral model of suicidality, *Suicide and Life Threatening Behavior*, 30: 18–33.

Russell, F. (2007) Portage in the UK: recent developments, *Child: Care, Health and Development*, 33: 677–83.

Russell, G.F.M., Szmukler, G.I., Dare, C. et al. (1987) An evaluation of family therapy in anorexia nervosa and bulimia nervosa, *Archives of General Psychiatry*, 44: 1047–56.

Russell, V.A., Sagvolden, T. and Johansen, E.B. (2005) Animal models of attention-deficit hyperactivity disorder, *Behavioral and Brain Functions*, 1: 9.

Russon, L. and Alison, D. (1998) Palliative care does not mean giving up, *British Medical Journal*, 317: 195–7.

Ryle, A. (1975) *Cognitive Analytic Therapy: Developments in Theory and Practice*. Chichester: Wiley.

Ryle, A. and Kerr, I.B. (2002) *Introducing Cognitive Analytic Therapy: Principles and Practice*. Chichester: Wiley Blackwell.

Sachs-Ericsson, N., Plant, E.A. and Blazer, D.G. (2005) Racial differences in the frequency of depressive symptoms among community dwelling elders: the role of socio-economic factors, *Aging and Mental Health*, 9: 201–9.

Sadeh, N. and Verona, E. (2008) Psychopathic personality traits associated with abnormal selective attention and impaired cognitive control, *Neuropsychology*, 22: 669–80.

Sagvolden, T., Johansen, E.B., Aase, H. et al. (2005) A dynamic developmental theory of attention-deficit/hyperactivity disorder (ADHD) predominantly hyperactive and combined subtypes, *Behavioral and Brain Sciences*, 28: 397–68.

Saiz, P.A., Garcia-Portilla, M.P., Florez, G. et al. (2009) Polymorphisms of the IL-1 gene complex are associated with alcohol dependence in Spanish Caucasians: data from an association study, *Alcoholism: Clinical and Experimental Research*, 33: 2147–53.

Sala, M., Caverzasi, E., Marraffini, E. et al. (2008) Cognitive memory control in borderline personality disorder patients, *Psychological Medicine*, 20 August: 1–9.

Salekin, R.T. (2002) Psychopathy and therapeutic pessimism: clinical lore or clinical reality?, *Clinical Psychology Review*, 22: 79–112.

Salkovskis, P. and Kirk, J. (1997) Obsessive-compulsive disorder, in D.M. Clark and C.G. Fairburn (eds) *Science and Practice of Cognitive Behaviour Therapy*. Oxford: Oxford University Press.

Salkovskis, P.M., Atha, C. and Storer, D. (1990) Cognitive-behavioural problem-solving in the treatment of patients who repeatedly attempt suicide: a controlled trial, *British Journal of Psychiatry*, 157: 871–6.

Salokangas, R.K. and McGlashan, T.H. (2008) Early detection and intervention of psychosis: a review, *Nordic Journal of Psychiatry*, 62: 92–105.

Samuels, J.F. (2009) Recent advances in the genetics of obsessive-compulsive disorder, *Current Psychiatry Reports*, 11: 277–82.

Sandberg, S. (2005) The biopsychosocial context of ADHD, *The Behavioral and Brain Sciences*, 28: 441–2.

Sanders, A.R., Duan, J., Levinson, D.F. et al. (2008) No significant association of 14 candidate genes with schizophrenia in a large European ancestry sample; implications for psychiatric genetics, *American Journal of Psychiatry*, 165: 497–506.

Sar, V., Akyuz, G., Kundakci, T. et al. (2004) Childhood trauma, dissociation, and psychiatric comorbidity in patients with conversion disorder, *American Journal of Psychiatry*, 161: 2271–6.

Saraceno, B., Levav, I. and Kohn, R. (2005) The public mental health significance of research on socio-economic factors in schizophrenia and major depression. *World Psychiatry*, 4: 181–5.

Sassi, R.B., Stanley, J.A., Axelson, D. et al. (2005) Reduced NAA levels in the dorsolateral prefrontal cortex of young bipolar patients, *American Journal of Psychiatry*, 162: 2109–15.

Satel, S.L. and Edell, W.S. (1991) Cocaine-induced paranoia and psychosis proneness, *American Journal of Psychiatry*, 141: 1708–11.

Sauter, C., Zebenholzer, K., Hisakawa, J. et al. (2008) A longitudinal study on effects of a six-week course for energy conservation for multiple sclerosis patients, *Multiple Sclerosis*, 14: 500–5.

Sayette, M.A. (1993) An appraisal-disruption model of alcohol's effect on stress responses in social drinkers, *Psychological Bulletin*, 114: 459–76.

Sayette, M.A. (1999) Does drinking reduce stress? *Alcohol Research and Health*, 23: 250–5.

Scheib, J.E., Gangestad, S.W. and Thornhill, R. (1999) Facial attractiveness, symmetry and cues to good genes, *Proceedings of the Royal Society of London*, 266: 1913–17.

Schell, T.L., Marshall, G.N. and Jaycox, L.H. (2004) All symptoms are not created equal: the prominent role of hyperarousal in the natural course of posttraumatic psychological distress, *Journal of Abnormal Psychology*, 113: 189–97.

Schenk, D., Barbour, R., Dunn, W. et al. (1999) Immunization with amyloidbeta attenuates Alzheimer-disease-like pathology in the PDAPP mouse, *Nature*, 400: 173–7.

Scherbaum, N., Kluwig, J., Specka, M. et al. (2005) Group psychotherapy for opiate addicts in methadone maintenance treatment – a controlled trial, *European Addiction Research*, 11: 163–71.

Schiffer, B., Peschel, T., Paul, T. et al. (2007) Structural brain abnormalities in the frontostriatal system and cerebellum in pedophilia, *Journal of Psychiatric Research*, 41: 753–62.

Schipper, H.M. (2009) Apolipoprotein E: Implications for AD neurobiology, epidemiology and risk assessment, *Neurobiology of Aging*, epub ahead of print.

Schmidt, U., Lee, S., Beecham, J. et al. (2007) A randomized controlled trial of family therapy and cognitive behavior therapy guided self-care for adolescents with bulimia nervosa and related disorders, *American Journal of Psychiatry*, 164: 591–8.

Schöning, S., Engelien, A., Bauer, C. et al. (2010) Neuroimaging differences in spatial cognition between men and male-to-female transsexuals before and during hormone therapy, *Journal of Sexual Medicine*, 7: 1858–67.

Schneider, A.J., Mataix-Cols, D., Marks, I.M. et al. (2005) Internet-guided self-help with or without exposure therapy for phobic and panic disorders, *Psychotherapy and Psychosomatics*, 74: 154–64.

Schooler, C., Caplan, L.J., Revell, A.J. et al. (2008) Brain lesion and memory functioning: short-term memory deficit is independent of lesion location, *Psychonomic Bulletin Review*, 15: 521–7.

Schotte, D.E. and Clum, G.A. (1987) Problem-solving skills in suicidal psychiatric patients, *Journal of Consulting and Clinical Psychology*, 55: 49–54.

Schubert, D.S. and Foliart, R.H. (1993) Increased depression in multiple sclerosis patients: a meta-analysis, *Psychosomatics*, 34: 124–30.

Schuckit, M.A., Tsuang, J.W., Anthenelli, R.M. et al. (1996) Alcohol challenges in young men from alcoholic pedigrees and control families: a report from the COGA project, *Journal of Studies in Alcohol*, 57: 368–77.

Schultz, T., Passmore, J.L. and Yoder, C.Y. (2003) Emotional closeness with perpetrators and amnesia for child sexual abuse, *Journal of Child Sexual Abuse*, 12: 67–88.

Schulze-Rauschenbach, S.C., Harms, U., Schlaepfer, T.E. et al. (2005) Distinctive neurocognitive effects of repetitive transcranial magnetic stimulation and electroconvulsive therapy in major depression, *British Journal of Psychiatry*, 186: 410–16.

Schwartz, C.E., Foley, F.W., Rao, S.M. et al. (1999) Stress and course of disease in multiple sclerosis, *Behavioral Medicine*, 25: 110–16.

Schwartz, D.M. and Thompson, M.G. (1981) Do anorexics get well? Current research and future needs, *American Journal of Psychiatry*, 138: 319–23.

Schwarz, T. (1981) *The Hillside Strangler: A Murderer's Mind*. New York: New American Library.

Schwitzer, A.M., Rodriguez, L.E., Thomas, C. et al. (2001) The eating disorders NOS diagnostic profile among college women, *Journal of the American College of Health*, 49: 157–66.

Scott, J. (2001) Cognitive-behavioral management of patients with bipolar disorder who relapse while on lithium prophylaxis, *Journal of Clinical Psychiatry*, 62: 556–9.

Scott, J., Garland, A. and Moorhead, S. (2001) A pilot study of cognitive therapy in bipolar disorders, *Psychological Medicine*, 31: 459–67.

Scott, J., Stanton, B., Garland, A. et al. (2000) Cognitive vulnerability in patients with bipolar disorder, *Psychological Medicine*, 30: 467–72.

Seedat, S. and Stein, M.B. (2004) Double-blind, placebo-controlled assessment of combined clonazepam with paroxetine compared with paroxetine monotherapy for generalized social anxiety disorder, *Journal of Clinical Psychiatry*, 65: 244–8.

Sel, R. (1997) Dissociation as complex adaptation, *Medical Hypothesis*, 48: 2205–8.

Seligman, M.E.P. (1970) On the generality of the laws of learning, *Psychological Review*, 77: 406–18.

Seligman, M.E.P. (1971) Phobias and preparedness, *Behavior Therapy*, 2: 307–20.

Seligman, M.E.P. (1975) *Helplessness*. San Francisco, CA: Freeman.

Sellman, J.D., Sullivan, P.F., Dore, G.M. et al. (2001) A randomized controlled trial of motivational enhancement therapy (MET) for mild to moderate alcohol dependence, *Journal of Studies in Alcohol*, 62: 389–96.

Semrud-Clikeman, M., Nielsen, K.H., Clinton, A. et al. (1999) An intervention approach for the children with teacher- and parent-identified attentional difficulties, *Journal of Learning Disabilities*, 32: 581–90.

Seto, M.C. and Barbaree, H.E. (1999) Psychopathy, treatment behavior, and sex offender recidivism, *Journal of Interpersonal Violence*, 14: 1235–48.

Seto, M.C., Harris, G.T., Rice, M.E. et al. (2004) The screening scale for pedophilic interests predicts recidivism among adult sex offenders with child victims, *Archives of Sexual Behaviour*, 33: 455–66.

Shahmanesh, M., Wayal, S., Cowan, F. et al. (2009) Suicidal behavior among female sex workers in Goa, India: the silent epidemic, *American Journal of Public Health*, 99: 1239–46.

Shallice, T. (1988) *From Neuropsychology to Mental Structure*. Cambridge: Cambridge University Press.

Shapiro, D.A. and Shapiro, D. (1983) Comparative therapy outcome research: methodological implications of meta-analysis, *Journal of Consulting and Clinical Psychology*, 45: 543–51.

Shapiro, F. (1995) *Eye Movement Desensitization and Reprocessing: Basic Principles*. New York: Guilford.

Sharpe, L. (2002) A reformulated cognitive-behavioral model of problem gambling: a biopsychosocial perspective, *Clinical Psychology Review*, 22: 1–25.

Sharpe, L., Tarrier, N., Schotte, D. et al. (1995) The role of autonomic arousal in problem gambling, *Addiction*, 90: 1529–40.

Shaw, M.E., Moores, K.A., Clark, R.C. et al. (2009) Functional connectivity reveals inefficient working memory systems in post-traumatic stress disorder, *Psychiatry Research: Neuroimaging*, 172: 235–411.

Shea, M.T., Elkin, I., Imber, S.D. et al. (1992) Course of depressive symptoms over follow-up: findings from the National Institute of Mental Health Treatment of Depression Collaborative Research Program, *Archives of General Psychiatry*, 49: 782–7.

Shea, S.C. (1998) *Psychiatric Interviewing: The Art of Understanding*, 2nd edn. Philadelphia, PA: Saunders.

Shea, T.M., Edelen, M.O., Pinto, A. et al. (2009) Improvement in borderline personality disorder in relationship to age, *Acta Psychiatria Scandinavica*, 119: 143–8.

Shean, G. (2004) *Understanding Schizophrenia: Contemporary Research, Theory, and Practice*. New York: Haworth Press.

Sheikh, S. and Furnham, A. (2000) A cross-cultural study of mental health beliefs and attitudes towards seeking professional help, *Social Psychiatry and Psychiatric Epidemiology*, 35: 326–34.

Shekharm, A. and Katnerm, J.S. (1995) Dorsomedial hypothalamic GABA regulates anxiety in the social interaction test, *Pharmacology Biochemistry and Behavior*, 50: 253–8.

Shelton, R.C., Haman, K.L., Rapaport, M.H. et al. (2006) A randomized, double-blind, active-control study of sertraline versus venlafaxine XR in major depressive disorder, *Journal of Clinical Psychiatry*, 67: 1674–81.

Sher, L. (2001) Genetic studies of seasonal affective disorder and seasonality, *Comprehensive Psychiatry*, 42: 105–10.

Sherer, M., Madison, C.F. and Hannay, H.J. (2000) A review of outcome after moderate and severe closed head injury with an introduction to life care planning, *Journal of Head Trauma and Rehabilitation*, 15: 767–82.

Sherman, J.J., LeResche, L., Huggins, K.H. et al. (2004) The relationship of somatization and depression to experimental pain response in women with temporomandibular disorders, *Psychosomatic Medicine*, 66: 852–60.

Shi, J., Hui, L., Xu, Y. et al. (2002) Sequence variations in the mu-opioid receptor gene (OPRM1) associated with human addiction to heroin, *Human Mutation*, 19: 459–60.

Shin, J.Y., Nhan, N.V., Lee, S.B. et al. (2009) The effects of a home-based intervention for young children with intellectual disabilities in Vietnam, *Journal of Intellectual Disability Research*, 53: 339–52.

Shinohara, K., Yanagisawa, A., Kagota, Y. et al. (1999) Physiological changes in Pachinko players: beta-endorphin, catecholamines, immune system substances and heart rate, *Applied Human Science*, 18: 37–42.

Siegert, R.J. and Abernethy, D.A. (2005) Depression in multiple sclerosis: a review, *Journal of Neurology Neurosurgery and Psychiatry*, 76: 469–75.

Siev, J. and Chambless, D.L. (2007) Specificity of treatment effects: cognitive therapy and relaxation for generalized anxiety and panic disorders, *Journal of Consulting and Clinical Psychology*, 75: 513–22.

Silove, D., Parker, G., Hadzi-Pavlovic, D. et al. (1991) Parental representations of patients with panic disorder and generalised anxiety disorder, *British Journal of Psychiatry*, 159: 835–41.

Silverman, W.K., Pina, A.A. and Viswesvaran, C. (2008) Evidence-based psychosocial treatments for phobic and anxiety disorders in children and adolescents, *Journal of Clinical Child and Adolescent Psychology*, 37: 105–30.

Simeon, D., Greenberg, J., Nelson, D. et al. (2005) Dissociation and posttraumatic stress 1 year after the World Trade Center disaster: follow-up of a longitudinal survey, *Journal of Clinical Psychiatry*, 66: 231–7.

Simon, A.E., Cattapan-Ludewig, K., Gruber, K. et al. (2009) Subclinical hallucinations in adolescent outpatients: an outcome study, *Schizophrenia Research*, 108: 265–71.

Simon, R. (1995) Gender, multiple roles, role meanings, and mental health, *Journal of Health and Social Behavior*, 36: 182–94.

Sinclair, J.D. (2001) Evidence about the use of naltrexone and for different ways of using it in the treatment of alcoholism, *Alcohol and Alcoholism*, 36: 2–10.

Singh, S.P. and Lee, A.S. (1997) Conversion disorders in Nottingham: alive, but not kicking, *Journal of Psychosomatic Research*, 43: 425–30.

Sinha, S., Anderson, J., John, V. et al. (2000) Recent advances in the understanding of the processing of APP to beta amyloid peptide, *Annals of the New York Academy of Science*, 920: 206–8.

Sinnakaruppan, I. and Williams, D.M. (2001) Head injury and family carers: a critical appraisal of case management programmes in the community, *Brain Injury*, 15: 653–72.

Sir, A., D'Souza, R.F., Uguz, S. et al. (2005) Randomized trial of sertraline versus venlafaxine XR in major depression: efficacy and discontinuation symptoms, *Journal of Clinical Psychiatry*, 66: 1312–20.

Sirey, J.A., Bruce, M.L., Alexopoulos, G.S. et al. (2001) Stigma as a barrier to recovery: perceived stigma and patient-rated severity of illness as predictors of antidepressant drug adherence, *Psychiatric Services*, 52: 1615–20.

Sivberg, B. (2002) Family system and coping behaviors: a comparison between parents of children with autistic spectrum disorders and parents with non-autistic children, *Autism*, 6: 397–409.

Skinner, B.F. (1953) *Science and Human Behavior*. New York: Macmillan.

Skokauskas, N. and Satkeviciute, R. (2007) Adolescent pathological gambling in Kaunas, Lithuania, *Nordic Journal of Psychiatry*, 61: 86–91.

Skre, I., Onstad., S., Torgersen, S. et al. (2000) The heritability of common phobic fear: a twin study of a clinical sample, *Journal of Anxiety Disorders*, 14: 549–62.

Skrzypek, S., Wehmeier, P.M. and Remschmidt, H. (2001) Body image assessment using body size estimation in recent studies on anorexia nervosa: a brief review, *European Child and Adolescent Psychiatry*, 10: 215–21.

Slade, P. and Brodie, D. (1994) Body-image distortion and eating disorder: a reconceptualization based on the recent literature, *European Eating Disorders Review*, 2: 32–46.

Slutske, W.S., Meier, M.H., Zhu, G. et al. (2009) The Australian Twin Study of Gambling (OZ-GAM): rationale, sample description, predictors of participation, and a first look at sources of individual differences in gambling involvement, *Twin Research and Human Genetics*, 12: 63–78.

Smith, A.J., Brown, R.T., Bunke, V. et al. (2002) Psychosocial adjustment and peer competence of siblings of children with attention-deficit/hyperactivity disorder, *Journal of Attention Disorder*, 5: 165–77.

Smith, C.A. and Lazarus, R.S. (1993) Appraisal components, core relational themes and the emotions, *Cognition and Emotion*, 7: 233–96.

Smith, M.L. and Glass, G.V. (1977) Meta-analysis of psychotherapy outcome studies, *American Psychologist*, 32: 752–60.

Smith, M.L., Glass, G.V. and Miller, T.I. (1980) *The Benefits of Psychotherapy*. Baltimore, MD: Johns Hopkins University Press.

Smith, T., Buch, G.A. and Gamby, T.E. (2000) Parent-directed, intensive early intervention for children with pervasive developmental disorder, *Research in Developmental Disabilities*, 21: 297–309.

Smith, Y.L.S., Van Goozen, S.H.M. and Cohen-Kettenis, P.T. (2001) Adolescents with gender identity disorder who were accepted or rejects for sex reassignment surgery: a prospective follow-up study, *Journal of the Academy of Child and Adolescent Psychiatry*, 40: 472–81.

Smoller, J.W., Gardner-Schuster, E. and Covino, J. (2008) The genetic basis of panic and phobic anxiety disorders, *American Journal of Medical Genetics: C Seminars in Medical Genetics*, 148: 118–26.

Smyth, B.P., O'Brien, M. and Barry, J. (2000) Trends in treated opiate misuse in Dublin: the emergence of chasing the dragon, *Addiction*, 95: 1217–23.

Sobanski, E. and Schmidt, M.H. (2000) 'Everybody looks at my pubic bone': a case report of an adolescent patient with body dysmorphic disorder, *Acta Psychiatrica Scandinavica*, 101: 80–2.

Sobczak, S., Riedel, W.J., Booij, I. et al. (2002) Cognition following acute tryptophan depletion: difference between first-degree relatives of bipolar disorder patients and matched healthy control volunteers, *Psychological Medicine*, 32: 503–15.

Sohlberg, M.M., Johnson, L., Paule, L. et al. (2001) *Attention Process Training-II: A Program to Address Attentional Deficits for Persons with Mild Cognitive Dysfunction*, 2nd edn. Wake Forest, NC: Lash & Associates.

Sohlberg, M.M. and Mateer, C.A. (2001) Improving attention and managing attentional problems: adapting rehabilitation techniques to adults with ADD, *Annals of the New York Academy of Sciences*, 931: 359–75.

Solari, A., Motta, A., Mendozzi, L. et al. (2004) Computer-aided retraining of memory and attention in people with multiple sclerosis: a randomized, double-blind controlled trial, *Journal of the Neurological Sciences*, 222: 99–104.

Soloff, P.H., Anselm, G., Nathan, R.S. et al. (1986) Paradoxical effect of amitriptyline on borderline patients, *American Journal of Psychiatry*, 143: 1603–5.

Solomon, R.L. (1980) The opponent-process theory of acquired motivation: the costs of pleasure and the benefits of pain, *American Psychologist*, 35: 691–712.

Sørensen, P., Birket-Smith, M., Wattar, U., Buemann, I. and Salkovskis, P. (2010) A randomized clinical trial of cognitive behavioural therapy versus short-term psychodynamic psychotherapy versus no intervention for patients with hypochondriasis, *Psychological Medicine*, 12: 1–11.

Spanos, N.P. (1994) Multiple identity enactments and multiple personality disorder: a sociocognitive perspective, *Psychological Bulletin*, 116: 143–65.

Spanos, N.P., Weekes, J.R. and Bertrand, L.D. (1985) Multiple personality: a social psychological perspective, *Journal of Abnormal Psychology*, 94: 362–76.

Sparks, D.L., Sabbagh, M.N., Connor, D.J. et al. (2005) Atorvastatin for the treatment of mild to moderate Alzheimer disease: preliminary results, *Archives of Neurology*, 62: 753–7.

Spector, A., Orrell, M., Davies, S. et al. (2000) Reality orientation for dementia, *Cochrane Database of Systematic Reviews*, 4: CD001119.

Spector, A., Thorgrimsen, L., Woods, B. et al. (2003) Efficacy of an evidence-based cognitive stimulation therapy programme for people with dementia: randomised controlled trial, *British Journal of Psychiatry*, 83: 248–54.

Spencer, T., Heiligenstein, J.H., Biederman, J. et al. (2002) Results from 2 proof-of-concept, placebo-controlled studies of atomoxetine in children with attention-deficit/hyperactivity disorder, *Journal of Clinical Psychiatry*, 63: 1140–7.

Spiegel, D. (1993) Multiple post-traumatic personality disorder, in R.P. Kluft and C.G. Fine (eds) *Clinical Perspectives on Multiple Personality Disorder*. Washington, DC: American Psychiatric Press.

Spiegel, D. (1999) Commentary: deconstructing self-destruction, *Psychiatry*, 62: 329–30.

Spiegel, D.A. and Barlow, D.H. (2000) Generalized anxiety disorders, in M.G. Gelder, J.J. López-Ibor Jr. and N.C. Andreasen (eds) *New Oxford Textbook of Psychiatry*. Oxford: Oxford University Press.

Spiegel, D.A., Bruce, T.J., Gregg, S.F. et al. (1994) Does cognitive behaviour therapy assist slow-taper alprazolam discontinuation in panic disorder?, *American Journal of Psychiatry*, 151: 876–81.

Spielberger, C.D. (1983) *Manual for the State-Trait Anxiety Inventory (STAI)*. Palo Alto, CA: Consulting Psychologists Press.

Srivareerat, M., Tran, T.T., Salim, S. et al. (2009) Chronic nicotine restores normal Abeta levels and prevents short-term memory and E-LTP impairment in Abeta rat model of Alzheimer's disease, *Neurobiology of Aging*, 20 May.

Stahl, S.M., Grady, M.M. et al. (2005) SNRIs: their pharmacology, clinical efficacy, and tolerability in comparison with other classes of antidepressants, *CNS Spectrum*, 10: 732–47.

Stanton, M.D. and Shadish, W.R. (1997) Outcome, attrition, and family-couples treatment for drug abuse: a meta-analysis and review of the controlled, comparative studies, *Psychological Bulletin*, 122: 170–91.

Startup, M., Jackson, M.C., Evans, K.E. and Bendix, S. (2005) North Wales randomized controlled trial of cognitive behaviour therapy for acute schizophrenia spectrum disorders: two-year follow-up and economic evaluation, *Psychological Medicine*, 35: 1307–16.

Steege, M.W., Wacker, D.P., Cigrand, K.C. et al. (1990) Use of negative reinforcement in the treatment of self-injurious behavior, *Journal of Applied Behavior Analysis*, 23: 459–67.

Steiger, H., Gauvin, L., Engelberg, M.J. et al. (2005) Mood- and restraint-based antecedents to binge episodes in bulimia nervosa: possible influences of the serotonin system, *Psychological Medicine*, 35: 1553–62.

Stein, K.F. and Corte, C. (2003) Reconceptualizing causative factors and intervention strategies in the eating disorders: a shift from body image to self-concept impairments, *Archives of Psychiatric Nursing*, 17: 57–66.

Steinberg, M., Cichetti, D., Buchanan, J. et al. (1993) Clinical assessment of dissociative symptoms and disorders: the Structured Clinical Interview for DSM-III dissociative disorders (SCID-D), *Dissociation*, 6: 3–15.

Steiner, H., Smith, C., Rosenkranz, R.T. et al. (1991) The early care and feeding of anorexics, *Child Psychiatry and Human Development*, 21: 163–7.

Steinhausen, H.C. and Glanville, K. (1983) Follow-up studies of anorexia nervosa: a review of research findings, *Psychological Medicine*, 13: 239–49.

Stella, L., D'Ambra, C., Mazzeo, F. et al. (2005) Naltrexone plus benzodiazepine aids abstinence in opioid-dependent patients, *Life Sciences*, 77: 2717–22.

Steptoe, A. and Noll, A. (1997) The perception of bodily sensations, with special reference to hypochondriasis, *Behaviour Research and Therapy*, 35: 901–10.

Sterling, R.C., Gottheil, E., Weinstein, S.P. et al. (2001) The effect of therapist/patient race and sex-matching in individual treatment, *Addiction*, 96: 1015–22.

Stewart, R.M. and Brown, R.I. (1988) An outcome study of Gamblers Anonymous, *British Journal of Psychiatry*, 152: 284–8.

Stewart, S.M., Kennard, B.D., Lee, P.W. et al. (2005) Hopelessness and suicidal ideation among adolescents in two cultures, *Journal of Child Psychology and Psychiatry*, 46: 364–72.

Stinson, F.S., Dawson, D.A., Chou, P. et al. (2007) The epidemiology of DSM-IV specific phobia in the USA: results from the National Epidemiologic Survey on Alcohol and Related Conditions, *Psychological Medicine*, 37: 1047–59.

Stockwell, T. (2004) Australian alcohol policy and the public interest: a brief report card, *Drug and Alcohol Review*, 23: 377–9.

Stoller, R.J. (1968) *Sex and Gender: Vol. 1. The Development of Masculinity and Femininity*. New York: Jason Aronson.

Story, T.J. and Craske, M.G. (2008) Responses to false physiological feedback in individuals with panic attacks and elevated anxiety sensitivity, *Behaviour Research and Therapy*, 46: 1001–8.

Strang, J., Sheridan, J., Hunt, C. et al. (2005) The prescribing of methadone and other opioids to addicts: national survey of GPs in England and Wales, *British Journal of General Practice*, 55: 444–51.

Strange, P.G. (1992) *Brain Biochemistry and Brain Disorders*. New York: Oxford University Press.

Strickland, B.R. (1992) Women and depression, *Current Directions in Psychological Science*, 1: 132–5.

Striegel-Moore R.H., Franko D.L., Thompson D. et al. (2004) Changes in weight and body image over time in women with eating disorders, *International Journal of Eating Disorders*, 36: 315–27.

Striegel-Moore, R.H. and Smolak, L. (2000) The influence of ethnicity on eating disorders in women, in R.M. Esler and M. Hersen (eds) *Handbook of Gender, Culture, and Health*. Mahwah, NJ: Erlbaum.

Strong, R.E., Marchant, B.K., Reimherr, F.W. et al. (2009) Narrow-band blue-light treatment of seasonal affective disorder in adults and the influence of additional nonseasonal symptoms, *Depression and Anxiety*, 26: 273–8.

Strosahl, K.D., Hayes, S.C., Wilson, K.G. and Gifford, E.V. (2004) An ACT primer: core therapy processes, intervention strategies, and therapist competencies, in S.C. Hayes and K.D. Strosahl (eds) *A Practical Guide to Acceptance and Commitment Therapy*. New York: Springer.

Struewing, J.P. and Gray, G.C. (1990) An epidemic of respiratory complaints exacerbated by mass psychogenic illness in a military recruit population, *American Journal of Epidemiology*, 132: 1120–9.

Stuart, S. and Noyes, R. (1999) Attachment and interpersonal communication in somatization, *Psychosomatics*, 40: 34–43.

Sukhodolsky, D.G. and Ruchkin, V.V. (2004) Association of normative beliefs and anger with aggression and antisocial behavior in Russian male juvenile offenders and high school students, *Journal of Abnormal Child Psychology*, 32: 225–36.

Sullivan, H.S. (1953) *The Interpersonal Theory of Psychiatry*. New York: Norton.

Sumaya, I., Rienzi, B.M., Deegan II, J.F. et al. (2001) Bright light treatment decreases depression in institutionalized older adults: a placebo-controlled crossover study, *Journal of Gerontology*, 56A: M356–M360.

Sundet, J.M., Skre, I., Okkenhaug, J.J. et al. (2003) Genetic and environmental causes of the interrelationships between self-reported fears: a study of a non-clinical sample of Norwegian identical twins and their families, *Scandinavian Journal of Psychology*, 44: 97–106.

Suppes, T., Baldessarini, R.J., Faedda, G.L. et al. (1991) Risk of recurrence following discontinuation of lithium treatment in bipolar disorder, *Archives of General Psychiatry*, 48: 1082–8.

Surtees, P.G., Wainwright, N.W., Willis-Owen, S.A. et al. (2006) Social adversity, the serotonin transporter (5-HTTLPR) polymorphism and major depressive disorder, *Biological Psychiatry*, 58: 451–6.

Sutherland, I. and Wilner, P. (1998) Patterns of alcohol, cigarette and illicit drug use in English adolescents, *Addiction*, 93: 1199–208.

Svartberg, M., Stiles, T.C. and Seltzer, M.H. (2004) Randomized, controlled trial of the effectiveness of short-term dynamic psychotherapy and cognitive therapy for cluster C personality disorders, *American Journal of Psychiatry*, 161: 810–17.

Swanson, M.C., Bland, R.C. and Newman, S.C. (1994) Antisocial personality disorders, *Acta Psychiatrica Scandinavica*, Suppl. 37: 63–70.

Swift, W., Maher, L. and Sunjic, S. (1999) Transitions between routes of heroin administration: a study of Caucasian and Indochinese heroin users in south-western Sydney, Australia, *Addiction*, 94: 71–82.

Szasz, T.S. (1960) The myth of mental illness, *American Psychologist*, 15: 113–18.

Szasz, T.S. (1971) From the slaughterhouse to the madhouse, *Psychotherapy Theory Research and Practice*, 8: 64–7.

Tadić, A., Victor, A., Başkaya, O. et al. (2008) Interaction between gene variants of the serotonin transporter promoter region (5-HTTLPR) and catechol O-methyltransferase (COMT) in borderline personality disorder, *American Journal of Medical Genetics B Neuropsychiatric Genetics*, 150B: 487–95.

Tallmadge, J. and Barkley, R.A. (1983) The interactions of hyperactive and normal boys with their fathers and mothers, *Journal of Abnormal Child Psychology*, 11: 565–79.

Tamam, L. and Ozpoyraz, N. (2002) Selective serotonin reuptake inhibitor discontinuation syndrome: a review, *Advances in Therapy*, 19: 17–26.

Tan, E., Marks, I.M. and Marset, P. (1971) Bimedial leucotomy in obsessive compulsive neurosis: a controlled serial inquiry, *British Journal of Psychiatry*, 118: 155–64.

Tandon, R. and Fleischhacker, W.W. (2005) Comparative efficacy of antipsychotics in the treatment of schizophrenia: a critical assessment, *Schizophrenia Research*, 79: 145–55.

Tang, T.Z. and DeRubeis, R. (1999) Sudden gains and critical sessions in cognitive–behavioral therapy for depression, *Journal of Consulting and Clinical Psychology*, 67: 1–11.

Tarrier, N., Kinney, C., McCarthy, E. et al. (2000) Two-year follow-up of cognitive–behavioral therapy and supportive counseling in the treatment of persistent symptoms in chronic schizophrenia, *Journal of Consulting and Clinical Psychology*, 68: 917–22.

Taylor, A., Goldberg, D., Hutchinson, S. et al. (2001) High risk injecting behaviour among injectors from Glasgow: cross-sectional community-wide surveys 1990–1999, *Journal of Epidemiology and Community Health*, 55: 766–7.

Taylor, B., Miller, E., Farringdon, C.P. et al. (1999) MMR vaccine and autism: no epidemiological evidence of a causal association, *Lancet*, 353: 2026–9.

Taylor, S., Thordarson, D.S., Maxfield, L. et al. (2003) Comparative efficacy, speed, and adverse effects of three PTSD treatments: exposure therapy, EMDR, and relaxation training, *Journal of Consulting and Clinical Psychology*, 71: 330–8.

Tcheremissine, O.V. and Lieving, L.M. (2006) Pharmacological aspects of the treatment of conduct disorder in children and adolescents, *CNS Drugs*, 20: 549–65.

Teasdale, J.D. (1993) Emotion and two kinds of meaning: cognitive therapy and applied cognitive science, *Behaviour Research and Therapy*, 31: 339–54.

Teasdale, J.D., Segal, Z.V., Williams, J.M.G. et al. (2000) Reducing risk of recurrence of major depression using Mindfulness-based Cognitive Therapy, *Journal of Consulting and Clinical Psychology*, 68: 615–23.

Teasdale, J., Segal, Z.V. and Williams, M.G. (1995) How does cognitive therapy prevent depressive relapse and why should attentional control (mindfulness training) help? *Behaviour Research and Therapy*, 33: 25–39.

Tee, S.F., Chow, T.J., Tang, P.Y. and Loh, H.C. (2010) Linkage of schizophrenia with TPH2 and 5-HTR2A gene polymorphisms in the Malay population, *Genetics and Molecular Research*, 9: 1274–8.

Telch, M.J., Jacquin, K., Smits, J.A. et al. (2003) Emotional responding to hyperventilation as a predictor of agoraphobia status among individuals suffering from panic disorder, *Journal of Behavior Therapy and Experimental Psychiatry*, 34: 161–70.

Terman, J.S., Terman, M., Lo, E.S. et al. (2001) Circadian time of morning light administration and therapeutic response in winter depression, *Archives of General Psychiatry*, 58: 69–75.

Terman, M. (1988) On the question of mechanism in phototherapy for seasonal affective disorder: considerations of clinical efficacy and epidemiology, *Journal of Biological Rhythms*, 3: 155–72.

Terr, L.C. (1991) *Unchained Memories*. New York: Basic Books.

Thapar, A., O'Donovan, M. and Owen, M.J. (2005) The genetics of attention deficit hyperactivity disorder, *Human Molecular Genetics*, 14 (Suppl. 2): R275–82.

Tharyan, P. (2002) Electroconvulsive therapy for schizophrenia, *Cochrane Database of Systematic Reviews*, 1.

Tharyan, P. and Adams, C.E. (2005) Electroconvulsive therapy for schizophrenia, *Cochrane Database of Systematic Reviews*, 2: CD000076.

Thomas, P.W., Thomas, S., Hillier, C. et al. (2006) Psychological interventions for multiple sclerosis, *Cochrane Database of Systematic Reviews*, 1: CD004431.

Thompson, C. and Briggs, M. (2000) Support for carers of people with Alzheimer's type dementia, *Cochrane Database of Systematic Reviews*, 2: CD000454.

Thompson, C., Raheja, S.K. and King, E.A. (1995) A follow-up study of seasonal affective disorder, *British Journal of Psychiatry*, 167: 380–4.

Tienari, P., Wynne, L.C., Moring, J. et al. (2000) Finnish adoptive family study: sample selection and adoptee DSM-III-R diagnoses, *Acta Psychiatrica Scandinavica*, 101: 433–43.

Timko, C., Moos, R.H., Finney, J.W. et al. (2000) Long-term outcomes of alcohol use disorders: comparing untreated individuals with those in Alcoholics Anonymous and formal treatment, *Journal of Studies in Alcohol*, 61: 529–40.

Tondi, L., Ribani, L., Bottazzi, M. et al. (2007) Validation therapy (VT) in nursing home: a case-control study. *Archives of Gerontology and Geriatrics*, 44 Suppl. 1: 407–11.

Toneatto, T. (1999) Metacognition and substance use, *Addictive Behaviors*, 24: 167–74.

Toneatto, T. and Ladouceur, R. (2003) Treatment of pathological gambling: a critical review of the literature, *Psychology of Addictive Behavior*, 17: 284–92.

Torgersen, S., Czajkowski, N., Jacobson, K. et al. (2008) Dimensional representations of DSM-IV cluster B personality disorders in a population-based sample of Norwegian twins: a multivariate study, *Psychological Medicine*, 38: 1617–25.

Torgersen, S., Kringlen, E. and Cramer, V. (2001) The prevalence of personality disorders in a community sample, *Archives of General Psychiatry*, 58: 590–6.

Torgersen, S., Lygren, S., Oien, P.A. et al. (2000) A twin study of personality disorders, *Comprehensive Psychiatry*, 41: 416–25.

Touchette, P.E., McDonald, R.F. and Langer, S.N. (1985) A scatter plot for identifying stimulus control of problem behavior, *Journal of Applied Behavior Analysis*, 18: 343–51.

Treasure, J., Todd, G., Brolly, M. et al. (1995) A pilot study of a randomised trial of cognitive analytical therapy vs educational behavioural therapy for adult anorexia nervosa, *Behaviour Research and Therapy*, 33: 363–7.

Treasure, T. (2001) *The Mental Health Act and Eating Disorders*. Institute of Psychiatry, Division of Psychological Medicine, Eating Disorders Research Unit. (www.iop.kcl.ac.uk)

Tremlett, H.L., Luscombe, D.K. and Wiles, C.M. et al. (2001) Prescribing for multiple sclerosis patients in general practice: a case-control study, *Journal of Clinical Pharmacy and Therapeutics*, 26: 437–44.

Troisi, A., Massaroni, P. and Cuzzolaro, M. (2005) Early separation anxiety and adult attachment style in women with eating disorders, *British Journal of Clinical Psychology*, 44: 89–97.

Trower, P., Birchwood, M., Meaden, A. et al. (2004) Cognitive therapy for command hallucinations: randomised controlled trial, *British Journal of Psychiatry*, 184: 312–20.

Truax, C.B. (1966) Reinforcement and nonreinforcement in Rogerian psychotherapy, *Journal of Abnormal Psychology*, 71: 1–9.

Trull, T.J. (2005) A dimensional view challenging DSM, *Journal of Personality Disorders*, 19: 262–82.

Tsai, S.J., Hong, C.J., Liou, Y.J. et al. (2009) Tryptophan hydroxylase 2 gene is associated with major depression and antidepressant treatment response, *Progress in Neuropsychopharmacology and Biological Psychiatry*, 33: 637–41.

Tsai, Y.F., Yeh, S.H. and Tsai, H.H. (2005) Prevalence and risk factors for depressive symptoms among community-dwelling elders in Taiwan, *International Journal of Geriatric Psychiatry*, 20: 1097–102.

Tsao, J.C.I., Mystkowski, J.L., Zucker, B.G. et al. (2002) Effects of cognitive behaviour therapy for panic disorder on comorbid condition: replication and extension, *Behaviour Therapy*, 33: 459–500.

Tsuang, M.T. (2000) Schizophrenia: genes and environment, *Biological Psychiatry*, 47: 210–20.

Tucker, T.K. and Ritter, A. (2000) Naltrexone in the treatment of heroin dependence: a literature review, *Drug and Alcohol Review*, 19: 73–82.

Turner, N.E., Preston, D.L., Saunders, C. et al. (2009) The relationship of problem gambling to criminal behavior in a sample of Canadian male federal offenders, *Journal of Gambling Studies*, 25: 153–69.

Turner, R.J., Lloyd, D.A. and Roszell, P. (1999) Personal resources and the social distribution of depression, *American Journal of Community Psychology*, 27: 643–72.

Turner, R.M. (1989) Case study evaluations of a bio-cognitive-behavioral approach for the treatment of borderline personality disorder, *Behavior Therapy*, 20: 477–89.

Tyrer, P. (2002) Practice guideline for the treatment of borderline personality disorder: a bridge too far, *Journal of Personality Disorders*, 16: 113–18.

Tyrer, P., Seivewright, N., Ferguson, B., Murphy, S. and Johnson, A.L. (1993) The Nottingham study of neurotic disorder: effect of personality status on response to drug treatment, cognitive therapy and self-help over two years, *British Journal of Psychiatry*, 162: 219–26.

Ueshima, H. (2005) Do the Japanese drink less alcohol than other peoples? The finding from INTERMAP, *Nihon Arukoru Yakubutsu Igakkai Zasshi*, 40: 27–33.

Uher, R., Huezo-Diaz, P., Perroud, N. et al. (2009) Genetic predictors of response to antidepressants in the GENDEP project, *Pharmacogenomics Journal*, 9: 225–33.

Uhlmann, V., Martin, C.M., Sheils, O. et al. (2001) Potential viral pathogenic mechanism for new variant inflammatory bowel disease, *Journal of Clinical Pathology: Molecular Pathology*, 55: 1–6.

Ullrich, S., Borkenau, P. and Marneros, A. (2001) Personality disorders in offenders: categorical versus dimensional approaches, *Journal of Personality Disorders*, 15: 442–9.

Ulvik, A., Kvåle, R., Wentzel-Larsen, T. et al. (2008) Quality of life 2–7 years after major trauma, *Acta Anaesthesiologica Scandinavica*, 52: 195–201.

US Department of Health and Human Services (1999) *Mental Health: A Report of the Surgeon General. Mental Health: Culture, Race, Ethnicity – Supplement.* Washington, DC: Office of the Surgeon General, SAMHSA.

van Apeldoorn, F.J., van Hout, W.J., Mersch, P.P. et al. (2008) Is a combined therapy more effective than either CBT or SSRI alone? Results of a multicenter trial on panic disorder with or without agoraphobia, *Acta Psychiatrica Scandinavica*, 117: 260–70.

Van den Bosch, L.M., Koeter, M.W., Stijnen, T. et al. (2005) Sustained efficacy of dialectical behaviour therapy for borderline personality disorder, *Behaviour Research and Therapy*, 43: 1231–41.

van der Feltz-Cornelis, C.M., van Oppen, P., Adèr, H.J. et al. (2006) Randomised controlled trial of a collaborative care model with psychiatric consultation for persistent medically unexplained symptoms in general practice, *Psychotherapy and Psychosomatics*, 75: 282–9.

Van der Sande, R., Buskens, E., Allart, E. et al. (1997) Psychosocial intervention following suicide attempt: a systematic review of treatment interventions, *Acta Psychiatrica Scandinavica*, 96: 43–50.

Van Elst, L. Tebartz, Hesslinger, B., Thiel, T. et al. (2003) Frontolimbic brain abnormalities in patients with borderline personality disorder: a volumetric MRI study, *Biological Psychiatry*, 54: 163–71.

Van Goozen, S.H.M., Cohen-Kettenis, P.T., Gooren, L.J.G. et al. (1995) Gender differences in behaviour: activating effects of cross-sex hormones, *Psychoneuroendocrinology*, 20: 343–63.

Van Hoeken, D., Veling, W., Sinke, S. et al. (2009) The validity and utility of subtyping bulimia nervosa, *International Journal of Eating Disorders*, 42: 595–602.

Van Oppen, P., de Haan, E., Van Balkom, A.J. et al. (1995) Cognitive therapy and exposure in vivo in the treatment of obsessive-compulsive disorder, *Behaviour Research and Therapy*, 33: 379–90.

Van Os, J. and Selten, J.P. (1998) Prenatal exposure to maternal stress and subsequent schizophrenia: the May 1940 invasion of The Netherlands, *British Journal of Psychiatry*, 172: 324–6.

van Straten, A., Cuijpers, P. and Smits, N. (2008) Effectiveness of a web-based self-help intervention for symptoms of depression, anxiety, and stress: randomized controlled trial, *Journal of Medical Internet Research*, 10: e7.

Van Trotsenburg, A.S., Vulsma, T. et al. (2005) The effect of thyroxine treatment started in the neonatal period on development and growth of two-year-old Down syndrome children: a randomized clinical trial, *Journal of Clinical Endocrinology and Metabolism*, 90: 3304–11.

Vaughn, C.E. and Leff, J.P. (1976) The influence of family and social factors on the course of psychiatric patients, *British Journal of Psychiatry*, 129: 125–37.

Veale, D., Gournay, K., Dryden, W., Boocock, A., Shah, F., Wilson, R. and Walburn, J. (1996) Body dysmorphic disorder: a cognitive behavioural model and pilot randomised controlled trial, *Behaviour Research and Therapy*, 9: 717–29.

Veletza, S., Samakouri, M., Emmanouil, G. et al. (2009) Psychological vulnerability differences in students – carriers or not of the serotonin transporter promoter allele S: effect of adverse experiences, *Synapse*, 63: 193–200.

Vernberg, E.M., Jacobs, A.K. and Hershberger, S.L. (1999) Peer victimization and attitudes about violence during early adolescence, *Journal of Clinical Child Psychology*, 28: 386–95.

Viken, R.J., Treat, T.A., Nosofsky, R.M. et al. (2002) Modeling individual differences in perceptual and attentional processes related to bulimic symptoms, *Journal of Abnormal Psychology*, 111: 598–609.

Vitaro, F., Arseneault, L. and Tremblay, R.E. (1999) Impulsivity predicts problem gambling in low SES adolescent males, *Addiction*, 94: 565–75.

Voisey, J., Swagell, C.D., Hughes, I.P. et al. (2009) The DRD2 gene 957C>T polymorphism is associated with posttraumatic stress disorder in war veterans, *Depression and Anxiety*, 26: 28–33.

Wade, T.D., Bergin, J.L., Tiggemann, M. et al. (2006) Prevalence and long-term course of lifetime eating disorders in an adult Australian twin cohort, *Australia and New Zealand Journal of Psychiatry*, 40: 121–8.

Wagenaar, A.C. and Crombag, H. (2005) *The Popular Policeman and Other Cases*. Chicago/Amsterdam: University of Chicago Press/Amsterdam University Press.

Wagner, A., Aizenstein, H., Venkatraman, V.K. et al. (2006) Altered reward processing in women recovered from anorexia nervosa, *American Journal of Psychiatry*, 164: 1842–9.

Wagner, A., Greer, P., Bailer, U.F. et al. (2006) Normal brain tissue volumes after long-term recovery in anorexia and bulimia nervosa, *Biological Psychiatry*, 59: 291–3.

Wahlberg, K-E., Jackson, D., Haley, H. et al. (2000a) Gene–environment interaction in vulnerability to schizophrenia: findings from the Finnish Adoptive Family Study of Schizophrenia, *American Journal of Psychiatry*, 154: 355–62.

Wahlberg, K.E., Wynne, L.C., Oja, H. et al. (2000b) Thought disorder index of Finnish adoptees and communication deviance of their adoptive parents, *Psychological Medicine*, 30: 127–36.

Wakefield, A.J., Murch, S.H., Anthony, A. et al. (1998) Ileal-lymphoid-nodular hyperplasia, non-specific colitis, and pervasive developmental disorder in children, *Lancet*, 351: 637–41.

Wald, J., Taylor, S. and Scamvougeras, A. (2004) Cognitive behavioural and neuropsychiatric treatment of post-traumatic conversion disorder: a case study, *Cognitive and Behavior Therapy*, 33: 12–20.

Waldron, H.B., Miller, W.R., and Tonigan, J.S. (2001) Client anger as a predictor of differential response to treatment, in R. Longabaugh and P.W. Wirtz (eds) *Project MATCH Hypotheses: Results and Causal Chain Analyses*. Project MATCH Monograph Series, Vol. 8. Bethesda, MD: National Institute on Alcohol Abuse and Alcoholism.

Waldron, H.B. and Turner, C.W. (2008) Evidence-based psychosocial treatments for adolescent substance abuse, *Journal of Clinical Child and Adolescent Psychology*, 37: 238–61.

Walker, E.F. and Diforio, D. (1997) Schizophrenia: a neural diathesis-stress model, *Psychological Review*, 4: 667–85.

Wallien, M.S. and Cohen-Kettenis, P.T. (2008) Psychosexual outcome of gender-dysphoric children. *Journal of the American Academy of Child and Adolescent Psychiatry*, 47: 1413–23.

Walsh, B.T., Agras, W.S., Devlin, M.J. et al. (2000) Fluoxetine for bulimia nervosa following poor response to psychotherapy, *American Journal of Psychiatry*, 157: 1332–4.

Walsh, B.T., Fairburn, C.G., Mickley, D. et al. (2004) Treatment of bulimia nervosa in a primary care setting, *American Journal of Psychiatry*, 161: 556–61.

Walshe, D.G., Lewis, E.J., Kim, S.I. et al. (2003) Exploring the use of computer games and virtual reality in exposure therapy for fear of driving following a motor vehicle accident, *Cyberpsychology and Behavior*, 6: 329–34.

Walters, E.E. and Kendler, K.S. (1995) Anorexia nervosa and anorexic-like syndromes in a population-based female twin sample, *American Journal of Psychiatry*, 152: 64–71.

Walters, S.T., Vader, A.M., Harris, T.R. et al. (2009) Dismantling motivational interviewing and feedback for college drinkers: a randomized clinical trial, *Journal of Consulting and Clinical Psychology*, 77: 64–73.

Wang, J.J. (2007) Group reminiscence therapy for cognitive and affective function of demented elderly in Taiwan, *International Journal of Geriatric Psychiatry*, 22: 1235–40.

Ward, A., Ramsay, R., Turnbull, S. et al. (2001) Attachment in anorexia nervosa: a transgenerational perspective, *British Journal of Medical Psychology*, 74: 497–505.

Ward, E. and Ogden, J. (1994) Experiencing vaginismus: sufferers' beliefs about causes and effects, *Sexual and Marital Therapy*, 9: 33–45.

Ward, T., Hudson, S.M. and Marshall, W.L. (1996) Attachment style in sex offenders: a preliminary study, *Journal of Sex Research*, 33: 17–26.

Ward, T. and Siegert, R.J. (2002) Toward a comprehensive theory of child sexual abuse: a theory knitting perspective, *Psychology, Crime, and Law*, 9: 319–51.

Wardle, J. and Marsland, L. (1990) Adolescent concerns about weight and eating: a social developmental perspective, *Journal of Psychosomatic Research*, 34: 377–91.

Warman, D.M., Grant, P., Sullivan, K. et al. (2005) Individual and group cognitive-behavioral therapy for psychotic disorders: a pilot investigation, *Journal of Psychiatric Practice*, 11: 27–34.

Warwick, H.M. and Salkovskis, P.M. (1990) Hypochondriasis, *Behaviour Research and Therapy*, 28: 105–17.

Warwick Daw, E., Payami, H., Nemens, E.J. et al. (2000) The number of trait loci in late-onset Alzheimer disease, *American Journal of Human Genetics*, 66: 196–204.

Watanabe, N., Churchill, R. and Furukawa, T.A. (2009) Combined psychotherapy plus benzodiazepines for panic disorder, *Cochrane Database of Systematic Reviews*, 1: CD005335.

Waters, A.M., Craske, M.G., Bergman, R.L. et al. (2008) Threat interpretation bias as a vulnerability factor in childhood anxiety disorders, *Behaviour Research and Therapy*, 47: 39–47.

Watson, D. and Pennebaker, J.W. (1989) Health complaints, stress, and distress: exploring the central role of negative affectivity, *Psychological Review*, 96: 234–54.

Watson, J.B. and Rayner, R. (1920) Conditioned emotional reaction, *Journal of Experimental Psychology*, 3: 1–14.

Watzlawick, P., Weakland, J.H. and Fisch, R. (1974) *Change: Principles of Problem Formulation and Problem Resolution*. New York: W.W. Norton.

Weich, S., Sloggett, A. and Lewis, G. (1998) Social roles and gender difference in the prevalence of common mental disorders, *British Journal of Psychiatry*, 173: 489–93.

Weiner, B. (1986) *An Attributional Theory of Motivation and Emotion*. New York: Springer-Verlag.

Weiner, H.L., Lemere, C.A., Maron, R. et al. (2000) Nasal administration of amyloid-beta peptide decreases cerebral amyloid burden in a mouse model of Alzheimer's disease, *Annals of Neurology*, 48: 567–79.

Wells, A. (1995) Meta-cognition and worry: a cognitive model of generalized anxiety disorder, *Behavioural and Cognitive Psychotherapy*, 23: 301–20.

Wells, A. (2000) *Emotional Disorders and Metacognition: Innovative Cognitive Therapy*. Chichester: Wiley.

Wells, A. and King, P. (2006) Metacognitive therapy for generalized anxiety disorder: an open trial, *Journal of Behavior Therapy and Experimental Psychiatry*, 37: 206–12.

Wells, A. and Matthews, G. (1996) Modelling cognition in emotional disorder: the S-REF model, *Behaviour Research and Therapy*, 34: 881–8.

Wells, A. and Sembi, S. (2004) Metacognitive therapy for PTSD: a preliminary investigation of a new brief treatment, *Journal of Behavior Therapy*, 35: 307–18.

Weltzin, T.E., Fernstrom, M.H., Fernstrom, J.D. et al. (1995) Acute tryptophan depletion and increased food intake and irritability in bulimia nervosa, *American Journal of Psychiatry*, 152: 1668–71.

Wender, P.H., Kety, S.S., Rosenthal, D. et al. (1986) Psychiatric disorders in the biological and adoptive families of adopted individuals with affective disorders, *Archives of General Psychiatry*, 43: 923–9.

Wender, P.H., Wolf, L.E. and Wasserstein, J. (2001) Adults with ADHD: an overview, *Annals of the New York Academy of Science*, 931: 1–16.

Wenzel, A., Brendle, J.R., Kerr, P.L. et al. (2007) A quantitative estimate of schema abnormality in socially anxious and non-anxious individuals, *Cognitive Behaviour Therapy*, 36: 220–9.

Werner, S., Malaspina, D. and Rabinowitz, J. (2007) Socioeconomic status at birth is associated with risk of schizophrenia: population-based multilevel study, *Schizophrenia Bulletin*, 33: 1373–8.

Wessels, C., Van Kradenberg, J., Mbanga, I. et al. (1999) Television as a medium for psychoeducation in South Africa: analysis of calls to a mental health information centre after screening of a TV series on psychiatric disorders, *Central African Journal of Medicine*, 45: 1–3.

Weyers, S., Elaut, E., De Sutter, P. et al. (2009) Long-term assessment of the physical, mental, and sexual health among transsexual women, *Journal of Sexual Medicine*, 6: 752–60.

Whalen, C.K., Henker, B. and Hinshaw, S.P. (1985) Cognitive-behavioral therapies for hyperactive children: premises, problems, and prospects, *Journal of Abnormal Child Psychology*, 13: 391–409.

Whitaker-Azmitia, P.M. (2005) Behavioral and cellular consequences of increasing serotonergic activity during brain development: a role in autism?, *International Journal of Developmental Neuroscience*, 23: 75–83.

Whitehouse, P.J., Struble, R.G., Clark, A.W. et al. (1982) Alzheimer disease: plagues, tangles, and the basal forebrain, *Annals of Neurology*, 12: 494.

Whitfield, J.B. (2005) Alcohol and gene interactions, *Clinical Chemistry and Laboratory Medicine*, 43: 480–7.

Whittal, M.L. and Zaretsky, A. (1996) Cognitive-behavioral strategies for the treatment of eating disorders, in M.H. Pollack, M.W. Otto and J.F. Rosenbaum (eds) *Challenges in Clinical Practice: Pharmacologic and Psychosocial Strategies*. New York: Guilford.

Wicki, W., Angst, J. and Merikangas, K.R. (1992) The Zurich Study, XIV: epidemiology of seasonal depression, *European Archives of Psychiatry and Clinical Neuroscience*, 241: 301–6.

Widiger, T.A. and Costa, P.T. Jr (1994) Personality and personality disorders, *Journal of Abnormal Psychology*, 95: 43–51.

Widiger, T.A., Frances, A. and Trull, T.J. (1987) A psychometric analysis of the social, interpersonal and cognitive-perceptual items for the schizotypal personality disorder, *Archives of General Psychiatry*, 44: 786–95.

Wiers, R.W. and Stacy, A.W. (eds) (2006) *Handbook of Implicit Cognition and Addiction*. London: Sage.

Wileman, S.M., Eagles, J.M., Andrew, J.E. et al. (2001) Light therapy for seasonal affective disorder in primary care, *British Journal of Psychiatry*, 178: 311–16.

Wilhelm, K., Boyce, P. and Brownhill, S. (2004) The relationship between interpersonal sensitivity, anxiety disorders and major depression, *Journal of Affective Disorders*, 79: 33–41.

Wilk, A.I., Jensen, N.M. and Havighurst, T.C. (1997) Meta-analysis of randomized control trials addressing brief interventions in heavy alcohol drinkers, *Journal of General Internal Medicine*, 12: 274–83.

Wilkinson, M. (1992) Income distribution and life expectancy, *British Medical Journal*, 304: 165–8.

Willemse-van Son, A.H., Ribbers, G.M., Verhagen, A.P. et al. (2007) Prognostic factors of long-term functioning and productivity after traumatic brain injury: a systematic review of prospective cohort studies, *Clinical Rehabilitation*, 21: 1024–37.

Willemsen-Swinkels, S.H., Buitlaar, J.K., Nijhof, G.J. et al. (1995) Failure of naltrexone hydrochloride to reduce self-injurious and autistic behavior in mentally retarded adults: doubleblind placebo-controlled studies, *Archives of General Psychiatry*, 52: 766–73.

Williams, D.R. (1999) Race, socioeconomic status, and health: the added effects of racism and discrimination, *Annals of the New York Academy of Science*, 896: 173–88.

Williams, G-J., Power, K.G., Millar, H.R. et al. (1993) Comparison of eating disorders and other dietary/weight groups on measures of perceived control, assertiveness, self-esteem, and self-directed hostility, *International Journal of Eating Disorders*, 4: 7–32.

Williams, J.G., Higgins, J.P. and Brayne, C.E. (2006) Systematic review of prevalence studies of autism spectrum disorders, *Archives of Diseases of Childhood*, 91: 8–15.

Williams, J.M., Alatiq, Y., Crane, C. et al. (2008) Mindfulness-based Cognitive Therapy (MBCT) in bipolar disorder: preliminary evaluation of immediate effects on between-episode functioning, *Journal of Affective Disorders*, 107: 275–9.

Willner, P. (2005) The effectiveness of psychotherapeutic interventions for people with learning disabilities: a critical overview, *Journal of Intellectual Disability Research*, 49: 73–85.

Wilson, B. (1989) Models of cognitive rehabilitation, in R.L. Wood and P.G. Eames (eds) *Models of Brain Injury Rehabilitation*. Baltimore, MD: Johns Hopkins University Press.

Wilson, B.A. (2001) Assessment and management of people with severe brain injury and reduced states of awareness, *Brain Impairment*, 2: 52.

Wilson, B.A. (2005) The effective rehabilitation of memory-related disabilities, in P.W. Halligan and D.T. Wade (eds) *Effectiveness of Rehabilitation for Cognitive Deficits*. New York: Oxford University Press.

Wilson, B.A., Emslie, H., Quirk, K. et al. (2005) A randomized control trial to evaluate a paging system for people with traumatic brain injury, *Brain Injury*, 19: 891–4.

Wilson, G.T. (1988) Alcohol use and abuse: a social learning analysis, in C.D. Chaudron and D.A. Wilkinson (eds) *Theories on Alcoholism*. Toronto: Addiction Research Foundation.

Wilson, G.T. (1996) Treatment of bulimia nervosa: when CBT fails, *Behaviour Research and Therapy*, 34: 197–212.

Wilson, G.T., Grilo, C.M. and Vitousek, K.M. (2007) Psychological treatment of eating disorders, *American Psychologist*, 62: 199–216.

Winters, K. and Karasik, D. (2009) *Gender Madness in American Psychiatry: Essays from the Struggle for Dignity*. Booksurge: Llc.

Winters, K.C. and Neale, J.M. (1985) Mania and low self-esteem, *Journal of Abnormal Psychology*, 94: 282–90.

Wiser, S. and Goldfried, M.R. (1998) Therapist interventions and client emotional experiencing in expert psychodynamic-interpersonal and cognitive-behavioral therapies, *Journal of Consulting and Clinical Psychology*, 66: 634–40.

Wisniewski, A.B., Prendeville, M.T. and Dobs, A.S. (2005) Handedness, functional cerebral hemispheric lateralization, and cognition in male-to-female transsexuals receiving cross-sex hormone treatment, *Archives of Sexual Behavior*, 34: 167–72.

Wistow, R. and Schneider, J. (2003) Users' views on supported employment and social inclusion: a qualitative study of 30 people at work, *British Journal of Learning Disabilities*, 31: 166–74.

Wittchen, H.U. and Essau, C.A. (1993) Epidemiology of panic disorder: progress and unresolved issues, *Journal of Psychiatric Research*, 27 (Suppl. 1): 47–68.

Wittchen, H-U. and F. Jacobi (2005) Size and burden of mental disorders in Europe – a critical review and appraisal of 27 studies, *European Neuropsychopharmacology*, 15: 357–76.

Wolfensberger, W. (1972) *The Principle of Normalization in Human Services*. Toronto: National Institutes of Mental Retardation.

Wolfensberger, W. (1983) Social role valorization: a proposed new term for the principle of normalization, *Mental Retardation*, 21: 234–9.

Wolfersdorf, M. (1995) Depression and suicidal behaviour: psychopathological differences between suicidal and non-suicidal depressive patients, *Archives of Suicide Research*, 1: 273–88.

Wolitzky-Taylor, K.B., Horowitz, J.D., Powers, M.B. et al. (2008) Psychological approaches in the treatment of specific phobias: a meta-analysis, *Clinical Psychology Review*, 28: 1021–37.

Wolpe, J. (1982) *The Practice of Behavior Therapy*, 3rd edn. New York: Pergamon.

Wong, S. and Hare, R.D. (2002) *Program Guidelines for the Institutional Treatment of Violent Psychopathic Offenders*. Toronto: Multi-Health Systems.

Wood, S.J., Yucel, M., Velakoulis, D. et al. (2005) Hippocampal and anterior cingulate morphology in subjects at ultra high-risk for psychosis: the role of family history of psychotic illness, *Schizophrenia Research*, 75: 295–301.

Woods, R. and Bird, M. (1999) Non-pharmacological approaches to treatment, in G.K.Wilcock, R.S. Bucks and K. Rockwood (eds) *Diagnosis and Management of Dementia: A Manual for Memory Disorders Teams*. Oxford: Oxford University Press.

Woods, R. and Roth, A. (1996) Effectiveness of psychological therapy with older people, in A. Roth and P. Fonagy (eds) *What Works for Whom? A Critical Review of Psychotherapy Research*. New York: Guilford.

Woodside, D.B., Bulik, C.M., Halmi, K.A. et al. (2002) Personality, perfectionism, and attitudes toward eating in parents of individuals with eating disorders, *International Journal of Eating Disorders*, 31: 290–9.

Woody, G.E., Luborsky, L., McLellan, A.T. et al. (1983) Psychotherapy for opiate addicts. Does it help?, *Archives of General Psychiatry*, 40: 639–45.

World Health Organization (WHO) (1979) *Schizophrenia: An International Follow-up Study*. Chichester: Wiley.

World Health Organization (WHO) (1992) *Tenth Revision of the International Classification of Diseases*. Geneva: WHO.

World Health Organization (WHO) (1996) *Ottawa Charter for Health Promotion*. Geneva: WHO.

Wupperman, P., Neumann, C.S. and Axelrod, S.R. (2008) Do deficits in mindfulness underlie borderline personality features and core difficulties? *Journal of Personality Disorder*, 22: 466–82.

Xu, K., Lichtermann, D., Lipsky, R.H. et al. (2004) Association of specific haplotypes of D2 dopamine receptor gene with vulnerability to heroin dependence in 2 distinct populations, *Archives of General Psychiatry*, 61: 597–606.

Yale, R. (1995) *Developing Support Groups for Individuals with Early Stage Alzheimer's Disease: Planning, Implementation and Evaluation*. Baltimore, MD: Health Profession Press.

Yalom, I.D., Green, R. and Fisk, N. (1973) Prenatal exposure to female hormones: effect on psychosocial development in boys, *Archives of General Psychiatry*, 28: 554–61.

Yamada, T., Hattori, H., Miura, A. et al. (2001) Prevalence of Alzheimer's disease, vascular dementia and dementia with Lewy bodies in a Japanese population, *Psychiatry and Clinical Neurosciences*, 55: 21–5.

Yang, C.F., Gray, P. and Pope, H.G. Jr. (2005) Male body image in Taiwan versus the West: Yanggang Zhiqi meets the Adonis complex, *American Journal of Psychiatry*, 162: 263–9.

Yang, L.H., Phillips, M.R., Licht, D.M. et al. (2004) Causal attributions about schizophrenia in families in China: expressed emotion and patient relapse, *Journal of Abnormal Psychology*, 113: 592–602.

Yatham, L.N., Kauer-Sant'Anna, M., Bond, D.J. et al. (2009) Course and outcome after the first manic episode in patients with bipolar disorder: prospective 12-month data from the systematic treatment optimization program for early mania project, *Canadian Journal of Psychiatry*, 54: 105–12.

Yerevanian, B.I., Koek, R.J., Feusner, J.D. et al. (2004) Antidepressants and suicidal behaviour in unipolar depression, *Acta Psychiatrica Scandinavica*, 110: 452–8.

Yoast, R., Williams, M.A., Deitchman, S.D. et al. (2001) Report of the Council on Scientific Affairs: methadone maintenance and needle-exchange programs to reduce the medical and public health consequences of drug abuse, *Journal of Addictive Diseases*, 20: 15–40.

Young, J.E. (1999) *Cognitive Therapy for Personality Disorders: A Schema-Focused Approach*. Professional Resource Exchange Inc.

Young, J.E. and Lindemann, M.D. (1992) An integrative schema-focused model for personality disorders, *Journal of Cognitive Psychotherapy*, 6: 11–23.

Zack, M. and Poulos, C.X. (2009) Parallel roles for dopamine in pathological gambling and psychostimulant addiction, *Current Drug Abuse Reviews*, 2: 11–25.

Zanarini, M.C., Frankenburg, F.R., Hennen, J. et al. (2005) The McLean Study of Adult Development (MSAD): overview and implications of the first six years of prospective follow-up, *Journal of Personality Disorders*, 19: 505–23.

Zanarini, M.C., Frankenburg, F.R. and Vujanovic, A.A. (2002) Inter-rater and test-retest reliability of the Revised Diagnostic Interview for Borderlines, *Journal of Personality Disorders*, 16: 270–6.

Zarros, A.C., Kalopita, K.S. and Tsakiris, S.T. (2005) Serotoninergic impairment and aggressive behavior in Alzheimer's disease, *Acta Neurobiologiae Experimentalis*, 65: 277–86.

Zerbe, K.J. (2001) The crucial role of psychodynamic understanding in the treatment of eating disorders, *Psychiatric Clinics of North America*, 24: 305–13.

Zhou, J-N., Hofman, M.A. and Black, K. (1995) A sex difference in the human brain and its relation to transsexuality, *Nature*, 378: 68–70.

Zilbergeld, B. (1992) *The New Male Sexuality*. New York: Bantam.

Zimmerman, J. and Grosz, H.J. (1966) 'Visual' performance of a functionally blind person, *Behaviour Research and Therapy*, 4: 119–34.

Zlomke, K. and Davis, T.E. 3rd (2008) One-session treatment of specific phobias: a detailed description and review of treatment efficacy, *Behavior Therapy*, 39: 207–23.

Zola, S.M. (1998) Memory, amnesia, and the issue of recovered memory: neurobiological aspects, *Clinical Psychology Review*, 18: 915–32.

Zucker, K.J. and Bradley, S.J. (1995) *Gender Identity Disorder and Psychosexual Problems in Children and Adolescents*. New York: Guilford.

Zucker, K.J., Green, R., Garofano, C. et al. (1994) Prenatal gender preference of mothers of feminine and masculine boys: relation to sibling sex composition and birth order, *Journal of Abnormal Child Psychology*, 22: 1–13.

Zweig-Frank, H. and Paris, J. (2002) Predictors of outcome in a 27-year follow-up of patients with borderline personality disorder, *Comprehensive Psychiatry*, 43: 103–7.